Wood.
Rethinking
Material

Editorial

„Wir müssen aus dem Betonbau raus!"[1] fordert der Klimaforscher Joachim Schellnhuber und mahnt eine bevorstehende, dringend notwendige Baurevolution an, in der CO_2-intensive Baumaterialien wie Stahl und Beton möglichst bald von Holz oder Bambus abgelöst werden sollten. Eine seiner aktuellsten Studien,[2] die er gemeinsam mit einem internationalen Forscherteam der Yale School of Forestry und dem Potsdam Institut für Klimaforschung durchgeführt hat, belegt, dass eine holzzentrierte Baukultur weltweit zu einer bedeutenden CO_2-Emissionssenkung und damit zu einer Klimastabilisierung führen würde. Dieses Szenario, in dem der Einsatz von Holz als Baumaterial deutlich gesteigert werden soll, ist jedoch nur dann möglich und sinnvoll, wenn auch die Wälder in Zukunft nachhaltig und sorgfältig bewirtschaftet werden. *GAM.17* stellt sich dieser Forderung und fragt, wie ein solcher Prozess des grundsätzlichen Umdenkens unserer Rohstoff- und Materialverwendung in der Architektur stattfinden kann.

Um die erweiterten ökologischen Zusammenhänge des Holzbaus mit den gegenwärtigen architektonischen Perspektiven auf das zukunftsträchtige (Bau-)Material Holz vereinen zu können, ist es aus dem Blickwinkel von *GAM.17* notwendig, zunächst einmal den Begriff des Materials von seinem eindimensionalen Verständnis als bloßer, überall und leicht verfügbarer materieller Rohstoff zu befreien. Holz als Material aufzufassen, vermag ohne die ökonomische, kulturelle und politische Dimension dieses Materials keinen zukunftsweisenden Sinn zu erzeugen, der über seine reine Verfügbarmachung hinausgehen

"We must stop building with concrete!"[1] demands the climate researcher Joachim Schellnhuber, calling for an imminent, direly needed revolution in architecture, the idea being to quickly replace CO_2-intensive building materials like steel and concrete with timber or bamboo. One of his most recent studies,[2] conducted in collaboration with an international team of researchers from the Yale School of Forestry and with the Potsdam Institute for Climate Impact Research, proves that a building culture focused on timber would lead to a significant drop in CO_2 emissions on a global scale and thus to a more stable climate. However, this scenario, in which the use of timber as a building material must to be greatly stepped up, is only possible and feasible when forests of the future are cultivated carefully and sustainably. *GAM.17* addresses this demand and examines how such a process of fundamentally rethinking our use of resources and materials can take place in the context of architecture.

In order to reconcile the expanded ecological contexts of timber construction with contemporary architectural perspectives on timber as a future-oriented (building) material, *GAM.17* finds it necessary to first liberate the concept of this material from the one-dimensional notion of it being a simple resource easily obtainable anywhere. Viewing timber as a mere material, without taking its economic, cultural, and political dimensions into account, does not in fact make sense in the

---

1   Joachim Schellnhuber im Interview mit Benedikt Narodoslawsky: „Klimaschutz wird nicht honoriert", *Falter*, 24. November 2020, 18–29, hier 19.

2   Vgl. Churkina, Galina/Organschi, Alan/Reyer, Christopher P. O./Ruff, Andrew/Vinke, Kira/Liu, Zhu/Reck, Barbara K./Graedel, T. E./Schellnhuber, Hans Joachim: „Buildings as a Global Carbon Sink", *Nature Sustainability* 3 (2020), 269–276.

1   Joachim Schellnhuber in conversation with Benedikt Narodoslawsky, "Klimaschutz wird nicht honoriert," *Falter,* November 24, 2020, 18–29, esp. 19.

2   See Galina Churkina, Alan Organschi, Christopher P. O. Reyer, Andrew Ruff, Kira Vinke, Zhu Liu, Barbara K. Reck, T. E. Graedel, and Hans Joachim Schellnhuber, "Buildings as a Global Carbon Sink," *Nature Sustainability* 3 (2020): 269–276.

würde. Aus diesem Grund geht *GAM.17* davon aus, dass das Material Holz wie seine Verwendung mit kulturellen Traditionen verbunden ist und Holz als Gegenstand einer eigenen Industrieform und ihrer Ökonomie auch eine politische Geschichte besitzt. Daraus folgt, dass hinsichtlich der architektonischen Verwendung von Holz durchaus die Wirtschaftskreisläufe von Belang sind, in die eine Produktion und Verwertung von Holz ökonomisch eingebunden ist. Es erscheint notwendig, die Industrialisierung der Waldbewirtschaftung zu hinterfragen, die zu einer höheren Anfälligkeit für klimawandelbedingte Wetterextreme geführt hat; sowie die Konjunktur, die der Baustoff Holz gegenwärtig auch bei Bauten im urbanen Kontext erlebt, durch eine historische Analyse seiner kulturellen Vereinnahmungen und Bedeutungszuschreibungen zu kontrastieren.

    GAM.17 stellt sich die weiterreichende Frage, ob mit dem Material und Baustoff Holz eine Dekarbonisierung der Bauwirtschaft erreicht werden könnte, die unter dem Begriff der Nachhaltigkeit derzeit diskutiert wird. Dabei gilt es ebenfalls zu hinterfragen, ob uns die Nachhaltigkeitsdebatte, die sich das Material Holz gerne auf ihre Fahne heftet, tatsächlich einen Schritt weiterbringt oder eher den Blick auf erweiterte Lösungsansätze verstellt. Die in dieser Ausgabe von *GAM* versammelten Beiträge haben somit gemeinsam, dass sie Holz als architektonisches Material einer Neubewertung unterziehen und seine Potenziale für eine nachhaltige Bauwirtschaft ausloten – aus kulturhistorischer, ökologischer, handelspolitischer, konstruktiver und ästhetischer Sicht.

    Eröffnet wird *GAM.17* mit Beiträgen, die sich mit der kulturgeschichtlichen Relevanz von Holz auseinandersetzen. **Stephan Trüby** nimmt das Thema Holz historisch und politisch in den Blick und richtet seinen kritischen Fokus auf die

long term, aside from the basic question of how to make it available. It is for this reason that *GAM.17* assumes that wood as a material, like its use, is tied to cultural traditions and that timber, as the object of its own industrial form and economy, also has a political history. It follows that, when it comes to the architectural use of wood, definite importance is placed on the business cycles in which the production and use of timber are economically integrated. It seems necessary to question the industrialization of silviculture, considering that it has led to a greater vulnerability to extreme weather conditions caused by climate change; but also to contrast the economic boom that timber as a building material is currently experiencing, even in urban contexts, with a historical analysis of its cultural appropriations and its attributions of meaning.

    GAM.17 raises the broader question of whether timber as a substance and building material is able to help achieve a decarbonization of the construction industry as is currently being discussed under the umbrella term of sustainability. It is also vital to question whether the sustainability discussion that is so often associated with wood as a material actually signifies a leap forward, or whether it in fact obscures other possible far-reaching solutions. The contributions compiled in this issue of *GAM* thus all reevaluate timber in its role as an architectural material and examine its potential for furthering a sustainable construction industry—from the vantage point of cultural history, ecology, trade policy, structural design, and aesthetics.

    GAM.17 opens with contributions that delve into the cultural-historical relevance of timber. **Stephan Trüby** ap-

„deutsche Silvapolitik", die sich in rechtspopulistischen (architekturtheoretischen) Ausprägungen des 19. Jahrhunderts über Heimatschutzbewegungen des 20. Jahrhundert bis hin zu zeitgenössischeren rechtsökologischen Projekten manifestiert. Anschließend zeigt der Cartoonist **Tom Körner** eine kleine, illustre Auswahl seiner traditionsreichen Comic-Serie aus der *TAZ*, in der sich die Liebe zum deutschen Wald in immer neuen und augenzwinkernden Varianten des Bäume-Umarmens artikuliert. **Anselm Wagner** beschreibt den allgemeinen Imagewandel, den der Holzbau von der Antike über das 19. Jahrhundert bis heute im mitteleuropäischen Raum vollzogen hat und argumentiert am Beispiel Peter Zumthors einen *material turn*, der Architektur nicht nur rein konzeptuell, sondern materialistisch denkt. Anschließend gibt **Reyner Banham** in seinem hier abgedruckten Konferenzbeitrag aus dem Jahre 1972 einen erkenntnisreichen, an manchen Stellen amüsanten Rückblick auf die Kultur- und Bedeutungsgeschichte von Holz und seinen bauwirtschaftlich effizienteren Nachfolger, das Holzimitat, in dessen „perfektionierten Reinkarnationen" er eine in der nordamerikanischen Kultur verankerte Sehnsucht nach dem verschwundenen „unzuverlässigen" Baumholz erkennt.

Banhams Text leitet zum zweiten Teil von *GAM.17* über, der sich mit den Materialeigenschaften von Holz und ihrer Bedeutung für die gegenwärtige Baupraxis beschäftigt. Die Frage, wann ein Holzbau überhaupt ein Holzbau ist, steht im Zentrum von **Anne Isopps** Text, die in Hybridbauten, d.h. der Verwendung von Holz mit anderen Materialien, das größte Zukunftspotenzial vor allem für den mehrgeschossigen Wohnbau erkennt und dies am Beispiel der Holz-Beton-Verbunddecke belegt. Im Anschluss setzt sich **Stefan Winter** mit sechs kritischen Kernfragen zum Baustoff Holz auseinander, deren Beantwortung zum Ziel haben, den Holzbau weiter voranzubringen und zu belegen, dass Holz den anderen Baustoffen auf eine spezifische Art überlegen ist. **Urs Hirschberg** zeigt anhand von an der TU Graz entwickelten Pavillons, inwiefern sich mithilfe digitaler Methoden eine Konstruktionslogik direkt aus dem Material ableiten lässt. Digitalisierung, so das Argument, trägt nicht nur zu einem besseren Verständnis der Materialeigenschaften von Holz bei, sondern ermöglicht auch eine Verfeinerung desselben in Entwurf und Fabrikation. Im nachfolgenden Interview mit **Kai Strehlke**, der die digitalen Prozesse der Schweizer Holzbaufirma Blumer Lehmann leitet, wird zudem deutlich, wie komplexe Freiformprojekte aus Holz, wie z.B. das neue Swatch Hauptgebäude in Biel von Shigeru Ban, materialgerecht entwickelt und umgesetzt werden. Anhand einer vom „verästelten Habitus des Waldes" abgeleiteten Astwerkdecke verdeutlicht **Jens Ludloff**, inwiefern Holzbau dazu in der Lage ist, ein neuartiges, nachhaltig-erfahrbares Raumvokabular zu generieren – ein Entwurfskonzept, das auf dem Zusammenwirken von Ökologie, Forst- und Bauwirtschaft

proaches the topic of wood from a historical and political perspective, placing a critical focus on "German silvipolitics," which has taken various forms—ranging from right-wing populist (architectural-theoretical) manifestations during the nineteenth century to *Heimatschutz* movements in the twentieth century to contemporary right-wing ecological projects. The cartoonist **Tom Körner** then presents a small, outstanding selection of his comic series from the daily newspaper *TAZ*. This series, steeped in tradition, articulates—through ever-new, cheeky variants of tree hugging—how loved German forests are. **Anselm Wagner** describes the general change in image experienced by timber construction in Central Europe from ancient times through the nineteenth century and also extending up to the present day. Citing the example of Peter Zumthor, he elucidates the *material turn* pursued by architecture, which understands the discipline no longer only conceptually but also in terms of materials. This is followed by a reprint of a conference paper by **Reyner Banham** from 1972, which offers an insightful, occasionally amusing retrospective view of timber's history of culture and meaning, while also touching on its more efficient successor in the construction industry, imitation wood. It is in the latter's "perfected reincarnations" that Banham sees a yearning anchored in North American culture for the disappearing, "unreliable" tree wood. This text leads into the second section of *GAM.17*, which deals with the material qualities of wood and its significance for the practice of contemporary architecture and building.

The question of when timber construction is actually timber construction is at the center of the text by **Anne Isopp**. She identifies hybrid buildings, that is, the use of timber combined with other materials, as holding the greatest potential for the future, especially for multistory architecture, and substantiates this claim by example of the timber-concrete composite ceiling. This is followed by a contribution by **Stefan Winter**, who discusses six key critical questions related to wood as a building material. The answers to these questions aim to further advance timber construction and to demonstrate how, in a certain way, timber is superior to other building materials. By example of pavilions developed at Graz University of Technology, **Urs Hirschberg** shows how digital methods can be used to derive a structural design logic directly from the material. He argues that digitalization not only leads to a better understanding of timber's material qualities but also facilitates the refinement of timber in terms of design and production. In the subsequent interview with **Kai Strehlke**, who is in charge of digital processes at the Swiss timber construction firm Blumer

beruht. Schließlich markiert die Fotostrecke von **Formafantasma** (**Andrea Trimarchi** & **Simone Farresin**) den Übergang zum dritten Teil dieser *GAM*-Ausgabe und verweist auf die ökologische und politische Verantwortung, die der architektonische Umgang mit Holz verlangt. Als Teil der umfangreichen Ausstellung „Cambio" erzählen ihre Fotografien von der komplexen Materialgeschichte der dreizehn Millionen Bäume, die 2018 durch die Sturmkatastrophe im italienischen Fleimstal zu Fall gebracht wurden und durch die lokale Bevölkerung verarbeitet werden mussten.

Der dritte Teil von *GAM.17* enthält Beiträge, die Holz als Material in ein breiteres Beziehungsgeflecht von Umweltschutz, Holzwirtschaft und Handelsketten stellt. Eröffnet wird dieser Teil durch eine Fotostrecke von **Don Fuchs**, die das zerstörerische Ausmaß des Gospers Mountain Buschfeuers im Nordwesten Sydneys abbildet und damit gleichzeitig die Fragilität wie auch die Regenerationskraft von Holz eindrucksvoll vor Augen führt. Welche bedeutsame Rolle der Wald als Ökosystem für die Architektur spielen kann, zeigt **Laila Seewang** in ihrem Beitrag, der im Nordwesten der USA ein sogenanntes „Timber Territory" lokalisiert, in dem Holz nicht bloß als Material, sondern vielmehr als komplexe Infrastruktur verstanden wird. Im Anschluss daran deckt **Francesca Zanotto** die globalen Ausbeutungsverhältnisse und undurchsichtigen Praktiken im Holzhandel auf und zeigt, wie Architektur ihr Handlungsfeld erweitern und zu einem fairen Gebrauch von Holz als Naturressource beitragen kann. Welche Rolle dabei makroskopische Analysen von Holz spielen, erklären **Alan Crivellaro** und **Flavio Ruffinatto**, die durch die Betrachtung der Zellstruktur von kommerziellen Holzproben deren tatsächliche Art und Herkunft identifizieren können. Holz besitzt demzufolge spezifische Charakteristika, die es genau zu analysieren gilt, um unser gegenwärtig vorherrschendes, eindimensionales Materialverständnis von Holz zu überdenken. In diesem Sinne wünschen wir eine anregende Lektüre. ∎

Lehmann, it becomes clear how complex free-form timber projects, such as the new Swatch headquarters in Biel by Shigeru Ban, were developed and implemented with a special eye to materials. Based on a branchwork roof derived from the "ramified resource of the forest," **Jens Ludloff** illustrates how timber construction is capable of generating an innovative, sustainably experienceable spatial vocabulary—a design concept founded on the synergy between ecology, forestry, and the construction industry. Lastly, the visual essay by **Formafantasma** (**Andrea Trimarchi** & **Simone Farresin**) marks the transition to the third section of this issue of *GAM*, referencing the ecological and political responsibility inherent to an architectural handling of wood. In the scope of the comprehensive exhibition *Cambio*, their photographs tell of the complex material history of the 13 million trees toppled by the 2018 catastrophic storm in Italy's Fiemme Valley, and of the local citizens' efforts to process all of the wood.

The third part of *GAM.17* contains contributions that situate wood as a material in a broader nexus of relations among environmental protection, the timber industry, and chains of commerce. This section is opened by a series of photos by **Don Fuchs** portraying the destructive magnitude of the Gospers Mountain bushfire northwest of Sydney, Australia. At the same time, it impressively visualizes both the fragility and the regenerative power of timber. **Laila Seewang**, in turn, writes about the vital role that forests as an ecosystem can play in the context of architecture, localizing a so-called "timber territory" in the Northwest of the United States, where wood is not seen merely as a material but rather as a complex infrastructure. This is followed by a contribution by **Francesca Zanotto**, who exposes the conditions of exploitation and questionable practices in the global timber trade, thus showing how architecture is able to expand its field of activity and contribute to a fair use of wood as a natural resource. The importance of the macroscopic analysis of wood is explained by **Alan Crivellaro** and **Flavio Ruffinatto**, which is able to identify the actual type and origin of commercial timber samples by evaluating their cell structure. Wood possesses specific characteristics that, when precisely analyzed, encourage us to rethink our one-dimensional understanding of timber as a material as is currently prevalent today. With this in mind, we hope you will have an inspiring reading experience. ∎

Tom Kaden/Daniel Gethmann/Petra Eckhard

(Translation: Dawn Michelle d'Atri)

Material Culture

Wald und Holz.
Architektur(-theorie) zwischen romantisch-völkischer Verklärung und wissenschaftlicher (Klimaschutz-)Aufklärung

Forest and Wood:
Architecture (Theory) between Romantic, Populist Idealizing and Scientific (Climate Change) Enlightenment

Stephan Trüby

1   Martin Heideggers Hütte | Martin Heidegger's hut, Todtnauberg, Deutschland | Germany
© Muesse, Wikimedia Commons

Vom Geigenbau abgesehen, gibt es wohl keine Kulturtechnik, die – jedenfalls in den allermeisten Klimazonen – so abhängig ist von Wäldern, Bäumen und Holz wie die Architektur. Und doch steht nach einer rund zweitausendjährigen Geschichte der Architekturtheorie ein systematischerer Versuch noch aus, die Geschichte des Waldes auf die Geschichte der Architektur zu beziehen. Die folgenden Ausführungen mögen hierzu einen – natürlich höchst fragmentarischen – Anfang bilden. Gleichzeitig stellen sie vor dem Hintergrund verbreiteter nationalistischer Lesarten von Wäldern zumindest passagenweise eine vertiefende Analyse (der Entstehungsbedingungen) von „rechten Räumen" dar, die der Verfasser an anderer Stelle unternommen hat.[1] In diesem Zusammenhang sind insbesondere die Epoche der Romantik, die Heimatschutzbewegung sowie die Idee des einsamen Hauses bzw. der ländlichen Siedlung als Brückenköpfe einer völkisch inspirierten Besiedelungstaktik zu erwähnen. Ein bekannt gewordener Vorschlag Reyner Banhams sei an den Anfang der folgenden Zeilen gestellt. In seinem Buch *The Architecture of the Well-Tempered Environment* unterscheidet der britische Architekturhistoriker mithilfe einer Parabel zwei Formen der Raumbildung, nämlich die konstruktive und die energie-gestützte. Eines Abends, so Banham, kommt ein „wilder Stamm" an eine Lagerstätte, an der wie durch ein Wunder Bauholz liegt: „Es gibt zwei Möglichkeiten, mit dem Umwelt-Potential Holz umzugehen: Es könnte entweder zur Errichtung eines Wind- und Regenschutzes genutzt werden – die konstruktive Lösung – oder um ein Feuer zu machen – die energiegestützte Lösung."[2] Banhams Doppeloption ist, wie zu zeigen sein wird, jedoch zu erweitern: Holz durchkreuzt die Architekturgeschichte nicht nur in der gesägten Form von Halbzeugen und nicht nur in der brennenden Form von Wärme; Holz taucht bereits in der antiken Architekturtheorie als Metaphernlieferant auf – und in jüngerer Zeit auch als wachsender Baustoff in lebenden Häusern, und zwar mit einem ökologisch inspirierten Begleitsound, der allerdings in einem besonders prominenten Fall deutlich ins Rechtsesoterische spielt.

I. Die Geburt des aufklärerischen Vorbilds „Urhütte" aus dem Geiste der „Holznot". In der antiken Architekturtheorie, die bis auf wenige marginale Namen im Grunde vom römischen Autor Vitruv (81–15 v. Chr.) repräsentiert wird, spielen im Gegensatz zu silvanen (also waldbezogenen) eher arboreale (also baumbezogene) Überlegungen eine Rolle. Die frühesten Formen von Häusern sind bei Vitruv daher „Nachahmungen von Naturformen (Laubhütten, Schwalbennester, Höhlen) gewesen, da *die Menschen von Natur zur Nachahmung geneigt* seien".[3] Die Nachahmungstheorie Vitruvs ist jedoch nicht nur auf den Ursprung der Architektur bezogen, sie zeigt sich auch in seiner Interpretation des griechischen – und hier insbesondere des dorischen – Tempels, dessen Steindetails er in einer Art vorweggenommenen „Stoffwechseltheorie"[4] auf hölzerne Zimmermanndetails zurückführt. Silvane Schilderungen

2

Charles Eisen: *Die Allegorie der Architektur zeigt dem menschlichen Genius die Urhütte*, aus: | from: Marc-Antoine Laugier: *Essai sur l'Architecture*, 2. Aufl., Paris 1755.

tauchen in der römischen Antike insbesondere außerhalb der Architekturtheorie auf, und zwar vor allem in den Beschreibungen von germanischen Wäldern aus antiker mediterraner Perspektive bei Cäsar, Plinius (er berichtet in seinen ca. 77 n. Chr. verfassten *Naturalis historiae* von „hallenartigen Wäldern") oder in Tacitus' *Germania*.[5] Tacitus berichtet darüber hinaus in seinen *Annales* von der siegreichen Schlacht des Germanenführers Arminius (Hermann der Cherusker) gegen den römischen Feldherr Varus im Teutoburger Wald. Derlei übernahm der deutsche Humanist Conrad Celtis (1459–1508) für die Neuzeit und kontrastierte in Fortschreibung antiker Spekulationen eine „in der wilden Sumpf- und Waldnatur begründete germanische Sinnlichkeit" gegenüber „einer römischen Dekadenz und Luxussucht aus dem Geiste der imperialen Weltstadt".[6] Dass hiermit

1 Trüby, Stephan: *Rechte Räume. Politische Essays und Gespräche*, Basel 2020.

2 Banham, Reyner: *The Architecture of the Well-Tempered Environment*, Chicago 1984, 19. (Übers. S.T.)

3 Kruft, Hanno-Walter: *Geschichte der Architekturtheorie*, München ³1991, 23.

4 Dieser Begriff ist stark mit Gottfried Semper verknüpft.

5 Vgl. Zechner, Johannes: *Der deutsche Wald. Eine Ideengeschichte zwischen Poesie und Ideologie 1800–1945*, Darmstadt 2016, 16–18.

6 Zechner: *Der deutsche Wald* (wie Anm. 5), 19.

Apart from violin making, there is probably no other cultural technique—in most climate zones, at least—that is as dependent on forest, trees, and wood as architecture. But even after the roughly two millennia of the history of architectural theory, no one has yet made a systematic attempt to relate the history of the forest to the history of architecture. The discussions that follow offer a start—though of course a highly fragmentary one. At the same time, at least in passages, against the backdrop of widespread nationalist readings they offer a closer analysis (of the conditions for creating) "proper spaces" than the one the author attempted elsewhere.[1] In this context, the Romantic era, the *Heimatschutz* (homeland protection) movement, and the idea of the isolated house or rural settlement should be mentioned as the bridgeheads of a folk-inspired tactic for settlement. One proposal by Reyner Banham that has become famous should preface what follows. In his book *The Architecture of the Well-Tempered Environment*, the British architectural historian distinguishes, with the aid of a parable, two ways of creating space, namely, the structural one and the power-operated one. One evening, according to Banham, a "savage tribe" arrives at a campsite, at which, as if by some miracle, wood for construction is lying around: "Two basic methods of exploiting the environmental potential of that timber exist: either it may be used to construct a wind-break or rain-shed—the structural solution—or it may be used to build a fire—the power-operated solution."[2] Banham's dual option should, as we will see, be expanded: wood crisscrosses the history of architecture not only in its sawn form as a semifinished product and not only in its burning form for heat. Wood is already a source of metaphors in the architectural theory of antiquity—and more recently also as a growing construction material in living buildings, and indeed with an ecologically inspired accompaniment that in one particularly prominent case clearly tends to a right-wing esotericism.

I. The Birth of the Enlightenment Model of the "Primitive Hut" Out of the Spirit of the "Timber Shortage."

In the architectural theory of antiquity, which, apart from a few marginal names, is essentially represented by the Roman author Vitruvius (81–15 BC), sylvan (i.e., forest related) reflections play less of a role than arboreal (i.e., tree-related) reflections. The earliest forms of dwellings in Vitruvius are therefore

"imitations of natural formations (leaf huts, swallows' nests, caves), since 'men are by nature given to imitation and ready to learn.'"[3] Vitruvius' theory of imitation, however, does not simply relate to the origin of architecture but is also revealed in his interpretation of the Greek—and especially the Doric—temple, the details of whose stones he traces back to details of carpentry, in a kind of anticipation of "metabolism theory."[4] In Roman antiquity, sylvan descriptions occur above all outside of architectural theory and specially in descriptions of Germanic forests from the perspective of the ancient Mediterranean in the writings of Caesar, Pliny the Elder (who speaks of "hall-like forests" in his *Naturalis historia*, written around AD 77), and in Tacitus' *Germania*.[5] Tacitus reports in his *Annales* on the victorious battle of Arminius (also known as Hermann the Cheruscan), the leader of the Germanic Cherusci tribe, against the Roman general Varus in the Teutoburg Forest. The German humanist Conrad Celtis (1459–1508) adopted this in the modern era and, continuing ancient speculations, contrasted a "Germanic sensibility founded in the nature of swamps and forests" with "Roman decadence and addition to luxury from the spirit of the cosmopolitan city of the empire."[6] Johannes Zechner makes it clear in *Der deutsche Wald* that this established a relative rock bottom for a modern, reactionary mythologizing of the forest: "Soon after Celtis' death, his selective interpretations of *Germania* found their way into the humanist canon and their sylvan references continued to influence consciousness in many ways."[7]

Vitruvius' wooden primitive hut was first promoted from a distant anecdote to an eternally valid architectonic role model during the Enlightenment and specifically by the *Essai sur l'architecture*, first published anonymously in 1753 and then under the name of its author, Marc-Antoine Laugier (1713–1769). It also contains a description of the human being

---

1 Stephan Trüby, *Rechte Räume: Politische Essays und Gespräche* (Basel, 2020).

2 Reyner Banham, *The Architecture of the Well-Tempered Environment* (Chicago, 1984), 19.

3 Hanno-Walter Kruft, *A History of Architectural Theory: From Vitruvius to the Present*, trans. Ronald Taylor, Elsie Callander, and Antony Wood (New York, 1994), 23.

4 This concept is closely associated with Gottfried Semper.

5 See Johannes Zechner, *Der deutsche Wald: Eine Ideengeschichte zwischen Poesie und Ideologie, 1800–1945* (Darmstadt, 2016), 16–18.

6 Zechner, *Der deutsche Wald* (see note 5), 19.

7 Ibid.

auch ein relativer Nullpunkt für eine reaktionäre moderne Wald-mythisierung gelegt wurde, macht Johannes Zechner in *Der deutsche Wald* deutlich: „Schon bald nach Celtis' Tod fanden seine selektiven *Germania*-Interpretationen Aufnahme in den humanistischen Kanon und wirkten auch in ihren silvanen Bezügen vielfach bewusstseinsprägend weiter."[7]

Vitruvs hölzerne Urhütte wurde erst in der Aufklä-rung von einer fernen Anekdote zu einem ewig gültigen archi-tektonischen Vorbild befördert, und zwar mit dem zuerst 1753 anonym, 1755 dann unter dem Namen des Autors Marc-Antoine Laugier (1713–1769) veröffentlichten *Essai sur l'architecture*. Darin findet sich auch eine Beschreibung des Menschen „in seinem ursprünglichen Zustand", wie er Schutz sucht vor der Sonne, daraufhin in den Wald geht, dort von einem Regen überrascht wird und in eine Höhle flieht, diese aber aufgrund des Gestanks und der Dunkelheit schnell wieder verlässt[8] – um dann eine Urhütte zu bauen, die Laugier nicht nur detailliert schildert, sondern sie auf dem Frontispiz der zweiten Auflage auch mit einem berühmt gewordenen Stich von Charles Eisen illustriert (Abb. 2): „Einige im Wald abgeschlagene Äste sind das für seine [des urspünglichen Menschen, S.T.] Zwecke ge-eignete Material. Er wählt die vier stärksten aus, die er senk-recht, im Quadrat angeordnet, aufstellt. Er verbindet sie mit vier anderen, die er quer über sie legt. Darüber breitet er von zwei Seiten Äste, die sich schräg ansteigend in einem Punkt berühren. Diese Art Dach wird mit Blättern so dicht bedeckt, dass weder Sonne noch Regen eindringen können, und so hat der Mensch jetzt eine Unterkunft. Allerdings werden ihm in seinem nach allen Seiten offenen Haus Kälte und Hitze sehr unangenehm; er wird also den Raum zwischen den Pfeilern ausfüllen und auf diese Weise geschützt sein."[9] Diesen Ur-sprungsmythos erklärte Laugier zur fortdauernden Norm, wenn er schreibt: „Diese kleine, rustikale Hütte [...] war das Modell, von dem alle Herrlichkeit der Architektur ihren Aus-gang nahm."[10] Laugier, von Jean-Jacques Rousseau (1712–1787) beeinflusst, stellt nicht nur die Architektur als eine waldgebore-ne, der Urhütte nacheifernde Disziplin dar, auch den zeit-genössischen Städtebau will er auf die Vorbildhaftigkeit des Waldes verpflichten: „Man muss eine Stadt unter dem gleichen Gesichtspunkt sehen wie einen Wald. Die Strassen der ersteren sind die Schneisen des letzteren und müssen auf die gleiche Art angelegt werden."[11]

Wie konnte es im französischen Spätabsolutismus zu dieser bemerkenswerten Natur- und Waldverehrung kom-men, für die Laugier steht und die Charles François Ribart de Chamoust auf die Spitze trieb, und zwar mit seiner Darstellung einer französischen Ordnung, die aus eng nebeneinander ste-henden Dreiergruppen von Säulen nach dem Vorbild angeblich locker in Gruppen bepflanzter französischer Wälder besteht (Abb. 3)? Hanno-Walter Krufts Verweis auf den Einfluss des englischen Landschaftsgartens[12] ist berechtigt, greift aber zu kurz. Zentral erscheint ein Blick auf den ökonomischen Status quo des französischen Waldes im 18. Jahrhundert, der in den

rund 150 Jahren zwischen der Krönung Ludwigs XIV. 1643 und der Französischen Revolution 1789 signifikant an Fläche ein-büßte, obwohl absolutistische Politik – ab 1661 wurde die Wald-wirtschaft zentral vom Finanzminister Jean-Baptiste Colbert dirigiert – alles daran setze, das Gegenteil zu bewirken; vor allem um den Schiffsbau zu unterstützen, der für Masten und Schiffsrumpf viel Holz verschlang. So durften in privaten Wäl-dern Bäume nur noch alle zehn Jahre gefällt werden; so muss-ten Besitzer von Wäldern, die bis zu 50 Kilometer vom Meer oder bis zu vier Kilometer von einem Fluss entfernt waren, eine Genehmigung für den Holzverkauf besorgen. Vor dem Hinter-grund einer „Holznot" gewinnen die weithin unverstanden gebliebenen Laugier-Ausführungen Manfredo Tafuris, der die ideologische Hülle des Naturalismus mit den Widersprüchen des *Ancien régime* erklärt,[13] beträchtlich an Luzidität: „Genau in dem Moment, in dem die bürgerliche Ökonomie beginnt, ihre Handlungsprinzipien und Denkkategorien zu entdecken und zu begründen [...], wird die Krise der antiken ‚Wertesyste-me' durch neue Sublimationen überdeckt und diese durch den Appell an die Universalität der Natur künstlich objektiviert."[14]

II. „Vaterlandswälder": Zur deutschen Silvapolitik im 19. Jahrhundert. Die Einschreibung des Waldmotivs in eine national gewendete Architekturtheorie, die zuerst in Frankreich im Kontext der Aufklärung stattfand, erreichte den deutsch-sprachigen Raum mit etwas Verzögerung, und zwar in der Epoche der Romantik. Bemerkenswerterweise machten derlei silvane Motive um die Architektur einen größeren Bogen – trotz aller gotisierenden Tendenzen im 19. Jahrhundert. Zwar defi-nierte der wichtigste deutsche Architekt in der ersten Hälfte des 19. Jahrhunderts, Karl Friedrich Schinkel (1781–1841), die Ar-chitektur mit Blick auf die Gotik als „Fortsetzung der Natur in ihrer constructiven Thätigkeit",[15] doch bei derlei blieb es im Grunde. Ganz im Gegenteil zur deutschen Literatur. Dort er-schien nun – vermittelt durch Celtis und auch durch Bühnen-stücke wie Friedrich Gottlieb Klopstocks *Hermanns Schlacht*

7 Ebd.

8 Laugier, Marc-Antoine: *Das Manifest des Klassizismus*, Zürich/ München 1989, 33.

9 Ebd., 34.

10 Ebd.

11 Ebd., 176.

12 Vgl. Kruft: *Geschichte der Architekturtheorie* (wie Anm. 3), 172.

13 Vgl. Tafuri, Manfredo: *Kapitalismus und Architektur: Von Corbusiers „Utopia" zur Trabantenstadt*, Hamburg 1977, 16.

14 Ebd.

15 Karl Friedrich Schinkel zit. nach Kruft: *Geschichte der Architekturtheorie* (wie Anm. 3), 341.

TYPE DE L'ORDRE FRANÇOIS.

L'ORDRE FRANÇOIS DÉVELOPPÉ.

3

Aus | From: Hanno-Walter Kruft: *Geschichte der Architekturtheorie*, Tafel Nr. | Plate number: 96.

"in his first origin," going into the forest to seek protection from the sun, being surprised by rain there and fleeing into a cave but then quickly leaving again because of its stench and darkness[8]—only to build a primitive hut, which is not only described in detail by Laugier but also illustrated in an engraving by Charles Eisen for the frontispiece that has become famous (fig. 2): "Some branches broken down in the forest are the proper materials for his [the primitive man's, S.T.] design. He chooses four of the strongest, which he raises perpendicularly and which he disposes into square. Above he puts four others across, and upon these he raises some that incline from both sides. This kind of roof is covered with leaves put together, so that neither the sun nor the rain can penetrate therein; and now the man is lodge. Indeed cold and heat will make him sensible of their inconveniences in his house, open on every part; but then he will fill up between the space of the pillars, and will then find himself secure."[9] Laugier declares this origin myth to be an enduring norm when he writes: "This little rustic cabin […] is the model upon which all the magnificences of architecture have been imagined."[10] Laugier, influenced by Jean-Jacques Rousseau (1712–1787), not only presented architecture as a forest-born discipline emulating the primitive hut but also wanted to oblige contemporaneous urban planning to follow

the example of the forest: "We should look upon a city as a forest. The streets of this are the roads of that, and ought to be entered into in the same manner."[11]

How could late absolutism in France arrive at this remarkable reverence for nature and the forest for which Laugier stands and that Charles François Ribart de Chamoust took to the extreme in his description of a French order that consists of closely set groups of three columns supposedly based on the model of French forests planted in loose groups (fig. 3)? Hanno-Walter Kruft's reference to the influence of the English landscape garden is justified, but it is reductive.[12] It seems crucial to look at the economic status quo of the French forest in the eighteenth century, which in the roughly 150 years between the coronation of Louis XIV in 1643 and the French Revolution in 1789 had been significantly reduced in size, although absolutist policy—from 1661 onward, forestry was controlled centrally by the minister of finance, Jean-Baptiste Colbert—had done everything to prevent that, above all to protect shipbuilding, which consumed a great deal of wood for masts and hulls. In private forests, therefore, trees could only be felled every ten years; the owners of forests who were up to fifty kilometers from the sea or up to four kilometers from a river had to apply for permission to sell wood. Against the backdrop of a "timber shortage," Manfredo Tafuri's often-misunderstood discussion of Laugier, in which he described the ideological cover of naturalism in terms of the contradictions of the *ancien régime*,[13] become considerable more lucid: "in exactly the moment when bourgeois economy began to discover and invent its own categories of action and judgment, […] the crisis of the old system of values was immediately hidden by recourse to new sublimations, rendered artificially objective by means of the call to the universality of Nature."[14]

II. "Fatherland Forests": On German Sylvan Policy in the Nineteenth Century. The inscribing of the motif

8 Marc-Antoine Laugier, *An Essay on Architecture* (London, 1755), 9–10.

9 Ibid., 10–11.

10 Ibid., 11.

11 Ibid., 248.

12 See Kruft, *A History of Architectural Theory* (see note 3), 153.

13 See Manfredo Tafuri, *Architecture and Utopia: Design and Capitalist Development*, trans. Barbara Luigia La Penta (Cambridge, MA, 1976), 8.

14 Ibid., 7.

(1769)[16] – das von römischen Ethnografen initiierte derbe Porträt von Germanen, die in wilden Wäldern Bier trinkend dahinvegetieren, bei vielen Literaten als „positiv gewendete Eigensicht".[17] Aus der deutschsprachigen, romantisch inspirierten Literaturperspektive wurde der (französischen) Aufklärung zunehmend eine „Waldfeindlichkeit"[18] unterstellt; insbesondere die Auflösung des Heiligen Römischen Reiches Deutscher Nation 1806 und die weitgehende französische Kontrolle deutschsprachiger Territorien bis zu den antinapoleonischen Befreiungskriegen 1813–1815[19] ließen, so Zechner, eine zunehmend sich radikalisierende deutsche Romantik entstehen, die „Silvaimaginationen mit patriotischen und nationalen Bedeutungszuschreibungen" erzeugte, „die später zunehmend nationalistische, rassistische und antisemitische Argumentationsmuster beinhalteten".[20] Der Schriftsteller Ludwig Tieck (1773–1853), der in seinen Texten eine umfängliche „Poetisierung und partiell[e] Politisierung des deutschen Waldes"[21] betrieb, muss beispielsweise in diesem Zusammenhang erwähnt werden. In seinen Briefen und Tagebüchern finden sich diverse „antijüdische Auslassungen, beispielsweise eine Polemik gegen die Judenemanzipation oder die diffamierende Charakterisierung ‚der verliederlichte Heine, dieser Juden-Messias'".[22]

Vor allem aber dem deutschen Schriftsteller, Historiker und Abgeordneten der Frankfurter Nationalversammlung Ernst Moritz Arndt (1769–1860) kommt eine zentrale Rolle in der mentalen Konstituierung von nationalistisch und antisemitisch aufgeladenen deutschen „Vaterlandswäldern" zu. Geprägt von der taciteischen *Germania* sah Arndt in den Deutschen die „Enkeln der Germanen"[23] und appellierte an sein Publikum: „Leset Tacitus und Plinius und schämet euch! Eure Väter in den Tierfellen waren viel klügere Männer als ihr."[24] Für Arndt, so Zechner, „hatten die Römer ihre Gottesdienste in kalten steinernen ‚Mauern' gefeiert, während die Germanen ihren uralten Göttern ‚im Athem der Natur und im Dunkel der Haine' nahegekommen seien".[25] „Germaniens alte Freiheit", formulierte Arndt, sei „unter Bäumen geboren" worden, „wohingegen die ‚sogenannte französische Freiheit' als abstraktrationales Prinzip keinerlei Naturbezug aufweise".[26] Ohne wissenschaftliche Grundlage wies Arndt die Eiche als „rechte[n] teutsche[n] Baum" aus; es wüchsen „wohl in keinem Lande so viele Eichen als in Deutschland".[27] Für seine deutsche Gegenwart hoffte er auf umfängliche „Waldgebiete als nationalen Wurzelgrund, den es für den Erhalt des Volkes unbedingt zu verteidigen gelte".[28] Als größte Gefahr für Deutschland machte Arndt den „waldverwüstenden Fabrikanten" aus, ebenso „Juden und Judengenossen": In diesem klaren Feindbild der Naturgegnerschaft, schreibt Zechner, zeigt sich eine frühe Verbindung der Denkmuster von Judenfeindschaft und (Proto-)Kapitalismuskritik, wie sie in der Folge mehrfach aufgegriffen werden sollte.[29]

Auch der Arndt-Schüler Wilhelm Heinrich Riehl (1823–1897), einer der einflussreichsten deutschen Publizisten

in der zweiten Hälfte des 19. Jahrhunderts, sollte sich folgenträchtig in den Narrativen seines Lehrers bewegen. Auch Riehl sah „weiland das deutsche Volk aus seinen Wäldern"[30] treten und empfahl seinen Zeitgenossen, angesichts der liberalen Verfehlungen der vergangenen Jahrzehnte dem Gemeinwesen der „Bärenhäuter in den germanischen Urwäldern" wieder eine Vorbildfunktion für die politische Kultur der Zeit[31] zukommen zu lassen. Riehl: „Wir müssen den Wald erhalten, nicht bloß damit uns der Ofen im Winter nicht kalt werde, sondern auch damit die Pulse des Volkslebens warm und fröhlich weiter schlagen, damit Deutschland deutsch bleibe."[32] Vor allem in seiner vierbändigen *Naturgeschichte des Volkes* (1851–1869) erhob Riehl den Wald „zum Hauptkriterium deutscher kollektiver Identität und stellte ihn den vermeintlichen Nationalnaturen anderer Völker gegenüber".[33] Nicht nur auf silvaner, sondern auch auf arborealer Ebene zog er Differenzen insbesondere zwischen Deutschland und Frankreich, dem er eine „napoleonische Vorliebe für die Pappel" als Alleebaum vorwarf, in der der militaristische und zentralistische Charakter des Nachbarlandes zum Ausdruck komme.[34] Der „französischen" Pappel stellte er die Linde gegenüber, „die er den ‚volksthümlichsten deutschen Waldbaume' nannte und der Eiche klar vorzog – anders als etwa Klopstock, Arndt[35] und andere deutsche Publizisten des 19. Jahrhunderts. Nicht nur haltlose Kontrastierungen von Deutschen gegenüber Franzosen durchziehen Riehls Werk, auch zwischen Deutschen und Juden glaubte der Autor differenzieren zu müssen. Vor allem in seiner Schrift *Die deutsche Arbeit* (1861) „postulierte er einen grundlegenden

16 Vgl. Zechner: *Der deutsche Wald* (wie Anm. 5), 22.

17 Ebd., 21.

18 Ebd., 13.

19 Vgl. ebd.

20 Ebd., 12.

21 Ebd., 26.

22 Ebd., 30.

23 Zit. nach ebd., 72.

24 Ernst Moritz Arndt, zit. nach Zechner: *Der deutsche Wald*, (wie Anm. 5), 73.

25 Zechner: *Der deutsche Wald*, (wie Anm. 5), 80.

26 Ebd.

27 Zit. nach ebd., 74.

28 Ebd., 80.

29 Ebd.

30 Wilhelm Heinrich Riehl, zit. nach ebd., 120.

31 Ebd.

32 Zit. nach ebd., 117.

33 Ebd., 115.

34 Wilhelm Heinrich Riehl, zit. nach ebd., 116.

35 Ebd.

of the forest into a nationalistically inclined theory of architecture, which occurred first in France in the context of the Enlightenment, reached the German-speaking realm with some delay, namely, in the Romantic era. Remarkably, such sylvan motifs gave architecture a wide berth—despite all the Gothicizing tendencies of the nineteenth century. Although the most important German architect in the first half of the nineteenth century, Karl Friedrich Schinkel (1781–1841), defined architecture, with an eye to the Gothic, as the "extension of Nature in her constructive activity,"[15] it was essentially left at that. Quite the reverse was true of German literature. There, mediated by Celtis and also plays such as Friedrich Gottlieb Klopstock's *Hermanns Schlacht* (1769)[16]—which for many writers turned the Roman ethnographers' portrait of coarse Teutons vegetating away drinking beer in wild woods into a "self-image with a positive twist."[17] From the perspective of German-language, Romantically inspired literature, the (French) Enlightenment was increasingly accused of "hostility toward forests";[18] the breakup of the Holy Roman Empire in 1806 in particular and German-speaking territories largely under French control until the anti-Napoleonic wars of liberation in 1813–1815[19] caused, according to Zechner, an increasingly radicalizing German Romanticism that produced "sylvan imaginations with patriotic and national attributions of meaning" that "later increasingly contained nationalistic, racist, and anti-Semitic modes of argumentation."[20] The writer Ludwig Tieck (1773–1853), who pursued in his texts a wide-ranging "poeticization and partial politicization of the German forest,"[21] must be mentioned in this context, for example. His letters and diaries contain diverse "anti-Jewish remarks, for example, a polemic against the emancipation of the Jews and the defamatory characterization of 'the dissolute Heine, that Messiah of the Jews.'"[22]

It was, however, above all the German writer, historian, and member of the National Assembly in Frankfurt Ernst Moritz Arndt (1769–1860) who played a central role in the mental constitution of nationalistically and anti-Semitically charged "fatherland forests" of Germany. Influenced by Tacitus' *Germania*, Arndt saw the Germans as the "grandchildren of the Teutons"[23] and appealed to his audience: "Read Tacitus and Pliny and feel ashamed of yourselves! Your fathers in animal skins were much cleverer than you."[24] In Arndt's view, according to Zechner, "the Romans celebrated their religious services within cold, stone 'walls,' whereas the Germanic tribes came close to their ancient gods "in the open air of nature and in the darkness of meadows."[25] "Germania's old freedom," as Arndt

put it, was "born under trees," whereas "'so-called French liberty' turned out to be an abstract, rational principle with no connection to nature."[26] With no scientific basis, Arndt identified the oak as the "true German tree," of which he claimed "probably in no other country do as many oaks grow as in Germany."[27] For his own era in Germany, he hoped for extensive "forested regions as national rooting soil that absolutely must be defended for the preservation of the people."[28] Arndt identified as the greatest danger to Germany "manufacturers devastating the forests," as well as "Jews and the comrades of the Jews." This portrait of the enemy as opposed to nature, Zechner writes, reveals an early connection of the thought patterns of hostility to the Jews and the (proto-)critique of capitalism that would subsequently be adopted again and again.[29]

Arndt's student Wilhelm Heinrich Riehl (1823–1897), one of the most influential German journalists of the second half of the nineteenth century would also operate consequentially in the narratives of his teacher. Riehl, too, believed "the German people once emerged from its forests"[30] and recommended to his contemporaries, in light of the liberal transgressions of recent decades, to make the "bear skinners in the Germanic primal forests" once again the role model for the polity in the political culture of that era.[31] Riehl: "We have to preserve the forest, not simply so our stoves do not grow cold in winter but also so that the pulses of the life of the people continue to beat warmly and joyfully, so that Germany remains

15 Karl Friedrich Schinkel, quoted in Kruft, *A History of Architectural Theory* (see note 3), 298.

16 See Zechner, *Der deutsche Wald* (see note 5), 22.

17 Ibid., 21.

18 Ibid., 13.

19 See ibid.

20 Ibid., 12.

21 Ibid., 26.

22 Ibid., 30.

23 Quoted in ibid., 72.

24 Ernst Moritz Arndt, quoted in Zechner, *Der deutsche Wald*, (see note 5), 73.

25 Zechner, *Der deutsche Wald*, (see note 5), 80.

26 Ibid.

27 Quoted in ibid., 74.

28 Ibid., 80.

29 Ibid.

30 Wilhelm Heinrich Riehl, quoted in ibid., 120.

31 Ibid.

Gegensatz zwischen ‚semitischer und arischer Arbeitsehre', der sich durch den jeweiligen Volkscharakter ergebe. In Aufnahme älterer Stereotype unterschied er vor allem einen vermeintlich jüdischen ‚Mammonsgeist' und ‚Schacher' von einer ehrlichen deutschen Arbeit als Bauer oder Handwerker."[36] Es liegt auf der Hand, dass derlei Riehl während der Zeit der NS-Herrschaft retroaktiv „zum ‚Seher, Künder und […] Kenner deutschen Wesens'" empfahl.[37]

III. „Ewiger Wald – Ewiges Volk": Vom Heimatschutz zum Nationalsozialismus.

Eine nationalistische, rassistische und antisemitische Silvapolitik kam in die Architektur des 20. Jahrhunderts nicht über die deutsche Architekturtheorie des 19. Jahrhunderts, sondern über die sich gegen Ende des 19. Jahrhunderts formierende Heimatschutzbewegung, die erst im 20. Jahrhundert in architekturtheoretische Konzeptionen integriert wurde. In diesem Zusammenhang ist insbesondere Ernst Rudorff (1840–1916) zu erwähnen, der deutsche Komponist, Musikpädagoge und Naturschutz-Aktivist, der mit seinem Buch *Heimatschutz* (1897) der gleichnamigen Bewegung zu ihrem Kampfslogan verhalf. Darin deklamiert er etwa: „[…] der armselige Moorbauer, der raue, zähe Waldbauer, das sind die Männer der Zukunft."[38] Nicht zuletzt motiviert von den für ihn offenbar recht traumatischen Verkoppelungen in den Dörfern seiner Jugend, verschrieb er sich der Anpflanzung von Waldrändern, Hecken und Galeriewäldern. Auch wehrte er sich gegen Abholzungen und rettet so beispielsweise eine Eichenallee hinter der Knabenburg im Weserland. „Mit seiner Publizistik", scheibt Zechner, „kritisierte Rudorff in scharfen Worten die nutzenorientierte Forstwirtschaft der Monokulturen und warnte in sexualisiertem Vokabular vor ‚Prostituierung', ‚Schändung' und ‚Vergewaltigung' einer feminin imaginierten Gesamtnatur".[39] Auch beteiligte er sich „am Kampf gegen naturnah aufgestellte Reklametafeln, in dem sich kapitalismuskritische oft mit antiamerikanischen und judenfeindlichen Denkmustern verbanden".[40] Zechner weiter: „Bei Rudorff zeigt sich damit zeitbedingt eine durchgängige Aktualisierung und rhetorische Radikalisierung älterer silvapolitischer Vorstellungen unter den gewandelten Umständen der Jahrhundertwende."[41] Im Jahre 1904 gründete er den Deutschen Bund Heimatschutz.[42] Dass auch Frauen und Juden den Gründungsaufruf unterzeichnen konnten, wusste Rudorff zeitlebens zu verhindern.

Was sich bereits im 19. Jahrhundert bei Tieck, Arndt, Riehl und vor allem Rudorff ankündigte, brach zunächst in der Weimarer Republik und dann im Nationalsozialismus vollends durch: „Vorrangiges Feindbild waren nicht mehr […] die europäischen Konkurrenznationen, sondern resultierend aus einer Umkehrung des Barbarenstereotyps die vermeintlich nomadisch-naturfernen Juden und Slawen."[43] Insbesondere Alfred Rosenberg (1892–1946), der Chefideologe der NSDAP, betrieb mit seiner „Amt Rosenberg" genannten Dienststelle für NS-Kulturpolitik die Differenz eines „deutschen Waldvolkes" von einem „slawischen Steppenvolk" und einem „jüdischen Wüsten-

4

„Ewiger Wald" (Eternal Forest), Berlin 1936. Regie | Directed by: Hanns Springer/Rolf von Sonjevski-Jamrowski; Montage: Stephan Trüby.

volk".[44] Die Geschichtsauffassungen Rosenbergs liegen beispielhaft in dem Film „Ewiger Wald" (1936) vor, einer esoterischen „silvapolitische[n] Interpretation und Inszenierung der gesamten germanisch-deutschen Geschichte".[45] Bereits zum Einstieg wird eine vermeintliche Nationalgeschichte der Deutschen mit Waldgeschichte parallelisiert: „Ewiger Wald – Ewiges Volk. Es lebt der Baum wie du und ich, er strebt zum Raum wie du und

36 Ebd., 111f.

37 Ebd., 107.

38 Rudorff, Ernst: *Heimatschutz*, St. Goar 1994, 48.

39 Zechner: *Der deutsche Wald*, (wie Anm. 5), 133.

40 Ebd.

41 Ebd.

42 Der Deutsche Bund Heimatschutz ist im noch heute existierenden Bund Heimat und Umwelt in Deutschland (BHU) mit Sitz in Bonn aufgegangen.

43 Zechner, *Der deutsche Wald*, (wie Anm. 5), 158.

44 Ebd., 191.

45 Ebd., 188.

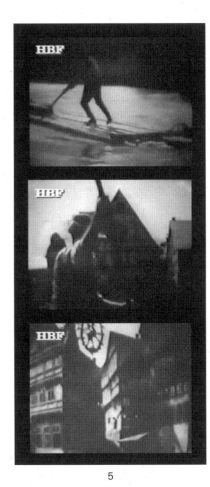

5

„Ewiger Wald" (Eternal Forest), Berlin 1936. Regie | Directed by:
Hanns Springer/Rolf von Sonjevski-Jamrowski; Montage: Stephan Trüby.

German."[32] Above all in his four-volume *Naturgeschichte des Volkes* (1851–69), Riehl emphasized the forest "as the main criterion of German collective identity and contrasted it with the supposed national natures of other peoples."[33] He made distinctions not just on the sylvan plane but also on the arboreal one, especially between Germany and France, which he accused of a "Napoleonic penchant for the poplar" to line boulevards, thereby expressing the militaristic and centralist character of the neighboring country.[34] He contrasted the "French" poplar with the linden, "which he called the 'the tree in the German forest closest to the people' and clearly preferred the oak—in contrast to, say Klopstock, Arndt,"[35] and other German writers of the nineteenth century. Not only do untenable contrasts between the German and the French run through Riehl's work, but the author also believed it necessary to differentiate between the Germans and the Jews. Above all in his book *Die deutsche Arbeit* (1861), "he postulated a fundamental contrast between the 'Semitic and Aryan honoring of work' that supposedly resulted from the national character

of each. Adopting older stereotypes, he distinguished above all a supposedly Jewish 'spirit of Mammon' and 'hagglers' from honest German work as farmers or craftsman."[36] It was only natural that under National Socialist rule Riehl was retroactively promoted as the "visionary, herald, and […] connoisseur of the German essence."[37]

III. "Eternal Forest, Eternal People": From *Heimatschutz* to National Socialism. A nationalistic, racist, and anti-Semitic sylvan policy influencing the architecture of the twentieth century came not only from the nineteenth-century German architectural theory but also from the Heimatschutz movement, which formed in the late nineteenth century but was not integrated into conceptions of architectural theory until the twentieth century. The German composer, music teacher, and nature conservation activist Ernst Rudorff (1840–1916) is particularly noteworthy in that context; his book *Heimatschutz* (1897) helped provide a battle cry for the eponymous movement. In it he declaimed, for example, that "the impoverished moorland farmer, the raw, tough forest farmer, are the men of the future."[38] Motivated not least by couplings in the villages of his youth that were obviously traumatic for him, he espoused the planting of forest borders, hedges, and riparian forests. He also combated deforestation; for example, he saved an oak-lined boulevard behind the Knabenburg in the Weser region. "In his writings," Zechner writes, "Rudorff criticized in harsh words the use-oriented forestry of monocultures and warned in sexualized vocabulary of the 'prostituting,' 'violation,' and 'rape' of Nature in general, which was imagined to be feminine."[39] He too participated "in the battle against billboards erected near nature, in which ideas critical of capitalism were often combined with anti-American and anti-Jewish ways of thinking."[40] Zechner continues: "Rudorff's writings thus reflect a thorough updating

32 Quoted in ibid., 117.

33 Ibid., 115.

34 Wilhelm Heinrich Riehl, quoted in ibid., 116.

35 Ibid.

36 Ibid., 111–112.

37 Ibid., 107.

38 Ernst Rudorff, *Heimatschutz* (St. Goar, 1994), 48.

39 Zechner, *Der deutsche Wald* (see note 5), 133.

40 Ibid.

ich. Sein ‚Stirb und Werde' webt die Zeit, Volk steht wie Wald in Ewigkeit."[46] Auch das von Rosenberg häufig verwendete Denkbild des „Waldes als Dom" (Abb. 4) taucht in den dem Mittelalter gewidmeten Passagen des Filmes auf: „Du warst, Wald, in Ahnentagen Vorbild hoher Meisterschaft für die Dome, die da ragen hoch wie deiner Stämme Macht."[47] Auch eine knappe Würdigung von Kulturtechniken wie der Holzschnitzerei und dem Fachwerkbau fehlt nicht, denn aus ihnen „grüßt und spricht der Wald als deutsches Angesicht" (Abb. 5).[48] Der Film „Ewiger Wald", fasst Zechner zusammen, „konstruierte […] nicht nur eine historische Parallele zwischen Wald und Volk durch die Jahrtausende germanisch-deutscher Geschichte. In der epochenübergreifenden Engführung von Baum und Mensch war der Film ebenso ein expliziter silvapolitischer Aufruf, eine überlegene Ordnung der Waldgemeinschaft zu derjenigen der Volksgemeinschaft zu erklären."[49]

Selbstverständlich betrieb die nationalsozialistische Silvapolitik nicht nur Volksmythologisierungen, sondern auch und vor allem konkret geplante, teilweise auch umgesetzte Anpflanzungs-Strategien. So wurde es ab 1933 unter linientreuen Förstern Mode, Hakenkreuzwälder anzulegen (Abb. 6). Kurz darauf wurden in Deutschland immer häufiger Wald-Betretungsverbote für Juden und Jüdinnen ausgesprochen (Abb. 7). Ab 1941 verfolgte das NS-Reichsforstamt unter der Leitung des „Reichsforstmeisters" Hermann Göring im Rahmen der „Blut und Boden"-Politik in Osteuropa das megalomane Projekt einer „der deutschen Seele wesensgemäß[en][50] „Wiederbewaldung des Ostens",[51] von der aufgrund des Kriegsverlaufes statt der geplanten 2,7 Millionen Hektar immerhin 7.000 Hektar aufgeforstet wurden.[52] Bereits 1940 war in diesem Zusammenhang der Münchner Architekt Alwin Seifert (1890–1972) zum „Reichslandschaftsanwalt" ernannt worden. In dieser Beraterfunktion wirkte er nicht nur bei der landschaftsdramaturgischen Absteckung von Autobahntrassen mit, er entwickelte auch Überlegungen, wie der von der Wehrmacht eroberte „Lebensraum im Osten" mit seinen als „undeutsch" empfundenen Steppenlandschaften durch entsprechende Pflanzungen „eingedeutscht" werden könnte. Nach dem Zweiten Weltkrieg als „unbelastet" eingestuft, machte Seifert in der Bundesrepublik Deutschland Karriere nicht nur als Professor für Landschaftspflege, Landschaftsgestaltung sowie Straßen- und Wasserbau an der TH München, sondern auch als Kompostierapostel: Sein erstmals 1967 publiziertes Buch *Gärtnern ohne Gift*[53] wurde ein großer Erfolg in der deutschen grün-ökologischen Bewegung – mit Neuauflagen bis heute. Die ersten Kompostierexperimente hatte Seifert wahrscheinlich in der anthroposophisch beeinflussten Heilkräuterplantage des KZ Dachau betrieben, auf der KZ-Häftlinge Zwangsarbeit verrichten mussten.[54]

IV. „Waldsterben", 1980ff: Deutsche Heimatschutzbewegungen, neue Folge. Die mit dem Nationalsozialismus recht kompatible Heimatschutzbewegung des ausgehenden 19. und frühen 20. Jahrhunderts endete nicht mit dem Ende des

6

Hakenkreuzwald nahe Zernikow, Aufnahme von 1965 | Trees form a swastika in a German forest near Zernikow, photograph taken in 1965, Datengrundlage | data basis: Hessische Verwaltung für Bodenmanagement und Geoinformation.

Nationalsozialismus 1945 – im Gegenteil. Auch und gerade die frühe Geschichte der deutschen Partei Die Grünen zeigt, dass zwischen Heimat- und Umweltschutz zuweilen ein schmaler Grat liegen kann. Gegründet in Karlsruhe im Jahre 1980 – also in dem Jahr, in dem das Thema „Waldsterben" erstmals von einer breiten Öffentlichkeit als ultimative Bedrohung wahrgenommen wurde – waren die ersten Monate und Jahre der Grünen von scharfen Auseinandersetzungen zwischen dem linken und rechten Flügel der Partei gekennzeichnet. Zu Letzterem zählte etwa Baldur Springmann (1912–2003), ein Ökobauer, Publizist sowie ehemaliges Mitglied der SA, SS und NSDAP, der später Mitglied der ersten Stunde bei den Grünen wurde – die er allerdings noch im Gründungsjahr aufgrund massiver Gegenproteste verließ. Kurz darauf – im Jahre 1982 – veröffentlichte er seinen Bestseller *Partner Erde. Einsichten eines Öko-*

46 Zit. nach ebd.

47 Zit. nach ebd., 189.

48 Zit. nach ebd.

49 Ebd., S. 191.

50 Vgl. ebd., 177f.

51 Vgl. ebd., 176.

52 Vgl. ebd.

53 Seifert, Alwin: *Gärtnern ohne Gift. Eine Fibel für Gartenfreunde und Bauern*, München 1967. Das Buch wurde 1971 neu aufgelegt unter dem Titel *Gärtnern, Ackern – ohne Gift*.

54 Vgl. Radkau, Joachim/Uekötter, Frank (Hg.): *Naturschutz und Nationalsozialismus*, Frankfurt am Main 2003, 276, 297 bzw. 304.

and rhetorical radicalizing of older ideas of sylvan policy that was characteristic of the time under the changed circumstances of the turn of the century."[41] In 1904, he founded the Deutscher Bund Heimatschutz (German Association of Homeland Protection).[42] Throughout his lifetime, Rudorff managed to prevent women and Jews from signing its founding appeal.

What had been heralded already in the nineteenth century in the writings of Tieck, Arndt, Riehl, and above all Rudorff had its total breakthrough first during the Weimar Republic and then under National Socialism: "The dominant picture of the enemy was no longer [...] that of competing European nations but rather, in an inversion of the stereotype of the barbarian, the Jews and Slavs, who were said to be nomadic and remote from nature."[43] In particular, Alfred Rosenberg (1892–1946), the head ideologue of the National Socialist Party, advocated at his department of National Socialist cultural policy, known as the "Rosenberg Office," distinguishing a "German people of the forest" from a "Slavic people of the steppes" and a "Jewish people of the desert."[44] Rosenberg's views of history are exemplarily presented in the film "Ewiger Wald" (1936), an esoteric "sylvan-policy interpretation and dramatization of the whole of Germanic and German history."[45] Already in the opening, parallels are drawn between a supposed national history of the German and the history of the forest: "Eternal forest, eternal people. The tree lives, like you and me; it strives toward space, like you and me. Its 'Die and Become' is woven by time; the people stand, like the forest, for ever and ever."[46] Rosenberg's frequently employed image of the "forest as cathedral" (fig. 4) also appears in the film in the sequences devoted to the Middle Ages: "You, forest, in the days of our forefathers were the model for the great master of the cathedrals, which loom high there like the power of your branches."[47] Nor did it fail to pay brief tribute to such cultural techniques as wood carving and the half-timber construction, since in them "the forest greets and speaks as a German visage" (fig. 5).[48] The film "Ewiger Wald," as Zechner summarizes it, "did not just construct [...] a historical parallel between forest and people through millennia of Germanic-German history. By bringing together tree and human being over centuries, the film represented an explicit appeal for a sylvan policy that declared the order of the community of the forest to be superior to that of the community of the people."[49]

National Socialist sylvan policy did, of course, leave it at mythologizing the German people but also pursued, specifically planned, and in part implemented strategies of planting.

From 1933 onward, for example, it became fashionable among foresters faithful to the Nazi party to plant forests in the form of a swastika (fig. 6). Soon thereafter, more and more bans were passed to prevent Jews from entering the forest (fig. 7). From 1941 onward, the National Socialist Reichsforstamt (Reich Department of Forestry), under the direction of "Reichsforstmeister" (Reich Forest Master) Hermann Göring, pursued, as part of Blood and Soil policies in Eastern Europe, the megalomaniacal project, "in keeping with the essence of the German soul,"[50] a "reforesting of the East,"[51] which owing to the course of the war only managed to plant 7,000 hectares of a planned 2,7 million hectares.[52] In that context, the Munich Alwin Seifert (1890–1972) had been appointed Reichslandschaftsanwalt (Reich Landscape Advocate) in 1940. In this advisory capacity, he not only contributed to lining autobahns with dramatic landscapes but also developed ideas for how the "Lebensraum in the East" that had been conquered by the German army, which was perceived as "un-German" steppe landscapes, could be "Germanized" by appropriate planting. Declared "exonerated" in the denazification program after World War II, Seifert not only had a career as a professor of landscape conservation, landscape design, and street and waterways construction at the Technische Hochschule München but also became an apostle of composting: His book *Gärtnern ohne Gift* (Gardening without Poison),[53] first published in 1967, was a great success with the German ecology movement and remains in print today. Seifert probably conducted his first experiments with composting at the anthroposophy-influenced

41 Ibid.

42 The Deutscher Bund Heimatschutz became what is now the Bund Heimat und Umwelt in Deutschland (BHU) with headquarters in Bonn.

43 Zechner, *Der deutsche Wald*, (see note 5), 158.

44 Ibid., 191.

45 Ibid., 188.

46 Quoted in ibid.

47 Quoted in ibid., 189.

48 Quoted in ibid.

49 Ibid., 191.

50 See ibid., 177–178.

51 See ibid., 176.

52 See ibid.

53 Alwin Seifert, *Gärtnern ohne Gift: Eine Fibel für Gartenfreunde und Bauern* (Munich, 1967). The book was reissued in 1971 under the title *Gärtnern, Ackern—ohne Gift*.

7

„Juden in Wäldern nicht erwünscht" aus | from: Zechner, Johannes:
Der deutsche Wald, Darmstadt 2016, 161.

Bauern im rechtsextremen Arndt Verlag. Dem rechten Partei-flügel der frühen Grünen war auch Herbert Gruhl (1921–1993) hinzuzurechnen, der 1978 seine ursprüngliche politische Heimat, die CDU, lautstark verließ – befremdet von der dort propagierten Wachstumspolitik. Im selben Jahr gründete er die Grüne Aktion Zukunft (GAZ), die 1980 in den Grünen aufging. Gruhls rechte Taktung wird bereits in seinem 1975 erschienen Bestseller *Ein Planet wird geplündert – Die Schreckensbilanz unserer Politik*[55] deutlich, in dem er die Einwanderungspolitik der „europäischen Völker" eine „sagenhafte Dummheit"[56] nennt. In seinem letzten, kurz vor seinem Tod erschienenen Buch *Himmelfahrt ins Nichts. Der geplünderte Planet vor dem Ende* (1993)[57] warnt Gruhl gar davor, „viele Kulturen in einem Raum [zusammenzumixen]", denn der Wert des Gemisches sinke „mit zunehmender Durchmischung".[58] Gruhl hatte die Grünen 1982 wieder verlassen und gründete im selben Jahr die noch heute als Kleinpartei existierende Ökologisch-Demokratische Partei (ÖDP) – unter Beteiligung von Springmann. Mit Blick auf Gruhl, Springmann und andere[59] schreibt Jutta Ditfurth in ihrem Buch *Entspannt in die Barbarei* (1996), dass derlei „Ökofaschisten" nur deshalb aus den Grünen hinaus gedrängt werden konnten, weil sich der linke Parteiflügel, der später seinerseits von den sogenannten „Realos" marginalisiert werden sollte, erfolgreich zu wehren verstand: „Auf diese Weise konnte die drohende Besetzung der Ökologie von rechts und ihre gesellschaftliche Wirkung als modernisierte Blut-und-Boden-Variante in und mit einer erfolgreichen grünen Partei vorläufig verhindert werden."[60]

Der linken politischen Umdeutung von Heimatschutzthemen zu antinationalistisch konnotierten Umweltschutzthemen kann auf akademischer Ebene der Versuch gegenübergestellt werden, rechte Themen gleichsam von links zu besetzen. Dies kann für den deutschsprachigen Architekturdiskurs

vor allem mit einer kurzen Phase der Zeitschrift *ARCH+* deutlich gemacht werden, die ab Ende der 1970er-Jahre den Ökologiediskurs entdeckte und im Zuge dessen mit diversen Beiträgen die Geschichte des Heimatschutzes, aber auch die der Stuttgarter Schule um Paul Schmitthenner und Paul Bonatz sowie Figuren wie Hugo Kükelhaus beleuchtete. In diesem Zusammenhang erschien 1985 in der *ARCH+* 81 „Vom landschaftsgebundenen zum ökologischen Bauen"[61] ein Aufsatz von Rolf Peter Sieferle mit dem Titel „Heimatschutz und das Ende der Utopie". Darin finden sich neben einer Apologie von Ernst Rudorff auch Sätze wie „Die Heimat ist von der modernen Gleichschaltung bedroht."[62] Derlei kulminiert im Aufruf zur Wiederentdeckung der Buchreihe *Kulturarbeiten* (1901–1917) des Architekten, Heimatschutz-Propagandisten und NSDAP-Politikers Paul Schultze-Naumburg (1869–1949): „Der Vorwurf ist absurd, solches habe ‚schon einmal' zum Nationalsozialismus geführt. Die Geschichte wiederholt sich nicht und schon gar nicht in gleichen Konstellationen. Nur weil Schultze-Naumburg für das ‚Deutsche Haus' plädiert hat, soll man für alle Zeiten so bauen wie in den fünfziger Jahren?"[63] Ungefähr zur gleichen Zeit führte Sieferle mit dem Historiker Joachim Radkau und anderen eine emotionale „Holznot-Debatte"[64], in der es um die wissenschaftliche Frage ging, ob es überhaupt eine für alle Bevölkerungsschichten gleichermaßen dramatische Holznot im Europa des 17. und 18. Jahrhunderts gab, die mit der Ölkrise der Gegenwart parallelisiert werden könnte. Die Rechtswende des Karl-Marx-Experten und ehemaligen SDS'lers Sieferle begann also nicht erst, wie gemeinhin angenommen, nach der Wiedervereinigung mit dem Buch *Epochenwechsel. Die Deutschen an der Schwelle zum 21. Jahrhundert* (1994), sondern mindestens rund zehn Jahre früher, nicht zuletzt mit seiner Verteidigung des Heimatschutz-Gedankens in der *ARCH+*.

55 Gruhl, Herbert: *Ein Planet wird geplündert – Die Schreckensbilanz unserer Politik*, Frankfurt am Main 1975.

56 Ebd.

57 Gruhl, Herbert: *Himmelfahrt ins Nichts. Der geplünderte Planet vor dem Ende*, München 1992.

58 Ebd.

59 Rudolf Bahro (1935–1997) etwa.

60 Ditfurth, Jutta: *Entspannt in die Barbarei. Esoterik, (Öko-) Faschismus und Biozentrismus*, Hamburg ²1997, 99.

61 Sieferle, Rolf Peter: „Heimatschutz und das Ende der Utopie", *ARCH+* 81 „Vom landschaftsgebundenen zum ökologischen Bauen" (1985), 38–42.

62 Ebd., 38.

63 Ebd., 42.

64 Vgl. dazu die Debattenbeiträge beispielsweise von Joachim Radkau („Holzverknappung und Krisenbewußtsein im 18. Jahrhundert", *Geschichte und Gesellschaft. Zeitschrift für historische Sozialwissenschaft* 9 (1983), 513–543) oder Rolf Peter Sieferle (*Der unterirdische Wald. Energiekrise und industrielle Revolution*, München 1982).

herbal medicine plantation at the Dachau concentration camp, which employed inmates as forced laborers.[54]

IV. "Forest Dieback" since 1980: German Homeland Protection Movements, New Series. The Heimatschutz of the late nineteenth and early twentieth centuries, which was quite compatible with National Socialism, did not end in 1945 when the latter did—on the contrary. The early history of the German political party Die Grünen (The Greens) also demonstrates, and particularly well, that sometimes the line between homeland protection and environmentalism can be quite thin. Founded in Karlsruhe in 1980—the year in which the theme of *Waldsterben* (forest dieback) was first perceived by a broad audience as a grave threat—the first months and years of the Greens were characterized by acrid debates between the party's left and right wings. One member of the latter, Baldur Springmann (1912–2003)—an organic farmer, writer, and former SA, SS, and Nazi Party member who then became a founding member of the Greens—though he left within its first year in the face of massive counterprotests—published his bestseller *Partner Erde: Einsichten eines Öko-Bauern* (Partner Earth: Views of an Organic Farmer) with the right-wing-extremist Arndt publishing house. Another member of the right wing of the early Greens was Herbert Gruhl (1921–1993), who in 1978 loudly left his original political home, the Christlich Demokratische Union Deutschlands (CDU; Christian Democratic Union of Germany), in 1978, having been alienated by the policies of growth it advocated. That same year, he founded the Grüne Aktion Zukunft (GAZ), which merged with the Green Party in 1980. Gruhl's rightist leanings are already clear in his bestseller *Ein Planet wird geplündert: Die Schreckensbilanz unserer Politik* (A Planet Is Plundered: An Accounting of the Horrors of Our Policy),[55] published in 1975, in which he refers to the immigrations policies of the "European nations" as "incredible stupidity."[56] In his final book, published shortly before his death, *Himmelfahrt ins Nichts: Der geplünderte Planet vor dem Ende* (Ascension into the Void: The Plundered Planet at an End) (1993),[57] Gruhl even warns against "many cultures [mixing] in one space," since the value of the mixture declines "with increasing mixing."[58] Gruhl had left the Greens in 1982 and founded that same year, with Springmann's participation, the Ökologisch-Demokratische Partei (ÖDP), which still exists as a small party. With Gruhl, Springmann, and others in mind,[59] Jutta Ditfurth writes in her 1996 book *Entspannt in die Barbarei* (Relaxed into Barbarism) that such "eco fascists" were forced out of the Green Party only because its left wing, which would itself later be marginalized by the so-called Realos (realists), was able to defend itself successfully: "In this way, the threat that ecology would be taken over by the right and its social effect as a modernized variation on Blood and Soil ideology could be blocked for a time by a successful Green Party."[60]

The leftist political reinterpretation of the themes of the Heimatschutz movement as environmental themes with antinationalistic connotations can be compared with the effort on the academic plane to co-opt right-wing themes from the left. In the case of the German-language discourse on architecture, that can be illustrated particularly well using the example of a brief phase in the history of the journal *ARCH+*, which from the later 1970s onward discovered the ecology discourse and in the wake of that published various articles shedding light on the history of the Heimatschutz movement but also that of the Stuttgart school around Paul Schmitthenner and Paul Bonatz and figures such as Hugo Kükelhaus. In that context, *ARCH+*, no. 81, a special issue in 1985 titled "Vom landschaftsgebundenen zum ökologischen Bauen" (From Landscape-Oriented to Ecological Building), published an essay by Rolf Peter Sieferle titled "Heimatschutz und das Ende der Utopie" (Homeland Protection and the End of Utopia).[61] It includes not only an apologia for Ernst Rudorff but also such sentences as "Homeland is threatened by the modern Gleichschaltung."[62] All this culminated in a call to rediscover the *Kulturarbeiten* (Cultural Works) book series (1901–1917) by the architect, Heimatschutz propagandist, and Nazi politician Paul Schultze-Naumburg (1869–1949): "It is an absurd reproach that such things have 'already once' led to National Socialism. History does not repeat itself and certainly not in the same constellations. Just because Schultze-Naumburg argued for the 'German house,' do we have to keep

---

54 See Joachim Radkau and Frank Uekötter, eds., *Naturschutz und Nationalsozialismus* (Frankfurt am Main, 2003), 276, 297, and 304.

55 Herbert Gruhl, *Ein Planet wird geplündert: Die Schreckensbilanz unserer Politik* (Frankfurt am Main, 1975).

56 Ibid.

57 Herbert Gruhl, *Himmelfahrt ins Nichts: Der geplünderte Planet vor dem Ende* (Munich, 1992).

58 Ibid.

59 Rudolf Bahro (1935–1997), for example.

60 Jutta Ditfurth, *Entspannt in die Barbarei: Esoterik, (Öko-) Faschismus und Biozentrismus* (Hamburg, 1997), 99.

61 Rolf Peter Sieferle, "Heimatschutz und das Ende der Utopie," in "Vom landschaftsgebundenen zum ökologischen Bauen," special issue, *ARCH+* 81 (1985): 38–42.

62 Ibid., 38.

In jüngerer Zeit finden sich im deutschsprachigen Raum diverse Versuche, an die verschiedenen Heimatschutzbewegungen des 20. Jahrhunderts anzuknüpfen, insbesondere jenseits der Architekturwelt im engeren Sinne. So ist in diesem Zusammenhang die zwischen 2007 bis 2019 erschienene Zeitschrift *Umwelt & Aktiv* zu erwähnen, die vom NPD-nahen Traunsteiner Verein Midgard e.V. herausgegeben wurde und neonazistischen AutorInnen aus dem Umfeld der Partei Der III. Weg eine Plattform bot. Der Untertitel der Zeitschrift lautete zunächst *Zeitschrift für gesamtheitliches Denken: Umweltschutz – Tierschutz – Heimatschutz*; später wurde aus „Umweltschutz" dann „Naturschutz". Das völkische Magazin versteht sich als Kampfansage gegen die Grünen, denen ökologischer „Verrat" vorgeworfen wird. In der Ausgabe 3/2017, die mit dem Aufmacher „Das große Sterben in Feld und Flur" aufwartet, findet sich in direkter Anknüpfung an nationalsozialistische Heimatschutzbestrebungen eine Würdigung des von den „Siegermächten zum Tode verurteilte[n] Hermann Göring", der sich als „Minister für Forst und Jagd" durch eine „starke innere Naturverbundenheit" sowie als „Treuhänder des deutschen Waldes und Schützer herrlicher Naturdenkmäler" ausgezeichnet habe.[65] In dem Heft finden sich auch Aufsätze mit Titeln wie „Ewiger Wald und ewiges Volk" oder „Wie die Migration unser Land auffrißt". Seit 2020 gibt es einen Nachfolger von *Umwelt & Aktiv: Die Kehre – Zeitschrift für Naturschutz*. Herausgegeben von dem Identitären Jonas Schick lässt sich das Blatt und der begleitende Blog dem extrem rechten Umfeld des Instituts für Staatspolitik (IfS) in Schnellroda und dem Verein „Ein Prozent" verorten. Der Magazinname ist dem Buch *Die Technik und die Kehre* (1962) von Martin Heidegger entliehen, in dem der antisemitische Philosoph, eine „Kehre" am Horizont ersehend, die moderne Technik als unabweisbare Gefahr ausweist. Vor diesem Hintergrund will *Die Kehre* laut Eigenbeschreibung „Ökologie aus ganzheitlicher Perspektive betrachten", um „der aktuell stattfindenden Verengung auf den ‚Klimaschutz'" entgegenzuwirken; eine „Lehre von der gesamten Umwelt" müsse „Kulturlandschaften, Riten und Brauchtum, also auch Haus und Hof" mit einschließen.[66] Zu dem Kreis potenzieller LeserInnen dieser Zeitschrift dürfte auch Alina Wychera gehören, eine Aktivistin der Identitären Bewegung, die unter dem Namen „Alina von Rauheneck" eine Zeit lang eine viel beachtete Tumblr-Seite betrieb, auf der sie sich mit selbst geschossenen und mit einem Sepia-Tool bearbeiten Fotos als „Tochter des Waldes" stilisierte.[67]

V. Naturbauten für Familienlandsitze: Der Fall Konstantin Kirsch.
Doch auch auf dem Feld der Architektur – gar auf dem Feld der *experimentellen* Architektur – gibt es Versuche, den Hausbau an das rechtsökologische Projekt einer romantischen Baum- und Waldverbundenheit von Menschengruppen zu binden. Hier ist vor allem der bekannte Architekt Konstantin Kirsch zu erwähnen, der sich mit diversen Naturbauten und nicht zuletzt auch seinem Buch *Naturbauten aus*

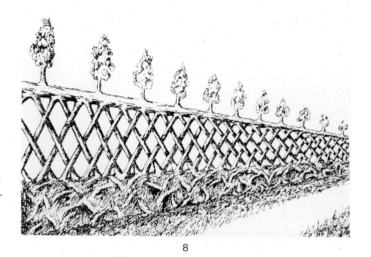

8

Wiechula Friedhofszaun | Cemeterial fence of living wood, aus | from: Kirsch, Konstantin: *Naturbauten aus lebenden Gehölzen* (Natural Buildings from Living Woods), Kevelaer 2012, 25.

lebenden Gehölzen (2003) einen Namen gemacht hat. In diesem Buch war die spätere Entwicklung Kirschs noch kaum auszumachen und vielleicht nur für die Allerhellhörigsten zumindest möglich – wenn er etwa in anti-emanzipatorischer Manier den zeitgenössischen Menschen als ein in ewigen natürlichen Ordnungen verfangenes Subjekt beschreibt: „Insgesamt entwickelt sich ein Lebensstil, in dem die Menschen ein integrierter Bestandteil des ‚Ökosystems Naturbau' sind."[68] Bereits auf dem Buchcover findet sich eine Zeichnung von Kirschs Vorbild Arthur Wiechula (1876–1941), der 1926 ein bemerkenswertes Buch mit dem Titel *Wachsende Häuser aus lebenden Bäumen entstehend* veröffentlichte, in welchem beschrieben wird, wie durch Pflanzschnitte, Biegungen und Verwachsungen aus lebenden Zweigen und Ästen Gebäude geschaffen werden können. Vermutlich errichtete Wiechula zeitlebens keinen seiner visionären Gebäude- und Zaunentwürfe aus lebenden Hölzern (Abb. 8); allerdings kam er gegen Ende der 1920er-Jahre in Kontakt mit der Deutschen Reichsbahn, für die er lebende Schneeschutzwände entlang von Eisenbahnlinien zu entwickeln versuchte. Wahrscheinlich wurde im Zuge dieser Kooperation eine 120 Meter lange Schutzwand aus kanadischen Pappeln bei Barleben im heutigen Sachsen-Anhalt errichtet (Abb. 9). Es ist unbekannt, womit Wiechula seinen Lebensunterhalt im Nationalsozialismus verdiente.

Seit 2006 versucht Kirsch vom sogenannten „WaldGärtnerHaus" im hessischen Nentershausen-Bauhaus unweit

65 Keil, Gerhard in *Umwelt & Aktiv* 3 (2017), zit. nach Röpke, Andrea/Speit, Andreas: *Völkische Landnahme. Alte Sippen, junge Siedler, rechte Ökos*, Berlin 2019, 99.

66 Vgl. Speit, Andreas: „Rechtes Öko-Magazin *Die Kehre*: Den Grünen den Naturschutz nehmen", *TAZ*, 2. Juni 2020, online unter: https://taz.de/Rechtes-Oeko-Magazin-Die-Kehre/!5690299/ (Stand: 31. Januar 2021).

67 Der Verfasser verdankt diesen Hinweis Philipp Krüpe.

68 Kirsch, Konstantin: *Naturbauten aus lebenden Gehölzen*, Xanten ³2003, 103.

building as in the 1950s for all eternity?"[63] Around the same time, Sieferle had an emotional "timber shortage debate" with the historian Joachim Radkau and others,[64] which concerned the scholarly question whether there was a timber shortage in the seventeenth and eighteenth centuries that was as dramatic for all strata of the population that it could be seen as a parallel to the oil crisis of that era. The rightward turn of Sieferle, an expert on Karl Marx and former member of the Sozialistischer Deutscher Studentenbund (SDS; Socialist German Student Union), did not therefore begin, as is often assumed, after German reunification with his book *Epochenwechsel: Die Deutschen an der Schwelle zum 21. Jahrhundert* (Epochal Change: The Germans on the Threshold to the Twenty-first Century) (1994), but at least about a decade earlier, not least with his defense of the Heimatschutz idea in *ARCH+*.

Recently, there have been various attempts in the German-speaking world to link to the various Heimatschutz movements of the twentieth century, especially outside of the world of architecture in the strict sense. For example, the magazine *Umwelt & Aktiv*, which was published from 2007 to 2019 by the Verein Midgard e.V. in Traunstein, which is close to the far-right Nationaldemokratische Partei Deutschlands (NPD; National Democratic Party of Germany), offered a platform to neo-Nazi authors from circles of the party Der III. Weg (The Third Path). The magazines subtitle was originally *Zeitschrift für gesamtheitliches Denken: Umweltschutz – Tierschutz – Heimatschutz* (Magazine for Holistic Thinking: Environmental Protection, Animal Protection, Homeland Protection); later *Umweltschutz* was changed to *Naturschutz* (Nature Conservation). This *völkisch* (ethnic nationalist) magazine saw itself as a challenge to the Greens, whom it accused of ecological "treason." In issue number 3/2017, with the cover headline "Das grosse Sterben in Feld und Flur" (The Great Extinction in Field and Meadow), in direct connection with National Socialist efforts in homeland protection, there is a tribute to "Hermann Göring, who was sentenced to death by the victorious powers," and who as "Forest and Hunting Minister" said to have distinguished himself with his "strong inner tie to nature" as well as a "trustee of the German forest and protector of magnificent natural monuments."[65] The issue also has articles with titles such as "Ewiger Wald und ewiges Volk" (Eternal Forest and Eternal People) and "Wie die Migration unser Land auffrisst" (How Migration Is Eating Up Our Country Up). Since 2020, it has had a successor magazine, *Umwelt & Aktiv: Die Kehre; Zeitschrift für Naturschutz* (Environment & Active: The Turn; Journal for Nature Conservation). Edited by the Identitarian Jonas Schick, the magazine and its associated blog belong to the far-right circles of the Institut für Staatspolitik (IfS; Insti-

tute for National Policy) in Schnellroda and the Verein "Ein Prozent" (One Percent Association). The name of the magazine is derived from the book *Die Technik und die Kehre* (Technology and the Turn) (1962) by Martin Heidegger, in which the anti-Semitic philosopher, seeing a "turn" on the horizon, identifies modern technology as an inevitable danger. Against that backdrop, *Die Kehre* seeks, by its own account, "to observe ecology from a holistic perspective" in order to counter "the reduction to 'climate protection' that is currently occurring"; a "theory of the entire environment" must include "cultural landscapes, rites, and customs, that is to say, house and home."[66] The circle of potential readers of that magazine presumably also included Alina Wychera, an activist from the Identitarian movement, who under the name Alina von Rauheneck had a popular tumblr page for a time, on which she stylized herself as a "daughter of the forest" with photographs she took herself and modified with a sepia tool.[67]

V. Natural Buildings for Family Estates: The Case of Konstantin Kirsch. But in the field of architecture—even in the field of *experimental* architecture—there have also been efforts to link housing construction to the right-wing ecological project of a romantic connection of certain groups of people to trees and forests. The famous architect Konstantin Kirsch deserves mention in this context. He made a name for himself with diverse natural buildings and not least with his book *Naturbauten aus lebenden Gehölzen* (Natural Buildings from Living Woods) (2003). Kirsch's later development could hardly have been predicted from that book or at least only by the most keenly alert, for example, from his anti-emancipatory description of the contemporary human being as a subject caught up in eternal natural orders: "In general, a lifestyle evolves in which people are an integrated component of the 'ecosystem of natural building.'"[68] The book's cover features a drawing by

63 Ibid., 42.

64 See the contributions to the debate, such as Joachim Radkau, "Holzverknappung und Krisenbewusstsein im 18. Jahrhundert," *Geschichte und Gesellschaft: Zeitschrift für historische Sozialwissenschaft* 9 (1983): 513–543, and Rolf Peter Sieferle, *Der unterirdische Wald: Energiekrise und industrielle Revolution* (Munich, 1982).

65 Gerhard Keil in *Umwelt & Aktiv* no. 3 (2017), quoted in Andrea Röpke and Andreas Speit, *Völkische Landnahme. Alte Sippen, junge Siedler, rechte Ökos* (Berlin 2019), 99.

66 See Andreas Speit, "Rechtes Öko-Magazin *Die Kehre*: Den Grünen den Naturschutz nehmen," *TAZ*, (June 2, 2020), https://taz.de/Rechtes-Oeko-Magazin-Die-Kehre/!5690299/ (accessed January 31, 2021).

67 The author is grateful to Philipp Krüpe for this reference.

68 Konstantin Kirsch, *Naturbauten aus lebenden Gehölzen* (Xanten 2003), 103.

von Bad Hersfeld aus das dazugehörige „Waldgartendorf" zu einem Zentrum für die rechtsesoterische Anastasia-Familienlandsitzbewegung auszubauen. Hervorgegangen aus der Romanserie *Anastasia – Die klingenden Zedern Russlands* des russischen Autors und Geschäftsmannes Wladimir Megre (geb. 1950), die in zehn Bänden zwischen 1996 und 2010 auf Russisch und zwischen 1999 und 2011 auf Deutsch erschienen war, entstanden zunächst in Russland, Weißrussland und der Ukraine, später dann auch in Australien, Litauen, Tschechien, Ungarn, den USA und Deutschland zahllose ländliche Wohnkommunen, in der nach den Idealen der angeblich real existierenden Anastasia gelebt werden soll: „in Harmonie mit der Natur" und ihrer vermeintlich natürlichen Geschlechterordnung, auf einem „Familienlandsitz" von etwa einem Hektar Fläche, gemäß einer patriarchalen, heteronormativen und auch antisemitischen Ideologie, bei der Jüdinnen und Juden selbst die Schuld an ihrer Verfolgungsgeschichte zugewiesen wird.[69] Das offizielle Register der Anastasia-Siedlungen listet derzeit mehr als 213 Siedlungen mit Internetadresse und ebenfalls mehr als 230 Siedlungen alleine in Russland auf. In Deutschland existieren derzeit 17 Siedlungen, in denen zwar nur etwa 50 Anhänger leben, aber auf Anastasia-Treffen kommen gerne auch mal 800 Menschen zusammen. Dass Kirsch eine zentrale Figur der Anastasia-Bewegung in Deutschland und darüber hinaus ist, kann als gesichert gelten: 2013 richtete er ein solches Treffen auf seinem Anwesen aus, für das er auch gezielt ein Reichsbürger-Publikum ansprach;[70] 2014 publizierte er gemeinsam mit Lutz Rosemann den *Anastasia-Index*, das Standard-Nachschlagewerk der deutschsprachigen Anastasia-Szene;[71] und 2018 wurde er auf der Frankfurter Buchmesse auf dem Anastasia-Stand vor 200 AnhängerInnen von Nina Megre interviewt, der Enkelin Megres.[72]

Schluss. Der Umgang mit Umwelt, Wäldern und Bäumen ist seit dem 18. Jahrhundert nicht nur von zweifellos gewonnenen wissenschaftlichen Erkenntnisgewinnen, sondern – wie zu zeigen versucht wurde – eben auch von antiaufklärerischen Mythisierungstendenzen geprägt worden. Dieses romantische bis esoterische Diskurserbe, das Menschen in eherne göttlich-natürliche Ordnungen von „Völkern" und anderen Schicksalskollektiven mit zumeist starr fixierten Geschlechterrollen einweist, stellt in Zeiten einer sich zuspitzenden Klimakrise eine große Herausforderung dar: Es steht zu erwarten, dass die notwendigen globalen Klimaschutzmaßnahmen in vielen Ländern zu signifikanten nationalistischen Gegenreaktionen mit entsprechenden Heimatschutzverklärungen führen. Wälder und ihr Holz dürften sowohl im Zentrum der romantischen Gegenaufklärung wie der wissenschaftlich fundierten Aufklärung über die drohende globale Klimakatastrophe stehen. Diese stellt insbesondere die Architektur vor einschneidende Veränderungen. Denn von der Transformation des Bausektors hängt es entscheidend ab, ob die beim Pariser Klimaschutzabkommen 2015 festgelegten globalen Klimaziele er-

9

Wiechula Bahnhecke | Living wall to protect a railway line, aus | from: Kirsch, Konstantin: *Naturbauten aus lebenden Gehölzen* (Natural Buildings from Living Woods), Kevelaer 2012, 25.

reicht werden können. Höchstwahrscheinlich wird es im Zuge der zu erwartenden Durchsetzung einer Low Carbon Economy, einer emissionsarmen Wirtschaft im Bereich des Bauwesens, nicht zuletzt dem „Wunderstoff Beton" an den Kragen gehen. Die Zementindustrie ist für rund acht Prozent der globalen CO_2-Emissionen verantwortlich,[73] und „beim Herstellen von einer Tonne Zement [steigen] rund 700 Kilogramm des Treibhausgases Kohlendioxid in die Luft".[74] Vor dem Hintergrund der Tatsache, dass jedes Holzprodukt den Kohlenstoff speichert, den der ursprüngliche Baum, aus dem das Produkt gefertigt wurde, der Atmosphäre entzogen hat, wird immer wieder der Vorschlag gemacht, „Beton im großen Stil durch Holz zu ersetzen"[75] und Städte so zu einem riesigen CO_2-Speicher zu machen.[76] Banhams Doppeloption dürfte sich in Anbetracht dieser Szenarien auf nur eine Möglichkeit reduzieren: nicht die Verbrennung, sondern nur die Verbauung von Holz. Ob in Form von Naturbauten oder in Form von Halbzeugen – dies dürfte eher eine untergeordnete Zeit- und Geschmacksfrage sein. ∎

69 Vgl. Kinsky, Carl/Hell, Sebastian: „Ökologie, Rassenlehre und Antisemitismus. Die ‚Anastasia-Bewegung' in Hessen", in: *Lotta* 77, 12. Februar 2020, online unter: http://www.lotta-magazin.de/ausgabe/78/kologie-rassenlehre-und-antisemitismus (Stand: 31. Januar 2021).

70 Vgl. ebd.

71 Kirsch, Konstantin/Lutz Rosemann: *Anastasia-Index. Gesamtindex für die „Anastasia"-Bände 1 bis 10*, Zürich 2014.

72 Vgl. Kinsky/Hell: „Ökologie, Rassenlehre und Antisemitismus" (wie Anm. 69).

73 Vgl. Weiß, Marlene: „Klimaschutz: Holz statt Beton", *Süddeutsche Zeitung*, 28. Januar 2020, online unter: https://www.sueddeutsche.de/wissen/holz-co2-klimaschutz-1.4775157 (Stand: 31. Dezember 2020).

74 Knauer, Roland: „Das große Beton-Problem", *Spektrum der Wissenschaft*, 20. August 2020, online unter: https://www.spektrum.de/news/warum-beton-klimaschaedlich-ist/1760122 (Stand: 31. Dezember 2020).

75 Weiß: „Klimaschutz: Holz statt Beton" (wie Anm. 73).

76 Vgl. ebd.

Kirsch's role model Arthur Wiechula (1876–1941), who published a remarkable book in 1926 titled *Wachsende Häuser aus lebenden Bäumen entstehend* (Growing Houses Resulting from Living Trees), in which he described how to create buildings by plants, bends, and deformities of living branches and twigs. Wiechula probably never built any of his visionary designs for buildings and fences of living woods (fig. 8), but in the late 1920s he came into contact with the Deutsche Reichsbahn (German Railway), for which he tried to develop living walls to protect railway lines from snow. This cooperation probably resulted in the construction of a 120-meter-long protective wall made from Canadian poplars, near Barleben in present-day Saxony-Anhalt (fig. 9). It is not known how Wiechula earned his living under National Socialism.

Since 2006, Kirsch has been working at the so-called WaldGärtnerHaus (Forest Gardener House) in Nentershausen-Bauhaus, Hesse, not far from Bad Hersfeld, to develop the Waldgartendorf (Forest Garden Village) there into a center for the right-wing, esoteric Anastasia kinship homestead movement. An outgrowth of the *Ringing Cedars of Russia* series of novels—known in German as *Anastasia*, after the title of the first volume—by the Russian writer and businessman Vladimir Megre (born 1950), which was published in ten volumes in Russian between 1996 and 2010, in German between 1999 and 2011 and in English between 2008 and 2016, numerous rural communes were formed, first in Russia, Belarus, and Ukraine and then later also in Australia, Lithuania, the Czech Republic, Hungary, the United States, and Germany, where the goal was to live according to the ideals of the supposedly actually existing Anastasia: "in harmony with nature" and its supposed natural hierarchy of the sexes on a "kinship homestead" on roughly one hectare of land, according to a patriarchal, heteronormative, and also anti-Semitic ideology, in which Jews are to blame for their own history of being persecuted.[69] The official register of the Anastasia settlements currently has more than 213 settlements with an Internet address and also more than 230 settlements in Russia alone. There are currently seventeen settlements in Germany, where only about fifty followers live, but as many as eight hundred people come to Anastasia meetings. It is certain that Kirsch is a central figure of the Anastasia movement in Germany and beyond: In 2013, he organized one such meeting at his property, for which he deliberately reached out to a Reichsbürger (Reich's Citizens) audience.[70] In 2014, he and Lutz Rosemann published the *Anastasia-Index*, the standard reference work of the German-speaking Anastasia scene.[71] And in 2018 he was interviewed by Nina Megre, the author's granddaughter, at the *Anastasia* stand at the Frankfurt Book Fair in front of 200 followers.[72]

Conclusion: The approach to the environment, forests, and trees has been characterized since the eighteenth century not only by unquestionably attained scientific knowledge but also, as I have tried to show, by anti-Enlightenment, mythologizing tendencies. This legacy of discourse ranging from the Romantic to the esoteric, which assigns people to ironclad divine-natural orders of "peoples" and other collectives of fates, usually with rigidly fixed gender roles, presents a big challenge in an era of a growing climate crisis: It is reasonable to expect that the necessary global measures to mitigate climate change will in many countries lead to significant nationalistic counterreactions with corresponding glorification of homeland protection. This confronts architecture especially with drastic changes. For the transformation of the construction industry depends crucially on whether the global climate goals set by the Paris Agreement of 2015 can be met. Very probably, in the way of the anticipated implementation of a low-carbon economy in the building industry, the "miraculous material concrete" will be in trouble. The cement industry is responsible for around eight percent of global CO_2 emissions,[73] and "producing a [metric] ton of cement [releases] around 700 kilograms of carbon dioxide into the air."[74] In light of the fact that every wood product stores the carbon that the original tree from which it was made removed from the atmosphere, it has been repeatedly proposed that "concrete be replaced by wood on a large scale,"[75] turning cities into enormous CO_2 reservoirs.[76] In light of such scenarios, Banham's two options can be reduced to just one possibility: not burning wood but building with it. Whether in the form of natural buildings or in the form of semifinished products, that is surely a minor question of time and taste. ∎

Translation: Steven Lindberg

69 See Carl Kinsky and Sebastian Hell, "Ökologie, Rassenlehre und Antisemitismus: Die 'Anastasia-Bewegung' in Hessen," *Lotta* 77 (2020), available online at: http://www.lotta-magazin.de/ausgabe/78/kologie-rassenlehre-und-antisemitismus (accessed January 31, 2021).

70 See ibid.

71 Konstantin Kirsch and Lutz Rosemann, *Anastasia-Index: Gesamtindex für die "Anastasia"-Bände 1 bis 10* (Zurich, 2014).

72 See Kinsky and Hell, "Ökologie, Rassenlehre und Antisemitismus" (see note 69).

73 See Marlene Weiss, "Klimaschutz: Holz statt Beton," *Süddeutsche Zeitung*, January 28, 2020, https://www.sueddeutsche.de/wissen/holz-co2-klimaschutz-1.4775157 (accessed December 31, 2020).

74 Roland Knauer, "Das große Beton-Problem," *Spektrum der Wissenschaft*, August 20, 2020, https://www.spektrum.de/news/warum-beton-klimaschaedlich-ist/1760122 (accessed December 31, 2020).

75 Weiss, "Klimaschutz: Holz statt Beton" (see note 73).

76 See ibid.

Die Baumumarmerin

Treehuggers

Tom Körner

Irgendwann 2001 las ich in einer Zeitschrift über Leute, die Bäume umarmen. Mein erster Gedanke war: „Die armen Bäume." Menschen sollten andere Spezies nicht betatschen, nur um sich selbst besser zu fühlen. Schon gar nicht welche, die weder beißen, stechen, kratzen, giftige oder übelriechende Flüssigkeiten versprühen oder nicht weglaufen können. Weil es mir so skurril vorkam, zeichnete ich ein paar Witze mit einer etwas abgedrehten Dame, die leidenschaftlich gerne Bäume umarmt. Mittlerweile gibt es die „Baumtante" seit fast 20 Jahren, und ihre Fans schicken mir regelmäßig Fundstücke aus der ganzen Welt über das Baumumarmen in allen denkbaren und undenkbaren Variationen.

„Tree Hugging" ist erschreckend populär geworden. Irgendwas muss ich falsch gemacht haben.

Die armen Bäume. ∎

Sometime back in 2001, I came across an article in a magazine about people who hug trees. My first thought was: "what poor trees." Surely, we humans shouldn't be allowed to grope another species just to feel better ourselves. Least of all those that aren't even able to run away or to bite, sting, scratch, or spray you with something toxic or foul-smelling. As it seemed so bizarre to me, I decided to make a joke of it and drew a somewhat eccentric cartoon of a lady who rather passionately hugs trees. The lady, named "Baumtante," has now been on the scene for 20 years, and her fans regularly send me all kinds of weird and wonderful things they find related to tree-hugging.

Tree-hugging has become frighteningly popular. I must have done it wrong.

What poor trees. ∎

Hauptsache Holz. Zu Imagewandel und kultureller Bedeutung eines zeitgemäßen Baustoffs

Wood Is the Main Thing: On the Change in the Image and Cultural Significance of a Contemporary Construction Material

Anselm Wagner

1   Jože Plečniks Version der Vitruvschen Urhütte |
Jože Plečnik's interpretation of the Vitruvian primitive hut,
Begunje/Slowenien | Slovenia, 1940 © Miran Kambic

Der folgende Beitrag versucht, die zeitgenössische Bedeutung von Bauen mit Holz architekturtheoretisch zu verstehen und in einen größeren kulturhistorischen Zusammenhang zu bringen. Neben ökologischen, technischen, finanziellen und praktischen Aspekten, die in der Debatte um den Holzbau[1] meistens dominieren und für ihn ins Treffen geführt werden, stellt das „Image" von Holzarchitektur einen zentralen, nicht zu unterschätzenden Faktor dar. Dieses Image macht derzeit einen tiefgreifenden Wandel durch, der an Bedeutung und Dimension durchaus mit dem Imagewandel von Stahlbeton in der Nachkriegszeit vergleichbar ist. Sollte dieser Imagewandel keine unvorhersehbaren Einbrüche oder Kehrtwendungen erleiden, dann wird Holz in wenigen Jahrzehnten zu einem der wichtigsten Baustoffe (wenn nicht *dem* wichtigsten Baustoff) des 21. Jahrhunderts werden.

Um gleich eine Einschränkung vorwegzunehmen: Ich spreche hier von einer mitteleuropäischen Perspektive aus und meine Ausführungen müssen sich aus praktischen Gründen auf diese beschränken. Kulturelle Bedeutungen können nur äußerst selten globale Gültigkeit beanspruchen und im konkreten Fall gelten sie nicht einmal für die gesamte westliche Welt. Regionen wie z.B. Skandinavien, in denen die Tradition des Holzbaus nie abgebrochen ist,[2] sind nicht mit den romanischen Ländern vergleichbar, in denen das Bauen mit Stein, Backstein und Zement seit Jahrtausenden die Regel darstellt. Der eingangs erwähnte Imagewandel konzentriert sich daher zunächst auf Mitteleuropa, ist aber keineswegs darauf beschränkt.

„Ländlich und primitiv" – das traditionelle Bild des Holzbaus. Um den Imagewandel zu verstehen, der sich gegenwärtig abspielt, ist es nötig, sich kurz das traditionelle Bild zu vergegenwärtigen, das mit dem Holzbau noch bis vor wenigen Jahrzehnten assoziiert worden ist. Die jahrhundertelang vorherrschende Konnotation lautete: Holzhäuser sind ärmlich, rückständig, ländlich und meist provisorisch. So meinte etwa der Münchner Akademieprofessor Moriz Carriere in seiner 1873 publizierten *Aesthetik*, Holzbauten besäßen „einen primitiven und ländlichen Charakter".[3] Die Ursachen für diese nicht nur im 19. Jahrhundert weit verbreitete Vorstellung gehen bis in die Antike zurück und bilden einen *locus classicus* der humanistischen Bildung. In seiner um 98 n. Chr. verfassten *Germania* berichtet Tacitus, dass die Germanen keine Städte mit aneinander gelehnten Gebäuden, sondern lediglich Dörfer mit freistehenden Häusern kennen würden: „Jeder umgibt sein Haus mit einem Freiraum, sei es als Schutz vor Feuer oder aus mangelnder Kenntnis im Bauen. Nicht einmal die Verwendung von Mauersteinen oder Dachziegeln ist bei ihnen üblich. Zu allem verwenden sie unförmiges Bauholz, das keinerlei Ansehen und Reiz besitzt."[4] Seither gilt: Dörfer aus Holz sind barbarisch, Städte aus Stein und Ziegel zivilisiert – obwohl Holzkonstruktionen ein mindestens ebenso hohes handwerkliches Können voraussetzen wie der Massivbau. Wie um das Urteil des Tacitus zu bestätigen, setzte sich nach dem Zusammenbruch der römischen Zivilisation der „germanische" Holzbau durch.[5] Im Frühmittelalter waren außerhalb Südeuropas sämtliche Siedlungen inklusive ihrer Verteidigungsanlagen, Kirchen und Burgen aus Holz errichtet. Holzhäuser mussten zwar alle paar Jahrzehnte erneuert werden, konnten aber bei Kriegs- oder Brandgefahr rasch abgebaut und auch transportiert werden,[6] was auch den Bedürfnissen einer mobileren Gesellschaft entsprach. Mit Beginn des Hochmittelalters und dem damit verbundenen wirtschaftlichen Aufschwung begannen Steinbauten schrittweise ihre hölzernen Vorgänger zu ersetzen. Die Mittelalterarchäologie ist voll von Beispielen, in denen eine ältere Schicht von Holzbauten den jüngeren Schichten von Steinbauten vorangeht.[7] So stellt 1991 der Hausforscher Konrad Bedal für Mitteleuropa fest, dass „insgesamt gesehen die Entwicklung auf eine Verdrängung des Holzbaus durch den massiven Steinbau seit dem Ende des Mittelalters hinausläuft, ein Prozess, der inzwischen größtenteils beendet ist".[8] Die Gründe für diesen Materialwechsel liegen vorwiegend in der größeren Brandgefahr für Holzbauten. In vielen Städten, wie etwa 1313 in Zürich, wurde nach einem Stadtbrand der Steinbau vorgeschrieben[9] oder zumindest die (stellenweise sogar subventionierte) Eindeckung mit Ziegeln statt mit Stroh verordnet, was aufgrund des höheren Gewichts massive Mauern voraussetzte.[10] Eine Mischform stellt der Fachwerkbau dar, der zunächst mit Flechtwerk oder Lehmflechtwerk, ab dem 15. Jahrhundert vereinzelt und ab Mitte des 19. Jahrhunderts

1   Unter Holzbauten werden im Folgenden nur jene verstanden, die zum überwiegenden Teil aus Holz bestehen. Selbstverständlich enthält auch jedes vormoderne Massivbauwerk größere Anteile aus Holz (meistens Decken, Dachstuhl, Türen und Fenster) und besitzen die meisten Holzbauten auch gemauerte Teile (Sockel, Kamine).

2   Nikula, Riitta: *Bebaute Landschaft. Finnlands Architektur im Überblick*, Helsinki 1993, 13, gibt den Anteil von Holzbauten in Finnland mit 80 Prozent an.

3   Carriere, Moriz: *Aesthetik. Die Idee des Schönen und ihre Verwirklichung im Leben und in der Kunst. Zweiter Teil: Die bildende Kunst. Die Musik. Die Poesie*, Leipzig ²1873, 129; zit. n. Rübel, Dietmar/Wagner, Monika/Wolff, Vera (Hg.): *Materialästhetik. Quellentexte zu Kunst, Design und Architektur*, Berlin 2005, 52.

4   „Suam quisque domum spatio circumdat, sive adversus casus ignis remedium sive inscitia aedificandi. Ne caementorum quidem apud illos aut tegularum usus: materia ad omnia utuntur informi et citra speciem aut delectationem." Tacitus: *De origine et situ Germanorum*. (Übers. A.W.)

5   Vgl. Sarti, Raffaela: „Ländliche Hauslandschaften in Europa in einer Langzeitperspektive", in: Eibach, Joachim/Schmidt-Voges, Inken (Hg.): *Das Haus in der Geschichte Europas. Ein Handbuch*, Berlin/Boston 2015, 175–194, hier 176.

6   Vgl. Hundsbichler, Helmut: „Wohnen", in: Kühnel, Harry (Hg.): *Alltag im Spätmittelalter*, Augsburg 2003, 254–269, hier 256.

7   Vgl. Fehring, Günter P.: *Die Archäologie des Mittelalters. Eine Einführung*, Darmstadt 2000, 68, 75, 90, 99ff, 106f, 110, 113, 170.

8   Bedal, Konrad: *Historische Hausforschung. Eine Einführung in Arbeitsweise, Begriffe und Literatur* (Quellen und Materialien zur Hausforschung in Bayern Bd. 6), Bad Windsheim ²1993, 43.

9   Vgl. Hundsbichler: „Wohnen" (wie Anm. 6), 255 (mit weiteren Beispielen).

10 Vgl. Kühnel, Harry: „Normen und Sanktionen", in: Kühnel: *Alltag* (wie Anm. 6), 17–48, hier 21–26.

The present essay attempts to understand the contemporary significance of building with wood in terms of the theory of architecture and to put it in a larger context of cultural history. In addition to the ecological, technological, financial, and practical aspects that usually dominate the debate over timber construction[1] and are presented as arguments for it, the "image" of wood architecture represents a central factor that should not be underestimated. This image is currently undergoing a profound change that is certainly comparable in significance and dimension to the change in image of reinforced concrete in the postwar era. If this transformation in image does not suffer any unforeseen setbacks or reversals, then in a few decades wood will be one of the most important building materials (if not *the* most important building material) of the twenty-first century.

One restriction should be stated right at the outset: I am speaking here from a Central European perspective, and for practical reasons my reflections have to be limited to this. Cultural significances can only extremely rarely claim global validity, and in the specific case they are not even valid for the whole of the Western world. Regions such as Scandinavia, where the tradition of timber construction is unbroken,[2] cannot be compared to the Romance countries, in which building with stone, brick, and cement has been the rule for millennia. The aforementioned change in image is therefore concentrated on Central Europe but is by no means limited to it.

"Rural and Primitive": The Traditional Image of Timber Construction. To understand the change in image it is undergoing today, it is necessary to call to mind briefly the traditional image associated with timber construction until just a few decades ago. For centuries, the dominant connotations of wood houses were poor, backward, rural, and usually temporary. Professor Moriz Carriere of the Akademie der Bildenden Künste in Munich opined in his *Aesthetik* of 1873 that wood buildings possess "a primitive and rural character."[3] The causes of this idea that was widespread not only in the nineteenth century can be traced back to antiquity and represent a locus classicus of humanistic education. In his *Germania*, written in AD 98, Tacitus reports that the Germans did not build cities with adjoining buildings but only villages with free-standing houses: "Every person surrounds his dwelling with an open space, either as a precaution against the disasters of fire, or because they do not know how to build. No use is made by them of stone or tile; they employ timber for all purposes, rude

masses without ornament or attractiveness."[4] Ever since then it has been claimed that villages of wood are barbaric, and cities of stone and brick civilized—even though wood constructions require at least as much craft skill as solid construction. As if to confirm the judgment of Tacitus, after the fall of Roman civilization, "Germanic" timber construction gained acceptance.[5] In the Early Middle Ages, all settlements outside of southern Europe were built of wood, including their defensive structures, churches, and fortresses. Wooden houses had to be renovated every couple of decades, but when war or fire threatened, they could be quickly disassembled and even transported,[6] which was also in keeping with the needs of a more mobile society. With the beginning of the High Middle Ages, and the associated economic upturn, stone buildings gradually began to replace their wooden predecessors. The archaeology of the Middle Ages is full of examples in which an older layer of wooden buildings precedes the more recent layer of stone buildings.[7] For example, the scholar Konrad Bedal noted of Central Europe in 1991 that "seen as a whole the evolution moved toward an edging out of wood construction by massive stone construction since the end of the Middle Ages—a process that has since largely ended."[8] The reasons for this change of material lie primarily in the greater risk of fire with wood buildings. In many cities, for example, in Zurich in 1313, stone construction was

1 "Timber Construction" is understood here to mean buildings made predominately of wood. Naturally, every premodern massive construction had larger components made of wood (usually ceilings, roof truss, doors, and windows), and most wood buildings also have masonry elements (base, chimneys).

2 Riitta Nikula, *Architecture and Landscape: The Building of Finland* (Helsinki, 1993), 13, indicates that eighty percent of the building stock in Finland is wood.

3 Moriz Carriere, *Aesthetik: Die Idee des Schönen und ihre Verwirklichung im Leben und in der Kunst*, part 2, *Die bildende Kunst, Die Musik, Die Poesie*, 2nd ed. (Leipzig, 1873), 129, reprinted in Dietmar Rübel, Monika Wagner, and Vera Wolff, eds., *Materialästhetik: Quellentexte zu Kunst, Design und Architektur* (Berlin, 2005), 52.

4 Tacitus, "Germany and Its Tribes," in *The Agricola and Germany of Tacitus*, trans. Alfred John Church and William Jackson Brodribb (London, 1868), 1–33, esp. 11–12; Tacitus, *De origine et situ Germanorum*, chap. 16: "Suam quisque domum spatio circumdat, sive adversus casus ignis remedium sive inscitia aedificandi. Ne caementorum quidem apud illos aut tegularum usus: materia ad omnia utuntur informi et citra speciem aut delectationem."

5 See Raffaela Sarti, "Ländliche Hauslandschaften in Europa in einer Langzeitperspektive," in *Das Haus in der Geschichte Europas: Ein Handbuch*, ed. Joachim Eibach and Inken Schmidt-Voges (Berlin, 2015), 175–194, esp. 176.

6 See Helmut Hundsbichler, "Wohnen," in *Alltag im Spätmittelalter*, ed. Harry Kühnel (Augsburg, 2003), 254–269, esp. 256.

7 See Günter P. Fehring, *Die Archäologie des Mittelalters. Eine Einführung* (Darmstadt, 2000), 68, 75, 90, 99ff, 106–107, 110, 113, 170.

8 Konrad Bedal, *Historische Hausforschung: Eine Einführung in Arbeitsweise, Begriffe und Literatur*, Quellen und Materialien zur Hausforschung in Bayern 6, 2nd ed. (Bad Windsheim, 1993), 43.

2

Jean de la Vallée, Schloss Fullerö | Fullerö Castle, Barkarö, Västmanland, Schweden I Sweden, 1656
© Olle Norling

durchgehend mit Ziegeln ausgefacht wird und sich somit der Massivbauweise angleicht.[11] Wer es sich leisten konnte, baute zunehmend in Stein (bzw. wo dieser nicht verfügbar war, in Backstein). Zur Bevorzugung der Massivbauweise trugen im Mittelalter wohl auch die Klöster und Bauhütten der Kathedralen sowie in der Neuzeit die am antiken Vorbild orientierten Architekten bei.[12] Massiv zu bauen diente der sozialen Distinktion: „Die Reichen bauen hoch aufragend mit Steinen und Mörtel: die Armen nur niedriger mit Lehm und Holz",[13] schreibt der Humanist Johannes Böhm über die deutschen Städte in seinem erstmals 1520 aufgelegten, viel gelesenen ethnografischen Standardwerk *Mores, leges et ritus omnium gentium*.[14] Und wenn Böhm von den Siedlungen der Bauern am Land und ihrem „elenden und harten Los"[15] berichtet, klingt das wie ein Reflex auf die Germanendörfer des Tacitus: „Sie wohnen abgesondert voneinander, schlicht mit ihren Angehörigen und ihrem Viehstand. Die Hütten bestehen aus Lehm und Holz, ragen wenig über die Erde empor, sind mit Stroh gedeckt: das sind ihre Häuser."[16] Das von Böhm beobachtete Stadt-Land-Gefälle lässt erkennen, dass zunehmende Urbanisierung zunehmende „Versteinerung" bedeutete, während das Land aus sowohl wirtschaftlichen als auch praktischen Erwägungen noch wesentlich länger am Holzbau festhielt. Daraus ergab sich die Assoziation des Holzbaus mit ländlich, traditionell, ärmlich und rückständig, während Massivbauten Urbanität, Modernität und Reichtum signalisierten. Belegt wird dieser Imageverfall des Holzbaus gerade in seinen Zentren, wie etwa in Skandinavien, wo es ab dem 16. Jahrhundert üblich wurde, Holzhäuser mit Ochsenblut bzw. Falunrot anzustreichen, um die Backsteinfassaden der reichen norddeutschen Städte zu imitieren (Abb. 2).[17] Ähnliches lässt sich bei US-amerikanischen Ständerbauten des 19. Jahrhunderts beobachten, die mittels natursteinfarbenen Schlämmen ein massives Aussehen bekamen.[18]

11 Vgl. Bedal: *Hausforschung* (wie Anm. 8), 45

12 Vgl. ebd., 70.

13 „Divites lapidibus caementoque superbe aedificant: pauperes luto et ligno tantum humilius." Böhm, Johannes: *Mores, leges et ritus omnium gentium*, Lyon 1541, 210 (1. Aufl. Augsburg 1520); online unter: http://mateo.uni-mannheim.de/camenahist/boehme1/jpg/s210.html

14 Vgl. Huber, Max: „Boemus, Johannes", in: *Neue Deutsche Bibliographie*, Bd. 2, 1955, 403, online unter: https://www.deutsche-biographie.de/pnd104230894.html#ndbcontent (Stand: 4. Februar 2021). Demnach erfuhr das Buch bis 1621 29 lateinische, zehn französische, zehn italienische, eine spanische, eine deutsche und zwei englische Auflagen.

15 „misera et dura conditio", Böhm: Mores (wie Anm. 13), 211.

16 „[…] seorsum ab aliis quisque cum familia et pecore suo humiliter vivit. Casae luto, lignoque e terra paululum eductae, et stramine contectae domus", ebd., Übers. nach Hundsbichler: „Wohnen" (wie Anm. 6), 256.

17 Vgl. Edenheim, Ralph: *The Red Houses*, Malmö 2005, 9–12, 118.

18 Vgl. Banham, Reyner: „Is There a Substitute for Wood Grain Plastic?", in: Anderson, Eric A./Earle, George F. (Hg.): *Design and Aesthetics in Wood*, New York 1977, 4–11, hier 6. Den Hinweis auf diesen Text und seine Interpretation verdanke ich Petra Eckhard und Christoph Tinzl.

prescribed by law after a fire in the city[9] or at least (in some cases even subsidized) covering with bricks rather than straw was required, which because of the greater weight presumed massive walls.[10] Half-timber represented a hybrid form, first with infill of wattle and daub and then from the fifteenth century occasionally and from the middle of the nineteenth century always brick, thus becoming more similar to massive construction.[11] Increasingly, anyone who could afford it built in stone (or, where it was not available, in brick). The preference for massive construction in the Middle Ages was probably reinforced by the monasteries and cathedral masonry works and in the modern era by architects following antique models.[12] Massive construction served social distinction: "The rich build tall with stones and mortar: the poor only lower with loam and wood,"[13] writes the humanist Johannes Böhm of German cities in his much-read ethnographic standard work *Mores, leges et ritus omnium gentium*, first published in 1520.[14] And when Böhm reports of the farmers' settlements in the country and their "miserable and hard situation,"[15] it sounds like a reflection of Tacitus's description of the villages of the ancient Germans: "They live separately from one another, simply with their family and cattle. Their huts are made of clay and timber, rising little above the earth and covered with straw."[16] The city-country divide observed by Böhm illustrates that increasing urbanization meant increasingly "turning to stone," whereas the countryside kept to timber construction for considerably longer for both economic and practical reasons. It resulted in timber construction being associated with rural, traditional, poor, and backward, whereas massive construction signaled urbanism, modernity, and affluence. This decline in the image of timber construction is documented especially in its centers, such as Scandinavia, where from the sixteenth century it became common to paint wooden houses with oxblood or falu red to imitate the brick façades of the wealthy northern German cities (fig. 2).[17] Something similar can be observed in the timber-frame houses of the nineteenth century in the United States, which were made to look like massive construction by applying stucco colored to look like natural stone.[18]

This development did not spare even those Western countries that had clung to timber construction in the city into the nineteenth century. The devastating urban fires of Turku in 1827 and of Chicago in 1871 led to the wood structures that had until then dominated[19] being banned from the centers of these cities.[20] This strengthened the identification of the city—and hence of architecture—and stone. (Richard Sennett logically titled his history of the body in the city of Western civilization

Flesh and Stone[21]—even in the United States, "flesh and wood" is something only for the village and the suburbs.) Just as logically, the history of architecture that became established at institutes of art history at universities during the nineteenth century concentrated on massive constructions, whereas research on timber construction was left to ethnologies, thus cementing the notorious antagonism of urban high culture and rural folk culture.

From the Truth of Nature to "German Wood."
In addition to the numerous negative connotations of the backward and poor, however, timber construction also has the positive ones of the original, genuine, and true—just as Tacitus saw in the ancient Germans not just barbarians but also "noble savages." A prominent ancient source is responsible for that as

9   See Hundsbichler, "Wohnen" (see note 6), 255 (with additional examples).

10 See Harry Kühnel, "Normen und Sanktionen," in Kühnel, *Alltag* (see note 6), 17–48, esp. 21–26.

11 See Bedal, *Hausforschung* (see note 8), 45.

12 Ibid., 70.

13 Johannes Böhm, *Mores, leges et ritus omnium gentium* (Lyon, 1541; orig. pub. Augsburg, 1520), 210, available online at: http://mateo.uni-mannheim.de/camenahist/boehme1/jpg/s210.html: "Divites lapidibus caementoque superbe aedificant: pauperes luto et ligno tantum humilius"; Böhm, *The Manners, Lawes and Customs of All Nations* (London, 1611), 261.

14 See Max Huber, "Boemus, Johannes," in *Neue Deutsche Bibliographie*, vol. 2 (1955), 403, available online at: https://www.deutsche-biographie.de/pnd104230894.html#ndbcontent (accessed February 4, 2021). By 1621, the book had been published in twenty-nine Latin, ten French, one Spanish, one German, and two English editions.

15 Böhm, *Mores* (see note 13), 211: "misera et dura conditio"; Böhm, *The Manners, Lawes and Customs* (see note 13), 262.

16 Böhm, *Mores* (see note 13), 211: "seorsum ab aliis quisque cum familia et pecore suo humiliter vivit. Casae luto, lignoque e terra paululum eductae, et stramine contectae domus"; Böhm, *The Manners, Lawes and Customs* (see note 13), 262.

17 See Ralph Edenheim, *The Red Houses* (Malmö, 2005), 9–12, 118.

18 See Reyner Banham, "Is There a Substitute for Wood Grain Plastic?" in *Design and Aesthetics in Wood*, ed. Eric A. Anderson George F. Earle (New York, 1977), 4–11, esp. 6. I am grateful to Petra Eckhard and Christoph Tinzl for the reference to this text and his interpretation.

19 Carl W. Condit, *The Chicago School of Architecture: A History of Commercial and Public Building in the Chicago Area, 1875–1925* (Chicago, 1966), 18, indicates that before the fire in Chicago in 1871 two-thirds of the buildings were all wood.

20 See Joseph Kirkland and John Moses, *The History of Chicago, Illinois* (Chicago, 1895), 219–220. In Turku, "Buildings along the main streets and squares were to be built exclusively of stone. Two-storey wooden houses and mansard roofs were strictly prohibited." Nikula, *Architecture and Landscape* (see note 2), 73.

21 Richard Sennett, *Flesh and Stone: The Body and the City in Western Civilization* (New York, 1994).

Diese Entwicklung machte auch vor jenen westlichen Ländern nicht halt, die bis ins 19. Jahrhundert am städtischen Holzbau festgehalten hatten. So führten die verheerenden Stadtbrände von Turku 1827 und von Chicago 1871 dazu, dass Holzbauten, welche bis dahin dominierten,[19] aus den Zentren dieser Städte verschwinden mussten.[20] Damit festigte sich die Identifikation von Stadt – und damit Architektur – und Stein (Richard Sennett übertitelte seine Geschichte des Körpers in der Stadt der westlichen Zivilisation folgerichtig mit *Fleisch und Stein*[21] – „Fleisch und Holz" ist selbst in den USA nur etwas für das Dorf und die *Suburbs*). Ebenso folgerichtig konzentrierte sich die von der universitären Kunstgeschichte im 19. Jahrhundert etablierte Architekturgeschichte auf den Massivbau, während die Erforschung des Holzbaus der Volkskunde überlassen wurde und damit den notorischen Antagonismus von urbaner Hoch- und ländlicher Volkskultur zementierte.

Von der Wahrheit der Natur zum „deutschen Holz".

Neben den zahlreichen negativen Konnotationen des Rückständigen und Ärmlichen besitzt der Holzbau aber auch die positiven des Urtümlichen, Echten und Wahren (wie schon Tacitus in den Germanen nicht nur Barbaren, sondern auch „edle Wilde" sah). Auch dafür ist eine prominente antike Quelle verantwortlich. So spekuliert Vitruv darüber, dass der Ursprung des Bauens, die sogenannte Urhütte (Abb. 1), aus Holz, Schilf, Laub und Lehm bestanden habe, wie man es auch seinerzeit noch bei den Hütten der Gallier, Hispanier, Lusitanier und Aquitanier, aber auch bei der strohgedeckten Hütte des Romulus auf dem Kapitol und anderen römischen Altertümern beobachten könne.[22] Entstanden seien diese Behausungen u.a. aus der Nachahmung tierischer Bauten.[23] Mit fortschreitender Kunstfertigkeit und der Entwicklung „von einem wilden und bäuerischen Leben zu sanftmütiger, höherer Bildung" wären die Menschen jedoch dazu übergegangen, „statt Hütten Häuser mit Grundmauern zu bauen, die Wände aus Ziegeln hatten oder aus Stein und Holz errichtet und mit Ziegeln gedeckt waren".[24] Der „wilde und bäuerische" Holzbau blieb aber als ursprüngliche „Wahrheit" (*veritas*) der Architektur erhalten, weil der steinerne Tempelbau, so Vitruv weiter, bis in die kleinsten Details dessen Nachahmung (*imitatio*) bzw. Abbild (*imago*) darstelle.[25] Die klassische, platonisch ausgerichtete Architekturtheorie hat die Ursachen für diesen Materialwechsel in der generellen Aufgabe jeglicher Kunst gesehen, die Natur – repräsentiert im Holz, das meist als das ursprünglichste Baumaterial betrachtet wurde[26] – nachzuahmen und in diesem Nachahmungsprozess zu idealisieren und zu veredeln (d.h. hier, in Marmor zu übertragen). „Stone as a material was in itself incapable of providing architecture with any rules – only through the process of imitation does architecture become an *art raisonné*", fasst Ákos Moravansky die Imitationstheorie des Klassizisten Quatremère de Quincy[27] zusammen. „If wooden buildings had only ever imitated other wooden buildings then the classical

column would never have emerged. It was the fact that the architect always had to interpret wood architecture as soon as he built with stone that led to the vast formal wealth of stone and brick architecture. The imitation of a wooden building in stone is an idealizing, interpretative process that generates both identity and difference – a distance between the original and the work of art like that between a person and their portrait."[28]

Mit dem Aufkommen neuer, industrieller Materialien im 19. Jahrhundert und der daraus entstehenden moralischen Abwertung von Materialimitationen als „Betrug"[29] und der Forderung nach „Materialgerechtigkeit" verliert der – ohnehin auf dem Rückzug befindliche – Holzbau seine Rolle als archaischer Urtypus und besitzt nur mehr als museales Relikt einer vorindustriellen Lebensform Existenzberechtigung. Während 1851 Friedrich Theodor Vischer, noch ganz im Bann der Urhüttenidee, dem Holzbau zugesteht, dass er „einen ländlich-patriarchalischen Charakter" entwickle, „durch seine primitive Stimmung, seine Ursprünglichkeit" erfreue und in ihm „das Einfache, Urgerüstartige, worin alles streng Constructive als solches hervortritt, [...] höhere, poetische Bedeutung" erhalte,[30] bedauert der kulturkonservative Politiker August Reichensperger 1860, dass „diese malerischen Holzbauten stets mehr und mehr verschwinden und die modernen saft- und kraftlosen Häuserkarikaturen auch in die Dörfer einwandern" und lediglich „im Schwarzwalde und dem ‚zurückgebliebenen' Schweizer- und

19 Condit, Carl W.: *The Chicago School of Architecture. A History of Commercial and Public Building in the Chicago Area, 1875–1925*, Chicago/London 1966, 18, gibt den Anteil der reinen Holzbauten in Chicago vor dem Stadtbrand von 1871 mit zwei Dritteln an.

20 Vgl. Kirkland, Joseph/Moses, John: *The History of Chicago, Illinois*, Chicago 1895, 219f. In Turku durften an „Hauptstraßen und Plätzen [...] nur Steinhäuser gebaut werden, der Bau von zweistöckigen Holzhäusern und Mansardendächern wurde verboten". Nikula: *Landschaft* (wie Anm. 2), 74.

21 Sennett, Richard: *Flesh and Stone. The Body and the City in Western Civilization*, New York/London 1994; dt.: *Fleisch und Stein. Der Körper und die Stadt in der westlichen Zivilisation*, Berlin 1995.

22 Vgl. Vitruv: *De architectura libri decem*, II, 34, 24f; 35, 20–22.

23 Vgl. ebd., II, 34, 8f.

24 „[...] e fera agrestique vita ad mansuetam perduverunt humanitatem. [...] non casas sed etiam domus fundatas et latericiis parietibus aut e lapide structas materiaque et tegula tectas perficere coeperunt [...]." Ebd., II, 36, 6f; 36, 10ff; überarb. Übers. nach Vitruv: *Zehn Bücher über Architektur*, übers. u. m. Anm. versehen v. Curt Fensterbusch, Darmstadt 1964, 83ff.

25 Vgl. Vitruv: *De architectura*, IV, 88, 19ff; 89, 6–11; 90, 1–17.

26 Vgl. Moravanszky, Ákos: *Metamorphism. Material Change in Architecture*, Basel/Berlin 2018, 167.

27 Vgl. Quatremère de Quincy, Antoine Chrysostôme: *Essai sur la nature, le but et les modes de l'imitation dans les Beaux Arts*, Paris 1823, Reprint, Brüssel 1980.

28 Moravanszky: *Metamorphism* (wie Anm. 26), 167.

29 Vgl. Ruskin, John: *The Seven Lamps of Architecture*, London 1849; dt.: *Die Sieben Leuchter der Baukunst*, Übers. Wilhelm Schölermann, Leipzig 1900, 65–66.

30 Vischer, Friedrich Theodor: *Aesthetik oder die Wissenschaft des Schönen. Dritter Teil: Die Kunstlehre*, Stuttgart 1851, 211; zit. n. Rübel et al.: *Materialästhetik* (wie Anm. 3), 46.

well. Vitruvius speculated about the origin of building—the so-called primitive hut (fig. 1) of wood, reeds, leaves, and mud—as could still be observed in his day in the huts of Gaul, Hispania, Lusitanian, and Aquitania but also in the straw-covered hut of Romulus on the Capitol and other Roman antiquities.[22] He argued that these structures had resulted from, among other things, imitating structures made by other animals.[23] As their skills improved and they evolved "from a rude and barbarous mode of life to civilization and refinement," people "gave up their huts and began to build houses with foundations, having brick or stone walls, and roofs of timber and tiles."[24] But "rude and barbarous" timber construction was preserved as the original "truth" (*veritas*) of architecture, because the stone construction of the temple, Vitruvius continued, represents down to the tiniest details its imitation (*imitatio*) or image (*imago*).[25] Classical Plato-oriented architectural theory saw the causes for this change in material in the general task of every art to imitate nature—represented by wood, which was usually seen as the most primeval building material[26]—and to idealize and ennoble it in this process of imitation (i.e., in this case, to apply it to marble). "Stone as a material was in itself incapable of providing architecture with any rules—only through the process of imitation does architecture become an *art raisonné*"—as Ákos Moravansky sums up the theory of imitation of the classicist Quatremère de Quincy.[27] "If wooden buildings had only ever imitated other wooden buildings then the classical column would never have emerged. It was the fact that the architect always had to interpret wood architecture as soon as he built with stone that led to the vast formal wealth of stone and brick architecture. The imitation of a wooden building in stone is an idealizing, interpretative process that generates both identity and difference—a distance between the original and the work of art like that between a person and their portrait."[28]

With the rise of new industrial material in the nineteenth century and the resulting moral dismissal of imitations of materials as "deceit"[29] and the call for "truth to materials," timber construction lost its role as the archaic, original type, which was already on the decline in any case, and the only justification for its existence was now as a museum relict of a pre-industrial way of life. Whereas Friedrich Theodor Vischer, still entirely under the sway of the idea of the primitive hut in 1851, admits that timber construction develops "a rural, patriarchal character," is pleasing "thanks to its primitive atmosphere, its originality," and preserves "its simple, primally structural quality in which everything that is per se strictly structural stands

out" and obtains "higher, poetic significance,"[30] the culturally conservative politician August Reichensperger regretted in 1860 that "these picturesque wooden buildings continue to disappear more and more, and modern, insipid, listless caricatures of houses are migrating even to villages" and only "in the Black Forest and the 'backward' Swiss and Tyrolean highlands does the art of timber construction live on in the people in all its freshness."[31] Here it is only about the literal farmer's house, which is supposed to be protected or revived as a picturesque prop of the countryside.

Especially in the German-speaking world, the identification of timber construction with rusticity is unbroken, that is, with a ruralness that has connotations ranging (depending on one's standpoint) from the positive to the negative. A Google image search for the German word "rustikal" turns up pages and pages of interiors with ceilings with wooden beams, wood paneling, plank floors, oak cabinets, and carved wood in farmhouses (fig. 3). The hits are similar for the English word "rustic" and the Czech "rustikální," whereas with the French word "rustique," the Croatian word "rustikalna," and above all the Italian word "rustico" (interestingly, also the Finnish word "maalaismainen"), the images are dominated instead by rubble-work masonry (albeit in combination with wooden country-house furniture) (fig. 4). A survey conducted in Styrian

22 See Vitruvius, *De architectura libri decem*, 2.34.24–25; 2.35.20–22; Vitruvius, *The Ten Books on Architecture*, trans. Morris Hicky Morgan (Cambridge, MA: 1914), 39–40.

23 See Vitruvius, *De architectura* (see note 22), 2.34.8–9; Vitruvius, *The Ten Books on Architecture* (see note 22), 38.

24 Vitruvius, *De architectura* (see note 22), 2.36.6–7; 2.36.10ff.: "e fera agrestique vita ad mansuetam perduverunt humanitatem. [...] non casas sed etiam domus fundatas et latericiis parietibus aut e lapide structas materiaque et tegula tectas perficere coeperunt"; Vitruvius, *The Ten Books on Architecture* (see note 22), 40–41.

25 See Vitruvius, *De architectura* (see note 22), 4.88.19–21; 4.89.6–11; 2.90.1–17; Vitruvius, *The Ten Books on Architecture* (see note 22), 107–109.

26 See Ákos Moravanszky, *Metamorphism: Material Change in Architecture* (Basel, 2018), 167.

27 See Antoine Chrysostôme Quatremère de Quincy, *Essai sur la nature, le but et les modes de l'imitation dans les Beaux Arts* (Paris, 1823); translated by J. C. Kent as *An Essay on the Nature, the End and the Means of Imitation in the Fine Arts* (London, 1837).

28 Moravanszky, *Metamorphism* (see note 26), 167.

29 See John Ruskin, *The Seven Lamps of Architecture* (London, 1849), 32–33.

30 Friedrich Theodor Vischer, *Aesthetik; oder, Die Wissenschaft des Schönen*, part 3, *Die Kunstlehre* (Stuttgart, 1851), 211; reprinted in Rübel, *Materialästhetik* (see note 3), 46.

31 August Reichensperger, *Die christlich-germanische Baukunst und ihr Verhältnis zur Gegenwart* (Trier, 1860), reprinted in Rübel, *Materialästhetik* (see note 3), 150.

Tyroler-Hochlande diese Kunst des Holzbaues noch in aller Frische im Volk fort[lebt]".[31] Hier geht es nur mehr um das buchstäbliche Bauernhaus, das als malerisches Landschaftsrequisit geschützt oder wiederbelebt werden muss.

Bis heute ist besonders im deutschen Sprachraum die Identifikation des Holzbaus mit Rustikalität ungebrochen, also einer (je nach Standpunkt) positiv bis negativ konnotierten Ländlichkeit. Die Google-Bildersuche unter dem Stichwort „rustikal" fördert seitenweise Innenräume mit Holzbalkendecken, Holzvertäfelungen, Schiffböden, Eichenholzschränken und geschnitzten Bauernstuben zutage (Abb. 3). Ähnlich fällt die Suche mit dem englischen „rustic" und dem tschechischen „rustikální" aus, während beim französischen „rustique", beim kroatischen „rustikalna" und vor allem beim italienischen „rustico" (interessanterweise auch beim finnischen „maalaismainen") zunehmend Bruchsteinmauerwerk (aber in Kombination mit hölzernen Landhausmöbeln) das Bild bestimmt (Abb. 4). Eine 1997 durchgeführte Umfrage unter steirischen Gemeinden ergab, dass 88 Prozent der Befragten die Anwendung des Baustoffes Holz mit dem landwirtschaftlichen Bereich assoziierten. Umgekehrt rangierte die Vorstellung, dass Holz ein städtischer Baustoff sei, bei den befragten ArchitektInnen der Steiermark weit abgeschlagen auf dem letzten Platz.[32]

Ab dem 19. Jahrhundert konnten aus der rustikalen Konnotation des Holzbaus nationale Identifikationsmuster geschnitzt werden, wenn etwa Henry D. Thoreau die Holzfällerhütte zum architektonischen Leitmotiv erklärte: „One of the most beautiful buildings in the country is a logger's hut in the woods",[33] schrieb er 1852 in sein Tagebuch, nachdem er zuvor zwei Jahre als Einsiedler in einer selbstgebauten Holzhütte verbracht hatte. In Deutschland nahm sich zuerst die Volkskunde mit ihrer Suche nach nationalen Haustypen[34] und später die Heimatschutzbewegung einem ideologisch überhöhten Holzbauprogramm an. Vor allem, als die Moderne das Bauen mit Stahl und Stahlbeton vom Industrie- in den Wohnungsbau übertrug und das Flachdach propagierte, reagierten Deutsch- und Heimattümler mit extra steilen Zimmermannsdächern auf biederen Blockhäusern im Retro-Stil. (Abb. 5) Nach Hitlers Machtergreifung errichteten die Stuttgarter Nazi-Architekten im Herbst 1933 mit der Kochenhofsiedlung (Abb. 6) ein Gegenprogramm zur Weißenhofsiedlung, die Paul Bonatz als „Vorstadt Jerusalems"[35] antisemitisch verunglimpft hatte, und ließen dort nicht von ungefähr alle Häuser aus „deutschem Holz"[36] errichten (um seinerseits als „Holzwurmsiedlung" verspottet zu werden). Holz wurde zum Nationalmaterial des Germanentums schlechthin erklärt: „Mit einem Materiale hat der germanische und hat späterhin der deutsche Mensch vorzugsweise gearbeitet: mit dem Holze", verkündete etwa der NS-Kunsthistoriker Alfred Stange.[37]

Obwohl hölzerne Wohnbauten für das NS-Regime höchstens einen Nebenschauplatz darstellten („Stein statt Eisen"

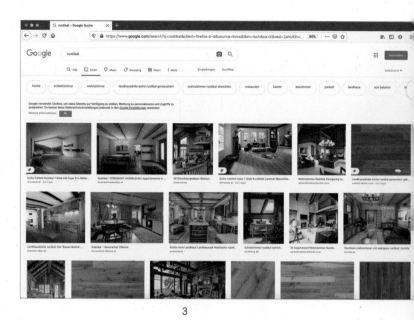

3

Google-Bildersuche zum Stichwort „rustikal" | Google image search for the word "rustikal" ("rustic"), Screenshot, 22.10.2020

lautete die Parole von Albert Speer),[38] haben Heimatschutz- und NS-Propaganda den Holzbau für Jahrzehnte diskreditiert. Dazu kam die Erinnerung an die von der Deutschen Wehrmacht in Brand gesteckten Holzsiedlungen und -städte Osteuropas und vor allem, dass während und nach den beiden Weltkriegen notdürftige Quartiere für Flüchtlinge, Ausgebombte, Kriegsgefangene und schließlich auch viele KZ-Bauten in Holzbauweise als sogenannte Baracken errichtet wurden (Abb. 7). Weniger das Material als Überbelegung, katastrophale hygienische Zustände und der Zusammenhang mit Vertreibung und Massenmord machten die Baracken zu einem Synonym für unbeschreibliches Elend. Millionen von Menschen erlebten die Übersiedlung von einer Holzbaracke in eine moderne Wohnsiedlung

31 Reichensperger, August: Die christlich-germanische Baukunst und ihr Verhältnis zur Gegenwart, Trier 1860; zit. n. ebd., 150.

32 Vgl. Schaffer, Rafaela: Imageanalyse des Baustoffes Holz und Ableitung von Konsequenzen für die Kommunikationspolitik von PROHOLZ, Dipl.-Arb. Universität Graz 1997, 40, 56.

33 Thoreau, Henry D.: Journal, Bd. 3, New York 1968, 181; zit. n. Kruft, Hanno-Walter: Geschichte der Architekturtheorie, München 2013, 404.

34 Vgl. Bedal: Hausforschung (wie Anm. 8), 12f, 42.

35 Bonatz, Paul: „Noch einmal die Werkbundsiedlung", Schwäbischer Merkur, 5. Mai 1926.

36 Die Kochenhofsiedlung entstand im Rahmen der „Bau-Ausstellung Deutsches Holz in Hausbau und Wohnung", die von 23.09.–29.10.1933 in Stuttgart stattfand.

37 Stange, Alfred: Die Bedeutung des Werkstoffes in der deutschen Kunst, Bielefeld/Leipzig 1940; zit. n. Rübel et al.: Materialästhetik (wie Anm. 3), 232.

38 Speer, Albert: „Stein statt Eisen", in: Der Vierjahresplan 1 Folge 3 (1937), 136–137; wieder abgedr. in: ebd., 221–224.

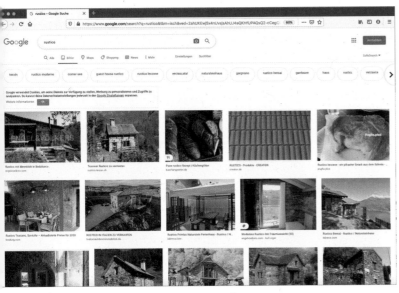

Google-Bildersuche zum Stichwort „rustico" | Google image search
for the word "rustico", Screenshot, 22.10.2020

communities in 1997 showed that 88 percent of respondents associated the use of wood as a building material with the agricultural sector. Conversely, the idea that wood is an urban building material came dead last among the architects in Styria surveyed.[32]

From the nineteenth century onward, models of national identification could be carved from the rustic connotations of timber construction, for example, when Henry David Thoreau declared the logger's hut to be the leitmotif for architecture: "One of the most beautiful buildings in the country is a logger's hut in the woods,"[33] he wrote in his diary in 1852, two years after he himself had lived as a hermit in a log cabin he built himself. In Germany, ethnologists searching for national house types[34] and later the Heimatschutz (Homeland Protection) movement adopted an ideologically superelevated program for timber construction. Especially when the modern architects transferred building with steel and reinforced concrete from industry to housing construction and advocated the flat roof, the proponents of the German and of *Heimat* responded with extra-steep *Zimmermannsdächer* (wood-frame roofs) on old-fashioned log cabins in the retro style (fig. 5). After Hitler seized power, Nazi architects in Stuttgart presented the Kochenhof housing development (fig. 6) in the autumn of 1933 as a counter-program to the Weissenhof housing development, which Paul Bonatz had disparaged with the anti-Semitic label "suburb of Jerusalem";[35] not coincidentally, all the houses were of "German wood"[36]—only to be mocked in turn as the "Woodworm housing development." Wood was declared to be the national material of Teutonism: "The Teutons and later the

Germans have worked with one material by preference: with wood," announced the Nazi art historian Alfred Stange, for example.[37]

Although wood houses were at most a sideshow for the Nazi regime ("stone instead of iron" was Albert Speer's slogan),[38] *Heimatschutz* and Nazi propaganda brought timber construction in disrepute for decades. The memory of the German Wehrmacht setting the wooden housing developments and cities of Eastern Europe on fire contributed to that as well, and above all the fact that during and after both world wars temporary housing for refugees, those left homeless by bombings, war prisoners, and also many concentration camp buildings were constructed as wooden barracks (fig. 7). It was not so much that material as overcrowding, catastrophic hygienic conditions, and the association with banishment and mass murder that made barracks synonymous with indescribable misery. Millions of people experienced relocation from wooden barracks to a modern housing development of bricks and concrete as an act of liberation from impoverished conditions and as the beginning of their good fortune and prosperity. It is reasonable to assume that hardly anyone moved willingly into a wooden house in the Europe of the 1940s, 1950s, and early 1960s.

The Parametric Forgetting of the Materials. How was timber construction able to enjoy a revival in the late twentieth century? Initially, it was part of the context of a new consciousness of materials in architecture that began with Brutalism (and, among other things, its penchant for the traces of rough-sawn shuttering boards)[39] and continued by movements

---

32 See Rafaela Schaffer, "Imageanalyse des Baustoffes Holz und Ableitung von Konsequenzen für die Kommunikationspolitik von PROHOLZ," diploma thesis, Universität Graz, 1997, 40, 56.

33 Henry David Thoreau, *Journal*, vol. 3 (Boston, 1906), 182–183 (January 11, 1852).

34 See Bedal, *Hausforschung* (see note 8), 12–13, 42.

35 Paul Bonatz, "Noch einmal die Werkbundsiedlung," *Schwäbischer Merkur*, May 5, 1926.

36 The Kochenhof housing development was built as part of the *Bau-Ausstellung Deutsches Holz in Hausbau und Wohnung*, held in Stuttgart from September 23 to October 29, 1933.

37 Alfred Stange, *Die Bedeutung des Werkstoffes in der deutschen Kunst* (Bielefeld, 1940), reprinted in Rübel, *Materialästhetik* (see note 3), 232.

38 Albert Speer, "Stein statt Eisen," *Der Vierjahresplan* 1, no. 3 (1937): 136–37, reprinted in Rübel, *Materialästhetik* (see note 3), 221–224.

39 See Le Corbusier, *Œuvre complète*, vol. 5, 1946–1952, ed. Willi Boesinger (Zurich, 1953), 191.

5

Otto Robert Trnik, Haus Wittmann, Graz, Österreich I Austria, 1935
© Anselm Wagner

aus Ziegel und Beton als Akt der Befreiung aus ärmlichen Umständen und Beginn ihres Wohlstandsglücks. Man kann davon ausgehen, dass im Europa der 1940er-, 50er- und frühen 60er-Jahre kaum jemand freiwillig in ein Holzhaus gezogen ist.

Parametrische Materialvergessenheit. Wie konnte der Holzbau Ende des 20. Jahrhunderts ein Revival erfahren? Zunächst steht dieser im Kontext eines neuen Materialbewusstseins, das in der Architektur mit dem Brutalismus (und u.a. seiner Vorliebe für die Spuren sägerauher Schalungsbretter)[39] einsetzt und sich über Strömungen wie den Kritischen Regionalismus[40] und den *Dirty Realism*[41] fortsetzt. In den späten 1980er- und 1990er-Jahren stehen aber dazu gegenläufige, dekonstruktivistische und sich daraus entwickelnde parametrische Tendenzen im Rampenlicht des Architekturdiskurses. Bei aller formalen Avanciertheit verfolgen diese Richtungen ein sehr traditionelles idealistisches Konzept, das auf der bis in die antike Philosophie zurückreichenden Idee des Primats der Form vor der Materie bzw. der Herrschaft der Kultur über die Natur beruht. Demnach bedarf die Kunst eines Stoffes,

um sichtbar werden zu können, aber dieser ist nur eine passive Masse, „roh und todt", wie Vischer in seiner *Aesthetik* sagt: „Der Stoff muß aber für den Zweck der darstellenden Phantasie roh sein in dem Sinne, daß die Form, die jene ihm aufdrückt, nichts zu schaffen hat."[42] Mit dem Aufkommen des digitalen Entwerfens konnte die Form soweit verselbstständigt werden, dass die bauliche Umsetzung in einem bestimmten Material nicht mehr am Beginn, sondern am Ende des Entwurfsprozesses stand und diesem somit weitgehend äußerlich war. In der unendlichen Möglichkeitswelt der Algorithmen konnte scheinbar alles nicht nur jede erdenkliche Form annehmen, sondern sich auch in jedem beliebigen Stoff materialisieren. Woraus die von Zaha Hadid oder Greg Lynn entworfenen Gebäude bestehen, ist an den Entwürfen weder ablesbar noch in irgendeiner Weise von Bedeutung. Spätestens die ökologische Krise, die während der 2010er-Jahre auch im Mainstream angekommen ist, hat die digitale Blase platzen lassen und die Fragen, mit welchem Material wir eigentlich bauen, von wem es unter welchen Bedingungen produziert wird und welche Wegstrecken es bis zum Bauplatz zurücklegen muss, zu zentralen Fragen der Architektur gemacht. Deshalb wirkt parametrische Architektur heute nicht nur wegen ihres modischen Gestus, sondern auch wegen ihres oft „materialvergessenen" Entwurfsansatzes nicht mehr ganz zeitgemäß.

Ähnliches gilt für jede Art konzeptueller, ausschließlich an der Form orientierter Architektur, wie sie etwa Peter Eisenman vertritt, für den Plan und Kartonmodell als ideelle, „anti-materielle" Medien das Eigentliche von Architektur ausdrücken, während reale Baumaterialien mit ihrem Eigenleben die Reinheit des architektonischen Konzepts verunklären. So stellte er etwa 2013 in einem Interview fest: „If there is a debate in architecture today, the lasting debate is between architecture as a conceptual, cultural, and intellectual enterprise, and architecture as a phenomenological enterprise – that is, the experience of the subject in architecture, the experience of materiality, of light, of color, of space and etc. I have always been on the side opposed to phenomenology. I'm not interested in Peter Zumthor's work or people who spend their time worrying about the details or the grain of wood on one side or the color of the material on the surface, etc. I couldn't care less. That having been said, it is still necessary to build. But the whole notion of the idea of ‚cardboard architecture' meant that the

39   Vgl. Le Corbusier: „L'unité d'Habitation in Marseille" [1952]; zit. n. Rübel et al.: *Materialästhetik* (wie Anm. 3), 82f.

40   Vgl. Frampton, Kenneth: „Towards a Critical Regionalism: Six Points for an Architecture of Resistance", in: Foster, Hal (Hg.): *The Anti-Aesthetic. Essays on Postmodern Culture*, Seattle 1983, 16–30; dt.: „Kritischer Regionalismus: moderne Architektur und kulturelle Identität", in: ders.: *Architektur der Moderne. Eine kritische Baugeschichte*, Stuttgart 2001, 263–273.

41   Vgl. Lefaivre, Liane: „Dirty Realism in European Architecture Today. Making the Stone Stony", in: *Design Book Review* 17 (1989), 17–20; dt.: dies.: „Dirty Realism' in der Architektur. Den Stein steinern machen!", in: *Archithese* 20 (1990), 1, 14–21.

42   Vischer: *Aesthetik* (wie Anm. 30), 8f; zit. n. Rübel et al.: *Materialästhetik* (wie Anm. 3), 44.

such as Critical Regionalism[40] and Dirty Realism.[41] In the late 1980s and 1990s, however, the contrary trends of Deconstructivism and, evolving from it, parametric design were in the limelight of the discourse on architecture. For all their advanced form, these movements pursued a very traditional, idealist concept based on the idea that can be traced back to ancient philosophy of the primacy of form over materials or of the dominance of culture over nature. In this view, art needs a material in order to become visible, but it is just a passive mass, "raw and dead," as Vischer says in his *Aesthetik*: "But the material has to be raw for the purpose of the depicting imagination in the sense that the form that the latter impresses on it has nothing to create."[42] With the rise of digital design, form could be made autonomous to such an extent that its architectural realization in a particular material no longer stood at the beginning of the design process but rather at the end and was thus largely external to it. In the world of the infinite possibilities of algorithms, apparently everything could not only adopt every conceivable form but also be materialized in any material at all.

7

Barackenlager in Kapfenberg | Wooden barracks in Kapfenberg, Österreich | Austria um | around 1950 © Stadtgemeinde Kapfenberg

What the buildings designed by Zaha Hadid or Greg Lynn are made of is neither evident from the designs nor significant in any way. At the latest, the ecological crisis, which entered mainstream consciousness as well in the second decade of the twenty-first century, caused the digital bubble to burst and made the questions of the material with which we build, who produces it and under what conditions, and the routes it takes to the construction site the central questions of architecture. For that reason, parametric architecture no longer seems entirely up-to-date, not just because of its fashionable gesture but also owing to its design approach often "forgetting the materials."

Much the same is true of any form of conceptual architecture oriented exclusively around form, like that represented by Peter Eisenman, for example, for whom the plan and the cardboard model as the "antimaterial" medium of ideas express the authentic aspect of architecture, whereas the real building materials with their lives of their own obscure the purity of the architectural concept. He observed in an interview

6

Hans Mayer, Haus Nr. 22, Kochenhofsiedlung | Kochenhof housing development Stuttgart, Deutschland | Germany, 1933 © Fyrtaarn/Wikimedia Commons

40 See Kenneth Frampton, "Towards a Critical Regionalism: Six Points for an Architecture of Resistance," in *The Anti-Aesthetic: Essays on Postmodern Culture*, ed. Hal Foster (Seattle, WA, 1983), 16–30.

41 See Liane Lefaivre, "Dirty Realism in European Architecture Today: Making the Stone Stony," *Design Book Review* 17 (1989): 17–20.

42 Vischer, *Aesthetik* (see note 30), 8–9; reprinted in Rübel, *Materialästhetik* (see note 3), 44.

materiality of the work was important as an ‚anti-material‘
statement."[43]

Offensichtlich bezieht sich Eisenman hier auf ein
1996 verfasstes Statement von Peter Zumthor, wo dieser (in
deutlicher Abgrenzung von den nicht namentlich erwähnten
„Papierarchitekten") sagt: „Architektur ist immer konkrete
Materie. Architektur ist nicht abstrakt, sondern konkret. Ein
Entwurf, ein Projekt, aufgezeichnet auf Papier, ist nicht Architektur, sondern nur eine mehr oder weniger mangelhafte Repräsentation von Architektur, vergleichbar mit den Noten in
der Musik. Die Musik bedarf der Aufführung. Architektur bedarf der Ausführung. Dann entsteht ihr Körper. Und dieser ist
immer sinnlich."[44] Dieser materialistische Ansatz steht somit
jenem von Eisenman diametral gegenüber. Da Zumthor nicht
nur eine ganze Generation von Architektinnen und Architekten geprägt hat, sondern auch im *material turn* in der Architektur, der dem gegenwärtigen Boom von Bauen mit Holz zugrunde liegt, eine zentrale Rolle spielt, lohnt sich ein genauerer
Blick auf sein Entwurfskonzept.

**Peter Zumthor und der *material turn* in der Archi-
tektur.** Das Credo des ausgebildeten Möbelschreiners Zumthor
lautet: „Die Wirklichkeit der Architektur ist das Konkrete, das
Form-, Masse- und Raumgewordene, ihr Körper. Es gibt keine
Idee, ausser in den Dingen."[45] Daraus folgt eine radikale Umkehrung des architektonischen Entwurfsprozesses, der gewissermaßen vom Kopf auf die Füße gestellt wird. Anstatt Raumprogramme zu entwerfen und Pläne zu zeichnen, die dann erst
an der Baustelle in einem konkreten Material umgesetzt werden, beginnt das von Zumthor 1996–2008 geleitete erste Jahr
des Architekturstudiums an der Accademia di architettura in
Mendrisio mit den Materialien: „In allen Übungen wird mit
wirklichen Materialien gearbeitet. Die Entwurfsarbeiten zielen
immer auf konkrete Gegenstände, Objekte, Installationen aus
wirklichen Materialien (Ton, Stein, Kupfer, Stahl, Filz, Stoff,
Holz, Gips, Ziegel …). Kartonmodelle gibt es nicht. Eigentlich
sollen gar keine ‚Modelle' im hergebrachten Sinn hergestellt
werden, sondern konkrete Objekte, plastische Arbeiten in
einem bestimmten Massstab."[46]

Auf den ersten Blick schließt Zumthor damit an den
berühmten Vorkurs des Bauhauses an, der – fußend auf dem
modernen Dogma der „Materialgerechtigkeit" – in der Erkundung spezifischer Materialeigenschaften bestand (und ohne solche Forschungen wären Erfindungen wie z.B. der Freischwin-
ger gar nicht möglich gewesen).[47] Zumthors Materialpalette ist
allerdings eingeschränkter als jene der Bauhauspädagogik: Sie
umfasst nur „wirkliche Materialien", also keinen Karton und
kein Papier, weil diese in realer Architektur nicht vorkommen,
und scheint natürliche Materialien gegenüber künstlichen zu
bevorzugen. Dies hat wohl mit der meist geringeren sinnlichen
Qualität letzterer zu tun: „Architektur konkret erfahren, das
heisst ihren Körper berühren, sehen, hören, riechen."[48] Zielten

8

Peter Zumthor, Schweizer Pavillon | Swiss Pavilion, Expo Hannover,
Deutschland | Germany, 2000 © Roland Halbe

die Materialforschungen der Moderne primär auf die funktionalen Potenziale des jeweiligen Materials, sodass dieses oft hinter seiner Funktion verschwand (das stützenlose Überspannen
weiter Räume war wichtiger als das Zeigen des Stahls, der dies
ermöglichte), geht es Zumthor, um mit dem Phänomenologen
Gernot Böhme zu sprechen, mehr um die Materialität als solche, d.h. die Erscheinungsform, den Charakter und den Insze-
nierungswert des Materials.[49] Das führt automatisch zu einer
Bevorzugung von Naturmaterialien gegenüber synthetischen,

43 Peter Eisenman zit. n. Ansari, Iman: „Eisenman's Evolution. Architecture,
Syntax, and New Subjectivity", in: *ArchDaily*, 23. September 2013, online
unter: https://www.archdaily.com/429925/eisenman-s-evolution-
architecture-syntax-and-new-subjectivity (Stand: 4. Februar 2021).

44 Zumthor, Peter: „Architektur lehren, Architektur lernen" [1996], in:
Architektur Denken, Basel/Boston/Berlin 2006, 65–69, hier 66.

45 Ders.: „Der harte Kern der Schönheit" [1991], in: ebd., 29–37, hier 37.

46 Ders.: „Architektur lehren, Architektur lernen" [1996], in: ebd., 65–69, hier 66.

47 Vgl. Bayer, Herbert/Gropius, Walter/Gropius, Ise (Hg.): *Bauhaus
1919–1928*, Teufen 1955, 30, 89, 114–118.

48 Zumthor: „Architektur lehren, Architektur lernen" (wie Anm. 44), 58.

49 Vgl. Böhme, Gernot: *Architektur und Atmosphäre*, München 2013, 156f.

in 2013, for example: "If there is a debate in architecture today, the lasting debate is between architecture as a conceptual, cultural, and intellectual enterprise, and architecture as a phenomenological enterprise—that is, the experience of the subject in architecture, the experience of materiality, of light, of color, of space and etc. I have always been on the side opposed to phenomenology. I'm not interested in Peter Zumthor's work or people who spend their time worrying about the details or the grain of wood on one side or the color of the material on the surface, etc. I couldn't care less. That having been said, it is still necessary to build. But the whole notion of the idea of 'cardboard architecture' meant that the materiality of the work was important as an 'anti-material' statement."[43]

Eisenman is clearly referring here to a statement written in 1996 by Peter Zumthor in which he (clearly distinguishing himself from unnamed "paper architects") says: "Architecture is always concrete matter. Architecture is not abstract, but concrete. A plan, a project drawn on paper is not architecture but merely a more or less inadequate representation of architecture, comparable to sheet music. Music needs to be performed. Architecture needs to be executed. Then its body can come into being. And this body is always sensuous."[44] This materialist approach is thus diametrically opposed to that of Eisenman. Because Zumthor influenced not only an entire generation of architects but also played a central role in the material turn in architecture on which the current boom in building with wood is based, it pays to take a closer look at his concept of design.

Peter Zumthor and the Material Turn in Architecture. The credo of Zumthor, who trained as a cabinetmaker, was: "The reality of architecture is the concrete body in which forms, volumes, and spaces come into being. There are no ideas except in things."[45] From that follows a radical inversion of the process of architectural design, turning it from its head onto its feet in a sense. Rather than designing space allocation programs and drawing plans that are first implemented in a specific material at the construction site, the first-year program in architecture at the Accademia di architettura in Mendrisio, of which Zumthor was in charge from 1996 to 2008, began with materials: "All the design work in the studio is done with materials. It always aims directly at concrete things, objects, installations made of real material (clay, stone, copper, steel, felt, cloth, wood, plaster, brick ...). There are no cardboard models. Actually, no 'models' at all in the conventional sense, but concrete objects, three-dimensional works on a specific scale."[46]

At first glance, Zumthor seems to be taking up the practice of the famous preliminary course at the Bauhaus, which—based in turn on the modern dogma of "truth to materials"—explored specific properties of materials (and inventions such as the cantilever chair would not even have been possible without such research).[47] Zumthor's palette of materials was, however, more limited than that of Bauhaus pedagogy, including only "real materials," that is, no cardboard and no paper, because they are not found in real architecture, and seems to prefer natural materials to artificial ones. That is probably because the latter have less of a sensuous quality: "To experience architecture in a concrete way means to touch, see, hear, and smell it."[48] If the material studies of the modern era focused primarily on the potential functions of the material in question, so that the latter often vanished behind its function (spanning large spaces without supports was more important than showing the steel that made that possible), Zumthor was concerned more with, to paraphrase the phenomenologist Gernot Böhme, materiality as such, that is, the forms of appearance, character, and theatrical value of the material.[49] This automatically leads to a preference for natural materials over synthetic but rather characterless ones such as chipboards, Formica, PVC, polyurethane foam, and so on, which in construction are either clad or themselves serve as indifferent cladding. Whereas contemporary materials sciences focus exclusively on the properties of materials with respect to processing and performance, architecture and design are increasingly concerned with appearance, that is, the image, of materiality and about the emotions and qualities associated with it. Being and appearance can diverge but they can also—as in Zumthor's case—reinforce each other. Examples include his thermal bath in Vals, his Swiss Pavilion at Expo 2000 in Hannover (fig. 8), and his Bruder-Klaus-Kapelle

43 Peter Eisenman quoted in Iman Ansari, "Eisenman's Evolution: Architecture, Syntax, and New Subjectivity," *ArchDaily*, September 23, 2013, available online at: https://www.archdaily.com/429925/eisenman-s-evolution-architecture-syntax-and-new-subjectivity.

44 Peter Zumthor, "Teaching Architecture, Learning Architecture" (1996), trans. Maureen Oberli-Turner (1996), in Zumthor, *Thinking Architecture*, 2nd ed. (Basel, 2006), 57–59, esp. 58.

45 Peter Zumthor, "The Hard Core of Beauty" (1991), trans. Maureen Oberli-Turner, in Zumthor, *Thinking Architecture* (see note 44), 27–34, esp. 34.

46 Zumthor, "Teaching Architecture, Learning Architecture" (see note 44), 58.

47 See Herbert Bayer, Ise Gropius, and Walter Gropius, eds., *Bauhaus 1919–1928*, exh. cat. (New York, 1938), 32, 91, 116–120.

48 Zumthor, "Teaching Architecture, Learning Architecture" (see note 44), 58.

49 See Gernot Böhme, *The Aesthetics of Atmospheres*, ed. Jean-Paul Thibaud (London, 2017), 142–143.

eher charakterlosen Werkstoffen wie Spanplatten, Resopal, PVC, Schaumstoff usw., die im Bau entweder verkleidet werden oder als indifferente Verkleidung dienen. Während die zeitgenössischen Materialwissenschaften alleinig auf die Bearbeitungs- und Belastbarkeitsqualitäten von Materialien ausgerichtet sind, geht es in Architektur und Design immer mehr um die Erscheinung, d.h. das Image, von Materialität und um die Gefühle und Qualitäten, die man damit verbindet. Dabei können Sein und Schein auseinanderfallen, sich aber auch – wie im Fall von Zumthor – wechselseitig aufladen. Beispiele wären seine Therme in Vals, der Schweizer Pavillon auf der Expo 2000 in Hannover (Abb. 8) oder die Bruder-Klaus-Kapelle in der Eifel, wo durch die Reduzierung der Form die jeweilige Materialität – Gneis bei der Therme, Lärchen- und Föhrenholz beim Pavillon und Stampfbeton bei der Kapelle – umso stärker den Eindruck bestimmt. Gewagtes Konstruieren und spektakuläre Raumbildung werden ersetzt durch bloßes Stapeln und Schichten von Material, das auf lapidare Weise nichts als seine bloße Materialität zeigt. Diese „Neue Einfachheit" beherrscht auch weite Teile der heutigen Holzarchitektur (Abb. 9) und wird gerne als minimalistisch apostrophiert. Die Dominanz der Materialität verbietet es aber eigentlich, von Minimalismus zu sprechen, da die historische *minimal art* jede Form von Materialität zu vermeiden suchte und ihre Objekte so abstrakt wie möglich (industriell gefertigt, ohne Bearbeitungsspuren, ohne Textur etc.) erscheinen ließ. Formale Reduktion ist hier auch weniger das Ziel als das Mittel, um das Material sprechen zu lassen. Insofern hat die heutige Architektur wesentlich mehr mit dem *material turn* der 2000er-Jahre als mit der *minimal art* der 1960er-Jahre zu tun.

Unter dem 2006 von Dan Hicks und Mary C. Beaudry ausgerufenen *material turn*[50] wird – in Anlehnung an den *linguistic turn* der 1960er- und den *iconic turn* der 1990er-Jahre – eine Denkschule verstanden, die sich, ausgehend von der Ethnologie, der Archäologie und der Kunstwissenschaft, mittlerweile in allen Kultur- und Geisteswissenschaften etabliert hat und in der die Materialität der Dinge im Fokus steht. Es geht dabei darum, Dinge der materiellen Kultur als Zeugen des Umgangs mit ihnen, als Objekte mit einer eigenen Biografie, ja sogar – im Sinne von Bruno Latours Akteur-Netzwerk-Theorie – als Akteure („Aktanten") zu verstehen.[51] In der Humangeografie ist von „nonhuman social partners", in der Literaturwissenschaft von „thing theory", in der Soziologie von der „Affordanz", dem Angebotscharakter der Dinge, in der Philosophie von „vital materialism" oder „speculative realism" die Rede. War die Kulturanalyse bisher sprach- bzw. symbolzentriert, erhalten nun – ganz im Sinne der Philosophie des *New Materialism* – die Dinge und mit ihnen ihre konkrete Materialität neues Gewicht.[52] Nachdem die vom *linguistic turn* beförderte Semiotik einen deutlichen Einfluss zumindest auf die Theoriebildung der postmodernen Architektur ausgeübt hat, scheint es

verführerisch, einen – wenn auch nicht kausalen – Zusammenhang zwischen dem *material turn* und der auf Materialität fokussierten zeitgenössischen Architektur herzustellen, also vom *material turn* in der Architektur als einem Parallelphänomen zu den Kulturwissenschaften zu sprechen. Gemeinsam ist den Kulturwissenschaften und der Architektur vor allem die Überzeugung, Material nicht als bloß passiv und dienend, als bloße Füllung von Form zu begreifen, sondern als aktiv, bestimmend und die Aussage prägend.

Materialität und ihre prominente Stellung sind in der Architektur aber kein Selbstzweck. „Materialität", so Gernot Böhme, „soll sich zeigen, heraustreten, sie soll das ihre zur Gestaltung von Lebensatmosphären leisten".[53] „Atmosphäre", einer der Schlüsselbegriffe der gegenwärtigen Architekturtheorie, ist deshalb auch für Zumthor zentral, die er im Anschluss an Böhme als „Wechselwirkung zwischen unseren Empfindungen und den Dingen, die uns umgeben",[54] definiert. Neben den Pflichtaufgaben des Architekten, Gebäude zu entwerfen, die hinsichtlich Funktion, Ökonomie, Innovation und Repräsentation alle Wünsche erfüllen, bestehe die Kür darin, „auch das zu entwerfen, was eine architektonische Atmosphäre wirklich ausmacht, diese einmalige Dichte und Stimmung, dieses Gefühl von Gegenwart, Wohlbefinden, Stimmigkeit, Schönheit".[55] Zumthor klingt dabei wie ein alchemistischer Meisterkoch, wenn er die materiellen Zutaten für eine gelungene Raumatmosphäre beschreibt: „Ich achte darauf, dass die Materialien zusammen klingen und zum Strahlen kommen, nehme eine bestimmte Menge von Eichenholz und eine andere von Tuffstein und gebe noch etwas hinzu: drei Gramm Silber, ein Griff zum Drehen, Flächen von glänzendem Glas, damit mit jeder Materialkomposition etwas Einmaliges entsteht."[56] Man mag diesen Materialfetischismus für elitär, übertrieben oder einfach unsympathisch halten, aber man muss anerkennen, dass er aus der zeitgenössischen Architektur kaum mehr wegzudenken ist. Dies ist umso bemerkenswerter, als das bewusste Erzeugen von Stimmungen mit dafür geeigneten Materialoberflächen bis heute als Kennzeichen des Unechten, Uneigentlichen und Unarchitektonischen, kurz: des Kitsches, gilt.

50 Vgl. Hicks, Dan/Beaudry, Mary C.: „Introduction: The Place of Historical Archaeology", in: dies. (Hg.): *The Cambridge Companion to Historical Archaeology*, Cambridge 2006, 1–9; dies.: „Introduction. Material Culture Studies: A Reactionary View", in: dies. (Hg.): *The Oxford Handbook of Material Culture Studies*, Oxford 2010, 1–21.

51 Vgl. Latour, Bruno: *Eine neue Soziologie für eine neue Gesellschaft*, Berlin 2009.

52 Vgl. Barad, Karen: „Agential Realism. How Material-Discursive Practices Matter", In: *Signs* 28 (2003), 3, 803–831; dt.: *Agentieller Realismus*, Berlin 2012.

53 Böhme: *Architektur* (wie Anm. 49), 156.

54 Zumthor, Peter: „Die Magie des Realen" [2003], in: ders., *Architektur* (wie Anm. 44), 83–87, hier 84.

55 Ebd., 85.

56 Ebd., 86.

9

Architekturwerk Christoph Kalb/Philipp Berktold Architekten, Volksschule Mariagrün | Elementary School Mariagrün, Graz, Österreich | Austria, 2012–2014
© Dominic Conrads

(Brother Klaus Chapel) in the Eifel, where reducing the form means that the given materiality—gneiss in the case of the thermal baths, larch and Scots pine in the case of the pavilion, and tamped concrete in the case of the chapel—determines the impression all the more. Daring construction and spectacular formation of space are replaced by mere stacking and layering of materials, which in its lapidary way shows nothing more than its mere materiality. This "New Simplicity" dominates broad swaths of today's wood architecture (fig. 9) and is often called minimalistic. The dominance of materiality, however, actually rules out speaking of minimalism, since historical minimal art tried to avoid any form of materiality and make its objects seem as abstract as possible (industrially produced, without traces of processing, without texture, etc.). Here, too, reduction of form is not so much the goal as the means to allow the material to speak. In that sense, today's architecture has considerably more to do with the material turn of the first decade of the twenty-first century than with the minimal art of the 1960s.

The material turn that Dan Hicks and Mary C. Beaudry announced in 2006[50]—in allusion to the linguistic turn of the 1960s and the iconic turn of the 1990s—is understood to mean a school of thought that started out from ethnology, archaeology, and art history and has since established in all cultural studies and the humanities and that focuses on the materiality of things. It understands things of material culture as evidence of the approach to them, as objects with their own biography, and even as actors (or actants) in the sense of Bruno Latour's Actor-Network-Theory.[51] Human geographers speak of "nonhuman social partners," literary scholars of "thing theory," sociologists of "affordance" (what things offer), and

50 See Dan Hicks and Mary C. Beaudry, "Introduction: The Place of Historical Archaeology," in The Cambridge Companion to Historical Archaeology, ed. Dan Hicks and Mary C. Beaudry (Cambridge, 2006), 1–9; Dan Hicks and Mary C. Beaudry, "Introduction. Material Culture Studies: A Reactionary View," in The Oxford Handbook of Material Culture Studies, ed. Dan Hicks and Mary C. Beaudry (Oxford, 2010), 1–21.

51 See Bruno Latour, Reassembling the Social: An Introduction to Actor-Network-Theory (Oxford, 2005).

Ökologisch, romantisch, bescheiden und moralisch: das heutige Image von Holzarchitektur. Der *material turn* der Architektur des frühen 21. Jahrhunderts bevorzugt Baustoffe mit einer ausgeprägten Haptik, Schwere und Dichte (also dem Gegenteil der digitalen Immaterialität, aber auch der modernen Transparenz), einer damit verbundenen Fähigkeit, atmosphärische Wirkungen zu erzielen und mit einer entsprechenden ökologischen Glaubwürdigkeit. Dies ist vor allem bei Naturstein, Lehm und Holz der Fall, die bis vor wenigen Jahrzehnten noch als Ausdruck des Vor- und Unmodernen, wenn nicht des Reaktionären galten (so beklagten die Organisatoren eines 1967 in New York abgehaltenen Holz-Symposions „our culture's blind rejection of wood because wood lacks novelty, inventiveness and imagination").[57] Der entscheidende Faktor in diesem Imagewandel liegt zweifelsohne in der Klimakrise und der öffentlichen Aufmerksamkeit, die ihr mittlerweile weltweit entgegengebracht wird. Holz kommt dabei eine Schlüsselrolle zu. Während CO_2-Schleudern wie Beton oder exotische Baustoffe, die um die halbe Welt transportiert werden müssen, zunehmend *material shaming* auslösen, beruhigt die Verwendung heimischer Hölzer das schlechte Gewissen der Bauwirtschaft, die für rund ein Drittel des weltweiten CO_2-Ausstoßes verantwortlich ist. Als nachwachsender Rohstoff verkörpert Holz den Wert der Nachhaltigkeit wie kein anderes Material. Damit sind die letzten Reste politischer Anrüchigkeit, die am Holz noch haften geblieben sein mögen, getilgt. Mit der Betonung der Regionalität des verwendeten Holzes lassen sich aber immer noch chauvinistische Diskurse bedienen, ohne dass dies weiter störend ins Gewicht fällt. Seine Eigenschaft, für progressive wie konservative, „grüne" wie rechtspopulistische, universelle wie regionalistische Werthaltungen anschlussfähig zu sein, macht Holz unangreifbar und zu *dem* Baumaterial der Gegenwart, in dem sich gegensätzliche Utopien bündeln. Verhießen Stahl, Beton und Glas eine hygienische und demokratische Zukunft, während man deren ungewohnte bis unheimliche Eigenschaften in Kauf nehmen musste, so verspricht Holz eine nicht minder gesunde und heilende Wirkung für den Planeten und kann zudem mit spontaner Vertrautheit und Heimeligkeit rechnen, während den Durchschnittsbürger bei den revolutionären Materialien der Moderne bis heute ein Gefühl der Entfremdung beschleicht.

Der zweifellos im Vordergrund stehende ökologische und im Windschatten mitsegelnde traditionalistische Faktor erklärt die zunehmende Beliebtheit von Holz aber nur zum Teil. Nicht zu unterschätzen ist eine (neo-)romantische Grundstimmung, die seit der Jahrtausendwende die *structure of feeling* der westlichen Gesellschaften beherrscht und, wie Timotheus Vermeulen und Robin van den Akker gezeigt haben,[58] zur Ablöse der von Ironie und Skepsis gekennzeichneten Postmoderne durch die heutige, wie sie es nennen, „Metamoderne" geführt hat. Zu den zahllosen Eigenschaften und Zuschreibungen der Romantik gehört nicht zuletzt der Hang zur Widerspiegelung

der eigenen Gefühle in der Natur (und vice versa die Bereitschaft, sich ihren „Stimmungen" hinzugeben – also für Atmosphärisches empfänglich zu sein). Als einziger organischer Baustoff von Belang bietet Holz hier das größte Identifikationspotenzial (auch jenseits esoterischer „Bäume sind unsere Brüder"-Affekte). Auf unübertroffene Weise hat dies der Kunsthistoriker August Schmarsow, ein Vertreter der um 1900 verbreiteten Einfühlungstheorie, hinsichtlich der besonderen Bedeutung des Materials Holz für den Menschen beschrieben: „Das Holz wächst wie unsere eigenen Glieder, streckt sich oder krümmt sich wie sie. [...] Auch der regelmäßig behauene Stamm, der diese Ähnlichkeit verleugnet, weil man ihm die Rinde abschält und seiner Rundung die ebenflächige kristallinische Form aufgenötigt hat, befremdet uns nur aus der Ferne und als Ganzes in dieser ungewohnten Erscheinung. Kommen wir ihm näher, entdecken wir die Spuren des Wachstums in dem Zug seiner Fasern oder Ringe, in der verschiedenen Färbung der Teile oder den dunklen Ansatzstellen, wo ein Zweig entsprungen ist. Er mutet uns bald lebendig an und warm, je mehr wir aus diesen Niederschlägen seine Geschichte lesen, die von Recken und Strecken, Leben und Weben erzählt wie unsere Erinnerung an gestern und unsere Absichten für morgen."[59] Aus Sicht heutiger *material culture studies* erkennt Schmarsow im Holz ein Material, das schon per se (und nicht erst durch seine kulturelle Überformung und Verwendung) über eine Biografie verfügt.

Zur gegenwärtigen *structure of feeling* gehört auch die Wiederentdeckung des Handwerks,[60] worin zweifellos eine (mehr oder weniger naive und romantische) Gegenbewegung zur allgegenwärtigen Digitalisierung zu erkennen ist, eine Sehnsucht nach Erdung, ursprünglicher Kreativität und haptisch-sinnlicher Erfahrung. Objekte aus Holz, auch wenn sie rein industriell produziert wurden, verbreiten immer eine handwerkliche Aura, während Stahl und Beton ihren industriellen Charakter nie verleugnen können. Die Vorstellung des manuellen Machens (bzw. Gemachtseins) unserer Behausung verleiht das Gefühl, ein Stück weit die Kontrolle über eine sonst anonyme und fremdbestimmte Umgebung zurückzuerlangen.

Schließlich wirkt Holz bescheiden (was ein Erbe seiner traditionellen Funktion als Baumaterial der Armen darstellt). „Man monumentalizes stone, the monarch of natural material, but wood he feels to be more intimate and democratic", stellten Eric A. Anderson und George F. Earle bereits 1972 fest.[61] Die aus Holz konstruierten Bauten lassen in der Regel

---

57 Anderson, Eric A./Earle, George F.: „Preface", in: dies., *Design* (wie Anm. 18), ix–x, hier x.

58 Vgl. van den Akker, Robin/Vermeulen, Timotheus: *Anmerkungen zur Metamoderne*, Uhlenhorst Bd. 2, Hamburg 2015, 33–47.

59 Schmarsow, August: *Grundbegriffe der Kunstwissenschaft. Am Übergang vom Altertum zum Mittelalter* [1905]; zit. n. Rübel et al.: *Materialästhetik* (wie Anm. 3), 123f.

60 Vgl. Sennett, Richard: *The Craftsman*, New Haven, Conn. 2008 (dt.: *Handwerk*, Übers. Michael Bischoff, Berlin 2008).

61 Anderson, Eric A./Earle, George F.: „Introduction", in: dies., *Design* (wie Anm. 18), xi–xiii, hier xiii.

philosophers of "vital materialism" or "speculative realism." Whereas the analysis of culture until now has centered on language or symbols, now—very much in the spirit of the philosophy of New Materialism—new weight is given to things and with them their specific materiality.[52] After the semiotics promoted by the linguistic turn had a clear influence at least on the theorizing of postmodern architecture, it seems tempting to make a connection—even if not a causal one—between the material turn and contemporaneous architecture focused on materiality—that is to say, to speak of the material turn in architecture as a parallel phenomenon to cultural studies. Cultural studies and architecture have in common above all the conviction that material should not be understood as merely passive and auxiliary—as merely the filling of the form—but as active, determinant, and forming the message.

Materiality and its prominent position in architecture are not ends in themselves. "Materiality," according to Gernot Böhme, "is supposed to show itself, to come forward, to help shape the atmospheres in which we live."[53] "Atmosphere," one of the key terms of current architectural theory, is therefore also central for Zumthor, who, following Böhme, defines it as an "intimate relationship between our emotions and the things around us."[54] In addition to the architect's obligatory tasks of designing buildings that satisfy all desires in terms of function, economy, innovation, and status symbols, the question is: "Can I, as an architect, invest what I design with whatever it is that actually constitutes the essence of an architectural atmosphere? Can I create that unique feeling of intensity and mood, of presence, well-being, rightness, and beauty?"[55] Zumthor sounds like an alchemical master chef when he describes the material ingredients for a successful spatial atmosphere: "I try to make sure that the materials are attuned to each other, that they radiate; I take a certain amount of oak and a different amount of *pietra serena* and add something to them: three grams of silver or a handle that turns or maybe surfaces of gleaming glass, so that every combination of materials yields a unique composition, becomes an original."[56] One can see this fetishism of materials as elitist, exaggerated, or simply off-putting, but one has to recognize that contemporary architecture is almost inconceivable without it. This is all the more remarkable given that the conscious production of atmospheres with suitable material surfaces is still today considered a sign of the ungenuine, inauthentic, and unarchitectural—in short, of kitsch.

Ecological, Romantic, Modest, and Moral: The Image of Wood Architecture Today. The material turn in the architecture of the early twenty-first century reflects a preference for building materials with pronounced haptics, heaviness, and density (that is, the opposite of digital immateriality but also of modern transparency), an associated ability to achieve atmospheric effects, and with a corresponding ecological credibility. The last of these is especially true of natural stone, clay, and wood, which until a few years ago were still regarded as expressions of the premodern and unmodern if not of the reactionary (the organizers of a symposium on wood held in New York in 1967 lamented "our culture's blind rejection of wood because wood lacks novelty, inventiveness and imagination").[57] The deciding factor in this change in image doubtless lies in the climate crisis and the public attention being paid to it internationally in the meanwhile. Wood plays a key role here. Whereas carbon dioxide sources such as concrete or exotic building materials that have to be transported around half the world increasingly trigger material shaming, the use of native woods eases the bad conscience of the construction industry, which is responsible for around a third of carbon dioxide emissions worldwide. As a renewable resource, wood embodies the value of sustainability like no other material. That eliminates the final remnants of any bad political reputation that may still cling to wood. By emphasizing that the wood used is local, one can still make use of chauvinistic discourses without seeming in any way disturbing. Its quality of being open to connection to both progressives and conservatives, "greens" and right-wing populists, universalist and regionalist values makes wood irreproachable and *the* building material of the present, in which antithetical utopias are combined. Whereas steel, concrete, and glass once promised a hygienic and democratic future, while its unfamiliar and even uncanny qualities had to be tolerated, wood promises a no less healthy and healing effect on the planet and can, moreover, count on spontaneous familiarity and hominess, whereas the average citizen still has a feeling of alienation toward the revolutionary materials of the modern era.

52 See Karen Barad, "Agential Realism: How Material-Discursive Practices Matter," *Signs* 28, no. 3 (2003): 803–831.

53 Böhme, *The Aesthetics of Atmospheres* (see note 49), 142.

54 Peter Zumthor, "The Magic of the Real" (2003), trans. Catherine Schelbert, in Zumthor, *Thinking Architecture* (see note 44), 83–87, esp. 85.

55 Ibid., 85.

56 Ibid., 86.

57 Eric A. Anderson and George F. Earle, "Preface," in Anderson and Earle, *Design* (see note 18), ix–x, esp. x.

10

Alexander Brodsky, 95 Degree Restaurant, Pirogovo, Russland I Russia, 2000–2002 © Yuri Palmin

keine spektakulären formalen Experimente zu, und wenn, führen sie eher zu einer Bewunderung des darin manifesten handwerklichen Könnens als der technischen Überlegenheit. Stattdessen demonstrieren sie Einfachheit, die soliden Kräfte des Tektonischen oder, wie bei den poetischen Bauten von Alexander Brodsky, eine anrührende Form von Hinfälligkeit und Fragilität (Abb. 10). Während Banken, Konzernzentralen und Regierungssitze nach wie vor auf das Stahl-Glashochhaus und Kulturtempel auf *signature buildings* setzen, sind Holzbauten vor allem im (sozialen) Wohnbau, bei Schulen, sozialen Einrichtungen, aber auch bei ihre Regionalität betonenden Hotels und Fertigungsbetrieben zu finden. Gesteigertes Machtbewusstsein und Protzertum lassen sich mit Holz nur schwer vermitteln. Bescheidenes Auftreten steht der krisengeschüttelten Gegenwart, die architektonisch mit dem weitblickenden Biennale-Slogan „Less Aesthetics More Ethics"[62] ins 21. Jahrhundert eingetreten ist, wohl besser zu Gesicht.

Alles in allem: Bauen mit Holz gilt als moralisch. Die Moralisierung des Architekturdiskurses, die mit John Ruskin einsetzt, in der Moderne einen Höhepunkt erlebt und in den autonomen Architekturdebatten der 1990er-Jahre nahezu verschwindet, erlebt in der Ära der *political correctness* ein kräftiges Comeback. Kaum ein Statement, kaum ein Text über Holz und Bauen kommt heute ohne moralische Wertung aus. Das Entscheidende dabei ist: Es lässt sich nichts dagegen sagen. Denn „das Moralische", wusste schon Friedrich Theodor Vischer, „versteht sich doch immer von selbst".[63] ∎

62 Vgl. Fuksas, Massimiliano (Hg.): *Less Aesthetics More Ethics. 7th International Architecture Exhibition*, Milano 2001.

63 Vischer, Friedrich Theodor: *Auch Einer. Eine Reisebekanntschaft*, Hamburg 2012, 19 (1. Aufl. Stuttgart/Leipzig 1879).

The doubtless primary ecological factor and the traditionalist one that sails along in its slipstream explain the increasing popularity of wood, but only partially so. One should not underestimate a fundamental (neo-)Romantic mood that dominates the structure of feeling of Western societies since the turn of the millennium and that, as Timotheus Vermeulen and Robin van den Akker have shown,[58] had led to postmodernism characterized by irony and skepticism being replaced by today's "metamodernism," as they call it. Not the least important of Romanticism's countless qualities and attributions is a penchant for one's own feelings being mirrored in nature (and, vice versa, the willingness to give in to its "moods"—that is, to be receptive to the atmospheric). As the only significant organic construction material, wood offers the greatest potential for identification here (even beyond New Age "trees are our brothers" affects). The art historian August Schmarsow, a proponent of the theory of empathy circulating around 1900, described this in an unparalleled way with regard to the particular importance of the material wood for human beings: "Wood grows like our own limbs, stretches out or bends like them. […] Even the regularly hewn trunk that denies this similarity, because one has peeled off its bark and imposed a smooth, crystalline form on its curving, strikes us as strange in this unfamiliar appearance only when seen from afar and as a whole. If we get closer to it, we discover the traces of growth in the character of its fibers or rings, in the different coloring of its parts, or in the dark places where a branch had emerged. Soon it seems alive and warm to us, the more we read from these deposits its story, which tells of cranking and stretching, of living and weaving, like our memory of yesterday and our intentions for tomorrow."[59] From the perspective of today's material culture studies, Schmarsow was recognizing in wood a material that already per se (and not only after its cultural reshaping and use) has a biography.

Part of the current structure of feeling is the rediscovery of the crafts,[60] which should no doubt be seen as a (more or less naive and romantic) countermovement to the omnipresent digitalization, a desire for grounding, original creativity, and haptic-sensuous experience. Objects of wood, even if they are produced entirely by industrial means, always disseminate an aura of the crafts, whereas steel and concrete can never deny their industrial character. The idea of the manual making (or of being made) of our houses lends the feeling of regaining some control over an otherwise anonymous and heteronomous environment.

In the end, wood seems modest (that represents part of the legacy of its traditional function as the building material of the poor). "Man monumentalizes stone, the monarch of natural material, but wood he feels to be more intimate and democratic," observed Eric A. Anderson and George F. Earle as early as 1972.[61] As a rule, buildings constructed of wood do not permit any spectacular formal experiments, and, when they do, they lead to admiration of the craft skills manifested therein rather than of technical superiority. They demonstrate instead simplicity, the solid powers of the tectonic, or, like the poetic buildings of Alexander Brodsky, a touching form of frailty and fragility (fig. 10). While banks, company headquarters, and seats of government still insist on the glass-and-steel high-rise and cultural temples on signature buildings, wood buildings are found above all in (social) housing, schools, and community institutions but also in hotels and factories that want to emphasize their regionality. A heightened awareness of power and showiness are difficult to convey with wood. A modest look surely better suits our crisis-shocked present, which entered the twenty-first century with the farsighted Biennale slogan "Less Aesthetics, More Ethics."[62]

All in all: building with wood is considered moral. The rise of morality in the discourse on architecture that began with John Ruskin experienced a peak in the modern era, then almost disappeared in autonomous debates on architecture of the 1990s, and is experiencing a powerful comeback in the era of political correctness. Scarcely any statement, scarcely any text on wood and building can get by without a moral assessment today. The crucial thing is: Nothing can be said against it. For "the moral," as Friedrich Theodor Vischer already knew, "always goes without saying."[63] ∎

Translation: Steven Lindberg

58 See Robin van den Akker and Timotheus Vermeulen, "Notes on Meta-modernism," *Journal of Aesthetics & Culture* 2, no. 1 (2010), available online at: https://www.tandfonline.com/doi/pdf/10.3402/jac.v2i0.5677 (accessed February 4, 2021).

59 August Schmarsow, *Grundbegriffe der Kunstwissenschaft: Am Übergang vom Altertum zum Mittelalter* (1905), reprinted in Rübel, *Materialästhetik* (see note 3), 123–124.

60 See Richard Sennett, *The Craftsman* (New Haven, CT, 2008).

61 Eric A. Anderson and George F. Earle, "Introduction," in Anderson and Earle, *Design* (see note 18), xi–xiii, esp. xiii.

62 See Massimiliano Fuksas, ed., *Less Aesthetics, More Ethics: Seventh International Architecture Exhibition* (Milan, 2001).

63 Friedrich Theodor Vischer, *Auch Einer: Eine Reisebekanntschaft* (Hamburg, 2012), 19 (1st ed. Stuttgart and Leipzig, 1879).

Is There a Substitute for Wood Grain Plastic?

Gibt es einen Ersatz für Holzimitat?

Reyner Banham

1 © Mike Rynearson/Los Angeles Times

In the remote and picturesque ghost-city of Port Townsend in the state of Washington, I lunched at the Bartlett House, possibly the most westerly example of the Hudson River Bracketed style, a handsome double-fronted mansion, built entirely of wood, full of ingenious and crafty carpenter's details, warmed and serviced by wood-burning stoves. From its front garden one could look out across the still waters of the Sound and see islands apparently still covered in aboriginal forest, except where thin horizontal wisps of wood smoke lay across the scene as neat and pretty as those in a Japanese wood engraving. And the smell of that smoke hung sharp and dramatic on the still afternoon air.

For a visitor like myself, born and brought up in a culture and a part of the world where a wood fire is a demonstrative luxury, where aboriginal forest must be preserved as jealously as rare birds or ancient buildings and where timber is a commodity that often has to be rationed in times of national stringency—with such a background I was bound to be somewhat impressed not only by the sheer abundance of trees, wood, and timber, but also by the sense of a whole way of life, a civilization almost, carved out of that abundance.

Then a neighbor looked in to ask for help in unloading the week's shopping from the station wagon. Almost the first commodity to be loaded into my arms from the tailgate of the wagon—which had plastic panels of simulated wood on its sides—was something I had never seen before: perfectly regular cylindrical logs of reconstructed wood, identical in length and diameter and packaged in standard bundles of eight.

"Where shall I put these?" I inquired.

"By the stove in the living room!"

I did so, but in the process I underwent what anthropologists call culture-shock—the sheet-steel jacket of the neighbor's stove was handsomely adorned with enameled wood graining!

The whole experience was culture-shock too in the contrast between past and present; a past in which tree-wood was a substance to burn and to build and to look upon, but was always one and indivisible, the same substance. And a present in which the real substance and fictive appearance of wood had drifted so far apart that not only was the appearance of wood-grain to be found on substances that had never at any stage of their history been tree products, but also that the substance of wood for burning had to be re-created in its own image, that fictional logs had to be made from the waste products of processes whose raw material had once been logs.

You may regard such a situation as farcical, derisory, hysterical, sinister, or schizophrenic, but you cannot fail to regard it if you observe the life of North America as it is lived at present. Nor can you fail to reflect it on the rest of the world, for in every nation and people that traditionally employed wood for construction and furnishing, this dichotomy between form and substance may be observed—there is hardly a modern hotel from Oslo to Osaka to Ottawa where you will not discover that seemingly wooden surfaces are in fact plastic or metal. But before we damn the whole situation out-of-hand as a modern aberration, we should remember that it does have historical antecedents.

In the ancient English fishing port of Whitby, from which Captain Cook sailed to discover most of what we know of the South Pacific, there is a spectacular church, roofed in with a structure like ship's wooden deck and lit by skylights identical with the glazed hatch of the local fishing cobbles. The internal space of the church contains about the maximum amount of woodwork compatible with human occupation and religious ceremony—the floor space is entirely subdivided by chest-high partitions into private pews with locking doors; galleries—also subdivided—bracket off every piece of solid wall, and a complex three-decker pulpit rises in carpenter-baroque fantasy to a height of perhaps eighteen feet in the center of the church. You would think it was carpentry rather than the Trinity that was worshipped there—especially as most of this wood has artificial wood graining painted on it!

In practice, this wood-grained paint has perfectly reasonable justifications. The wood must be painted to preserve it, especially in that corrosive seaside atmosphere, and the graining of the paint serves to reassert the nature of the material beneath it. Or even enhance its nature, for quite often on top of wood one knows to be perfectly ordinary, boring, straight-grain yellow pine, appears such an efflorescence of figuring and knots as never grew on any tree in heaven or earth. Indeed, the grainer's art became quite independent of the wood beneath in the nineteenth century in England, and expressive figuring spread from the woodwork of exposed window frames and door cases to the cheap stucco that commonly surfaced

In der abgelegenen malerischen Geisterstadt Port Townsend im Bundesstaat Washington war ich zum Mittagessen im Bartlett House, möglicherweise dem westlichsten Beispiel des „Hudson River Bracketed"-Stils[1]: einem hübschen, symmetrisch gegliederten Landhaus, komplett aus Holz, voller einfallsreicher, ausgetüftelter Tischlerdetails und mit Holzöfen ausgestattet und beheizt. Vom Vorgarten konnte man über die stillen Wasser des Sunds scheinbar noch immer von Urwald bewachsene Inseln sehen, wenn der Blick nicht durch dünne horizontale Holzrauchschwaden verschleiert war, so feinsäuberlich verteilt wie in einem japanischen Holzschnitt. Und der Geruch dieses Rauchs hing scharf und dramatisch in der ruhigen Nachmittagsluft.

Als Besucher, der in einer Kultur und Weltgegend geboren und aufgewachsen ist, in der ein Holzfeuer als demonstrativer Luxus gilt und Urwälder so sorgsam geschützt werden müssen wie seltene Vögel oder alte Gebäude, und in der Holz ein Gut ist, das in nationalen Notzeiten oft rationiert werden muss, war ich unweigerlich ziemlich beeindruckt nicht nur von dem schieren Überfluss an Bäumen, Wäldern und Holz, sondern auch von der gesamten, von diesem Überfluss geprägten Lebensweise, ja vielleicht sogar Zivilisation.

Dann kam ein Nachbar vorbei und bat um Hilfe beim Ausladen des Wocheneinkaufs aus seinem Kombi. Unter den ersten Artikeln, die mir aus der Hecktür des seitlich mit Paneelen aus Holzimitat verkleideten Wagens herausgereicht wurden, war etwas, das ich nie zuvor gesehen hatte: vollkommen regelmäßig geformte zylindrische Holzfaserscheite, alle gleich lang und dick und in genormte Bündel zu acht Stück verpackt.

„Wo sollen die hin?", fragte ich.

„Neben den Ofen im Wohnzimmer!"

Ich tat wie geheißen und erlebte dabei, was Anthropologen einen Kulturschock nennen – der Stahlmantel dieses Ofens war nämlich mit einer hübschen brennlackierten Holzmaserung verziert!

Ein Kulturschock war dieses Erlebnis auch hinsichtlich des Kontrasts von Vergangenheit und Gegenwart: einer Vergangenheit, in der Baumholz eine Substanz zum Verbrennen, Bauen *und* Betrachten war, jedoch stets und untrennbar ein- und dieselbe Substanz; und einer Gegenwart, in der die reale Substanz und das fiktive Aussehen von Holz so weit auseinandergedriftet waren, dass Holzmaserung nicht nur auf Materialien auftreten konnte, die zu keinem Zeitpunkt ihrer Geschichte ein Produkt von Bäumen gewesen waren, sondern sogar die Substanz von Brennholz nach seinem eigenen Ebenbild neu geschaffen werden musste, fiktive Holzscheite aus den Abfallprodukten von Produktionsverfahren, deren Rohmaterial einmal Baumstämme gewesen waren.

Man kann eine derartige Situation für absurd, lächerlich, komisch, unheimlich oder verrückt halten, aber man kann nicht umhin, sie zur Kenntnis zu nehmen, wenn man sich mit dem heutigen Leben in Nordamerika beschäftigt. Noch kann man umhin, sie auf den Rest der Welt zu übertragen, denn diese Dichotomie zwischen Form und Substanz ist mittlerweile überall dort zu beobachten, wo Häuser und Möbel traditionellerweise aus Holz gebaut wurden – von Oslo bis Osaka und Ottawa wird man kaum ein Hotel finden, in dem scheinbare Holzflächen nicht aus Plastik oder Metall bestehen. Doch bevor wir diese gesamte Situation kurzerhand als Verirrung der Moderne abtun, sollten wir bedenken, dass sie historische Vorläufer hat.

Im alten englischen Fischereihafen Whitby, von dem aus sich Kapitän Cook auf seine Entdeckungsfahrt in den Südpazifik aufmachte, befindet sich eine spektakuläre Kirche mit einer Dachkonstruktion, die an das Holzdeck eines Schiffes erinnert, erhellt von Oberlichten, die wie verglaste Ladeluken der lokalen Fischerboote aussehen. Der Innenraum der Kirche beinhaltet die wohl größtmögliche Menge an Holzarbeiten, die sich noch mit menschlicher Betätigung und religiösem Zeremoniell vereinbaren lässt: die gesamte Bodenfläche ist durch brusthohe Trennwände in private Betstühle mit verschließbaren Türen unterteilt; die ebenfalls untergliederten Galerien verstellen jedes Stück fester Wand, und in der Kirchenmitte ragt eine komplexe dreistöckige tischlerbarocke Fantasiekanzel sechs Meter in die Höhe. Man könnte fast meinen, hier würde weniger die Dreifaltigkeit als die Tischlerei verehrt – zumal der Großteil des Holzes mit einer künstlichen Maserung überstrichen ist!

In der Praxis gab es für diese Maserierung absolut verständliche Gründe. Das Holz bedarf – vor allem in der salzhaltigen Meeresluft – eines schützenden Anstrichs, und die Maserierung dient dazu, auf die Natur des darunterliegenden Materials zu verweisen, ja diese sogar zu verbessern: Denn häufig sprießt auf Holz, bei dem es sich mit ziemlicher Sicherheit um eine gewöhnliche, langweilige, längsgemaserte Gelbkiefer handelt, ein derartiges Dickicht an Linien und Astknoten, wie es in keinem Baum im Himmel und auf Erden je wachsen könnte. Tatsächlich erlangte die Kunst des Maserierens im England des 19. Jahrhunderts eine relative Unabhängigkeit vom Holz und expressive Musterungen breiteten sich von der Außenseite der Fenster- und Türrahmen hin zu dem billigen Stuck aus, der zumeist das allgegenwärtige Ziegelmauerwerk überdeckte, geradeso wie sich in den USA zur selben Zeit steinfarbene Schlämme[2] über das Holzskelett vieler Gebäude ausbreiteten.

---

1 A.d.Ü.: Der „Hudson River Bracketed"-Stil verdankt seine Bezeichnung dem gleichnamigen Roman von Edith Wharton aus dem Jahr 1929 (dt.: *Ein altes Haus am Hudson River*). Der Architekturstil wird auf Alexander Jackson Davis zurückgeführt, der ab Mitte der 1830er-Jahre zahlreiche pittoreske Villen im italienisierenden und tudorgotischen Stil entwarf. Prototyp ist das von Davis 1839 und 1849 umgebaute Bronson House in Hudson.

2 A.d.Ü.: Den korrekten Begriff aus der deutschen Fachterminologie verdanke ich Christoph Tinzl.

extremely common brickwork, much as the imitation sanded stonepainting spread over the wooden carcasses of many buildings of the same period in the U.S.A.

In both cases, the primary need is to give some form of weather-protection to a common constructional material, but in both cases artifice seizes the opportunity to make the material appear less common; to disguise stucco as wood and wood as stone. Stern moralists from Ruskin onwards have found either subterfuge intolerable, have damned stucco, and insisted that wood look like the wood it really is, and brick like brick. So, the generation of architects—Le Corbusier, Mies Van der Rohe—who in the 1920s covered concrete in stucco and white paint to make it look more like concrete and waxed indignant at Frank Lloyd Wright's use of steel to help seemingly wooden cantilevers carry well beyond the possibilities of wooden construction—such men, when they used wood in their interiors as a visual relief from the austerities of steel and glass, frequently finished up using woods as expensive as they were impractical in order to get figurings strong enough to register visually.

So, if Le Corbusier hoped to make these "materials friendly to man" available to all mankind with his common universal generosity, he was going to need exotic woods or at least exotic veneer, on the cheap. And they were to become available, sure enough—though somewhat later—printed by the yard on paper and either pasted on to the wall or bonded into the surface of plastic laminates. Which he, and most architects, now profess to find disgusting.

It quite often happens that, in discussion with architects or interior decorators of my acquaintance, we argue this way and that over the ideal qualities required of a kitchen work-surface or something similar and in the end, when all aspects of durability, cleaning, heat resistance, and appearance have been totted up, I have to say "admit it, the answer to your problem is wood-grain, Formica-faced block board—but you haven't got the guts to use it!"

In my turn, I should admit that "guts" is an unkind way of putting the matter. Most architects would say that they have a moral scruple against employing such a deception on the public. But I think we should notice that this has now become a very *nice* scruple, in the Shakesperian use of *nice*, and the morality involved has to be sliced very fine. For these same architects would probably accept, without moral difficulty, such a material as exterior grade, mahogany-faced plywood, in which the face veneer is apt to be a misrepresentation of the substance of the plies behind, and in which there may be quite as much

miscellaneous plastics for bonding and weathering purposes as there is in avowedly plastic-faced block boards or chipboards.

The difference between the morally intolerable and the morally tolerable may only be the difference between paper (made from wood) with a grain printed on it and wood (paper-thin) with a grain grown in it. I wouldn't like to try and explain this situation to an intelligent Martian or even an intelligent four-year-old human being. Both would certainly find more interest and more profit in discussing what is behind the paper-thin surface graining.

For what does lie behind is an avowal of the useless-ness of wood as nature provides it. Plywood, laminates, block board, chipboard and, indeed, paper too—are all ways of re-moulding wood nearer to heart's desire, structural need, or green-backed profit. The pressing up of veneer into plies and laminates has grown from a way of making expensive figures cover more dull grain—the original use of veneers—into a way of making a continuous, wooden, thin sheet-material with better performance, utility, and range of sizes than regular match-boarding could ever offer. And the materials rolled out from chips and assembled from blocks seem to have started as ways of reusing the vast quantities of fairly homogeneous offcuts that arise from the mechanical working of raw wood—but grew into a way of producing wood substitutes with better strength-weight ratios, stiffness-weight ratios, or better dimensional stability.

Technical historians of the wood-processing indus-tries may want to quarrel with me about the intentions or outcomes of these developments—and I must admit myself a layman in the history of such techniques—but any observant layman must see that these are the effective practical outcomes of the transformation of wood. It emerges as a material at last freed from the immemorial faults of shake, split, warp, shrink, and the rest of it. The layman who "does it himself" knows that any normal tree wood he uses is apt to do any of these things and that he will rarely buy a parcel of lumber that does not contain some pieces too faulty to be used. But if he buys ply, "compo," or other made-up boards, he can at least be sure of avoiding any of these traditional faults critical to his struc-tural intentions.

In beiden Fällen geht es in erster Linie darum, ein gebräuchliches Baumaterial mit einem Wetterschutz zu versehen, und in beiden Fällen wird die Gelegenheit dazu genutzt, das Material weniger gewöhnlich aussehen zu lassen; Stuck als Holz, und Holz als Stein zu verkleiden. Strenge Moralisten fanden seit Ruskin beide Täuschmanöver unerträglich, verdammten Stuck und beharrten darauf, dass Holz wie das Holz, das es ist, und Backstein wie Backstein auszusehen habe. So endete die Architektengeneration von Le Corbusier und Mies van der Rohe – die in den 1920er-Jahren Beton mit Stuck und weißer Farbe bearbeitete, um ihn mehr nach Beton aussehen zu lassen, und sich darüber entrüstete, dass Frank Lloyd Wright das Tragvermögen scheinbar aus Holz bestehender Träger mithilfe von Stahl weit über das einer Holzkonstruktion hinaus steigerte – bei ihrer eigenen Verwendung von Holz im Innenausbau, mit der sie die Härte von Stahl und Glas visuell abzumildern suchte, meist bei Hölzern, die gleichermaßen kostspielig wie untauglich waren, weil sich nur damit eine Textur erreichen ließ, die visuell stark genug war.

Wenn Le Corbusier also hoffte, diese „Materialien menschenfreundlich", sie in seiner bekannten universellen Großzügigkeit für alle Menschen verfügbar zu machen, so benötigte er dazu billige exotische Hölzer oder wenigstens exotische Furniere. Und diese sollten schließlich auch – wiewohl erst später – allgemein verfügbar werden: meterweise auf Papier gedruckt und an die Wand geklebt oder in Kunststofflaminate eingeschweißt. Dinge, die er – wie fast alle Architekten – heute ganz abscheulich fände.

In Gesprächen mit Architekten und Innenausstattern aus meinem Bekanntenkreis streiten wir nicht selten auf ähnliche Art und Weise über die idealen Eigenschaften etwa einer Küchenarbeitsplatte, und am Ende, wenn alle Aspekte wie Haltbarkeit, Reinigbarkeit, Hitzebeständigkeit und Aussehen in Rechnung gestellt wurden, muss ich dann meist sagen: „Gib es zu, die Lösung für dein Problem ist eine resopalbeschichtete Tischlerplatte mit Holzmaserung, aber du hast nicht den Mumm, sie einzusetzen!"

Ich meinerseits muss zugeben, dass es nicht die feine Art ist, das auf fehlenden „Mumm" zurückzuführen. Die meisten Architekten würden eher sagen, dass sie moralische Skrupel haben, einen derartigen Betrug an der Öffentlichkeit zu begehen. Aber mir scheint, wir sollten festhalten, dass dies mittlerweile äußerst erlesene Skrupel sind und die damit verbundene Moral sehr fein geschnitten werden muss. Denn die gleichen Architekten würden vermutlich ohne moralische Probleme ein Material wie wetterfestes Mahagony-Sperrholz akzeptieren, bei dem die Deckschicht wohl kaum die Substanz der darunterliegenden Schichten wiedergibt und in dem sich wahrscheinlich gleich viel Kunststoff für Binde- und Wetterschutzzwecke befindet wie in offensichtlich mit Kunststoff beschichteten Tischler- oder Spanplatten.

Der Unterschied zwischen dem moralisch Erträglichen und Unerträglichen läuft vielleicht lediglich auf den Unterschied zwischen aus Holz erzeugtem, mit einer Maserung bedrucktem Papier und papierdünn geschnittenem Holz mit einer gewachsenen Maserung hinaus. Ich würde nicht den Versuch machen wollen, dies einem intelligenten Marsianer oder auch nur einem intelligenten Vierjährigen zu erklären. Beide fänden es bestimmt interessanter und nützlicher zu erörtern, was hinter der Maserung der papierdünnen Oberfläche steckt.

Denn was wirklich dahintersteckt, ist nichts anderes als ein Eingeständnis der Nutzlosigkeit von Holz in seinem Naturzustand. Sperrholz, Laminate, Tischlerplatten, Spanplatten und selbst Papier sind nämlich lauter Versuche, Holz nach den eigenen Herzenswünschen, baulichen Notwendigkeiten oder aus Profitabilitätsgründen umzuformen. Das Pressen von Furnieren zu Schichtholz oder Laminat entwickelte sich aus einer Methode zum Überdecken eintönig gemaserter Hölzer mit einer edleren Textur – so der ursprüngliche Einsatz von Furnieren – hin zu einem Herstellungsverfahren für ein nahtloses, hölzernes Plattenmaterial mit besseren Eigenschaften, Einsatzmöglichkeiten und Abmessungen, als sie mit Spundbrettern je erreichbar wären. Und die aus Spänen gepressten und aus Stabholz zusammengesetzten Platten scheinen als eine Möglichkeit zur Wiederverwendung der Unmengen relativ homogenen Verschnittmaterials entstanden zu sein, das bei der mechanischen Bearbeitung von Rohholz anfällt, wurden dann aber zu einer Möglichkeit, Holzersatz mit besserer spezifischer Festigkeit und spezifischer Steifheit, oder genauer gesagt: dimensionaler Stabilität, zu produzieren.

Historiker der holzverarbeitenden Industrie mögen mir bezüglich der Intentionen oder Ergebnisse dieser Entwicklungen widersprechen – und ich gebe zu, dass ich in der Geschichte dieser Techniken ein Laie bin –, aber jeder aufmerksame Laie wird erkennen, dass sie das effiziente, praktische Resultat der Transformation von Holz sind. Es erscheint als ein Material, das endlich befreit ist von seiner Neigung zu reißen, zu splittern, sich zu verziehen, zu schrumpfen usw. Der Heimwerker weiß, dass jedes Schnittholz für all das anfällig ist und dass man selten einen Stapel erwischt, der nicht einige unbrauchbare Stücke enthält. Kauft man aber Sperrholz-, Komposit- oder anderweitig künstlich hergestellte Platten kann man zumindest sicher sein, dass einem bei der Umsetzung des eigenen Bauvorhabens keiner dieser traditionellen Mängel in die Quere kommt.

Und spricht man mit Leuten, die zum Beispiel in der Möbelerzeugung tätig sind, wird man zu hören bekommen, dass es geradezu eine Frage des wirtschaftlichen Überlebens ist, nicht mit Holz zu arbeiten, so wie es die Natur bereitstellt. Ohne die Austauschbarkeit von Teilen gäbe es keine Massenproduktion, und diese Austauschbarkeit ist nur möglich, wenn die Teile dimensional stabil sind. Terence Conran, ein englischer

And if he talks to friends in, say, the furniture industry, he will hear that their very economic survival depends on their not using wood as nature provides it. There can be no mass production, they point out, without interchangeability of parts, and there can be no interchangeability of parts that are not dimensionally stable. Terence Conran, English furniture manufacturer, once said to me, "What is the use of my making up stocks of wooden components if they come out of stock a different size to what they went in, just because the weather has changed? We would love to mass-produce and mechanize, but as things are we always finish up with so much hand fitting to pay for, that we never accumulate the capital to buy a mechanical plant, even if we could use it." Part of his trouble, indeed, is that he makes "well-designed" furniture and sells it therefore to a restricted and educated clientele who feel—like architects—that the use of chipboard and such are dishonest practices, without realizing that without such practices they could never afford well-designed furniture at all.

Or to put it another way, without such practices we might, in a true mass-producing society, have to give up using wood altogether. On the other hand, for quasimass-producing industries and ones where the required dimensional tolerances are fairly sloppy, and the housebuilding industry fulfills both requirements, wood obviously has a long future. In the most sophisticated of architectural housing practice the ultimate production process and the ultimate arbiter of dimensional tolerances is he whom Serge Chermayeff once described as "the same old eighteenth-century carpenter with his mouth full of nails." And a house structure, once up, is allowed to settle, shift, take up, creak, and go bang in the night, in a manner that would be intolerable in a yacht hull, an aircraft propellor, or a normally jointed chair or table.

For each of these more specialized uses, Mother Nature's tree-wood is a "nonstarter," or nearly so, and we all of us increasingly know it. And as natural treewood has increasingly faded from our tangible and structural environment, so we have come increasingly to value its appearance, real or fictitious. And it is not only the ignorant and allegedly cultureless with their fake wood-grain station wagons and knotty-pine wallpaper and embossed-grain aluminum roll-away garage doors who hunger after the sight of wood. Many a cultured household is proud to display upon its coffee table a wooden bowl by Prestini's (or some other less cunning) hand. So this is real wood, not applied graining, but it is wood used in a context that would have been rare a generation ago, and unknown

three generations since—our grandfathers would have relegated a wooden bowl to the kitchen, if they had possessed them at all.

Along side such semi-fine-art objects, the fine arts too have developed a new passion for wood and its grainy structure. But, by a splendid irony, the tremendous revival of interest in wood—as a carver's material in the generation of Henry Moore, and as a printmaker's material in the sense of changing from end-grain boxwood, which is neutral in the finished print, to side-grain softwood which registers its grain—in both these cases the revaluation of wood was preceded by George Braque's joking use of wood-grain paper in Cubist collages from 1911 onwards. In historical fact, those wood-grain decorator's papers are the almost exact halfway stage between the hand-painted grainer's art of the nineteenth century and the applied-printed grains of today, so this was an extremely suitable point for modern art to join the cult.

I do not use the word *cult* rashly—I mean it to be taken seriously, with those religious overtones that the word retains, say, in French, even if they are largely lost in English. What is rash here is that I propose to change from historical exposition to psychological speculation. Obviously, though, it is a fact that we regret the passing of something valuable in the disappearance of natural tree-wood from our practical surroundings and wish it back in simulation and in art. What is it that we feel we have lost?

Le Corbusier, I think, was not kidding when he listed wood among those "materials friendly to man." We actively like wood. We pick up and handle wooden objects in a way in which we rarely do with other materials. Indeed we expect the handle-end of a tool or weapon to be of wood and regard other materials as poor substitutes. He that "set his hand to the plow, and looked not back," expected his hand to touch wood—and so does the man who gets into a racing car and puts his hand to the wheel. The butt of a gun and the grip of a screwdriver, the baseball bat and haft of an axe are all, in our expectation, wooden. And for good reasons—many of the qualities possessed by wood make it a natural for handles; the ease with which it can be shaped, its resilience under impact and its poor conductivity of heat, which brings it to comfortable hand temperature almost as soon as it is grasped.

Möbelbauer, erklärte mir einmal: „Was nützt es mir, Lagerbestände von Holzbauteilen anzulegen, wenn ich sie nicht in der gleichen Größe entnehmen kann wie ich sie hineingetan habe, einfach nur, weil sich das Wetter geändert hat. Wir würden gern mechanisieren und serienmäßig produzieren, aber wie die Dinge nun mal stehen, müssen wir am Ende immer so viel in kostspieliger Handarbeit angleichen, dass wir nie das nötige Kapital zum Kauf einer mechanischen Anlage aufbauen können, selbst wenn wir Verwendung dafür hätten." Ein Teil des Problems ist tatsächlich, dass Terence „Designer"-Möbel baut und sie also an eine ausgewählte, gebildete Klientel verkauft, die wie Architekten der Meinung ist, dass die Verwendung von Faserplatten und dergleichen unehrlich sei, ohne zu erkennen, dass sie sich Designermöbel ohne solche Verfahren gar nicht leisten könnte.

Anders gesagt, in einer wahrhaft massenproduzierenden Gesellschaft müssten wir ohne derartige Verfahren den Gebrauch von Holz wohl vollkommen aufgeben. Dagegen ist Holz in quasi-massenproduzierenden Industriezweigen und solchen mit relativ saloppen Maßtoleranzen – und auf das Wohnbaugewerbe trifft beides zu – zweifellos eine lange Zukunft beschieden. Selbst im raffiniertesten architektonischen Hausbau ist der ultimative Produktionsprozess und der ultimative Gradmesser der Maßtoleranz noch immer der „des guten alten Tischlers mit seinem Mund voller Nägel", wie es Serge Chermayeff einmal ausgedrückt hat. Und ein Bauwerk, wenn es einmal steht, darf sich auch setzen, bewegen, ansaugen und des Nachts knarren und knacken wie wir es bei einem Jachtrumpf, einem Flugzeugpropeller oder einem ordentlich gebauten Stuhl oder Tisch niemals tolerieren würden.

Für all diese spezialisierteren Einsatzbereiche ist Baumholz, wie es Mutter Natur hervorbringt, praktisch ungeeignet, wie wir alle immer deutlicher sehen. Und während das natürliche Baumholz immer mehr aus unserer realen und gebauten Umwelt verschwindet, lernen wir zunehmend sein Erscheinungsbild zu schätzen, ob real oder fiktiv. Und es sind nicht nur die Ahnungs- und vermeintlich Kulturlosen mit ihren Kombis mit falschen Holzpaneelen und ihren Astkiefer-Tapeten und Aluminiumgaragentoren mit eingeprägter Maserung, die sich nach dem Anblick von Holz sehnen. Auch so mancher kultursinnige Haushalt stellt auf dem Wohnzimmertisch gern eine von Prestini (oder einem weniger geschickten Handwerker) gefertigte Holzschüssel zur Schau. Dabei handelt es sich zwar um echtes Holz und nicht um eine Applikation, jedoch in einem Kontext, der noch vor einer Generation höchst selten und vor drei gänzlich unbekannt gewesen wäre: Unsere Großväter hätten eine Holzschüssel, falls sie überhaupt eine hatten, allenfalls in der Küche eingesetzt.

Neben derartigen angewandten Kunstobjekten hat aber auch die schöne Kunst eine neue Leidenschaft für Holz und seine Textur entwickelt. Ironischerweise jedoch ging diesem wiederaufflammenden Interesse an Holz – sei es als skulpturales Material in der Generation Henry Moores oder als Material der Druckgrafik im Wechsel vom Buchsbaumstirnholz, das im Druck neutral bleibt, zum längsgeschnittenen Weichholz, dessen Maserung im Druck zu sehen ist – die scherzhafte Verwendung von mit Holzmaserung bedruckten Papieren in Georges Braques kubistischen Collagen voraus (ab 1911). Historisch gesehen liegen diese mit Holzmaserung bedruckten Deko-Papiere ziemlich genau auf halbem Weg zwischen der handgefertigten Maserierung des 19. Jahrhunderts und den heutigen angewandten Holzmaserdrucken, waren also für die Kunst ein sehr treffender Einstiegspunkt in den Kult.

Ich verwende das Wort „Kult" nicht vorschnell – ich möchte, dass es ernstgenommen wird, mit allen religiösen Konnotationen, die es etwa im Französischen noch besitzt, auch wenn sie im Englischen weitgehend verloren gegangen sind. Etwas plötzlich kommt nur mein Vorschlag, von der historischen Exposition zur psychologischen Spekulation überzugehen. Allerdings ist wohl offensichtlich, dass wir das Verschwinden des natürlichen Baumholzes aus unserer Alltagsumgebung als den Verlust von etwas Wertvollem erleben und es uns im Imitat und in der Kunst zurückzuholen versuchen. Aber was glauben wir eigentlich verloren zu haben?

Le Corbusier war es, denke ich, ernst damit, Holz unter die „menschenfreundlichen Materialien" zu zählen. Wir lieben Holz. Wir ergreifen und handhaben Holzobjekte wie kaum ein anderes Material. Beim Griff eines Werkzeugs oder einer Waffe erwarten wir geradezu, dass er aus Holz ist, und betrachten andere Materialien als schwachen Ersatz. Wer „die Hand an den Pflug gelegt und niemals zurückgeblickt hat", erwartete, Holz zu berühren – und das erwartet noch, wer in einen Rennwagen steigt und die Hand aufs Lenkrad legt. Auch vom Gewehrkolben, vom Griff eines Schraubenziehers, vom Baseballschläger und vom Stiel einer Axt erwarten wir, dass sie aus Holz sind. Und aus gutem Grund – viele der Eigenschaften von Holz machen es zu einem natürlichen Material für Handgriffe: die leichte Formbarkeit, die Fähigkeit, Schläge zu absorbieren, und die geringe Hitzeleitfähigkeit, die es bei Berührung sofort auf angenehme Handtemperatur bringt.

So wurden unsere Hände seit Menschengedenken auf das Berühren von Holz konditioniert und es hat für uns eine alte Vertrautheit angenommen, die uns vielleicht zu Sentimentalität verleitet, aber auch auf einem objektiven menschlichen Bedürfnis beruht: nur das anzufassen, was sich gut anfühlt. Man beachte etwa, wie im letzten Jahrzehnt trotz der unerbittlichen Rituale moderner Hygiene Besteck mit Holzgriffen wiederaufgekommen ist. Das Angreifen von Holz ist für die menschliche Kultur vielleicht ebenso grundlegend wie das Feuermachen und die Sprachaufzeichnung – ein marodierender Wikinger könnte im 10. Jahrhundert einem irischen Stammesführer mit einem zufällig herumliegenden Stück Holz den Schädel eingeschlagen und es danach ins Feuer geworfen

And so our hands become immemorially conditioned to the grasp of wood and it has acquired for us an ancient familiarity which may encourage us to sentimentality, but depends on an objective human need—to grasp only that which may comfortably be grasped. Notice how wooden-handled cutlery has come back in the last ten years, in defiance of the unrelenting rituals of modern hygiene. The grasp of wood is probably as basic to human culture as the making of fire and the writing of language—a Viking marauder in the tenth century might have brained an Irish chieftain with a lump of wood that came to hand and then added it to the fire, without knowing that some valued historical record was notched in its edge in Ogham script.

But, in general practice within the culture we inhabit, valuable records have been carved in stone, not wood. Partly because stone is more durable, but more perhaps, because stone is the dominant material of the Mediterranean basin—poor in wood in all historic time—from which our conscious culture derives. Masonry, statuary, Latinate languages, Greek philosophy, Roman law—these are the cultural concepts we have consciously cultivated in universities, the courts of princes and judges, and have illuminated with that Christian religion which is in so many ways the distilled wisdom of settled Mediterranean peasant communities. This is our superculture, so to speak, so that for both the king of England and the president of the United States we built imitations of the masonry mansions of Mediterranean noblemen and we regard the progress of Abraham Lincoln from wooden log cabin to the stone White House as an *upward* movement.

Maybe it was, but if a wooden building represents, in economic fact, the bottom end of the scale, why does the top end have to be a stone one? The Norwegian royal family have a sizeable masonry palace in Oslo and an equally impressive one in wood in Trondheim. But this is rare; wood is generally the symbolic material of our underculture and disregarded so. But it is nonetheless symbolic of very valuable parts of our culture. It is the material of tools and trade; until recently it was the material of transportation and movement in boats and carts and early aeroplanes; it was—and is—the material of the dwellings of the humble, the pioneers, the adventurers. Above all, it was and is the material of the northern forests where most of us come from, the original environment of our human stock and many of our most valued social concepts, such as practical equality and universal democracy.

I know that for many cultured people, talk about the forests of Northern Europe conjures embarrassing or downright sinister visions of Nazis capering about in torchlit Walpurgisnacht orgies. The point is well taken, the forests and democracy are not inevitably linked. And on the other hand, the vain and inhumane pomposities of Mussolini's regime were acceptable to a number of cultured people just because they seemed to sustain the traditions of masonry architecture, marble statuary, and Roman law. It should also be added however that the democratic Scandinavians caper about in torchlit orgies from time to time and this leads to nothing more ominous than a lot of harmless jollity and new scenarios for Ingmar Bergmann.

I will refrain from generalizing too extensively from what may be a unique personal experience, but I must testify that the most sustainedly and deafeningly good-natured party I was ever at was conducted in full Viking vigor in a wooden ski hut in a Norwegian forest to celebrate the broaching of the spring beer. Merry peasants come in all flavours and many different kinds of party gear. You can have innocent fun in a forest clearing or a paved piazza, by the harvest moon or the midnight sun. But we do not seem to concede that one can have a valid higher culture in the context of a forested landscape and a wooden-built environment.

And whether this exclusive preference for a Mediterranean culture is right or wrong, the fact remains that most of us Anglo-Saxon or Nordic peoples came from a wooden environment and originally steered around the world in wooden ships and largely lived in wooden houses. We speak a language full of wood-words or wooden-type meanings even when the words are ultimately Latin. What, for instance, do we do with our proudest contribution to human justice, the jury of twelve good men and true? We empanel them. Where do we (or did we until recently) cast our universal democratic vote? In a wooden box (whereas the vote of the more limited democracy of Athens was cast in a pottery urn). Hospitably, we offer bed and board, and for both justice and refreshment we are called to an originally wooden bar. And there is probably some good reason why bastard means "son of a wooden bench!"

The Germans, Norwegians, Ukrainians, Danes, Swedes, Finns, Russians, Poles, and English (if not Irish and Welsh) who came to colonize North America came mostly from wood-built farms and woodbuilt towns. They had, in some cases, worshipped in wooden churches and wooden synagogues, they had in nearly all cases cooked at wood fires and eaten from wooden bowls and even wooden spoons. They

haben, ohne zu merken, dass an seiner Kante in Ogham-Schrift ein wertvolles historisches Zeugnis eingekerbt war.

Im Allgemeinen jedoch wurden wertvolle Zeugnisse in der Kultur, in der wir leben, in Stein gemeißelt und nicht in Holz geschnitten. Zum Teil deshalb, weil Stein haltbarer ist, mehr aber noch, weil Stein das vorherrschende Material des von alters her holzarmen Mittelmeerbeckens ist, von wo unsere bewusste Kultur herkommt. Baukunst, Bildhauerei, romanische Sprachen, griechische Philosophie, römisches Recht sind lauter kulturelle Errungenschaften, die an Universitäten, Fürsten- und Gerichtshöfen bewusst gepflegt wurden, illuminiert durch die christliche Religion, die in vieler Hinsicht aus der Weisheit sesshafter mediterraner Bauerngemeinschaften destilliert wurde. Das ist gewissermaßen unsere Überkultur, weshalb wir für den König von England wie für den Präsidenten der Vereinigten Staaten die Steinvillen mediterraner Fürsten nachbauen und den Weg Abraham Lincolns von der Blockhütte ins steinerne Weiße Haus als Aufstieg betrachten.

Vielleicht war es sogar einer, doch wenn ein Holzbau ökonomisch gesehen am unteren Ende der Skala rangiert, warum muss es dann am oberen ein Steinbau sein? Die norwegische Königsfamilie besitzt einen mächtigen Steinpalast in Oslo, aber in Trondheim auch einen ebenso ansehnlichen aus Holz. Das ist freilich selten; Holz ist gewöhnlich das materielle Inbild unserer Unterkultur und wird darum geringgeschätzt. Zugleich symbolisiert es auch sehr wertvolle Teile unserer Kultur. Es ist das Material für Werkzeug und Gewerbe; bis vor Kurzem war es das des Transports und der Fortbewegung, das Material von Schiffen, Fuhrwerken und den frühen Flugzeugen; es war und ist das Material der Behausungen der armen Leute, der Pioniere und Abenteurer. Vor allem aber war und ist es das Material der Wälder des Nordens, wo die meisten von uns herkommen, der ursprünglichen Umwelt unserer Vorfahren und vieler unserer meistgeschätzten Gesellschaftsideen wie praktische Gleichheit und allgemeine Demokratie.

Mir ist bewusst, dass die Rede von den Wäldern Nordeuropas bei den meisten Gebildeten beklemmende oder richtig finstere Bilder von herumhüpfenden Nazis in fackelerleuchteten Walpurgisnachtorgien heraufbeschwört. Da ist etwas dran, denn Wälder und Demokratie hängen nicht zwangsläufig zusammen. Andererseits war der eitle, menschenverachtende Pomp des Mussoliniregimes für eine ganze Reihe gebildeter Menschen durchaus akzeptabel, nur weil es die Tradition der Steinarchitektur, der Marmorbildhauerei und des römischen Rechts fortzuführen schien. Auch sollte nicht vergessen werden, dass die demokratisch gesonnenen Skandinavier ebenfalls mitunter in fackelerleuchteten Orgien herumhüpfen und das nichts Schlimmeres als harmlose Fröhlichkeit und neue Szenarien für Ingmar Bergmann gebiert.

Ich will eine vielleicht einmalige persönliche Erfahrung nicht zu sehr verallgemeinern, muss aber doch berichten, dass das ausdauerndste, lauteste, herzerwärmendste Fest, dem ich je beiwohnte, in einer Holzschihütte in einem norwegischen Wald stattfand, wo mit wikingischer Inbrunst das Anzapfen des Frühjahrsbiers gefeiert wurde. Fröhliches Landvolk gibt es in vielen Ausformungen und in vielen verschiedenen Festtrachten. Unschuldig vergnügen kann man sich auf einer Waldlichtung ebenso wie auf einer steingepflasterten Piazza, zum Erntemond ebenso wie zur Mitternachtssonne. Dass es aber in einer Waldlandschaft und einer aus Holz gebauten Umwelt eine echte höhere Kultur geben könnte, räumen wir nicht so leicht ein.

Ob nun dieses exklusive Beharren auf einer mediterranen Kultur richtig oder falsch ist, fest steht, dass die meisten von uns Angelsachsen oder Nordländern aus einer von Holz geprägten Umwelt stammen, die Welt einst in Holzschiffen umsegelten und weitgehend in Holzhäusern lebten. Wir sprechen eine Sprache voller Wörter, die auf Holz oder Holzobjekte referieren, selbst wenn sie aus dem Lateinischen kommen. Was müssen wir zum Beispiel tun, wenn wir ein schwieriges Problem zu lösen haben? Ein dickes Brett bohren. Wohin werfen wir (oder warfen wir bis vor Kurzem) unsere allgemeindemokratische Stimme? In eine Holzkiste, die wir Urne nennen, weil sie in der weniger allgemeinen Demokratie Athens in ein Tongefäß geworfen wurde. Wenn wir ein Schiff oder Flugzeug betreten, gehen wir an Bord, vom Recht werden wir in die Schranken gewiesen, und zum Trinken betreten wir eine Bar, die ebenfalls der Rest eines ehemaligen Holzbalkens ist. Ja vermutlich gibt es sogar einen guten Grund, weshalb ein Bastard der „Sohn einer Holzbank"[3] ist.

Die Deutschen, Norweger, Ukrainer, Dänen, Schweden, Finnen, Russen, Polen und Engländer (wenn auch nicht die Iren und Waliser), die Nordamerika kolonisierten, kamen größtenteils von aus Holz erbauten Bauernhöfen, Dörfern und Städten. Sie hatten zum Teil in Holzkirchen und Holzsynagogen gebetet und fast immer auf Holzfeuern gekocht und mit Holzlöffeln aus Holzschüsseln gegessen. Sie kamen aus Waldlandschaften, die seit dem Mittelalter abgeholzt wurden oder vor dem Abholzen standen oder aber bis heute nicht abgeholzt sind, und fanden sich in einer anderen Waldlandschaft wieder, die darauf wartete, abgeholzt zu werden. Sie blickten auf Amerikas Wälder und sahen eine ungeheure Menge Holz, die im Überfluss einige uralte, atavistische Instinkte – oder zumindest tief verwurzelte Gewohnheiten – befriedigte. Bis vor Kurzem beruhten die Lebensweise und Ökonomie Nordamerikas auf einer Orgie zügellosen Holzverbrauchs, die historisch wahrscheinlich ihresgleichen sucht, und dies hat, so meine ich, eine Kultur hervorgebracht, die unbewusst „holzsüchtig" ist.

---

3 A.d.Ü.: Banham bezieht sich hier offenbar auf die Etymologie, wonach Bastard von altfranz. *bast* (Pack-Sattel) abgeleitet ist, der etwa in der Redewendung *fils de bast* für ein Notbett stehen soll. Einige der vorausgegangenen Beispiele wurden nicht übersetzt, sondern durch deutsche Analogien ersetzt.

came from a landscape that had been cleared of forests since the middle ages, or even awaited clearing, or is still not cleared today, and on arriving in North America found themselves frequently in another forested landscape that still awaited clearing. They looked out upon America's trees and enjoyed an incredible abundance of wood, and some very old and atavistic instincts—or at least, *ingrained* habits—were fulfilled in overplus. Until recently the life and economy of North America has enjoyed an orgy of wooden self-indulgence which is probably without precedent or previous equal, and I believe this has created a culture which is, unknowingly, "hooked" on wood.

What I am suggesting is less that North America as a culture is suffering from wooden withdrawal symptoms, than that it is now in the condition of the drinker who discovers that the bottle he thought nearly half full is nearly three-quarters empty. With natural woodland fast disappearing from the areas within the reach of the ordinary citizen, and with natural wood fast vanishing from his built environment, he overreacts and begins to fight desperately to keep every scenic drive through the redwood country or to ornament every nonwooden object with simulated wood grain.

Perhaps the situation should be phrased even more mildly than that. I would settle for something like the following summary of what I have been hinting at so far: that the use and experience of wood is an essential and basic part of the cultural inheritance of all northern, non-Mediterranean peoples.

Though they have cultivated Mediterranean arts, architecture, and design, the constant presence of wood in their working environment, both indoors and out, satisfied whatever cultural needs they had for contact with this material. *As long as the wood was there.* Once the real presence of natural tree-wood began to be withdrawn, then their cultural situation began to be thrown off balance and overcompensations began to appear—men began to exaggerate the nature of natural wood, invent wood where none was, refabricate wood products to look more like wood, cultivate a mystique of carpentry, woodcarving and do-it-yourself, and finally, to prepare symposia on aesthetics and design in wood.

For it is inconceivable to me that a culture that was at home with wood and comfortable with it, would ever feel any need to discuss wood at this high intellectual level. It was this thought that prompted me to approach the matter in the way I have done. I am sure many writers will address themselves to the topic under discussion in a bluff and practical way, explaining how they use wood to contrive that structure or this visual effect. But it takes two to make a structure—the builder as well as the material. And it takes two to make an aesthetic—the observer as well as the observed object.

To me the builder and the observer and the carver and the engraver are as interesting as the common material they all perform upon. What is it that they see in wood, what gratifications do they derive from working on it, why are they sufficiently "hung up" about it to talk and argue about it? For, let us face it, we are not considering the structural, operational, and visual exploitations of a mere natural resource, a raw material like any other. We are considering a material that is loaded with meanings, a material which inspires strong feelings in most of us.

We are here concerned with a material which is not brewed up at the behest of our own immediate will in vats and furnaces, nor laid down by geological process millions of years ago, but a material which commonly grows at a speed comparable to the speed at which we grow, so that a man who plants a seedling tree in middle age can just about expect to see it outtop himself before he dies. A material which, like man, grows upright and at right angles to the surface of the earth—a growth habit unique to man among the primates and unique to wood among his structural materials. No wonder we can identify so closely that we see men as trees walking, or mistake wind-shaken trees for men waving. No wonder they say that where a tree won't grow, a man won't grow.

And little wonder that we crave the presence of wood so deeply and so indiscriminately that we will settle for its painted or printed appearance even when its substance is present. And no wonder that every one has a ready answer to the rhetorical question which is the title of this paper.

Yes, Virginia, there is a substitute for wood-grain plastic—it is wood itself. But let us face the fact that for most employments and deployments, natural wood is a poor physical substitute for the many and sundry processed and perfected reincarnations of wood which now come coolly and unemotionally to hand.

Rationally and reasonably, the future lies with wood products, we must all suspect, rather than wood as it grows, but in our hearts we know that we will always prefer the old unreliable, twisty, shaky, knotty random lengths from the lumber yard—and *because* of those imperfections, not in spite of them. ∎

This text has previously been published in *Design and Aesthetics in Wood*, edited by Eric A. Anderson and George F. Earle, State University of New York, in 1972 and has been reprinted here with the permission of the Reyner Banham Estate and Shelley Power Literary Agency.

Ich will damit nicht sagen, dass die nordamerikanische Kultur an Entzugssymptomen leidet, sondern eher, dass sie sich in der Situation eines Trinkers befindet, der bemerkt, dass die Flasche, die er eben noch für halbvoll hielt, fast dreiviertel leer ist. Der rasche Rückzug des Waldlands aus Gegenden, die in Reichweite des Durchschnittsbürgers liegen, und das rasche Verschwinden von Naturholz aus seiner gebauten Umwelt lässt ihn überreagieren und er beginnt, verzweifelt um jede Panoramastraße durch Rotholzwälder zu kämpfen und jedes nicht aus Holz bestehende Objekt mit simulierter Holzmaserung zu überziehen.

Vielleicht sollte man die Situation sogar noch diskreter beschreiben. Ich könnte mit folgender Zusammenfassung des bisher Gesagten leben: Der Gebrauch von und das Leben mit Holz sind ein wesentliches und grundlegendes kulturelles Vermächtnis aller nördlichen, nicht-mediterranen Völker. Wiewohl sie Kunst, Architektur und Design des Mittelmeerraums fortgeführt haben, hat die ständige Gegenwart von Holz in ihrer Arbeitsumgebung – ob im Haus oder im Freien – all ihre kulturellen Bedürfnisse nach Kontakt mit diesem Material befriedigt. *Solange Holz vorhanden war.* Als die reale Gegenwart natürlichen Baumholzes zu schwinden begann, brachte das die kulturelle Situation ins Wanken und es kam zu Anzeichen einer Überkompensation – der Mensch fing an, die Natur von Holz überzubetonen, Holz zu erfinden, wo keines war, Holzprodukte stärker nach Holz aussehen zu lassen, einen Mythos um das Tischlern, Schnitzen und Heimwerken zu erzeugen und Symposien zum Thema „Holz: Ästhetik und Gestaltung"[4] abzuhalten.

Ich kann mir nämlich nicht vorstellen, dass eine Kultur, für die Holz etwas Selbstverständliches ist, je die Notwendigkeit empfinden würde, darüber auf einem solchen intellektuellen Niveau zu diskutieren. Diese Überlegung hat mich auch dazu veranlasst, das Thema auf die Art und Weise zu behandeln, wie ich es hier getan habe. Zweifellos werden es manche Autoren direkter und praktischer angehen, erklären, wie sie mit Holz dies oder jenes bauen oder diese oder jene optische Wirkung erzielen. Es gehören aber zwei dazu, etwas zu bauen – der Bauende und das Material. Und es gehören zwei dazu, eine Ästhetik zu kreieren – der Betrachtende und das Betrachtete.

Für mich sind Bauender und Betrachtender, Schnitzer und Holzschneider so interessant wie das Material, mit dem sie arbeiten. Was sehen sie im Holz, welche Befriedigung ziehen sie aus der Arbeit mit ihm? Warum sind sie so davon „besessen", dass sie darüber reden und diskutieren wollen? Denn, seien wir mal ehrlich, wir sprechen ja nicht von den strukturellen, funktionalen und visuellen Einsatzmöglichkeiten eines x-beliebigen natürlichen Rohstoffs. Wir sprechen von einem Material, das aufgeladen ist mit Bedeutung, einem Material, das bei den meisten von uns starke Gefühle hervorruft.

Wir haben es mit einem Material zu tun, das nicht nach unserem eigenen Willen in Fässern und Öfen zusammengebraut wird oder vor Jahrmillionen durch geologische Prozesse geformt wurde, sondern das häufig mit einer vergleichbaren Geschwindigkeit wächst wie wir selbst, sodass ein Mensch, der in der Mitte seines Lebens einen Setzling pflanzt, gerade mal erwarten kann, dass er bis zu seinem Tod zu einem halbwegs stattlichen Baum heranwächst. Es ist ein Material, das, wie der Mensch, aufrecht, im rechten Winkel zur Erdoberfläche wächst – ein Wuchsverhalten, das unter den Primaten allein dem Menschen und unter seinen Baumaterialien allein dem Holz vorbehalten ist. Kein Wunder also, dass wir uns so stark mit ihm identifizieren, dass wir Menschen als wandelnde Bäume betrachten oder windgebeutelte Bäume für Winkende halten. Kein Wunder, dass man sagt: Wo kein Baum wächst, da wächst auch kein Mensch.

Und so nimmt auch nicht groß wunder, dass wir uns so sehr und so unterschiedslos nach der Gegenwart von Holz sehnen, dass wir uns sogar in Anwesenheit seiner Substanz mit einer gemalten oder gedruckten Version begnügen. Noch ist verwunderlich, dass jeder eine fertige Antwort auf die rhetorische Frage hat, mit der dieser Artikel überschrieben ist.

Ja, Virginia, es gibt einen Ersatz für Holzimitat[5] – Holz. Aber schauen wir auch der Tatsache ins Auge, dass Naturholz in den meisten Anwendungsgebieten physikalisch ein schlechter Ersatz für die zahlreichen unterschiedlich produzierten und perfektionierten Reinkarnationen von Holz ist, auf die man heute kühl und gelassen zurückgreifen kann.

Rational betrachtet – so müssen wir wohl alle annehmen – gehört die Zukunft den Holzprodukten und nicht dem Holz wie es gewachsen ist, doch unser Herz sagt uns, dass wir immer die alten unzuverlässigen, verzogenen, rissigen, astübersäten zufälligen Stücke vom Holzplatz bevorzugen werden – und zwar *wegen*, nicht *trotz* ihrer Unvollkommenheit. ■

Übersetzung: Wilfried Prantner

Dieser Text wurde erstmals in *Design and Aesthetics in Wood*, herausgegeben von Eric A. Anderson und George F. Earle, State University of New York, 1972 veröffentlicht und ist hier mit freundlicher Genehmigung des Reyner Banham Estate und der Shelley Power Literary Agency abgedruckt.

4 A.d.Ü.: Anspielung auf den Titel des Symposions, auf dem der Autor diesen Vortrag hielt.

5 A.d.Ü.: Paraphrase auf die berühmte Antwort der *New York Sun* auf die Frage der 8-jährigen Virginia, ob es den Weihnachtsmann gibt.

Material Practice

Sortenrein oder gemischt? Zur Hybridität im Holzbau

Monomaterial or Mixed Varieties? On Hybridity in Timber Construction

Anne Isopp

1

Wohnbau Esmarchstraße 3 in Berlin | Residential building at Esmarchstraße 3 in Berlin. Planung | Planning:
Kaden Klingbeil Architekten, Statik | Statics: Julius Natterer mit | with Tobias Linse, Berlin, 2008 © Photo: Bernd Borchardt

In ländlichen Bereichen hat man schon immer mit Holz gebaut, nun hält der Holzbau auch vermehrt in den Städten Einzug. Hier wird naturgemäß höher und größer gebaut, deshalb bedienen sich ArchitektInnen vermehrt einer hybriden Bauweise, meist einer Kombination von Holz und Beton. In vielen Fällen lassen die Brandschutzverordnungen auch gar nichts anderes zu. Die Frage, ob man diese Hybridbauten überhaupt als Holzbau bezeichnen kann, wird in Fachkreisen unterschiedlich beantwortet. Dabei hat die Kombination mit anderen Materialien das mehrgeschossige Bauen mit Holz erst salonfähig gemacht. Was heißt es eigentlich, sortenrein mit Holz zu bauen und welche Mischungsverhältnisse sind üblich?

Was ist ein Holzbau? Oder anders gefragt: ab wann ist ein Haus ein Holzhaus? Diese Frage ist nicht leicht zu beantworten und erhitzt in Diskussionen immer wieder die Gemüter. Ein Gebäude, an dem sich diese Diskussion gerne entzündet, ist das „HoHo Wien", das derzeit mit seinen 84 Metern als höchstes Holzhaus Österreichs gelistet wird. Die einen sagen: „Das ist ja kein richtiger Holzbau!" und argumentieren mit dem Erschließungskern aus Stahlbeton, den Randträgern aus Beton und den Holz-Beton-Verbunddecken. Die anderen sagen: „Ohne eine hybride Bauweise gäbe es dieses Hochhaus nicht!" und führen an, dass es im Hinblick auf die Erfüllung der Brand- und Schallschutzanforderungen durchaus Sinn mache, unterschiedliche Materialien miteinander zu kombinieren und dabei materialimmanente Nachteile zu kompensieren.

Eine Vielzahl an Kriterien wie Ort, Budget, Funktion, die individuelle Architektursprache, Gewohnheit und auch Überzeugung bestimmen, welche Materialien ArchitektInnen für Konstruktion und Ausbau auswählen. Gewöhnlich bauen sie im mehrgeschossigen Segment mit Stahlbeton und Ziegel, der Holzbauanteil ist noch relativ gering, dennoch steigend, da die Nachfrage nach nachhaltigem und ressourcenschonendem Bauen zunimmt. Vielleicht gerade wegen dieser ökologischen Überlegenheit des Holzes als nachwachsender und CO_2 speichernder Baustoff scheint es, dass für den Holzbau höhere Maßstäbe angelegt werden als für andere Bauweisen.

Ein echtes Holzhaus müsse doch auch von außen als solches erkennbar sein, heißt es immer wieder, sprich, es muss eine Holzfassade haben. Für den Vorarlberger Architekten Hermann Kaufmann ist diese Forderung nicht nachvollziehbar: „Für Holz gilt das Gleiche wie für alle anderen Materialien. Ein Gebäude zeigt in der Regel nicht, aus welchen Materialien es gebaut ist. So hat ein Haus, das konstruktiv aus Beton besteht, in der Regel auch keine Sichtbetonfassade oder ein Ziegelbau keine Sichtziegelfassade. Es gibt Situationen, in denen naturbelassenes Holz als Haut die einzige richtige Antwort ist. Ebenso gibt es Umgebungen, in die das nicht passen würde."[1] Es geht aber auch anders herum. Soll einem Stahlbetonhaus ein wärmeres und nachhaltigeres Erscheinungsbild gegeben werden, wird es gerne mit einer Holzfassade verkleidet. Was hinter der Fassade liegt, ist oft schwer zu erkennen.

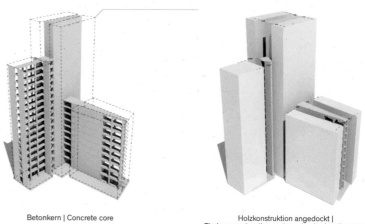

Angedockte Holzkonstruktion | Timber construction system attached to the core
Holz-Beton-Verbunddecken | Timber-concrete composite ceilings

Betonkern | Concrete core

Holzkonstruktion angedockt |
Timber construction system attached to the core

2

Tragwerkskonzept des HoHo Wien | Load-bearing concept for HoHo Wien.
Planung | Planning: RLP Rüdiger Lainer + Partner Architekten,
Statik | Statics: Woschitz Group, 2019 © RLP

Monomaterialität – Hybrid. Der Tragwerksplaner Konrad Merz stellt sich unserer Frage, ab wann ein Bau ein Holzbau ist, pragmatisch: „Es gibt eigentlich keinen reinen Holzbau. Jedes Gebäude ist ein Hybridbau."[2] Im Grunde gibt es immer einen mineralischen Keller oder zumindest eine mineralische Bodenplatte. In dieselbe Kerbe schlägt auch Richard Woschitz, der mit seinem Team für die Tragwerksplanung des „HoHo Wien" (Abb. 2) verantwortlich war: „Ich kenne keinen reinen Holzbau. Ich glaube, dass es ideologische Vorurteile sind, die dazu führen, so viel wie möglich in Holz zu machen, auch in Bereichen, wo andere Baustoffe logischer wären."[3]

Beide sind der Meinung, dass man die Materialen doch dort einsetzen solle, wo sie ihre Stärken haben. Die Schweizer Holzbauingenieure von Timbatec hingegen versuchen in ihren Bauwerken, soviel Holz wie möglich und nur soviel Stahlbeton wie nötig einzusetzen. Sind die einen nun Pragmatiker, die anderen Idealisten? Gerade der Holzbau bietet eine große Bandbreite an Bauweisen und Detaillösungen an, dass es nur logisch ist, dass sich darin auch unterschiedliche Denkweisen widerspiegeln.

Nähern wir uns der Eingangsfrage daher wissenschaftlich: In der Studie „Holzbauanteil in Österreich", die Alfred Teischinger, Robert Stingl und Marie Louise Zukal von der Universität für Bodenkultur in Wien für proholz Austria erstellten, schreiben sie, dass der Begriff des Holzbaus in den

1 Isopp, Anne: „Gespräch mit Architekt Hermann Kaufmann", in: B&O Gruppe (Hg.): *Wie wir heute für die Welt von morgen bauen*, Bad Aibling 2020, 20–21.

2 Merz, Konrad im persönlichen Gespräch, September 2020.

3 Kaiser, Gabriele: „Gespräch mit Richard Woschitz über das Konstruktionsprinzip des HoHo Wien", in: Cetus Baudevelopment GmbH (Hg.): *HoHo Wien*, Wien 2019, 73.

Wood has always served as a building material in rural areas, but timber construction is now starting to make inroads into cities. In this setting, structures are naturally built bigger and higher, which is why architects are increasingly using hybrid construction methods, often a combination of wood and concrete. In many cases, fire codes permit no other options. The question of whether such hybrid designs can even be deemed timber construction is addressed by specialists in different ways. In fact, combining wood with other materials has made multistory timber construction acceptable in the first place. What does all-timber construction actually involve? And which blending ratios are common?

What is a timber construction? Or to phrase it differently: When does a structure become a timber building? This question is not easy to answer, and it never fails to cause heated discussions. A building that frequently ignites such discourse is HoHo Wien, which at a height of 84 meters is currently listed as the tallest timber structure in Austria. Some say: "That's not really a timber building!" They pursue this line of argumentation due to the building core of reinforced concrete, the edge beams of concrete, and the timber-concrete composite ceilings. Others say: "This high-rise wouldn't exist without hybrid construction!" They argue that, in view of fire safety and sound insulation regulations, it makes perfect sense to combine different materials in order to compensate for the disadvantages inherent to each individual material.

A variety of criteria—including location, budget, function, individual architectural language, habits, and also beliefs—determine which materials architects choose for construction and development. They usually build multistory architecture, using reinforced concrete and brick; the share of timber construction is still relatively low, yet it is rising, as demand for sustainable and resource-friendly building increases. It seems that higher standards are applied to timber construction than to other building methods, perhaps precisely because of this ecological superiority of wood as a renewable and CO_2-retaining building material.

A real timber building, it is widely believed, really should be identifiable as such from the outside, meaning that it must have a wood façade. Hermann Kaufmann, an architect from the Vorarlberg region of Austria, however, finds this assumption illogical: "Wood is no different than any other material. A building rarely shows its structural materials. For instance, a house with a structural core of concrete will not usually have an exposed concrete façade, nor will a brick building have an exposed brick façade. There are situations in which a skin of natural wood is the only right answer, but there are also environs where this would not be appropriate."[1] Indeed, it also works the other way around. If a reinforced-concrete building is to be given a warmer and more sustainable appearance, then it is often clad with a wood façade. It really is hard to determine what lies behind a façade.

Monomateriality: The Hybrid. The structural engineer Konrad Merz has taken a pragmatic approach to addressing our question of when a building is a timber construction: "There is really no such thing as an all-timber construction. Every building is a hybrid."[2] Basically, there is always a mineral basement or at least always mineral slab foundation. Richard Woschitz, who with his team was responsible for the structural design of HoHo Vienna (fig. 2), also takes the same view: "I have never encountered an all-timber construction. It seems that ideological prejudices lead people to use as much wood as possible, even in areas where other materials would be more logical."[3]

Both are of the opinion that one should employ materials in ways that underpin their strengths. The Swiss timber engineers at the company Timbatec, in contrast, try to use as much wood as possible in their buildings and only as little reinforced concrete as absolutely necessary. Are the first ones pragmatists and the others idealists? Timber construction in particular offers a wide range of building methods and detail solutions, so it is only logical that it also reflects different mentalities.

Let's take a scientific approach to our initial question. In the study "Holzbauanteil in Österreich" (Share of Timber Construction in Austria), conducted by Alfred Teischinger, Robert Stingl, and Marie Louise Zukal from the University of Natural Resources and Life Sciences in Vienna for proholz Austria, the researchers write that, in most cases, the concept of timber construction is very broadly defined. For example:

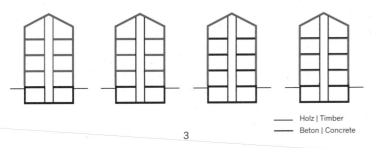

       —— Holz | Timber
       —— Beton | Concrete

3

Holzhybrid-Variationen | Timber hybrid variations © Anne Isopp

1   Anne Isopp, "Gespräch mit Architekt Hermann Kaufmann," in *Wie wir heute für die Welt von morgen bauen*, ed. B&O Gruppe (Bad Aibling, 2020), 20–21.

2   Merz, Konrad in a personal conversation, September 2020.

3   Gabriele Kaiser, "Gespräch mit Richard Woschitz über das Konstruktionsprinzip des HoHo Wien," in *HoHo Wien*, ed. Cetus Baudevelopment GmbH (Vienna, 2019), 73.

meisten Fällen sehr allgemein formuliert wird. Zum Beispiel: „Holzbau = Verwendung von Holz als Baustoff für tragende Konstruktionen." Deshalb konkretisieren sie für ihre Studie die Definition wie folgt: „Gebäude mit einem Holzanteil ab 50 Prozent gelten als Holzbauten, wobei nur die statisch tragenden Teile (Wand, Decke, Dach) zur Beurteilung herangezogen wurden. Fundamente und Kellerwände hat man für diese Berechnung gleich ausgeschlossen, da diese größtenteils aus Beton und Stahlbeton sind."[4]

Welche Formen von Hybridbauten gibt es? Folgen wir also der Definition, dass nur statisch relevante Bauteile für die Definition eines Holzhauses zählen und konzentrieren uns auf die Verbindung von Holz und Beton. Dann gibt es im Grunde genommen vier unterschiedliche Kombinationsarten, die von einem sehr hohen Holzanteil bis zu einem geringen reichen. Noch einigermaßen sortenrein geht es zu, wenn ein Holzbau auf einem Fundament oder einem Kellergeschoss aus Beton errichtet wird. Öfters wird der Holzbau hingegen um einen zentralen Treppenhaus- und Liftkern aus Stahlbeton angeordnet. Im dritten Fall wird der Stahlbetonbau mit Außenwänden aus Holz ummantelt, meist mit vorgefertigten Holzrahmenbauwänden. Bei der vierten Variante gehen die Materialien dann schon eine engere Bindung ein. Neben einem Stahlbetonkern wird hier mit hybriden Bauteilen, den Holz-Beton-Verbunddecken gearbeitet. Die Varianten unterscheiden sich zum einen in ihrem Anteil an Holz und Beton, und zum zweiten, wie eng die beiden Materialien miteinander verbunden sind. Bei der vierten Variante (Holz-Beton-Verbunddecken) ist die Verbindung zwischen den beiden Materialien am engsten. Das hat im Hinblick auf Schallschutz und Brandschutz seinen Vorteil. Einen späteren Rückbau und die damit verbundene notwendige Trennung der Materialien erschwert diese Variante aber im Vergleich zu den anderen. Für jedes Projekt muss den jeweiligen Rahmenbedingungen entsprechend ein adäquates Konstruktionssystem und die richtige Materialkombination gefunden werden. Eine eher ungewöhnliche Kombination haben Architektur Lischer Partner gemeinsam mit dem Holzbauingenieur Pirmin Jung bei einem Ferienhaus im schweizerischen Vitznau gewählt. Um einen reinen Holzbau herum wurde eine Schale aus Ortbeton erstellt, die wie ein schützender Vorhang den weichen Kern umschließt.

Ein Hybrid ist laut Wörterbuch etwas zwitterhaftes, etwas von zweierlei Herkunft. Betrachtet man den Holz- und den Stahlbetonbau näher, erkennt man, dass sich diese nicht nur in ihrer Materialität unterscheiden, sondern auch in ihren Bau- und Planungsweisen. Der Holzbau zeichnet sich durch seine trockene Bauweise und seinen hohen Vorfertigungsgrad aus. Wird bei einer Kombination mit Beton vor Ort betoniert, erhöht sich durch die Trocknungszeiten und Schalungsarbeiten die Bauzeit. Außerdem ist das Bauen mit Holz wesentlich präziser als das Bauen mit Beton und das jeweilige Setzungsverhalten unterschiedlich. So beschreiben die Tragwerksplaner Julius Natterer und Tobias Linse den damaligen Entwurfsprozess für

ein siebengeschossiges Holzhaus wie folgt: „Der erste Tragwerksentwurf ging davon aus, dass das Treppenhaus aus Stahlbeton und das Wohnhaus aus Holz in einem Gesamtsystem zusammenwirken. Es zeigte sich jedoch, dass ein Zusammenspiel der zwei Konstruktionen nur schwer zu verwirklichen ist."[5]

Es war in Deutschland der erste höhere Wohnbau aus Holz, den die Architekten Tom Kaden und Tom Klingbeil für eine Berliner Baulücke entwickelten (Abb. 1). Hinter der weißen Putzfassade versteckt sich ein Holzskelettbau mit Holz-Beton-Verbunddecken. Davon etwas abgerückt steht das Treppenhaus in Sichtbeton. Dazwischen eine präzise gesetzte Fuge. „Die unterschiedlichen Verformungsverhalten der beheizten Holzkonstruktion und der unbeheizten Stahlbetonkonstruktion [...] stellten eine Herausforderung dar. Daher wurden das Treppenhaus und das Wohnhaus komplett voneinander getrennt. Dies erwies sich als wirtschaftlicher, ‚konstruktiv sauberer' und einfacher in der Ausführung."[6] Im Nachhinein stellen die beiden Tragwerksplaner die Ausgliederung vom Treppenhaus aus Kostengründen aber selbst wieder zur Diskussion. Zum damaligen Zeitpunkt war die Trennung für die Lösung der Brandschutzproblematik von zentraler Bedeutung. Zum Errichtungszeitpunkt waren hier nur Gebäude mit einem Fluchtniveau von maximal 13 Metern in Holzbauweise erlaubt. Da das Gebäude mit einer Fußbodenhöhe von 19,4 Metern erheblich über der maximal zulässigen Höhe lag, musste ein genehmigungsfähiges Brandschutzkonzept mit Zustimmungen im Einzelfall ausgearbeitet werden. Durch die Trennung von Wohnhaus und Treppenhaus ist im Brandfall ein gut belüfteter und kurzer Fluchtweg sichergestellt. Etwa zeitgleich mit Kaden Klingbeil bauten auch Waugh Thistleton Architects in London sogar ein fast 30 Meter hohes Holzhaus. Da die Brandschutzbestimmungen in Großbritannien liberaler waren als in Deutschland, errichteten sie über dem Sockelgeschoss aus Stahlbeton einen reinen Holzbau, bei dem sogar Treppenhaus und Liftschacht aus Holz sind.

Die Holz-Beton-Verbunddecke. Ein hybrides Bauteil. „Sieht man von den aus der Römerzeit überlieferten Versuchen zu zusammengesetzten Holz-Verbundbauteilen ab, so wurden die ersten Untersuchungen an Holz-Beton-Verbundkonstruktionen in den 20er- und 30er-Jahren des 20. Jahrhunderts durchgeführt",[7] so Stefan Winter, Heinrich Kreuzinger

---

4   Teischinger, Alfred/Stingl, Robert/Zukal, Marie Louise: „Holzbauanteil in Österreich. Statistische Erhebung von Holzbauvorhaben", in: proholz Austria (Hg.): *att Zuschnitt*, Wien 2011, o.S.

5   Linse, Tobias/Natterer, Julius: „Ein 7-Geschosser (fast) ganz aus Holz. Konstruktive Details eines Pilotprojekts", *Bauingenieur* 83 (2008), 532.

6   Ebd.

7   Winter, Stefan/Kreuzinger, Heinrich/Mestek, Peter: „Flächen aus Brettstapeln, Brettsperrholz und Verbundkonstruktionen", in: TU München, Lehrstuhl für Holzbau und Baukonstruktion (Hg.): *Holzbau der Zukunft*, Teilprojekt 15, München 2009, 182.

"timber construction = use of wood as a building material for load-bearing structures." Hence, they phrase the definition in more specific terms for their study: "Buildings with a wood share of 50 percent or more are considered timber constructions, whereby only the statically load-bearing parts (walls, ceiling, roof) were considered in this assessment. Foundations and basement walls were excluded from this calculation, as they are largely made of concrete and reinforced concrete."[4]

What Kinds of Hybrid Buildings Exist? So let's concentrate on combining timber and concrete, adhering to the definition that only statically relevant structural elements pertain to the definition of a timber building. There are basically four different types of combinations, ranging from a very high share of wood to a low one. First, using a single material still reasonably applies when a timber construction is erected on a concrete foundation or basement. Second, more often than not the timber construction is arranged around a central reinforced-concrete core that houses the stairwell and elevator. In the third instance, a reinforced-concrete structure is encased in exterior walls made of wood, usually in prefabricated timber-frame walls. In the fourth case, the materials are more closely combined, featuring, aside from a reinforced-concrete core, hybrid structural elements and timber-concrete composite ceilings. The variants differ firstly in their share of timber and concrete, and secondly in how closely the two materials are connected. In the fourth version (timber-concrete composite ceilings), the connection between the two materials is the closest. This has advantages when it comes to fire safety and sound insulation. However, this version makes any later dismantling, as well as the unavoidable separation of materials, more difficult as compared to the others. For each project, the appropriate construction system and the right combination of materials must be found and tailored to the respective framework conditions. The architectural firm Lischer Partner, together with the timber engineering firm Pirmin Jung, arrived at a rather unusual combination for a vacation home in the Swiss village of Vitznau. A shell of in-situ concrete was built around an all-timber construction, enclosing the soft core like a protective curtain.

According to the dictionary, a hybrid is something hermaphroditic, something of dual origin. If we take a closer look at timber and reinforced-concrete construction, it is clear that they differ not only in their materiality, but also in their building and planning methods. Timber construction is characterized by its dry building method and its high degree of prefabrication. If the two materials are combined on site, which involves the pouring of concrete, then the actual construction

period increases due to drying time and formwork. Also, building with wood is much more precise than building with concrete, and the respective setting properties are different. The structural engineers Julius Natterer and Tobias Linse describe their process of having designed a seven-story timber building as follows: "The initial structural design assumed that the stairwell made of reinforced concrete and the residential building made of timber would interact in an overall system. As it turned out, however, interplay of the two structures is very difficult to achieve."[5]

The first residential timber building of considerable height in Germany was developed by the architects Tom Kaden and Tom Klingbeil for a vacant lot in Berlin (fig. 1). Hidden behind the white plaster façade is a timber-frame construction with timber-concrete composite ceilings. Somewhat removed from this is the exposed-concrete stairwell, and there is a precisely positioned gap in between. "The deviant deformation behavior of the heated timber construction and the unheated reinforced-concrete structure … posed a challenge. It was for this reason that the stairwell and the residential building were erected completely separate from each other. This proved to be more economical, 'structurally cleaner,' and easier to carry out."[6] In retrospect, however, the two structural engineers reexamined their idea of separating the stairwell from the rest of the building with an eye to cost considerations. During the planning period, the separation of the two had been of central importance in addressing fire safety issues. But later, during the building period, only structures with a maximum escape level of 13 meters were permitted in timber constructions. Since the building, at a floor height of 19.4 meters, was considerably taller than the maximum permissible height, an approvable fire safety concept had to be drawn up subject to approval on a case-by-case basis. Separating the stairwell from the residential building ensures a well-ventilated and short escape route in case of fire. Around the same time as Kaden Klingbeil were developing this building, Waugh Thistleton Architects in London erected an even taller timber structure, nearly 30 meters high. Because fire safety regulations in Great Britain were more liberal than in Germany, they built an all-timber construction

4   Alfred Teischinger, Robert Stingl, and Marie Louise Zukal, "Holzbauanteil in Österreich: Statistische Erhebung von Holzbauvorhaben," in *att Zuschnitt*, ed. proholz Austria (Vienna, 2011), n.p.

5   Tobias Linse and Julius Natterer, "Ein 7-Geschosser (fast) ganz aus Holz: Konstruktive Details eines Pilotprojekts," *Bauingenieur* 83 (2008), 532.

6   Ibid.

und Peter Mestek von der TU München. „Vor allem bedingt durch den Mangel an Bewehrungsstahl zur Zeit des Zweiten Weltkrieges wurden alternative Tragkonstruktionen erforscht. So meldete Otto Schaub im Jahre 1939 ein Patent auf Verbunddecken aus Holzrippen und einer Deckschicht aus Beton an. Nach dem Ende des Zweiten Weltkrieges rückte das Interesse an Holz-Beton-Verbundkonstruktionen zunächst wieder in den Hintergrund."[8] In den 1980er-Jahren begann man verschiedene Schubverbindungen und Berechnungsmethoden zu entwickeln. Bauingenieur Julius Natterer, der von 1978 bis 2004 Professor an der Eidgenössisch Technischen Hochschule Lausanne (EPFL) war und dort das Institut für Holzkonstruktionen (Ibois) leitete, trug wesentlich zur Weiterentwicklung und Verbreitung der Holz-Beton-Verbundkonstruktionen bei.

Heute ist die Holz-Beton-Verbunddecke aus dem mehrgeschossigen Bauen mit Holz nicht mehr wegzudenken. Dennoch war zu Beginn die Verwunderung groß: „Warum bitte soll man auf ein trockenes Holz einen nassen Beton geben und damit die Vorteile des Holzbaus, der trockenen Bauweise und des hohen Vorfertigungsgrades zunichte machen?"[9] Ein anderes Gegenargument lautete: „Warum sollte man zusätzliches Gewicht aufbringen, der Holzbau kann das auch alleine – vom Schallschutz bis hin zum Brandschutz."[10] Inzwischen hat sich die Erkenntnis durchgesetzt, dass die Holzdecke, genauso wie die Betondecke, die Anforderungen alleine erfüllen kann, dass beide in der Kombination aber noch besser sind.

Bei einer Holz-Beton-Verbunddecke wird eine Holzplatte oder Holzbalken mit einer dünnen Betonplatte kraftschlüssig verbunden. Hierbei übernimmt das Holz die Zugkräfte und der Beton die Druckkräfte. Für den Beton ist weniger Bewehrung notwendig, im Vergleich zu einer reinen Holzdecke kommt man mit einer geringeren Konstruktionshöhe aus und die Anforderungen an den Schallschutz und den Brandschutz sind leichter zu erfüllen. Die Kombination ermöglicht eine Gewichtseinsparung gegenüber einer reinen Betondecke und hat den Mehrwert einer sichtbaren Holzdeckenuntersicht. Vorfertigung und Schnelligkeit wie beim Holzbau können je nach gewähltem Vorfertigungsgrad trotzdem gegeben sein. Nicht zu vergessen ist die vertrauensbildende Funktion, die der Beton in Bezug auf den Brandschutz einbringt. Der Entwurf der Architekten Kaden Klingbeil eines Siebengeschossers in Berlin wäre zum Beispiel ohne Holz-Beton-Verbunddecken nie genehmigt worden. Auch der achtgeschossige Holzturm in Dornbirn wäre ohne die Kombination mit Beton nicht denkbar gewesen. Der sogenannte Life Cycle Tower von Hermann Kaufmann Architekten besteht aus einem Betonkern mit Stiegenhaus und Lift und einem angrenzenden hölzernen Skelettbau. Die Holz-Beton-Verbunddecken waren dabei der Schlüssel dafür, dass hier nicht – wie damals erforderlich – die gesamte Holzkonstruktion hinter Gipskartonschichten versteckt werden musste. Die tragenden Holzstützen sowie die Untersichten der Holzdecken konnten sichtbar belassen werden. Natürlich ist Beton nicht das einzige Material, mit dem Holz gelungene

Verbindungen eingeht. Die Kombination unterschiedlicher Materialien ermöglicht es, auf intelligente Weise materialimmanente Nachteile des Holzbaus zu kompensieren. Inzwischen gibt es zahlreiche Arten an Verbindungsmitteln und Berechnungsmethoden. Und nach wie vor ist die Holz-Beton-Verbunddecke Thema laufender Forschungsprojekte. So erforscht zum Beispiel die Woschitz Group gemeinsam mit Wood K plus derzeit unterschiedliche Verbindungstechniken sowie das Verhalten von einzelnen Klebern und die dazugehörigen Simulationen von Holz-Hybridelementen, um ein reales Verhalten zukünftig schneller vorherzusagen können.

Während die einen daran interessiert sind, das Bauen mit Holz effizienter und wirtschaftlicher zu gestalten, tendieren andere zum sortenreinen, weil noch ökologischerem Bauen: Das Holzbauingenieurbüro Timbatec, mit drei Standorten in der Schweiz und einem in Wien, hat seine eigene Definition von Holzbau: "Ein Holzbau ist erst dann ein richtiger Holzbau, wenn er ohne Beton auskommt."[11] Auf ihrer Webseite ist zu lesen, dass sie seit 2013 konsequent auf Holz-Beton-Verbunddecken verzichten. Sie verwenden stattdessen auf den Holzdecken elastisch gebundene Splittschüttungen. Begründet wird dies mit dem ökologischen Vorteil, so wenig Beton wie möglich zu verbauen und der Gewichtseinsparung von bis zu 50 Prozent gegenüber Beton. Ebenso würden sie gerne auch Treppenhäuser und Liftschächte möglichst ohne Stahl und Beton bauen. Deshalb haben sie bei dem erst kürzlich fertiggestellten Wohnbau in Winterthur die gängige Bauweise – erst den Stahlbetonkern zu errichten und dann den Holzbau – umgedreht. Das Wohnhaus mit 254 Wohnungen, das sich „Krokodil" nennt, wurde von den Architekten Baumberger & Stegmeier und KilgaPopp gemeinsam mit den Holzbauingenieuren von Timbatec geplant. Dafür wurde auf einem Sockel zuerst der Holzbau errichtet und dann die Erschließungskerne betoniert, wobei das Holz als verlorene Schalung diente. Diese Vorgehensweise beschleunigte den Bauprozesses, reduzierte den Materialverbrauch und folgte im Grunde der Logik des Holzbaus, der präzise die Form des zu gießenden Betons bestimmte (Abb. 4–6).

Wie geht es weiter? In Bayern hat man den nächsten Schritt bereits gewagt und Wohnhäuser aus nur einem Material gebaut. ArchitektInnen und IngenieurInnen hatten sich an der TU München zusammengefunden, um über Forschung und Lehre eine neue Entwicklung in Richtung einer einfacheren

8   Ebd.

9   Isopp, Anne: „Editorial", in: *Zuschnitt* 45 (2012), 3.

10 Ebd.

11 o.A.: „Trockene Schüttung statt HBV", *Timbatec. Timber and Technology*, online unter: www.timbatec.com/at/Innovation-Lab/referenzen/ 2020-03-31-Gebundene-Schuetteung.php (Stand: 20. Januar 2021).

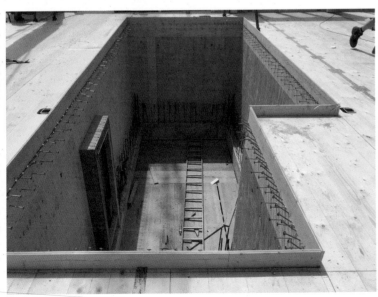

4–6

Beim Wohnbauprojekt „Krokodil" in Winterthur drehte man den üblichen Bauablauf um: Erst wurde der Holzbau errichtet, danach die Treppenhäuser betoniert. |
In the case of the Krokodil residential building in Winterthur, the conventional sequence was reversed: first the timber construction was erected and then the stairwells were cast in concrete. Planung | Planning: Baumberger & Stegmeier Architekten und KilgaPopp Architekten, Statik | Statics: Timbatec, Winterthur, 2020
© Baumberger & Stegmeier AG

7

Forschungshäuser in Bad Aibling: drei Häuser aus Beton, Holz und Ziegel |
Research architecture in Bad Aibling: three residential buildings made of concrete, wood, and masonry respectively.
Planung | Planning: Florian Nagler Architekten, 2020 © Sebastian Schels

on a reinforced-concrete base floor, in which even the stairwell and elevator shaft are made of wood.

Timber-Concrete Composite Ceilings: A Hybrid Structural Element. "If we disregard the experiments with composite timber elements handed down from Roman times, the first investigations involving timber-concrete composite structures were carried out in the twenties and thirties of the twentieth century," as Stefan Winter, Heinrich Kreuzinger, and Peter Mestek from the Technical University of Munich explain.[7] "Mainly due to a lack of reinforcing steel around the Second World War, alternative load-bearing structures were researched. In 1939, for example, Otto Schaub applied for a patent on composite ceilings made of wooden ribs and a concrete surface layer. After the Second World War, interest in timber-concrete composite structures initially receded into the background again."[8] The 1980s saw the advent of various shear connections and calculation methods. The civil engineer Julius Natterer, a professor at the Swiss Federal Institute of Technology Lausanne (EPFL) from 1978 to 2004 who headed the Laboratory for Timber Constructions (Ibois) there, made an essential contribution to the further development and dissemination of timber-concrete composite structures.

Today, multistory timber buildings are inconceivable without timber-concrete composite ceilings. Yet they seemed quite amazing at the outset: "Why on earth should we put wet concrete on top of dry wood, thus negating the advantages of timber construction, dry building methods, and the high degree of prefabrication?"[9] Another counterargument wondered: "Why add extra weight unnecessarily when timber construction itself is perfectly capable—from sound insulation to fire safety."[10] Meanwhile, it is widely acknowledged that timber ceilings alone can meet the same demands as concrete ceilings, but that a combination of both is even more favorable.

In the case of a ceiling made of a timber-concrete composite, a wooden panel or beam is force-fitted to a thin concrete slab. Here, the wood takes over the tensile forces and the concrete the compressive forces. Less reinforcement is needed for the concrete, a lower construction height is possible as compared to an all-timber ceiling, and the requirements for sound insulation and fire safety are easier to meet. The combination saves weight as compared to a concrete-only ceiling and has the added value of a wood ceiling visible from below. The advantages of prefabrication and speed are, in fact, comparable to timber construction depending on the degree of prefabrication

chosen. It is also important to remember the confidence-building function that concrete brings to the table in terms of fire safety. The design of a seven-story building in Berlin by the architects Kaden Klingbeil, for example, would never have been approved without timber-concrete composite ceilings. The eight-story timber tower in Dornbirn would likewise have been inconceivable without a concrete composite. The Life Cycle Tower by Hermann Kaufmann Architekten has a concrete core with stairwell and elevator, and an adjacent timber-frame construction. Indeed, timber-concrete composite ceilings were the key to ensuring that the whole timber construction did not have to be hidden behind layers of plasterboard, as was necessary at the time. The load-bearing timber supports could remain in view, as could the wood ceilings visible from below. Of course, concrete is not the only material that can enter into successful combinations with timber. Bringing together different materials makes it possible to intelligently compensate for the disadvantages of timber construction inherent to this particular material. Meanwhile, there are numerous calculation methods and types of joining. And timber-concrete composite ceilings still remain the subject of ongoing research projects. For example, the Woschitz Group has teamed up with Wood K plus to investigate different joining techniques, along with the behavior of individual adhesives and the associated simulations of wood hybrid elements, in order to be able to predict actual behavior more quickly in the future.

While some are interested in making it more efficient and economical to build with wood, others tend more toward timber-only architecture for ecological reasons. The timber engineering firm Timbatec, with three offices in Switzerland and one in Vienna, has developed its own definition of timber construction: "A timber construction is only a real timber construction if it can do without concrete."[11] On their website,

---

7   Stefan Winter, Heinrich Kreuzinger, and Peter Mestek, "Flächen aus Brettstapeln, Brettsperrholz und Verbundkonstruktionen," in *Holzbau der Zukunft*, Teilprojekt 15, ed. TU München, Lehrstuhl für Holzbau und Baukonstruktion (Munich, 2009), 182.

8   Ibid.

9   Anne Isopp, "Editorial," *Zuschnitt* 45 (2012), 3.

10 Ibid.

11 Anon., "Trockene Schüttung statt HBV," Timbatec: Timber and Technology, available online at: www.timbatec.com/at/Innovation-Lab/referenzen/2020-03-31-Gebundene-Schuetteung.php (accessed January 23, 2021).

und zugleich robusteren Architektur anzustoßen und damit eine Gegenbewegung zu den immer komplexeren und zugleich fehleranfälligeren Baupraktiken, mit denen PlanerInnen und BauherrInnen tagtäglich konfrontiert sind. Doch wie kann man langlebiger und weniger fehleranfällig bauen? Ihre Hypothese lautete: Nur wer einschichtig baut, kann robuster bauen. So können Wohngebäude mit einer hochwertigen und zugleich suffizienten Architektur, einer robusten Baukonstruktion und einer reduzierten Gebäudetechnik errichtet werden, die dann über einen Lebenszeitraum von 100 Jahren hinsichtlich Ökobilanz und Lebenszykluskosten der Standardbauweise überlegen sind. Auf Grundlage dieses Forschungsprojektes setzte Architekt Florian Nagler in diesem Jahr die Strategien des einfachen Bauens erstmals um und errichtete auf dem Firmengelände der B&O-Gruppe in Bad Aibling drei Wohnhäuser (Abb. 7).

Die drei Häuser mit Satteldach und niedrigem Anbau schauen nur auf den ersten Blick identisch aus. Auf den zweiten erkennt man die Unterschiede in ihrer Materialität und ihrem Fassadenbild. Alle drei Häuser wurden konsequent monomateriell, einmal aus Beton, aus Holz und aus Mauerwerk errichtet. Alle Außenwände sind einschalig und erzielen durch Einkapselung von Luft eine hohe Dämmleistung. Der Beton ist ein Dämmbeton, das Mauerwerk sind Hochlochziegeln und das Massivholz hat eingefräste Lufteinschlüsse. Auf die Frage, ob diese Bauweisen das Potenzial zum Standard haben, antwortet Florian Nagler: „Der Dämmbeton ist noch zu experimentell und damit sehr teuer. Das Mauerwerk bietet sich hervorragend für eine Standardbauweise an. Die Massivholzplatte mit den Lufteinschlüssen halte ich für ein gutes Produkt. Mit 30 Zentimetern Wanddicke ist die Holzwand sogar etwas überdimensioniert im Hinblick auf die Anforderungen der deutschen Energieeinsparverordnung. Dieses Produkt ist schon jetzt sehr konkurrenzfähig, da es einen geringen Flächenbedarf hat."[12]

Während auf der einen Seite eine Etablierung des Holzbaus im mehrgeschossigen Wohnbau stattfindet, einhergehend mit einer immer effizienteren Verzahnung von Holz und Betonbau, gibt es auf der anderen Seite das Bestreben, einfacher und sortenreiner zu bauen. So vielfältig der Holzbau ist, so unterschiedlich sind auch die Richtungen, den Holzbau weiterzuentwickeln. Will der Holzbau sich weiter als gleichberechtigter Baustoff neben den gängigen mineralischen Baustoffen etablieren, wird die pragmatische Sichtweise, die Materialien dort einzusetzen, wo sie ihre Stärken haben, fürs erste obsiegen. Und doch eröffnet jede Produktentwicklung, neue Bau- und Konstruktionsweisen ungeahnte Möglichkeiten. ∎

12 Isopp, Anne: „Gespräch mit Architekt Florian Nagler", in: B&O Gruppe (Hg.): *Wie wir heute für die Welt von morgen bauen*, Bad Aibling 2020, 14–15.

they claim to have been building totally without timber-concrete composite ceilings since 2013. Instead, they use elastically bonded chippings on the timber ceilings. This is justified by the ecological advantage of using as little concrete as possible during the building process and by a weight savings of up to 50 percent as compared to concrete. The company also aims to build stairwells and elevator shafts without steel and concrete wherever possible. This is why, in the case of the recently completed residential building in Winterthur, they reversed the usual construction method of erecting the reinforced-concrete core before implementing the timber construction. The residential building with 254 apartments, called Krokodil (Crocodile), was designed by the architects Baumberger & Stegmeier and KilgaPopp together with timber engineers from Timbatec. First, a timber construction was erected on a base and then the building cores cast in concrete, with the wood serving as the missing formwork. This approach accelerated the building process, reduced material consumption, and basically followed the logic of timber construction, which precisely determined the shape of the concrete to be poured (figs. 4–6).

How Bright Is the Future? In Bavaria, the next step has already been taken, with residential buildings constructed from a single material only. Architects and engineers at the Technical University of Munich have come together to develop, through research and teaching, simpler yet more robust architecture, and thus to initiate a countermovement to the increasingly complex and also error-prone building practices with which planners and clients are confronted on a daily basis. But how can we build in a way that is more durable and less fault-prone? Their hypothesis is: Only those who build with a single layer can build more robustly. This enables residential buildings to be erected that have high-quality and sufficiency-oriented architecture, solid structural design, and reduced building technology—buildings that are superior to standard construction methods in terms of ecological footprint and life-cycle costs over a life span of 100 years. Based on this research project, the architect Florian Nagler implemented, in 2020, the strategies of simple construction for the first time and built three residential buildings on the premises of the B&O Group in Bad Aibling (fig. 7).

The three buildings with gabled roofs and low extensions seem identical only at first glance. When looking twice, we see differences in materiality and façade appearance. All three buildings were constructed with a consistent, mono-material approach: concrete, timber, and masonry respectively. All exterior walls feature a single skin and achieve high insulation performance by encapsulating air. The concrete is an insulating concrete, the masonry consists of vertically perforated bricks, and the solid timber has milled-in air pockets. When asked if these construction methods have the potential to become the norm, Florian Nagler replied: "The insulating concrete is still rather experimental and therefore very expensive. The masonry is excellently suited to normed construction. The solid timber slab with air pockets is a good product, in my opinion. At a thickness of 30 centimeters, the timber wall is even slightly oversized with regard to Germany's energy-saving regulations. This product is already very competitive because it has a low space requirement."[12]

Although timber construction is becoming well established in the context of multistory housing on the one hand, accompanied by an ever-efficient dovetailing of timber and concrete construction, there is, on the other hand, an evident desire to build more simply, with just a single material. Timber construction is extremely diverse, as are all the ways in which it can be developed further. If timber construction is to continue to establish itself as a building material on an equal footing with conventional mineral building materials, then the pragmatic view of implementing materials according to their strengths will prevail for the time being. Yet any new product design or building and construction methods open up unimagined possibilities. ∎

Translation: Dawn Michelle d'Atri

12 Anne Isopp, "Gespräch mit Architekt Florian Nagler," in *Wie wir heute für die Welt von morgen bauen*, ed. B&O Gruppe (Bad Aibling, 2020), 14–15.

Wood Is Good! – Alles gut! Wirklich?

Wood Is Good! – All Good! Really?

Stefan Winter

2
Mjøstårnet, Brumunddal, Norwegen | Norway, 2018, Voll Arkitekter, Trondheim
© Stefan Winter/TUM

Vor lauter positiven Nachrichten könnte man daher zu unreflektierter Euphorie neigen, wenn es nicht auch ein paar wenige, aber durchaus kritische Punkte gäbe. Bitte aber nicht falsch verstehen – der Autor ist ein absolut überzeugter Holzwurm von Kindesbeinen an. Die nachfolgenden Anmerkungen basieren auf den Tätigkeiten als Wissenschaftler, Tragwerksplaner, Sachverständiger, Prüfingenieur, der Mitarbeit an vielen Normen und der gelegentlichen Waldarbeit und reflektieren die persönlichen Erfahrungen mit dem Werkstoff Holz. Die folgenden Überlegungen befassen sich vom Rohstofflieferanten Wald über Forschung, Standardisierung, (Fertigungs-)Kapazitäten des Holzbaus, der möglichen Industrialisierung bis hin zu Brand- und Feuchteschutz mit sechs Kernfragen, deren gemeinsame Bearbeitung und Lösung den Holzbau noch weiter voran bringen kann. Sie werden jeweils am Ende der Kapitel in einem kurzen Fazit zusammengefasst.

Der Wald. Am Anfang steht ein Problemfall, für den wir nur indirekt etwas können, an dem wir aber alle je nach Eigenverhalten mehr oder weniger beteiligt sind: Der klimabedingte Patient Wald. Die damit verbundene Frage lautet: Dürfen wir denn überhaupt noch mit Holz bauen? Oder sollte nicht besser der alte Slogan der 1970er-Jahre „Baum ab? Nein Danke!" wieder gelten?

Um die Antwort vorwegzunehmen: Na klar sollten – besser noch müssen – wir weiter und vermehrt mit Holz bauen, um das jetzt bereits vorhandene Kohlenstoffspeicherpotenzial des nun durch Trockenheit und Käferbefall geschädigten

Das Bauen mit Holz erlebt derzeit zweifelsohne eine nicht erwartete Renaissance. Und zwar weit, sehr weit entfernt von Alpenstilromantik, Blockhütten oder einfachen Ingenieurholzbauten. Heute ist im Holzbau alles möglich: Vielgeschossige Wohnungs- oder Hotelbauten (Abb. 2), öffentliche und gewerbliche Gebäude mit für den Holzbau außergewöhnlichen Abmessungen (Abb. 3) bis hin zu einer Serie von Kleinodien (Abb. 4) oder profanen Hochregallagern. Die Erwartungen bezüglich der positiven Eigenschaften sind überall hoch. BauherrInnen erwarten ein tolles Wohn- oder Betriebsklima gepaart mit gutem Gewissen, was die klimatischen Auswirkungen ihres Tuns angeht. Die öffentliche Hand entdeckt den Holzbau als ein wirksames Mittel, um auf der Basis des Kohlenstoff-Speicherpotenzials von langfristig verbautem Holz die CO_2-Bilanzen wenigstens ein wenig besser in den Griff zu bekommen und der Holzsektor – vom Baustoffproduzenten bis hin zu den Zimmerer- und Fertigbaubetrieben – ist ohnehin davon überzeugt, dass der Holzbau mit seiner trockenen, schnellen, vorgefertigten Bauweise den anderen Baustoffen eigentlich überlegen ist.

3
Skellefteå Kulturhuset, Schweden | Sweden, 2020, White Arkitekter, Göteborg
© Stefan Winter/TUM

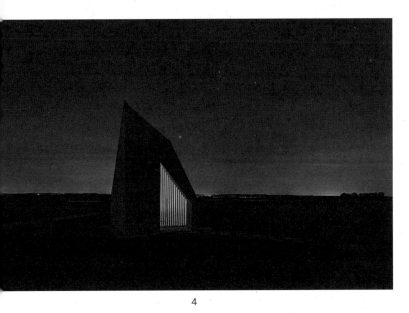

4

Kapelle nahe Oberbechingen | Chapel near Oberbechingen, lattkearchitekten, Augsburg
© Siegfried und Elfriede Denzel Stiftung, Photo: Eckhart Matthäus, Wertingen

There is no doubt that building with wood is currently experiencing an unexpected renaissance. One that is removed—very far removed—from a romantic Alpine style, from log cabins, or from simple engineered timber-frame constructions. Everything is possible in timber construction today: from multi-story apartment buildings or hotels (fig. 2), to public and commercial buildings with dimensions unusual for timber structures (fig. 3), so far as a series of architectural gems (fig. 4) or mundane high-bay warehouses. Expectations regarding the positive qualities are ubiquitously high. Builders expect an exceptional living or work environment paired with a clear conscience when it comes to the climatic implications of their work. The public sector is discovering timber construction as an effective tool for gaining slightly more control of their carbon footprint through drawing on the carbon sequestration capacities of durable, long-lasting timber, while the wood industry—from the manufacturers of building materials to carpenters and companies working in prefabrication—is already convinced that wood, with its fast, dry and prefabricated construction methods, is actually superior to other building materials.

So much positive news might lead one to mindless euphoria, if it were not for a few (definitively critical) points. Please don't misunderstand, however: this author has been a thoroughly convinced wood enthusiast since childhood. The following remarks are based on experiences as a scientist, structural engineer, expert, check engineer, collaborator on numerous building standards, and occasional forestry worker, and reflect personal experience with wood as a material. The following considerations address topics ranging from the forest as raw material source to research, standardization, the (manufacturing) capacities of timber construction, the potential for industrialization, and fire and moisture protection, examining these through six key questions—the joint handling and resolution of which can continue to further advance timber construction. They will be summarized in a short conclusion at the end of each section.

The Forest. At the outset we find a problem that we can address only indirectly, yet in which we are all, depending on our behavior, either more or less involved: the climate-conditioned patient that is the forest. The related question is: can we still build with wood? Or should the old slogan from the 1970s—"*Baum ab? Nein Danke!*" (Tree down? No, thank you!)—be applied once again? To anticipate the answer: Of course we should—better yet, we must—continue to build with wood, and increasingly so, in order to preserve the existing carbon storage potential of trees now damaged by drought and beetle infestation through long-term and sustainable material use. Additionally, due to the high demand for raw wood we can at least slightly curb its drop in price. One's heart does of course bleed upon seeing vast areas of naturally fallen trees when driving through Germany or other neighboring countries such as the Czech Republic—especially the so-called "bread and butter tree," the spruce. This is partly reminiscent of the dramatic loss of forest in northern Canada (beetle pine). But just as in Canada this wood, if harvested even halfway on time, must and can be used unproblematically for structural purposes in the form of modern timber products—solid structural timber, glulam timber, or cross-laminated timber—so long as it is not part of visible building components with high visual requirements. The mechanical properties of the timber products are not negatively affected if the dead trees are harvested in good time. Those trees with still-active bark beetle infestations must of course be felled and debarked or removed from the forest as quickly as possible. Even if the effect of the bark beetles' tunneling has a certain aesthetic appeal (fig. 5), it is in fact a pestilence.

5

Fraßbild des Borkenkäfers | Tunnels created by the bark beetle
© Stefan Winter/TUM

Baumbestandes durch die langfristige stoffliche Nutzung weiter zu erhalten. Zudem können wir durch eine hohe Nachfrage den Preisverfall für das Rohholz wenigstens ein wenig dämpfen. Natürlich blutet einem das Herz, wenn man bei Fahrten quer durch Deutschland oder einige angrenzende Nachbarländer, wie z.B. Tschechien, riesige, trocken gefallene Bestände – insbesondere des Brot- und Butterbaums Fichte – sieht. Das erinnert teilweise an die dramatischen Waldverluste im Norden Kanadas (*beetle pine*). Aber ebenso wie inzwischen auch in Kanada muss und kann dieses Holz bei halbwegs rechtzeitiger Ernte für tragende bauliche Zwecke in Form der modernen Holzbaustoffe Konstruktionsvollholz, Brettschichtholz oder Brettsperrholz unproblematisch genutzt werden, soweit es sich nicht um sichtbare Bauteile mit hohen optischen Anforderungen handelt. Die mechanischen Leistungseigenschaften der Holzprodukte werden bei rechtzeitiger Ernte der abgestorbenen Bäume nicht negativ beeinflusst. Natürlich müssen insbesondere die Bäume mit noch aktivem frischen Borkenkäferbefall schnellstmöglich gefällt und entrindet oder aus dem Wald verbracht werden. Auch wenn das Fraßbild des Borkenkäfers durchaus eine gewisse Ästhetik aufweist (Abb. 5), er ist eine echte Plage.

Aber in jeder Krise steckt auch eine Chance! In diesem Fall die Chance, den ohnehin erforderlichen Waldumbau weiter zu beschleunigen und bei den erforderlichen Aufforstungen gegenüber Hitze und Trockenheit robustere Baumarten, wie die Schwarzkiefer, Douglasie oder Flaumeiche zu pflanzen und somit möglichst robuste Mischwälder aufzubauen. Von der zunehmenden Trockenheit ist aber nicht nur die Fichte betroffen, sondern auch einige Laubbaumarten – wie an einigen Standorten in Deutschland die Buche. Dadurch, und natürlich durch den ja schon vor langer Zeit begonnenen Waldumbau, fallen inzwischen neben den großen Mengen Nadelholz zusätzlich bereits erhebliche Mengen an Laubholz an, deren stoffliche Verwendung im Bauwesen im Vergleich zu den Nadelhölzern mengenmäßig deutlich hinterherhinkt.

Fazit Eins. Das Waldsterben beeinflusst unsere Rohstoffquelle. Da aber in Mitteleuropa immer noch deutlich mehr Zuwachsmenge gegenüber der Entnahme zu verzeichnen ist, können wir auf Basis unserer dauerhaft nachhaltigen Forstwirtschaft jedenfalls davon ausgehen, dass wir auch bei einer deutlichen Ausweitung des Holzbaus genügend nachhaltig erzeugte Holzmenge zur Verfügung haben. Man bedenke dabei auch, dass wir derzeit wieder einmal große Mengen Schnittholz, beispielsweise in die USA, exportieren,[1] die bei Bedarf genauso gut innereuropäisch verwendbar wären. Ergänzend könnten wir wieder viel mehr Laubholz im Bauen verwenden.

Die Forschung. Das zuvor beschriebene, sich verändernde Holzangebot führt uns unmittelbar zu einem weiteren kritischen Punkt im Bereich der Holzwirtschaft – den Aufwendungen für Forschung. Zwar hat erfreulicherweise in Deutschland die öffentliche Hand die Forschungsmittel deutlich erhöht, z.B. über die Programme der Fachagentur Nachwachsende Rohstoffe (FNR) oder das Innovationsprogramm „Zukunft Bau", und auch in europäischen Ausschreibungen wird eine deutliche Zunahme der auf die Holzwirtschaft zugeschnittenen Programme beobachtet. Hier helfen vor allen Dingen wiederum die positiven umweltrelevanten Eigenschaften von Holz. Der angekündigte „Green Deal" der EU-Kommission lässt eine weitere Ausweitung in diesem Bereich erwarten. Aber in den meisten Fällen ist eine Mitfinanzierung der Wirtschaft in erheblichen Mengen (bis zu 50 Prozent) erforderlich. Die Forschungsinvestitionen der Betriebe der Holzwirtschaft aber hinken dem oft als sinnvoll bezeichneten Maß von ca. drei Prozent des Umsatzvolumens deutlich hinterher. Dabei wäre es gerade jetzt wichtig, z.B. bei der Entwicklung von Holzwerkstoffen, auf das zu verändernde Rohstoffangebot zu reagieren

1 Vgl. o.A.: *Holz-Zentralblatt* 146, 38 (2020), 675.

Yet in every crisis there is also an opportunity! In this case it is the chance to further accelerate the transformation of the forest, an endeavor that is in any case necessary, and to plant tree species that are more resistant to heat and drought (such as the black pine, Douglas fir, or downy oak) and thus to build up mixed forests that are as robust as possible. It is not only the spruce that is affected by increasing drought but also several deciduous tree species, such as the beech in some parts of Germany. As a result, and due also of course to the forest transformation that began already long ago, considerable amounts of deciduous wood, sources of hardwood, are now also accumulating in addition to coniferous wood, or softwood. The use of hardwood as a building material is clearly lagging far behind that of softwood.

Conclusion One. Forest dieback affects our raw material supply. However, as there is still significantly more growth than removal in Central Europe, based on our lasting, sustainable forest management we can still assume that we will have enough sustainably-produced wood available even with a significant expansion in timber construction. Also of note is the fact that we are now once again exporting large amounts of sawn timber—to the United States, for example—which could just as easily be used within Europe if required.[1] In addition, we could again use significantly more hardwood in our construction projects.

Research. The changing wood supply described above brings us directly to another critical point of the wood industry: Research costs. Fortunately, the public sector in Germany has significantly increasing research funding—as in programs of the *Fachagentur Nachwachsende Rohstoffe* (FNR) (Agency for Renewable Raw Materials) or the *"Zukunft Bau"* (Future Building) innovation program—while a significant increase in programs tailored to the timber industry can be observed in European invitations to tender. The positive, environmentally relevant properties of wood are of particular help here. The "Green Deal" announced by the EU Commission suggests that there will be further expansion in this area. In most cases, however, substantial co-financing (up to 50 percent) is required. Research investments by companies in the wood industry lag well behind the measure often referred to as meaningful, around three percent of a company's sales volume. In this current moment it would be important—in the development of raw materials, for example—to react to changing raw material supplies, or to better integrate fast-advancing digitalization practices in planning, manufacturing and optimization processes. Figures 6–7 show an example of the development of new wood-based materials, that are today often hybrid. In the case shown here, beech veneers are combined with spruce glulam timber ("wood-reinforced wood").[2]

Conclusion Two. The future development of timber construction will be incredibly exciting. There are numerous challenges to face, and with them many new approaches. It is hoped that we will continue to succeed in intriguing many young scientists with this topic, and in using their potential for innovation and imagination. The wood industry should more widely support these efforts. The emphasis here lies on "breadth" and universality, as there are of course already several highly innovative companies and associations that understand research not as a playground for universities but rather

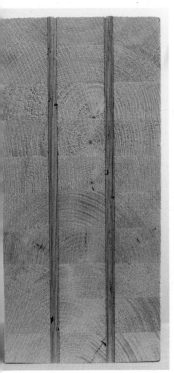

6–7

„Holzbewehrtes Holz" – Brettschichtholz mit schräg verlaufenden, innenliegenden Buchenholzfurnieren | "Wood-Reinforced Wood" – Glulam timber with sloping, internal beech wood veneers (6) Querschnitt | section (7) Furnierlagen | veneer layers
© Markus Lechner/Lehrstuhl für Holzbau und Baukonstruktion, TUM

1   See Anon., *Holz-Zentralblatt* 146, no. 38 (2020): 675.

2   "Holzbewehrtes Holz" ("Wood-Reinforced Wood") is an ongoing research project at the Technical University of Munich and part of the *Zukunft Bau* research initiative.

oder die rasant fortschreitende Digitalisierung noch stärker in Planungs- und Fertigungs- sowie Optimierungsprozesse zu integrieren. Abbildungen 6–7 zeigen ein Beispiel für die Entwicklung neuer, heute häufig hybrider Holzwerkstoffe, im gezeigten Fall aus hochfesten Buchenfurnieren in Kombination mit Fichten-Brettschichtholz („Holzbewehrtes Holz"[2]).

Fazit Zwei. Die zukünftige Entwicklung wird im Holzbau unglaublich spannend. Es gibt vielfältige Herausforderungen und damit auch viele neue Ansätze. Es bleibt zu hoffen, dass es uns weiterhin gelingt, viele junge WissenschaftlerInnen dafür zu begeistern und ihr Innovations- und Fantasiepotenzial zu nutzen. Die Holzindustrie sollte diese Bemühungen breiter unterstützen. Dabei liegt die Betonung auf „Breite" und Allgemeingültigkeit, denn natürlich gibt es bereits einige hochinnovative Unternehmen und Verbände, welche Forschung nicht als Spielwiese der Universitäten, sondern als das begreifen, was sie tatsächlich ist – Dienst an der Zukunft der gemeinsamen Sache. Für die Verbesserung des Zusammenspiels zwischen Wissenschaft und Praxis besteht aber durchaus weiteres Optimierungspotenzial.

Die Standardisierung. Ein mindestens ebenso großes Optimierungspotenzial besteht in der Standardisierung des Holzbaus. Denn ein Aspekt des heutigen Holzbaus ist einerseits positiv, andererseits extrem behindernd: Die Vielfalt im Holzbau! Konrad Merz, ein hochrespektierter Kollege aus der Holzbau-Tragwerksplanung, hat einmal die schöne Übung unternommen, alle unterschiedlichen Deckenaufbauten der Projekte eines Jahres hinter seinem Schreibtisch an die Wand zu pinnen. Nicht einer hat sich wiederholt! Die gleiche Situation würde wohl eintreten, wenn man dazu die Außenwände, die Innenwände und die Dachaufbauten ergänzt – vermutlich würde das zum Tapezieren der Wände eines mittleren Büros ausreichen. Alle unterschiedlich!

Es ist ja richtig, dass der Holzbau insgesamt etwas komplexere Aufbauten der Bauteilquerschnitte erfordert. Beispielsweise muss die fehlende Masse zur Erzielung eines hinreichenden Schallschutzes durch eine sinnvolle Schichtung ausgeglichen werden. Ähnliches gilt für den Brandschutz. Wir benötigen für einige Gebäudeklassen zusätzliche brandschutztechnisch wirksame, nichtbrennbare Bekleidungen. Wir können heute mit Holzbauweisen die baurechtlichen Anforderungen und die Komfortansprüche der NutzerInnen gleichermaßen befriedigen, aber eben nicht mit monolithischen Lösungen. Die zugrundeliegenden Forschungen basieren meist auf öffentlichen Mitteln und führen damit zu allgemein verwendbaren technischen Nachweisen. Alleine daraus resultiert schon eine gewisse Vielfalt. Gleichzeitig haben die großen Baustoffproduzenten von Gips über Holzwerkstoffe bis Brettsperrholz durch umfangreiche Prüfungen mit ihren spezifischen Baustoffen baurechtliche Verwendbarkeitsnachweise, wie allgemeine bauaufsichtliche Prüfzeugnisse für den Feuerwiderstand oder für die

Schallschutzeigenschaften, erwirkt. Zwar ist es verständlich, dass die Baustoffproduzenten diese zum Teil recht hohen Ausgaben für ihre spezifischen Marketingmaßnahmen nutzen wollen – und für eine gewisse Übergangzeit war das auch durchaus sinnvoll – nun aber ist wohl der Zeitpunkt gekommen, auf eine gemeinsame Standardisierung zu setzen. Das fällt schwer und wird wohl einige Überzeugungskraft der technischen Experten bei den CEOs erfordern, aber wenn wir den Holzbau weiter in die Breite entwickeln wollen, ist dieser Schritt dringend erforderlich.

Ein Beispiel: Wenn ArchitektenInnen und IngenieurInnen gemeinsam einen Wohnungsbau in Beton-Halbfertigbauteilen (für Wand und Decke) realisieren wollen, dann greifen sie dabei auf Standarddetails zurück und können sich sicher sein, dass praktisch jedes beliebige Betonfertigteilwerk in der näheren Umgebung die entsprechenden Bauteile ohne weitere Änderungen liefern kann. Entscheiden sich PlanerIn und BauherrIn für die weitgehende Verwendung von Brettsperrholz, so liegen der Bemessung spezifische, herstellergebundene Nachweise zugrunde. Sie beruhen auf nationalen oder europäischen Zulassungen sowie nationalen oder europäischen Prüfungen. Und diese gehören „einem Produzenten". Kommt nun nach der Ausschreibungsphase dieses Produkt nicht zum Einsatz, weil z.B. aus Kostengründen ein anderes Brettsperrholzprodukt verwendet wird, so sind in den technischen Spezifikationen häufig zwar oft nur leicht variierende Angaben zu finden, die aber dennoch alle Beteiligten zu einer Umplanung und Umbemessung zwingen. Das kostet Geld, wird meist vom Bauherr bzw. der Bauherrin nicht monetär gewürdigt und führt eher zu Unmut, insbesondere wenn es sich um Newcomer auf PlanerInnen- und BauherrInnenseite handelt. Beim Brettsperrholz ist der Nachteil bereits erkannt und die Entwicklung einer Produktnorm wurde vorangetrieben (EN 16351[3]). Leider wurde diese europäische Norm aber bisher noch nicht harmonisiert und steht daher europaweit noch nicht zur Verfügung. Zumindest ist es aber ein Schritt in die richtige Richtung. Das Beispiel ist ebenso auf andere Produkte übertragbar, bis hin zu den heute viel verwendeten Voll- und Teilgewindeschrauben. Eine weitergehende Standardisierung ist aber nicht nur im Bereich der Holzbauprodukte erforderlich, sondern sollte auch für Detaillierungen gelten, z.B. den Einbau von Fenstern oder die Ausbildung eines Attikabereichs. Es ist einfach nicht sinnvoll, jedes Mal fünf neue Details zu „erfinden".

Fazit Drei. Um dem Holzbau eine noch breitere Anwendung in der Baupraxis zu ermöglichen, sind die begonnenen Prozesse der Standardisierung der Holzbauprodukte, der Bauteilquerschnitte und der Detaillierungen weiter voran zu treiben. Einen großen Beitrag dazu liefert schon seit Jahren

2   „Holzbewehrtes Holz", laufendes Forschungsprojekt TU München, Forschungsinitiative Zukunft Bau.

3   EN 16351:2015-12 Holzbauwerke – Brettsperrholz – Anforderungen

for what it truly is: Serving the future of the common cause. In improving the interaction between science and practice, however, there is definitely potential for further optimization.

Standardization. A potential for optimization that is at least equally as great lies in the standardization of timber construction. This arises from one aspect of timber construction today that is both positive, on the one hand, and extremely hindering on the other: The diversity of timber construction! Konrad Merz, a highly respected colleague in the field of structural design for timber construction, once carried out the exercise of pinning all the different floor structures from the projects of one year on the wall behind his desk. Not one was repeated! The situation would likely be the same if the outer walls, the inner walls and the roof structures were added—and it would probably be enough to paper the walls of a medium-sized office. All of them different!

It is true that the cross-sectional profiles of components in timber construction generally require somewhat more complex structures. For example, the lower mass must be compensated for by an appropriate layering in order to achieve sufficient sound insulation. The same applies to fire protection. Some building classes require additional, non-combustible cladding in this regard. With timber construction today we can both satisfy building regulations and meet the comfort requirements of users, but not by implementing monolithic solutions. The underlying research draws primarily on public funds and thus leads to broadly applicable technical results. This alone produces a certain variety. At the same time, major manufacturers of building materials—from plaster to wood-based materials and cross-laminated timber—have obtained evidence of their specific materials' usability and adherence to building regulations through extensive testing, gaining general certifications of technical approval for fire resistance or properties of sound insulation, for example. It is understandable that building material manufacturers want to put these at times very significant expenditures towards their specific marketing strategies, and for a certain transitional period this made sense—but the time has now come to focus on collective standardization. This is difficult and will likely require the persuasiveness of experts in addressing CEOs, but this step is urgently required if we want to further develop timber construction.

As an example: If architects and engineers want to build a residential building using semi-prefabricated concrete components for the walls and floor plates, they resort to using standard details, and thus can be assured that practically any precast concrete plant in the vicinity will be able to produce the necessary components without additional changes. If the planner and client decide on the extensive use of cross-laminated timber, the dimensioning is based on precise, manufacturer-specific specifications. These are based on national or European certifications as well as national or European testing. And these belong to "a single manufacturer." If this product is not used after the tendering phase, for example if another cross-laminated is instead used for reasons of cost, the technical specifications often contain only slightly varying instructions; this nevertheless forces all involved to alter both scheduling and dimensions. This costs money, is not usually acknowledged in monetary terms by the client, and tends to lead to resentment, especially when it involves newcomers on the part of designers and clients. With cross-laminated timber this disadvantage has already been recognized and the development of a product standard has been pushed forward (EN 16351[3]). Unfortunately, this European norm has not yet been harmonized and is therefore not yet available across Europe. But it is at least a step in the right direction. This example can also be applied to other products, so far as to the fully and partially threaded screws that are widely used today. Further standardization is required not only in the area of timber construction products, however, but also in detailing—in the installation of windows, for example, or the outfitting of a flat roof. It simply doesn't make sense to "invent" five new details each time.

Conclusion Three. In order to enable an even broader use of timber construction in building practices, the processes—already in motion—of standardizing wood products, component cross-sections, and details must be further advanced. For years now, a significant contribution has been found in dataholz.com, the database of *Holzforschung Austria* (The Austrian Forest Products Research Society), which has been further developed as dataholz.eu as part of a joint Austrian-German project.[4] The database system is freely accessible to the public and makes work much easier, especially for beginners. This database system is of course continuously updated. The major goal of providing a completely product-neutral usability that adheres to building regulations has not yet been achieved, for example. In some areas, product-specific certification is still used.

In the past, the contribution made by building material manufacturers to the development of timber construction has been valuable and significant. Now, however, a further

---

3   *Timber structures – Cross-laminated timber – Requirements,* EN 16351:2015-12.

4   See www.dataholz.eu.

dataholz.com, die Datenbank der Holzforschung Austria, die inzwischen im Rahmen eines gemeinsamen österreichisch-deutschen Projekts in dataholz.eu[4] weiterentwickelt wurde. Das Datenbanksystem ist frei öffentlich zugänglich und erleichtert die Arbeit insbesondere für Einsteiger wesentlich. Selbstverständlich wird dieses Datenbanksystem immer weiter aktualisiert. Das große Ziel einer völlig produktneutralen baurechtlichen Verwendbarkeit ist z.B. noch nicht erreicht. In einigen Bereichen wird weiter auf produktspezifische Nachweise zurückgegriffen.

Der Beitrag der Baustoffhersteller zur Entwicklung des Holzbaus war in der Vergangenheit wertvoll und bedeutsam. Jetzt aber ist eine weitere Neutralisierung für die Entwicklung des Holzbaus als Regelbauweise zum Wohl aller Beteiligten voran zu treiben. Was inzwischen wirklich aus der Zeit gefallen ist und verschwinden sollte, sind sogenannte „firmenspezifische Bausysteme". Die Erfahrungen der letzten Jahre zeigt, dass diese meist zu unvollständig sind und zudem in Ausschreibungsverfahren keinen Bestand haben. Wir brauchen allgemein gültige Lösungen!

Das industrialisierte Bauen. Wenn uns eine weitere Standardisierung der Bauprodukte und Bauteile gelingt, dann wird auch der nächste Schritt einfacher, den wir allerdings bereits parallel vorantreiben müssen. Es ist der Schritt zum echten industrialisierten Bauen. Er wird es uns ermöglichen, in bestimmten Bauwerkstypologien zu einer schnelleren und preiswerteren Umsetzung zu kommen. Denn nach wie vor ist die sogenannte „Anpassungsplanung" einer der Kostentreiber im Holzbau. Unter Anpassungsplanung verstehen wir die Notwendigkeit, die Ausführungsplanung der PlanerInnen in Werkstattzeichnungen (landläufig Werkplanung genannt) umzusetzen. Holzbauunternehmen beziffern die Aufwendungen auf bis zu 25 Prozent der Angebotspreise. Vergleichbare Aufwendungen bei einem Betonbauunternehmen werden hingegen auf max. drei bis fünf Prozent geschätzt. Denn diese erhalten z.B. auf der Basis genormter Details und jahrzehntelanger gemeinsamer Übung Schal- und Bewehrungspläne, die sie auf der Baustelle unmittelbar umsetzen.

Im Holzbau muss daher der nächste Schritt eine weitergehende, echte Industrialisierung im Bauen sein. Sie ist durch Baukastensysteme unter Einsatz der heute verfügbaren digitalen Methoden realisierbar, wie beispielsweise das Forschungsprojekt „Bauen mit Weitblick"[5] gezeigt hat. Dabei bedeutet ein Baukastensystem nicht zwangsweise das Bauen mit 3D-Modulen. Ein Baukastensystem kann ebenso mit flächigen Elementen oder mit einer Mischung aus flächigen und dreidimensionalen Elementen realisiert werden. Die Forschung hat jedoch gezeigt, dass je Baukastensystem immer nur eine bestimmte Bauweise, z.B. Holztafelbau in Verbindung mit Holzmassivbau oder Holztafelbau in Verbindung mit Betonbau,

abgebildet werden kann, da die sonst entstehende Variationsvielfalt selbst durch moderne digitale Werkzeuge nicht mehr zu bewältigen ist. Die Ergebnisse des Vorhabens sind selbstverständlich öffentlich zugänglich.[6]

Baukastensysteme enthalten standardisierte Dach-, Wand- und Deckenaufbauten, die von vielen Herstellern produziert werden können. Eine Standardisierung der technischen Gebäudeausrüstung kann ergänzend erfolgen. Die Baugruppen für Wohnungen oder Büros werden durch Ergänzungsbaugruppen zur Erschließung oder für Balkonanlagen ergänzt. Eine weitere Individualisierung ist durch eine Vielfalt an möglichen Fassaden sowie die Variation von Öffnungen in einem verhältnismäßig breiten Spektrum möglich. Abbildung 8 zeigt eine mögliche Konfiguration von Baugruppen für eine hybride Mischbauweise aus Holztafel- und Betonfertigteilen. Es konnte der Nachweis geführt werden, dass aus wenigen Grundelementen sehr unterschiedliche Gebäude entstehen können. „Building Information Modelling" (BIM)-basiert sind die Baugruppen und ihre Schnittstellen komplett definiert, da würde BIM auch endlich mal richtig Sinn machen. Mit dieser Art zu planen, müsste sich allerdings die Architektur bereits in der Ausbildung intensiver auseinandersetzen. Wir sind überzeugt, dass dann trotz einer Industrialisierung gute nachhaltige Architektur entstehen kann. Die zunehmende Standardisierung kann zudem helfen, die ständige Spirale zu immer höheren Anforderungen gerade im Wohnungsbau zu durchbrechen. Das gilt natürlich nicht für den Brandschutz, da gelten die gesetzlichen Schutzziele ohne Einschränkungen. Aber für den Schall- und Wärmeschutz kann man vom baurechtlich gefordertem Mindestniveau bis zum Luxuswohnen klare Stufen definieren und diese dann auch preislich eindeutig definieren.

Die Baukastensysteme könnten web-basiert, ähnlich wie Airbnb oder Uber, nachgefragt und angeboten werden. Klar definierte Bauteile, für die bis hin zu digitalen Daten zur Fertigung alles vorliegt, werden netzbasiert nachgefragt und wer Fertigungskapazitäten frei hat, bietet an. Entwurf, Ausschreibung und Bauprojektmanagement wiederum ist und bleibt Kernaufgabe der ArchitektenInnen und der beteiligten PlanerInnen. Die Montage auf der Baustelle übernehmen darauf spezialisierte Unternehmen. Eine solche Entwicklung könnte zu einer wesentlichen Verbesserung der Angebotssituation führen, u.a. da die produzierenden Unternehmen dann eben nicht mehr mit Anpassungsplanung beschäftigt sind, sondern die freiwerdenden Kapazitäten in die Optimierung ihrer Produktions-, Liefer- und ggf. Montageprozesse investieren können. Der Beton-Fertigteilbau lässt grüßen!

4 Vgl. dazu www.dataholz.eu

5 „Bauen mit Weitblick. Systembaukasten für den industrialisierten sozialen Wohnungsbau", TU München, Bundesministerium f. Umwelt, Naturschutz, Bau und Reaktorsicherheit; Forschungsinitiative Zukunft Bau, Abschluss 2017.

6 Vgl. ebd.

neutralization in the development of timber construction as a standard construction method should be sought after for the benefit of all those involved. In the meantime, the elements that have truly become outdated and should disappear are the so-called "company-specific building systems." Experience gained over last few years has shown that these are most often too incomplete and, moreover, have no place in the tendering process. We need universal solutions!

Industrialized Building. If we are successful in further standardizing building products and components then the next step, which we will have to advance in parallel, will become easier as well. It is the step towards truly industrialized building processes; it will enable us to achieve faster and cheaper implementation in certain building typologies. This, as so-called "adaptation planning" is still one of the drivers of costs in timber construction. By adaptation planning we refer to the necessity of transforming designers' construction documents into shop drawings (commonly known as *Werkplanung*, or execution planning). Timber construction companies estimate these expenses at up to 25 percent of the bid price. Comparable expenses for a concrete construction company, meanwhile, are estimated at a maximum of three to five percent. This arises, for example, from receiving formwork and reinforcement drawings that are implemented directly on the construction site, drawing on standardized details and decades of joint practice.

In timber construction, the next step must be towards the further and veritable industrialization of construction. This can be realized through modular systems, using the digital methods available today—as shown, for example, in the *"Bauen mit Weitblick"* (Building with Vision) research project.[5] A modular system does not necessarily mean building with 3D modules. A modular system can also be implemented with flat elements or with a mixture of flat and three-dimensional elements. Research has shown, however, that only one type of construction can be mapped out per modular system (such as wood panel systems in connection with solid wood construction or wood panel systems in connection with concrete), as it would be otherwise impossible to cope with the resulting scope of possible variations, even with modern digital tools. The results of the project are of course publicly available.[6]

Modular systems contain standardized roof, wall, and floor structures that can be produced by many manufacturers. Technical building systems can also be standardized. The modular units for apartments or office buildings are supplemented by additional modules for circulation or balcony

systems. Further individualization is facilitated by a diversity of possible façades and variation of openings along a relatively broad spectrum of possibilities. Figure 8 shows a possible configuration of modular units for a hybrid mixed construction made of wood panels and precast concrete parts. The conclusion can be drawn that very different buildings can be created from a few basic elements. Based on Building Information Modeling (BIM), the modular units and their interfaces are completely defined (meaning that BIM also finally makes sense). This would have to be addressed more intensively in architectural education, however, in order to design in this way. Good, sustainable architecture can then emerge, despite industrialization. Increasing standardization can also help break the cycle of ever stricter requirements, especially in residential construction. This of course doesn't apply to fire protection, as in this case the legal regulations apply without restrictions. For sound and thermal insulation, however, degrees of insulation can be clearly defined—from the minimum required by building regulations to that of luxury housing—along with a clear definition of each in terms of price.

The modular systems could be ordered and offered online, similar to Airbnb or Uber. Clearly defined components for which everything is available, including digital data for manufacturing, would be ordered through a network and offered by those with available manufacturing capacity. Design, tendering, and project management, on the other hand, are and will remain a core task of the architects and planners involved in a project. Specialized companies would take care of the assembly on the construction site. Such a development could lead to a marked improvement in terms of supply since, among other things, manufacturing companies would then no longer be busy transforming construction drawings and could instead invest their freed-up energy into optimizing their production, delivery, and (if necessary) assembly processes. Precast concrete sends its regards!

Conclusion Four. Planning and building with modules in specific building typologies can lead to a veritable industrialization of the building process and can make it both

---

5   "Bauen mit Weitblick – Systembaukasten für den industrialisierten sozialen Wohnungsbau" [Building with Vision – Modular System for Industrialized Social Housing], Technical University of Munich, Federal Ministry for the Environment, Nature Conservation and Nuclear Safety; part of the *Zukunft Bau* research initiative concluded in 2017.

6   See ibid.

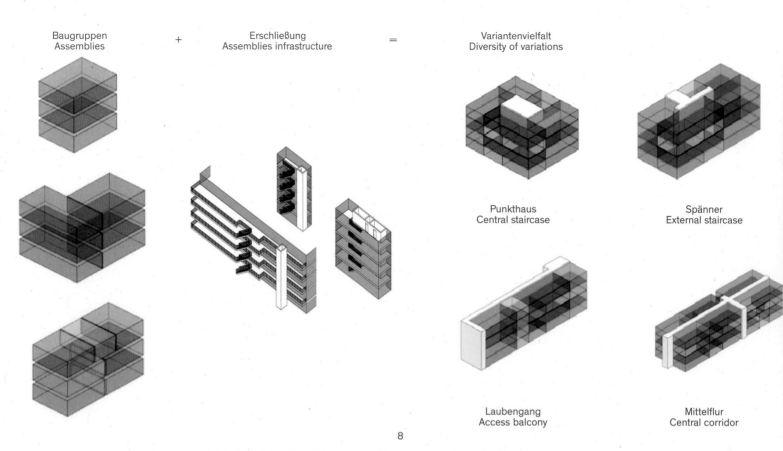

| Baugruppen Assemblies | + | Erschließung Assemblies infrastructure | = | Variantenvielfalt Diversity of variations |

Punkthaus
Central staircase

Spänner
External staircase

Laubengang
Access balcony

Mittelflur
Central corridor

8

Gebäudekonfiguration mit Baugruppen | Configuration of modules for individual buildings
© Stefan Winter/TUM

Fazit Vier. Das Planen und Bauen mit Baugruppen in definierten Gebäudetypologien kann zu einer echten Industrialisierung des Bauens führen und dieses preiswerter und qualitätsrobuster machen. Der Holzbau kann hier durch seine ohnehin schon weit fortgeschrittene Integration digital basierten Planens und Fertigens eine Vorreiterrolle einnehmen. Aber das löst auch Ängste aus. Denn diese Zeichen der Zeit haben erste Baustoffproduzenten im Holzbaubereich bereits erkannt und beginnen eigene Wand- oder Deckenbauteilfertigungen – sicher eine gewisse Bedrohung für die mittelständischen Holzbaubetriebe. Hier ist in naher Zukunft ein Dialog gefordert, wer in Zukunft welche Rolle übernimmt. Denn die pure Größe oder Finanzmacht hilft da nicht zur Durchsetzung am Markt. Den BaustoffproduzentInnen sei zur Beurteilung der Gefährdung ihrer Marktposition die Lektüre der Dissertation von Matti Kairi[7] zur Markteinführung des Werkstoffs LVL (Kerto) empfohlen – Stichwort: Wer kauft schon gerne bei der Konkurrenz? Klar ist: Zur Einführung industrialisierten Bauens ist ein Paradigmenwechsel von allen Baubeteiligten gefordert! Der Holzbau kann hier führend sein!

Die Kapazität des Holzbaus. Die angesprochene Veränderung der Abläufe von Planung und Bauausführung würde zudem helfen, andere, derzeit für den Holzbau sehr hinderliche Entwicklungen zu überwinden. Das ist einerseits die zunehmend spürbare Begrenzung der Kapazität des (Holz-)Baus. An allen Ecken und Enden fehlen qualifizierte HandwerkerInnen, insbesondere im Ausbau und in der technischen Gebäudeausrüstung. Eine zunehmende Vorfertigung verschafft hier durch die wesentlich besseren Arbeitsbedingungen Vorteile. Der Holzbau selbst hat derzeit allerdings ebenfalls eine begrenzte Kapazität in der Vorfertigung. Aus Sicht der BauherrInnen wäre daher die oben beschriebene Entwicklung hin zu einer weitergehenden Industrialisierung durchaus willkommen, weil dann mehr Betriebe die standardisierten Bauteile produzieren könnten. Was auch zu einer gewissen preislichen Entspannung führen wird. Es ist eine Tatsache, dass wir immer mal wieder Holzbauten „verlieren", weil die Bauherrschaft trotz des ursprünglichen Willens mit Holz zu bauen einfach an die Grenzen ihrer finanziellen Möglichkeiten kommt. Es geht hier nicht um „billig bauen" sondern um „preiswert" unter Berücksichtigung der Lebenszykluskosten.

Eine weitere Behinderung des Holzbaus besteht darin, dass viele BauherrInnen vorzugsweise mit Generalunternehmen, manchmal sogar Generalübernehmern bauen wollen.

7   Kairi, Matti: *Interaction of R&D and Business Development in the Wood Products Industry, Case Kerto®– Laminated Veneer Lumber (LVL)*, Diss., Aalto University, Helsinki 2005.

more affordable and more robust in terms of quality. Timber construction can play a pioneering role in this regard due to its already well-advanced integration of digitally-based planning and manufacturing. This, however, also triggers fears. Some manufacturers of building materials in the wood industry have already recognized these signs of the times and are starting their own production of prefabricated wall or floor systems—a certain threat to medium-sized timber construction companies. A dialogue will be necessary in the near future as to who will take on which role, as size or financial power alone do not decide this on the market. It is suggested that building material manufacturers might read Matti Kairi's dissertation[7] on the market launch of the material LVL (Kerto). Catchphrase: Who likes to buy from the competition? One thing is clear: the introduction of industrialized building requires a paradigm shift on the part of all those involved in the building process! Timber construction can be a leader here!

The Capacities of Timber Construction. The aforementioned change in planning and construction processes would also help to overcome other developments that are currently holding timber construction back. For one thing, overcoming the increasingly noticeable limitation that is the capacity for (timber) construction. There is a lack of qualified craftsmen on all sides, especially in areas of expansion and technical building systems. Increasing prefabrication creates advantages in this regard in leading to significantly improved working conditions. Timber construction itself, however, currently has a limited capacity for prefabrication. From the developer's point of view, the advancement described above—the move towards further industrialization—would therefore be welcome, as it would allow more companies to be able to produce standardized components. This would also lead to a certain lowering of prices. It is a fact that we sometimes "lose" wood buildings because the client, despite their original intention to build with wood, simply reach the limits of what is financially feasible. It isn't about "building cheaply" but rather "cost-effectively," taking into account life-cycle costs.

Another obstacle faced in timber construction is that many developers prefer to work with general contractors with their own in-house team of workers, or sometimes even with construction managers responsible for hiring subcontractors. It remains to be seen whether this always makes sense. This approach is by no means cheaper due to risk and management surcharges. The advantage is more likely in the fact that there is only one responsible company. In any case, the general contractor (or construction manager) must have sufficient capacities in terms of finances and personnel in order for them to assume responsibility. Both of these capacities are relatively restricted within established timber construction companies in comparison to those of large concrete and masonry construction companies. And the latter have so far felt little desire to actively bring their supposed competition to the table. Meanwhile many large buildings—including public buildings—continue to be built using primarily concrete.

Conclusion Five. Timber construction must noticeably expand its capacities in every respect in order to meet increasing demand. When opportunity knocks, you must open the door! New alliances are required and along with them the desire to change familiar processes and behavior patterns, taking into consideration the possibilities for standardization and industrialization mentioned above. If the aforementioned web-based offer works, and building materials and components are advertised and offered in a product- and manufacturer-neutral way, then general contractors will no longer be needed. A planning and design team appointed by the builder will take over coordination. Alternatively, enough "green" capital will be found and timber construction companies will become general contractors themselves. A simple "Keep it up!" will not work, as the upward trend in timber construction would then quickly run into a gray wall.

Fire and Moisture Protection. In regard to fire protection, there are still obstacles that arise due to the building regulations of many countries. But there has also been a noticeable improvement. In many countries, fire protection regulations have now been adapted so that wood can be used so far as to construct high-rise buildings, in many cases with

7   Matti Kairi, *Interaction of R&D and Business Development in the Wood Products Industry, Case Kerto®– Laminated Veneer Lumber (LVL)*, Diss., Aalto University (Helsinki, 2005).

Ob das immer sinnvoll ist, sei dahingestellt. Aus unserer Erfahrung wird das nämlich keineswegs billiger, schließlich fallen Risiko- und Management-Zuschläge an. Der Vorteil liegt wohl eher darin, dass es nur ein verantwortliches Unternehmen gibt. Jedenfalls ist aber zur Übernahme der Generalunter- oder -übernehmerschaft hinreichende Finanz- und Personalkapazität erforderlich. Beides ist bei den etablierten Holzbauunternehmen im Vergleich zu den großen Massivbauunternehmen eher begrenzt. Und letztere verspüren bisher wenig Lust, die vermeintliche Konkurrenz aktiv ins Boot zu holen. Und damit werden viele große – auch öffentliche – Bauten immer noch überwiegend aus Beton gebaut.

Fazit Fünf. Der Holzbau muss seine Kapazitäten in jeder Hinsicht spürbar erweitern, um die steigende Nachfrage zu befriedigen. Wenn es Brei regnet, braucht man Löffel! Es sind neue Allianzen gefragt und unter Berücksichtigung der zuvor genannten Möglichkeiten zur Standardisierung und Industrialisierung der Wille, gewohnte Prozesse und Verhaltensmuster zu ändern. Wenn das oben beschriebene webbasierte Angebot funktioniert und die Baustoffe und Bauteile produkt- und herstellerneutral ausgeschrieben und angeboten werden, dann braucht es auch keine Generalunternehmer mehr. Die Koordination übernimmt das vom Bauherren bzw. der Bauherrin eingesetzte PlanerInnenteam. Oder man findet genügend „grünes" Kapital und die Holzbauunternehmen werden zu Generalunternehmen. Ein einfaches „Weiter so!" wird nicht funktionieren, der Aufwärtstrend des Holzbaus läuft sonst zu schnell gegen eine graue Wand.

Der Brandschutz und der Feuchteschutz. Im Bereich des Brandschutzes bestehen tatsächlich noch Behinderungen durch die Bauordnungen vieler Länder. Aber es gibt auch eine klare Verbesserung. In vielen Ländern sind inzwischen die Brandschutzvorschriften so angepasst worden, dass zumindest bis zur Hochhausgrenze geregelt mit Holz gebaut werden kann – in vielen Fällen mit teilweise sichtbaren Oberflächen von Massivholzbauteilen. Zwar gibt es immer noch keine völlige Gleichbehandlung der Bauweisen und es wäre sehr wünschenswert, dass bei den weiteren Diskussionen die reinen Vorurteile („Holz brennt halt!") der nüchternen Betrachtung der vorliegenden wissenschaftlichen Ergebnisse weichen. Aber der Holzbau sollte auch nicht überziehen: Eine vollständig sichtbare Holzoberfläche aller Bauteiloberflächen hat beispielsweise auch nach unserem Verständnis im vielgeschossigen Holzbau einfach nichts verloren, weil dadurch nachweisbar eine deutlich beschleunigte Brandausbreitung erfolgen kann. Ein Holztafelbau benötigt eben eine hinreichende brandschutztechnisch wirksame, nichtbrennbare Bekleidung, um Hohlraumbrände sicher zu vermeiden. Dazu müssen Fugen so ausgebildet werden, dass sie so rauchdicht sind wie ein Massivbau, alles kein Problem. Andererseits spricht nichts gegen einen Treppenraum aus Brettsperrholz mit rundum nichtbrennbarer Bekleidung in Brandwandqualität. Der Brandschutz ist jedenfalls nicht (mehr) das Hauptproblem des Holzbaus.

Eher ein dauerhaft wirksamer Feuchteschutz der Bauteile, der bei der Montage beginnt und während der gesamten Nutzungsdauer gewährleistet sein muss. Im Regelfall für mindestens 50 Jahre, bei nichttragenden Fassadenbauteilen und Fassaden zumindest 25 Jahre. Das gilt nicht nur für Außenbauteile sondern auch für Innenbauteile. Wir brauchen also bereits für die Montage ein wirksames Feuchteschutzkonzept, ein dauerhaftes Abdichtungskonzept für innere Leckagen (Wasserleitungen, Waschmaschinen, Fliesenanschlüsse in Bädern, …), eine wirksame Schlagregendichtigkeit und für alles eine klar durchdachte, standardisierte Detaillierung der relevanten Anschlüsse, die dann in der Fertigung und auf der Baustelle auch umgesetzt wird. Klar – alles nicht neu, und es gibt viele Vorschläge für Detaillierungen, die ja gleichzeitig auch die brand- und schallschutztechnischen Eigenschaften sicherstellen müssen. Aber die Praxis zeigt, dass hier Verbesserungspotenzial vorhanden ist und die erprobten Lösungen leider nicht immer angewendet werden. Im mehrgeschossigen Holzbau tauchen zudem ergänzende Fragestellungen auf. So ist z.B. während der Bauphase bei Massivholzdecken alleine durch das Klima während der Bauzeit eine Feuchteerhöhung auf bis zu zwanzig Prozent mittlerer Holzfeuchte kaum zu vermeiden. Im Endzustand liegt die Decke dann bei zehn Prozent, was eine Höhendifferenz von ca. vier Millimetern bei einer Decke mit 200 Millimetern Deckendicke ergibt. Über zwei Geschosse sind das schon acht, usw. Das sieht man dann an den Differenzsetzungen zum Treppenraum aus Beton, der Spalt zur Fußleiste wird immer größer.

Fazit Sechs. Im Brandschutz für eine echte Gleichstellung zu kämpfen, ist weiterhin erforderlich. Lösungen liegen auf dem Tisch. Der Wille bei vielen Akteuren einschließlich der Feuerwehr zur offenen Diskussion ist vorhanden. Es braucht einfach noch ein wenig Geduld und bis dahin weiter das Bauen mit Abweichungen. Das eigentliche Risiko liegt im Feuchteschutz. Der verursacht zwar keinen Totalverlust wie ein Vollbrand, aber die Mangelbeseitigung ärgert die BauherrInnen und ist aufwändig. Hier muss der Holzbau mit seinen Partnern noch sorgfältiger werden. Das gilt auch für den Schallschutz, wo kleine Mängel in der Ausführung schon zu Beschwerden führen können. Und die treten dann sofort nach Einzug auf. Alles lösbar, Standardisierung hilft - siehe oben!

Zum guten Schluss. Jetzt aber bloß nicht abhalten lassen, vom Holzbau! Erfahrene KollegInnen einbinden, nicht alles neu erfinden und mit ein bisschen Übung entsteht dann das, was immer wieder fasziniert: Bauwerke, welche die wunderbaren Eigenschaften des Holzes reflektieren, von der Optik über die Haptik bis zum Raumklima. Und erfahrungsgemäß sehr viele sehr zufriedene NutzerInnen hat. Wood is good! ∎

partially visible solid wood components. There is however still no completely equal consideration of different building methods, and it would be very desirable that in future discussions evident prejudices ("Wood burns!") concede to the rational deliberations of available scientific results. But timber construction should also not overreach: Using fully visible wood surfaces for all component surfaces, for example, has no place in a multi-story timber construction (also from my understanding), as this can verifiably lead to an accelerated spread of fire. Wood panel construction requires adequate fire rated, non-combustible cladding in order to prevent fires in wall cavities. Connection and joints must also be designed to meet this end, so that they are as impervious to smoke as a solid construction, no problem whatsoever. On the other hand, nothing speaks against a stairwell made of cross-laminated timber with all-around non-combustible cladding suitable for use in a firewall. Fire protection is not (or is no longer) the main problem in timber construction.

Instead, the problem lies in the permanent and effective protection of building components from moisture, which begins with assembly and must be guaranteed for the entire service life of a building. As a general rule this means a period of at least fifty years, or at least twenty-five years for non-load bearing façade components and façades. This applies not only to exterior building elements, but also to interior elements. We thus need an effective plan for moisture protection at the time of assembly, a durable waterproofing plan for interior leakages (water pipes, washing machines, tile connections in bathrooms ...), an effective impermeable barrier to driving rain, and—for everything—a clearly thought out, standardized detailing of the relevant joints, which is then realized in manufacturing phases and on the construction site. Of course: this isn't all new and there are many proposals for detailing that also address properties of fire protection and sound insulation at the same time. Practice shows, however, that there is potential for improvement and that tried and tested solutions are unfortunately not always applied. Multi-story timber construction brings further questions to light. In the construction phases of massive timber floor systems, for example, an increase in humidity of up to twenty percent in mean wood moisture content is difficult to avoid due to climate alone. In the end this floor system then has a mean moisture content of ten percent, which leads to a height difference of about four millimeters for a slab with a thickness of two hundred millimeters. Over two stories this amounts to eight millimeters, and so on. This becomes noticeable in settling differences in concrete stairwells, where the gap to the baseboard becomes increasingly bigger.

Conclusion Six. It is still necessary to fight for true equality in fire protection. Solutions are on the table. Many stakeholders, including the fire service, are open to discussion. It will simply take a little patience and, until then, continuing to work with variations in the building process. The real risk lies in moisture protection. Moisture doesn't lead to a complete loss, as an extensive fire would, but remedial action is cumbersome and an annoyance to the client. It is here that timber construction and its partners must become even more careful. This also applies to soundproofing, where even small defects in execution can lead to grievances. And these appear immediately after moving in. All resolvable, and standardization helps—see above!

To Conclude. Don't let this deter you, however, from building with wood! Bring in experienced colleagues, do not reinvent everything from scratch, and with a little practice you can create something that never fails to fascinate: Buildings that reflect the wonderful properties of wood, from look and feel to interior atmosphere—and that have many very satisfied users, as experience has shown. Wood is good! ▪

Translation: Katie Filek

Wood, Digitally Refined

Holz, digital verfeinert

Urs Hirschberg

1 Twist Pavilion in the campus park of Alte Technik | Twist Pavilion im Park der Alten Technik, Graz University of Technology, 2018–2019
© Florian Fend

Refinement adds value. We can add value to a material by treating it with artistry and skill. It may sound a bit like alchemy, but it's hardly a novel idea. In fact the idea is as old as humanity; it encapsulates the way homo sapiens gradually set themselves apart from the rest of the animal kingdom. Our distant forbears practiced the art of refinement when they turned stones into tools and weapons, clay into pots and vases or animal skin into shoes and garments. It's these and many other practices of refinement that launched us on our journey towards becoming the dominant species on the planet. The refinement of wood is very much part of this history. From the primitive axe to the first forms of manmade shelter to the boats that allowed us to travel to distant continents, wood has been a companion to our species and often played a pivotal role in the ingenious material refinements we are so prolific at inventing. Of course the amount of value we add through these transformative activities varies. We can burn wood to keep us warm or we can build Stradivari violins out of it—in both cases the material used is the same, but the value added could hardly be more different.

What constitutes refinement in architecture? Is there an equivalent to Stradivari violins in buildings? Probably not. Yet, there are different levels of refinement in the way we have learned to build and in the way we are still learning to make use of materials in construction. This is where the digital comes in. Arguably, digital design and fabrication have started a transformation in the construction industry. The digital repertoire is in itself refining the ways in which architectural design adds value. This text traces the notion of refinement in architecture with a focus on wood and on the digital. It presents recent digital timber fabrication projects that are based on a sophisticated understanding of this complex material and the use of advanced robotic tools. Rather than imposing arbitrary forms (as early digital design projects tended to), these projects tap into and bring out timber's intrinsic qualities. The argument, in short, is that when dealing with wood, digital technology, despite its reputation to the contrary, has great potential for subtlety and finesse.

Digital Refinement. In the long history of refinements that characterize human culture, digital technology is a recent development. It is a game changer, not only, but also for wood construction. While many aspects of timber construction have been developing rapidly in recent years and some novel technologies, for example cross laminated timber, have enabled entirely new kinds of structures—arguably no development is as consequential to wood construction as digital technology.

What sets it apart from other technical advancements is its all-encompassing nature. Digitally controlled machines redefine the way we build with wood; increasingly sophisticated software dramatically raises the levels of complexity we can handle in design. Last not least: a growing number of digital measuring and analysis methods are giving us a much better understanding of the material we work with. In short: digital technology reshapes fabrication as well as design as well as material analysis. The full potential for digital refinement results from the synergies of these three.

Surprisingly the first—the introduction of digital machinery into the wood production and fabrication industry—and to some extent also the last—the integration of material analysis—are already well advanced in practice, while the second—designing in a way that takes maximal advantage of this sophisticated machinery—is actually still in its infancy. Somehow the current situation in practice is the opposite of what conventional wisdom has led us to expect: It's not the designers who have to compromise their vision because technology isn't advanced enough for their soaring ideas—it's the machines that have to settle for much less than they are capable of, because architects and designers don't take advantage of their potential.

A case in point illustrates the current situation in Austria. The Landesberufsschule (LBS) Murau is one of the schools where future carpenters in the Austrian province of Styria learn their trade. The most remote district of Styria, Murau has few inhabitants and Austria's highest density of forest. Besides tourism, the wood industry is the region's main economic pillar. In the school's own joinery workshop, the young apprentices see the many traditional tools of their craft on display, but most of them only as reminiscences of times past. These youngsters train on a state of the art Hundegger CNC joinery machine which is placed prominently in the hall. Ironically, though, the roof structures they build look just like they did in times when the historic tools were used.

What's true in the Murau school is true in practice in the region. The potential of CNC-based wood construction is available at many of the local woodworking companies. They could allow non-standard geometries and details to be realized at affordable cost throughout the region. But this potential is not being realized. There are some exceptions, but for the most part the most remarkable wood structures locally are the historical ones. In other words: digitally controlled machinery is firmly established as a way to perform conventional work more

Verfeinerung erzeugt Wert. Man kann den Wert eines Materials steigern, indem man es mit Kunstfertigkeit und Geschick bearbeitet. Es klingt ein bisschen nach Alchemie, aber es ist eigentlich keineswegs eine neue Idee. Vielmehr ist sie so alt wie die Menschheit: sie umschreibt die Art und Weise, wie sich Homo Sapiens Schritt für Schritt vom Rest des Tierreiches absonderte. Unsere entfernten Vorfahren übten sich in der Kunst des Verfeinerns, wenn sie aus Steinen Werkzeuge und Waffen, aus Lehm Töpfe und Vasen, aus Tierhäuten Schuhe und Gewänder machten. Diese und viele weitere Verfeinerungspraktiken waren es, die sie auf den Weg brachten, die dominante Spezies des Planeten zu werden. Die Verfeinerung von Holz ist ein fester Bestandteil dieser Geschichte. Von der primitiven Axt zu den ersten Formen menschlicher Behausung zu den Schiffen, die uns erlaubten zu entfernten Kontinenten zu reisen – Holz war immer ein Begleiter unserer Art und spielte oftmals eine entscheidende Rolle in den einfallsreichen Materialverfeinerungen, die wir immer wieder erfunden haben. Wie groß die Wertsteigerung ist, die durch diese transformativen Aktivitäten entsteht, ist natürlich sehr verschieden. Wir können Holz verbrennen, um uns daran zu wärmen oder wir können Stradivari-Geigen daraus bauen – in beiden Fällen ist das Ausgangsmaterial das gleiche, aber der entstandene Wert könnte kaum unterschiedlicher sein.

Wann kann man in der Architektur von Verfeinerung sprechen? Gibt es unter Gebäuden auch solche, die mit Stradivari Violinen vergleichbar sind? Wahrscheinlich nicht. Dennoch gibt es unterschiedliche Grade von Verfeinerung in der Art, wie wir zu bauen gelernt haben und darin, wie wir Materialien konstruktiv einsetzen. Damit sind wir schon bei der Digitalisierung. Digitale Entwurfs- und Fabrikationsmethoden haben im Bauen eine Transformation ausgelöst. Das digitale Repertoire verfeinert die Art und Weise, wie architektonische Gestaltung Wert erzeugt. Dieser Artikel diskutiert den Begriff der Verfeinerung in der Architektur, mit besonderem Augenmerk auf Holz und Digitalisierung. Er präsentiert aktuelle Holzbauprojekte, die auf einem detaillierten Verständnis dieses komplexen Materials und der Verwendung von robotischen Werkzeugen basieren. Statt auf die Umsetzung möglichst spektakulärer Formen (wie man das bei früheren digitalen Projekten häufig beobachten konnte), setzen diese Projekte auf die dem Material innewohnenden Qualitäten und auf Formen, die sich aus diesen Qualitäten ableiten. Kurz gesagt, der Text möchte zeigen, dass die Digitalisierung, trotz gegenteiliger Reputation, im Umgang mit Holz ein großes Potenzial für Subtilität und Finesse eröffnet.

Digitale Verfeinerung. In der langen Reihe der Verfeinerungen, welche die Kulturgeschichte prägen, ist die Digitaltechnik eine jüngere Entwicklung. Sie verändert vieles grundlegend, nicht nur, aber auch für die Holzbearbeitung. Es gab in letzter Zeit viele wichtige Entwicklungen in der Holzindustrie. Einige neue Technologien, etwa Brettsperrholz, haben zu ganz neuen Konstruktionsweisen geführt. Dennoch hat keine Neuentwicklung so weitreichende Folgen wie die Digitalisierung. Was sie von anderen technischen Neuerungen unterscheidet, ist, dass sie so allumfassend ist. Digital gesteuerte Maschinen definieren ganz neu, wie wir mit Holz bauen; immer raffiniertere Software erhöht auf dramatische Weise die Komplexität, die wir im Entwurf bewältigen können. Durch neuartige Mess- und Analyseverfahren eröffnet die Digitalisierung uns zudem ein immer besseres Verständnis des Materials, mit dem wir arbeiten. Kurz: digitale Technologien verändern sowohl die Fabrikation als auch den Entwurf als auch die Materialanalyse von Grund auf. Das volle Potenzial der digitalen Verfeinerung entsteht aus den Synergien dieser drei Aspekte.

Überraschenderweise sind der erstgenannte, also die Einführung digitaler Maschinen in der Holzindustrie, und zum Teil auch schon der zuletzt genannte, also die Integration von digitalen Materialanalyseverfahren, in der Praxis schon sehr weit fortgeschritten, während der zweite Aspekt, also das Entwerfen, welches diese neuartigen Möglichkeiten wirklich zur Gänze ausnutzt, noch in den Kinderschuhen steckt. Die gegenwärtige Situation in der Praxis ist sozusagen das Gegenteil von dem, was man gemeinhin erwarten würde. Es sind nicht die Entwerferinnen und Entwerfer, die Kompromisse machen müssen, weil die technischen Möglichkeiten nicht mit ihren hochfliegenden Ideen mithalten können. Es sind die Maschinen, die ihr Potenzial nicht entfalten können, weil das, was Architektinnen und Architekten von ihnen fordern, viel weniger ist, als das, was sie in der Lage wären, zu leisten.

Ein Beispiel illustriert die gegenwärtige Situation in Österreich. Die Landesberufsschule (LBS) Murau ist einer der Orte, an denen angehende Zimmerleute in der Steiermark ihr Handwerk erlernen. Murau ist der entlegenste Bezirk des Bundeslandes, mit wenigen Einwohnern und dem österreichweit höchsten Waldanteil. Neben dem Tourismus ist die Holzindustrie der wichtigste Wirtschaftszweig der Region. In der schuleigenen Abbundhalle sehen die Lehrlinge die vielen traditionellen Werkzeuge ihrer Zunft, die meisten allerdings nur als Ausstellungsstücke, als Reminiszenzen an vergangene Zeiten. Eine prominent platzierte brandneue Hundegger-Abbundmaschine ist das wichtigste Gerät, das bei ihrer praktischen Schulung zum Einsatz kommt. Ironischerweise sehen die Dachstühle, für deren Erstellung diese digital gesteuerte Maschine verwendet wird, kaum anders aus als zu Zeiten, als noch die historischen Werkzeuge verwendet wurden.

In der Praxis ist das Bild nicht anders. Viele holzverarbeitenden Betriebe der Region sind mittlerweile mit CNC-gesteuerten Maschinen ausgerüstet, mit denen man sogenannte Non-Standard-Geometrien und Details mit wenig Mehraufwand umsetzen könnte. Von wenigen Ausnahmen abgesehen sind die bemerkenswertesten Holzbauten der Region die historischen.

Joinery workshop with CNC joinery machine at LBS Murau | Abbundhalle mit Abbundanlage an der Landesberufsschule Murau, Master Studio "Break It Till You Make It," WS 2017/18 © Tom Lamm

efficiently. As a way to add refinement it has not yet been discovered. At the TU Graz Institute of Architecture and Media (IAM) we are striving to change this. The LBS Murau was kind enough to let us use their brand new Hundegger joinery machine for a studio project (fig. 2). The designs our master students fabricated on it served to illustrate some of the machine's potential to both the construction school and the architecture students. In a second studio project we were invited to make use of an industrial robot at the Holzinnovationszentrum (HIZ) in Zeltweg, another small town in the same region (figs. 3–6). These two projects are described later in the text. However, since this text hinges on the term refinement, let's first come to a clearer definition of what we mean by the word.

What's Refined, What's Not? According to definitions provided by the Oxford Dictionary, refinement can be understood as "the process of removing impurities or unwanted elements from a substance" as well as "the improvement or

clarification of something by the making of small changes."[1] Furthermore refinement also signifies "cultured elegance in behavior or manner" as well as "sophisticated and superior good taste."[2] Not all of these definitions apply directly to woodworking. Nevertheless the refinement of wood is not as straightforward as for example that of crude oil, which is a purely technical process. When it comes to wood, the cultural overtones of the term refinement are relevant. In any case refinement is something that builds on what is already there. It makes an existing quality finer. Any refinement requires a degree of inventiveness, but more importantly perhaps, an understanding of the material at hand and its potential.

---

1   "Refinement," via Lexico powered by Oxford, available online at: https://www.lexico.com/en/definition/refinement (accessed February 26, 2021).

2   Ibid.

3–6

The Engineering Center Wood (ECW) at the Wood Innovation Center in Zeltweg (HIZ). The industrial robot at ECW was used during the master studio "Lusthaus" (WS 2016/17) to cut the parts for the Cocoon Pavilion. | Das ECW (Engineering Center Wood) am Holzinnovationszentrum Zeltweg (HIZ). Mit dem Industrieroboter wurden im Entwurfsstudio „Lusthaus" (WS 2016/17) die Teile für den Cocoon Pavillon zugeschnitten. © IAM, TU Graz

Mit anderen Worten: Digital gesteuerte Maschinen haben sich durchgesetzt, als effizientere, schnellere Art, konventionelle Bauformen umzusetzen. Als Möglichkeit, Bauten zu verfeinern, sind sie noch nicht entdeckt worden. Am Institut für Architektur und Medien (IAM) der TU Graz versuchen wir das zu ändern. Die LBS Murau war so freundlich, uns ihre neue Abbundmaschine in einem kürzlich abgehaltenen Entwurfsstudio verwenden zu lassen. Die Entwürfe, die unsere Studierenden auf dieser Maschine gebaut haben, dienten dazu, sowohl den Studierenden als auch der Berufsschule deren Potenzial vor Augen zu führen (Abb. 2). In einem zweiten Entwurfsstudio durften wir den Industrieroboter des Holzinnovationszentrums (HIZ) in Zeltweg, einem Ort in der selben Gegend, verwenden (Abb. 3–6). Diese beiden Projekte werden gegen Ende dieses Textes vorgestellt. Da unsere Argumentation sich sehr stark um den Begriff der Verfeinerung dreht, ist es sinnvoll, zunächst zu einer etwas klareren Bestimmung zu kommen, was damit gemeint ist.

Was ist verfeinert, was nicht? Das englische Wort *refinement* kann im Deutschen mit „Verfeinerung" oder auch mit „Veredelung" übersetzt werden. Das Deutsche kennt auch das Wort „raffiniert", das die im Englischen bestehende, aber im Deutschen fehlende Nähe zum Wort „Raffinerie" (engl. *refinery*) nachvollziehbar macht. Die Bedeutung von *refinement* ist laut Oxford Dictionary „der Prozess, mit dem Unreinheiten oder ungewollte Elemente aus einer Substanz entfernt werden" oder „die Verbesserung oder Klärung einer Sache durch kleine Veränderungen".[1] Weitere Bedeutungen sind „kultivierte Eleganz in Verhalten und Sitten" und „raffinierter und hoch entwickelter guter Geschmack".[2] Nicht alle dieser Bedeutungen können direkt auf die Holzbearbeitung angewendet werden. Allerdings ist die Verfeinerung von Holz ein

1 „Refinement", via Lexico powered by Oxford, online unter: https://www.lexico.com/en/definition/refine (Stand: 26. Februar 2021). (Übers. U.H.)

2 Ebd.

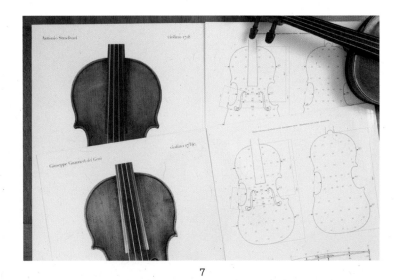

7

Cartella Antonio Stradivari violino 1718 "San Lorenzo" and Cartella Giuseppe Guarneri del Gesù Violino 1734c. "Spagnoletti," published by the Fondazione "A. Stradivari" Museo del Violino, Cremona. The detailed measurements show distinct differences between the two master violins. The Guarneri del Gesù also features surprising asymmetries and irregularities. | Cartella Antonio Stradivari violino 1718 „San Lorenzo" und Cartella Giuseppe Guarneri del Gesù Violino 1734c. „Spagnoletti," herausgegeben von der Fondazione „A. Stradivari" Museo del Violino, Cremona. Die detaillierten Maßangaben zeigen erstaunlich große Unterschiede zwischen diesen Meistergeigen, wobei die Guarneri del Gesù auch überraschende Asymmetrien und Unregelmäßigkeiten aufweist. © Photo: GAM.Lab, TU Graz

To come to a working definition of the term, let's consider an extreme example. We mentioned violin making as perhaps the most refined of crafts, resulting in staggering increases of value. The finest examples, violins created by Stradivari or by Guarneri del Gesù, are now typically owned by foundations that loan them to the world's leading violinists. Their multimillion price tags put purchasing them firmly out of reach of all but the very wealthiest. Even experts struggle to explain what sets these instruments apart. At the violin museum in Cremona, the Italian city where in the 16th to 18th centuries most of the world's top violins were built and both these legendary violin makers had their ateliers, violin aficionados can buy 1:1 plans of their most famous creations, along with plans of the forms used in their making (fig. 7). As the detailed dimensions on these plans reveal, the differences between just these two violinmakers' creations, whose work was informed by the local tradition going back to Amati, are surprisingly large. Not only the length and placement of the f-holes, the shape of the bulge of both the top and the bottom piece of the body, even the thickness of these pieces, which varies throughout, are quite differently proportioned. For example the Stradivari *San Lorenzo* is five millimeters longer overall, while its f-holes are four millimeters shorter than those of the Guarneri del Gesù *Spagnoletti*. So it seems clear that to make an instrument of comparable quality is not just a matter of getting the form exactly right. When compared with Stradivari's perfect specimens,

Guarneri del Gesù's violins sometimes display asymmetries and surprising details. Indeed, within the tight constraints of his craft, Guarneri del Gesù experimented rather wildly with forms. Yet in terms of sound, many violinists consider his instruments to be even superior to Stradivari's. It appears that he had an incredible intuition about what it takes to make an instrument sound good.

The question how violin making and architecture might be related was discussed at a recent symposium held at TU Graz in honor of the late Ferdinand Schuster's 100th birthday.[3] Schuster was a professor at the TU Graz Faculty of Architecture, but had trained as a violinmaker in his father's atelier before he went on to study architecture. The consensus at the symposium was that formal analogies are problematic at best, yet that at the level of craftsmanship and care of details, the two disciplines can perhaps indeed learn from each other. Schuster's violinmaker's diary bore the motto: *Dum vixi, tacui: mortua dulce cano*.[4] It is an abbreviated version of a Latin inscription that goes back to one of the earliest violinmakers, Caspar Tieffenbrucker (who is also known as Gasparo Duiffopruggar or Gaspard Duiffoprugcar as he left his native Germany to learn and practice his art first in Italy, then in France).[5] The full quote is: *Viva fui in sylvis. sum dura occisa securi. Dum vixi, tacui: mortua dulce cano*. (I was alive in the woods; I was cut down by the cruel axe. While I lived I was silent; In death I sweetly sing.)[6] Tieffenbrucker wrote it along the ribs or onto the fingerboards of his fine and often very ornate instruments. It has become an often-quoted classic among instrument makers. What's remarkable about the quote is the attitude it conveys. The wood used for making the violin is not the object, but the subject. What's more, the wood doesn't say: "now people can make music with me," but "In death I sweetly sing."

Architecture That Sings, Materials That Speak. In his Socratic dialogue *Eupalinos or The Architect*[7] Paul Valéry evokes the idea of an architecture that sings. Socrates tells his disciple Phaidros about Eupalinos, an architect, who sometimes achieves this quality in his work: it sings. Eupalinos describes

3   See Daniel Gethmann, ed., *Ferdinand Schuster (1920–1972). Das architektonische Werk: Bauten, Schriften, Analysen*, (Zurich, 2020).

4   Ibid., 19.

5   See Edmund Schebeck, "Duiffopruggar," *Allgemeine Deutsche Biographie* 5 (1877): 454–455, available online at: https://www.deutsche-biographie.de/pnd138793409.html#adbcontent (accessed February 26, 2021).

6   Ibid.

7   Paul Valéry, *Eupalinos oder der Architekt. Eingeleitet durch Die Seele und der Tanz*, trans. Rainer Maria Rilke (Berlin, 2017). Title of the French original: *Eupalinos ou l'Architecte, précédé par L'Ame et la Danse* (Paris, 1923).

nicht ganz so technischer Vorgang wie etwa das Raffinieren von Öl. Bei Holz sind auch die kulturellen Konnotationen des Begriffs relevant. In jedem Fall ist Verfeinerung etwas, das auf dem Vorhandenen aufbaut. Es macht eine bestehende Qualität feiner. Jede Verfeinerung setzt Erfindungsgabe voraus, aber vielleicht noch wichtiger: ein Verständnis des Materials und seiner Möglichkeiten.

Um zu einer für unsere Zwecke brauchbaren Definition des Begriffs zu kommen, wollen wir ein besonders extremes Beispiel von Verfeinerung näher betrachten. Wir haben den Geigenbau als die vielleicht am höchsten entwickelte handwerkliche Tätigkeit bereits erwähnt. Sie führt zu verblüffenden Wertsteigerungen. Die hervorragendsten Beispiele, die Violinen von Stradivari und Guarneri del Gesù, sind heute meist im Besitz von Stiftungen, welche sie an die weltbesten Geigenvirtuosen verleihen, denn durch ihren Marktwert in Millionenhöhe sind sie nur für extrem Begüterte erschwinglich. Auch ExpertInnen tun sich schwer damit, zu erklären, was diese Instrumente so außergewöhnlich macht. Im Museo del Violino in Cremona, der italienischen Stadt in welcher zwischen dem 16. und 18. Jahrhundert die meisten der besten Geigen der Welt gebaut wurden und wo auch diese beiden legendären Geigenbauer ihre Ateliers hatten, können Geigenliebhaber 1:1 Fotos und Pläne der berühmtesten Instrumente erstehen, ebenso von den Formen, welche für ihre Fertigung verwendet wurden (Abb. 7). Wie man den detaillierten Vermaßungen auf diesen Plänen entnehmen kann, sind die Unterschiede zwischen den Violinen dieser beiden Geigenbauer, deren Werk fest in der auf Amati zurückgehenden lokalen Tradition stand, erstaunlich groß. Nicht nur die Gesamtlänge, auch die Größe und Platzierung der F-Löcher, die Wölbung von Boden und Decke, sogar die durchwegs unterschiedliche Dicke dieser Teile sind sehr verschieden. Die Stradivari *San Lorenzo* ist beispielsweise fünf Millimeter länger, ihre F-Löcher hingegen vier Millimeter kürzer als die der Guarneri del Gesù *Spagnoletti*. Es scheint klar, dass es beim Bau eines vergleichbaren Instruments nicht nur darum gehen kann, die Form ganz genau hinzubekommen. Im Vergleich mit Stradivaris perfekteren Erzeugnissen, weisen die Violinen von Guarneri del Gesù oftmals Asymmetrien und überraschende Details auf. Innerhalb der engen Grenzen seines Handwerks hat Guarneri del Gesù recht wild experimentiert. Was den Klang betrifft, stufen viele Geigerinnen und Geiger seine Instrumente aber sogar noch höher ein als die von Stradivari. Es scheint, dass er ein außergewöhnliches Gespür dafür hatte, was es braucht, damit ein Instrument vollendet klingt.

Die Frage, was Architektur und Geigenbau miteinander verbindet, ist unter anderem an einem Symposium diskutiert worden, welches an der TU Graz anlässlich Ferdinand Schusters hundertstem Geburtstag stattfand.[3] Schuster (1920–1972) war Professor an der Architekturfakultät der TU Graz, aber er hatte im väterlichen Atelier das Geigenbauerhandwerk erlernt, bevor er eine erfolgreiche Laufbahn als Architekt einschlug. Der Konsens unter den ReferentInnen am Symposium war, dass formale Analogien bestenfalls problematisch sind, dass es aber auf der Ebene des Handwerks und der Liebe zum Detail durchaus Anknüpfungspunkte zwischen den sehr unterschiedlichen Disziplinen gibt. Schusters Werkstattbuch trug das Motto „*Dum vixi, tacui, mortua dulce cano*".[4] Es ist eine gekürzte Version einer lateinischen Inschrift, die auf einen der frühesten Geigenbauer zurückgeht, Caspar Tieffenbrucker (bekannt auch als Gasparo Duiffopruggar, bzw. als Gaspard Duiffoprugcar, denn er verließ seine deutsche Heimat, um in Italien und später in Frankreich sein Handwerk zu lernen und zu praktizieren).[5] Das vollständige Zitat lautet: „*Viva fui in sylvis. sum dura occisa securi. Dum vixi, tacui: mortua dulce cano*" („Ich lebte im Wald. Ich wurde durch die Axt getötet. Solange ich lebte, schwieg ich, im Tode singe ich süß".)[6] Tieffenbrucker schrieb den Spruch auf die Zargen oder Fingerbretter seiner vornehmen und oftmals stark verzierten Instrumente. Unter InstrumentenbauerInnen ist der Spruch ein oft zitierter Klassiker. Das Bemerkenswerte daran ist die Haltung, die er vermittelt: Das Holz, das zum Bau der Violine verwendet wird, ist nicht das Objekt, sondern das Subjekt. Außerdem sagt das Holz nicht: „Nun können Menschen mit mir Musik machen", sondern „im Tode singe ich süß".

Architektur die singt, Materialien die sprechen. In seinem sokratischen Dialog *Eupalinos oder der Architekt*,[7] evoziert Paul Valéry die Idee von einer Architektur, die singt. Sokrates erzählt seinem Schüler Phaidros von Eupalinos, einem Architekten, der es manchmal schafft, diese Qualität in seinen Bauten zu erreichen: sie singen. Eupalinos beschreibt den „zarten Tempel", in den er „die Erinnerung an einen lichten Tag [s]eines Lebens untergebracht" hat. Er nennt ihn „das mathematische Bildnis eines Mädchens", das er geliebt habe. Der kleine und einfache Tempel „wiederholt getreu die besonderen Verhältnisse ihres Körpers [...] O süße Verwandlung!" Deswegen ist der Tempel „von so unerklärlicher Anmut".[8] Valéry beschreibt hier das höchste Maß der Verfeinerung, die Architektur erreichen kann. Aber die Verfeinerung, von welcher er spricht, ist eine immaterielle, eine, die sich aus mathematischen Proportionen ergibt. Von Guarneri del Gesù können wir hingegen ableiten, dass es nicht ausreicht, geometrischen Proportionen exakt

3 Vgl. Gethmann, Daniel (Hg.): *Ferdinand Schuster (1920–1972) Das architektonische Werk. Bauten, Schriften, Analysen*, Zürich 2020.

4 Ebd., 19.

5 Vgl. Schebeck, Edmund: „Duiffopruggar", *Allgemeine Deutsche Biographie* 5 (1877), 454–455, online unter: https://www.deutsche-biographie.de/pnd138793409.html#adbcontent (Stand: 24. Februar 2021).

6 Ebd. (Übers. U.H.)

7 Valéry, Paul: *Eupalinos oder der Architekt. Eingeleitet durch Die Seele und der Tanz*, Übers. Rainer Maria Rilke, Berlin 2017. Titel der französischen Originalausgabe: *Eupalinos ou l'Architecte, précédé par L'Ame et la Danse*, Paris 1923.

8 Ebd., 56.

the small temple in which he managed to capture the memory of one of the brightest days of his life. He calls it the mathematical image of a girl he loved. The small and simple temple faithfully repeats the special proportions of her body—"o sweet transformation." That's why the temple is of such inexplicable beauty.[8] In many ways, Valéry describes the ultimate refinement architecture can achieve. But his is an immaterial refinement, one of mathematical proportions. From the example of Guarneri del Gesù we might conclude that to make material truly sing, just following geometrical proportions is not enough. (It may be worth noting that also for Valéry, the geometry alone is not enough. For him, geometry is "nothing without the word."[9] But that would be another discussion.)

Imposing an ideal geometry, ideal proportions, onto a material is, of course, a quintessentially architectural attitude. Proportional systems have been used throughout architectural history, from Vitruvius to Le Corbusier: architects impose their plans, their geometric ideals onto the material they build with. But there is also another tradition, one that sees the material not just as an object, but as a subject. In this tradition you don't impose your design onto a material, but the design results from a dialogue with the material. This attitude is famously captured by Louis Kahn who reportedly used to tell his students to ask their materials for advice if they were stuck for inspiration: "You say to a brick, 'What do you want, brick?' And brick says to you, 'I like an arch.' And you say to brick, 'Look, I want one, too, but arches are expensive and I can use a concrete lintel.' And then you say: 'What do you think of that, brick?' Brick says: 'I like an arch.'"[10] It's a beautiful anecdote. It reveals a deep understanding of brick as a material. Arches are pure compression forms and bricks are notable for their ability to sustain great compression stress. What's more: one of the intriguing qualities of arches created from bricks is that each of the bricks is essential: You take one away and it all breaks down. Being part of an arch is a proud function and making a brick part of one is a way to honor it. Of course, what Kahn told his students doesn't contradict the notion that proportions matter. Likewise, Guarneri's violins are always beautifully proportioned, even if they display some slight deviations from convention. So the takeaway from our excursion into the meaning of refinement in architecture could be that "the improvement or clarification of something by the making of small changes" is best achieved by an attitude that is mindful of the particularities of the material used.

The Inner Composition of Wood. Wood is a famously anisotropic material: it exhibits different materials along different axes. The natural growth of a tree, which adds a layer of early wood and one of late wood that together form an annual ring, results in the characteristic concentric pattern found in the cross section of any tree. Wood consists of cells that are composed of micro-fibrils of cellulose (40–50 percent) and hemicellulose (15–25 percent), impregnated with lignin (15–30 percent). Its microstructure can be described as a natural composite of cellulose fibers embedded in a matrix of lignin. The cellulose fibers are strong in tension, while the lignin resists compression. As a result, the orientation of wood fibers greatly affects the mechanical characteristics of lumber, both locally and globally along the whole trunk. In general, the fibers spiral along the axis of the tree trunk, gradually changing grain angle with each growth ring. Furthermore the proximity of natural growth anomalies such as knots or branches can alter the orientation of fibers significantly.[11]

The wood industry has long taken the differing qualities of timber into account. The grading process traditionally involves two different approaches. Visual inspection is of course the oldest method. Checking for branch and knot accumulation, fiber orientation, and annual growth ring width allows a wood expert to make a primary selection. Machine strength grading, which involves 2D scanning, X-ray scanning and ultrasonic tests, measures qualities such as density and elasticity that allow the classification of lumber into different strength classes. Digital technology is currently opening up a third kind of material grading. Computer tomography (CT) is already used by some wood processing facilities as a way to improve strength grading and to achieve better exploitation of available timber qualities. The CT scans used today are not yet very detailed, but as technology progresses, higher resolutions will become standard. The higher the resolution, the more detailed the nondestructive analysis of the timber that can be done before processing. More potential uses of more parts of a tree can eventually be taken into account. In this same spirit of resource efficiency there are already projects that make use of crotches or

---

8   Ibid., 56 (Trans. U.H.).

9   Ibid., 77 (Trans. U.H.).

10 Louis Kahn, quoted from the documentary *My Architect: A Son's Journey*, directed by Nathaniel Kahn, USA 2003. The quote is from a master class at the University of Pennsylvania, 1971.

11 See Anton Pech, ed., *Holz im Hochbau: Theorie und Praxis* (Berlin, 2016).

zu folgen, wenn man Material wirklich zum Singen bringen will. (Es ist vielleicht erwähnenswert, dass auch für Valéry die Geometrie allein nicht genug ist. Für ihn ist Geometrie nichts „ohne das Wort".[9] Aber das wäre eine andere Diskussion.)

Einem Material eine ideale Geometrie, ideale Proportionen aufzuerlegen, ist natürlich eine ganz grundlegende architektonische Haltung. Proportionssysteme wurden in der gesamten Architekturgeschichte verwendet, von Vitruv bis Le Corbusier: Architektinnen und Architekten bestimmen mit ihren Plänen, mit ihren geometrischen Idealen, in welche Form ein Material gebracht werden soll. Daneben gibt es aber auch noch eine andere Tradition, eine, welche im Material nicht nur ein Objekt, sondern ein Subjekt sieht. In dieser Tradition wird nicht eine Gestaltung einem Material auferlegt, sondern die Gestaltung selbst ist das Resultat eines Dialoges mit dem Material. Louis Kahn war bekannt dafür, dass er seinen Studierenden diese Haltung vermitteln wollte, indem er ihnen riet, das Material um Rat zu fragen, wenn sie beim Entwurf nicht weiterwussten: „Du sagst zum Backstein: ‚Was willst Du, Backstein?' Und Backstein sagt zu Dir: ‚Ich mag einen Rundbogen.' Und Du sagst zum Backstein: ‚Schau, ich will auch einen, aber Rundbögen sind teuer und ich kann einen Zementsturz verwenden.' Und dann sagst Du: ‚Was meinst Du dazu, Backstein?' Backstein sagt: ‚Ich mag einen Rundbogen.'"[10] Es ist eine wunderschöne Anekdote und zeugt von einem tiefen Verständnis des Materials Backstein. Rundbögen sind reine Kompressionsformen und Backstein ist bekannt dafür, dass er hohen Druckbelastungen standhalten kann. Vielleicht noch wichtiger: Bögen, die aus Backsteinen gebildet werden, haben die faszinierende Eigenschaft, dass jeder einzelne Stein darin wichtig ist. Sobald einer fehlt, bricht die ganze Konstruktion zusammen. Es ist eine stolze Aufgabe für einen Backstein, Teil eines Rundbogens zu sein. Einen Backstein in einen Rundbogen einzubauen, ist eine Art ihn zu ehren. Natürlich widerspricht das, was Kahn seinen Studierenden gesagt hat, nicht der Auffassung, dass Proportionen wichtig sind. Genauso wie auch Guarneris Violinen immer meisterhaft proportioniert sind, auch wenn sie von den Konventionen leicht abweichen. Was wir von dieser kurzen Exkursion in mögliche Bedeutungen von Verfeinerung in der Architektur mitnehmen können, ist vielleicht, dass die erwähnte „Verbesserung oder Klärung einer Sache durch kleine Veränderungen" am besten mit einer Haltung zu erreichen ist, welche auf die Besonderheiten des verwendeten Materials achtet.

Der innere Aufbau von Holz. Holz ist bekanntlich ein anisotropes Material, das heißt, es verfügt über unterschiedliche Eigenschaften entlang unterschiedlicher Achsen. Das natürliche Wachstum eines Baumes, bei welchem sogenanntes Frühholz gefolgt vom dichteren Spätholz gemeinsam einen Jahresring bildet, führt zum charakteristischen konzentrischen Muster, welches man im Querschnitt jedes Baumes findet. Holz besteht aus Mikrofasern aus Cellulose (40–50 Prozent)

und Hemicellulose (15–25 Prozent), imprägniert von Lignin (15–30 Prozent). Seine Mikrostruktur kann als natürliche Verbindung aus Cellulosefasern, eingebettet in eine Matrix aus Lignin beschrieben werden. Cellulosefasern weisen eine besonders hohe Zugfestigkeit auf, während Lignin besonders druckfest ist. Daraus ergibt sich, dass die Faserrichtung in hohem Maße die mechanischen Eigenschaften beeinflusst, sowohl lokal als auch global entlang des ganzen Stammes. Im Allgemeinen folgen die Fasern der Achse des Stammes in einer leichten Spirale um das Zentrum, wobei sich der Faserwinkel mit jedem Jahrring graduell ändert. Außerdem kann die Nähe zu natürlichen Wachstumsanomalien, wie zum Beispiel Knoten oder Ästen, die Orientierung der Fasern signifikant verändern.[11]

Die Holzindustrie berücksichtigt die Unterschiede in der Holzqualität schon lange. Die Sortierung von Holz in verschiedene Qualitätsklassen erfolgt traditionell auf zwei unterschiedliche Arten. Die visuelle Inspektion ist die älteste Methode. Indem sie Ast- und Knotenakkumulationen, Faserausrichtung und Jahresringbreite bewerten, können HolzexpertInnen eine erste Selektion vornehmen. Maschinelle Stärkesortierung, bei welcher 2D-Scan, Röntgenbilder und Ultraschalltests zum Einsatz kommen, messen Eigenschaften wie Dichte und Elastizität und erlauben die Einteilung von Bauholz in verschiedene Stärkeklassen. Digitale Verfahren eröffnen derzeit eine dritte Art der Holzsortierung. Computertomografie (CT) wird in manchen Holzbearbeitungsfabriken schon eingesetzt, um die Sortierung zu verbessern und eine optimale Ausnutzung der vorhandenen Holzqualitäten zu erreichen. Die CT-Scans, die derzeit gemacht werden, sind noch nicht sehr detailliert, aber die technische Entwicklung schreitet voran, sodass höhere Auflösungen wohl bald üblich werden. Je höher die Auflösung, desto detaillierter die nicht-destruktive Analyse, die man schon vor jeglicher Verarbeitung vornehmen kann. Das bedeutet, dass mehr potenzielle Verwendungsmöglichkeiten von mehr Bestandteilen jedes Baumes in Betracht gezogen werden können. Den Geist der gesteigerten Ressourceneffizienz, der hinter diesen Entwicklungen steht, kann man auch bereits an einzelnen Projekten beobachten, welche Astgabeln oder gebogene Teile in digital geplanten Non-Standard-Konstruktionen verwenden. In vorindustriellen Zeiten war die

9 Ebd., 77.

10 Kahn, Louis zitiert nach dem Dokumentarfilm „My Architect: A Son's Journey", USA 2003, Regie: Nathaniel Kahn. Das Zitat stammt ursprünglich aus einer Master Class an der University of Pennsylvania von 1971. (Übers. U.H.)

11 Vgl. Pech, Anton (Hg.): *Holz im Hochbau, Theorie und Praxis*, Berlin 2016

8–9

Steampunk Pavilion, winner of the | Siegerbeitrag der Tallinn Architecture Biennale 2019 installation competition | Wettbewerbsinstallation. Design by | Entwurf von Gwyllim Jahn, Cameron Newnham, Soomeen Hahm and | und Igor Pantic © Peter Bennets, Hanjun Kim

bent wood in non-standard construction. A common tradition in pre-industrial joinery could thus see a digitally enabled revival.[12]

Digital Design and Wood: Some Recent Advances. Irregular forms have been a hallmark of digital fabrication, although not necessarily in response to the nature of the material. Rather than the shapes in which wood naturally grows, the shapes that have been the most prominent in digital fabrication were those that were easy to design in Computer Aided Design (CAD) tools. CAD has famously made it very easy to work with NURBS (Non-Uniform Rational B-Splines). As a consequence, digital design is now mostly associated with free-form structures. When such double-curved forms are realized with wood, the timber is usually either milled or bent—often both. Given the anisotropic characteristics of wood as a material, bending has enormous structural benefits. Some specialized woodwork companies have risen to the challenge of this CAD-inspired desire for curved forms. They have mastered the production and subsequent high-precision milling of double-curved glue-lam beams to the point where they can now be used to build very large freeform structures such as the recently completed Swatch Headquarters by Shigeru Ban Architects.[13]

Bending of wood for architectural constructions is of course not a new idea. In fact, the weaving of branches is a part of traditional hut building and may well be considered one of the oldest building methods. It has also been taken advantage of in multiple recent digital design projects. The Steampunk Pavilion, the winning entry of the 2019 Tallinn Architecture Biennale was designed by Soomeen Hahm, Igor Pantic, Gwyllim Jahn and Cameron Newnham, tutors from UCL's Bartlett School of Architecture, in collaboration with the Australian company Fologram and software of the same name,

which was key to getting the structure built as it facilitates the use of Augmented Reality during construction. Steaming the many curved pieces into their proper shape was only possible because the software allowed the 3D design to be viewed holographically during the bending (figs. 8–9). A different kind of bending is employed in the Urbach tower (2019, ICD Stuttgart, Achim Menges, Jan Knippers et al): here, the bending of components is the result of natural forces at play during the drying of timber (figs. 10–11) An earlier project by Menges, the playfully dynamic HygroSkin-Meteorosensitive Pavilion (2012), took advantage of the natural bending and unbending of timber elements due to different air humidity levels during the day or in changing weather conditions (figs. 12–14).

12 See for example: Robotically Fabricated Wood Chip Barn, Hooke Park, AA School of Architecture described in Martin Self and Emmanuel Vercruysse, "Infinite Variations, Radical Strategies," in *Fabricate 2017*, ed., Achim Menges, Bob Sheil, Ruairi Glynn, and Maria Skavara (London 2017), 30–35, available online at: https://doi.org/10.2307/j.ctt1n7qkg7.8 (accessed February 26, 2021).

13 See the interview with Kai Strehlke in this *GAM* issue on pp. 110–129.

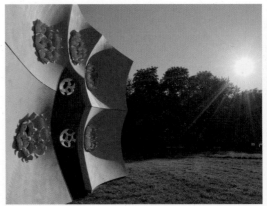

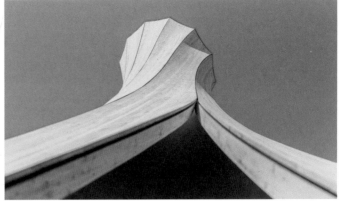

10–11

Urbach tower, 2019, ICD/ITKE University of Stuttgart, Achim Menges, Jan Knippers © ICD/ITKE University of Stuttgart

Verwendung krummer Balken im Zimmerhandwerk durchaus üblich. Nun eröffnet die Digitalisierung dieser Bauweise die Chance auf ein unerwartetes Revival.[12]

Digitales Entwerfen und Holz: einige aktuelle Entwicklungen. Unregelmäßige Formen waren von Anfang an ein Markenzeichen des digitalen Entwerfens, allerdings zumeist nicht als Antwort auf die Eigenschaften des Materials. Statt der Formen, in denen Holz natürlicherweise wächst, waren im digitalen Entwurf vor allem diejenigen Formen beliebt, die sich besonders leicht mit Computer Aided Design (CAD) modellieren ließen. CAD hat es bekanntermaßen sehr einfach gemacht, mit sogenannten NURBS (Non-Uniform Rational B-Splines) zu arbeiten. Deswegen wird das sogenannte digitale Design heute zumeist mit Freiformen assoziiert. Wenn solche mehr-

fach gekrümmten Formen aus Holz erbaut werden, wird das Bauholz üblicherweise entweder gefräst oder gebogen – oftmals beides. Aufgrund der anisotropischen Eigenschaften von Holz hat das Biegen enorme Vorteile. Einige Holzbauer haben auf das CAD-inspirierte Verlangen nach kurvigen Formen reagiert und sich auf das Herstellen und millimetergenaue Fräsen gekrümmter Brettschichtträger spezialisiert. Die Technik ist bei einzelnen Firmen schon so weit fortgeschritten, dass auf diese Weise bereits riesige Freiformtragwerke hergestellt werden können, wie zum Beispiel der neue Hauptsitz der Firma Swatch in Biel von Shigeru Ban Architects.[13]

Das Biegen von Holz ist natürlich keine neue Idee. Das Flechten von Zweigen ist Teil der meisten traditionellen Bauweisen und kann wohl als eine der ältesten Bautechniken überhaupt gelten. Es wurde auch in einigen digital entwickelten Projekten in letzter Zeit verwendet. Der Steampunk Pavillon, der Siegerbeitrag der Tallinn Architecture Biennale von 2019 wurde von Soomeen Hahm, Igor Pantic, Gwyllim Jahn und Cameron Newnham entworfen, die an der Bartlett School des University College London (UCL) unterrichten. Die Zusammenarbeit mit der Australischen Firma Fologram und deren gleichnamiger Software war der Schlüssel zur baulichen Umsetzung des Projekts. Fologram erlaubt die Verwendung von Augmented Reality beim Bauen. Das präzise Dampfbiegen der vielen Einzelteile in die vorgesehene Krümmung ebenso wie deren komplexe Montage waren nur möglich, weil man mit der Software den 3D-Entwurf holografisch der Wirklichkeit überlagern konnte (Abb. 8–9). Eine ganz andere Form des Biegens kam beim Urbach Tower (2019, ICD Stuttgart, Achim Menges, Jan Knippers, et al.) zum Einsatz. Hier ist die Biegung der Teile das Resultat der natürlichen Kräfte, welche beim Trocknen des Bauholzes auftreten (Abb. 10–11). Ein früheres Projekt der Forschungsgruppe um Achim Menges, der spielerisch dynamische HygroSkin Meteorosensitive Pavillon (2012), nutzte die natürliche Biegung und Glättung von dünnen Holzmembranen aufgrund von unterschiedlicher Luftfeuchtigkeiten im Laufe eines Tages oder bei unterschiedlichen Wetterverhältnissen (Abb. 12–14).

12 Vgl. z.B. Robotically Fabricated Wood Chip Barn, Hooke Park Gelände der AA School of Architecture, beschrieben in Self, Martin/Vercruysse, Emmanuel: „Infinite Variations, Radical Strategies" in: Menges, Achim/ Sheil, Bob/Glynn, Rauiri/Skavara, Marilena (Hg.): *Fabricate 2017*, London 2017, 30–35, online unter: https://doi.org/10.2307/j.ctt1n7qkg7.8 (Stand: 26. Februar 2021).

13 Siehe dazu das Interview mit Kai Strehlke auf den Seiten 110–129 dieser *GAM*-Ausgabe.

12–14

HygroSkin-Meteorosensitive Pavilion, 2012, Institute for Computational Design and Construction (ICD), University of Stuttgart (A. Menges, O. Krieg, S. Reichert) © ICD University Stuttgart

These projects give an idea of the kinds of research investigations into timber construction that are currently taking place. Whether they are still experimental or have already found their way into real-world projects, they are examples of a new and hopeful trend: They are trying to push the envelope of digital timber design, yet they do so not by maximizing formal spectacle, but instead by inventing construction methods that are mindful of wood's inherent characteristics and qualities. In this sense they can be said to tap into the spirit of craftsmanship we find epitomized in violin making, though, to be clear: not in the sense that they're nostalgically looking back. (The pioneer violin makers of Cremona didn't, either!) Rather, they arrive at new levels of refinement by using digital technology to radically explore the material's potential. These high profile projects are inspiring, yet the fact remains that they are still the rare exception. And they really shouldn't be. Which brings us back to the joinery machine at the LBS Murau. The projects we were able to fabricate at this facility and at the HIZ in Zeltweg show that a more refined use of timber in construction is indeed possible even for modest undertakings, such as the two studio projects described below.

1:1 Studio Projects in Digital Fabrication. Over the past decade, the building of 1:1 digital design studio projects has been an important part of the educational strategy at the Institute of Architecture and Media (IAM). The real-world hands-on construction experience is critical to our approach. The organizational overhead, cost and time involved in building a complete project from start to finish is daunting, especially when such a project takes place within a single fifteen-week semester, but at IAM we believe 1:1 projects are worth the trouble when it comes to digital fabrication. The advent of CNC controlled machinery in many construction fields, but in particular the timber industry, has made such 1:1 studios not only more relevant, but also more doable. Digital technology challenges us to think through every aspect of a fabrication and construction process. As a result it also greatly simplifies even ambitious projects, because high volume, high precision tasks can be delegated to the machine. Furthermore, because we need to use industrial facilities, and typically involve various industry players not only as sponsors, but also as partners in the construction, these projects also lead to a welcome transfer of

know-how. The collaborations with industry that take place as part of such studios are modest. They typically consist of material sponsorship and free use of machines, tools and work clothing as well as protective gear, such as helmets. All combined, sponsoring usually remains well below 10,000 euros. We have worked with different partners and used various facilities in the past ten years. The following two studios were carried out between 2016 and 2018. Both studios resulted in the construction of pavilions that were erected for a limited time on the TU Graz campus. For the second project we were given access to the joinery machine at LBS Murau. It led to the commission of nine similar pavilions that were installed throughout the Murau region in 2020.

Our studios follow a common pattern. For the first two months, students work individually or in groups of two to develop designs in response to a brief, usually building many scale models and 1:1 or 1:2 details of their ideas. Team building is an important part of this initial period: in both studios discussed here, we spent a week in Günther Domenig's Steinhaus at Ossiachersee, where students explored emerging ideas in a remote and inspiring architecture and landscape. Back on campus students develop their projects using parametric design programs as well as the workshops and digital fabrication facilities. Our winter semester starts on October 1st, the midterm takes place in early December. It's at this point that teachers and students collectively decide which of the projects will be built. It's a bit like a competition: all designs should be developed in such a way that building them would be possible, but of course in the end only one of them gets the honor. Surprisingly perhaps, in our experience this isn't a problem for the group dynamics. The students rally behind the chosen project, develop it further collectively, with many ideas from other projects influencing the development. At this stage, students are put into different teams that take over specific tasks in the building preparation. Construction then takes place in the last two weeks of semester. So far we have always managed to finish construction on time before (or on) the last day of the semester.

Cocoon Pavilion (2017): Exploring the Rhetoric of Joinery. "Lusthaus," the German word for folly, was the title we chose for the Masterstudio 2016/17. Even though we used an industrial robot rather than the Hundegger joinery machine at LBS Murau, exploring novel concepts of joinery was the main theme of the studio. To understand the topic in more depth and to get to know the material, students built Japanese

Diese Projekte geben einen Einblick in aktuelle Forschungsansätze und technische Entwicklungen im konstruktiven Holzbau. Unabhängig davon, ob es sich dabei noch um Experiment handelt oder ob sie bereits Eingang in die Baupraxis gefunden haben, stehen sie beispielhaft für einen hoffnungsvollen Trend: Sie versuchen die Möglichkeiten des digitalen Bauens mit Holz zu erweitern, aber sie tun dies nicht, indem sie auf willkürliche Formen setzen, sondern indem sie Konstruktionsmethoden entwickeln, welche auf die spezifischen Eigenschaften und Qualitäten des Baustoffes Holz eingehen. In diesem Sinne kann man sagen, dass ihre Haltung verwandt ist mit jenem Geist der Handwerklichkeit, den wir an den berühmten Geigenbauern beobachtet haben. Allerdings ist dies keineswegs als rückwärts gewandte, nostalgische Referenz zu verstehen. (Die Geigenbaupioniere von Cremona waren ja auch in keiner Weise rückwärts gewandt!) Vielmehr eint sie mit jenen die radikale Haltung, mit der sie das Potenzial des Materials ausforschen, um so zu noch höherer Verfeinerung vorzudringen. Diese international bekannten Projekte sind inspirierend, aber Tatsache ist auch, dass sie immer noch seltene Ausnahmen sind. Und eigentlich sollten sie das nicht sein. Womit wir wieder zu der Abbundmaschine der LBS Murau zurückkommen. Die Projekte, die wir dort und am HIZ in Zeltweg gefertigt haben, zeigen, dass ein digital verfeinerter Umgang mit Holz auch bei einfachsten Rahmenbedingungen und bescheidenen Budgets möglich ist.

1:1 Studio-Projekte in digitaler Fabrikation. Während des letzten Jahrzehnts war das Bauen von 1:1 Entwurfsstudio-Projekten zum Thema „Digitale Fabrikation" ein wichtiger Teil der Lehre am Institut für Architektur und Medien (IAM). Die Umsetzung im Maßstab 1:1 und die Erfahrungen, welche die Studierenden auf diesem Weg sammeln können, ist ein wesentlicher Teil unseres Ansatzes. Organisatorisch bedeutet das einen enormen Mehraufwand für unsere Betreuerteams. In nur einem Semester, also in 15 Wochen, von den ersten Entwurfsskizzen bis zum fertig ausgeführten Projekt zu kommen, gelingt nur, wenn alle – Studierende ebenso wie Lehrende – bereit sind, sich weit über das normale Maß hinaus einzusetzen. Am IAM sind wir der Meinung, dass solche Projekte den Aufwand wert sind, wenn sie sich innovativ mit den Möglichkeiten der digitalen Fabrikation auseinandersetzen. Die Einführung von CNC-Maschinen in vielen Bausparten, insbesondere aber im Holzbau, hat solche 1:1-Entwurfsstudios nicht nur relevanter, sondern auch leichter umsetzbar gemacht. Die Digitalisierung der Bauprozesse zwingt uns dazu, jeden Schritt des Fertigungs- und Bauprozesses genau durchzudenken – bis hin zu jedem Werkzeug, welches zum Einsatz kommt. Ein Resultat dieses genauen Durchdenkens ist aber, dass auch recht ambitionierte Konstruktionsweisen auf einmal machbar werden, weil Arbeiten, welche viele Bearbeitungsschritte oder höchste Genauigkeit erfordern, an die Maschinen delegiert werden können. Diese Projekte, die wir oft mit Unterstützung von Industriepartnern oder als Gast auf deren Maschinen durchführen,

haben weiter den Vorteil, dass sie zu einem wertvollen Wissenstransfer führen.

Das Sponsoring der Kooperationen, die im Rahmen von solchen kurzen Projekten stattfinden, besteht meistens aus Materialspenden, der kostenlosen Verwendung von Maschinen, Werkzeugen, Arbeitskleidung und Schutzausrüstung wie Helmen. Es ist also recht bescheiden – alles zusammen üblicherweise deutlich unter 10.000 Euro. Über die letzten zehn Jahre haben wir mit verschiedenen Partnern gearbeitet und unterschiedliche Einrichtungen und Maschinen genutzt. Die im Folgenden beschriebenen Entwurfsstudios fanden zwischen 2016 und 2018 statt. In beiden Fällen wurden Pavillons erbaut, welche für eine beschränkte Zeit im Park der Alten Technik, auf dem Gelände der TU Graz, standen. Im zweiten Projekt wurde die eingangs erwähnte Abbundmaschine der LBS Murau verwendet. Es führte zum Auftrag, weitere neun ähnliche Pavillons in der Region Murau zu bauen, welche 2020 fertiggestellt wurden.

Unsere Studios folgen einem gemeinsamen Muster: In den ersten beiden Monaten arbeiten die Studierenden einzeln oder in kleinen Gruppen an der Entwicklung eines Entwurfs, wobei sie auch schon sehr viel mit großen Modellen im Maßstab 1:2 oder 1:1 arbeiten, um die Machbarkeit ihrer Ideen zu überprüfen. Eine gute Gruppendynamik ist von Anfang an ein wichtiger Faktor bei solchen Projekten. Mit manchen Studiogruppen gehen wir zum Semesterauftakt für eine Woche in Günther Domenigs Steinhaus am Ossiachersee. An diesem relativ entlegenen Ort können die Studierenden umgeben von inspirierender Landschaft und Architektur ihre ersten Ideen erproben und sich kennenlernen. Zurück auf dem Campus entwickeln sie ihre Projekte weiter, wobei parametrische Software ebenso wie Werkstatt und Digitalwerkstatt intensiv genutzt werden. Unser Wintersemester beginnt am ersten Oktober, die „Midterm Review", die Kritik zur Semesterhalbzeit, findet jeweils Anfang Dezember statt. Zu diesem Zeitpunkt entscheiden Studierende und Lehrende gemeinsam, welches der Projekte umgesetzt wird. Es ist also ein bisschen wie ein interner Wettbewerb: jedes der Projekte wird im Hinblick auf die realistische Machbarkeit im Rahmen des Semesters entwickelt, aber natürlich kann am Ende nur einem diese Ehre zuteil werden. Überraschenderweise führt das in unserer Erfahrung nie zu Problemen in der Gruppendynamik. Im Gegenteil, die Studierenden engagieren sich für das ausgewählte Projekt, entwickeln es gemeinsam weiter, wobei viele gute Ideen von anderen Projekten einfließen. Jetzt werden auch Gruppen gebildet, welche mit bestimmten Aufgaben in der Bauvorbereitung betraut werden. Die eigentliche bauliche Umsetzung findet dann meist in den letzten beiden Semesterwochen statt. Bisher hat es jedes Mal geklappt, dass wir am letzten Semestertag gemeinsam die Fertigstellung feiern konnten.

Cocoon Pavilion (2017): die Rhetorik des Fügens. „Lusthaus" nannten wir das Semesterthema des Masterstudios

· Cocoon mit textiler Verspannung innen | Cocoon with textile finish, June | Juni 2017 © Simon Oberhofer

joinery details by hand, without the use of digital tools. In parallel they were asked to develop the overall shape of their folly out of clay. To let the students develop the massing in clay was deliberate. It allowed them to forget about the limitations of traditional joinery and conceive of their structures as sculptures. This led them to explore forms they would not have otherwise considered for a construction in timber. In a subsequent step, these monolithic objects were turned into skeletal structures, whereby we introduced them to structural optimization methods and parametric design tools. For this translation from monolith to skeleton to be successful, students had to invent a joinery system, which captured the expressiveness of their sculpture. They had to find ways to let the joinery speak. The winning project, named "Cocoon" by its designer team, had already been a successful clay sculpture. It led to a structure that was more regular and symmetric than most, but still proved

challenging to build, not least of all due to the very cold temperatures during construction. Our studio was allowed to use the industrial robot at the HIZ Zeltweg to make the unorthodox joinery cuts in the timber. The structure was then assembled by the students on site. At one point the structure needed to be lifted into place, with almost the entire group and several bystanders joining in the effort.

Twist Pavilion (2018): Exploring the Inner Composition of Wood. If in the Cocoon project we already engaged in material studies by letting the students cut joinery details by hand, we wanted to take this aspect of our pedagogy even further. For the Masterstudio 2017/18 we therefore chose the motto "Break It Till You Make It." We encouraged the students to experiment rather wildly with wood. Even though the LBS had agreed to let us use their joinery machine, we left the type

2016/17. Obwohl wir einen Industrieroboter und nicht die im Jahr darauf verwendete Abbundmaschine nutzten, war ein Hauptthema des Semesters, neue Fügekonzepte für Stabwerke zu entwickeln. Um ein besseres Verständnis des Themas zu entwickeln und auch um das Material kennenzulernen, bauten die Studierenden in der ersten Übung japanische Holzverbindungsdetails nach – von Hand, ganz ohne digitale Werkzeuge. Parallel dazu sollten sie die Form ihres Lusthauses aus Lehm formen. Die Wahl von Lehm zur Formfindung war bewusst gewählt. Er erlaubte ihnen, einen skulpturalen Zugang zum Thema zu finden, ohne sich durch die Vorstellung von traditionellen Stab- oder Rahmenkonstruktionen ablenken oder einschränken zu lassen. Im nächsten Schritt wurden diese skulpturalen Formen allerdings in skelettartige Strukturen übersetzt, wobei strukturelle Optimierungsverfahren als auch parametrische Entwurfswerkzeuge zum Einsatz kamen. Um ihren Monolith erfolgreich in ein Skelett zu übersetzen, mussten die Studierenden ein sowohl gestalterisch als auch konstruktiv überzeugendes Fügeprinzip entwickeln. Sie mussten einen Weg finden, wie sie das Stabwerk zum Sprechen bringen. Das zum Bau ausgewählte Projekt, von seinen Entwerfern „Cocoon" genannt, war schon als Lehmskulptur überzeugend. Die resultierende Struktur war regelmäßiger und symmetrischer als die meisten anderen. Sie war aber dennoch nicht einfach zu realisieren, nicht zuletzt aufgrund der eisigen Temperaturen beim Bau. Die unorthodoxen Fügeschnitte in die Stäbe wurden auf der Roboteranlage des HIZ Zeltweg umgesetzt. Die halbfertige Struktur musste mit vereinten Kräften auf den Fundamentkranz gehoben werden, wobei fast die ganze Gruppe und auch einige PassantInnen mit anpackten.

Twist Pavillon (2018): der innere Aufbau von Holz.

Schon beim „Lusthaus" Studio hatten wir Materialstudien betrieben, indem wir die Studierenden Holzverbindungsdetails von Hand ausschneiden ließen. Im darauffolgenden Jahr wollten wir diesen Aspekt unserer Pädagogik noch verstärken. Für das Masterstudio 2017/18 wählten wir das Motto „Break It Till You Make It" und ermutigten die Studierenden recht wild mit Holz zu experimentieren. Obwohl die LBS Murau uns die Nutzung ihrer Abbundmaschine in Aussicht gestellt hatte, wollten wir die Konstruktionsart diesmal viel offener lassen. Im Geiste von Kahns Dialog mit dem Backstein forderten wir die Studierenden dazu auf, eine Konstruktionslogik aus ihrer Interaktion mit dem Material abzuleiten. Brechen, ausbessern, kerben, biegen, weben und viele weitere Arten, mit Holz zu arbeiten, wurden in zahllosen Modellen und Mockups ausprobiert. Am Ende gewann das „Twisten" den Wettbewerb. Eine der Gruppen hatte entdeckt, dass Bretter durch Verdrehen deutlich an Steifigkeit und damit an Tragfähigkeit gewinnen. Sie schlugen eine Lamellenstruktur aus dünnen, tragenden Brettern als Konstruktionsmotiv ihres Pavillons vor. Für die Umsetzung dieses Projekts wurde die Abbundmaschine am Ende nur benötigt, um CNC-gesteuert präzise Schlitze in Basis und Deckenplatten zu schneiden. Um die Bretter zunächst in die oberen Schlitze und dann verdreht in die Basisplatten einstecken zu können, musste ein Gerüst aufgebaut werden, auf dem die Deckenplatte während der Montage lagern konnte (Abb. 20). Wir hatten einige Belastungstests durchgeführt und die Konstruktion auch von den Statikern des Büros Bollinger+Grohmann berechnen lassen, dennoch war es ein spannender Moment, als das Gerüst entfernt und das gesamte Gewicht des Daches nur mehr von den dünnen verdrehten Brettern getragen wurde.

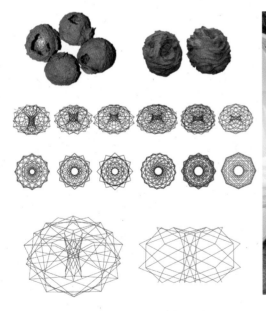

16–18

(16) Cocoon design development: conceptual idea, clay model, parametric variations of the conceptual model, final scheme as wireframe | Cocoon Entwurfsentwicklung: Konzeptidee, Lehmmodell, parametrische Variationen des Stabwerkmodells, endgültige Version als Wireframe © IAM, TU Graz
(17) Cocoon interior with textile finish and hammocks | Cocoon Innenraum mit Hängematten, 2017 © Simon Oberhofer
(18) Cocoon Pavillon, 2017 © IAM, TU Graz

of construction much more open. In the spirit of Kahn's dialogue with a brick we asked students to derive a construction logic from their interactions with the material. Breaking, mending, grooving, bending, weaving and many other ways of working with timber were explored in countless models and mockups at different scales. In the end twisting won the day. One of the groups had discovered that boards considerably gain in stiffness when they are twisted. They proposed a lamella-structure of load-bearing twisted boards as the signature construction motive of their pavilion.

The use of the jointing machine was rather limited for this project: precisely cut slots in the ceiling and in the base plate needed to be CNC-cut. In order to be able to insert and bend the individual boards into place, a scaffold had to be erected first onto which the roof could be placed (fig. 20). We had done various load tests and also consulted the structural engineers Bollinger+Grohmann to check the structure for stability. Nevertheless it was a tense moment, when the scaffolding was removed and the weight of the entire roof rested only on the skinny twisted boards.

For this studio we actually had a client. The regional tourism organization "Holzwelt Murau" was interested in our work and commissioned us to come up with a proposal for the design of touristic information pavilions to be set up in their region. Murau is known for its timber industry as well as its landscape. The pavilions were to present information about touristic sites as well as signal the region's competence in tim-

ber construction. While the students largely ignored the brief's limitations in terms of size and budget, our clients were very pleased with the result. It led to the tourism board more than doubling their original budget and commissioning IAM with the design of nine different pavilions to be built in the region (figs. 22–24). This time, local contractors carried out the construction. Bollinger+Grohmann again were the structural engineers, while a team recruited from the studio and led by Florian Fend at IAM was responsible for the different designs and respective digital fabrication codes.

Digital Refinement and Sustainability. Obviously, the student-built pavilions are relatively modest, temporary constructions. Their relevance lies in the attitude towards digital construction we hope to teach the students. They signal that even within the constraints of small budgets and limited time and experience it is possible to endow simple structures with the additional value that comes from thoughtful, original design and from a thorough engagement with the material. Our students will carry this experience with them into their professional lives. We believe that design often fails to take advantage of the full potential of timber construction. We are convinced that this will change as architects develop a deeper understanding of the digital repertoire. Education is key. Architecture schools have an important role to play in teaching the use of digital tools and the understanding of materials as well as setting the right priorities. In striving for higher refinement in

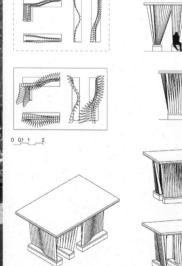

19–21

(19) Twist Pavilion, construction detail of twisted loadbearing boards | Detailansicht der verdrehten, tragenden Lärchenbretter, 2018 © KUBIZAPHOTO
(20) Twist Pavilion, construction with scaffolding | Aufbau mit Gerüst, 2018 © IAM, TU Graz
(21) Twist Pavilion, drawings of the finalized parametric design | Pläne des finalisierten parametrischen Entwurfsmodells © IAM, TU Graz

22

Holzwelt Murau information pavilion, type 1 | Infopavillon Typ1, Standort | Location Murau © Florian Fend

Für dieses Studio hatten wir sogar einen Auftraggeber. Der Verein für Regionalentwicklung des Bezirks Murau, der sich „Holzwelt Murau" nennt, war an unserer Arbeit interessiert und beauftragte uns, im Rahmen eines Studios Vorschläge für die Gestaltung von touristischen Infopavillons für die Region zu entwickeln. Murau ist sowohl für seine Holzindustrie als auch für seine Landschaft bekannt. Die Pavillons sollten Informationen über das touristische Angebot der Region anbieten und zugleich deren Kompetenz im Holzbau signalisieren. Obwohl wir gegenüber den Studierenden die Vorgaben des Vereins sehr lose formuliert hatten, waren unsere Auftraggeber vom Resultat sehr angetan. Der Verein erhöhte sein ursprüngliches Budget auf mehr als das Doppelte und beauftragte das IAM mit der Umsetzung von neun unterschiedlichen Pavillons in der Region. Diesmal wurden die Arbeiten von einer Holzbaufirma aus der Region ausgeführt. Bollinger+ Grohmann übernahmen wieder die Statik und ein Team von Studierenden unter der Leitung von Florian Fend am IAM war für den Entwurf der verschiedenen Varianten und für die digitale Fertigung verantwortlich (Abb. 22–24).

Digitale Verfeinerung und Nachhaltigkeit. Bei den vorgestellten Projekten handelt es sich offensichtlich um recht bescheidene, temporäre Bauten. Ihre Relevanz liegt in der Haltung gegenüber digitalen Konstruktionsweisen, die wir den Studierenden damit zu vermitteln hoffen. Sie zeigen, dass es sogar innerhalb der engen Beschränkungen eines kleinen Budgets und mit wenig Zeit und Erfahrung möglich ist, eine einfache Struktur mit dem zusätzlichen Wert auszustatten, der aus einer sorgfältigen, originellen Gestaltung und aus einer gründlichen Auseinandersetzung mit dem Material und der Bautechnik entsteht. Unsere Studierenden werden diese Erfahrung mit sich tragen, wenn sie in ihre eigene professionelle Praxis eintreten. Wir sind der Ansicht, dass Entwürfe heute allzu oft nicht das ganze Potenzial des konstruktiven Holzbaus ausnutzen. Wir sind überzeugt, dass sich das ändern wird, wenn Architektinnen und Architekten ein tieferes Verständnis des digitalen Repertoires entwickeln. Die Ausbildung spielt dabei eine Schlüsselrolle. Architekturschulen sind wichtige Vermittler: für die technischen Kenntnisse, für die Haltung gegenüber dem Material und für das Setzen der richtigen Prioritäten. Im Streben

107

23

Holzwelt Murau information pavilion, type 2 | Infopavillon Typ 2, Standort | Location Oberwölz © Florian Fend

wood architecture, the use of digital technology takes on a cultural dimension.

History teaches us that objects with a high identification value, that were created with a lot of loving care, are the ones most likely to gain dignity and increase in value with age. This holds as true for architecture as it does for violins. In pre-industrial times, when manual labor was still affordable, this loving care was the result of traditional craftsmanship. While industrial production favored standardization over bespoke design, digital fabrication has opened possibilities up again. Digital technology now allows us to create unique objects with sophisticated geometries and details as well as economic use of materials at affordable cost. Moreover, it enables a deep engagement with a material's properties, and refined ways of designing that bring out a material's inherent qualities. We believe that the notion of digital refinement can serve as an inspiration as well as a guideline towards not only a more sophisticated but also a more culturally, environmentally and socially sustainable future practice. ∎

Acknowledgements: The "Lusthaus" studio (WS 2016/17) was taught by Florian Fend, Martin Kaftan, Urs Hirschberg and Michael Stadler, assisted by Theresa Fink and Julian Jauk. Students: Sayna Abbasaliyan, Primož Brglez, Julia Bruckmüller, Xaver Burkart, Michael Deutsch, Lukas Gosch, Sabrina Patricia Kullmaier, Paul Christoph Lindheim, Stefan Neumann, Daniel Plazza, Victoria Postlmayr, Georg Scherrer, Daniel Seiwald, Christoph Thambauer, Corinna Wassermann, Lukas Wokatsch, Nuša Zupanc. The "Break It Till You Make It" studio (WS 2017/18) was taught by Florian Fend, Urs Hirschberg, José Paixão and Matthew Tam, assisted by Theresa Fink and Julian Jauk. Students: Aaron Leonard Haase, Armin Baumgartner, Armin Karner, Clemens Sebastian Wolte, Daniel Huber, Doris Rainer, Eleni Chatzatoglou, Emina Lozo, Gabriel Severin Sieghartsleitner, Kathrin Bräuer, Michela Freri, Matthias Steinscherer, Parimala Venkatesh, Raphael Martinz, Renata Proença Tarran Gomes, Youjung Song. Many other members of the Institute of Architecture und Media have contributed to the success of the presented projects. For feedback on this text I want to thank Albert Wiltsche, Milena Stavrić and Thomas Bogensperger.

24

Holzwelt Murau information pavilion, type 3 | Infopavillon Typ 3, Standort | Location St. Lamprecht © Florian Fend

nach Verfeinerung in der Holzarchitektur bekommt die Verwendung von digitaler Technik auch eine kulturelle Dimension.

Aus der Geschichte lernen wir, dass Objekte mit einem hohen Identifikationswert, die mit Liebe und Sorgfalt gestaltet wurden, auch zumeist diejenigen sind, die mit der Zeit an Würde und gesellschaftlicher Wertzuschreibung gewinnen. Dies gilt für Architektur genauso wie für Geigen. In vorindustriellen Zeiten, als Handarbeit noch leistbar war, war diese Sorgfalt das Merkmal hochwertiger Handwerkskunst. Während die Industrieproduktion die Standardisierung gegenüber dem besonderen Einzelstück bevorteilte, hat die Digitalisierung wieder neue Möglichkeiten eröffnet. Digitaltechnik erlaubt uns heute, einzigartige Artefakte zu erzeugen, mit raffinierten Geometrien und Details, aber ebenso mit ressourcenschonender Materialnutzung und zu erschwinglichen Preisen. Darüber hinaus ermöglicht sie uns eine vertiefte Auseinandersetzung mit Materialeigenschaften und unterstützt Gestaltungsmethoden, welche die einem Material innewohnenden Qualitäten hervorkehren. Wir glauben, dass der Begriff der digitalen Verfeinerung als Inspiration dienen und uns die Richtung weisen kann – nicht nur in eine raffiniertere, sondern auch in eine sozial, ökologisch und kulturell nachhaltigere zukünftige Praxis. ∎

Übersetzung: Urs Hirschberg

Danksagung: Das „Lusthaus"-Masterstudio (WS 2016/17), aus dem der Twist Pavillon hervorging, wurde von Florian Fend, Martin Kaftan, Urs Hirschberg und Michael Stadler geleitet, assistiert durch Theresa Fink und Julian Jauk. Die Studierenden waren Sayna Abbasaliyan, Primož Brglez, Julia Bruckmüller, Xaver Burkart, Michael Deutsch, Lukas Gosch, Sabrina Patricia Kullmaier, Paul Christoph Lindheim, Stefan Neumann, Daniel Plazza, Victoria Postlmayr, Georg Scherrer, Daniel Seiwald, Christoph Thambauer, Corinna Wassermann, Lukas Wokatsch, Nuša Zupanc. Das „Break It Till You Make It"-Masterstudio (WS 2017/18) wurde von Florian Fend, Urs Hirschberg, José Paixão und Matthew Tam geleitet, assistiert durch Theresa Fink und Julian Jauk. Die Studierenden waren Aaron Leonard Haase, Armin Baumgartner, Armin Karner, Clemens Sebastian Wolte, Daniel Huber, Doris Rainer, Eleni Chatzatoglou, Emina Lozo, Gabriel Severin Sieghartsleitner, Kathrin Bräuer, Michela Freri, Matthias Steinscherer, Parimala Venkatesh, Raphael Martinz, Renata Proença Tarran Gomes, Youjung Song. Viele weitere MitarbeiterInnen des Instituts für Architektur und Medien haben zum Gelingen der hier vorgestellten Projekte beigetragen. Für Hinweise zu diesem Text sei insbesondere Albert Wiltsche, Milena Stavrić und Thomas Bogensperger gedankt.

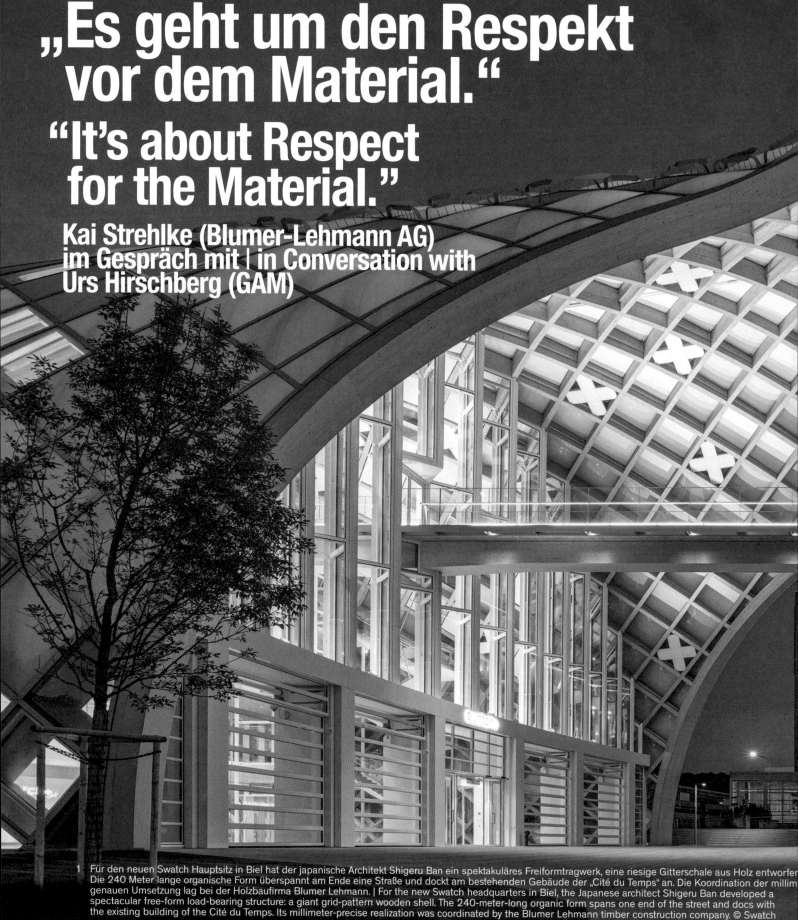

„Es geht um den Respekt vor dem Material."

"It's about Respect for the Material."

**Kai Strehlke (Blumer-Lehmann AG)
im Gespräch mit | in Conversation with
Urs Hirschberg (GAM)**

1 Für den neuen Swatch Hauptsitz in Biel hat der japanische Architekt Shigeru Ban ein spektakuläres Freiformtragwerk, eine riesige Gitterschale aus Holz entworfen. Die 240 Meter lange organische Form überspannt am Ende eine Straße und dockt am bestehenden Gebäude der „Cité du Temps" an. Die Koordination der millimetergenauen Umsetzung lag bei der Holzbaufirma Blumer Lehmann. | For the new Swatch headquarters in Biel, the Japanese architect Shigeru Ban developed a spectacular free-form load-bearing structure: a giant grid-pattern wooden shell. The 240-meter-long organic form spans one end of the street and docs with the existing building of the Cité du Temps. Its millimeter-precise realization was coordinated by the Blumer Lehmann timber construction company. © Swatch

Der Architekt **Kai Strehlke** leitet seit fünf Jahren die digitalen Prozesse in der CAD/CAM-Produktion der Schweizer Holzbaufirma Blumer Lehmann. Davor war er zehn Jahre als Head IT beim Architekturbüro Herzog & de Meuron tätig. Bei Herzog & de Meuron hat er an vielen international bekannten Projekten des Büros mitgearbeitet. Er kennt also die Architekturpraxis nicht nur aus dem speziellen Blickwinkel des Holzbaus, auf den er sich inzwischen spezialisiert hat. Blumer Lehmann ist ein traditionsreiches ostschweizerisches Familienunternehmen. Der Erlenhof, wo 1875 das erste Sägewerk gegründet wurde und bis heute mit dem zweiten Standort im Ort die gesamte Produktion stattfindet, liegt idyllisch gelegen bei Gossau (Abb. 2). Für zeitgenössische Holzarchitektur, insbesondere im Bereich Freiformgeometrien, ist Blumer Lehmann eine international profilierte erste Adresse. In jüngster Vergangenheit hat Kai Strehlke unter anderem am neuen Swatch Hauptgebäude (Architektur: Shigeru Ban Architects, Paris/Tokio) und an der Moschee in Cambridge (Architektur: Marks Barfield Architects, London) maßgeblich mitgearbeitet. Die meisten Abbildungen im Beitrag stammen von diesen beiden Projekten. Das Gespräch mit Kai Strehlke, der vor seinem Engagement bei Blumer Lehmann im Jahr 2015 ein Semester lang als Gastprofessor an der TU Graz unterrichtete, fand im September 2020 per Videokonferenz statt.

2

Der Erlenhof bei Gossau ist das Werkgelände von Blumer Lehmann. Hier wurde 1875 das erste Sägewerk gegründet. | The Erlenhof, near Gossau, is the site of Blumer Lehmann's factory. The first sawmill on this site opened in 1875.
© Blumer-Lehmann AG

Urs Hirschberg (GAM): Du arbeitest jetzt seit fünf Jahren bei Blumer Lehmann, einem Familienbetrieb. Angesichts deiner langen Zeit bei einem der weltweit führenden Architekturbüros wundert man sich vielleicht, dass du bei einer Holzbaufirma im ländlichen Raum gelandet bist. Aber bei Blumer Lehmann kannst du ebenfalls an äußerst spannenden Projekten arbeiten, die nachher weltweit umgesetzt werden. Der Firma gelingt das Kunststück, als produzierender Betrieb im Hochlohnland Schweiz international kompetitiv zu sein. Ihr fertigt Bauteile in der teuren Schweiz und verfrachtet sie nach England, sogar ins Holzland Norwegen, ja sogar ins weit entfernt gelegene und für deutlich niedrigere Lohnkosten bekannte Korea. Wie geht das? Was macht Blumer Lehmann so viel besser als die Konkurrenten vor Ort?

Kai Strehlke (KS): Die Firma hat eine lange Tradition. Sie wurde 1875 als Sägerei gegründet. Wir haben eine lange Holzbautradition und verfügen über ein enormes Wissen über den Werkstoff Holz. Im Unternehmen legen wir großen Wert auf die Ausbildung von Fachkräften und bilden Lernende aber auch StudentInnen aus Fachhochschulen aus. Gleichzeitig sind wir unglaublich daran interessiert, was Holz heute und in der Zukunft für Potenziale bietet. Außerdem sind wir sehr gut mit Universitäten wie jener in Stuttgart, der EPFL Lausanne, der ETH

Zürich und mit der EMPA (Eidgenössische Materialprüfungs- und Forschungsanstalt) vernetzt. Wir haben viele Projekte, bei denen man verstehen lernt, was man mit Holzfasern auch in Zukunft machen kann. Der Blick einerseits in die Vergangenheit aber auch das Offensein für die Zukunft, das zeichnet die Firma aus. Aber nochmals zu deiner Frage. Im Ausland sind wir vor allem mit unseren Freiformen wettbewerbsfähig, da wir dort über einen Know-how-Vorsprung zu unseren Mitbewerbern verfügen. Unser Hauptmarkt ist aber nach wie vor die Schweiz.

GAM: Du erwähnst den Forschungskonnex. Ist der das Geheimnis? In vielen Branchen ist die Produktion ja schon lange nach China abgewandert. Gelingt es euch, die Schweizer Personalkosten in der Produktion durch besseres Know-how im Engineering wettzumachen?

KS: Die Forschungswidmung ist wichtig. Es ist wichtig, sich mit potenten Forschungspartnern zu vernetzen und auch im Haus selbst Forschung zu betreiben. Die Projekte, die wir ins Ausland verkaufen sind meist Leuchtturmprojekte. Andere Firmen sind oft gar nicht in der Lage, diese zu bauen. Da gibt es nur wenige, die das können. Blumer Lehmann hat dafür die Kompetenz, nicht unbedingt, weil wir extreme SpezialistInnen haben, sondern weil wir intern als Team sehr gut aufgestellt sind und über viel Fachwissen verfügen: Zimmerleute, StatikerInnen, Holzbau-IngenieurInnen, Leute, die in der Lage sind, die komplexe Logistik zu bewältigen und auch Leute wie ich, die mit den digitalen Prozessen sehr gut klarkommen, damit solche komplexen Entwürfe auch gefertigt werden können. Das, was uns ausmacht, ist das Team.

Ein weiterer Grund, warum wir erfolgreich sind, ist Katharina Lehmann, unsere CEO, sie ist mutig, unternehmerische

For the past five years, the architect **Kai Strehlke** has been in charge of digital processes in CAD/CAM production for the Swiss timber construction company Blumer Lehmann. Before that, he worked as head of IT for ten years at the architectural firm Herzog & de Meuron. At Herzog & de Meuron, he worked on many of the firm's internationally famous projects. He is familiar with the practice of architecture and not just from the perspective of timber construction that has since become his specialty. Blumer Lehmann is a family business in eastern Switzerland with a rich tradition. The Erlenhof, where its first sawmill was founded in 1875, and where, together with a second site nearby, the entire production takes place, is an idyllic rural location near Gossau (fig. 2). For contemporary architecture in wood, especially in the area of freeform geometries, Blumer Lehmann is a prime address with an international profile. In the recent past, Kai Strehlke has been a crucial collaborator on projects such as the new Swatch headquarters (architecture: Shigeru Ban Architects, Paris/Tokyo) and the mosque in Cambridge (architecture: Marks Barfield Architects, London). Most of the illustrations that follow are from these two projects. This interview with Kai Strehlke, who, before being hired by Blumer Lehmann, taught for a semester in 2015 as a visiting professor at Graz University of Technology, was conducted via video conference in September 2020.

Urs Hirschberg (GAM): You've been working at Blumer Lehmann, a family-owned company, for five years. In view of the long time you spent at one of the leading international architecture firms, it is perhaps surprising that you ended up at a timber construction company in a rural area. But at Blumer Lehmann you can also work on extremely exciting projects that are then built worldwide.

The company pulls off the trick of remaining internationally competitive as a production operation in the high-wage country of Switzerland. You manufacture construction parts in expensive Switzerland and ship them to England, even to the timber country Norway, indeed, even to Korea which is far away and famous for considerably lower wage costs. How does that work? What makes Blumer Lehmann so much better than the local competition in those countries?

Kai Strehlke (KS): The company has a long history. It was founded as a sawmill in 1875. We have a long tradition of timber construction and have enormous knowledge about wood as a material. We in the company attach great importance to upskilling our workers and teaching apprentices and students from technical colleges about wood's potential today and in the future. Moreover, we are well networked with universities such as Stuttgart, the EPFL Lausanne, the ETH Zurich, and the EMPA (Swiss Federal Laboratories for Materials Science and Technology). We have many projects from which we are learning what wood fibers could do in the future. Looking at the past, on the one hand, and being open to the future, on the other, distinguishes this company. But to return to your question: We are competitive abroad, above all with our freeform constructions, because we are a step ahead of our competitors in terms of know-how. Our main market, however, is still Switzerland.

GAM: You mention your research focus. Is that the secret? In many sectors, production has long since moved to China. Do you manage to compensate for the personnel costs in production in Switzerland with better know-how in engineering?

KS: Dedication to research is important. It's important to network with powerful research partners and to do your own

3–5

(3) Timber Code, eine eigens für das CNC-Fräsen von sehr großen Freiformbauteilen erbaute Werkhalle | Timber Code, a factory hall specially built for the CNC milling of very large, free-form construction parts
(4) CNC-Fräskopf und Werkstück auf der Timber Code-Anlage | CNC milling head and workpiece at the Timber Code facility
(5) Mehrfach gekrümmte Bauteile für das Swatch Projekt in Biel in der Timber Code Halle | Multiply-curved construction parts for the Swatch project in Biel in the Timber Code hall
© Blumer-Lehmann AG

Schritte zu gehen, wobei diese oft mit relativ viel Risiko verbunden sind. Sie nimmt Projekte an, bei denen man eventuell am Anfang noch nicht weiß, wie man sie fertigen wird. Aber sie hat das Vertrauen in ihr Team, das in der Lage sein wird, Lösungen zu finden. Das ist das, was uns als Firma auszeichnet.

Diese internationalen Projekte könnte man auch kritisch sehen. Es ist nicht besonders nachhaltig, in der Schweiz das Holz zu fertigen und mit Lkws nach England oder mit Schiffen nach Korea zu transportieren, um sie dort aufzubauen. Aber ich glaube, dass diese Projekte, diese Leuchtturmprojekte, dem Holzbau generell einen unglaublich guten Dienst leisten. Sie treiben den Holzbau auch in anderen Ländern voran. Gerade England ist ein sehr backsteinlastiges Land. Dort hat ein Projekt wie die Moschee in Cambridge eine Signalwirkung. Auch in der Schweiz hat der Holzbau erst in der letzten Zeit, gerade im Wohnungsbau, wieder an Bedeutung gewonnen. Diese Leuchtturmprojekte helfen dem Material, wieder mehr Aufschwung zu bekommen.

GAM: Diese Leuchtturmprojekte haben viel mit der digitalen Fabrikation zu tun, auf die du dich spezialisiert hast. In Bezug auf Digitalisierung und Robotisierung des Bauwesens passiert ja derzeit sehr viel. Andererseits ist Holz als nachhaltiger Baustoff stark im Trend. Als Firma profitiert ihr sicher davon, dass Holzverarbeitung und Digitalisierung so gut zusammenpassen. Es gibt im Holzbau ein hohes Potenzial für die Vorfertigung. Man kann damit Bauprozesse beschleunigen. Wie beobachtest du die allgemeine Entwicklung in Richtung Holzbau, sowohl in Bezug auf die Digitalisierung aber auch im Zusammenhang mit dem Nachhaltigkeitsthema?

KS: Du sprichst zwei Themen an: Nachhaltigkeit und Digitalisierung. Die Nachhaltigkeit ist ein hochaktuelles Thema, vor allem, wenn man sich Bewegungen wie Fridays for Future anschaut und die allgemeine CO_2-Debatte, die gerade sehr stark in der Politik behandelt wird, oder nach Corona wieder behandelt werden wird. Holz ist ein Material, das in dieser Debatte eine wichtige Rolle spielt. Holz bindet CO_2, Beton verbraucht CO_2. Holz kann eine Antwort liefern auf die Diskussion der Nachhaltigkeit im Bauwesen. Das Bauwesen ist bekanntlich für 35 bis 40 Prozent des CO_2-Ausstoßes verantwortlich. Dass Holz in Bezug auf die CO_2-Bilanz so ein sinnvolles Material ist, hilft natürlich dem Holzbau.

Bei der Digitalisierung gibt es zwei große Tendenzen: die Vorfabrikation und das Bauen in situ, also das Bauen auf der Baustelle. Beton gibt es auch in der Vorfabrikation, aber viel Beton oder Stein wird vor Ort verbaut. Beim Holz hat die Vorfabrikation eine lange Tradition. Schon die deutschen Fachwerkhäuser wurden auf Plätzen vor den Dörfern abgebunden. Es gab eine Logistiklösung, um die Teile nachher in die Dörfer zu bringen und dort wieder zusammenzubauen. Das sind Erfindungen, die schon vor hunderten Jahren gemacht worden

sind, die schon immer dem Holz einen Vorteil gegeben haben in der Vorfabrikation. Die Digitalisierung ist nur die logische Weiterentwicklung dieser Praktiken mit den heutigen technischen Möglichkeiten. Holz hat hier große Vorteile. Dass man sich eine Zeit lang vom Holz abgewendet hat, hatte vor allem damit zu tun, dass Holz brennen kann. Viele Dörfer und Städte sind wegen Bränden in Holzhäusern fast oder gänzlich vernichtet worden. Den Brandschutz haben wir heute im Griff. Das heißt, es macht heute wieder Sinn, das Holz in die Städte hinein zu bringen.

Für Baustellen in der Stadt ist die Vorfabrikation ein enormer Vorteil: Man ist in der Lage, vor der Stadt hochkomplexe Teile vorzufertigen, die dann in der Stadt legomäßig zusammengebaut werden können. Man hat kurze Bauzeiten, kleine Baustellen. Holz ist perfekt für die Vorfabrikation geeignet. Es ist auch nicht so schwer wie Stein oder Beton. Die Städte wachsen, wir brauchen immer mehr Wohnraum. Wir können nicht nur neu bauen, mit einem leichten Material wie Holz können wir auch aufstocken und an Gebäude anbauen. Holz ist dafür ein sinnvolles Material. Ich glaube, Holz ist das Material der Zeit.

Was ich im Augenblick erlebe, ist eine Art Pionierhaltung im Holzbau, die ich ähnlich empfinde wie zu den Zeiten von Mies van der Rohe in Berlin oder den USA in den 1920er-Jahren. Ich habe das Gefühl, Holz ist im Augenblick so interessant, wie es damals Glas und Stahl waren. Interessant ist, dass es ein uraltes Material ist, welches wir dabei sind, neu zu entdecken.

GAM: Liegen die Ursachen für diese Neuentdeckung nicht auch in einer anderen Wertschätzung des Materials Holz?

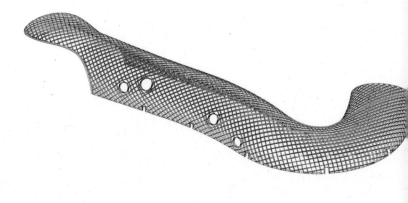

6

Das Swatch Hauptgebäude von Shigeru Ban im CAD-Modell. Der längste Träger (orange markiert) ist 130 Meter lang. Er steht entlang seiner gesamten Länge senkrecht zur Dachfläche und ist deswegen mehrfach in alle Richtungen gekrümmt. | The CAD model of the Swatch headquarters by Shigeru Ban. The longest beam (marked in orange) is 130 meters long. Along its entire length, it is perpendicular to the roof and is therefore curved in all directions several times. © Blumer-Lehmann AG

research in house. The projects we sell abroad are usually light-house projects. Other companies are often not even in a position to build them. There are only a few that can. Blumer Lehmann has the competence to do that, not necessarily because we have "extreme specialists," but because we are set up internally very well as a *team* and have a lot of specialized knowledge: carpenters, structural engineers, timber-construction engineers—people who are in a position to master the complex logistics and also people like me who understand digital processes very well. It's thanks to this team that complex designs can be built. What makes us distinctive is the team.

Another reason we are successful is Katharina Lehmann, our CEO; she is bold about taking the entrepreneurial steps, even though they are often tied to relatively large risk. She takes on projects in which, perhaps, no one knows at the start how they will be completed. But she has faith in her team, that it will be able to find solutions. That is why we stand out as a company.

These international projects can also be regarded critically. It isn't especially sustainable to prepare the wood in Switzerland and transport it by truck to the United Kingdom or by ship to Korea to assemble it there. But I believe that these projects, these lighthouse projects, provide an unbelievably good service to timber construction. They advance timber construction in other countries as well. The United Kingdom

in particular is a very brick-heavy country. A project like the mosque in Cambridge has a signal effect there. Even in Switzerland, wood construction has regained importance only recently, especially in residential architecture. These lighthouse projects are helping the material achieve a boom again.

GAM: These lighthouse projects have a lot to do with digital manufacturing, in which you have specialized. A lot is happening right now with digitalization and robotics in the construction business. At the same time, there is a strong trend toward wood as a sustainable building material. As a company, you surely profit from woodworking and digitalization going together so well. Timber construction has lots of potential for prefabrication. You can accelerate construction processes that way. How do you see the general evolution toward timber construction in terms of digitalization and also in connection with the theme of sustainability?

KS: You are talking about two themes: sustainability and digitalization. Sustainability is a highly topical subject right now, if you consider movements such as Fridays for Future and the general CO_2 debate, which is a big political issue right now, or at least will be again after the pandemic. Wood is a material that plays an important role in this debate. Wood absorbs CO_2; concrete uses CO_2. Wood can provide an answer to the discussion of sustainability in the construction business. Famously, the construction business is responsible for 35 to 40 percent of CO_2 emissions. That wood makes so much sense as a material in terms of the CO_2 balance naturally benefits timber construction.

There are two big trends in digitalization: prefabrication and building in situ, that is, building on the construction site. Concrete is also used in prefabrication, but lots of concrete and stone are built on site. Wood has a long tradition in prefabrication. German timber-framed buildings were preassembled on locations outside of the villages. That was a logistical solution so that the parts could be brought into the village and reassembled there. Those were inventions made already hundreds of years ago that have always given wood an advantage in prefabrication. Digitalization is merely a logical further development of these practices using today's technological possibilities. Wood has great advantages here. The primary reason

7

Montage in Biel: Die 240 Meter lange Gitterschale wird aus 4.600 unterschiedlichen Hauptträgern zusammengesetzt. Die Konstruktion verlangt höchste Präzision: die maximale Abweichung liegt bei zwei Millimetern. | Assembly in Biel: The 240-meter-long grid shell is composed of 4,600 different main beams. Its construction requires the greatest precision: maximum deviation is two millimeters. © Blumer-Lehmann AG

8

Innenraum der Moschee in Cambridge (Architektur: Marks Barfield Architects, London). „Das Bild eines Baumhaines lieferte die Grundidee"
erklärt die Architektin Julia Barfield. | Interior of the mosque in Cambridge (architecture: Marks Barfield Architects, London).
"The image of a grove of trees provided the basic idea," explains the architect Julia Barfield. © Morley von Sternberg

KS: Ich weiß nicht, ob das die Sache zu sehr vereinfacht, aber für mich ist es so: im Zuge der Industrialisierung in den 1950er-, 1960er- und 1970er-Jahren hat man versucht, möglichst standardisiert zu arbeiten. In den Fabriken wollte man deswegen homogene Materialien haben. Die Krönung dieser Entwicklung war, dass man die Faser, die anisotropen Eigenschaften des Holzes, also das, was Holz als Material ausmacht, komplett zerstört hat, indem man es zermahlen und mit Leim wieder zusammengeklebt hat. Das ist eigentlich eine Vergewaltigung des Werkstoffes. Man bekommt dann ein Material, das man „MDF" nennt, ein homogenes Material, das in alle Richtungen die gleichen Eigenschaften hat. Aber es sind die gleichen *schlechten* Eigenschaften, denn die Faser, die das Holz so unglaublich kräftig macht, hat man dadurch zerstört. Gerade ist man dabei zu erkennen, dass man besser nicht *gegen* die Faser, sondern *mit* der Faser arbeitet.

GAM: Unser Heftthema ist ja „Rethinking Material". Du hast gerade dargelegt, dass neu denken auch heißen kann, dass man jene Dinge wieder neu erkennt und zu schätzen lernt, die frühere Generationen schon gewusst haben. Du erwähnst die Nachkriegszeit. Dieses „dumbing down" des Materials Holz, also diese Faserplatten, die hat man ja auch deswegen gemacht, weil damit alles einfacher wurde. Man musste sich weniger Gedanken machen, man konnte alles einfacher berechnen. Es wird ja alles komplizierter, wenn man den Baustoff so nimmt wie er gewachsen ist, aber man bekommt eben dadurch auch weitere Möglichkeiten. Reden wir jetzt von diesen Möglichkeiten. Bei Blumer Lehmann seid ihr bereit, Neues auszuprobieren und ihr betont auch, dass ihr möglichst früh mit den ArchitektInnen zusammenarbeiten wollt, damit euer Expertenwissen in den Entwurf einfließen kann. Findet das auch statt? Läuft das immer so, dass ArchitektInnen früh auf euch zukommen, wenn sie ein Projekt entwickeln, das auf virtuose Weise mit Holz umgeht?

KS: Ich würde sagen, wenn die hochkomplexen Projekte erfolgreich sind, dann ist es so gelaufen. Es gibt ja die verschiedenen Leistungsphasen, die sind je nach Land etwas unterschiedlich geregelt, aber sowohl in Deutschland als auch in der Schweiz

people turned away from wood for such a long time was that wood can burn. Many villages and towns had been almost or totally destroyed by fires in wooden buildings. Today, we have a handle on fire safety. That means it makes sense again to bring wood into cities.

Prefabrication is an enormous advantage for construction sites in the city: Very complicated parts can be prefabricated outside of the city and then assembled, Lego-like, in the city. You have short construction times and small construction sites. Wood is perfectly suited to prefabrication. Moreover, it is not as heavy as stone or concrete. Cities are growing; we need more and more residential space. We can not only build new buildings; with a light material like wood, we can also add new floors and add to existing buildings. Wood makes sense as a material for that. I believe that wood is the material for our time.

What I am experiencing at the moment is a kind of pioneering attitude in timber construction, which seems to me similar to that of Mies van der Rohe in Berlin or of the United States in the 1920s. I have the feeling that wood is as interesting at the moment as glass and steel were then. It is interesting that it is an ancient material that we are in the process of rediscovering.

GAM: Don't the reasons for this rediscovery also lie in a different appreciation of wood as a material?

KS: I don't know whether it oversimplifies the matter, but this is how I see it: In the course of industrialization in the 1950s, 1960s, and 1970s, there was an effort to work in standardized

ways. For that reason, people wanted to have homogeneous materials in factories. The culmination of this development was that wood—or rather what distinguishes wood as a material, namely, fibers, the anisotropic qualities of wood were completely destroyed by grinding it up and gluing it back together. That is truly a mutilation of wood. The resulting material is called MDF: a homogeneous material that has the same properties in all directions. But they are the same *bad* properties, because the fibers that make wood so incredibly strong have been destroyed in the process. Now people are recognizing that it is better not to work *against* the fibers but with them.

GAM: The theme of this issue is "Rethinking Material." You have just shown that rethinking can also mean learning to recognize and appreciate the things that earlier generations already knew. You mention the postwar period. This dumbing down of the material wood, that is, into fiberboards, was also done because it made everything simpler. You didn't have to think as much; it was much easier to calculate everything. Everything gets more complicated when you take the construction material just as it grew, but it also provides other opportunities. Let's talk about these opportunities now. At Blumer Lehmann, you are willing to try out new things, and you also emphasize that you like to work together with the architects from as early on as possible, so your expert knowledge can contribute to the design. Does that happen? Is it always the case that architects come to you early when they are developing a project that treats wood in a virtuosic way?

KS: I would say that when highly complex projects are successful, that was how it happened. There are, of course, various work phases that are regulated a little differently depending on

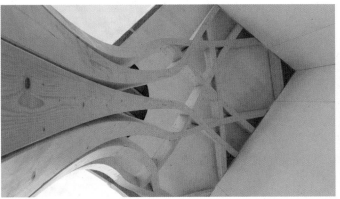 

9–10

(9) Mockup für die Moschee in Cambridge. Für engere Radien müssen die gebogenen Träger aus dünneren Stäben zusammengesetzt sein. Da diese deutlich teurer sind, werden sie nur in den stark gebogenen Abschnitten des Trägers verwendet. Im Mockup wird unter anderem überprüft, ob der Wechsel im Holzaufbau auch ästhetisch funktioniert. | Mockup of the mosque in Cambridge. For narrower radiuses, the curved beams are composed of thinner frames. Because the latter are considerably more expensive, they are used only in the parts of the beam that are very curved. The mockup is used to test, among other things, whether the changing structure of the wood works aesthetically.
(10) Detail des Mockups: aus der Nähe wird der unterschiedliche Holzaufbau der Trägerteile erkennbar. | Detail of the mockup: seen from up close, the differences in the structure of the wood of the parts of the beam are visible.
© Blumer-Lehmann AG

ist es so, dass die ausführenden Unternehmen erst nach der Ausschreibung ins Spiel kommen. Die ArchitektInnen entwickeln das Projekt davor mit FachplanerInnen usw. Die Unternehmen kommen erst danach dazu.

Was wir propagieren und sehr erfolgreich machen, vor allem bei privaten Freiformprojektes, ist, dass wir vor der Ausschreibung einen Piloten, ein Mockup bauen (Abb. 9–10). In diesem Mockup testen wir die Herstellung, die Ästhetik und wir sehen auch, was die Kostentreiber im Projekt sind und wie man diese eventuell reduzieren kann, z.B. indem man Krümmungen reduziert oder leichte Änderungen an der Architektur macht. Es geht nicht darum, die Architektur zu ändern. Es geht darum, die Konsequenzen aus einem Entwurf für die Ausführung aufzuzeigen. Bei privaten Projekten ist das sehr erfolgreich. Bei öffentlichen Ausschreibungen haben wir das Problem, dass wir als Unternehmen erst danach ins Spiel kommen können. Das führt dann oft zu Projektes, die unglaublich schwierig auszuführen sind. Die Projekte werden dann auch wesentlich teurer.

GAM: Das heißt, man müsste eigentlich diese Richtlinien ändern, um das auch bei öffentlichen Ausschreibungen zu ermöglichen. Oder das Mockup müsste schon als Teil der Vorplanungsphase akzeptiert werden und abrechenbar sein. Du sagst, die Richtlinien verhindern ein vernünftiges Vorgehen, das noch dazu Kosten sparen könnte?

KS: Ja!

GAM: Das heißt, ihr seid mit eurem Ansatz eigentlich im Nachteil bei öffentlich ausgeschriebenen Projekten?

KS: Ich glaube nicht, dass wir im Nachteil sind. Oft ist es ja so, dass die Firmen, die billig anbieten, ohne die Konstruktion wirklich auszuloten, sich dann übernehmen. Bei den Blobs, den Freiformarchitekturen, die Ende der 1990er-Jahre aufgekommen sind, konnte man das oft beobachten. Man hat den günstigsten Anbieter genommen, der dann aber nicht in der Lage war, das Projekt umzusetzen. Wenn dann eine Firma pleite gegangen ist, und manchmal ist ja auch noch eine zweite Firma pleite gegangen, hat das sicher nicht die Kosten reduziert. Im Gegenteil, das hat die Kosten in die Höhe getrieben. Es wäre in solchen Fällen viel besser, jemanden zu nehmen, der die Kosten von Anfang an seriös abgeschätzt hat.

Gerade bei Freiformen, also bei komplexeren Bauaufgaben, ist das aus meiner Sicht ein großes Problem in den aktuellen Leistungsphasen. Ich würde absolut dafür plädieren, dass eine zusätzliche Leistungsphase eingebaut wird, die eine Mockup-Phase ist, die vor der Ausschreibung stattfindet, wo auch der Architekt bzw. die Architektin selber noch im Entwurf ist und wo auch sein bzw. ihr Wissen mit dem Wissen des Unternehmers in das Projekt miteinfließen kann.

GAM: Das Mockup als Schlüssel, sehr interessant! Mir fällt dazu die Anekdote ein, die mir Peter Cook zur Entstehung des Grazer Kunsthauses erzählt hat. Das 1:1 Mockup der Fassade, das sie damals gebaut und auf der Biennale in Venedig gezeigt haben, hat für die Realisierung ebenfalls eine Schlüsselrolle gespielt …

KS: Man versucht oft, sich das Mockup zu ersparen, aber das ist genau der falsche Ansatz! Für ArchitektInnen ist es das erste Mal, dass sie praktisch, physisch erleben, was sie entwerfen. Das ist ein unglaublich schöner Moment, nicht nur für die ArchitektInnen, auch für die Bauherrschaft, weil sie das erste Mal spüren, was sie bekommen werden. Eine zweite Erfahrung, die wir gemacht haben, ist, dass Mockups die Entscheidungsprozesse beschleunigen, weil Fragen fundierter geklärt werden können. Damit spart man am Ende sogar Zeit.

GAM: Bei manchen Architekturbüros, mit denen ihr öfter zusammenarbeitet, müsst ihr diesbezüglich wohl keine Überzeugungsarbeit leisten. Mit Shigeru Ban beispielsweise habt ihr ja schon eine ganze Reihe an Projekten gemacht. Ich nehme an, dass Mockups da eine wichtige Rolle spielen. Wie läuft die Zusammenarbeit mit dem Büro Shigeru Ban?

KS: Wir haben nicht nur Projekte mit Shigeru Ban gemacht, sondern auch sehr viele mit Norman Foster. Diese Büros kommen sehr früh in der Entwicklung ihrer Projekte auf uns zu und machen dann meistens nicht nur ein Mockup, wenn der Entwurf mehr oder weniger fertig ist. Nein, diese Büros kommen früh, um zu testen, was mit Holz möglich ist, wie weit sie gehen können, um ihre Architektur damit umzusetzen. Da stehen auch die Bauherren dahinter, dass die Mockups gemacht werden, bis der Entwurf fix ist und auch die technologischen Möglichkeiten detailliert abgeklärt sind. Oft probieren wir mit diesen Büros neue Technologien aus.

GAM: Das gilt eindeutig auch für das neue Swatch Hauptgebäude in Biel, das ihr mit Shigeru Ban entwickelt habt. Das Projekt gehört zu den größten, auch umfangmäßig, die ihr je realisiert habt. Ich denke, es war 2015, als wir euch mit einer Studierendengruppe besucht haben. Da habt ihr uns damals schon ein beeindruckendes Mockup von diesem Swatch Projekt gezeigt. Das Projekt war also schon eine Zeit lang in Vorbereitung. 2019 ist es dann fertig gestellt worden. Was waren bei dem Projekt die größten Herausforderungen? Hast du das Projekt von Anfang an mitbetreut?

KS: Ich habe die Produktion von Anfang an mitbetreut. Ich habe 2015 angefangen und ich glaube im Herbst/Winter 2015 ist der Zuschlag gekommen, dass wir das Projekt bauen können.

GAM: Davor gab es aber schon das Mockup.

the country, but in both Germany and Switzerland the companies implementing the project come into play only after the call for bids. The architects develop the project first with specialized planners, etc. The companies get involved only thereafter.

What we are advocating and doing very successfully, especially in private freeform projects, is that we build a pilot, a mockup, *before* the call for bids (figs. 9–10). In such a mockup, we test the production and the aesthetic, and we also see what drives up the costs in the project, and how they can perhaps be reduced, for example, by reducing curvatures or making slight changes to the architecture. It's not about changing the architecture. It's about determining a design's consequences for its realization. With private projects, that's very successful. For public tenders, the problem is that we as a company can only come into play after the contract is awarded. That often leads to projects that are incredibly difficult to implement. Then the projects also become substantially more expensive.

GAM: That means that the guidelines for public contracts really have to be changed. The mockup would have to be part of the preliminary planning phase. You're saying that the guidelines get in the way of a rational approach that could also reduce costs?

KS: Yes!

GAM: That means that you're in fact at a disadvantage when it comes to public tenders with your approach to projects?

KS: I don't believe we're at a disadvantage. It's often the case, after all, that the companies that make cheap bids without really assessing the construction then take on more than they can handle. You saw that a lot with the blobs, the freeform architecture, that emerged in the late 1990s. They took the lowest bidder, who was then not able to implement the project. When a company goes bankrupt, and sometimes even a second company goes bankrupt, that certainly does *not* reduce costs. On the contrary, costs increase. In such cases, it would have been better to take someone who had seriously estimated the costs from the outset.

Especially with free forms, that is, with more complex architectural tasks, that's the biggest problem with the current stages of contract, in my view. I would absolutely argue for introducing an additional phase, a mockup phase, that occurs before the construction bid, when the architect is still in the design stage, so his or her knowledge and the company's knowledge can be incorporated into the project.

GAM: The mockup as key, very interesting. That reminds me of an anecdote that Peter Cook told me about the building of the Kunsthaus Graz. The full-scale mockup of the façade that was built at the time and shown at the Venice Architecture Biennale also played a key role in its building …

KS: People often try to skip the mockup, but that's precisely the wrong approach! It is the first opportunity for architects to experience in practice, physically, what they are designing. That's an incredibly beautiful moment, not only for the architects but also for the client, because for the first time they sense what they will get. A second thing we have learned is that mockups accelerate the decision-making processes, because issues can be clarified in a more grounded way. In the end, you even save time.

GAM: Presumably, when it comes to the architectural firms with which you work often, you don't have to work to convince them. With Shigeru Ban, for example, you have already done a whole series of projects. I assume that mockups play an important role there. How does your collaboration with Shigeru Ban's office work?

KS: We have done projects not only with Shigeru Ban but also many with Norman Foster. These firms come to us very early in the development of their projects. We don't just do one mockup when the design is more or less finished. No, these offices come early in order to test what is possible with wood and how far they can go with it to realize their architecture. Their clients understand the importance of these mockups as part of the design process and in clarifying technical possibilities in detail. Often, we try out new technologies with these firms.

GAM: That was clearly true of the new main headquarters for Swatch in Biel, which you developed with Shigeru Ban. The project is one of the largest, also in terms of sheer size, that you have ever realized. I think it was 2015 when we visited you with a group of students. Already at that time you showed us an impressive mockup from the Swatch project. So that project was in preparation for a very long time. It was completed in 2019. What were the biggest challenges of that project? Were you involved in the project from the beginning?

KS: I was involved in production from the beginning. I started in 2015, and I believe it was the autumn/winter of 2015 when we were awarded the contract to build the project.

GAM: But there was already a mockup.

KS: Davor war das Mockup. Diese Freiformprojekte haben meistens eine relativ lange Vorlaufzeit. Ich weiß nicht genau, wie viele Jahre schon vergangen waren, bis die Produktion startete. Ich bin in dieses Projekt in dem Moment reingekommen, als die Produktion startete. Es war klar, dass wir das als Blumer Lehmann nicht alleine stemmen können. Wir haben in einem Verbund mit fünf verschiedenen Holzbaufirmen an diesem Projekt gearbeitet. In Deutschland, in Frankreich und auch in der Schweiz waren Holzbaufirmen beteiligt, um die insgesamt 4.600 Teile fristgerecht zu fertigen. Ein Novum und damit auch eine Herausforderung war, das zu organisieren. Durch die räumliche Distanz konnte man den Aufbau vorher nicht testen. Die Teile sind alle direkt auf die Baustelle gekommen und mussten auf den Millimeter genau passen.

GAM: Wer hat das Ganze dann koordiniert?

KS: Die Fäden sind bei uns zusammengelaufen, aber es war eine Zusammenarbeit von SJB Kempter Fitze AG als Statiker, der Firma Design-to-Production, die die Daten vorbereitet haben und uns, die die Logistik und die ganze Projektplanung, und Organisation sowie das Risiko übernommen haben. Design-to-Production haben unterschiedliche Daten unterschiedlichen Holzbauern geschickt, je nachdem wie deren Produktion eingerichtet war. Wir haben die Daten im Rhino-Format bekommen, also als reine Geometriedaten und haben dann aus diesen Geometriedaten den kompletten Maschinensteuerungscode geschrieben oder programmiert und gescriptet.

Es gab verschiedene Herausforderungen. Eine Herausforderung war der Verbund von den verschiedenen Firmen. Eine andere war die Konstruktion selbst. Im Holzbau unterscheidet man den Stababbund und Platten und Träger. Bei dem Gebäude in Biel ist es so, dass wir lauter gebogene Träger haben. Das sind keine Stäbe und es sind auch keine Platten. Das heißt, die industriellen Prozesse, die es gibt, die Platten zuzuschneiden und zu verarbeiten, funktionieren nicht. Wir mussten für dieses Gebäude diese Prozesse komplett neu entwickeln. Das ist natürlich ein Risiko gewesen.

Ganz entscheidend ist der Faktor Zeit. Wenn wir ein Bauteil berechnen mit einer Zeit X und einen gewissen Puffer haben, dann ist das immer ein Stück weit Spekulation. Es kann sein, dass wir etwas nicht bedacht haben und dieses Bauteil nur in der drei- oder vierfachen Zeit hergestellt werden kann. Wir haben über ein Jahr jeden Tag 24 Stunden ohne Pause gearbeitet. Unsere Fräsmaschinen standen nie still. Wenn wir uns verschätzt hätten, dann hätte das Projekt auch ein, zwei oder drei Jahre länger dauern können. Das ist natürlich eine riesige Herausforderung, eine hohe Kunst, sich da nicht zu verschätzen.

Die Prozesse, das heißt diese verschiedenen Verbindungen im Holz, die wir für das Projekt entwickelt haben, waren völlig neu. Am Anfang hat es ca. 45 Minuten gedauert, bis wir

die rausgefräst hatten. Wir haben diese Prozesse im Projekt runterreduzieren können auf drei bis fünf Minuten. Wenn man das hochskaliert, dann sieht man, was für eine Herausforderung es ist, so ein Projekt so zu kalkulieren, dass man es danach auch fristgerecht produzieren kann.

GAM: Dieser Zeitfaktor wird ja leicht unterschätzt. Wir erleben das auch bei unseren 1:1 Projekten, die wir mit Studierenden erstellen. Aber bei einem so gewaltigen Projekt wie dem Swatch Hauptquartier ist man natürlich in einer ganz anderen Dimension.

KS: Ganz kurz dazu: Wenn man sich das „Bird's Nest" – das Olympiastadion von Herzog & de Meuron in Peking – anschaut, dann hatte das natürlich auch einen strikten Zeitplan. Aber dort konnten sie einfach die Anzahl der Arbeiter auf der Baustelle multiplizieren. Da waren dann Tausende von Arbeitern auf der Baustelle. Bei vielen Architekturprojekten geht das: die kann man beschleunigen, indem man einfach mehr Leute aufbietet. Wir konnten das nicht, denn wir mussten die Sachen auf unserer Maschine fräsen.

GAM: Ihr hättet aber eine zweite Fabrik oder eine dritte noch daneben stellen können und das parallel machen, wenn Geld keine Rolle spielt.

KS: Das geht aber nicht innerhalb des Zeitrahmens. Wenn auf einer Baustelle Leute Fenster montieren, kannst du ohne weiteres 20 Fenstermonteure von einem Tag auf den anderen organisieren, die dir dann helfen, die Baustelle zu beschleunigen. Aber eine Fabrik baust du nicht innerhalb von zwei Wochen. Und die Maschinen, die wir zum Fräsen verwenden, sind ja auch keine Massenprodukte. Die bekommst du nicht in diesem Zeitrahmen gebaut. Deswegen ist der Zeitfaktor in unseren Projekten mit so viel Risiko behaftet. Und Geld spielt immer eine Rolle, denn schließlich sollte jedes unserer Projekte auch betriebswirtschaftlich funktionieren.

GAM: Zurück zu den Besonderheiten der Konstruktion beim Swatch Projekt. Dass Holz ein anisotroper Werkstoff ist, hast du schon erwähnt. Für die doppelt gekrümmten Stäbe, die dann eben keine Stäbe mehr sind, ist das natürlich höchst relevant. Sie sollen ja möglichst in Faserrichtung belastet werden. Kannst du erklären, wie man diese doppelt gekrümmte Faserrichtung beim Swatch-Projekt erreicht hat?

KS: Am einfachsten lässt sich das mithilfe von Bildern erläutern. Auf Abbildung 13 sieht man, dass Holz extrem gute Eigenschaften aufweist, wenn Druck und Zug entlang der Faser wirken. Die Eigenschaften von Druck und Zug werden schlechter, wenn man von dieser Richtung abweicht – bis ca. fünf Grad sind sie noch O.K. Quer zur Faser sind die Eigenschaften extrem schlecht.

KS: There was already a mockup. These freeform projects usually have a relatively long run-up time. I don't remember exactly how many years it took before production started. I joined this project when production was starting. It was clear that we at Blumer Lehmann could not manage it alone. We worked on that project as an alliance of five different timber construction companies. Timber construction companies in Germany, in France, and in Switzerland worked to manufacture a total of 4,600 parts on schedule. Organizing that was a novelty and hence also a challenge. Because of the geographical distances, it was not possible to test assembly ahead of time. The parts all went directly to the construction site and had to fit down to the millimeter.

GAM: Who coordinated the whole thing?

KS: We were holding the reins, but it was a collaboration between SJB Kempter Fitze AG as the structural engineers, the firm Design-to-Production, which prepared the data and us. We were responsible for the overall project planning, the organization, and the risk. Design-to-Production prepared the data for the various wood manufacturers in accordance with the requirements of their production facilities. We got the data in Rhino format, that is, as pure geometric data, and based on that geometric data we wrote, programmed, and scripted all of the code to control our machines.

There were various challenges. One challenge was the alliance of different companies. Another was the construction itself. In timber construction, one distinguishes between frames and panels and beams. With the building in Biel, we have nothing but curved beams. That means that the existing industrial processes for cutting and milling panels and straight beams do not work. We had to develop completely new processes for this building. That was a risk, of course.

The time factor is crucial. When we calculate a construction part with time X and have a certain buffer, there is always a little speculation involved. It may be that we have not considered something, and it takes three or four times longer to produce that construction part. We were working twenty-four hours daily without a break for more than a year. Our milling machines never stopped. If we had misjudged, the project could have taken one, two, or even three years longer. That is, of course, a great challenge; not to misjudge is a high art.

The processes—that is, these different wood joints we developed for the project—were completely new. In the beginning, it took about forty-five minutes to mill them. During the project we were able to reduce these processes to three to five minutes. If you scale that up, you see what a challenge it is to calculate such a project in a way that it can be produced on schedule.

GAM: It's easy to underestimate this time factor. We also experience that in our full-scale projects that we build with students. But with a project as enormous as the Swatch headquarters, you are in an entirely different dimension, of course.

KS: About that, quickly: If you look at the Olympic stadium by Herzog & de Meuron in Beijing, the "Bird's Nest," that had a strict time plan, too, of course. But in that case we could simply increase the number of workers on the construction site. So there were thousands of workers on the construction site. That works with many architectural projects: you can speed things up simply by having more people. We couldn't do that because we had to mill these things on our machine.

GAM: But you could build a second or even a third factory next to it and work in parallel, when money plays no role.

KS: But that doesn't work within the time frame. When people are installing windows on a construction site, it's easy to organize another twenty window installers from one day to the next, who can then help you speed up construction. But you can't build a factory in two weeks. And the machines we use to mill are not mass produced either. You can't get them in that time frame. That is why the time factor is associated with so much risk in our projects. And money always plays a role, since in the end every single one of our projects has to work in terms of economics as well.

GAM: Let's return to the unusual characteristics of construction in the Swatch project. You've already mentioned that wood is an anisotropic material. For the doubly curved beams, which are then no longer beams, that is, of course, highly relevant. They should be stressed in the direction of the grain as much as possible. Can you explain how this doubly curved fiber direction was achieved in the Swatch project?

KS: It can be explained mostly simply with the aid of pictures. In figure 13 you see that wood has very good properties when

11–12

(11) Anlage zur Erstellung von einfach gekrümmten Brettschichtträgern. Einfach gekrümmte Träger können auf solchen Anlagen effizient und präzise hergestellt werden. | The set-up for producing single-curved glulam beams. Single-curved beams can be produced efficiently and precisely with this system. (12) Anlage zur Erstellung von doppelt gekrümmten Brettschichtträgern. Im Vergleich mit einfach gekrümmten Trägern sind mehrfach gekrümmte deutlich aufwändiger in der Herstellung. Im Bild sieht man das Verfahren, bei dem ein einfach gekrümmter Brettschichtträger in Bretter geschnitten und dann in der zweiten Richtung gekrümmt und erneut verleimt wird. Alternativ werden auch Stäbe verleimt, wobei dann nur ein Verformungs- bzw. Verleimungsschritt notwendig ist. | The set-up for producing double-curved glulam beams. In comparison to single-curved beams, multiply curved glulam beams are considerably more difficult to manufacture. The picture shows the process by which a single-curved glulam beam is cut into boards and then curved in a second direction and glued again. Alternatively, there is a system where thin sticks are bent and glued together in a single step.
© Blumer-Lehmann AG

GAM: Also bis zu fünf Grad ist gerade noch O.K.?

KS: Ja, das ist noch O.K. Das ist relativ wenig. Das bedeutet, dass man beim Fräsen eines Bauteils genau darauf achten muss, dass der Kräfteverlauf immer entlang dieser Faser geht. Wir sprechen hier vom Faseranschnittswinkel. Auf Abbildung 11 sieht man einen einfach gekrümmten Träger. Theoretisch könnte man den auch aus einem riesigen Stück Holz herausfräsen. Aber die statischen Eigenschaften wären dann ganz schlecht, weil die Kräfte darin nicht entlang der Faser laufen. Die Lösung dafür ist, dass man das Holz in einzelne Bretter schneidet und dann biegt und im gebogenen Zustand verleimt. Für einfach gekrümmte Träger geht das recht effizient, das kann man komplett maschinell machen.

Für doppelt gekrümmte Träger ist das allerdings viel komplizierter (Abb. 12). Man kann ein Brett ja nur in eine Richtung biegen. Deswegen muss man das ganze Verfahren zweimal machen. Wenn der einfach gekrümmte Träger fertig ist, schneidet man ihn in der anderen Richtung in Bretter und krümmt und verleimt ihn in diese zweite Richtung. Da kann man sich vorstellen, wie viel komplizierter es ist, dieses Holz wirklich in die richtige Form zu kriegen. Wenn man die Abbildung genauer betrachtet, sieht man, dass es keine normalen Bretter mehr sind. Das sind gekrümmte Bretter, die hier ein zweites Mal gekrümmt wurden. Die Idee ist immer die gleiche. Man versucht, das Holz so hinzubekommen, dass der Kräfteverlauf der Faser folgt. Wenn ich Holz biege, dann versucht es, sich elastisch wieder zurückzuformen. Das heißt, in dem Moment, wo ich das Holz biege und miteinander verleime, habe ich einen Zustand, der stabil ist. Aber jede dieser Lamellen ist unter Spannung. Das ist also ein ganzes Bauteil, in dem unglaublich viele Spannungen drinstecken.

GAM: Diese gekrümmten oder doppelt gekrümmten Träger sind dann aber nur die Rohlinge, aus denen dann die endgültigen Träger präzise herausgefräst werden. Sind diese Rohlinge beim Swatch-Projekt auch bei den einzelnen Holzbaufirmen erstellt worden?

KS: Bei Swatch haben wir mit der Firma Hess zusammengearbeitet, die haben das anders gemacht. Das, was ich dir vorher gezeigt habe, war, dass man die Lamellen in eine Richtung krümmt, dann salamimäßig aufschneidet und dann in die andere Richtung krümmt.

GAM: Das „Salamiprinzip". Daneben gibt es aber auch noch das sogenannte „Spaghettiprinzip" …

KS: Genau. Die Firma Hess hat nach dem „Spaghettiprinzip" gearbeitet. Die haben statt Brettern einfach Stäbchen genommen. Die Stäbchen haben die Möglichkeit, dass man sie in beide Richtungen krümmen kann. Die Stäbchen hat man gebündelt in eine Form hineingelegt und verleimt. Dadurch hat man sich einen der beiden Prozesse gespart.

GAM: Und die Firma Hess hat das auch für die anderen Betriebe gemacht?

KS: Genau!

GAM: Dann war sozusagen nur mehr der Feinschliff zu machen?

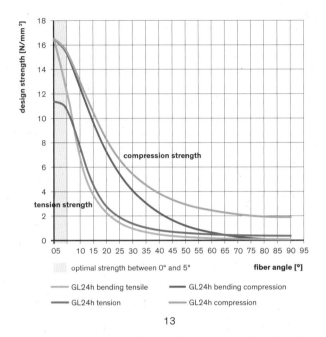

13

Faseranschnittswinkel als Festigkeitsparameter: Festigkeit auf Zug und Druck eines Brettschichtträgers der Festigkeitsklasse GL24h in Abhängigkeit des Faseranschnittswinkel. Bei einem Winkel von 0 bis 5 Grad sind die Werte am besten. | Fiber angle as a parameter of strength: tensile and compressive strength of a glulam beam of strength class GL24h in relation to the fiber angle. An angle of zero to five degrees produces the best values. © Blumer-Lehmann AG

compressive or tensile stress runs along the grain. Its properties under compression and tension get worse when deviating from this direction—up to about five degrees, it's still OK. At right angles to the grain, its properties are extremely poor.

GAM: So up to five degrees is still OK?

KS: Yes, that's still OK. That is relatively slight. That means that when milling a construction part you have to be very certain that the path of forces always moves along the grain. We talk about the fiber-cutting angle. In figure 11 you see the production of a single-curved glue laminated beam. Theoretically, you could also mill it out of a single, enormous piece of wood. But the structural properties would then be very bad, because the forces would no longer run along the grain. The solution is to cut the wood into single boards, curve them, and glue them in a curved state. For single-curved beams, that is very efficient; you can make them entirely by machine.

For double-curved beams, however, it is much more complicated (fig. 12). You can only bend a board in one direction, after all. For that reason, the whole procedure has to be

done twice. When the single-curved beam is finished, it is cut in the other direction into boards and glued together in this second direction. You can imagine how much more complicated it is to get this wood really into the right form. If you look at the illustration more closely, you will see that they are no longer normal boards. They are curved boards that were curved a second time here. The idea is always the same. You try to get the wood so that the lines of force follow the grain. When I bend wood, it tries to bend back elastically. That means that when I bend the wood and glue it together, then I have a state that is stable. But every one of these lamellae is under tension. It is a whole construction part in which there are an incredibly large number of tensions.

GAM: These single- or double-curved beams, however, are just the "raw parts" from which the beams are ultimately precisely milled. Were these raw parts for the Swatch project also manufactured by the various timber-construction companies?

KS: For Swatch, we worked with the firm Hess; they did it differently. What I just showed you was bending the laminations in one direction then cutting them up like a salami and bending them in the other direction.

Relationship between Radius and Lamella Thickness in Curved Glue Laminated Timber

t = Lamella Thickness?

Formula: Rmin / 200 = t Lamella

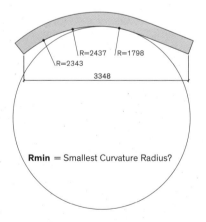

Rmin = Smallest Curvature Radius?

14

Der engste Krümmungsradius bestimmt die maximale Stärke der Lamellen eines gebogenen Brettschichtträgers. Als Faustregel gilt: die maximale Lamellenstärke ist 1/200 des kleinsten Radius. | The smallest curving radius determines the maximum laminate thickness of a bent glulam beam. The rule of thumb is that the maximum laminate thickness is 1/200th of the smallest radius. © Blumer-Lehmann AG

KS: Ja. Man versucht natürlich so sparsam wie möglich mit dem Material umzugehen. Ideal wäre, wenn man überhaupt nichts mehr abfräsen müsste in der Längsbearbeitung, aber mit dem ganzen Leim schafft man das nicht.

Wir schaffen auch nicht, die Krümmung perfekt hinzubekommen. Auch bei diesen Spaghettiträgern gibt es Rückstellungskräfte, das heißt, das Holz versucht, wieder gerade zu werden. Das ist nicht immer perfekt vorhersehbar. Meistens lassen wir ein Übermaß von zwei Zentimetern bei dieser Längsbearbeitung und diese zwei Zentimeter fräsen wir ab. Daraus ergibt sich dann noch eine andere Schwierigkeit. Manchmal ergibt es sich, dass ich beim Abfräsen genau auf der Ebene des Übergangs zwischen zwei Lamellen lande. Es kann sogar sein, dass die Schnittebene alle drei Zentimeter vom oberen Stab in den unteren Stab und dann wieder in den oberen Stab wechselt. Das sieht ästhetisch schwierig aus. Deshalb versuchen wir möglichst mit einer Längsbearbeitung innerhalb einer Lamelle oder innerhalb einer Schicht zu bleiben, um auch wirklich die ästhetisch schönen Faserverläufe zu haben. Wenn die einzelnen Stäbe dicker sind, dann ist das leichter, aber das kann man sich nicht immer aussuchen. Auf der Abbildung 14 sieht man, wie dick die Lamellen in Abhängigkeit von der Krümmung sein müssen. Es gibt unterschiedliche Richtwerte, aber meistens sprechen wir von einem Verhältnis von 1:200 von der Lamellendicke zum kleinsten Krümmungsradius im Träger. Wenn ich einen Radius von zwei Metern habe, ergibt das eine Lamellendicke von einem Zentimeter. Brettschichtholzträger haben normalerweise 40 Millimeter starke Lagen. Das lässt sich am günstigsten herstellen. Daraus ergibt sich, dass ein Krümmungsradius von acht Metern ein wirtschaftlich optimaler Radius ist.

Gekrümmtes Holz schlägt sich erheblich auf die Kosten nieder. Wenn ich einen Preis X habe für gerades Holz, dann ist in der Regel ein einfach gekrümmtes Holz zwei bis fünfmal teurer. Bei einer stärkeren Krümmung muss ich dünnere Lamellen nehmen und dann wird das bei den einfach gekrümmten Trägern teurer (Abb. 15). Bei doppelt gekrümmtem Holz wird es sogar bis zu fünfzehnmal teurer. Wir probieren, ein Gebäude so zu segmentieren, dass wir möglichst viel mit einem Krümmungsradius von acht Metern herstellen können, um weniger von dem sehr teuren Holz zu verwenden.

Auf den Abbildungen 9 und 10 sieht man ein Mockup, das wir für die Moschee in Cambridge gebaut haben (Abb. 8). Im unteren Bereich haben wir einfach gekrümmte BSH Träger verwendet, die bis in die Krone reichen. Oben mussten wir doppelt gekrümmte BSH Träger verwenden, bei welchen wir auch einen Wechsel der Lamellenschichtung haben. Dieses Mockup haben wir gemacht, um zu sehen, ob man den Wechsel von der Lamellenrichtung oder vom Holz von einem zum anderen sieht. Wenn man genau hinschaut, dann sieht man das natürlich, aber es funktioniert trotzdem.

GAM: Das heißt, es ist eine Optimierungsaufgabe, bei der auch die Ästhetik immer mit hineinspielt. Es ist ja schöner, die dickeren Querschnitte zu haben, rein optisch. Je dünner die „Spaghetti" werden, desto mehr entfernt man sich auch von dem, was man von der Anmutung her mit Holz verbindet. Letztlich geht es ja fast wieder in die Richtung einer Faserplatte, auch wenn die Faserrichtung noch stimmt. Das ist alles wirklich sehr beeindruckend und spannend auch als Optimierungsaufgabe. Aber angesichts dieses enormen Aufwands stellt man sich doch die Frage, ob das noch verhältnismäßig ist. Wäre so eine Struktur mit einem homogeneren Baustoff, zum Beispiel in Stahl, nicht einfacher und letztlich vielleicht auch materialgerechter herzustellen?

KS: Bei der Moschee haben wir zum Schluss relativ dünne und elegante Träger hinbekommen. Das heißt, wir schaffen es wirklich, mit der Faser zu arbeiten und die Faser so zu aktivieren, dass wir das Holz optimal in den Bauwerken anwenden können. Diese Freiformen sind Leuchtturmprojekte. Bei diesen Projekten geht es nicht darum, ein möglichst günstiges Projekt herzustellen. Leuchtturmprojekte braucht jede Gesellschaft, jedes Land, jede Stadt braucht seine kleinen Leuchtturmprojekte. Keine Stadt in Europa möchte einfach nur banale 08/15 Architektur haben. Wir brauchen das für den Tourismus, wir brauchen das für das Selbstbewusstsein und für die Identität der Städte. Ich glaube, das ist eine zentrale Aufgabe von Architektur.

Was wir mit Holz heutzutage machen, ist die Speerspitze, die zeigt, was mit Holz machbar ist. Es geht nicht darum, einfach nur billig mit Holz zu bauen, Holz zu verwenden, weil es ein billiger Baustoff ist. Es geht darum, Holz zu verwenden, weil es ein besserer Baustoff ist.

GAM: Bei der Moschee in Cambridge sprecht ihr in Bezug auf die Tragstruktur von Bäumen. Und das ist auch wirklich eine schöne Analogie. Dennoch liegt eine gewisse Absurdität darin, dass in der industriellen Holzproduktion erst mal alle gekrümmten Teile aussortiert werden. Die Bäume, die nicht gerade wachsen, die kann man da nicht brauchen. Und dann macht ihr, aus all diesen geraden Teilen, nach zahlreichen, logistisch komplexen High-Tech-Bearbeitungsschritten wieder etwas, das elegant und mehrfach gekrümmt ist und uns an die Form eines natürlich gewachsenen Baumes erinnert. Wäre es nicht eleganter, wenn man von Anfang an natürlich gewachsene, krumme Teile nehmen würde?

KS: Du hast in einem unserer Vorgespräche die Analogie mit der Geige gebracht. Bei der Geige geht es um eine enorme Veredelung vom Holz selbst. Man geht in einen Wald, man sucht sich genau den Baum aus, den man haben möchte für seine Geige, man lässt das Holz jahrelang trocknen, damit man möglichst alle Spannungsrisse herausbekommt, um dann schließlich daraus eine Geige zu bauen, als höchsten Schritt der Veredelung. Diese Geige ist in keiner Weise zu vergleichen mit einer Plastikgeige, die man im Supermarkt kauft. Da sind Welten dazwischen. Es geht da um den Respekt vor dem Material. Diesen

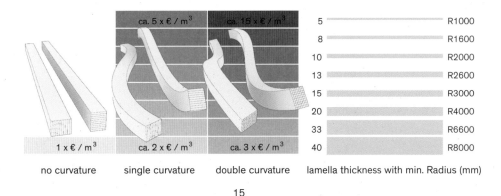

Geometry vs. Cost of Glue Laminated Timber

	ca. 5 x € / m³	ca. 15 x € / m³

1 x € / m³	ca. 2 x € / m³	ca. 3 x € / m³

no curvature	single curvature	double curvature

5	R1000
8	R1600
10	R2000
13	R2600
15	R3000
20	R4000
33	R6600
40	R8000

lamella thickness with min. Radius (mm)

15

Krümmung als Kostenfaktor: mehrfache Krümmung ist deutlich teurer als einfache, außerdem steigt der Preis, je enger der Radius ist, da immer dünnere Holzquerschnitte verleimt werden müssen. | Curving as a factor in costs: multiple curving is considerably more expensive than single curving; moreover, the price increases as the radius grows smaller, because thinner cross sections of wood have to be glued together. © Blumer-Lehmann AG

GAM: The "salami principle." But there is also the "spaghetti principle" …

KS: Precisely. The Hess firm worked using the "spaghetti principle." Rather than boards, they simply used "sticks." The sticks were bundled and placed into a form and glued. That skipped one of the two procedures.

GAM: And Hess did that for the other companies as well?

KS: Exactly!

GAM: Then you only have to do the finishing work, so to speak?

KS: Yes. Naturally, you try to be as economical with the material as possible. The ideal would be not milling anything off at all in the longitudinal processing, but with all the glue it's not possible. Nor do we manage to achieve the curvature perfectly. Even with these spaghetti beams, there are springback forces, that is to say: the wood tries to become straight again. That cannot always be predicted perfectly. Usually, we leave an excess of two centimeters in this longitudinal processing, and then we mill off these two centimeters. That results in yet another difficulty. Now it may be that when milling I end up precisely at the transition between two lamellae. It may be that the cut level alternates every three centimeters from the upper lamella to the lower lamella and then back to the upper one. That looks very problematic aesthetically. So during the longitudinal processing we try as much as possible to remain within

one lamella or within one layer, which also results in aesthetically beautiful grain patterns. That's easier if the individual layers are thicker, but you can't always have that. In figure 14 you see how thick the laminations have to be in relation to the curving. There are different benchmarks, but usually we speak of a ratio of 1:200 between lamella thickness and the smallest curvature radius in the beam. If I have a radius of two meters, that gives a lamella thickness of one centimeter. Glulam beams normally have laminations 40 millimeters thick. Those are the cheapest to produce. Thus, a curvature radius of eight meters is economically optimal.

Curving wood has a considerable effect on costs. If I have a price X for straight wood, a single-curved beam will, as a rule, be two to five times more expensive. With a sharper curve, I need thinner laminations, and then single-curved beams become even more expensive. Double-curved wood can cost up to fifteen times as much (fig. 15). We try to segment a building to produce as much as possible with a curvature radius of eight meters in order to use less of the very expensive wood.

Figures 9 and 10 show a mockup we built for the Cambridge mosque (fig. 8). In the lower area, we used single-curved glulam beams, which reach up into the crown. Up above, we had to use double-curved glulam beams, for which we also alternated the lamination thickness. We made this mockup to check whether one sees the alternations in the direction of lamination or from one wood to another. If you look closely, you see it, of course, but it works anyway.

Respekt würde ich auch für unsere Arbeit reklamieren. In meinen Augen liegt bei unserer Arbeit der Respekt vor dem Material darin, wie wir mit der Faser umgehen. Für mich ist das ein riesiger Unterschied, ob ich die Faser aktiviere, oder ob ich die Faser nicht aktiviere.

Es ist natürlich auch eine Frage der Perspektive. Wenn meine Perspektive ist, dass man Holz möglichst so, wie es aus dem Wald kommt, also ohne fremde Stoffe, ohne Leim usw. verwenden sollte, dann kommt man zu einer anderen Architektur. Da kommt man aber auch nicht unbedingt zu einer Geige. Aber ich will das eine nicht gegen das andere stellen. Es gibt den Stababbund, Hochhäuser aus CLT (Cross-Laminated Timber), den Modulbau, den normalen Holzbau und die Freiform. Holz ist vielfältig, es ermöglicht viele Ansätze und es geht nicht darum zu sagen, der eine Ansatz ist der richtige und der andere ist falsch. Sondern es geht darum, dass das Material vielseitig nutzbar ist. Es ist genauso in Ordnung, eine Cambridge Moschee mit gebogenen Trägern zu bauen, wo diese Technologie ausgelotet wird, wie es in Ordnung ist, ein Haus mit Mondholz zu bauen, das nur in bestimmten Momenten geschlagen wird und wo für die Verbindungen nur Holznägel verwendet werden. Zum Beispiel beim CLT, da baut man jetzt Hochhäuser. Es gibt Entwürfe, die bis zu 300 Meter hoch sind. Die Frage ist für mich nicht: „Macht es Sinn, 300 Meter hoch in Holz zu bauen?" Ausprobieren, wieviel geht, was möglich ist, das ist etwas sehr Menschliches. Dass diese Speerspitzenprojekte realisiert werden, dass jemand ein bisschen höher baut als jemand anderes, das gehört in der Welt der Architektur einfach dazu.

GAM: Wie weit haben diese Speerspitzen, wie Du sie nennst, das Potenzial irgendwann im Mainstream zu landen? Im Bereich der IT finden wir das normal, dass wir alle in unseren Taschen Geräte tragen, die vor wenigen Jahrzehnten noch Supercomputer gewesen wären. Glaubst Du, dass in der Holzarchitektur etwas Ähnliches passieren könnte? Werden die Leute sich irgendwann mal aus doppelt gekrümmten und gefrästen Hölzern gebaute Gazebos in ihren Garten stellen, die sie im Baumarkt gekauft haben? Oder glaubst du, dass in diesem Bereich so etwas nicht stattfinden kann?

KS: Ich glaube, dass es Nischenprojekte und spezielle Projekte und Aufgaben bleiben werden. Wenn ich jetzt nur den normalen Wohnungsbau betrachte, wo kann ich denn die Freiform einsetzen? Im Fußboden kann ich sie nicht einsetzen, in der Wand ist es meistens unpraktisch und die meisten Freiformprojekte, die wir haben, ob das Swatch oder die Moschee sind, sind Kuppelbauten und komplexe Dachkonstruktionen. Wir haben eine Villa in der Türkei für Norman Foster gebaut, in der wir auch ein Dach mit einer fliegenden Geometrie über einem relativ rechtwinkeligen Grundriss gebaut haben.

Wie gesagt, ich glaube diese Projekte werden zum größten Teil wirklich Leuchtturmprojekte bleiben. Es kann aber sein, dass es zunehmend auch kleinere Leuchtturmprojekte geben wird. Wir haben jetzt für das Kulturhaus in Böttstein ein Kuppeldach für den Gemeindesaal realisiert und das ist eine relativ günstige Freiform (Abb. 16). Bei diesem Projekt haben wir auch ohne Mockup gearbeitet. Es ist ein Tonnendach, wobei die Konstruktion einem Zollingerdach ähnelt. Das sieht jetzt allerdings nur aus wie ein Geflecht, in Wirklichkeit laufen die Träger nur in einer Richtung bis zum First. In der anderen haben wir kleine Träger, die einfach nur dazwischen gehängt sind. Man musste nur zwei Teile programmieren und diese dann in einer größeren Stückzahl herstellen.

GAM: Wie ist in diesem Fall die Zusammenarbeit mit den Architekten gewesen? Kannst Du Dich da in den Entwurf einbringen? Kannst Du das kurz beschreiben?

KS: Das kann ich nicht beschreiben, weil ich da nicht involviert war. Bei Herzog & de Meuron hatte ich 10 Jahre wirklich in den ersten Entwurfsphasen gearbeitet und jetzt bin ich sozusagen in der allerletzten Entwurfsphase dabei. Ich bin nur dann integriert, wenn es ganz am Anfang vom Entwurf darum geht, ob man etwas dieser Art technisch überhaupt herstellen kann. Also bei der Frage: Kriegen wir die Sachen gefräst?

GAM: Fehlt Dir das, bei der Konzeptfindung dabei zu sein?

KS: Nein, nicht unbedingt. Es gibt manchmal einen sehr großen Leidensweg bei ArchitektInnen, bis man ein Projekt wirklich auf den Weg bringt. Auch bei Herzog & de Meuron gab es Projekte, die haben viele Jahre gedauert, bis man wirklich in die Realisierung, in die Bauphase gekommen ist. Jetzt bekomme ich Projekte auf den Tisch, die unter einem enormen Kosten- und Zeitdruck stehen, aber die sind dann auch nach ein paar Monaten wieder weg. Dann kommen wieder neue Projekte. Ich glaube die Zeit, die ich jetzt habe, ist stressiger, aber spannender. Es ist eine enorme Befriedigung zu sehen, wenn unsere Arbeit das Werk verlässt. Wenn man weiß, da gehen jetzt 60 Lkws nach England. Wenn man diese riesigen Teile auf der Autobahn sieht und man weiß, die gehen nach Rotterdam, nach Korea oder woanders hin. Das ist für mich nach wie vor ein unglaublich faszinierender Moment.

Vor vielen Jahren bei Herzog & de Meuron habe ich mich einmal mit Pierre de Meuron darüber unterhalten, wo ich eigentlich hin möchte in meinem Leben mit der Architektur. Ich habe gesagt, ich sehe drei Bereiche: Den Bereich Design vom Architekten, den Entwurf; ich sehe den Bereich der Akademie, der Ausbildung und diesen Bereich der Produktion. Mich hat im Architekturbüro eigentlich gestört, dass ich in die Produktion nie hineinschauen konnte. Da war es für mich ein logischer Schritt, mal aus dem Büro hinaus und in die Produktion zu gehen. Ich hatte das Glück, zum richtigen Zeitpunkt bei Blumer Lehmann anzukommen, als gerade diese Projekte in der heißen Phase waren. Das war für mich ein sehr spannender Moment.

GAM: That means there is an optimization task in which aesthetics always plays a role. It is, after all, more beautiful to have the thicker cross sections—simply visually. The thinner the "spaghetti," the further one is from the "look" one associates with timber. Ultimately, it's almost like fiberboard, except that the correct fiber orientation has been preserved. All of that is really very impressive and exciting, also as an optimization task. But faced with this enormous effort, one has to ask if it's really worth it. Couldn't a structure of a more homogenous material, such as steel, be produced in a way that is simpler and finally, perhaps, truer to the material?

KS: For the mosque, in the end we managed relatively thin and elegant beams. That means we truly manage to work with the fibers and to activate them in a way that uses wood optimally in building. These free forms are lighthouse projects. The goal for these projects is not to produce the most affordable project possible. Every society needs lighthouse projects; every country, every city, needs its small lighthouse projects. No city in Europe wants to have only banal cookie-cutter architecture. We need something more for tourism; we need it for self-confidence and for the identity of cities. I believe that is a central task of architecture.

What we are doing with wood today is at the forefront of technology. It shows what is possible with wood. It is not just simply about building cheaply with wood, about using wood because it is the cheaper construction material. It is about using wood because it is a better construction material.

GAM: You speak of the mosque in Cambridge in relation to the load-bearing structure of trees. And that is truly a nice analogy. Nevertheless, it is also in a sense absurd that industrial timber production first sorts out all of the curvy parts. Trees that do not grow straight are useless. And then, in a number of logistically complex steps of high-tech processing you make something from all these straight parts that is elegantly and multiply curved and that reminds us of the form of a tree that has grown naturally. Wouldn't it be even more elegant if from the outset you could use naturally grown curved parts?

KS: In our preliminary conversations, you made the analogy to the violin. A violin is an enormous refinement of the wood itself. You go into a forest, search for exactly the tree you want to have for your violin, let the wood dry for years, during which all sorts of tension cracks might result, and then finally you build a violin from it, as the ultimate step of refinement. This violin can in no way be compared to a plastic violin you buy in the supermarket. There are worlds between them. It is about respect for the material. I would claim this respect for our work as well. In my eyes, in our work the respect for the material lies in how we deal with the fibers. For me, it is an enormous difference whether I activate the fibers or whether I don't activate the fibers.

It is, of course, also a question of perspective. If my perspective is that the wood should, as much as possible, be used as it comes from the forest, without foreign materials, without glue, and so on, then you will get a different architecture. But then you won't necessarily get a violin either. I don't want to set one against the other. There is frame joinery, high-rises of CLT (Cross-Laminated Timber), modular construction, normal timber construction, and free form. Wood is diverse; it permits many approaches, and the point is not to say that one approach is the right one and the other wrong. Rather, the point is that the material can be used in diverse ways. It is just as acceptable to build a mosque in Cambridge with curved beams in which this technology is explored, as it is to build with moon wood, which is from trees that are only felled at certain times, and where only wooden nails are used for joints. Take CLT, for example: now people are building high-rises with it. There are designs for building as tall as 300 meters. The question for me is not whether it makes sense to build in wood up to 300 meters. Trying out how far we can go, what is possible, that is something very human. That these spearhead projects are being built, that someone builds a little higher than someone else, that is simply part of the world of architecture.

GAM: To what extent do these spearhead projects, as you call them, have the potential to end up in the mainstream at some point? When it comes to IT, we find it normal that we carry around in our pockets devices that would have been supercomputers just a few decades ago. Do you believe that something similar could happen in wood architecture? Will people someday have gazebos in the garden that are made of doubly curved and milled timber parts that they bought at a home improvement store? Or do you believe that that won't happen in this sector?

KS: I believe these will continue to be niche projects and special projects and tasks. When I look at normal housing construction now, where can I employ free form? I can't use it for the floor; it's usually not practical for walls, and most of the freeform projects we have, whether for Swatch or the mosque, are dome

16

Das Tonnendach des Kulturhauses in Böttstein (Architektur: Haefeli Architekten, Döttingen) ähnelt einem Zollingerdach. Tatsächlich ist die Tragstruktur aus zwei Typen von jeweils einfach gekrümmten Brettschichtträgern zusammengesetzt: in einer Richtung reichen sie bis zum First, in der anderen sind es kurze Teile, die zwischen die Rippen eingesetzt wurden. | The barrel roof of the cultural center in Böttstein (architecture: Haefeli Architekten, Döttingen) resembles a Zollinger roof. The load-bearing structure is in fact a combination of two types of singly-curved glulam beams: in one direction, they extend to the ridge; in the other, they are short parts inserted between the ribs. © Andreas Buschmann

GAM: Kommen wir nochmals etwas allgemeiner auf die Zukunft des Holzbaus zu sprechen. Du hast ja eingangs schon gesagt, dass das Bauen mit Holz derzeit eine Blüte erlebt, vergleichbar damit, wie Anfang des 20. Jahrhunderts in der klassischen Moderne das Bauen mit Stahl und Glas entdeckt wurde. Wie wird sich das längerfristig entwickeln? Wie lang wird dieser Boom aus deiner Sicht noch anhalten?

KS: Ich glaube leider und Gott sei Dank lange. Leider, weil Holz wirklich ein adäquates Material ist, in der heutigen Zeit mit der Klimakrise, in die wir gerade hineinrutschen oder schon drin sind. Diese Klimakrise ist kein Hype, das ist kein Trend, der in zehn oder fünfzehn Jahren zu Ende gehen wird. Sondern das ist eine neue Realität, mit der wir uns in Zukunft auseinandersetzen müssen.

Gott sei Dank ist Holz ein gutes Material. Es ist nicht nur in der Lage, CO_2 zu binden, es hat auch sehr viele bautechnische Möglichkeiten. Deswegen glaube ich und wir bei Blumer Lehmann fest daran, dass das Bauen mit Holz jetzt nicht nur ein zeitlich kurzer Trend, ein Hype ist, dem man nachgeht und den man dann wieder verlässt. Ich glaube, dass das Material in der Architektur schon jetzt eine große Rolle spielt, und in Zukunft noch eine größere Rolle spielen wird.

GAM: Was empfiehlst Du ArchitektInnen in Bezug auf das Bauen mit Holz?

KS: Ich würde jungen Architektinnen und Architekten empfehlen, in ihrer Ausbildung einen Holzbauer zu besuchen oder noch besser ein Praktikum bei einem Holzbauer zu machen. Ich glaube, wenn ich mein Studium nochmals wiederholen könnte, hätte ich wahrscheinlich kein Praktikum in Architekturbüros gemacht, sondern bei einem Holzbauer. Ich glaube, das ist für einen jungen Architekten bzw. eine junge Architektin eine unglaubliche wertvolle Erfahrung.

GAM: Vielen Dank für das Gespräch! ∎

buildings and complex roof constructions. We worked on a villa in Turkey for Norman Foster in which we built a roof with a floating geometry over a relatively rectangular floor plan.

As I said, I believe these projects will for the most part truly remain lighthouse projects. But it may be that increasingly there are more smaller lighthouse projects as well. For the cultural center in Böttstein, we recently built a barrel roof for the community hall, and that is a relatively inexpensive free form (fig. 16). We worked without a mockup on that project. It is a barrel roof, though its construction resembles a Zollinger roof. It looks like wickerwork, but in reality, the beams extend to the roof ridge only in one direction. In the other direction, we have small beams that are simply placed between them. We only had to program two parts and then produce them in large quantities.

GAM: What was it like working with the architects in that case? Can you bring your own design ideas into it? Could you describe that briefly?

KS: I can't describe it, because I wasn't involved in the design of that one. At Herzog & de Meuron, I worked for ten years in the early design phases, but now I am involved in the very last design phase, as it were. I am only integrated at the very beginning of the design if there is a question about whether something is technically possible at all. That is, when the question is: Will we be able to mill this?

GAM: Do you miss being involved in conceptual design?

KS: No, not necessarily. Sometimes, it is a very long ordeal for architects before a project is really underway. Even at Herzog & de Meuron, there were projects that took many years before they were actually realized, before they made it to the construction phase. Now, the projects that land on my desk are under enormous pressure in terms of costs and time, but a few months later they are gone. There are always new projects. I believe that the time I have now is more stressful but also more exciting. It is an enormous satisfaction to see our work leaving the factory. When you know that, now, sixty trucks are leaving for England. When you see these enormous parts on the highway and know they are going to Rotterdam, to Korea, or somewhere else. That is still an incredibly fascinating moment for me.

At Herzog & de Meuron many years ago, I was talking to Pierre de Meuron about where I wanted to go with architecture in my life. I said I see three areas: the area of architectural design; I see the area of the academy, of education, and this area of production. It actually bothered me that in the architectural firm I could never get to see the production. That was a logical step for me, to get out of the office and into production. I had the good fortune to arrive at Blumer Lehmann right at the point when these projects were in a hot phase. That was a very exciting moment for me.

GAM: Let's get back to talking more generally about the future of timber construction. You said at the beginning that building with wood is currently experiencing a heyday, comparable to the beginning of the twentieth century when building with steel and glass was discovered by High Modernism. How will that evolve over the long term? How long will this boom last, in your view?

KS: I believe for a long time—unfortunately and thank God. Unfortunately, because wood is truly an appropriate material in the present time of climate crisis into which we are sliding or maybe in which we already find ourselves. This climate crisis is no hype; it's not a trend that will end in ten or fifteen years. Rather, it is a new reality that we will have to confront in the future.

But, thank God, wood is a good material. It's not only able to store CO_2 but also offers very many possibilities in terms of construction technology. For that reason, I believe, and we at Blumer Lehmann firmly believe, that building with wood is not just a brief trend, a hype that you chase and then abandon. I believe that this material already plays a big role in architecture and will play an even greater role in the future.

GAM: What do you recommend to architects about building with wood?

KS: I would recommend that young architects visit a timber construction company during their studies or, even better, do an internship with a timber construction company. If I could do my studies over again, I believe I probably wouldn't have done an internship in an architectural firm but rather at a timber construction company. I believe that's an incredibly valuable experience for a young architect.

GAM: Thank you for the interview! ∎

Translation: Steven Lindberg

Holzbau. Eine Überlebensstrategie

Timber Construction: A Strategy for Survival

Jens Ludloff

1   Ophelis Ausstellungshalle | Showroom for Ophelis, Bad Schönborn, Deutschland | Germany, 2018–2020 © Ludloff Ludloff, Photo: Jan Bitter

Holzbau kann als Methode begriffen werden, die aus tolerierbaren Ungenauigkeiten nachhaltig erfahrbare Architektur generiert. Holzbau kann ein andersartiges Raumvokabular und ein neues Raumverständnis hervorbringen. So kann Bauen mit Holz nicht zuletzt einen wesentlichen Beitrag zum Diskurs über nachhaltiges Handeln liefern.

Vorab. Nachhaltiges Handeln hat sich im aktuellen Diskurs vom vorausschauenden Agieren zu einer Anleitung zur Bewältigung von Krisen gewandelt. Mit dieser „Anerkennung", die der Ursprungsdefinition „vom nachhaltenden Handeln" von Carl von Carlowitz,[1] dem Oberbergmann August des Starken wieder näher kommt, erleben wir Nachhaltigkeit im Krisenmodus, als einen faktischen Zustand der Normalität. Daher wundert es nicht, dass der aktuelle gesellschaftliche Diskurs zu keiner echten Veränderung führt. Zwar wird in diesem Zusammenhang im politischen Feld immer wieder eine gesellschaftliche Wende angemahnt, also das Verlassen der bisher eingeübten Rituale. Aber von einer Umsetzung konkreter Handlungen kann weiterhin kaum die Rede sein. Durch ständigen folgenlosen Gebrauch sind selbst die Begriffe „Wende" oder eben auch „Nachhaltigkeit" bereits verbraucht, annektiert und weichgespült. Und doch ist das Wissen um die Notwendigkeit einer radikalen Veränderung des Handelns angesichts der Klimakrise allgegenwärtig.

Kultur. Höchstleistungen der Kulturen sind scheinbar untrennbar mit einem Maximum an Ressourcenverbrauch verbunden. Dies gilt historisch und aktuell für Rohstoffe, Energieträger und „Human Resources" gleichermaßen. Diese Erkenntnis scheint heute so interpretiert zu werden, dass kulturell asketische Zeiten auch besonders nachhaltige Epochen gewesen seien. Müssen wir also alle barocken Hüllen und jeden berauschend sinnlichen Lustgewinn, ja jeden ästhetischen Anspruch aufgeben, hilft nur die Askese, um eine „wirkliche Nachhaltigkeit" zu erreichen? Von der Aufklärung über den Humanismus zum Anthropozän[2] hat sich das menschliche Selbstbild radikal verändert – vom Lebensgefühl des „in der Welt sein" zum „an Bord sein".[3] Was ist notwendig, da uns die Götter verlassen haben, weil wir nicht mehr an sie glauben, damit wir selbst den Steuerknüppel in die Hände nehmen?

Steuern wir los. Ende der 1960er-Jahre hat Richard Buckminster Fuller die Erde in seinem Buch *Spaceship Earth*[4] mit einem Raumschiff verglichen und dargelegt, dass wir keine Gebrauchsanweisung zur Steuerung benötigen, da es sich um ein robustes Flugobjekt handelt. Es ist mit einer schützenden Hülle, der Atmosphäre, und mit einem Energielieferanten, der Sonne, ausgestattet, die mehr Energie bereitstellt als wir auf der Erde je verbrauchen könnten. Einschränkend weist er darauf hin, dass wir unseren Erkenntnissen folgen und gegensteuern müssen, falls es eines Gegensteuerns bedürfe. Dass

dieser Bedarf nunmehr besteht, ist offenkundig. Warum also ist die Spaltung von Erkenntnis und Handlung, d.h. Steuerung, so groß? Wenn das Steuern, also unser Verhalten, sich unter dem Eindruck neuer Erkenntnisse verändern würde, hätte es die Klimakrise von heute nie gegeben.

Raum- statt Weltraumerfahrung. Aktuell können wir feststellen, dass in der Corona-Pandemie konkrete wissenschaftliche Erkenntnisse als Handlungsanweisung unmittelbar in den politischen Raum gelangen und binnen kürzester Zeit in Gesetzesform lebensgestaltend wirksam werden. Es fragt sich, warum dieser „neue" Zusammenschluss von Wissenschaft und Politik nicht auch im Bezug auf die globale Erwärmung gelingt. Wo liegt der Unterschied? Was treibt uns jeweils an? Maßgebend für unser individuelles Handeln scheinen stets unsere Sinneserfahrungen und Wahrnehmungen im Sinne der „leiblichen Betroffenheit"[5] zu sein. Dagegen scheint die primär kognitive Verarbeitung einer Situation, wie jene der Klimaerwärmung, kein verantwortliches Handeln nach sich zu ziehen. Hier wird eine Spaltung zwischen Erleben und Wissen deutlich, gehören doch die uns global bedrohenden Symptome mittlerweile zu unserem selbstverständlichen Wissensbestand.

Was ist und was sein könnte. Der Architektur kommt im Erleben von leiblicher und damit auch ästhetischer Betroffenheit eine Schlüsselrolle zu. Auf die Ausstattung der Menschen, die neben dem „Wirklichkeitssinn", auch einen „Möglichkeitssinn" besitzen, hat uns Robert Musil in *Der Mann ohne Eigenschaften* aufmerksam gemacht.[6] Wir können nicht nur wahrnehmen was ist, sondern wir sind in der Lage uns vorzustellen, was sein könnte oder geschehen müsste – ein Denken, das im Entwurf und der Planung von Architektur seit jeher eine besondere Rolle spielt.

Jeder ist ein Entwerfer. Wenn wir den Gedanken vom „Anthroprozän" aufnehmen, so ist die bestehende Welt bereits von uns Menschen entworfen worden. Das Entwerfen ist eine Kulturtechnik, die der Mathematiker und Designtheoretiker Horst Rittel als eine Kompetenz des Alltags beschrieben hat.[7] Beispielsweise zeigt sich das Entwerfen im Alltag

1 Vgl. von Carlowitz, Carl: *Sylvicultura Oeconomica. Haußwirthliche Nachricht und Naturmäßige Anweisung zur wilden Baum-Zucht*, Leipzig 1713.

2 Vgl. Crutzen, Paul J.: „Geology of Mankind", *Nature* 415 (2002), 23.

3 Sloterdijk, Peter: „Wie groß ist ‚groß'", *Peter Sloterdijk – Philosoph und Schriftsteller*, online unter: https://petersloterdijk.net/2015/04/wie-gross-ist-gross/ (Stand: 19. Januar 2021).

4 Fuller, R. Buckminster: *Operating Manual for Spaceship Earth*, Carbondale 1969.

5 Böhme, Gernot: *Ethik leiblicher Existenz*, Frankfurt am Main 2008, 126.

6 Musil, Robert: *Der Mann ohne Eigenschaften*, Lausanne 1943, 16.

7 Vgl. Rittel, Horst W.J.: *Thinking Design. Transdisziplinäre Konzepte für Planer und Entwerfer*, neu herausgegeben von Rolf D. Reuter und Wolfgang Jonas, Basel 2013.

Timber construction is a method that utilizes tolerable imprecisions to create sustainable architecture. Timber construction produces a distinct vocabulary of space and a new understanding of space. Most importantly, building with wood makes an essential contribution to the discourse on sustainability.

First of All. Sustainable action has been transformed in the current discourse from prescient action to a way of handling crises. With this "recognition," which once again moves closer to the original eighteenth-century definition of "sustainable action" by Carl von Carlowitz, the head miner of Elector August the Strong of Saxony, we experience sustainability in a crisis mode, as a factual state of normality.[1] It is therefore unsurprising that current discourse does not lead to any real change in our society. Although in the political field there are repeated calls for society to change, that is, to abandon the rituals it has practiced thus far, very few concrete actions have actually been undertaken. Due to their constant but inconsequential use, terms such as "turnaround" and even "sustainability" have been worn out, annexed, and watered down. Yet awareness of the necessity of a radical change in action is omnipresent in the face of the climate crisis.

Culture. Great cultural achievements are believed to be inseparably associated with maximum consumption of resources. Both historically and in the present, this applies to raw materials, energy sources, and human resources in equal measure. This insight is interpreted today as meaning that culturally ascetic periods were especially sustainable eras. Does this mean that we have to abandon all Baroque façades, every intoxicatingly sensuous feeling of pleasure, and every aesthetic ambition? Is asceticism the only thing that can help us achieve "true sustainability"? Our self-image as human beings has radically changed from the Enlightenment by way of humanism to the Anthropocene[2]: from the feeling of "being in the world" to that of being "on board."[3] What is necessary—since the gods have abandoned us due to the fact that we no longer believe in them—for us to seize the controls ourselves?

Let's Take Control. In the late 1960s R. Buckminster Fuller compared the earth to a spaceship in his book *Operating Manual for Spaceship Earth*, explaining that since it is a robust flying object we do not need an instruction manual to steer it.[4] Equipped with a protective shell, the atmosphere, it also has a supplier of energy, the sun, that provides more energy than we could ever use on earth. He qualified this by pointing out that we have to follow our insights and steer in another direction when it becomes necessary. It is obvious that it is now necessary to do this. So why is there such a large division between insight and action—that is, in our steering? If we had changed our steering, or our behavior, when we gained new insights, today's climate crisis would never have occurred.

Experiencing Our Space Rather Than Outer Space. During the current coronavirus pandemic we have realized that specific scientific insights directly made their way into political space as instructions for taking action and within a very short time had an effect on our lives in the form of laws. The question remains why this "new" coalition of science and politics is unable to deal with global warming. What is the difference? What drives each of us? A crucial factor in our individual action invariably comes from our sensory experiences and perceptions, in the sense of having been "physically affected."[5] Conversely, processing a situation such as global warming in a primarily cognitive way does not necessarily lead to responsible action. This clearly reveals a division between life experience and knowledge, since the symptoms that threaten us globally have since become knowledge that we take for granted.

What Is and What Could Be. Architecture plays a key role in our experience of being affected physically and also aesthetically. In *The Man without Qualities*, Robert Musil pointed out that human beings are equipped not only with a "sense of reality" but also with a "sense of possibility."[6] Not only can we perceive what is but we are also in a position to imagine what could be or what would have to happen—thinking that has always played a special role in designing and planning architecture.

1 Carl von Carlowitz, *Sylvicultura Oeconomica: Hausswirthliche Nachricht und Naturmässige Anweisung zur wilden Baum-Zucht* (Leipzig, 1713).

2 See Paul J. Crutzen, "Geology of Mankind," *Nature* 415 (2002): 23.

3 Peter Sloterdijk, "Wie gross ist 'gross'?," *Peter Sloterdijk – Philosoph und Schriftsteller*, April 1, 2015, available online at: https://petersloterdijk.net/2015/04/wie-gross-ist-gross/ (accessed January 19, 2021).

4 R. Buckminster Fuller, *Operating Manual for Spaceship Earth* (Carbondale, 1969).

5 Böhme, Gernot: *Ethik leiblicher Existenz*, Frankfurt am Main 2008, 126 (Transl. S.L.).

6 Robert Musil, *The Man without Qualities*, trans. Sophie Wilkins and Burton Pike, vol. 1 (New York, 1995), 10–11.

bei der Zubereitung eines Essens mit der Einkaufsplanung. Die Planung denkt das, was sein kann und auch das, was sein wird, voraus. Folglich sind alle Menschen geübte Entwerferinnen und Entwerfer, einige von uns sind darüber hinaus Architektinnen und Architekten geworden.

Wissenschaft und Demokratie. Bezogen auf den Klimawandel beruht unser Verständnis seit den Aufzeichnungen Alexander von Humboldts auf wissenschaftlicher Erkenntnis, Kartierungen und physikalischen Gesetzmäßigkeiten. Die Physik duldet Ungenauigkeiten, die sich statistisch egalisieren lassen, aber keine Kompromisse. Die Grundlage der Demokratie hingegen ist der Kompromiss. Die Protagonistinnen und Protagonisten der Bewegung „Fridays for Future"[8] fordern hingegen das Primat der Wissenschaft. Was brauchen wir in dieser Situation? „Urteilskraft!" würde Hannah Arendt sagen,[9] aber wie wir feststellen müssen, reicht diese in aktuellen demokratischen Gesellschaften nicht aus, um den Wandel tatsächlich in Gang zu setzen.

Urteilskraft und leibliche Betroffenheit, das Analoge in der digitalen Welt. In seiner Bauhauslehre stellte Josef Albers die Aufgabe, aus einem Blatt Papier einen Raum zu erzeugen – einen Raum in der Fläche zu „entdecken" statt ihn zu erfinden.[10] Das verbindet Albers' Forschungen zu Raum und Scheinraum[11] unmittelbar mit den Forschungen Frei Ottos[12] zu Minimalflächen aus Seifenhäuten. Beide Entwurfstechniken besitzen eine direkte Verbindung zum parametrischen Entwerfen. Bei diesem werden Parameter definiert und damit ein Modell, das sich dynamisch entwickelt. Albers hat auf das Denken in analogen Farbräumen hingewiesen und uns geholfen, zwischen physischem und psychischem Raum zu unterscheiden, um den dreidimensional erlebten Raum im real zweidimensionalen Bild nutzen zu können. Die Konstruktionen Frei Ottos auf Grundlage der Minimalflächenforschung wie auch die 1972 in Mannheim realisierte Multihalle gaben und geben einen Vorgeschmack, wie viel Emotion, Ausschweifung und Ekstase der konsequenten Reduktion der Mittel innewohnen kann. Wir benötigen also, entgegen dem eingangs zitierten Carlowitz'schen Nachhaltigkeitsbegriff, kein protestantisches Maßhalten, sondern Parameter, die unsere Lebensgrundlage auf eine neue emotionale Basis stellen. Dies wird keine Frage des Stils, sondern zwingend eine der Methode sein.

Holz kann eine Antwort sein. 1914, also vor über 100 Jahren, publizierte Le Corbusier seinen Entwurf des „Maison Dom-Ino".[13] Als Architektinnen und Architekten müssen wir uns fragen lassen, was seit der Entwicklung dieses genialen Prototyps des Stahlbetonbaus eigentlich passiert ist? Weltweit, zumindest für das Gros der Bauproduktion, nicht viel. Le Corbusiers räumlich-konstruktive Einheit steht nach wie vor für ein kaum einholbares Erfolgsmodell, das jedoch allein aufgrund der Endlichkeit der Ressourcen zwingend eines Nachfolgers bedarf.

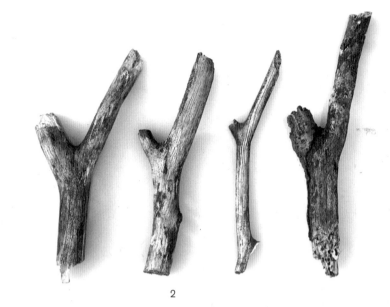

2

Astgabeln aus Buchenholz | Forked beech branches, Fundort | located at Brandenburg Werbellinsee © Ludloff Ludloff

Hat die Moderne, bis auf wenige Ausnahmen, die Chancen des Holzbaus verkannt? Holz kann eine Antwort sein. Aus dem Holzbau eine Methode zu machen wäre die Aufgabe. Bäume bilden vornehmlich linear gegliederte Wuchsformen aus, hieraus konnten historisch nur stabförmige Bauteile geschnitten werden. Seit Einführung des Sperrholzes 1858 durch Bruno Harras in Thüringen und spätestens seit 1932 nach der Patentierung der Spanplatte durch Max Himmelheber, hat die Holzverarbeitung zahlreiche Weiterentwicklungen und -nutzungen erfahren. Die Nutzung von Zellbestandteilen und die Holzverarbeitung zum Kompositwerkstoff gehören dazu.

Auf der Suche nach Methoden für neue Prototypen des Holzbaus, in Anerkennung des Erfolgsmodells „Maison Dom-Ino", beschäftigen wir uns in Forschungsprojekten an der Universität Stuttgart und in unserem Berliner Büro mit bewusst profanen Konstruktionen, die eine verblüffende Faszination des Einfachen hervorrufen. Die im weiteren beschriebenen Denkansätze sind Praxistests unter aktuellen Marktbe-

8 Vgl. Thunberg, Greta: „Natürlich bin ich privilegiert", Interview mit Greta Thunberg geführt von Bernd Ulrich, *Zeit Online*, 27. August 2020, online unter: https://www.zeit.de/2020/36/greta-thunberg-angela-merkel-klimakrise-klimabewegung-fridays-for-future?utm_referrer=https%3A%2F%2Fwww.google.com%2F (Stand: 19. Januar 2021).

9 Arendt, Hannah: *Vita activa oder Vom tätigen Leben*, Stuttgart 1960.

10 Vgl. Kühnlein, Andreas: „Der Künstler als Entdecker", *Bauhaus. Zeitschrift der Stiftung Bauhaus Dessau* 1 (2011), 27.

11 Vgl. Albers, Josef: *Interaction of Color*, New Haven 2006.

12 Vgl. Schriftenreihe IL 1 und IL 13, Institut für Leichtbau Entwerfen und Konstruieren, Stuttgart 1971/1978.

13 Le Corbusier: *Le Corbusier et Pierre Jeanneret. Oeuvre complète. 1910–1929*, Bd. 1, Zürich 1929.

3

Ophelis Ausstellungshalle | Showroom for Ophelis, Bad Schönborn
2018–2020 © Ludloff Ludloff, Photo: Jan Bitter

Everyone Is a Designer. If we accept the idea of the "Anthropocene," the existing world is already one designed by us human beings. Design is a cultural technology that the mathematician and design theorist Horst Rittel has described as a quotidian competency.[7] One example of everyday design is preparing a meal by planning the shopping. Planning thinks ahead about what can be and also what will be. Consequently, everyone is a trained designer; some of us have even become architects.

Science and Democracy. With respect to climate change, ever since Alexander von Humboldt's field notes our understanding has been based on scientific insight, mapping, and physical laws. Although physics tolerates imprecisions that balance each other out statistically, it does not tolerate compromises. The foundation of democracy, by contrast, is compromise. The protagonists of the Fridays for Future movement, by contrast, call for the primacy of science.[8] What do we need in this situation? "Judgment!" would be Hannah Arendt's response.[9] However, in our current democratic societies we are forced to acknowledge that this is not enough to truly set transformation in motion.

Judgment and Physical Impact: The Analogue in the Digital World. In his preliminary course at the Bauhaus, Josef Albers set the task of creating a space with a sheet of paper—"discovering" a space in the plane rather than inventing it.[10] That directly connects Albers's research on space and the appearance of space[11] to Frei Otto's research into creating minimal surfaces with soap film.[12] Both design techniques have a direct connection to parametric design, which defines parameters that result in a dynamically evolving model. Albers alluded to thinking in analogous color spaces and thus helped us distinguish between physical and psychological space so that we could use the space that we experience three-dimensionally in the actual two-dimensional image. Frei Otto's constructions based on his research on minimal surfaces—such as the Multihalle built in Mannheim in 1972—once offered and in fact still offer a foretaste of how much emotion, excess, and ecstasy can be inherent in a project of such rigorous reduction. Contrary to Carlowitz's concept of sustainability quoted at the beginning of this essay, instead of Protestant restraint we need parameters that create a new emotional foundation for our lives. It will not be a question of style but rather necessarily one of method.

Wood Might Be the Answer. In 1914, more than a hundred years ago, Le Corbusier published his design for the Maison Dom-Ino.[13] As architects, we have to ask ourselves what has really happened since this brilliant prototype for reinforced-concrete construction was developed—and we have to conclude that not a lot has happened worldwide, at least for the majority of buildings produced. Le Corbusier's spatial-constructive unity is still a unique model of success that urgently needs a successor, not just due to our limited resources. Did modernism generally underestimate the opportunities of building with wood? Wood might be the answer. The challenge would be to make a method of timber construction. Due to the fact that trees grow for the most part in forms articulated by lines, only beam-shaped construction parts could be cut from them historically. Since Bruno Harras introduced plywood in Thuringia in 1858 and at least since 1932, when pressboard

7   See Horst W.J. Rittel, *Thinking Design: Transdisziplinäre Konzepte für Planer und Entwerfer*, ed. Rolf D. Reuter and Wolfgang Jonas (Basel, 2013).

8   Greta Thunberg, "Natürlich bin ich privilegiert," interview by Bernd Ulrich, *Zeit Online*, August 27, 2020, available online at: https://www.zeit.de/2020/36/greta-thunberg-angela-merkel-klimakrise-klimabewegung-fridays-for-future?utm_referrer=https%3A%2F%2Fwww.google.com%2F (accessed January 19, 2021).

9   Hannah Arendt, *The Human Condition* (Chicago, 1958).

10 See Andreas Kühnlein, "Der Künstler als Entdecker," *Bauhaus: Zeitschrift der Stiftung Bauhaus Dessau* 1 (2011): 27.

11 See Josef Albers, *Interaction of Color*, rev. ed. (New Haven, CT, 2006).

12 See Schriftenreihe IL 1 and IL 13, Institut für Leichtbau Entwerfen und Konstruieren (Stuttgart, 1971 and 1978).

13 See Le Corbusier, *Le Corbusier and Pierre Jeanneret: Oeuvre complete*, vol. 1, 1910–1929 (Zurich, 1929).

4

Ophelis Ausstellungshalle | Showroom for Ophelis, Bad Schönborn
2018–2020 © Ludloff Ludloff, Photo: Jan Bitter

dieser holzsparenden Bauweise in ganz Europa. Die Zollinger-bauweise kann als eine, wenn auch nicht geradlinige, Weiter-entwicklung zu einem räumlichen Tragwerk angesehen werden. Rund 100 Jahre nach Gilly wurde so, wiederum aus Gründen der Holzersparnis, mit kurzen Brettern ein rautenförmiges Stabnetzwerk ausgebildet. Diese Dachkonstruktion, ebenso wie die hölzerne Gitterschale der Multihalle von Frei Otto in Mannheim erleben aktuell eine Renaissance, wie an Beispielen wie dem Centre Pompidou Metz oder der Werkhalle für Elite Holzbau bei Berlin deutlich wird.

Ein Merkmal verbindet all diese materialoptimier-ten, ein- oder zweiachsig gekrümmten Konstruktionen: die Schwäche des Knotens. Das Schwinden und Kriechen der Hölzer verringert auf Dauer die notwendige Biegesteifigkeit der Knoten, ein sich durch die gesamte Konstruktionsgeschich-te ziehendes Problem. Zwei Lösungsmöglichkeiten bieten sich hier an: Entweder man findet den universalen Knoten, wie ihn Konrad Wachsmann mit den zeittypischen Methoden der se-riellen Fertigung untersuchte, oder man verzichtet, im Sinne der Reduktion der Mittel, gänzlich auf den Knoten.

Analogie und Abstraktion 1: Die einachsig ge-spannte Astwerkdecke. Die Tragfähigkeit einer kreuzweise verleimten, 49 Millimeter starken Furnierschichtholzplatte, Kerto Q genannt, weckte unser Interesse beim Projekt einer Mensa[16] als Erweiterungsbau einer Schule auf dem Tempelhofer Feld in Berlin. Dieses als Hochleistungsprodukt aus Leim und Holzfurnier beworbene, scheibenförmige Element bildete die Basis unseres Gedankens, konstruktive Merkmale der Stahlbe-tondecke in eine Holzbaukonstruktion zu transformieren. Die einfache Frage, die wir gemeinsam mit den Tragwerksplanern Carsten Hein und Tim Göckel von Arup Berlin vor 12 Jahren diskutierten, war: Unter welchen Umständen können Träger ihre Tragwirkung entfalten, obwohl sie unterbrochen sind und somit ihre Last nicht direkt von Auflager zu Auflager transpor-tieren können? Die Übergreifungslängen der Stabstähle bei

dingungen und sollen helfen, Denkräume zu öffnen und die Rationalität und Urteilskraft in einen sinnlich wahrnehmba-ren Kontext zu setzen.

Prototypen und Methoden. Die faszinierend ein-fachen Konstruktionen des französischen Architekten Philibert de l'Orme (um 1510–1570) sind der Ausgangspunkt zahlreicher Lehrbuchpublikationen[14] und dürfen daher als Grundwissen jeder Holzbauerin und jedes Holzbauers angesehen werden. Die Entwicklung seines Bohlenbinders, eines weitgespannten Tragwerks aus kurzen, minderwertigen Brettern, war dem Raubbau an Wäldern und damit dem Mangel an großformati-gen Balkenquerschnitten im Frankreich der Mitte des 16. Jahr-hunderts geschuldet. 200 Jahre später leistete der Baureformer David Gilly in seinen in Berlin veröffentlichten Schriften[15] ei-nen wesentlichen Beitrag zur Propagierung und Verbreitung

14 Vgl. L'Orme, Philibert de: *Architecture de Philibert de l'Orme: oeuvre entière contenant unze livres*, Rouen 1648.

15 Folgende Aufsätze von Gilly wurden in Berlin publiziert: „Ueber Erfindung, Construction und Vortheile der Bohlen-Dächer" (1797), „Von den Bohlen-dächern überhaupt" (1800), „Etwas über die Bohlendächer und deren Construction" (1800), „Etwas über Bohlendächer" (1801), „Anleitung zur Anwendung der Bohlen-Dächer bey ökonomischen Gebäuden und insbesondere bey den Scheunen" (1801), „Über die Wiedererbauung der Kuppel der sogenannten Halle-au-bled in Paris" (1805).

16 Berliner Holzbaupreis 2019, Senatsverwaltung für Stadtentwicklung Berlin; vgl. dazu ludloff + ludloff/Kammleithner, Christa: „Über die Zusam-mensetzung von Atmosphären", *ARCH+ features 6. ludloff + ludloff, ARCH+* 189 (2008), 206–7; Haberle, Heiko: „Zerschnitten, zerstreut und zusammengeklebt", *Bauwelt* 7–8 (2010), 36–37; Fritzen, Klaus: „Neue Wege im Holzbau", *Bauen mit Holz* 9 (2009), 23–25; Göckel, Tim/Ludloff, Jens: „Gleichklang: Form & Konstruktion", *Bauen mit Holz* 9 (2009), 22–26; Schnittich, Christian (Hg.): *Einfach Bauen 2. Nachhaltig, kostengünstig, lokal*, Editon Detail, Basel 2012; Hartmann, Jonis: *Wiederkehr und Mehr-deutigkeit: Entwurfswerkzeuge der Architektur*, Wiesbaden 2016.

was patented by Max Himmelheber, the processing of wood has evolved in numerous ways. New uses include cellular components and processing to make composite materials.

In our search for methods to create new prototypes of timber construction and in recognition of the success of the Maison Dom-Ino model, we are conducting research projects at the University of Stuttgart and in our Berlin office to develop deliberately profane constructions that elicit an astonishing fascination in their simplicity. The approaches described in the following are practical tests under current market conditions; they are intended to help open up spaces for thought and to put rationality and power of judgment in a context that can be perceived by the senses.

Prototypes and Methods. The intriguingly simple constructions of the French architect Philibert de l'Orme (ca. 1510–1570) are the point of departure for numerous published textbooks and can therefore be considered basic knowledge for anyone who builds with wood.[14] The development of the plank roof truss—a broad, load-bearing structure composed of short, low-grade boards, was developed as a consequence of the despoliation of forests and the resulting shortage of beams of large cross section in France in the mid-sixteenth century. Two hundred years later, the writings of the architectural reformer David Gilly, published in Berlin, made an essential contribution to propagating and disseminating this wood-saving method of building throughout Europe.[15] The Zollinger system can be seen as a further development of a three-dimensional load-bearing structure. Roughly a century after Gilly, and once again in order to save wood, this system consists of a diamond-shaped network of short boards. Similar to the wooden lattice shell of Frei Otto's Multihalle in Mannheim, this roof construction is currently enjoying a renaissance, with examples including the Centre Pompidou in Metz or the workshop for Elite Holzbau in Berlin.

One feature shared by all of these material-optimized, uni- or biaxially curved constructions is the weakness of the nodes. Over time the shrinkage and creepage of the wood reduces the necessary bending resistance of the nodes—a problem that runs through the whole history of construction. There are two possible solutions: either developing a universal connector, as Konrad Wachsmann explored with methods of serial manufacturing that were typical at the time, or doing without nodes, in the spirit of reducing materials.

Analogy and Abstraction 1: The Uniaxially Spanned Branchwork Roof. The load-bearing capacity of a 49-millimeter-thick veneered laminated board that is glued crosswise, called Kerto Q, caught our interest during a school expansion project for a cafeteria at Tempelhofer Feld in Berlin.[16] This panel-shaped element, which had been advertised as a high-performance product made of glue and wood veneer, inspired us to transform certain features of the reinforced-concrete roof construction into a timber construction. The simple question that we discussed twelve years ago with the structural engineers Carsten Hein and Tim Göckel of Arup Berlin was: under what conditions can load-bearing members still perform that function even when there is an interruption that prevents them from transferring their load directly from support to support? The overlapping lengths of steel rods in load-bearing structures of reinforced steel would be the suitable analogy because when subjected to a tensile load, the steel rods inside the concrete transfer the load by means of overlapping lengths, without the rods themselves being connected to one another. Using this concept, we developed a lamella ceiling in a series of experiments with Arup, consisting of lamellae applied to plywood boards by pressure gluing on simple solid constructional timber that serve as T-beams without interconnecting nodes. Every lamella is required to bend, and the overlapping rods are sufficient to transfer the shear forces via the laminated-wood board to the next lamella. The 49-millimeter-thick roof panel with lamellae glued beneath it spans the 9.4-meter-wide cafeteria and resembles branchwork. The design of the joints in the bearing area of the roof was equally simple. Here there was no need for joining supports and beams; the roof panel, which helps bear the load, was placed on the supports of the post-and-beam façade and secured only to prevent it from shifting.

14 See Philibert de L'Orme, *L'architecture de Philibert de l'Orme*, 11 vols. (Rouen, 1648).

15 The following writings were published by Gilly in Berlin: *Ueber Erfindung, Construction und Vortheile der Bohlen-Dächer* (On the Invention, Construction, and Advantages of Plank Roofs), 1797; "Von den Bohlendächern überhaupt" (On Plank Roofs in General), 1800; "Etwas über die Bohlendächer und deren Construction" (Regarding Plank Roofs and Their Construction), 1800; "Etwas über Bohlendächer" (Regarding Plank Roofs), 1801; *Anleitung zur Anwendung der Bohlen-Dächer bey ökonomischen Gebäuden und insbesondere bey den Scheunen* (Directions for the Use of Plank Roofs for Outbuildings and Especially Barns), 1801; and "Über die Wiedererbauung der Kuppel der so-genannten Halle-au-bled in Paris" (On the Reconstruction of the Dome of the So-Called Halle-au-bled in Paris), 1805.

16 Berliner Holzbaupreis 2019, Senatsverwaltung für Stadtentwicklung Berlin. See also ludloff + ludloff and Christa Kammleithner, "Über die Zusammensetzung von Atmosphären," *ARCH+* 189 (2008): 206–207; Heiko Haberle, "Zerschnitten, zerstreut und zusammengeklebt," *Bauwelt* 7–8 (2010): 36–37; Klaus Fritzen, "Neue Wege im Holzbau," *Bauen mit Holz* 9 (2009): 23–25; Tim Göckel and Jens Ludloff, "Gleichklang: Form & Konstruktion," *Bauen mit Holz* 9 (2009): 22–26; Christian Schnittich, *Einfach Bauen 2: Nachhaltig, kostengünstig, lokal*, Edition Detail (Basel, 2012); Jonis Hartmann, *Wiederkehr und Mehrdeutigkeit: Entwurfswerkzeuge der Architektur* (Wiesbaden, 2016).

Tragwerken aus Stahlbeton waren die passende Analogie, denn bei diesen findet die Lastabtragung der zugbelasteten Stähle innerhalb des Betons mittels Übergreifungslängen statt, ohne dass die Stähle selbst kraftschlüssig miteinander verbunden wären. Mit diesem Konzept haben wir in Versuchsreihen mit Arup eine Lamellendecke entwickelt, deren Lamellen, die mittels Pressverleimung aus einfachem KVH auf die Sperrholzplatte aufgebracht werden, eine Plattenbalkenwirkung entfalten, ohne dass sie untereinander mit Knoten verbunden sind. Jede Lamelle wird hier auf Biegung beansprucht. Die Übergreifungslängen reichen aus, um die Querkräfte über die Furnierschichtholzplatte auf die nächstliegende Lamelle weiterzuleiten. Die 49 Millimeter starke Dachscheibe mit untergeleimten Lamellen überspannt den 9,50 Meter tiefen Mensaraum, wodurch das Bild eines Astwerks entstand. Die Fügung des Deckentragwerks im Auflagerbereich gestaltete sich ebenso einfach. Hier konnte auf die Fügung von Stütze und Träger verzichtet werden, die mittragende Dachscheibe wurde auf die Stützen der Pfostenriegelfassade aufgelegt und nur gegen Verschieben gesichert.

Analogie und Abstraktion 2: Die Sterndecke.

Ebene, zweiachsig gespannte Deckenkonstruktionen sind im Holzbau selten. Dies leisten z.B. Kassettendecken, die in Form von Brettstapeln konstruiert sein müssen, wie das Werk von Julius Natterer schlüssig nachweist. Als eine gelungene Alternative kann die Decke in der päpstlichen Aula im Palazzo Piccolomini in Pienza, ein Hebelstabwerk, betrachtet werden. Den statischen Luxus einer gleichwertig tragenden Zweiachsigkeit, wie es sich die heute im Bürobau weit verbreitete Flachdecke aus Stahlbeton leistet, bieten die aktuell verfügbaren Plattenwerkstoffe (KLH, Furnierschichtplatten) der Holzindustrie erstaunlicherweise nicht. Dabei hilft dieses Lastverhalten bei einem geringeren Materialeinsatz auch dabei, die Durchbiegung zu reduzieren. Die aus dem Gussmaterial Beton heute verbreitete Flachdecke wurde aus der unterzuglosen Pilzkopfdecke (Robert Maillart, Zürich 1910) so lange weiter entwickelt, bis die Pilzköpfe in der Plattenebene verschwunden waren und, zumindest räumlich, ein langweiliges Produkt entstanden war. Die Zulieferindustrie des Holzbaus bietet heute auch für diesen Bereich Metallverbindungen als „Durchstanzbewehrungen" an, eine fehlverstandene analogische Schlussfolgerung.

Wir hatten die Aufgabe, für den baden-württembergischen Büromöbelhersteller ophelis eine 1.500 Quadratmeter große Ausstellungshalle zu entwerfen. Diese Halle sollte mit einer reduzierten Anzahl von Stützen flexibel für wechselnde Ausstellungen nutzbar sein. Hier bot sich die Gelegenheit, unseren Ansatz der für die Mensa entwickelten „Astwerkdecke" mit dem Ingenieurbüro Külich als knotenlose Lamellendecke unter Ausnutzung der Tragfunktion des Plattenbalkens weiter

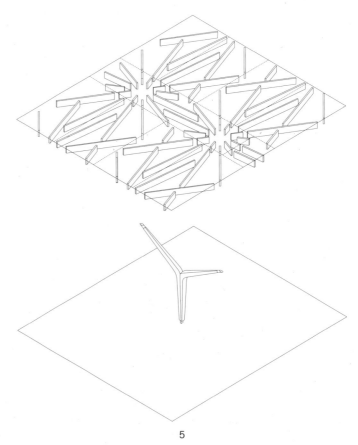

5

Sprengisometrie, Ophelis Ausstellungshalle | Exploded isometric view, showroom for Ophelis, Bad Schönborn 2018–2020 © Ludloff Ludloff

zu entwickeln. Als Deckenscheibe wurde 16 Zentimeter starkes Kreuzlagenholz verwendet und das Deckentragwerk mit sternförmig aufgeleimten BSH-Lamellen in die Lage versetzt, mehrachsig zu spannen. Anders als im Stahlbeton ist die Deckenplatte nicht monolithisch gegossen. Dies ist für das Plattentragwerk auch nicht notwendig, da alle Plattenstöße in den Bereich der Momentennullpunkte gelegt wurden. In den Plattenstößen werden nur Schubkräfte übertragen, was durch eine einfache Verschraubung gewährleistet wird.

Errichtet wurde das Tragwerk, indem zunächst zwei Stützenreihen der Y-förmigen Träger und der zugehörigen Deckenplatten mit den pressverleimten Lamellen aufgestellt wurden. Im Anschluss wurden diese Deckenstreifen dann mit den Zwischenelementen zu einem mehrachsig gespannten Tragwerk zusammengefügt. Da die Stöße der Deckenelemente keine Momente aufnehmen müssen, ist es nicht notwendig, die Lamellen über den Elementstoß zu führen. Damit ist das Zusammenfügen vorgefertigter tragender Deckenelemente zu einer mehrachsig gespannten Plattenbalkendecke möglich. Die aus zwei transportfähigen Halbrahmen zusammengesetzten Y-Stützen, im Abstand von 14 Metern, sind als Pendelstützen ausgebildet. Die Außenfassade mit gläsernem Oberlichtband und schneckenförmig eingeschriebenem Konferenzsaal steift das Gebäude aus. Aus der geschlossenen, ringförmig angelegten Holztafelbaufassade kragen die Pfosten als eingespannte

Analogy and Abstraction 2: The Star Roof. Flat, biaxially spanned roof constructions are rarely built with wood. Coffered ceilings, which must be constructed in the form of stacks of boards, are an exception, as the work of Julius Natterer convincingly demonstrates. The reciprocal frame of the ceiling of the papal auditorium of Palazzo Piccolomini in Pienza is a marvelous alternative. The structural luxury of biaxiality that provides equal support in both directions—as is common today, for example, in office buildings with flat roofs of reinforced concrete—is, surprisingly, not offered by industrial board material currently on the market (cross-laminated timber, or CLT, and laminated veneer lumber, or LVT). Yet this load behavior can help reduce deflection with a minimal use of materials. The now common flat roof made of poured concrete gradually evolved from the beamless mushroom roof (developed by Robert Maillart in Zurich, 1910) until the column capitals disappeared into flat plate, producing a boring effect, at least in terms of the space. The ancillary industry of timber construction now offers metal connectors as "punching reinforcements"—an inference by analogy based on a misunderstanding.

We were given the task of designing a 1,500-square-meter showroom for the office furniture manufacturer Ophelis in Baden-Württemberg. To provide flexibility for changing displays, the showroom was to have a reduced number of supports. This provided an opportunity to continue developing the "branchwork ceiling" we had created for the cafeteria in collaboration with the Külich engineering firm, now as a jointless lamella ceiling using the load-bearing function of the T-beam. Sixteen-centimeter-thick cross-laminated timber was used for the roof panel, and BSH lamellae were glued in a radial pattern to the roof truss to make multiaxial spanning possible. Unlike reinforced concrete, the T-beam is not cast in one piece. Nor is that necessary for the roof panel, since all of the joints were located at points of zero bending moment. Only shear forces are transferred to the plate joints, which was achieved simply by bolting.

The load-bearing structure was assembled by first erecting two rows of Y-shaped supports and the corresponding roof panel with press-glued lamellae. Then these ceiling strips were joined by elements in between to form a multiaxially spanned load-bearing structure. Because the joints of the ceiling elements did not have to absorb any moments, it was not necessary to continue the lamellae across the element joint. This made it possible to join prefabricated, load-bearing ceiling elements together to form a multiaxially spanned T-beam ceiling. The Y-supports, which were assembled from two transportable half-frames, are designed as hinged columns fourteen

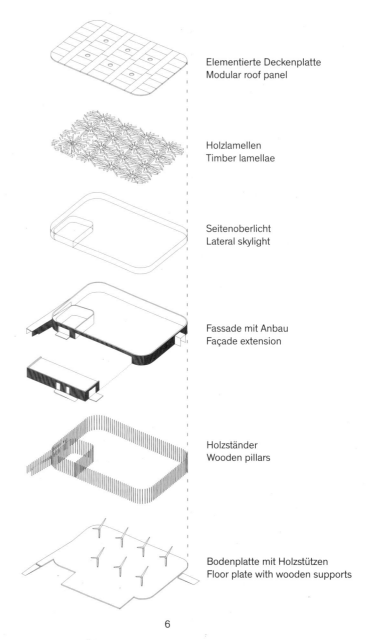

Elementierte Deckenplatte
Modular roof panel

Holzlamellen
Timber lamellae

Seitenoberlicht
Lateral skylight

Fassade mit Anbau
Façade extension

Holzständer
Wooden pillars

Bodenplatte mit Holzstützen
Floor plate with wooden supports

6

Sprengisometrie, Ophelis Ausstellungshalle | Exploded isometric view, showroom for Ophelis, Bad Schönborn 2018–2020 © Ludloff Ludloff

meters apart. The exterior façade, with a ribbon window skylight and a conference room inscribed into a snail shape, reinforces the building. Projecting 1.3 meters beyond the closed, ring-shaped, wood-paneled façade are posts that function as tied supports, on which the roof panel rests in the façade area. Skylights placed here and there cast shadowy light entering through openings in the ceiling onto artificial treetops, creating a world inside that deliberately evokes associations with natural spaces. It is against this atmospheric backdrop—and not in a white cube—that the models of this furniture maker are now presented for future working environments and homes.

Stützen 1,30 Meter aus, auf der die Deckenplatte im Bereich der Fassaden aufgelagert ist. Punktuell angeordnete Oberlichter werfen schattiges Licht durch Deckenöffnungen in künstliche Baumkronen und so entsteht eine Innenwelt, die bewusst Assoziationen an Naturräume wachruft. Nicht in einem „white cube", sondern vor diesem atmosphärischen Hintergrund werden die Modelle des Möbelherstellers für zukünftige Arbeits- und Lebenswelten präsentiert.

Der digitale Wald. Die Waldwirtschaft hat den zwingend notwendigen Umbau längst verstanden, Forstwirte denken in längeren Zeiträumen, aus Monostrukturen entstehen längst wieder diverse, artenreiche Lebensräume. Individuelle Holzentnahmen sind durch die umfängliche Digitalisierung des Waldes problemlos möglich. Diese Digitalisierung wird uns eine ähnliche Revolution wie die Entwicklung der Sägewerke bescheren. Industrielle Bretter halfen dabei, die Balloon-Frame-Konstruktion als einfache Hausform in Nordamerika zu verbreiten. Studierende der AA-London haben die digitale Abbildbarkeit des Waldes im Rahmen eines Design-Build-Projekts in einem Wald im südenglischen Dorset herausgearbeitet.[17] Im Hooke Park wurden Astgabeln gescannt und mit digitaler Unterstützung für die Nutzung als Tragwerk analysiert und zum Bau einer Scheune, „Wood Chip Barn", ausgewählt. Die biegesteifen Naturverbindungen der Astgabeln konnten dank dreidimensionaler Scans und digitaler Frästechnik in ihrer naturbelassenen Wuchsform genutzt und miteinander verbunden werden. Bereits dieses kleine Projekt zeigt, welche Entwicklungsmöglichkeiten in digitaler Forstwirtschaft, Planung und Holzbearbeitung stecken.

Wissen. Eine Klimakrise hätte es nie gegeben, wenn ein neuer Wissensstand unser Verhalten verändern würde. Lernprozesse werden weniger durch Argumente und Fakten angestoßen als durch gelebte Beispiele, also das gelungene Experiment, das Realisierte des so nie Vorstellbaren. Die Gewohnheit zementiert die Verhältnisse, in der Krise sind unsere Gewohnheiten auf den Prüfstand gestellt. Aus der Reflexion aktueller Diskurse müssen Prototypen nachhaltiger Handlungsdisziplin entwickelt werden, die als Modelle einer forschenden und produzierenden Praxis umsetzbar sind. Wir erkennen, dass das Geschehen auf der Makroebene vom Zustand auf der Mikroebene abhängt.

Holzbau als Methode. Holz und damit den Holzbau als Methode einer neuen Raumstruktur zu verstehen, begreift Bauen als eine komplett neue Form der Ökonomie, in der Ökologie, Forst- und Bauwirtschaft untrennbar verbunden sind und Architektur vom Rohstoff aus gedacht, mit dem Pflanzen von Bäumen beginnt. Damit kann es gelingen, Bauen als einen umfassenden Prozess der Teilhabe zu etablieren, der Ökonomie und Nachhaltigkeit auf eine neue Basis stellt.

Dabei wird nicht verkannt, dass Architektinnen und Architekten im Spannungsfeld divergierender Interessen arbeiten, in dem sie „alternative Zukünfte" entwerfen können. Unser methodischer Ansatz als Architektinnen und Architekten muss darin bestehen, Erfahrungen aus dem Raum der Einzelphänomene und der flüchtigen Kreativität in eine, wie oben skizziert, neue, gemeinsam durchsetzbare Bewegung nachhaltig erfahrbarer Architektur zu überführen.

Physik und Raum. Wenn wir für Wissenschaftlerinnen und Wissenschaftler planen, müsste die Nähe zum Faktischen am dichtesten sein. Das von Konrad Wachsmann 1929 für Albert Einstein in Caputh am Templiner See errichtete Sommerhaus aus Holz scheint hier die real existierende Gegenthese. Zwar lagen der Wahl des Baustoffs Holz physikalische Überlegungen zugrunde, doch war es der Wunsch des Bauherrn, ein „Schweizer Blockhaus" zu errichten. Die sichtbaren Köpfe der Deckenbalken erinnern noch heute an diesen Wunsch, dem Wachsmann als modern gesinnter Architekt nur ungern nachkam, indem er diese, konstruktiv nicht notwendig, als Ornament in der Fassade verankerte. Es dürfte keine Katastrophe darstellen, wenn sich die Physik betrügen lassen will, und dies emotionale Anforderungen befriedigt. „Physikalisch ausgedrückt" handelt es sich um eine tolerierbare Ungenauigkeit.

Neugierde und Empathie. Es wird keine Bauanleitungen aus der Natur geben. Je unveredelter wir jedoch mit den nachwachsenden Rohstoffen umgehen, um so reduzierter sind alle weiteren notwendigen energetischen Prozesse. Der Holzbau bietet die Chance, das Verständnis der Konstruktion vom Rohstoff her neu zu denken. Dabei bietet der stabförmige und verästelte Habitus der Ressource Wald ein noch zu entdeckendes Spektrum. Ein völlig andersartiges Raumvokabular kann entstehen. Zukünftig wird keiner Analogie des gegossenen, abgeformten Betons mehr bedürfen. Durch ein Holztragwerk, das sich von den profanen physikalischen Grundlagen der Schwerkraft zu emanzipieren scheint und uns zu einem neuen Raumverständnis führt, kann die Transformation vom Relief zum Raum gelingen. Wie dies aussehen kann, zeigt bis heute Frei Ottos Multihalle in Mannheim aus dem Jahr 1975.

Wissenschaftliche Praxis, die auf Empathie gründet, schöpft neue Methoden aus „tolerierbaren Ungenauigkeiten" und lotet diese bewusst in den Betrachtungen des Faktischen aus. Vergleichbar mit dem Phänomen der Atmosphäre, die zwischen uns und unserer Umgebung aufgespannt ist,[18] können wir auch den erweiterten digitalen Raum als Raum einer menschgemachten Weltkonstruktion begreifen und den Platz am Steuer mit Lust annehmen. ∎

17 Vgl. „Hooke Park" – AA School's Woodland Campus, online unter: http://hookepark.aaschool.ac.uk/ (Stand: 19. Januar 2021).

18 Vgl. Böhme, Gernot: *Atmosphäre. Essays zur neuen Ästhetik*, Frankfurt am Main 1995.

The Digital Forest. The urgent need for restructuring has long been an issue in forestry: foresters think in the long term, and monocultures are being changed back into diverse habitats for many species. Harvesting of individual trees is no longer a problem due to extensive digitization of the forest. The revolution that this digitization will bring is comparable to the rise of sawmills. Industrially produced boards helped spread balloon-frame construction as a simple form of housing in North America. As part of a design-build project in a forest in Dorset in southern England, students from the AA School in London have worked out how to represent the forest with digital means.[17] In Hooke Park, forked branches were scanned and, with the help of computers, analyzed for use as supports and selected to build a structure called the Wood Chip Barn. Forked branches are natural connectors that are resistant to bending, and, thanks to three-dimensional scans and digital milling technology, they could be used in the form in which they had grown naturally and then connected to one another. Even this small project demonstrates the potential for developments in digital forestry, planning, and wood projects.

Knowledge. There would never have been a climate crisis if new knowledge actually changed our behavior. Learning processes are motivated less by arguments and facts than by real-life examples such as the successful experiment of making something previously unimaginable a reality. Habits cement relationships, and our habits are put to the test in crises. Prototypes for sustainable disciplined action that can be implemented as models for research and production have to be developed through reflection on current discourses. We recognize that what happens on the macrolevel depends on the state of the microlevel.

Timber Construction as Method. Understanding wood and timber construction as a method for creating a new spatial structure means understanding building as a completely new form of economy in which the ecology, forestry, and the construction business are inseparably connected and architecture is conceived from its raw materials outward, beginning with the planting of trees. In this way, building can be successfully established as a comprehensive process of participation in a new foundation of efficiency and sustainability. This does not ignore the fact that architects work in the area of tension between divergent interests in which they can design "alternative futures." Our methodological approach as architects must be to transfer experiences from the space of individual phenomena and fleeting creativity into a new, jointly achievable movement, like the one described above, for architecture that can be experienced as sustainable.

Physics and Space. When designing for scientists, it is important to stick very close to the fact. The wooden summer house that Konrad Wachsmann built for Albert Einstein in 1929 in Caputh near Potsdam would appear to represent the very antithesis of this. Although the choice of wood as the construction material was based on physical considerations, the client wished to build a "Swiss log cabin." The visible heads of the ceiling beams still remind us of that wish today, which the modern-minded architect Wachsmann fulfilled only unhappily, by anchoring this structurally unnecessary element in the façade as an ornament. Surely it is no catastrophe if one wishes to deceive the laws of physics, and it even satisfies emotional requirements. "Expressed in terms of physics," it is a tolerable imprecision.

Curiosity and Empathy. Nature will not provide building instructions. But the more we work with unprocessed renewable resources, the more we will reduce all other necessary energy processes. Timber construction offers an opportunity to reassess our understanding of construction from the raw materials outward. The stick-like and ramified resource of the forest offers a spectrum of possibilities that remains to be discovered. A completely different spatial vocabulary can result. In the future, we will no longer need any analogy to poured and shaped concrete. A load-bearing structure in wood that appears to emancipate itself from the profane physical laws of gravity and to lead us to a new understanding of space achieves the transformation from relief to space. Even today, Frei Otto's Multihalle in Mannheim from 1975 demonstrates to us what that might look like.

Scientific practice based on empathy creates new methods of "tolerable imprecisions" and consciously explores them in observations of the factual. Similar to the phenomenon of atmosphere, which is stretched between us and our environment, we can also perceive expanded digital space as a human-made world construction and happily take control.[18] ∎

Translation: Steven Lindberg

17 See Hooke Park—AA School's Woodland Campus, available online at: http://hookepark.aaschool.ac.uk/ (accessed January 19, 2021).

18 Gernot Böhme, *Atmosphäre* (Frankfurt am Main, 1995).

"Cambio": Val di Fiemme

Formafantasma | Andrea Trimarchi & Simone Farresin

The following series of photographs has been taken from our multidisciplinary project "Cambio," (lat. *cambium*: change, exchange) an investigation into the governance of the timber industry, exhibited in the form of a video installation at the Serpentine Galleries in London from March 4 to May 17, 2020. The installation documents the topography of Val di Fiemme, a valley in Northern Italy whose forest was ravaged by the storm "Vaia" in 2018 and during which more than thirteen million trees were blown down. This natural disaster required an immediate response from the local community who had been managing the forest since the middle ages. Several factors had to be considered in the urgency of this effort: to prevent the wood from decaying and releasing unanticipated amounts of carbon dioxide into the atmosphere, to safeguard the community's livelihood, and finally, to learn from the disaster by reintroducing a larger variety of species into the valley.

One of the felled trees provided the wood for all of the displays and seating designed for the exhibition at the Serpentine Gallery. This decision followed our belief that in design materials should be chosen not only on the basis of aesthetic reasons but also on the basis of their original context and method of extraction. ■

Die nachfolgenden Aufnahmen entstanden im Rahmen unseres multidisziplinären Projekts „Cambio" (lat. *cambium*: Wandel, Austausch), das Steuerungs- und Lenkungsformen der Holzindustrie näher in den Blick nimmt und dessen Ergebnisse von 4. März bis 17. Mai 2020 in den Serpentine Galleries in London ausgestellt wurden. Die Installation dokumentiert die Topografie des im Norden Italiens gelegenen Fleimstals, in dem 2018 das Sturmtief „Vaia" mehr als dreizehn Millionen Bäume zu Fall brachte. Die Katastrophe verlangte eine sofortige Reaktion der lokalen Bevölkerung, die den Waldbestand der Region seit dem Mittelalter forstwirtschaftlich nutzt. Die Dringlichkeit der Lage erforderte dabei die Berücksichtigung unterschiedlicher Faktoren: das Schadholz musste vor Zersetzung bewahrt, der unerwartete Ausstoß von großen Mengen CO_2 in die Atmosphäre verhindert und die Existenzgrundlage der Gemeinde musste gesichert werden; als Lehre aus dem Unglück galt es zudem, im Ökosystem des Tals wieder eine größere Artenvielfalt anzusiedeln.

Einer der durch den Sturm entwurzelten Bäume lieferte das Baumaterial für die für „Cambio" entworfenen Ausstellungsdisplays und Sitzgelegenheiten. Diese Entscheidung gründet auf unserer Überzeugung, dass die Wahl des Materials für einen Entwurf nicht ausschließlich aufgrund von ästhetischer Wirkung, sondern auch unter Berücksichtigung von ursprünglichem Kontext und der Methode seiner Erzeugung getroffen werden sollte. ■

Übersetzung: Petra Eckhard

2

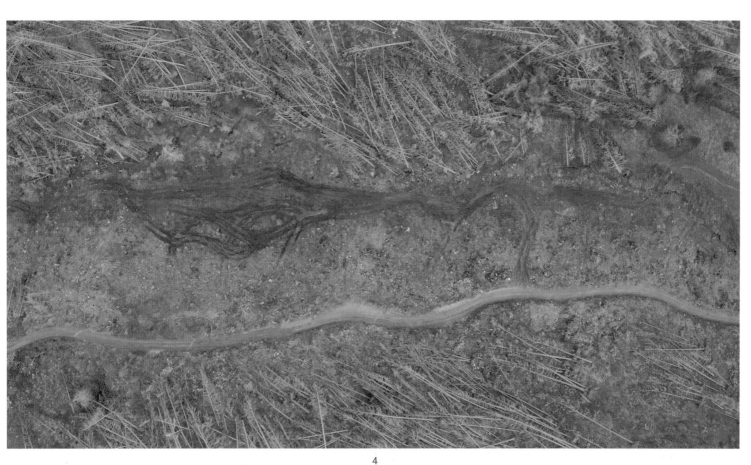

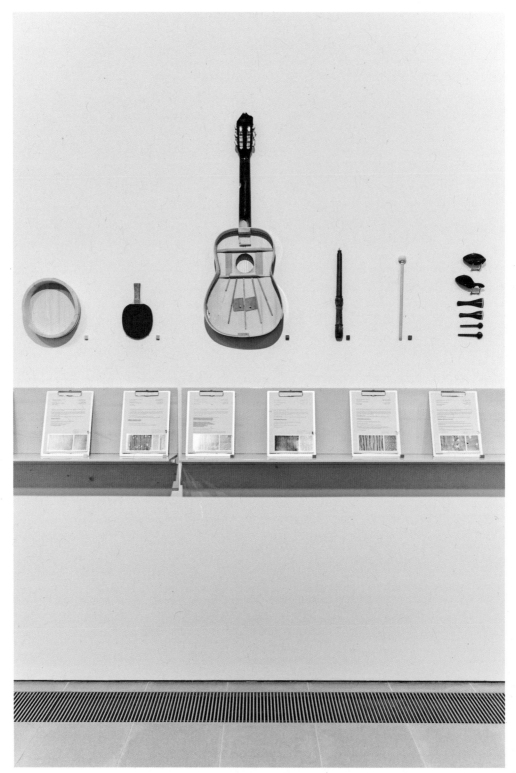

Material Territory

Fireground

Don Fuchs

On the 26th of October 2019, a lightning strike set a eucalyptus tree ablaze and started the Gospers Mountain fire in Wollemi National Park, north-west of Sydney. The blaze lasted 79 days, destroyed 10,000 km² bushland and over 100 houses and is now seen as one of the biggest bushfires in Australian history. In January 2020, after the fire finally run its course, Australia-based German photographer Don Fuchs began a long-term project documenting the regeneration of the devastated forests. His stark images tell the story of unimaginable destruction but also hope. Soon after the fire catastrophe, delicate shoots broke through the blackened bark of trees, much needed rain triggered the growth of eucalyptus and grass trees on the charred ground. His collection of photographs, taken over a time span of 12 months will be published in a book for the Australian Geographic Society in 2021. ∎

Am 26. Oktober 2019 schlug ein Blitz in einen Eukalyptusbaum des Wollemi Nationalparks ein und verursachte damit das verheerende Gospers Mountain Buschfeuer im Nordwesten Sydneys. Das Feuer wütete 79 Tage und zerstörte 10.000 Quadratkilometer Buschland sowie über 100 Häuser. Es gilt damit als eines der größten Buschfeuer in der Geschichte Australiens. Im Januar 2020, als der Brand schließlich eingedämmt werden konnte, begann der deutsche, in Australien wohnhafte Fotograf Don Fuchs damit, die Regeneration der verwüsteten Waldlandschaft zu dokumentieren. Seine im folgenden Beitrag gezeigten Fotografien erzählen eine Geschichte der unfassbaren Zerstörung aber auch der Hoffnung. Kurz nachdem das Feuer erlosch, bahnten sich zarte Triebe durch die geschwärzten Rinden, und erlösende Regenfälle ließen Eukalyptus- und Grasbäume erneut aus dem verkohlten Boden sprießen. Die Sammlung an Fotografien, die über den Zeitraum von zwölf Monaten entstanden sind, werden 2021 in Buchform im Auftrag der Australian Geographic Society veröffentlicht. ∎

Übersetzung: Petra Eckhard

Timber Territory: Salvaging a Resilient Timber Architecture in the Pacific Northwest

Timber Territory. Territoriale Aspekte der Holzwirtschaft im Nordwesten der USA

Laila Seewang

2

Blowdown | Wurf- und Bruchschaden, Mount St. Helens, 1980 © Lyn Topinka, United States Geological Society

The volcanic eruption that blew off most of Mount St. Helens' north face on May 18, 1980, also produced the largest landslide ever recorded (fig. 2). The blowdown consisted of over four billion board feet of Douglas Fir lying on the ground, and buyers of whole, damaged, logs needed to be found quickly before logs rotted or became infested with insects. From one day to the next, the nature of lumber exports in the Pacific Northwest of the USA changed direction.[1] While an export industry for unprocessed logs had been supplying the Pacific Rim since the nineteenth-century, it was by now largely a supplement to the domestic lumber mills for which most timber was destined. Suddenly the enormous salvage operation turned the market to China, which had recently opened up to trade with the USA and imported logs to use as concrete formwork or scaffolding. For local lumber mills, this event opened a decade that would see most of them close. They had already experienced a decline as automation changed the timber industry and by

June 22, 1990, environmental efforts to stop the rapid over-cutting of old-growth forest would result in the listing of the Spotted Owl as an endangered species that lived in them. Immediately, logging on Federal lands almost ceased. It was the final blow: a timber industry based on clear-cutting that outpaced young, plantation-style regrowth, aimed at producing the light-weight timber framing for most American housing, and an entire way of life based upon this, was blown down too.

Old-growth is the mythical center around which both the timber industry and environment science, for different reasons, revolved: trees older than 200 years, up to 1,000, years old that support entire forest eco-systems and that largely disappeared from continental Europe centuries ago. Trees of this

1 Like the Tillamook Burn(s) of the 1930s–1940s or the Columbus Day Storm of 1962, the blowdown forced everyone's hand, demanding near instantaneous public-private decision making about the fate of the downed trees before they rotted.

Der Vulkanausbruch vom 18. Mai 1980 sprengte fast die ganze Nordflanke des Mount St. Helens ab und verursachte damit den größten je verzeichneten Bergrutsch (Abb. 2). Der Bruch- und Wurfschaden belief sich auf rund eine Million Festmeter Douglastannen, und es mussten eilig Käufer für das beschädigte Rundholz gefunden werden, ehe dieses verrottete oder von Insekten befallen wurde. Von einem Tag auf den anderen wechselte der Holzexport im pazifischen Nordwesten damit die Richtung.[1] Eine Exportindustrie, die seit dem 19. Jahrhundert den gesamten pazifischen Raum mit unbearbeitetem Rundholz beliefert hatte, war damals bereits weitgehend zu einem Versorger der heimischen verarbeitenden Holzindustrie geworden. Nun aber verschob die Bergung der gewaltigen Materialmenge den Markt plötzlich in Richtung China, das sich gerade für Importe aus den USA geöffnet hatte und das Holz für Verschalungs- und Einrüstungszwecke importierte. Für die lokalen Sägewerke an der Nordwestküste der USA markierte der Vulkanausbruch den Beginn eines Jahrzehnts, an dessen Ende viele von ihnen vor der Schließung standen. Die zunehmende Automatisierung hatte sie bereits vor große Herausforderungen gestellt, und schließlich wurde am 22. Juni 1990 – im Zuge der Bemühungen von UmweltschützerInnen, die rasche Abholzung des Urwaldbestands zu bremsen –, der darin lebende Fleckenkauz auf die Liste der bedrohten Arten gesetzt. Dies bedeutete nicht nur das Ende einer Holzwirtschaft, die auf der Basis von Kahlschlag, der durch den Nachwuchs junger Plantagenwälder nicht kompensiert werden konnte, sondern auch das Ende eines ganzen, darauf beruhenden ländlichen Lebensstils.

Der in Europa bereits seit Jahrhunderten weitgehend verschwundene Urwald – zweihundert bis tausend Jahre alte Bäume, die ganze Waldökosysteme erhalten – bildet im Nordwesten der USA den mythischen Kern sowohl der Holzwirtschaft als auch der Umweltwissenschaften. Bäume dieser Größenordnung sind wesentlich effizienter zu verarbeiten als kleine Bäume, und ihr Verschwinden beschleunigte sich nach 1950, als im Bundesbesitz befindliche Wälder für den Hausbauboom der Nachkriegsjahre abgeholzt wurden.[2] Privates Waldland wurde häufig durch altersgleiche, dreißigjährige Monokulturen aus Douglastannen ersetzt, die das beliebteste Bauholz in Nordamerika und Asien sind und an der Westküste über 100 Meter hoch werden können. Bis 1990 wurde der Urwald so auf 13 bis 18 Prozent des ursprünglichen Bestands reduziert, und vom Restbestand befinden sich 78 Prozent in Bundesforsten. Vermutlich ist es sogar noch weniger.[3] Aber seit Ankunft der Europäer im Nordwesten der USA galt der Urwald mit seinen Douglastannen und seiner in Sekundärwäldern unerreichten Biodiversität, auch als ein letztes Stück Wildnis. Während der 1970er- und 1980er-Jahre, als diese Bäume immer rascher verschwanden, begann die Öffentlichkeit in ihnen mehr als nur Nutzholz zu sehen. „Aus dieser kleinen Veränderung entwickelte sich eine epische Schlacht, die zuerst den Nordwesten und dann das ganze Land erfasste."[4] Irgendwo zwischen Automatisierung, einem neuen Bewusstsein von der Bedeutung des Urwalds für die Ökologie des Planeten, einem Vulkanausbruch, Holzexporten und einer zurückgezogen lebenden Eulenart waren bis 1990 die „Timber Wars" entflammt.[5]

Sobald der Fleckenkauz auf die Liste der vom Urwald abhängigen gefährdeten Arten gekommen war, wurde der Kahlschlag in den Bundesforsten gestoppt. Die Reaktion folgte auf dem Fuß: Brandstiftungen machten Notverkäufe erforderlich; AktivistInnen ketteten sich an Bäume; Holzverkäufe wurden frühmorgens am Ostersonntag bekanntgegeben, damit die Öffentlichkeit nicht Wind davon erhielt; Fleckenkäuze wurden geschossen und angeblich sogar verspeist.[6] Das Ganze entwickelte sich zu einem Konflikt zwischen Stadt und Land, der die letzten zwanzig Jahre kultureller Gegensätze in Oregon und den Vereinigten Staaten insgesamt kennzeichnete. Aber auch wenn er fast durchgehend als einer zwischen ForstarbeiterInnen und UmweltschützerInnen, zwischen Menschen auf der einen und Eulen und alten Bäumen auf der anderen Seite charakterisiert wurde – in Wirklichkeit ging das komplexe, von der Holzindustrie geprägte Beziehungsgefüge auf die Verhältnisse des 19. Jahrhunderts zurück, in denen Holzarbeiter ebenso ausgebeutet wurden wie Bäume. Das auf den Nordwesten begrenzte Problem wirkte sich sogar auf die Präsidentschaftswahlen von 1992 aus, und als Bill Clinton zum Präsidenten gewählt worden war, flogen er, Vizepräsident Al Gore und das halbe Kabinett in dem Versuch, Frieden zu stiften, zu einem Holzgipfel nach Portland. Dieser führte zum „Northwest Forest Plan", eine Reihe von Bundesrichtlinien, deren Entwicklung noch nicht abgeschlossen ist. Lose auf den Ideen der „New

1 Wie die Tillamook Waldbrände der 1930er- bis 1940er-Jahre oder der Sturm am Columbus Day 1962 brachte der Wurf durch den Vulkanausbruch alle in Zugzwang und verlangte nach sofortigen Entscheidungen zwischen öffentlicher und privater Seite über das Schicksal der umgefallenen Bäume, ehe sie verrotteten.

2 Diese Abholzung war keineswegs umstritten, sondern folgte der damals üblichen Praxis. Im Rückblick wurde der Vorwurf erhoben, die Forstverwaltung habe eine „Orgie unnachhaltiger Abholzung" angeführt. Hirt, Paul W.: *A Conspiracy of Optimism: Management of National Forests since World War Two*, Lincoln, NE/London 1994, 294. (Übers. W.P.)

3 Laut einer Schätzung von 2006, da die U.S.-Forstverwaltung erst vor relativ Kurzem begonnen hat, Buch über den Zustand des „Altbestands" (älter als fünfzig Jahre) zu führen. Vgl. dazu LeGue, Chandra: *Oregon's Ancient Forests*, Seattle 2019, 20–24; Strittholt, James R./Dellasala, Dominick A./Jiang, Hong: „Status of Mature and Old-Growth Forests in the Pacific Northwest", *Conservation Biology* 20, 2 (2006), 363–374.

4 Scott, Aaron: „The Timber Wars", Episode 1, Oregon Public Broadcasting, online unter: https://www.opb.org/show/timberwars/ (Stand: 30. November, 2020).

5 Mit diesem Begriff wird umgangssprachlich die Auseinandersetzung darüber beschrieben, wozu der Wald dienen sollte: dem Erhalt von Arbeitsplätzen in der Forst- und Holzwirtschaft oder von gefährdeten Arten und Urwaldbäumen. „The Timber Wars" ist auch der Titel eines kürzlich gestarteten investigativen Rechercheprojekts von Oregon Public Broadcasting und der Leitung von Aaron Scott (wie Anm. 4).

6 Beim North Roaring Devil Timber Sale von 1989 ging es um ein 25–27 Hektar großes Stück Bundeswald mit jahrhundertealten Bäumen, das am Osterwochenende abgeholzt wurde, um eine Auseinandersetzung mit UmweltaktivistInnen zu vermeiden. Vgl. dazu „Protesters Halt Logging in Friendly Standoff; 13 Arrested", Associated Press, 26. März 1989; „The Timber Wars" (wie Anm. 4).

size are much more efficient for lumber production than smaller trees and their demise only accelerated after 1950 when national forestlands were utilized for the postwar housing boom.[2] Private forestlands were often replaced by Douglas Fir monoculture plantations, one of the most popular construction timbers in North America and Asia, that were harvested after thirty years. By 1990, old-growth forests had been logged back to 13–18 percent of their historical coverage and 78 percent of what is left is in the National Forests. There is likely even less.[3] But ever since Europeans arrived in the Northwest, old-growth, and the Douglas Fir in particular, has also represented the last of the wilderness and an ecological diversity unmatched in plantation forests. During the 1970s and 1980s, as these trees disappeared at an accelerating pace, their ecological value began to outweigh their value as timber. "This small shift turned into an epic battle that engulfed the Northwest then spilled out across the rest of the country."[4] By 1990, somewhere between automation, a new awareness of what old-growth meant for the ecology of our planet, a volcanic eruption, log exports, and a reclusive owl, the Timber Wars were born.[5]

Clear-cutting on Federal land had previously been the backbone of a regional economy. Now, the backlash was immediate. The backlash was immediate—arson produced "salvage" sales and activists chained themselves to trees, timber sales were announced at dawn on Easter Sundays to avoid public knowledge, and spotted owls were killed and purportedly eaten.[6] The battle became one between rural and urban and has defined the last twenty years of cultural antagonism in the Northwest and the United States at large. But as much as the wars were almost universally characterized as pitching loggers against environmentalists—owls and old trees versus humans—in reality, the complex set of relationships defined by the timber industry had stemmed from nineteenth-century circumstances that exploited loggers as much as trees. The distinctly Northwest issue influenced the 1992 presidential election and, after elected, President Bill Clinton, his Vice President Al Gore, and half his cabinet flew to Portland to sit down for an unprecedented timber summit to try and broker peace. The result was the "Northwest Forest Plan"—a collection of federal guidelines, loosely based upon the ideas of New Forestry and whose development is still in progress. Informed by the practical lessons of Structure-Based Management (SMB) that analyze forests as dynamic systems and not just stands of timber, it cemented the new approach to forestry in the Northwest. From renewable timber would emerge ecological resilience: a concern

for healthy trees, but also healthy water, fish, birds, soil, and communities.[7]

Despite the fact that the construction industry is, and has always been, the main driver of the timber industry, this radical shift in how timber arrived at the construction site went almost completely unnoticed by architects and homeowners. There was a slight shift in construction costs: after the eruption, when timber flooded the market, timber prices went down. Once a solid trade relationship was established with China, they went up again. When logging in National Forests slowed, wood from Canada or the southern states began to replace Northwest timber, and architectural production continued as before. Nonetheless, what did end was the ability to produce the kind of architecture the region is most noted for: old-growth was essential in defining a regional architecture that began in the interwar years and fueled the desire for the tight-grained, knot-free cabin interiors of Northwest Modernism. In Oregon, this is the architecture of A.E. Doyle, Pietro Belluschi, John Yeon, Van Evera Bailey and, more recently, John Storrs. In architectural history, from Lewis Mumford to Kenneth Frampton to Mark Treib, the defining characteristic of this architecture that opposed it to international modernism was its sense of "place," which has been consistently attributed to the use of pitched rooves, a sensitivity to landscape, and most of all, the use of exposed, old-growth timber.

2   This logging was in no way controversial but followed what was then standard practice. In hindsight, it has been charged that the Forest Service during the 1970s and 1980s presided over "an orgy of unsustainable logging." Paul W. Hirt, *A Conspiracy of Optimism: Management of National Forests Since World War Two* (Lincoln and London, 1994), 294.

3   This is an estimate from 2006 since the U.S. Forestry Service only relatively recently began producing inventories on the status and condition of "old" growth (older than 150 years). See Chandra LeGue, *Oregon's Ancient Forests* (Seattle, 2019), 20–24; James R. Strittholt, Dominick A. Dellasala and Hong Jiang, "Status of Mature and Old-Growth Forests in the Pacific Northwest," *Conservation Biology* 20, no. 2 (2006): 363–374.

4   Aaron Scott, "The Timber Wars," Episode 1, Oregon Public Broadcasting, available online at: https://www.opb.org/show/timberwars/ (accessed November 30, 2020).

5   This term is used colloquially to describe the battle over what the forest should support: logging and milling jobs or endangered species and old-growth trees. Additionally, "The Timber Wars" is the title of a recent investigative research project conducted by Oregon Public Broadcasting under the leadership of Aaron Scott (see note 4).

6   The North Roaring Devil Timber Sale of 1989 was a 63- to 68-acre site of centuries-old trees on National Forest land logged over Easter Weekend in the hopes of avoiding confrontation with environmental activists. See "Protesters Halt Logging in Friendly Standoff; 13 Arrested," Associated Press, March 26, 1989; "The Timber Wars" (see note 4).

7   Official United States Department of Agriculture, Forest Service documents outlining the plan, available online at: https://www.fs.usda.gov/detail/r6/landmanagement/planning/?cid=fsbdev2_026990 (accessed December 2, 2020). A review of the plan by four of the scientists responsible for the original plan: Jack Thomas, Jerry Franklin, John Gordon and Norman Johnson, "The Northwest Forest Plan: Origins, Components, Implementation Experience, and Suggestions for Change," *Conservation Biology* 20, no. 2 (2006), 297–305; Gail Wells, *The Tillamook: A Forest Comes of Age* (Corvallis, 1999).

Forestry" beruhend und von den praktischen Methoden des „Structure-Based Management" (SMB) ausgehend, die die Wälder als dynamische Systeme und nicht als bloße Holzbestände analysieren, begründet der Plan einen neuen Ansatz der Forstwirtschaft im Nordwesten der USA. Holz, das sich regeneriert, würde die ökologische Resilienz fördern: ein Interesse an gesunden Bäumen, aber auch an gesundem Wasser und Erdreich, gesunden Fischen, Vögeln, und Communities.[7]

Obwohl das Baugewerbe die größte Triebkraft der Holzwirtschaft ist und immer schon war, ist diese radikale Veränderung für den Weg des Holzes zur Baustelle von ArchitektInnen und HausbesitzerInnen kaum bemerkt worden. Sie schlug sich in leichten Schwankungen der Baukosten nieder: Als der Markt nach dem Vulkanausbruch mit Holz geflutet wurde, fielen sie. Sobald eine solide Handelsbeziehung mit China etabliert war, stiegen sie wieder. Als sich der Einschlag in den Bundesforsten verlangsamte, wurde das Holz aus dem Nordwesten allmählich durch Holz aus Kanada oder den Südstaaten ersetzt, und das Architekturschaffen ging wie gehabt weiter. Zu einem Ende kam allerdings die Architektur, für die die Region am meisten bekannt ist: Urwaldholz war ein wesentliches Kennzeichen einer regionalen Spielart der Moderne, die ihren Anfang in der Zwischenkriegszeit nahm und mit ihrer hüttenartigen Innengestaltung aus feinmaserigem, astfreiem Holz begeisterte. In Oregon versteht man darunter die Architektur von A.E. Doyle, Pietro Belluschi, John Yeon, Van Evera Bailey oder – in neuerer Zeit – John Storrs. Die Architekturgeschichte von Lewis Mumford bis Kenneth Frampton und Mark Treib nennt als definierendes Merkmal dieser regionalen Moderne, die sie von der internationalen unterscheidet, ihre Ortsverbundenheit, die durchgehend mit der Verwendung von Satteldächern, ihrer Anpassung an die Landschaft und vor allem dem Einsatz von altwüchsigem Sichtholz assoziiert wird.

Die Anomalie an den Urwaldbeständen der Region besteht darin, dass sie – wiewohl repräsentativ für die regionale Architektur von der Blockhütte bis zur Moderne – in der Praxis großteils zu dem kleindimensionierten Bauholz für die ortlosen, massenproduzierten Leichtrahmenkonstruktionen typisch amerikanischer Häuser verarbeitet wurde – Holz, das problemlos auch aus jungen Plantagenbäumen hätte gewonnen werden können. Der Markt tendiert zu diesem ortsungebundenen, massenhaft produzierten Leichtrahmenbau, und die in der regionalen Architektur so geschätzten alten Douglastannen gehen heute meist nach Japan, wo sie als Ersatz für die in japanischen Interieurs verwendete Sugikiefer oder als Trägermaterial von Sugi-Furnieren zur Schaffung typisch japanischer Architektur dienen.[8] Der „Ort" wird zu einem komplizierten Begriff, wenn die Realitäten einer Holzregion mit Narrativen zusammenprallen, die noch zu einer früheren Ära gehören.

„Framework" und sein Rahmen. 2015 stellte in Portland, Oregon, ein Kollektiv aus Bauträger, Entwicklungsfirma, Architektur-, Landschaftsarchitektur- und Ingenieurbüros sowie ausführendem Bauunternehmen „Framework" vor: den ersten Holzhochhausbau in den USA (Abb. 3). Neben Lever Architects, den Entwerfern des Gebäudes, wird ein sechzig Personen umfassendes Projektteam genannt, das über eine Million Dollar in Forschung, Prüfung und Zertifizierung des Holzhaushochbaus gemäß den Bau- und Brandschutzvorschriften der USA steckte. „Die Grundkonstruktion besteht aus einem Skelettbau aus Brettschichtholz mit einem massiven Kern und Decken aus Brettsperrholz."[9] Mit seinem kippfähigen Brettsperrholzkern ist es das erste 12-stöckige Holzbauwerk, das den Erdbebensicherheits- und Brandschutzvorschriften in den USA genügte. Die Entwicklerin Anyeley Hallová positionierte das Projekt als einen Vorboten der Zukunft – „Die Stadt der Zukunft besteht aus Holz" – und betonte, dass das Gebäude, auch wenn es sich von außen betrachtet nicht groß von anderen Hochhausbauten unterscheide, auf mehrere bedeutende Änderungen in der Schaffung von Architektur vorausweise.[10] „Framework" setzt das wenig überraschend in einem größeren Rahmen um: Das Architekturprojekt ist eingebettet in eine Vision von staatlich verwalteten Wäldern, wiederbelebten Sägewerken, innovativen Holzwerkstoffen, hohen Holzgebäuden, gesunden Städten und wirtschaftlich lebensfähigen Landgemeinden (Abb. 4). So wird „Framework" zu einem Projekt der Rettung und Erhaltung, diesmal nicht von umgeworfenen Bäumen, sondern von Menschen und Wäldern. „Framework" ist eigentlich der Entwurf eines ganzen Territoriums: Innovation auf einem Gebiet, die auf andere Gebiete übergreift und eine ganze resiliente Holzinfrastruktur schafft.

7 Official United States Department of Agriculture, Forest Service Documents, online unter: https://www.fs.usda.gov/detail/r6/ landmanagement/planning/?cid=fsbdev2_026990 (Stand: 2. Dezember 2020). Eine Evaluierung wurde von vier für den Originalplan verantwortlichen WissenschaftlerInnen durchgeführt: Thomas, Jack/ Franklin, Jerry/Gordon, John/Johnson, Norman: „The Northwest Forest Plan: Origins, Components, Implementation Experience, and Suggestions for Change", *Conservation Biology* 20, 2 (2006), 297–305; Wells, Gail: *The Tillamook: A Forest Comes of Age* (Corvallis, 1999).

8 Diese Charakterisierung der Regionalarchitektur im Nordwesten der USA zieht sich durch alle bedeutenderen Werke zu dem Thema, wie Mock, Elizabeth (Hg.): *Built in the USA*, New York 1944; Mumford, Lewis: „The Skyline: Status Quo", *The New Yorker*, 11. Oktober 1947, 104–110; McMath, George: „Emerging Regional Style" und „Buildings and Gardens", in: Vaughan, Thomas (Hg.): *Space, Style and Structure: Building in Northwest America*, Portland 1974; Frampton, Kenneth: „Prospects for a Critical Regionalism", *Perspecta* 20 (1983), 147–162; Miller, David: *Toward a New Regionalism: Environmental Architecture in the Pacific Northwest*, Seattle/London 2005; Treib, Marc: *John Yeon: Modern Architecture and Conservation in the Pacific Northwest*, San Francisco 2016. Zum U.S.-Holzexport und zu den Anforderungen der japanischen Hausbauindustrie vgl. Cox, Thomas: „Coping with Gaizai: Japanese Forest Cooperatives and Imported American Timber", *Environmental Review* 11, 1 (1987), 35–54. Die japanische Nachfrage ist hauptsächlich eine Folge der Entwaldung Japans. Vgl. dazu Iwamoto, Junishi: „The Development of Japanese Forestry", in: Iwai, Yoshiya (Hg.), *Forestry and the Forest Industry in Japan*, Vancouver 2007.

9 O.A.: „Wood Skyscraper", Framework, online unter: www.frameworkportland. com/#/wood-skyscraper/ (Stand: 21. Februar 2021) (Übers. W.P.)

10 Hallová, Anyeley: „The City of the Future is Made from Wood", *TEDx Talks*, 10. Januar 2017.

The anomaly of the old-growth forests in the region is that while they were representative of regional architecture, from the pioneer log cabin to Regional Modernism, in practical terms they were mostly transformed into small-dimensioned lumber for constructing the placeless, mass-produced, light-weight-framed American home—lumber that could easily have been provided by young plantation trees. The market is oriented towards a placeless, mass-produced, construction framing, and the large Douglas Firs so revered in regional architecture are now mostly sent to Japan to be used as a replacement for Sugi timber in Japanese interiors, or hidden below Sugi veneer, producing characteristic Japanese architecture.[8] "Place" becomes a more complicated concept when the realities of timber territory conflict with narratives that still belong to a prior era.

Framework's framework. In 2015, a design collective of client, developer, architect, landscape architect, engineer, and contractor in Portland, Oregon, announced "Framework": the USA's first timber high-rise (fig. 3). While Lever Architects are the architects of the building, a collaborative of sixty people is listed as the authors who chaperoned the one million dollar project to research, test and certify the structural and fire-resistant code compliancy of high-rise timber construction in the USA. "The structural design is a glue-laminated (Glulam) post-and-beam structure, surrounding a cross-laminated timber (CLT) central core, and topped by CLT floor panels."[9] Utilizing a CLT rocking wall core, it is the first time that a 12-story timber structure has passed seismic and fire codes in the USA. Developer Anyeley Hallová positioned the project as a harbinger of the future, "The city of the future is made from wood," and highlighted that although the building may not look so different from other high-rises on the exterior, it would most importantly indicate several changes to how architecture is produced.[10] "Framework" has, not surprisingly, a framework for doing this, a way of situating the architectural project into a vision of state-managed forests, resuscitated lumber mills, engineered wood products, tall wood buildings, healthy cities, and economically healthy rural communities (fig. 4). This would amount to another salvaging project. But this time, instead of salvaging logs, it is people and forests that would be salvaged. What "Framework" proposes a territorial design project—innovation at one scale producing a resilient timber infrastructure at other scales.

Timber territory is a way of talking about the region within which wood circulates. It simultaneously describes a living organism, a resource, a commodity, a building material,

and a livelihood. But wood is able to be all of these things because it is also an infrastructure even if wood's material flow is not always visible. While certain locations such as mills and ports are fixed parts of the infrastructure chain, logs and lumber move across vast landscapes. Timber territory describes a variety of agents: different trees such as Port Orford cedar, Western red cedar, Western hemlock, Ponderosa pine, white oak and, most famously, Douglas fir (which is not in fact a fir, but a false hemlock, Pseudotsuga menziesii), all of which have different needs and motivations within native forests; the earth within which these forests grow and the violent and legal steps that have wrested it away from indigenous populations and placed it into a variety of private, state, and federal ownership, in turn subjecting trees to a variety of different silvicultural practices; the forest owners and managers; timber brokers; sawmills and mill cooperatives; mill workers; the transport networks that move logs and lumber. This territory is subject to the caprices of the housing market for which most timber is destined. But into this mix projects another, less quantifiable force, which is the set of narratives we tell ourselves about what these component pieces, as well as the overall confederate body, that make up timber infrastructure mean. And at any moment, there looms the possibility of major external environmental or economic events that have the ability to upend this precarious balance of timber infrastructure at any moment—drought, flood, fire, earthquake, eruption.

"Framework" represents therefore not just a new architecture, but the first articulation of what Pacific Northwest timber territory could be since the Timber Wars and since the Northwest Forest Plan. By tying together timber joinery, the mill, silviculture trends, environmental conditions and narratives of wilderness and frontier, to volcanic eruptions, to traditions of craft, this essay hopes to speculate upon what we might

8   The characterization of Northwest regional architecture in this way runs through all the major works on the subject. See Elizabeth Mock, ed., *Built in the USA* (New York, 1944); Lewis Mumford, "The Skyline: Status Quo," *The New Yorker*, October 11, 1947, 104–110; George McMath, "Emerging Regional Style," and "Buildings and Gardens," in *Space, Style and Structure: Building in Northwest America*, ed. Thomas Vaughan (Portland, 1974); Kenneth Frampton, "Prospects for a Critical Regionalism," *Perspecta* 20 (1983):147–162; David Miller, *Toward a New Regionalism: Environmental Architecture in the Pacific Northwest* (Seattle and London, 2005); Marc Treib, *John Yeon: Modern Architecture and Conservation in the Pacific Northwest* (San Francisco, 2016); For United States log exports and the demands of the Japanese housing industry see: Thomas Cox, "Coping with Gaizai: Japanese Forest Cooperatives and Imported American Timber," *Environmental Review* 11, no. 1 (1987): 35–54. Most of the Japanese demand is a response to Japanese deforestation, see Junishi Iwamoto, "The Development of Japanese Forestry," in *Forestry and the Forest Industry in Japan*, ed. Yoshiya Iwai (Vancouver, B.C., 2007).

9   Anon., "Wood Skyscraper," Framework, available online at: www.frameworkportland.com/wood-skyscraper (accessed February 21, 2021).

10 See Anyeley Hallová, "The City of the Future is Made from Wood," *TEDx Talks*, January 10, 2017.

Der Begriff „Timber Territory" bezeichnet eine Region, in der Holz zirkuliert und beschreibt zugleich einen lebenden Organismus, einen Rohstoff, eine Ware, ein Baumaterial und einen Lebensunterhalt. Holz vermag das alles zu sein, weil es auch eine Infrastruktur darstellt, selbst wenn der Materialfluss von Holz nicht immer sichtbar ist. Während gewisse Orte wie Sägewerke und Häfen feste Punkte der Infrastrukturkette sind, verteilen sich Baumstämme und Bauholz über weite Landschaften. Zum „Timber Territory" gehören eine Fülle von Akteuren: verschiedene Baumarten wie die Oregonzeder, die Riesenthuja, die Westamerikanische Hemlocktanne, die Gelbkiefer, die Oregoneiche und, wohl am berühmtesten, die Douglastanne (die eigentlich keine Tanne, sondern eine falsche Hemlocktanne oder genauer eine Kiefer ist), die alle verschiedene Ansprüche an die heimischen Wälder stellen; den Grund und Boden, in dem diese Wälder wachsen, und die gewaltsamen und legalen Maßnahmen, mit denen er den indigenen Völkern entrissen und in Privat-, Staats- und Bundesbesitz überführt wurde, was die Bäume wiederum unterschiedlichen forstwirtschaftlichen Praktiken unterwirft; die WaldbesitzerInnen und ForstverwalterInnen, die HolzhändlerInnen, Sägewerke und Sägewerkkooperativen, die SägewerkarbeiterInnen und die Transportnetzwerke, die das Rund- und Schnittholz bewegen. Das alles unterliegt wiederum den Launen den Hausbaumarkts, für den das meiste Nutzholz

3

"Framework," the USA's first timber high-rise | Der erste Holzhochhausbau in den USA, 2016 © Courtesy LEVER Architecture

bestimmt ist. Überlagert wird dieser Mix dann von einer weiteren, weniger quantifizierbaren Kraft, nämlich von dem Ensemble an Narrativen, die wir einander über diese Elemente und den ganzen, die Holzinfrastruktur bildenden Verband erzählen. Über alledem steht schließlich drohend die Möglichkeit größerer externer Umwelt- oder Wirtschaftskatastrophen, die dieses prekäre Gleichgewicht der Holzinfrastruktur jederzeit kippen lassen können – Dürren, Überflutungen, Feuer, Erdbeben, Vulkanausbrüche.

Bei „Framework" handelt es sich also nicht nur um neue Architektur, sondern auch um den ersten Ausdruck dessen, was aus dem „Timber Territory" im Nordwesten der USA nach den „Timber Wars" und dem „Northwest Forest Plan" werden könnte. Durch die Verknüpfung von Zimmerei, holzverarbeitender Industrie und Handwerkstraditionen mit forstwirtschaftlichen Trends, Umweltbedingungen und Narrativen der Wildnis bis hin zu Vulkanausbrüchen hoffe ich, in diesem Essay ein Bild davon zeichnen zu können, was von so einem Territorium zu erwarten ist.[11] Ein resilientes Territorium der Massivholzerzeugung geht mit vielen kleinen Veränderungen bei Holzverbindungen, Holzverarbeitungsbetrieben und Forstwirtschaft einher, die derzeit alle in die Konstruktion unserer

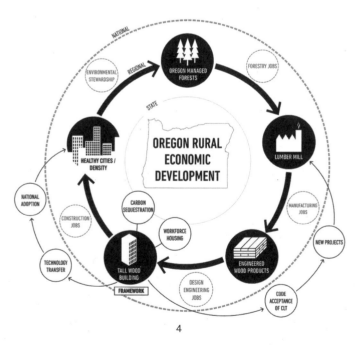

4

This diagram shows how the architectural project "Framework" is situated into a vision of state-managed forests, resuscitated lumber mills, engineered wood products, tall wood buildings, healthy cities, and economically healthy rural communities. | Das Architekturprojekt „Framework" ist eingebettet in eine Vision von staatlich verwalteten Wäldern, wiederbelebten Sägewerken, innovativen Holzwerkstoffen, hohen Holzgebäuden, gesunden Städten und wirtschaftlich lebensfähigen Landgemeinden. © Courtesy LEVER Architecture

11 Dieser Essay hat wesentlich von der Großzügigkeit einer ganzen Reihe von Menschen profitiert, die in Oregon an diesem „Timber Territory" arbeiten. An erster Stelle habe ich Rick Zenn, Senior Fellow am World Forestry Center und den WaldbesitzerInnen Peter und Pam Hayes von Hyla Woods zu danken. Viel profitiert habe ich auch von Gesprächen mit Ben und Sarah Deumling von Zena Forests; John Cole von SDS Lumber; Laurie Schimleck, Professorin für Holzwissenschaft an der Oregon State University; John Wilkinson, ehemaliger stellvertretender Vorstandsvorsitzender bei Weyerhaeuser, einem der größten privaten Forstunternehmen der USA; Dan Bowden von Port Blakely; Thomas Robinson von Lever Architects; Entwicklerin Anyeley Hallová von Project PDX; Sarah und Preston Browning von Salvage Works; Levi Huffman von D.R. Johnson Lumber; und Randy Gragg von der Parks Foundation Portland.

expect from such a territory.[11] A resilient mass timber territory will revolve around many small changes to joints, mills and silviculture, all of which are currently responsible for constructing the narratives we tell about architecture. With a new timber territory comes a new architectural narrative.

Joint. "A man and a boy can now attain the same results, with ease, that twenty men could on an old-fashioned frame."[12] The origin and propagation of the platform frame across the Midwest in the mid-nineteenth century is often tied to the invention of the mass-produced nail (fig. 5).[13] This invention produced a series of ripple effects. The nail allowed for the assembly of small-dimensioned lumber members to be assembled by laymen on the construction site. Previously, braced frame housing consisted of large dimension lumbers, which had to be fitted together on-site by skilled carpenters using mortise and tenon joints. In the mill, workers precisely cut joints with augers before timber was delivered on site. Constructing braced-framed houses was laborious, requiring "a thousand auger holes and a hundred days' work."[14] Platform framing was attractive both for supplier and builder. The platform frame boom in the Midwest coincided with the arrival of rail connections between the Midwest and the West Coast in 1869. Northwest mills that relied on railways embraced the change to platform framing because the smaller dimension lumber could be freighted over large distances by rail at lower freight costs than large-braced framing members. Freed from precise manufacturing, the mill became a place to cut down a standardized set of lumber dimensions. As housing production industrialized and the timber industry scaled up, the lumber mill became the backbone of a regional economy, cutting down as much wood as it could, as quickly as possible. The replacement of mortise and tenon "tree-nails" with mass-produced iron nails introduced a division and displacement of labor inside the Northwest lumber mill. But the same was true at the construction site, where skilled labor was no longer needed. In architectural history, this change is couched in terms of frontier independence, the man and boy being able to do on their own what previously had been the work of a crew of carpenters. The rise of the Midwest platform frame as the standard in construction up until today has been attributed to the lack of skilled labor on the frontier itself, the deforestation that had already occurred in the immediate region, but also to the perceived independence of life on the frontier.

Mass timber, whether in the form of Glulam beams, CLT panels, or Mass Plywood, exchanges nail joints for an array of glue or dowel joints and steel connecting plates. Joinery

is a combination of skilled trade gluing together of different dimension lumbers inside the CLT plant and fitting large, prefabricated pieces on the job site with steel plates. The construction independence and material immediacy of earlier timber architectures, so imbedded with the way in which timber architecture has historically been perceived in the Northwest, is nowhere to be found. Rather, a complicated fabrication process now stands between the tree and the building and places the CLT plant directly in conversation with architect and client over custom pieces. It is a process that demands significant, and precise, fabrication before panels of mass timber arrive, premade, on site, shifting the joinery from the job site to the

11 This essay has benefitted immensely from the generosity of a number of people active in this timber territory in Oregon. First and foremost, I have to thank Rick Zenn, Senior Fellow at the World Forestry Center and forest owners Peter and Pam Hayes of Hyla Woods. In addition, I have benefitted from conversations with: Ben and Sarah Deumling of Zena Forests; John Cole of SDS Lumber; Laurie Schimleck, professor of wood science at OSU; John Wilkinson, ex-Vice-President at Weyerhaeuser, one of the largest private timberland owners in the USA; Dan Bowden of Port Blakely; Thomas Robinson of Lever Architects; Developer Anyeley Hallová of Project PDX; Sarah and Preston Browning of Salvage Works; Levi Huffman at D.R. Johnson timber; Randy Gragg, Parks Foundation Portland.

12 George E. Woodward quoted in Sigfried Giedion, "The Invention of the Balloon Frame," *Space, Time and Architecture: The Growth of a New Tradition* (Cambridge, MA, 1941), 349. Giedion here quotes from *Woodward's Country Homes* (New York, 1869), 152–164, establishing the narrative amongst historians and setting up "a Giedion school of thought."

13 Ibid.

14 Paul Sprague, "Chicago Balloon Frame: The Evolution During the 19th Century of George W. Snow's System for Erecting Light Frame Buildings from Dimension Lumber and Machine-Made Nails," in *The Technology of Historic American Buildings: Studies of the Materials, Craft Processes and the Mechanization of Building Construction*, ed. H. Ward Jandl (Washington D.C., 1983), 41.

5

Platform frame | Platform-Rahmenbau, Omaha Reservation, Nebraska, 1877
© BAE GN 04042, National Anthropological Archives, Smithsonian Institution

Narrative über den Ausdruck von Architektur einfließen. Mit einem neuen „Timber Territory" wird auch ein neues Architekturnarrativ entstehen.

Holzverbindungen. „Ein Knabe und ein Mann können jetzt die gleichen Resultate mit Leichtigkeit erzielen, die zwanzig Arbeiter mit der alten Zimmermannskonstruktion zuwege brachten."[12]

Der Ursprung des Platform-Rahmenbaus und dessen Verbreitung über den gesamten Mittelwesten seit Mitte des 19. Jahrhunderts wird häufig mit der maschinellen Produktion von Nägeln in Verbindung gebracht (Abb. 5).[13] Die Erfindung hatte beträchtliche Folgen. Der Nagel ermöglichte den Zusammenbau kleindimensionierter Gliedteile auf der Baustelle durch Laien. Der zuvor übliche ausgesteifte Fachwerkbau bestand aus großdimensionierten Teilen, die vor Ort durch gelernte Zimmerleute mittels Zapfverbindungen zusammengefügt werden mussten. Vor der Anlieferung mussten die Zapfen und Zapflöcher in der Zimmerei präzise ausgestemmt werden. Der Bau von Fachwerkhäusern war aufwändig, erforderte „tausend Zapfenlöcher und hundert Tage Arbeit".[14] Das Platform Framing war sowohl für die Holzlieferanten als auch die Erbauer attraktiv. Der Boom des Platform Frame im Mittelwesten fiel mit der Fertigstellung der Eisenbahnlinie an die Westküste im Jahr 1869 zusammen. Die Sägewerke im Nordwesten, die von der Bahn abhängig waren, begrüßten den Wechsel zum Platform-Rahmenbau, weil die kleiner dimensionierten Teile zu geringeren Frachtkosten über große Entfernungen transportiert werden konnten als die großen Fachwerkteile. Befreit von der Notwendigkeit zur präzisen Vorfertigung, wurde das Sägewerk zu einem Ort für den Zuschnitt eines standardisierten Sortiments an Schnittholz. Mit der Industrialisierung der Produktion und der Aufskalierung der Holzindustrie entwickelte sich diese zum Rückgrat einer regionalen Ökonomie, die so viel und so schnell Holz schlägerte, wie sie nur konnte. Die Ersetzung der Zapfverbindungen durch massenproduzierte Eisennägel führte zu Arbeitsteilung und zum Verschwinden von Aufträgen in den Sägewerksbetrieben des Nordwestens. Dasselbe passierte auch auf den Baustellen, wo gelernte Arbeitskräfte überflüssig wurden. In der Architekturgeschichte wird dieser Wandel im Sinne eines Unabhängigkeitsgewinns dargestellt, dass ein Mann und ein Knabe nun etwas zu erledigen vermochten, wozu es früher einer ganzen Partie von Zimmerleuten bedurfte. Der Aufstieg der Platform Frame-Konstruktion des Mittelwestens zur bis heute gängigen Standardbauweise wurde dem Mangel an gelernten Arbeitskräften in der Pioniergesellschaft, der bereits bestehenden Entwaldung der Region, aber auch der Unabhängigkeit des Pionierlebens zugeschrieben.

Massivholz – ob in Form von Balkenbrettschichtholz, Brettsperrholzplatten oder Massivsperrholz – ersetzt Nagelverbindungen durch eine Matrix an Leim- und Dübelverbindungen sowie Anschlussplatten aus Stahl. Die Tätigkeit des Zimmerns besteht heute aus dem fachkundigen Verleimen verschiedener Dimensionshölzer im BSH-Werk und dem Zusammenbau großer, vorfabrizierter Teile auf der Baustelle mithilfe von Stahlplatten. Die konstruktive Unabhängigkeit und materielle Unmittelbarkeit früherer Holzbauwerke, die so eng mit dem historischen Verständnis von Holzarchitektur im Nordwesten der USA verbunden ist, ist heute nirgendwo mehr zu finden. Vielmehr steht nun ein komplizierter Fabrikationsprozess zwischen Baum und Gebäude, bei dem sich das BSH-Werk direkt mit ArchitektInnen und BauherrInnen über maßgefertigte Teile verständigt. Es ist ein Prozess, der wichtige und hochpräzise Fabrikationsschritte erfordert, ehe die vorgefertigten Massivholzteile an der Baustelle eintreffen, sodass sich die Tätigkeit des Zimmerns von der Baustelle in die Fabrik verschiebt. Auch der Zusammenbau vor Ort ist eine komplexe Angelegenheit, bei der riesige Teile mit Kränen in Position gebracht werden müssen. Produzierte das Sägewerk eine Ware, für die die Verantwortung endete, sobald das Dimensionsholz das Werk verließ, so wird das BSH-Werk zu einem Partner, dessen Produkt an einen Vertrag gebunden ist und der einen Konstruktionsdienst erbringt. Bestand die Rückversicherung gegen Konstruktionsungenauigkeiten beim Platform Framing in der Fähigkeit von Vater und Sohn ein Stück mit der Handsäge zuzuschneiden oder zusätzliche Nägel zu verwenden, so ist das bei Massivholz eine Frage von Maßtoleranzen.

Maßtoleranz meint die zulässige Abweichung eines Bauteils von der Fabrikationszeichnung – ein weiterer im Werk durchzuführender Prozess – von einem Glied der Werkstoffkette zum nächsten. Das Bauen mit einem bis vor Kurzem lebenden Material erfordert außerdem Toleranz für Ausdehnung, Schrumpfung und Bewegung. Maßtoleranz beschreibt aber auch die Nähe zwischen den Gliedern der Werkstoffkette, die mit der Popularisierung des Platform Framing voneinander getrennt wurden. Ermöglichte der Nagel die Produktion von Dimensionsholz in Tausenden Kilometern Entfernung von der Baustelle, so erfordert die Hinwendung zu Leim und zu Stahlplatten die Einigung auf gemeinsame Maßtoleranzen durch Entwurfs-, Fabrikations- und Montage-Teams, was diese einander

12 G.E. Woodward zit. n. Giedion, Sigfried: „Der Ballonrahmen und die Industrialisierung", in: *Raum, Zeit, Architektur: Die Entstehung einer neuen Tradition* [1941], Basel 1996, 233. Giedion zitiert hier aus Woodwards *Woodward's Country Homes* (New York 1869), 152–164, und etabliert damit ein Narrativ unter HistorikerInnen und „eine Giedion'sche Denkschule".

13 Ebd.

14 Sprague, Paul: „Chicago Balloon Frame: The Evolution During the 19th Century of George W. Snow's System for Erecting Light Frame Buildings from Dimension Lumber and Machine-Made Nails", in: Jandl, H. Ward (Hg.), *The Technology of Historic American Buildings: Studies of the Materials, Craft Processes and the Mechanization of Building Construction*, Washington D.C. 1983, 41. (Übers. W.P.)

manufacturing plant. Assembly is also a sophisticated operation on site, with large panels lifted into place with cranes. Whereas the lumber mill produced a commodity, its custody of wood ending when dimension lumber went out the door, the CLT workers become partners whose product is beholden to a contract, they are responsible for fulfilling a design service. If the platform frame's insurance against construction inaccuracy was low-tech—the ability for father and son to cut down lumber with a handsaw or use extra nails—in mass timber, it becomes a question of acceptable tolerances.

Tolerance articulates the range of acceptable deviation from the fabrication drawings—another new process undertaken at the mill—between one part of the material chain and the next. Building with a recently-living material itself also requires tolerance for expansion and contraction, and movement. But tolerance also describes a kind of proximity between two parts of the material chain that had been severed with the popularization of the platform frame. If the nail had allowed the production of dimension lumber to be separated by thousands of miles from the construction site, the turn to glue and steel plates requires tolerances to be agreed upon by the design, fabrication, and construction teams and brings them together physically. Accepted tolerance requires articulation in contracts, but also helps to construct a chain of custody, where wood remains in custody of one part of the design team until it can be safely delivered to the other.

The nail also defines the other end of the timber construction chain. It requires a lot of labor to remove, which has a significant impact on the ability, and desire, to re-use dimension lumber. This was never a problem when the infrastructure chain "ended" in the building and demolition costs were externalized. But in 2016, Portland City Council adopted an ordinance that required the construction industry to shift from *demolition to deconstruction.* Currently, any single-family house built before 1940 must be deconstructed, largely by hand, in order to salvage material. While large old-growth timbers can be profitably resold, there is little demand for the recycled two-by-four.[15] Material scientists at Oregon State University's Forestry School have successfully produced CLT and Glulam from this recycled material, but the nail joint, so useful for simplifying construction, becomes the weak link in these efforts since the removal of nails from lightweight framing is time-consuming and creates structural weaknesses.[16] Lumber mills have mechanized towards one simple output and do not have the manpower or technology to produce members from salvaged wood in any economical way. CLT plants find it difficult to certify a laminated product that uses recycled material, on top of which there are issues with bonding layers of recycled materials. The potentially enormous benefit that recycling timber from houses could have on the timber cycle could, in a sense, all be brought to a halt by the nail gun.

Mill. "The early history of the Balloon Frame, is somewhat obscure [...] It may, however, be traced back to the early settlement of our prairie countries where it was impossible to obtain heavy timber and skillful mechanics."[17]

While the re-use of a two-by-four riddled with nails is difficult from both an economic and structural standpoint, the main barrier to scaling up the OSU experiments to make deconstructed wood part of the material cycle is the lack of a middleman that can perform the same function in the chain as the lumber mill does today. Mills have always acted more like merchants than manufacturers in their key position in the material chain, buying a fixed and predictable resource—timber—before selling a commodity—lumber. In between these moments, despite being the most concentrated location of capital and labor in the material cycle, they are susceptible to both the fluctuations caused by environmental conditions and trade markets that affect timber prices and the fluctuations of housing markets. In Oregon, where regional mills provided the economic backbone of an entire region geared towards timber extraction, precarity, not stability, undergirded this arrangement. Being more competitive usually meant employing fewer people, something that mill automation facilitated rapidly after World War II. After 1990, logging restrictions on federal land reduced the workforce even more. And while "regional architecture" is a term that has generally been interpreted within architectural history as the relationship of structure to site, it nonetheless is also a term that aptly describes a region *produced by* a construction industry aimed at the single-family house built from dimension lumber. As architects, we are complicit.

If projects like "Framework" aim to address regional jobs through local production, there is another reason the mill's

15 The wording is actually: "All single-dwelling structures (houses or duplexes)." For clarity, I have used single-family house. Available online at: https://www.portland.gov/bps/decon/deconstruction-requirements (accessed October 12, 2020). The ordinance aimed at making the industry more environmentally conscious by limiting waste production and encourage renovation instead of new construction during Portland's most recent housing boom which peaked in 2018.

16 See Arbelaez Raphael, Laurence Schimleck and Arijit Sinha, "Salvaged Lumber for Structural Mass Timber Panels: Manufacturing and Testing," *Wood and Fiber Science* 52 (2020): 178–190.

17 Giedion, "The Invention of the Balloon Frame" (see note 12), 349.

physisch wieder näher bringt. Maßtoleranzen müssen vertraglich festgelegt werden und helfen eine Produktkette aufzubauen, bei der das Holz so lange in der Verantwortung eines Mitglieds des Bauteams bleibt, bis es sicher an das nächste übergeben werden kann.

Der Nagel bestimmt auch das entgegengesetzte Ende der Konstruktionskette von Holzbauten. Ihn zu entfernen ist überaus arbeitsaufwändig, was erhebliche Auswirkungen auf die Möglichkeit – und das Bedürfnis – hat, Dimensionsholz wiederzuverwenden. Das war kein Problem, solange die Kette mit dem Gebäude endete und die Kosten für den Abriss externalisiert wurden. Aber im Jahr 2016 verabschiedete der Stadtrat von Portland eine Verordnung, die die Bauindustrie dazu verpflichtet, vom *Abreißen zum Abtragen* überzugehen. Gegenwärtig muss jedes vor 1940 gebaute Einfamilienhaus (weitgehend von Hand) abgetragen werden, um Material rückzugewinnen. Während große Bauteile aus Urwaldholz profitabel weiterverkauft werden können, hält sich die Nachfrage nach recycelten *Two-by-Fours* in Grenzen.[15] MaterialwissenschaftlerInnen der Forstwirtschaftsfakultät an der Oregon State University haben aus diesem Material mit Erfolg Brettsperr- und Brettschichtholz produziert, aber die für die Vereinfachung des Bauens so nützliche Nagelverbindung bleibt das schwache Glied dabei, weil die Entfernung von Nägeln aus Leichtrahmen zeitaufwändig ist und Strukturmängel hervorruft.[16] Sägewerke haben sich auf die Produktion eines einfachen Outputs spezialisiert und verfügen weder über das Personal noch die Technologie, um wirtschaftlich Bauteile aus Altholz herstellen zu können. BSH-Werken fällt es schwer, Schichtholzprodukte aus Recyclingmaterial zertifizieren zu lassen. Dazu kommen bei Altmaterial Probleme mit der Bindeschicht. Der enorme Nutzen, den recyceltes Bauholz potenziell für den Holzkreislauf haben könnte, könnte gewissermaßen durch die Nagelpistole aufgehalten werden.

Sägewerk. „Die Frühgeschichte des balloon frame [liegt] im dunkeln […]. Früheste Spuren findet man jedoch in jenen ersten Siedlungen in den Prärieregionen, wo es sowohl an Holz als auch an gelernten Handwerkern mangelte."[17]

Abgesehen von den wirtschaftlichen und strukturellen Gründen, die gegen die Wiederverwendung eines mit Nägeln gespickten *Two-by-Four* sprechen, liegt das Haupthindernis für eine Skalierung der an der OSU durchgeführten Versuche zur Wiedereinspeisung von Holz aus abgetragenen Häusern in den Materialkreislauf, im Fehlen einer Mittlerinstanz, die dieselbe Funktion in der Werkstoffkette erfüllen könnte wie sie heute das Sägewerk innehat. Sägewerke haben in der Werkstoffkette immer eher als Händler denn als Hersteller fungiert; sie kaufen einen fixen, berechenbaren Rohstoff – Rundholz – und verkaufen eine Ware – Schnittholz. Dazwischen

sind sie, auch wenn sie im Werkstoffkreislauf den Ort mit der höchsten Kapital- und Arbeitskonzentration bilden, sowohl anfällig für Fluktuationen aufgrund von Umweltbedingungen und Handelsmärkten, die Auswirkungen auf den Holzpreis haben, als auch für Fluktuationen des Wohnungsmarktes. In Oregon, wo die Sägewerksbetriebe das ökonomische Rückgrat einer Region bilden, die ganz auf Holzgewinnung ausgerichtet ist, wurde dieses Arrangement nicht durch Stabilität, sondern durch Prekarität gestützt. Wettbewerbsfähiger zu sein, hieß meist, weniger Personal zu beschäftigen, was die Automatisierung nach dem Zweiten Weltkrieg rasch möglich machte. Die Beschränkung der Abholzung in den Bundesforsten nach 1990 brachte einen sogar noch größeren Personalabbau mit sich. Und auch wenn der Begriff „regionale Architektur" in der Architekturgeschichte meist im Sinn der Beziehung des Bauwerks zu seinem Standort verstanden wird, so beschreibt er eine Region auch sehr gut als *Produkt* einer Bauindustrie, die auf die Errichtung von Einfamilienhäusern aus Dimensionsholz ausgerichtet ist. Als ArchitektInnen sind wir daran nicht unbeteiligt.

Wenn es Projekten wie „Framework" um die Schaffung regionaler Jobs durch Produktion vor Ort geht, so ist das ein weiterer Grund, die Rolle des Sägewerks in der Infrastrukturkette zu aktualisieren. Das BSH-Werk wird auch dazu gebracht werden müssen, die Nachhaltigkeitsagenda dieses neuen „Timber Territory" mitzutragen, an einer „Kultur" mitzuwirken, „die sich von einer Umwelt und Menschen ausbeutenden hin zu einer regenerativen, respektvollen und fairen entwickelt".[18] Die Zertifizierung, die sich am besten durchgesetzt hat, ist die des Forest Stewardship Council (FSC), doch obwohl es in Oregon eine Reihe von FSC-zertifizierten Wäldern gibt und die Architekturcommunity bereit ist, sich auf Produkte daraus festzulegen, gibt es im Staat nicht genügend FSC-zertifizierte Werke, um das Holz zu verarbeiten. Für andere Massivholzprojekte von Lever Architects wurde das Holz darum zur Verarbeitung nach Kanada und zum Verbauen wieder nach Oregon zurückgebracht. Viele einheimische Holzbetriebe weisen darauf hin, dass seit der Verabschiedung des Northwest Forest Plan die Bewirtschaftung des öffentlichen Forstlands in Oregon und Washington einigen der strengsten Umweltvorschriften in den Vereinigten Staaten unterliegt. Sie schlagen vor, der Staat solle einen eigenen Zertifikationsprozess für kleinere

15 In der Verordnung heißt es eigentlich „Alle Einzelwohnungsbauten (Häuser oder Doppelhäuser)". Der Einfachheit halber habe ich Einfamilienhäuser daraus gemacht. Vgl. https://www.portland.gov/bps/decon/deconstruction-requirements (Stand: 12. Oktober 2020). Ziel der Verordnung war, im jüngsten Portlander Hausbauboom, der 2018 seinen Höhepunkt erreichte, durch Abfallbegrenzung und Anreize zu Renovierung statt Neubau die Umweltfreundlichkeit der Branche zu heben.

16 Vgl. Arbelaez, Raphael/Schimleck, Laurence/Sinha, Arijit: „Salvaged Lumber for Structural Mass Timber Panels: Manufacturing and Testing", *Wood and Fiber Science* 52 (2020), 178–190.

17 Giedion: *Raum, Zeit, Architektur* (wie Anm. 12), 235 [Text leicht modifiziert, W.P.].

18 Peter Hayes im Gespräch am 9. Oktober 2020.

role in the infrastructure chain will have to be updated. The mill will also be asked to collaborate in the sustainable agenda of this new timber territory, to participate in "a culture that is moving from environmentally extractive and humanly exploitive to one that is regenerative, respectful, and fair."[18] The certification that has gained the most traction is Forest Stewardship Council (FSC) Certification and while Oregon has a number of FSC-certified forests, and there is a willingness from within the architectural community to specify products from them, there is a dearth of FSC-certified mills in the state to process the timber in state. For other Lever mass timber projects, Oregon logs were sent to Canada for processing and brought back to Oregon for construction because the local mills would not provide this service. Many mills point out that since the adoption of the Northwest Forest Plan, public lands in Oregon and Washington are now subject to some of the most rigorous environmental logging practices in the United States. They suggest the state should structure its own certification process on behalf of small mills, and there are indeed significant efforts underway to provide alternate routes to certification.[19]

Physically, the mill will have to be reorganized to separate and track timber from sustainable sources—strangely termed "legal wood" in ASTM standards language—and other sources once they arrive at the mill. Certification adds costs for the mill, but it also alters a basic premise in the commodification of natural materials. Traditionally, wood from a specific place goes into the mill, joins wood from other places, and a specified, graded, placeless, commodity comes out.[20] The mill is now being asked to reverse this basic premise of industrialization: to become the custodian for a log from the moment it arrives to the moment it leaves the CLT plant or lumber yard. It is being asked to steward material, not commodify it, and in doing so put the place back into the construction material, allowing architects to track the material from the forest to the frame. Today's mill has already incorporated much of this work: each board that ends up on a construction site has a 50- to 100-megabyte data file in the mill, from scans, tests, and processing. "Where did your wood come from?" is a question that variable-retention foresters like the Deumlings of Zena Forest ask, and it is one that architects want to answer for clients. But without the mill's cooperation, that question is impossible to answer.[21]

Mass timber is a form of mechanized craft requiring custom fabrication, specialized trades, and more equipment, likely introducing more job training, and hence employment stability, to rural communities. The mill will be asked to incorporate this, and even more change if it is to accept deconstructed material. There are many lamination plants in the Northwest already turning in this direction. D.R. Johnson, in Riddle, Oregon, was the first mill to incorporate facilities for mass timber production utilizing a government grant, running a specialized lamination fabrication plant side-by-side with its sawmill. There are ever more sophisticated plants mills, like Katerra in Spokane, Washington, that have essentially cornered the entire fabrication chain from production, to design, and construction. The "mill" is not just a mill anymore.

Craft. "It began with an idea—a simple, yet ingenious idea—the brainchild of a small group of rough and ready wood workers. They were rugged fellows in a rugged era, these hardy millmen; inventors in an inventive period of American history [...] Their brawny arms contained great strength and their eyes were bright with visions which knew no horizons. The American Dream was their inspiration, success and wealth their goal. They had as companions courage and tenacity, those essential helpers of successful enterprise [...] They cut down the giant fir tree and hauled it to the mill. They put it in a rotary lathe and cut it into thin sheets of wood. Then, they glued pieces of those sheets together and let them set under pressure. That's how the fir plywood industry was born."[22]

There is a need within the new timber territory for exactly this kind of middleman that can physically take in wood, refashion it, and produce timber construction materials. But the shift from mercantilism, based on the subsidized extraction of natural resources, to manufacturing, based on shared custody, is not simple. In regional Oregon at least, delaminating the milling process from raw forest products is hard to imagine. It is this change in basic principle from commodification to custody—or trade to stewardship—behind how the mill was set up that makes many suspect that the mills that currently exist simply cannot transform into the new middleman situated between the tree and the construction material. And the conceptual difference between commodity and custody

18 Peter Hayes, conversation on October 9, 2020.

19 Jon Cole, SDS Lumber, conversation on October 19, 2020; Levi Huffman, D.R. Johnson, conversation on October 21, 2020.

20 Cronon examines this moment inside the grain elevators of Chicago in great historical specificity. See William Cronon, "Pricing the Future: Grain," *Nature's Metropolis: Chicago and the Great West* (New York and London, 1991): 97–147.

21 Presentation by Ben Deumling for the Build Local Alliance on September 24, 2020.

22 Robert M. Cour, *The Plywood Age: A History of the Fir Plywood Industry's First Fifty Years* (Portland, OR, 1955), 1.

Betriebe einführen, und es wurden auch bereits erhebliche Anstrengungen unternommen, alternative Wege der Zertifikation zu ermöglichen.[19]

Physisch muss das Sägewerk so reorganisiert werden, dass es in der Lage ist, Holz aus nachhaltigen Quellen – von ASTM Standards seltsamerweise als „legales Holz" bezeichnet – von Holz aus anderen Quellen zu trennen und nachzuverfolgen. Die Zertifizierung verursacht zwar zusätzliche Kosten für den Betrieb, ändert aber auch das Grundprinzip der Kommodifikation natürlicher Materialien. Herkömmlicherweise gelangt Holz von einem bestimmten Ort in ein Werk, verbindet sich dort mit Holz von anderen Orten, und heraus kommt eine spezifizierte, normierte, ortlose Ware.[20] Vom Betrieb wird nun verlangt, dieses Grundprinzip der Industrialisierung umzukehren: von seiner Ankunft im BSH-Werk bis zum Verlassen desselben zum Hüter eines Baumstamms zu werden. Statt das Material zur Ware zu machen, soll es Verantwortung dafür übernehmen, und ihm nebenbei wieder seinen Herkunftsort zurückgeben, sodass es ArchitektInnen vom Wald bis zum Bauteil nachverfolgen können. Heutige Holzbetriebe haben viel davon bereits umgesetzt: Für jedes Brett, das auf einer Baustelle landet, fällt dort mittlerweile ein 50–100 MB großer Satz mit Scan-, Test- und Verarbeitungsdaten an. „Woher stammt dein Holz?" ist eine Frage, die nachhaltige Forstwirte wie die Deumlings von der Firma Zena Forest stellen und die ArchitektInnen ihren AuftraggeberInnen gern beantworten würden. Aber ohne Mitwirkung des BSH-Werks ist das ein Ding der Unmöglichkeit.[21]

Massivholzerzeugung ist eine Art mechanisiertes Handwerk, das über die Fähigkeit zur Auftragsfertigung, spezialisiertes Fachpersonal und zusätzliche Maschinen verfügen muss, und damit auch eine bessere Berufsausbildung und folglich mehr Arbeitsplatzsicherheit in ländliche Gemeinden bringt. Säge- und BSH-Werke werden alles das miteinbeziehen und sogar noch weitere Änderungen vornehmen müssen, wenn sie auch mit Altmaterial umgehen können sollen. Im Nordwesten gehen viele Schichtholzerzeuger bereits in diese Richtung. D.R. Johnson, in Riddle, Oregon, war das erste Unternehmen, das mithilfe staatlicher Zuschüsse Anlagen zur Massivholzerzeugung eingeführt hat, und nun neben dem Sägewerk eine spezialisierte Schichtholzfabrik betreibt. Mittlerweile werden die Holzerzeugungswerke immer komplexer. Katerra in Spokane, Washington, vereinigt zum Beispiel den gesamten Fabrikationsprozess von der Produktion über den Entwurf bis hin zur Konstruktion unter einem Dach. Das „Sägewerk" ist keine bloße Säge mehr.

Technik. „Es begann mit einer Idee – einer einfachen, aber geistreichen Idee – dem Einfall einer kleinen Gruppe robuster Holzarbeiter. Es waren raue Kerle einer rauen Zeit, diese zähen Sägewerker; Erfinder in einer erfinderischen Periode der amerikanischen Geschichte […]. Ihre muskulösen Arme steckten voller Kraft und ihre Augen glänzten vor Visionen, die keine Grenzen kannten. Der amerikanische Traum war ihre Inspiration, Erfolg und Reichtum ihr Ziel. Zu ihren Gefährten zählten Mut und Ausdauer, diese unverzichtbaren Gehilfen erfolgreichen Unternehmertums […]. Sie fällten die Riesentanne und schleiften sie zum Sägewerk. Sie spannten sie in eine Drehmaschine und schnitten sie in dünne Holzblätter. Diese leimten sie zusammen und ließen sie unter Druck trocknen. So entstand die Douglastannen-Sperrholzindustrie."[22]

Im neuen „Timber Territory" bedarf es genau einer solchen Mittlerinstanz, die in der Lage ist, Holz physisch einzuholen, umzuwandeln und zu Konstruktionsholz zu verarbeiten. Doch das Umsatteln vom Handel, der auf subventionierter Ausbeutung natürlicher Ressourcen beruht, zu einer Produktion, die auf gemeinsamer Obhut beruht, ist nicht so einfach. Im ländlichen Oregon jedenfalls ist die Ablösung der Holzverarbeitung von der Rohholzproduktion schwer vorstellbar. Es ist dieser vom Sägewerk zu vollziehende prinzipielle Wandel von der Kommodifikation zur Obsorge – oder vom Handel zur Verwaltung –, der viele daran zweifeln lässt, dass die bestehenden Sägewerke zu dieser neuen Mittlerinstanz zwischen Baum und Baumaterial werden können. Der konzeptuelle Unterschied zwischen einer Ware und einem verantwortlich verwalteten Gut zeigt sich außerdem in den verschiedenen handwerklichen Ansätzen, die seit über einem Jahrhundert in die Holzarchitektur des pazifischen Nordwestens eingeschrieben sind.

1905 fand in Portland die Lewis and Clark Exposition statt, mit der das Hundertjahrjubiläum der „Entdeckung" des Westens nach dem Lousiana Purchase durch Thomas Jeffersons Corps of Discovery gefeiert wurde. Holz war schon vor der Ankunft von Meriwether Lewis und William Clark eine Triebkraft für die Besiedlung Oregons, und bei dieser Ausstellung machten zwei Exponate unmissverständlich klar, dass Holz auch das kulturelle Hauptprodukt der neuen Stadt sein

19 Jon Cole, SDS Lumber, im Gespräch am 19. Oktober 2020; Levi Huffman, Levi und D.R. Johnson im Gespräch am 21. Oktober 2020.

20 Cronon untersucht diesen Prozess historisch sehr genau an den Getreidespeichern von Chicago. Vgl. dazu Cronon, William: *Nature's Metropolis: Chicago and the Great West*, New York und London 1991, 97–147.

21 Präsentation von Ben Deumling für die Build Local Alliance am 24. September 2020.

22 Cour, Robert M.: *The Plywood Age: A History of the Fir Plywood Industry's First Fifty Years*, Portland, OR 1955, 1. (Übers. W. P.)

is also reflected in different approaches to craft that have been imbedded in the timber architectures of the Northwest for over a century.

In 1905, Portland hosted the Lewis and Clark Exposition to celebrate the centennial of the "discovery" of the West after the Louisiana Purchase by Thomas Jefferson's Corps of Discovery. Timber was the logic that drove Oregon's settlement even before Meriwether Lewis and William Clark arrived and, at the 1905 exhibition, two exhibitions made it clear that wood was also to be considered the new city's main cultural product. The Forestry Building was the world's largest log cabin, and it encapsulated the narrative of pioneer settlement (figs. 6–7). It scaled-up the rough and purportedly honest architecture made from entire trunks of old-growth Douglas Fir that loggers had established on the West Coast in the early nineteenth-century. In the shadow of the log cabin was another less imposing timber story. The recently established Portland Manufacturing Company, a company that specialized in making baskets and crates, displayed what might have been the world's first plywood panels.[23] Plywood would first be used in architecture as doors and panels for interior carpentry, but it would expand to become sub-flooring and lateral wall bracing, and formwork for concrete.[24]

These two different architectures represented Portland on the national stage. If the log cabin's claim to craft lay in its material immediacy to the forest—the logs were authentic because they were still recognizable as trees and spoke of a pioneer history—craft in the plywood panels resided with the workers who had used machinery to produce a new product. Compared to the log cabin, the plywood exhibition certainly appeared less representative of place. In its fabrication, it was not authentic; in its amalgamation of different woods and glue, it was not representative of any one place; in its procurement, despite what company biographies claim, very little brawn was required. In 1905 these ideas of craft—material immediacy and skilled labor—represented separate directions that craft would take in the face of modernization. The two notions were certainly fused together in the historiography of regional architecture in the Northwest, but the disruptions to timber territory that began with a volcanic eruption and ended with a spotted owl, are beginning to split these two ideas of craft apart again.

Mass timber is a form of mechanized craft that would build upon the plywood history of the region and could arguably be the most authentic form of "place" in northwest architecture.[25] But mass timber, like plywood before it, certainly does not demand a silviculture based on mature trees. The association with old-growth, with romantic ideas of wilderness

6

Exterior of Forestry Building, Lewis and Clark Centennial, Portland, Oregon, 1905 © Oregon Historical Society, Neg. 64423

and self-made log cabins and frontier houses—in short, everything which defines the cultural narratives of timber architecture in the Northwest—is gone. Instead of lumberjacks in forests selling logs to a mill which is then sold to a wholesaler, the mass timber plant collaborates with architects and contractors and clients who care about what this product looks like and how it performs. The sophisticated custom fabrication does not fit into narratives of the independence and immediacy built into the histories of timber architecture in the United States. But it does attempt to redirect an infrastructure geared towards quantity towards one of value-added quality. Rather than suggesting that mass timber has no place in genealogy of craft so central to histories of Northwest architecture, it would seem that it instead has to replace the log cabin's notion of craft-as-material immediacy and build upon plywood's emphasis on craft-as-skilled-labor. Beyond addressing aesthetics, this narrative will have to change how architecture sees itself in relation to the forests themselves, a change from wilderness to stewardship as the context for timber architecture. This is a reversal of earlier narratives that were similarly manufactured, designed to commodify the land itself in the first place or designed to create

23 See Thomas Jester, "Plywood," in Thomas Jester ed., *Twentieth-Century Building Materials: History and Conservation* (Los Angeles, 2014), 101–104; Thomas Perry, "Rolling off a Log," *Scientific American* 166 (1942): 125–128.

24 See Plywood Pioneers Association, *Plywood in Retrospect: Portland Manufacturing Company* (Tacoma, WA, 1967), 2–3.

25 Oregon is still the United States' largest producer of plywood.

7

Interior of Forestry Building, Lewis and Clark Centennial,
Portland, Oregon, 1905
© Oregon Historical Society, Gifford Collection, Neg. 2602

sollte. Das Forstwirtschaftsgebäude war der größte Blockbau der Welt und erzählte die Geschichte von der ursprünglichen Besiedlung (Abb. 6–7). Es war eine Vergrößerung der rauen und vermeintlich ehrlichen Architektur aus ganzen Stämmen urwüchsiger Douglasien, die die Holzfäller an der Westküste im frühen 19. Jahrhundert eingeführt hatten. Im Schatten dieses Blockhauses war eine andere, weniger auftrumpfende Holzgeschichte zu sehen. Die frisch gegründete Portland Manufacturing Company, eine Firma die sich auf die Erzeugung von Körben und Kisten spezialisiert hatte, zeigte die vielleicht ersten Sperrholzplatten der Welt.[23] Sperrholz wurde in der Architektur zuerst für Türen und Vertäfelungen verwendet, wurde aber bald auch als Bodenuntergrund, zur Wandversteifung und als Betonverschalung eingesetzt.[24]

Diese beiden architektonischen Ansätze repräsentierten Portland auf der nationalen Bühne. Aufgrund seiner unmittelbaren materiellen Nähe zum Wald beruhte das Blockhaus auf einer Handwerkstechnik – die Blöcke wirkten authentisch, weil sie noch als Bäume erkennbar waren und an die Pioniergeschichte erinnerten. Diese handwerkliche Fähigkeit wandelte sich im Fall der Sperrholzplatten zu einer Fertigungstechnik der Arbeiter, die mithilfe von Maschinen ein neues Produkt geschaffen hatten. Verglichen mit dem Blockhaus waren die Sperrholzexponate zweifellos weniger ortstypisch. In seiner Fabriziertheit war es nicht authentisch; als Amalgam von verschiedenen Hölzern und Leim war es nicht repräsentativ für einen Ort; zu seiner Herstellung wurde, ungeachtet der Behauptungen von Firmengeschichten, wenig Muskelkraft benötigt. 1905 standen diese zwei Auffassungen von Technik – materielle Unmittelbarkeit und fachmännische Arbeit – für verschiedene Richtungen, die das Handwerk im Zuge der Moder-

nisierung einschlagen würde. Waren diese beiden Handwerksauffassungen in der Geschichte der regionalen Architektur des Nordwestens miteinander verbunden, so werden sie von den Erschütterungen des „Timber Territory", die mit einem Vulkanausbruch begannen und beim Fleckenkauz endeten, nun allmählich wieder getrennt.

Die mechanisierte Erzeugung von laminiertem Massivholz [KLT, Kreuzlagenholz, oder Brettsperrholz] könnte auf die Geschichte des Sperrholzes in der Region aufbauen und so wohl die authentischste Form von Ortsverbundenheit in der Architektur des Nordwestens sein.[25] Aber Massivholz bedarf – wie das Sperrholz vor ihm – keiner auf alten Bäumen beruhenden Forstwirtschaft. Die Assoziation mit dem Urwald, mit romantischen Vorstellungen von Wildnis und selbstgebauten Blockhütten und Pionierhäusern – also mit allem, was die kulturellen Narrative der Holzarchitektur des Nordwestens ausmacht – ist damit Vergangenheit. Hat es das Sägewerk mit Holzfällern im Wald zu tun, von denen es Baumstämme kauft, um sie an Großhändler weiterzuverkaufen, arbeitet das Schichtholzwerk mit ArchitektInnen, Baufirmen und BauherrInnen zusammen, die sich dafür interessieren, wie das Produkt aussieht und was es kann. Die ausgeklügelte Maßfertigung passt nicht in das Narrativ von Unabhängigkeit und Unmittelbarkeit, das den Geschichten der Holzarchitektur in den Vereinigten Staaten innewohnt. Aber sie versucht, eine auf Quantität getrimmte Infrastruktur zu einer auf qualitative Wertschöpfung ausgerichteten umzubauen. Statt Massivholz einen Platz in der Genealogie des in der Architekturgeschichte des Nordwestens so hoch gehandelten Handwerks zu verweigern, sollte man lieber das mit dem Blockhaus assoziierte Handwerk-als-materielle-Unmittelbarkeit durch das mit Sperrholz verbundene Handwerk-als-Arbeit ersetzen. Abgesehen von ästhetischen Fragen muss sich in diesem Narrativ auch das Verhältnis der Architektur zum Wald selbst ändern, muss sich der Kontext der Holzarchitektur von der Wildnis zur Waldpflege verschieben. Das ist eine Umkehrung früherer, ähnlich fabrizierter Narrative – Narrative, die darauf abzielten, vor allem das Land selbst zur Ware zu machen oder in Bundesforsten Inseln der Wildnis zu schaffen, die einem Land, das sonst durch das Zusammenspiel von Zimmerei, Sägewerk, Architektur und Wald geprägt ist, den Stachel ziehen.

23 Vgl. Jester, Thomas: „Plywood", in: ders. (Hg.): *Twentieth-Century Building Materials: History and Conservation*, Los Angeles 2014, 101–104; Perry, Thomas: „Rolling off a Log", *Scientific American* 166 (1942), 125–128.

24 Vgl. Plywood Pioneers Association, *Plywood in Retrospect: Portland Manufacturing Company*, Tacoma, WA 1967, 2–3.

25 Oregon ist immer noch der größte Sperrholzproduzent der Vereinigten Staaten.

islands of wilderness within National Forests that mitigated a territory otherwise defined by the interactions of join, mill, architecture, and forest.

Land. I asked Peter Hayes, a fourth-generation forester, if the "variable retention forestry," required to produce the kind of framework suggested by "Framework" could ever yield enough material to supply the growing demand for timber in the United States. "That is the wrong question," he replied. "The right question is, we have to make it work. What do we have to do to make it work?"[26] Large private timberland owners point out that it is not economically viable, that "single tree selection" over clear-cutting as a way to ensure ecological complexity is time-consuming and thus expensive.[27] Hayes says that kind of answer is only possible because society still accepts an industry that is allowed to externalize costs by excluding certain subsidies, processes, and non-financial costs from timber territory. One may argue that industrial modernity, in general, was built on this externalization. To rectify this, to expand the understanding of timber territory in time and geography, it is necessary to look at the land that supports the forests.

The impossibility of resolving the myth of a virginal wilderness to be transformed by hard work with the violent politics required to produce free land has built into the timber territory a number of seemingly irresolvable conflicts and externalities. Most forest land in the Pacific Northwest was granted free to railroad companies by the federal government. The largest give away was signed by Abraham Lincoln in 1864, conditionally granting public lands to the Northern Pacific railway company "for the purpose of building and maintaining a railroad from Lake Superior to the Pacific Ocean." Railways were granted public lands for a railroad right-of-way upon which to lay the tracks and 40 million acres (an area slightly smaller than Washington state) to raise capital needed to build and maintain the railroad. The land was granted in alternative square miles, which created a "checkerboard" pattern of ownership still visible from the air.[28] The reason it is still visible is that while this granted land was intended to be sold to family farmers, most of it went to large timber companies moving out west after having cleared all the timber in the Midwest.

The standard practice on private land was to clear-cut, then stop paying taxes on the land once it was barren and worthless, and move on. Only like this is it possible to see the tree, an investment that may have taken 500 years to mature, as almost-free. From the perspective of indigenous communities who had used these trees for likely over a thousand years, the forest, like everything in the land, needs to be accounted for seven generations into the future. Re-incorporating this time frame into silviculture also would make it impossible to treat the land in this way. Rising costs of land certainly compelled forestry practice to focus on replacing clear-cutting with plantations from mid-century, instead of clear-cutting and moving on leaving a wasteland behind it. But accounting for the full costs of forestland would change silviculture, by making the labor costs for variable retention and management less significant by comparison, and would reposition this land as part of the public trust that the National Forests were set up to protect. And there are still outstanding legal petitions to have the railroad lands that were illegally sold to private forest owners returned to the public.[29]

Nonetheless, the myth that the trees are a free resource on the land still supports the myths of freedom and independence that pervade the ways in which we discuss both timber architecture and its history, regional economies, rural development, and regulation. Of course, the freedom associated with forest land is a myth. Beyond the railroad's direct costs there were other costs borne by humans that were externalized. Initially the disease, death, and relocation of indigenous communities who lived on that land, though European colonizers also bore the financial costs of a century-long battle against indigenous peoples in terms of men, weapons, provisions, infrastructures, and health. The longer-term costs are the placing into private hands of the public resources of the United States and the resulting impoverishment of its ecological complexity.

26 Peter Hayes, conversation (see note 18).

27 Conversation with John Wilkinson, ex-Senior Vice President, Weyerhaeuser on October 1, 2020.

28 See Derrick Jensen and George Draffan, *Railroads and Clearcuts: Legacy of Congress's 1864 Northern Pacific Railroad Land Grant* (Spokane, WA, 1995), 3.

29 Ibid.

Land. Ich fragte Peter Hayes, einen Forstwirt in der vierten Generation in Oregon, ob eine Forstwirtschaft nach der variablen Retentionsmethode, die für die Schaffung des von Framework vorgeschlagenen Rahmens nötig ist, jemals genug Ertrag bringen würde, um die Holznachfrage in den Vereinigten Staaten zu befriedigen. „Das ist die falsche Frage", lautete seine Antwort. „Wir müssen das erreichen. Die richtige Frage ist, was müssen wir tun, um es zu erreichen?"[26] Große private Waldbesitzer sagen, dass das wirtschaftlich nicht möglich ist, dass die Einzelbaumentnahme zur Erhaltung der ökologischen Vielfalt zeitaufwändig und deshalb zu kostspielig ist.[27] Für Hayes ist diese Argumentation nur möglich, weil die Gesellschaft immer noch eine Wirtschaft akzeptiert, die Kosten externalisieren kann, indem sie gewisse Zuschüsse, Prozesse und Sachkosten aus dem Holzterritorium ausschließt. Man könnte sagen, dass die Industriemoderne ganz allgemein auf dieser Externalisierung beruht. Um zurechtzurücken, das Verständnis des „Timber Territory" zeitlich und geografisch zu erweitern, müssen wir uns das Land ansehen, das die Wälder nährt.

Die Unmöglichkeit, den Mythos einer durch harte Arbeit zu transformierende jungfräuliche Wildnis mit der zur Schaffung von freiem Land nötigen Gewaltpolitik zu lösen, hat dem „Timber Territory" scheinbar unlösbare Konflikte und Externalitäten eingeschrieben. Das meiste Waldland im Nordwesten der USA wurde von der Bundesregierung in der Mitte des 19. Jahrhunderts den Eisenbahngesellschaften umsonst überlassen. Die größte derartige Schenkung, die der Northern Pacific Railroad Company öffentliches Land „zum Zweck der Errichtung und Erhaltung einer Eisenbahnlinie vom Lake Superior bis zum Pazifischen Ozean" zusagte, wurde 1864 von Abraham Lincoln unterzeichnet. Die Eisenbahngesellschaften erhielten das Land als Baugrund für die Errichtung der Schienenwege, aber auch gut 16 Millionen Hektar (ein Fläche fast von der Größe des Staates Washington), um das Kapital für den Bau und die Erhaltung der Eisenbahnlinie aufzubringen. Das Land wurde in wechselnden Quadratmeilen vergeben, wodurch ein Schachbrettmuster der Eigentümer entstand, das noch heute aus Luft zu erkennen ist.[28] Das Schachbrettmuster ist deshalb noch sichtbar, weil das Land, das eigentlich an kleine Farmer verkauft werden sollte, vorwiegend an große Forstunternehmen ging, die nach der Abholzung des Mittelwestens weiter westwärts zogen.

Das übliche Verfahren privater Besitzer war, das Land kahlzuschlagen, und wenn es nutz- und wertlos geworden war, die Zahlung der Grundsteuer einzustellen und weiterzuziehen. Nur so ist es möglich, den Baum – eine Investition, die bis zu ihrer Fälligkeit vielleicht 500 Jahre gebraucht hat – als fast kostenlos anzusehen. Aus der Perspektive der indigenen Völker, die diese Bäume wohl über tausend Jahre lang genutzt hatten, ist für den Wald, wie für überhaupt alles im Land, sieben Generationen in die Zukunft Rechenschaft abzulegen. Mit der Wiederaufnahme dieses Zeithorizonts in die Forstwirtschaft würde es auch unmöglich, das Land auf diese Weise zu behandeln. Wegen steigender Bodenpreise musste die Forstwirtschaft zwar seit Mitte des letzten Jahrhunderts zur Plantagenwirtschaft übergehen, statt weiter Kahlschlag zu betreiben und Ödland zu hinterlassen. Doch erst ein Einstehen für die vollen Kosten von Waldland würde die Forstwirtschaft von Grund auf ändern, ließe es doch die Arbeitskosten für die nachhaltige Bewirtschaftung vergleichsweise günstig erscheinen, und würde dieses Land wieder zu einem Teil des öffentlichen Guts machen, zu dessen Schutz die U.S.-Bundesforste eingerichtet wurden. Bei Gericht sind immer noch Klagen anhängig, die die Restitution des Eisenbahnlands, das illegal an private Waldbesitzer verkauft wurde, an die öffentliche Hand verlangen.[29]

Gleichwohl nährt die Mär vom Baum als Gratisressource noch immer den Mythos von Freiheit und Unabhängigkeit, von dem unsere Art über Holzarchitektur und ihre Geschichte, über regionale Ökonomien, ländliche Entwicklung und Regulierungen zu sprechen, zutiefst durchdrungen ist. Die Freiheit, die wir mit dem Waldland verbinden, ist in der Tat ein Mythos. Zu den direkten Kosten der Bahn kamen andere, externalisierte Kosten, die von Menschen beglichen wurden. Da ist zunächst einmal der Zoll, den die auf diesem Land lebenden indigenen Völker entrichteten – Krankheit, Tod und Umsiedlung –, wiewohl auch die europäischen KolonistInnen ihr Scherflein zu dieser ein Jahrhundert währenden Schlacht beitrugen: Männer, Waffen, Verpflegung, Infrastruktur und Gesundheit. Zu den längerfristigen Kosten gehört die Überführung der öffentlichen Ressourcen der Vereinigten Staaten in Privatbesitz und die daraus folgende Reduktion ihrer ökologischen Komplexität. Dennoch wurde das freie Land bald mit Freiheit für die europäischen Kolonisten gleichgesetzt, und Wildnis bedeutete alsbald unentgeltliche Ressourcen und die Freiheit, sich ihrer ohne Einschränkungen zu entledigen. Diese Idee vom freien Land ist auch der Grund, weshalb Forst- und Holzbetriebe ihre Firmengeschichten allesamt auf einen Mann

---

26 Peter Hayes im Gespräch (wie Anm. 18).

27 Gespräch mit John Wilkinson, früherer stellvertretender Vorstandsvorsitzender von Weyerhaeuser, am 1. Oktober 2020.

28 Vgl. Jensen, Derrick/Draffan, George: *Railroads and Clearcuts: Legacy of Congress's 1864 Northern Pacific Railroad Land Grant*, Spokane, WA 1995, 3.

29 Ebd.

Nonetheless, free land quickly became equated with freedom for European colonizers and wilderness grew to mean both free resources and a freedom from constraints on how to dispose of them. It is this free land that allows histories of timber companies and manufacturers to begin their biographies alike, with one man buying some land and, merely by working hard, building up a large, successful family timber business. Undoubtedly cutting down a 500-year-old tree is hard work, but hard work alone would not make it a successful venture.

It is not surprising that developments in laminated timber construction paralleled the disappearance of easy to reach old-growth timber. It utilizes many small pieces of timber. Mass timber will probably sever the association between architecture and wilderness that long defined regional architecture. This architecture would not be rooted in a forest but assembled from a plantation. "Framework's" challenge is to build a new identity for timber architecture in the Northwest. It seems the best way we can imagine this is to focus on the arrows that join "Framework's" framework instead of the points (tall wood building, healthy cities, Oregon managed forests, lumber mill, engineered wood products) in the chain. While all those agents may be in place, it is the nature of these relationships that will determine the outcome of the new timber territory. A new narrative focused on the people that maintain this infrastructure would replace "wilderness" with "stewardship" just as it replaces "forest" with "plantation." But stewardship, like joints, like forests, like buildings, has to be designed carefully.

Design. To achieve "Framework's" framework is not a difficult task, but it is still a complicated one. All the pieces are there, but pulling them together will be a design project, synthesizing processes and agents currently each focused on their own specialized part of the commodity chain. The benefit of seeing timber territory not as a war but as a design project is that architecture has the opportunity to make some design changes to it. By seeing the timber territory as a relationship between multiple agents that was for a long time driven by unchanging narratives (even as it was feeling the shocks of external environmental, economic, or cultural change) allows us to question other ways in which the pieces *could* be put together. If the old narrative began to crumble in 1980, maybe 2015 was the beginning of a new one. To create a more sustainable city of wood means to re-design the material flows that define the production of the built environment. Currently, the infrastructure that ties together the production of much of the United States' single-family housing—a whole other narrative that may need to be questioned—is driven by large-scale environmental extraction and industrial production. Underneath this was the premise that wood was a trade commodity and not a local resource. That original premise pulled together a variety of conditions into an infrastructure that has been hard to change, pulling land infrastructure and owners, merchants, millers, builders, and designers, not to mention housing customers, or consumers, into a seemingly inflexible relationship supported by cultural narratives, perhaps the most intransigent of agents in this assemblage. An infrastructure that worked in an era of free or almost-free land, seemingly endless timber resources, a frontier economy, and growing single-family housing demand is not well suited to accept new values. Resilience, not just for the material but those whose livelihoods depend upon it; conservation, or preservation, of forests for other reasons than material use; the need to densify human settlement patterns in this country for both environmental reasons and costs of infrastructure. The material flow of wood has, over two hundred years, crystallized into something that no longer works for the values we are asking it to accommodate today, but the economic scale of this infrastructure is what makes decisions today completely dependent upon the decisions of yesterday. "Framework" asks us to collaborate in designing this territory. Part of that work will be to tell new stories about how forests, houses, and people can steward the territory together and reframe the conventional narratives of free land, without calling it a war. ∎

zurückführen können, der etwas Land gekauft und allein durch seine harte Arbeit ein großes erfolgreiches Familienunternehmen aufgebaut hat. Das Fällen eines 500 Jahre alten Baums ist zweifellos harte Arbeit, aber damit allein entstünde noch kein erfolgreiches Unternehmen.

Es ist wenig überraschend, dass die Entwicklung auf dem Schichtholzsektor mit dem Verschwinden von leicht verfügbarem Urwaldholz einherging. Schichtholz verwendet viele kleine Holzteile. Es wird die Verbindung von Architektur und Wildnis, die die Regionalarchitektur so lange definierte, vermutlich kappen. Die neue Architektur wäre nicht mehr im Wald verwurzelt, sondern käme von einer Plantage. Das Ziel von „Framework" ist, eine neue Identität für Holzarchitektur im Nordwesten zu schaffen. Die bestmögliche Art dies zu tun, ist es, den Fokus auf die Vektoren im Rahmen von „Framework" zu legen, und nicht auf die einzelnen Glieder der Kette (Holzhochhausbau, gesunde Städte, verwaltete regionale Wälder, Sägewerke, Holzwerkstoffe). Denn auch wenn all diese Glieder existieren, so wird das Ergebnis des neuen „Timber Territory" doch durch die Art ihrer Beziehung bestimmt. Ein neues Narrativ, das den Schwerpunkt auf die Personen legt, die diese Infrastruktur erhalten, würde „Wildnis" durch „Ressourcen und Produktverantwortung" ersetzen, so wie es den „Wald" durch die „Plantage" ersetzt. Aber Ressourcen- und Produktverantwortung müssen wie Holzverbindungen, Wälder und Gebäude sorgfältig geplant werden.

Entwurf. Den Rahmen von „Framework" zu schaffen ist nicht besonders schwer, aber auch nicht unkompliziert. Die Einzelteile sind alle vorhanden, aber sie zusammenzufügen ist ein Entwurfsprojekt: eine Synthese von Prozessen und Kräften, die im Augenblick alle auf ihr eigenes Spezialgebiet in der Produktionskette fokussiert sind. Das „Timber Territory" nicht als Konflikt, sondern als Entwurfsprojekt zu verstehen, hat den Vorteil, dass die Architektur damit die Möglichkeit erhält, es teilweise umzugestalten. Betrachtet man das „Timber Territory" als Beziehungsgeflecht zwischen einer Vielzahl von Akteuren, das lange Zeit von scheinbar unveränderlichen Narrativen geprägt wurde (sogar noch, als die Erschütterungen durch den ökologischen, ökonomischen und kulturellen Wandels bereits spürbar waren), kann man andere Möglichkeiten in Betracht ziehen, diese Einzelteile zusammenzusetzen. Begann das alte Narrativ um 1980 zu bröckeln, so markierte 2015 vielleicht den

Beginn eines neuen. Die Schaffung einer nachhaltigen Stadt aus Holz impliziert den Umbau der Materialflüsse, die die Produktion der gebauten Umwelt bestimmen. Die aktuelle Infrastruktur, die die Produktion der meisten Einfamilienhäuser in den USA zusammenhält – übrigens ein ganz anderes Narrativ, das infrage gestellt werden müsste – ist von Umweltausbeutung und industrieller Produktion im großen Stil geprägt. Dabei wurde vorausgesetzt, dass Holz ein Handelsgut und nicht eine lokale Ressource ist. Diese Voraussetzung verband eine Reihe von Akteuren zu einem schwer veränderlichen Gebilde, verknüpfte ländliche Infrastruktur und LandbesitzerInnen, HändlerInnen, SägewerksbetreiberInnen, BauunternehmerInnen und ArchitektInnen, aber auch AuftraggeberInnen oder HausbewohnerInnen zu einem scheinbar starren Beziehungsgefüge, dessen wohl unbeugsamste Elemente die es stützenden kulturellen Narrative waren. Aber was in einem Zeitalter kostenlosen oder fast kostenlosen Landes, scheinbar endloser Holzreserven, einer Pionierökonomie und einer steigenden Nachfrage nach Einfamilienhäusern funktionierte, ist nicht dazu angetan, neue Werte zu akzeptieren: Resilienz, nicht nur für das Material, sondern auch für diejenigen, deren Lebensunterhalt auf ihm beruht; Erhaltung von Wäldern nicht nur um ihres materiellen Nutzens willen; Notwendigkeit zur Verdichtung menschlicher Siedlungsmuster in diesem Land, und zwar aus ökologischen Gründen ebenso wie aus Gründen der Infrastrukturkosten. Der Materialfluss von Holz hat im Lauf von über zweihundert Jahren eine Form angenommen, die nicht mehr den Werten zu genügen vermag, die wir ihm heute auferlegen, aber aufgrund der ökonomischen Größe dieser Infrastruktur hängen heutige Entscheidungen vollkommen von den Entscheidungen von gestern ab. „Framework" fordert zur Zusammenarbeit bei der Gestaltung dieses „Timber Territory" auf. Zum Teil wird diese Zusammenarbeit darin bestehen, neue Geschichten über Wälder, Häuser und Menschen zu erzählen und darüber nachzudenken, wie wir gemeinsam Verantwortung dafür übernehmen können – und zwar entkoppelt von traditionalistischen Freiheitsdiskursen und ohne es einen Krieg nennen zu müssen. ∎

Übersetzung: Wilfried Prantner

Nonexploitative Architecture: Beyond an Utilitarian Perspective on Wood

Architektur ohne Ausbeutung. Jenseits einer zweckorientierten Auffassung von Holz

Francesca Zanotto

1   Formafantasma, *Seeing the Wood for the Trees*, film still, 2020 © Formafantasma

Last year's public debate instigated fervent political discourse around the use of natural resources, the origins of goods and the sustainability—intended as environmental but also as social and cultural—of global production and consumption patterns. Consumers not only increasingly demand for cleaner processes behind their goods, but also for fairer supply chains, along which no exploitation is perpetrated and the rights of involved communities and living beings are safeguarded. Besides humans, these concerns are generally expressed for other animal species, whose bodies are turned into commodities by the global market and whose by-products are goods to sell and buy. Based on the zoocentrism of classic evolutionary literature and liberation causes,[1] movements advocating for non-humans' rights focus indeed on animals. However, thanks to the recent growth and diffusion of posthuman studies, the common understanding of the scope of non-humans is also broadening, and beginning to include other beings: plants, trees, as well as complex entities such as ecosystems. Their interest is starting to be a matter of concern within production and consumption processes aiming at fairness.

The discussion around non-humans as right-holders—involving a scope of beings broader than animals—is framed in modern terms by Christopher D. Stone in the seminal work "Should Trees Have Standing? Towards Legal Rights for Natural Objects,"[2] published in 1972 in reference with the legal fight *Sierra Club v. Morton*, seeing the environmental organization Sierra Club trying to block the approval of an extensive skiing development in the Mineral King Valley in the Sequoia National Forest.[3] Within the debate sparked by the case, the idea to legally personify inanimate objects—and, in this case, natural entities—providing them with rights for their own protection takes roots, despite that environmental regulations were—and mostly still are—built with a homocentric perspective, around potential loss of profits or benefits for humans. The personification of the environment has recently seen sentences granting rights to inanimate objects, such as in the case of the river Whanganui in New Zealand[4] and the rivers Ganga and Yamuna in India,[5] whereby legal personhood with fundamental rights was subsequently extended by the Uttarakhand high court to the connected rivers, streams, air, meadows, dales, jungles, forests wetlands, grasslands, springs, and waterfalls. Many of these advances have been made possible by the commitment of indigenous communities: in his essay "Nonhuman Rights," Paulo Tavares draws the attention to the case of the BP oil spill in the Gulf of Mexico in 2010, an environmental disaster to which legal response came from a lawsuit filed "in defense of the rights of the sea"[6] in the Constitutional Court of Ecuador, signed by the main indigenous organizations of the country, international NGOs and activists. The spiritual and cultural relationship between indigenous cultures and nature is part of the conversation as a driving force able to safeguard the interest of natural entities in legal disputes and, above all, reflects a perspective able to uproot the vision of nature imposed by the power: "a universal condition, [...] reducing the diversity of forms of entanglement between society and environment to an univocally utilitarian perspective."[7]

In this framework of renewed attention for the complex systems behind products and objects—"entanglements of materials, technologies, labor, interests, history, and ideals"[8]—and embracing a widespread political mindset on inanimate entities and their rights, the architecture domain has started to expand its perspective on the materials employed within the industry. Beside questioning their environmental impact, under reconsideration is the fairness of their production in relation to people, heritages, non-human entities, and ecosystems involved. Even the very idea of sustainable materials is challenged, as it is becoming increasingly clear how some of them—as "organic materials"—end up being sustainable just from a human perspective, while the survival or well-being of other involved species may be endangered. The bodies of other species—animals and non-animals—have been an essential tool for human evolution: "For the first million years or so after his appearance, man used essentially five materials to make all his tools and objects and structures: wood, rock, bone, horn, and

---

1 See Emanuele Coccia, *The Life of Plants: A Metaphysics of Mixture* (Cambridge, UK, 2018), 4.

2 Christopher D. Stone, "Should Trees Have Standing? Towards Legal Rights for Natural Objects," in *Southern California Law Review* 45 (1972): 450–501.

3 See "Sierra Club v. Morton, 405 U.S. 727," 1972, available online at: https://supreme.justia.com/cases/federal/us/405/727/ (accessed December 6, 2020).

4 See Jeremy Lurgio, "Saving the Whanganui: Can *Personhood* Rescue a River?" *The Guardian*, November 29, 2019, available online at: https://www.theguardian.com/world/2019/nov/30/saving-the-whanganui-can-personhood-rescue-a-river (accessed December 6, 2020).

5 See Kevin Schneider, "Why You Should Be Excited About India's 'Rivers with Rights' Ruling," in *Nonhuman Rights Blog* (2017), available online at: https://www.nonhumanrights.org/blog/rivers-with-rights/ (accessed December 6, 2020).

6 Lawsuit on Behalf of the Rights of Nature under the Principle of Universal Jurisdiction, filed November 26, 2010 in the Constitutional Court of Ecuador, at 1. in Paulo Tavares, "Nonhuman Rights," in *Forensis: The Architecture of Public Truth*, ed. Eyal Weizman, Anselm Franke, and Forensic Architecture (Berlin, 2014), 553–572, esp. 557.

7 Tavares, "Nonhuman Rights" (see note 6), 555.

8 Paola Antonelli, "Design and the Politics of Wood," in *Formafantasma: Cambio*, ed. Riccardo Badano and Rebecca Lewin (Cologne, 2020), 35–45.

Der öffentliche Diskurs des vergangenen Jahres war u.a. von leidenschaftlichen politischen Auseinandersetzungen über die Verwendung natürlicher Rohstoffe, den Ursprung von Waren und die Nachhaltigkeit – im ökologischen wie im sozialen und kulturellen Sinn – globaler Produktions- und Verbrauchszyklen geprägt. KonsumentInnen verlangen zunehmend nach Waren, die sauber produziert sind und auf fairen Lieferketten beruhen, entlang derer keine Ausbeutung stattfindet und die Rechte der daran beteiligten Gruppen und Lebewesen geachtet werden. Dieser Anspruch wird im Allgemeinen nicht nur in Bezug auf Menschen, sondern auch auf andere (nicht-menschliche) Arten erhoben, deren Körper oder Nebenprodukte vom globalen Markt zur Ware gemacht werden. Im Einklang mit dem Zoozentrismus der klassischen Evolutionsliteratur und Befreiungsanliegen[1] geht es Bewegungen, die sich für die Rechte von Nicht-Menschen einsetzen, zwar in erster Linie um Tiere, doch mit der jüngsten Ausbreitung des Posthumanismus weitet sich der Begriff dessen, was wir allgemein unter Nicht-Menschen verstehen, nun ebenso auf andere Lebewesen aus: auf Pflanzen und Bäume und sogar auf komplexe Gebilde wie Ökosysteme. Das Interesse daran wird zunehmend auch zu einem Anliegen in Produktions- und Konsumptionsprozessen, die auf Fairness setzen.

In moderne Rechtskategorien übersetzt und in einem über das Tierreich hinausgehenden Sinn wurde die Diskussion über Nicht-Menschen als Rechtssubjekte erstmals von Christopher D. Stone in seinem wegweisenden Text „Should Trees Have Standing? Towards Legal Rights for Natural Objects" eingeführt.[2] Der Text erschien 1972 im Zusammenhang mit dem Rechtsstreit *Sierra Club v. Morton*, mit dem die Umweltschutzorganisation Sierra Club die Baugenehmigung für ein riesiges Skigebiet im Mineral King Valley im Sequoia-Nationalpark zu verhindern versuchte.[3] Im Zuge der Debatte, die durch den Fall entfacht wurde, entstand die Idee, unbelebte – und in diesem Fall auch natürliche – Objekte zu Rechtspersonen zu machen; sie mit Rechten auszustatten, die ihrem eigenen Schutz dienen, im Gegensatz zum damals – und meist auch heute noch – gültigen anthropozentrischen Ansatz der Umweltgesetzgebung, die vom potenziellen Profit- oder Nutzenverlust für den Menschen ausgeht. Die Personifizierung der Umwelt hat in letzter Zeit zu Gerichtsurteilen geführt, die unbelebte Objekte wie dem Fluss Whanganui in Neuseeland[4] oder dem Ganges und der Yamuna in Indien[5] den Status von Rechtspersonen mit Grundrechten zuerkannten, wobei dieser im Fall der beiden letzteren vom Höchstgericht in Uttarakhand noch auf die angrenzenden Flüsse und Bäche, die Luft, die Wiesen, die Täler, den Dschungel, die Wälder, die Auen, das Grasland, die Quellen und Wasserfälle ausgeweitet wurde. Viele dieser Fortschritte wurden durch das Engagement indigener Communities ermöglicht: In seinem Essay „Nonhuman Rights" lenkt Paulo Tavares das Augenmerk auf den Fall der 2010 von BP verursachten Ölpest im Golf von Mexiko, einer Umweltkatastrophe, gegen die juristisch mit einer am Verfassungsgericht von Ecuador eingereichten und von den bedeutendsten Indigenenorganisationen des Landes sowie internationalen NGOs und AktivistInnen unterzeichneten Klage „zur Verteidigung der Rechte des Meeres"[6] vorgegangen wurde. Die spirituelle und kulturelle Beziehung indigener Kulturen zur Natur ist eine treibende Kraft bei der Wahrung der Interessen natürlicher Entitäten in juristischen Auseinandersetzungen, und reflektiert eine Weltsicht, die imstande ist, das herrschende Bild von der Natur als einem „universellen Zustand, der […] die Vielfalt an Verflechtungen zwischen Gesellschaft und Umwelt auf ein reines Nutzverhältnis reduziert",[7] zu zerschlagen.

Im Zuge dieser erneuten Aufmerksamkeit für die Produkten und Objekten zugrundeliegenden komplexen Systeme – „Verflechtungen von Materialien, Technologien, Arbeit, Interessen, historischen Gegebenheiten und Idealen"[8] – und der sich verbreitenden politischen Einstellung gegenüber unbelebten Entitäten und ihren Rechten hat auch die Architektur begonnen, ihren Standpunkt in Bezug auf die verwendeten Materialien zu überdenken. Auf dem Prüfstand steht neben ihrer Umweltbelastung auch, was ihre Produktion mit Menschen, dem kulturellen Erbe, nicht-menschlichen Entitäten und Ökosystemen anrichtet. Sogar die Idee nachhaltiger Materialien selbst wird infrage gestellt, da zunehmend deutlich wird, dass einige davon – etwa „organische Materialien" – lediglich von einem menschlichen Standpunkt aus nachhaltig sind, während

1 Vgl. Coccia, Emanuele: *The Life of Plants: A Metaphysics of Mixture*, Cambridge, UK, 2018, 4.

2 Stone, Christopher D.: „Should Trees Have Standing? Towards Legal Rights for Natural Objects", in: *Southern California Law Review* 45 (1972), 450–501.

3 Vgl. „Sierra Club v. Morton, 405 U.S. 727", 1972, online unter: https://supreme.justia.com/cases/federal/us/405/727/ (Stand: 6. Dezember 2020).

4 Vgl. Lurgio, Jeremy: „Saving the Whanganui: Can *Personhood* Rescue a River?", *The Guardian*, 29. November 2019, online unter: https://www.theguardian.com/world/2019/nov/30/saving-the-whanganui-can-personhood-rescue-a-river (Stand: 6. Dezember 2020).

5 Vgl. Schneider, Kevin: „Why You Should Be Excited About India's ‚Rivers with Rights' Ruling", in: *Nonhuman Rights Blog* (2017), online unter: https://www.nonhumanrights.org/blog/rivers-with-rights/ (Stand: 6. Dezember 2020).

6 Lawsuit on Behalf of the Rights of Nature under the Principle of Universal Jurisdiction, filed November 26, 2010 in the Constitutional Court of Ecuador, 1. Zit. n. Tavares, Paulo: „Nonhuman Rights", in: Weizman, Eyal/Franke, Anselm/Forensic Architecture (Hg.): *Forensis: The Architecture of Public Truth*, Berlin 2014, 553–572, hier. 557.

7 Tavares, „Nonhuman Rights" (wie Anm. 6), 555 (Übers. W.P.).

8 Antonelli, Paola: „Design and the Politics of Wood", in: Badano, Riccardo/Lewin, Rebecca (Hg.): *Formafantasma: Cambio*, Köln 2020, 35–45 (Übers. W.P.)

leather."[9] Just one out of five elements in the group summarized by John Thackara does not come from the body of another living being. After exploiting them for millennia to avoid labor, for leisure and entertainment, for sustenance, shelter, and clothing, humans have now started to question this state of things, trying to re-design highly exploitative industries. Many steps towards a less-exploitative market have been taken, as well as protocols to guarantee the transparency of supply chains. However, projects such as *PIG 05049*[10] by Christien Meindertsma, recounted in a 185-page-book reconstructing all the unexpected by-products extracted from a single pig, unveil how the exploitation of other species perpetrated by humans is pervasive and deeply rooted in the capitalistic global market. This cogitation on materials' fairness is boosting fervent research for alternatives in the design domain, of which the most radical results expand the spectrum of organic materials, including products of human origin: designers employ blood, hair, urine, and bodily fluids to mold items, make furniture and derive coatings and finishes, as in "The New Age of Trichology"[11] by Sanne Visser and "Urine Ware"[12] by Sinae Kim, employing waste products from human body as renewable resources.

These experiments, as far as radical, outline a dismantling of the exploitative structures existing among species: they entail a shift from an anthropocentric perspective towards a more equitable condition, where humans switch from exploiting non-human bodies to employing matter derived from their own to shape the shared living environment. They raise a crucial issue for contemporary architectural design, especially in the age of humanity where we are beginning to challenge our right to put ourselves at the center of the universe: how much interspecies exploitation is behind architecture?

A promising domain to consider in order to adopt a broader perspective on the sustainability of materials employed within architectural and construction processes is wood, recently the focus of renewed attention devoted by the industry as a climate-friendly construction solution. Wood is a renewable resource, harvested from trees that regenerate slowly but, however, according to time spans which are "just a blink on any geological time scale, i.e. the time scale for the replenishment of the Earth's resources (rocks, ores and soils) required in the supply chain of other construction materials."[13] Wood is back in the architectural debate as a sustainable material, light,

adaptable, with a low carbon impact and low embodied energy: "the benefits in the ecological and environmental aspects of wood-based constructions are indisputable."[14] Technological advances in construction techniques make timber suitable for high-rise buildings and large scale projects: in 2017, the construction of the student residence building Brock Commons Tallwood House was completed in Vancouver, back then providing the city with the tallest building (53 meters) with a timber structure in the world.[15] In 2019, this primacy passed to Mjøstårnet, a 85,4 meters-high mixed-use building completed in Brumunddal, Norway,[16] while Zaha Hadid Architects obtained the permission to realize the world's first wooden football stadium in Gloucestershire, England.[17] However, the renewed popularity of wood may also be related to the emerging of an independent, "smaller dimension" of the architectural practice: individuals or small offices practicing self-building as a way to reconnect with the ancestral building craft and, at the same time, performing an act of resistance "to the reduction of architecture to a rentable commodity";[18] the multiplication of recurring architectural exhibitions around the world, showcasing experimental and innovative agencies producing prototypal

9   John Thackara, *In the Bubble: Designing in a Complex World* (Cambridge, MA, 2005), 188.

10 See Christien Meindertsma, *PIG 05049* (Rotterdam, 2007).

11 See Sanne Visser, "The New Age of Tricology," in *Sanne Visser Studio* (2016), available online at: https://sannevisser.com/The-New-Age-of-Trichology (accessed September 25, 2020).

12 See Sinae Kim Studio, "Urine-Glaze," in *Material District* (2020), available online at: https://materialdistrict.com/material/urine-glaze/ (accessed December 6, 2020).

13 Michael H. Ramage et al., "The Wood From the Trees: The Use of Timber in Construction," in *Renewable and Sustainable Energy Reviews* 68 (2017): 333–359, esp. 340, available online at: https://www.sciencedirect.com/science/article/pii/S1364032116306050 (accessed September 25, 2020).

14 Jozef Svajlenka and Maria Kozlovska, "Evaluation of the Efficiency and Sustainability of Timber-Based Construction," in *Journal of Cleaner Production* 259 (2020): 1–12, esp. 11, available online at: https://www.sciencedirect.com/science/article/abs/pii/S0959652620308829 (accessed September 25, 2020).

15 See Zoya Gul Hasan, "Inside Vancouver's Brock Commons, the World's Tallest Mass Timber Building," *Archdaily* (2017), available online at: https://www.archdaily.com/879625/inside-vancouvers-brock-commons-the-worlds-tallest-timber-structured-building (accessed September 25, 2020).

16 See Moelven, "Mjøstårnet," *Moelven* (2019), available online at: https://www.moelven.com/mjostarnet/ (accessed January 28, 2021).

17 See India Block, "Zaha Hadid Architects Wins Approval for World's First All-Timber Stadium," in *Dezeen* (2019), available online at: https://www.dezeen.com/2019/12/27/worlds-first-timber-stadium-zaha-hadid-architects/ (accessed September 25, 2020).

18 Alejandro Zaera-Polo, "Well Into the 21st Century. The Architectures of Post-Capitalism?," in *El Croquis* 187 (2016): 252–287, esp. 256.

das Überleben oder Wohlergehen anderer beteiligter Arten gefährdet werden darf. Die Körper anderer Arten, tierischer wie nicht-tierischer, waren zentrale Mittel der menschlichen Entwicklung: „Während der ersten Million Jahre seiner Geschichte waren es im Wesentlichen fünf Materialien, aus denen der Mensch sämtliche Werkzeuge, Gegenstände und Bauwerke erzeugte: Holz, Stein, Knochen, Horn und Leder."[9] Lediglich eines dieser von John Thackara genannten Materialien stammt nicht vom Körper eines anderen Lebewesens. Nachdem wir sie jahrtausendelang zu Zwecken der Arbeitserleichterung, der Unterhaltung, des Lebensunterhalts, des Wohnens und der Bekleidung ausgebeutet haben, stellen wir diesen Zustand nun langsam infrage und versuchen, ausbeutende Industrien neu aufzustellen. Viele Schritte in Richtung eines weniger exploitativen Marktes wurden bereits unternommen, und es wurden Protokolle eingeführt, um Lieferketten transparent zu machen. Allerdings zeigen Projekte wie *PIG 05049*[10] von Christien Meindertsma, eine Rekonstruktion sämtlicher aus einem einzigen Schwein gewonnener Produkte, wie umfassend und tief verwurzelt die Ausbeutung anderer Spezies durch den Menschen im globalisierten kapitalistischen Markt ist. Derartige Überlegungen zur Fairness von Materialien haben im Designsektor zu einer eifrigen Suche nach Alternativen geführt, deren radikalste Ergebnisse das Spektrum organischer Materialien auf solche menschlichen Ursprungs ausdehnen. Designerinnen und Designer wie z.B. Sanne Visser mit „The New Age of Trichology"[11] oder Sinae Kim mit „Urine Ware"[12] verwenden Abfallprodukte des menschlichen Körpers als erneuerbare Ressourcen, schaffen Konsumartikel, Möbel und Glasuren aus Blut, Haar, Urin und anderen Körperflüssigkeiten.

In ihrer Radikalität deuten diese Experimente an, wie Ausbeutungsverhältnisse zwischen den Arten abgebaut werden könnten: Sie bedeuten eine Verschiebung von einem anthropozentrischen Weltbild zu gerechteren Verhältnissen, in denen der Mensch bei der Gestaltung der gemeinsamen Umwelt von der Ausbeutung nicht-menschlicher Körper zur Benutzung von aus dem eigenen Körper gewonnenen Materialien übergeht. Sie werfen eine fundamentale Frage für die zeitgenössische Architektur in einem Zeitalter auf, in dem wir das Recht des Menschen, ein Haus zu bauen und sich im Zentrum des Universums zu verorten, zunehmend infrage stellen: Wieviel Ausbeutung anderer Arten steckt in Architektur?

Ein gut geeigneter Bereich, um die Nachhaltigkeit der in Architektur und Bauwesen verwendeten Materialien unter diesem breiteren Gesichtspunkt betrachten, ist Holz, das als klimafreundliches Baumaterial neuerdings wieder in den Fokus der Aufmerksamkeit gerückt ist. Holz ist eine erneuerbare Ressource, gewonnen aus Bäumen, die sich zwar langsam, aber immerhin in Zeitspannen erneuern, die „nach erdgeschichtlichen Maßstäben, d.h. den Zeiträumen, die die in der Lieferkette anderer Baumaterialen enthaltenen Erdressourcen (Steine, Erze, Erden) zur Regeneration benötigen, lediglich einen Wimpernschlag darstellen".[13] Als nachhaltiges, leichtes, anpassungsfähiges Material mit guter CO_2-Bilanz und geringer grauer Energie steht Holz im Architekturdiskurs jedenfalls wieder verstärkt auf der Agenda: „[D]ie Vorteile holzbasierter Bauten in Hinblick auf Ökologie und Umweltbelastung sind unbestreitbar."[14] Dank bautechnischer Fortschritte eignet sich Holz heute auch für Hochhäuser und Großprojekte: 2017 wurde in Vancouver das Studierendenwohnheim Brock Commons Tallwood House fertiggestellt, das der Stadt das damals weltweit höchste Gebäude in Holzbauweise (53 Meter) bescherte.[15] 2019 ging dieser Titel auf das Mjøstårnet, ein Gebäude mit Mischnutzung in Brumunddal, Norwegen,[16] über, und Zaha Hadid Architects erhielten in Gloucestershire, England, die Genehmigung zur Errichtung des ersten Fußballstadions aus Holz.[17] Doch die neue Beliebtheit von Holz lässt sich auch mit der Entstehung einer unabhängigen, „kleiner dimensionierten" Architekturpraxis in Verbindung bringen: Individuen oder kleinen Büros, die den Selbstbau als eine Möglichkeit praktizieren, an die Baukunst der Vorfahren anzuschließen und zugleich einen Akt des Widerstands gegen die „Reduzierung der Architektur auf eine (ver)mietbare Ware"[18] zu leisten; die aus dem Boden schießenden Architekturausstellungen in aller Welt, die prototypische

9 Thackara, John: *In the Bubble: Designing in a Complex World*, Cambridge, MA 2005, 188 (Übers. W.P.).

10 Vgl. Meindertsma, Christien: *PIG 05049*, Rotterdam 2007.

11 Vgl. Visser, Sanne: „The New Age of Tricology", in: *Sanne Visser Studio* (2016), online unter: https://sannevisser.com/The-New-Age-of-Trichology (Stand: 25. September 2020).

12 Vgl. Kim, Sinae Studio: „Urine-Glaze", in: *Material District* (2020), online unter: https://materialdistrict.com/material/urine-glaze/ (Stand: 6. Dezember 2020).

13 Ramage, Michael H., et al.: „The Wood From the Trees: The Use of Timber in Construction", in: *Renewable and Sustainable Energy Reviews* 68 (2017): 333–359, hier: 340, online unter: https://www.sciencedirect.com/science/article/pii/S1364032116306050 (Stand: 25. September 2020).

14 Svajlenka, Jozef/Kozlovska, Maria: „Evaluation of the Efficiency and Sustainability of Timber-Based Construction", in: *Journal of Cleaner Production* 259 (2020), 1–12, hier 11, online unter: https://www.sciencedirect.com/science/article/abs/pii/S0959652620308829 (Stand: 25. September 2020).

15 Vgl. Zoya Gul, Hasan: „Inside Vancouver's Brock Commons, the World's Tallest Mass Timber Building", *Archdaily* (2017), online unter: https://www.archdaily.com/879625/inside-vancouvers-brock-commons-the-worlds-tallest-timber-structured-building (Stand: 25. September 2020).

16 Vgl. „Mjøstårnet", in: *Moelven* (2019), online unter: https://www.moelven.com/mjostarnet/ (Stand: 28. Januar, 2021).

17 Vgl. Block, India: „Zaha Hadid Architects Wins Approval for World's First All-Timber Stadium", in: *Dezeen* (2019), online unter: https://www.dezeen.com/2019/12/27/worlds-first-timber-stadium-zaha-hadid-architects/ (Stand: 25. September 2020).

18 Zaera-Polo, Alejandro: „Well into the 21st Century. The Architectures of Post-Capitalism?", in: *El Croquis* 187 (2016); 252–287, hier 256.

designs; the fervent experimentations on temporary architecture and material reuse. Timber is cheap and easily accessible; the simplicity of timber construction techniques makes wood the favorite material of self-builders, innovators, activists, and any designer aiming to practice a "mild-mannered,"[19] low-impact architecture.

Under a political perspective, the use of wood in the construction industry poses several questions, all of them set by the different angles decisionmakers and stakeholders have on wood. Wood is the biological ensemble of cells produced by the tree as structural element. Wood is the flesh of a living being, an individual part of a complex ecosystem. Wood is an asset with a commercial value and a dedicated regulation. In reference to the establishment of a new Constitution for Ecuador in 2008, through the words of ecologist Esperanza Martínez, Tavares recounts the efforts to break up the regime established by the heritage of colonialism by choosing a specific term referring to nature: "*Pachamama*—usually interpreted as *Madre Tierra*, 'Mother Earth,' a mythical deity entity that is omnipresent in Andean indigenous cultures—was the chosen concept to guarantee that Amerindian cosmologies were politically represented within constitutional law. 'If modernity has adopted a single paradigm, one single rationality, one sole model of nature,' Martínez concluded, 'what we are saying is that there is not only one but many, as many as there are cultures.'"[20] In the case of the Ecuadorian Constitution, the adoption of an inclusive view on nature, able to comprise and express a multitude of possible perspectives on wood, trees, and forests, tries to overcome merely techno-scientific or capitalistic notions of nature and environment which continue to inform regulations on wood in most parts of the world, as far as they are aimed to safeguard the environment.

One of the tools employed globally to ensure a fair use of wood is the regulation on logging. In comparison to many other raw materials employed in the industry, timber is a fast-renewing resource, and regulations allow the coupling of the commercial exploitation of this feature with its regeneration cycles and with the main task performed by trees: absorbing CO_2 from the atmosphere. However, illegal logging is still widespread, often intruding the legal timber market with unregulated products. In 2014, Europe still imported roundwood and sawnwood at high risk of illegality for a value of 453,9 millions of USD, equivalent to the 7,2 percent of the total export value generated globally from source regions at risk.[21] The impacts of illegal logging are multiple and severe: it directly and indirectly affects socially, economically, politically, and environmentally the areas targeted, as well as the global dimension, for example contributing to the process of deforestation. Direct social impacts involve the lack of social control over forest assets undermining the authority of local institutions, while indirect impacts include the development of external forms of control over the use of forests performed locally by smallholders, indigenous and other communities; cumulative impacts include a diminished resilient capacity of interested communities to adapt to economic change and climate change.[22] The European Union issued the Regulation 995/2010 to prohibit traders in EU timber market to trade illegally harvested timber and products and requires them to exercise the necessary due diligence to guarantee the legal activity of their suppliers.

Illegal logging especially targets rare and endangered species: they hold higher economic value based on the desirability of their physical features and cultural values,[23] generating incentives for illegal trade. Their availability depends on location and climate, and their wood may become a potential tool of domination and exploitation. Jennifer L. Anderson[24] recounts how the high request of West Indian mahogany in Europe and North America throughout the seventeenth century drove an intense trade of the precious wood, harvested by African slaves undertaking the "brutal, hazardous labor of downing and transporting the massive trees"[25] that consumers' imaginations transformed into "newly important emblems of refinement."[26] The Atlantic mahogany trade resulted in permanent ecological damage on the West Indies perpetrated by

19 Rowan Moore, "Why Wood Is Back at the Top of the Tree for Architects," *The Guardian* (2018), available online at: https://www.theguardian.com/artanddesign/2018/jan/28/wood-engineered-timber-housing-needs (accessed September 25, 2020).

20 See Tavares, "Nonhuman Rights" (see note 6), 568.

21 See Daniela Kleinschmit, Stephanie Mansourian, Christoph Wildburger and Andre Purret, eds., *Illegal Logging and Related Timber Trade – Dimensions, Drivers, Impacts and Responses. A Global Scientific Rapid Response Assessment Report* (Vienna, 2016), 49, available online at: https://www.iufro.org/fileadmin/material/publications/iufro-series/ws35/ws35-high-res.pdf (accessed January 28, 2021).

22 See ibid., 103.

23 See ibid., 38.

24 Jennifer L. Anderson, "Nature's Currency: The Atlantic Mahogany Trade and the Commodification of Nature in the Eighteenth Century," in *Formafantasma: Cambio*, ed. Riccardo Badano and Rebecca Lewin (Cologne, 2020), 77–90.

25 Ibid., 80.

26 Ibid., 86.

Entwürfe experimenteller und innovativer Büros zeigen; das unablässige Experimentieren mit temporärer Architektur und der Wiederverwendung von Materialien. Holz ist preiswert und leicht verfügbar; wegen der einfachen Techniken des Holzbaus ist es das bevorzugte Material für SelbstbauerInnen, InnovatorInnen, AktivistInnen und all jene PlanerInnen, die eine „sanfte",[19] umweltfreundliche Architektur anstreben.

Politisch gesehen wirft die Verwendung von Holz im Baugewerbe eine Reihe von Fragen auf, die mit dem Gesichtspunkt der damit befassten EntscheiderInnen und StakeholderInnen variieren. Holz ist eine vom Baum als Traggerüst entwickelte Anordnung biologischer Zellen. Es ist der Leib eines lebenden Wesens, einer individuellen Komponente eines komplexen Ökosystems. Holz ist ein Gut mit einem Handelswert und einer spezifischen Regulierung. Im Zusammenhang mit der Erstellung einer neuen Verfassung für Ecuador im Jahr 2008 berichtet Tavares in den Worten der Umweltschützerin Esperanza Martínez vom Versuch, das vom Erbe des Kolonialismus geprägte Regime durch den Rückgriff auf einen bestimmten Naturbegriff zu brechen: "*Pachamama* – meist als *Madre Tierra*, ‚Mutter Erde', eine in den indigenen Andenkulturen omnipräsente mythische Gottheit, verstanden – war der Begriff der Wahl, der für die politische Repräsentation amerindianischer Kosmologien im Verfassungsrecht sorgen sollte. Wenn sich die Moderne ein einziges Paradigma, eine einzige Rationalität, ein einziges Modell der Natur zu eigen gemacht hat, so Martinez' Schlussfolgerung, ‚so sagen wir, dass es nicht nur eine, sondern viele Naturen gibt, so viele wie Kulturen.'"[20] Die Ecuadorianische Verfassung versucht mithilfe dieses inklusiven Naturbegriffs, der imstande ist, eine Vielfalt möglicher Auffassungen von Holz, Bäumen, Wäldern abzudecken und auszudrücken, rein techno-wissenschaftliche oder kapitalistische Vorstellungen von Natur und Umwelt zu überwinden, wie sie in den meisten Teilen der Welt auch noch dem Umweltschutz dienenden Regulierungen des Umgangs mit Holz zugrunde liegen.

Eines dieser auf globaler Ebene eingesetzten Instrumente zur Gewährleistung einer fairen Verwendung von Holz ist die Regulierung des Holzeinschlags. Verglichen mit vielen anderen im Baugewerbe verwendeten Rohstoffen erneuert sich Holz relativ schnell, und die Regulierungen ermöglichen es, die kommerzielle Nutzung dieser Eigenschaft mit den Regenerationszyklen und der Hauptfunktion von Bäumen – der Absorption von CO_2 aus der Atmosphäre – zu verbinden. Gleichwohl ist illegaler Holzeinschlag noch immer weitverbreitet und bricht mit seinen unregulierten Produkten oft in den legalen Holzmarkt ein. 2014 wurde in Europa noch immer mit hohem Illegalitätsrisiko behaftetes Rund- und Schnittholz im Wert von 453,9 Mio. USD eingeführt, was 7,2 Prozent des gesamten Exportwerts riskanter Ursprungsregionen entspricht.[21] Die Auswirkungen illegalen Holzeinschlags sind vielfältig und

schwerwiegend: Er beeinträchtigt die betroffenen Regionen direkt und indirekt in sozialer, ökonomischer, politischer und ökologischer Hinsicht, hat aber auch globale Folgen, insofern er zur Entwaldung beiträgt. Direkte soziale Auswirkungen sind z.B. die Unterminierung der Autorität lokaler Institutionen durch den Verlust der gesellschaftlichen Kontrolle über Waldbestände; indirekte Auswirkungen sind die Entstehung externer, lokal von KleinbesitzerInnen, indigenen oder sonstigen Gemeinschaften ausgeübten Formen der Kontrolle über die Waldverwendung; kumulativ äußert sich das u.a. in einer verminderten Widerstandsfähigkeit interessierter Gemeinschaften gegen wirtschaftlichen und klimatischen Wandel.[22] Um den Handel mit illegal geschlagenem Holz und darauf beruhenden Holzerzeugnissen in der EU zu verhindern, wurde von der EU die Verordnung 995/2010 erlassen, die MarktteilnehmerInnen Sorgfaltspflichten in Bezug auf die Legalität der Tätigkeiten ihrer Lieferanten auferlegt.

Illegaler Holzeinschlag trifft besonders seltene und gefährdete Arten: Sie erzielen aufgrund der Begehrtheit ihrer physischen Eigenschaften und ihrem kulturellen Wert[23] einen höheren Preis, was Anreize für den illegalen Handel schafft. Ihre Verfügbarkeit ist standort- und klimaabhängig, und ihr Holz kann zu einem Herrschafts- und Ausbeutungsmittel werden. Jennifer L. Anderson[24] berichtet, wie die hohe Nachfrage nach Mahagoni von den Westindischen Inseln, die während des 17. Jahrhunderts in Europa und Nordamerika herrschte, einen intensiven Handel mit dem von afrikanischen Sklaven geernteten Edelholz antrieb. Diese führten nämlich die „brutale, gefährliche Arbeit des Fällens und Transportierens der gewaltigen Bäume"[25] aus, welche die Einbildungskraft der KonsumentInnen in „neu zu Bedeutung gelangte Embleme der Kultiviertheit"[26] verwandelte. Der von englischen und spanischen Imperialisten betriebene atlantische Mahagonihandel hinterließ einen permanenten ökologischen Schaden und führte fast zum Aussterben der Art auf den Westindischen Inseln. Ein heutiges Pendant zum atlantischen Holzhandel und zur Ausbeutung des

19 Moore, Rowan: „Why Wood Is Back at the Top of the Tree for Architects", *The Guardian*, 28. Januar 2018, online unter: https://www.theguardian.com/artanddesign/2018/jan/28/wood-engineered-timber-housing-needs (Stand: 25. September 2020).

20 Vgl. Tavares, „Nonhuman Rights" (wie Anm. 6), 568 (Übers. W.P.)

21 Vgl. Kleinschmit, Daniela/Mansourian, Stephanie/Wildburger, Christoph/Purret Andre (Hg.): *Illegal Logging and Related Timber Trade – Dimensions, Drivers, Impacts and Responses. A Global Scientific Rapid Response Assessment Report*, Wien 2016, 49, online unter: https://www.iufro.org/fileadmin/material/publications/iufro-series/ws35/ws35-high-res.pdf (Stand: 28 Januar 2021).

22 Vgl. ebd., 103.

23 Vgl. ebd., 38.

24 Anderson, Jennifer L.: „Nature's Currency: The Atlantic Mahogany Trade and the Commodification of Nature in the Eighteenth Century", in: Badano/Lewin: *Formafantasma: Cambio* (wie Anm. 8), 77–90.

25 Ebd., 80.

26 Ebd., 86.

English and Spanish imperialists and the near-extinction of the species. Atlantic wood trades and the exploitation of the West Indies' natural capital find a contemporary counterpart in the material and cultural appropriation happening today within the reclaimed wood market. Reclaimed wood has gained enthusiastic popularity within the domains of architectural, interior and product design. Usually it is cheap and often pleasant to look at: its worn appearance fulfills a "desire for sustainability."[27] The employment of reclaimed wood in projects is a supposedly sustainable, virtuous practice which, anyway, may lead to affect faraway economies through the destruction of housing and heritage, dismantled to mine reclaimed timber. Within their contribution to the 2013 Oslo Architecture Triennale entitled *Behind the Green Door*,[28] Rotor unveiled the activity of TerraMai, an American company founded in 1991 with the purpose to re-sell wood reclaimed around the world on the US market "to help offset the demand for new lumber."[29] The company, which successfully sells wood sourced mostly in Asia to Americans, re-milled to produce flooring, decking, countertops, staircases and cabinetry,[30] claims to trade reclaimed teak coming from unused real estate properties: wooden houses that would end up in waste anyway, under the blows of the unstoppable development of South-East Asia where old wooden structures are replaced with Western-style brick or concrete buildings. TerraMai's activities—as well as those of similar companies—raise concerns about the incentives that the commodification of local second-hand wood may generate to destroy sourcing areas' cultural heritage: the sums payed by TerraMai and counterparts to the owners of wooden houses are extremely high, reaching over $50,000 for an entire house. The Western demand for reclaimed teak is so high and its trade is so profitable that houses and teak structures are often used "like a bank: […] if you need cash and you have teak in your floor, you just sell it."[31]

Beside the wood trade, the natural capital of trees and forests is exploited through another tool. Green economy is a system to place "an economic value on what the earth 'does' for humans, [not only material goods but also] the processes of nature, such as a forest's ability to capture and store carbon."[32] Indeed, since 2005 the EU has been developing a carbon market through the European Union Emission Trading Scheme (EU ETS), putting a price on CO_2 per metric ton. This financial tool is an instrument for "reducing greenhouse gas emissions cost-effectively"[33] but it turns an ecologic issue into economic terms. The EU ETS overlooks main actors in the CO_2 circulation process, whose "appropriation still continues":[34] plants and trees, absorbing CO_2, are not counted in for their labor of CO_2 processing and oxygen producing. EU ETS thus "perpetuates the established economic tradition of environmental 'externalities,'"[35] transferring the price of human activities on the environment and future generations. Once again, the regulation of the ETS focuses on companies accounts rather than on the actual costs of greenhouse gas emissions to the environment. Indeed, EU ETS and similar emission trading systems unlocked the practice of carbon offset: the possibility for individuals and companies to invest in environmental projects—usually conducted in developing countries—to balance out their carbon footprints.[36] Besides being highly controversial as tools employed above all to relieve consciences and buy the right not to face environmentally-reprehensible behaviors directly, many forms of carbon offsetting reveal themselves to be indirectly harming, if not the atmosphere, far-away ecosystems from different angles. A popular form of carbon offsetting practiced by companies and public entities is the planting of trees, with the purpose to absorb CO_2 from the atmosphere. Unfortunately, this practice may create the space and conditions for exploitation and oppression. In the framework of the CAMBIO exhibition and research project, Formafantasma referred[37] to

27 Lionel Devlieger and Marteen Gielen, "Architettura e desiderio di sostenibilità," in *Abitare* 535 (2013): 102–103, esp. 102.

28 See Rotor, *Behind the Green Door* (Oslo, 2013).

29 TerraMai, "Sustainability and Reclaimed Wood," in *TerraMai*, available online at: https://www.terramai.com/ (accessed September 25, 2020).

30 See Luke Jerod Kummer, "Old-Growth Finds the New World," *The New York Times*, March 15, 2007, available online at: https://www.nytimes.com/2007/03/15/garden/15teak.html (accessed September 25, 2020).

31 Ibid.

32 Formafantasma Instagram Account (2020), available online at: https://www.instagram.com/p/B72×O5YJUxR/ (accessed September 25, 2020).

33 EU, "EU Emissions Trading System (EU ETS)," available online at: https://ec.europa.eu/clima/policies/ets_en (accessed September 25, 2020).

34 Mirko Nikolić, "Carbon Dioxide," in *New Materialism* (2018), available online at: https://newmaterialism.eu/almanac/c/carbon-dioxide.html (accessed September 25, 2020).

35 Ibid.

36 See Duncan Clark, "A Complete Guide to Carbon Offsetting," *The Guardian*, September, 16, 2011, available online at: https://www.theguardian.com/environment/2011/sep/16/carbon-offset-projects-carbon-emissions (accessed September 25, 2020).

37 See Formafantasma Instagram Account (2020), available online at: https://www.instagram.com/p/B72×O5YJUxR/ (accessed September 25, 2020).

Naturkapitals der Westindischen Inseln ist die materielle und kulturelle Aneignung, die gegenwärtig auf dem Altholzmarkt stattfindet. Altholz ist im Bereich der Architektur, der Innenausstattung und des Produktdesigns zu einer ungeheuren Popularität gelangt. Es ist meist billig und angenehm anzuschauen: Sein abgenutztes Aussehen erfüllt den „Wunsch nach Nachhaltigkeit".[27] Diese vermeintlich nachhaltige, tugendhafte Praxis der Altholzverwendung kann sich allerdings auf weit entfernte Ökonomien auswirken, wenn dort zur Gewinnung von Altholz Wohnhäuser zerlegt werden und kulturelles Erbe zerstört wird. Rotor haben 2013 im Rahmen ihrer Ausstellung *Behind the Green Door*[28] bei der Architekturtriennale Oslo u.a. die Aktivitäten von TerraMai offengelegt, einer 1991 gegründeten amerikanischen Firma, die vornehmlich in Asien gewonnenes Altholz auf dem U.S.-amerikanischen Markt weiterverkauft, um dabei zu „helfen", „den Bedarf an neuem Bauholz [zu] reduzieren".[29] Die Firma, die das Holz für Bodenbeläge, Dielen, Tischplatten, Treppen und Möbelbau zuschneidet,[30] behauptet, ihr altes Teakholz von nicht mehr genutzten Immobilien zu beziehen: Holzgebäuden, die unter dem Druck der unaufhaltsamen Entwicklung Südostasiens zunehmend durch Ziegel- oder Betonbauten im westlichen Stil ersetzt werden und ohnedies auf dem Müll landen würden. Die Aktivitäten von TerraMai und ähnlichen Unternehmen werfen aber Bedenken hinsichtlich der Anreize zur Zerstörung des kulturellen Erbes auf, die die Kommodifizierung des Gebrauchtholzes in den Herkunftsgebieten schafft: Die Summen, die Firmen wie TerraMai den HausbesitzerInnen bieten, sind extrem hoch, oft über 50.000 Dollar für ein ganzes Haus. Kurzum, die westliche Nachfrage nach Teak ist so groß und der Handel damit so profitabel, dass Häuser und Teakteile oft „wie eine Bank" genutzt werden: „Wenn du Cash benötigst und Teak in deinem Fußboden hast, verkauf es einfach."[31]

Das Naturkapital von Bäumen und Wäldern wird aber nicht nur vom Holzhandel, sondern auch mit anderen Mitteln ausgebeutet. Die grüne Ökonomie ist ein System, das „dem, was die Erde für den Menschen ‚tut', [u.zw. nicht nur materiellen Gütern, sondern auch] natürlichen Prozessen, wie der Fähigkeit des Waldes, CO_2 aufzunehmen und zu speichern, einen ökonomischen Wert beilegt".[32] So ist etwa in der Europäischen Union seit 2005 mit dem EU-Emissionshandelssystem (EU-EHS) ein Kohlenstoffhandel entwickelt worden, der die Tonne CO_2 mit einem Preis versieht. Dieses Finanzinstrument zur „kostenwirksamen Verringerung von Treibhausgasemissionen"[33] drückt ein ökologisches Problem in ökonomischen Begriffen aus. Das EU-EHS übersieht wesentliche Akteure im Prozess der CO_2-Zirkulation und setzt damit „deren Appropriation fort":[34] Pflanzen und Bäume werden mit ihrer Arbeit der CO_2-Absorbtion und der Sauerstoffproduktion

nicht einkalkuliert. Der EU-EHS „perpetuiert damit die herrschende ökonomische Tradition der ‚Externalisierung' der Umwelt",[35] verschiebt die Kosten menschlicher Aktivitäten auf die Umwelt und künftige Generationen. Beim Emissionshandelssystem geht es also erneut in erster Linie um die Kontostände von Unternehmen und nicht um die tatsächlichen Umweltkosten von Treibhausgasemissionen. Emissionshandelssysteme wie das EU-EHS haben überdies die Praxis der Klimakompensation hervorgebracht, die Individuen wie Firmen die Möglichkeit gibt, ihren CO_2-Rucksack durch Investitionen in – meist in Entwicklungsländern durchgeführte – Umweltprojekte zu verringern.[36] Abgesehen davon, dass es sich dabei um höchst umstrittene Instrumente handelt, mit denen man hauptsächlich sein Gewissen entlastet und sich das Recht erkauft, für umweltschädigendes Verhalten nicht direkt geradestehen zu müssen, erweisen sich viele Formen der Klimakompensation auch indirekt als schädlich wenn schon nicht für die Atmosphäre so doch für Ökosysteme in anderen Teilen der Welt. Eine bei Firmen wie öffentlichen Einrichtungen beliebte Form der Klimakompensation ist das Pflanzen von Bäumen, um das in der Atmosphäre befindliche CO_2 zu binden. Leider schafft diese Praxis oft auch Räume und Bedingungen für Ausbeutung und Unterdrückung. Im Rahmen des Ausstellungs- und Forschungs-

27 Devlieger, Lionel und Gielen, Marteen: „Architettura e desiderio di sostenibilità", in: *Abitare* 535 (2013), 102–103, hier: 102.

28 Vgl. Rotor: *Behind the Green Door*, Oslo 2013.

29 TerraMai: „Sustainability and Reclaimed Wood", in: *TerraMai*, online unter: https://www.terramai.com/ (Stand: 25. September 2020).

30 Vgl. Kummer, Luke Jerod: „Old-Growth Finds the New World", in: *The New York Times*, 15 März 2007, online unter: https://www.nytimes.com/2007/03/15/garden/15teak.html (Stand: 25. September 2020).

31 Ebd. (Übers. W.P.)

32 Formafantasma Instagram Account (2020), online unter: https://www.instagram.com/p/B72×O5YJUxR/ (Stand: 25. September 2020).

33 EU, „EU Emissionshandelssystem (EU-EHS)", online unter: https://ec.europa.eu/clima/policies/ets_de (Stand: 25. September 2020).

34 Nikolić, Mirko: „Carbon Dioxide", in: *New Materialism* (2018), online unter: https://newmaterialism.eu/almanac/c/carbon-dioxide.html (Stand: 25. September 2020).

35 Ebd. (Übers. W.P.)

36 Vgl. Clark, Duncan: „A Complete Guide to Carbon Offsetting", in: *The Guardian*, 16. September 2011, online unter: https://www.theguardian.com/environment/2011/sep/16/carbon-offset-projects-carbon-emissions (Stand: 25. September 2020).

an investigation[38] by Camilla Ziedorn, journalist at Sweden's TV4 Kalla Fakta program, illustrating the case of the area of Kachung in Uganda, where the government of Sweden offsets part of its CO_2 emission through the planting of pine forests, affecting local communities which are exploited of their land and struggle in the growing of food and farming.

Regulations on logging, timber trade, and murky carbon offset practices are necessary tools to regulate the market and safeguard the conservation of forests and the regeneration of trees; however, the perspective of regulation is to maintain the "environmental services"[39] provided by forests, "to conserve them for us—for the greatest good of the greatest number of human beings; [...] to conserve and guarantee our consumption and our enjoyment of these other living things."[40] The acknowledgement of these environmental services' cruciality and the safeguarding of the conditions enabling them are essential components of sustainable agencies, but a broader perspective on nature and environment and a less "human-centric concept of injury"[41] are urgent tools to globally adopt for a fair use of wood and natural resources.

The fervor around this broader perspective on the sustainable use of wood in architectural design is part of the effort made by this domain to expand its field of action, overcoming commodification to become a device to address environmental issues as well as inequalities, unveiling them in its dynamics or actively defeating them within its design and construction processes. The materialization phase of the architectural design process is often overlooked: that is the phase where the negotiation with materials happens and supply chains behind products and materials intertwine with architecture. Buildings can mask hidden forms of exploitation perpetrated by humans on other species, as well as on the human one, happening along different nodes and to actors along the chain: unpaid work, gender-based discrimination, undeclared animal-based finishes and adhesives, illegally-harvested wood-based

products and much more. An essential tool in the practice of architecture and construction holds the potential to become an effective way to unveil hidden forms of exploitation in architecture and construction: the bill of quantities. Created and devoted to predict and control the overall cost of construction, it can serve as a map to conversely deconstruct material supply chains behind buildings, unveiling the level of interspecies exploitation involved in these processes. The bill of quantities must be extended, partially re-written and integrated with anti-exploitation measures, in order to become an operative tool to support the recognition of both humans' and non-humans' rights. In this perspective, architecture as built entity would deeply support and enhance a fair multi-species cohabitation. ∎

The topics covered here are related to the ongoing research at the research unit at Università Iuav di Venezia (Iuav University of Venice), conducted as part of the 2017 PRIN call (Research Projects of National Interest) initiated by the Italian Ministry of Education, University and Research (MIUR). The research project is titled: "Rethink the Sylvan: Towards a New Alliance Between Biology and Artificiality, Nature and Society, Wilderness and Humanity." Principal Investigator: Claudio Cerreti—Università degli Studi Roma Tre (Roma Tre University, Rome). Associated Investigator, scientific director of the research unit at Università Iuav di Venezia (Iuav University of Venice): Sara Marini.

38 See TV4, "Kalla Fakta: The Forbidden Forest – TV4," 2015, available online at: https://www.youtube.com/watch?v=COoPVXlNbqQ&ab_channel=TV4 (accessed December 6, 2020).

39 EU, "REGULATION (EU) No 995/2010," 2010, available online at: https://eur-lex.europa.eu/legal-content/EN/TXT/?uri=celex%3A32010R0995 (accessed September 25, 2020).

40 Stone, "Should Trees Have Standing?" (see note 2), 463.

41 Tavares, "Nonhuman Rights" (see note 6), 562.

projekts „Cambio" verwies Formafantasma[37] auf einen investigativen Bericht der Journalistin Camilla Ziedorn für das Programm Kalla Fakta des schwedischen Fernsehsenders TV4,[38] der am Beispiel der Region Kachung in Uganda, wo die schwedische Regierung einen Teil ihres CO_2-Emissionen durch die Pflanzung von Kiefernwäldern kompensiert, zeigt, wie die lokale Bevölkerung dadurch ihres Landes beraubt wird und ihr nun die Flächen für den Nahrungsmittelanbau fehlen.

Die gesetzliche Regelung des Holzeinschlags, des Holzhandels und undurchsichtiger Praktiken der Klimakompensation sind notwendige Instrumente zur Regulierung des Marktes und zur Bewahrung der Wälder und der Regeneration von Bäumen; allerdings erfolgt sie mit dem Ziel, die von Wäldern erbrachten „Umweltleistungen"[39] zu erhalten, „sie für uns zu bewahren – zum größten Wohl für die größtmögliche Anzahl von Menschen; [...] unseren Konsum und unseren Genuss dieser anderen Lebewesen zu bewahren und sicherzustellen".[40] Die Anerkennung der Bedeutsamkeit dieser „Umweltleistungen" und der Schutz der sie ermöglichenden Bedingungen sind wichtige Komponenten nachhaltiger Politik, doch um global zu einem fairen Gebrauch von Holz und anderen Naturressourcen zu gelangen, bedarf es einer breiteren Auffassung von Natur und Umwelt und eines weniger „anthropozentrischen Verletzungsbegriffs".[41]

Die Bemühungen um diese breitere Auffassung einer nachhaltigen Verwendung von Holz gehören mit zu dem Versuch von Architektur, ihr Handlungsfeld zu erweitern, die Kommodifikation zu überwinden und zu einer Instanz zu werden, die auch Umweltprobleme und Ungleichheiten ansprechen, sie in ihrer Dynamik sichtbar machen oder sie mit ihren Entwurfs- und Bauprozessen aktiv bekämpfen kann. Die Materialisierungsphase wird im architektonischen Entwurfsprozess oft übersehen: Es ist die Phase, in der die Auseinandersetzung mit dem Material stattfindet und sich die Lieferketten hinter Produkten und Materialien mit der Architektur verbinden. Gebäude können die von Menschen gegenüber anderen Arten und auch gegenüber der eigenen Spezies verübte Formen

der Ausbeutung verschleiern, die entlang der gesamten Wertschöpfungskette stattfinden: unbezahlte Arbeit, Geschlechterdiskriminierung, Lacke und Klebstoffe mit unausgewiesenen tierischen Bestandteilen, aus illegal geschlagenem Holz bestehende Holzerzeugnisse usw. Es gibt ein wichtiges Instrument in Architektur und Bauwesen, das das Potenzial hat, versteckte Formen der Ausbeutung auf diesen Gebieten wirksam aufzudecken: das Leistungsverzeichnis. Dazu geschaffen und erdacht, die Gesamtkosten eines Bauwerks vorauszuberechnen und im Griff zu behalten, kann es auch dazu dienen, die Lieferketten des Materials von Gebäuden zu dekonstruieren und damit den daran beteiligten Grad an Ausbeutung anderer Arten zu enthüllen. Das Leistungsverzeichnis muss erweitert, teilweise umgeschrieben und in Anti-Ausbeutungsmaßnahmen integriert werden, so dass es ein wirksames Mittel zum Schutz von Menschenrechten wie den Rechten von Nichtmenschen wird. Damit könnte gebaute Architektur ein faires Zusammenleben zwischen den Arten maßgeblich fördern und erweitern. ∎

Übersetzung: Wilfried Prantner

Die hier angesprochenen Themen sind Teil eines laufenden Forschungsprojekts an der Forschungsabteilung der Università Iuav di Venezia, durchgeführt im Rahmen des vom italienischen Ministerium für Bildung, Universitäten und Forschung (MIUR) veranstalteten PRIN-Calls 2017 (Research Projects of National Interest). Der Titel des Forschungsprojekts lautet: „Rethink the Sylvan: Towards a New Alliance between Biology and Artificiality, Nature and Society, Wilderness and Humanity". Forschungsleiter: Claudio Cerreti – Università degli Studi Roma Tre. Assoziierte Forschungsleiterin: Sara Marini, wissenschaftliche Leiterin der Forschungsabteilung der Università Iuav di Venezia.

37 Vgl. Formafantasma Instagram Account (2020), online unter: https://www.instagram.com/p/B72×O5YJUxR/ (Stand: 25. September 2020).

38 Vgl. TV4, „Kalla Fakta: The Forbidden Forest – TV4", 2015, online unter: https://www.youtube.com/watch?v=COoPVXINbqQ&ab_channel=TV4 (Stand: 6. December 2020).

39 Europäische Union, „VERORDNUNG (EU) Nr. 995/2010", 2010, online unter: https://eur-lex.europa.eu/legal-content/DE/TXT/PDF/?uri=CELEX:32010R0995&from=EN (Stand: 25. September 2020).

40 Stone, „Should Trees Have Standing?" (wie Anm. 2), 463 (Übers. W.P.).

41 Tavares, „Nonhuman Rights" (wie Anm. 6), 562 (Übers. W.P.).

From Trees to Wood and Beyond: A Brief Look Into Wood Structure

Vom Baum zum Wald und darüber hinaus. Ein kurzer Ausflug in die Holzstruktur

Alan Crivellaro | Flavio Ruffinatto

1   What can we learn by looking at wood through the lenses? From the image of a thin section we learn that this willow suffered from extreme cold and was growing tilted, not upright. | Was kann man durch die mikroskopische Betrachtung von Holz lernen? Diesem Schnitt ist zu entnehmen, dass diese Weide unter extremer Kälte gelitten hat und verdreht gewachsen ist. © Crivellaro A.

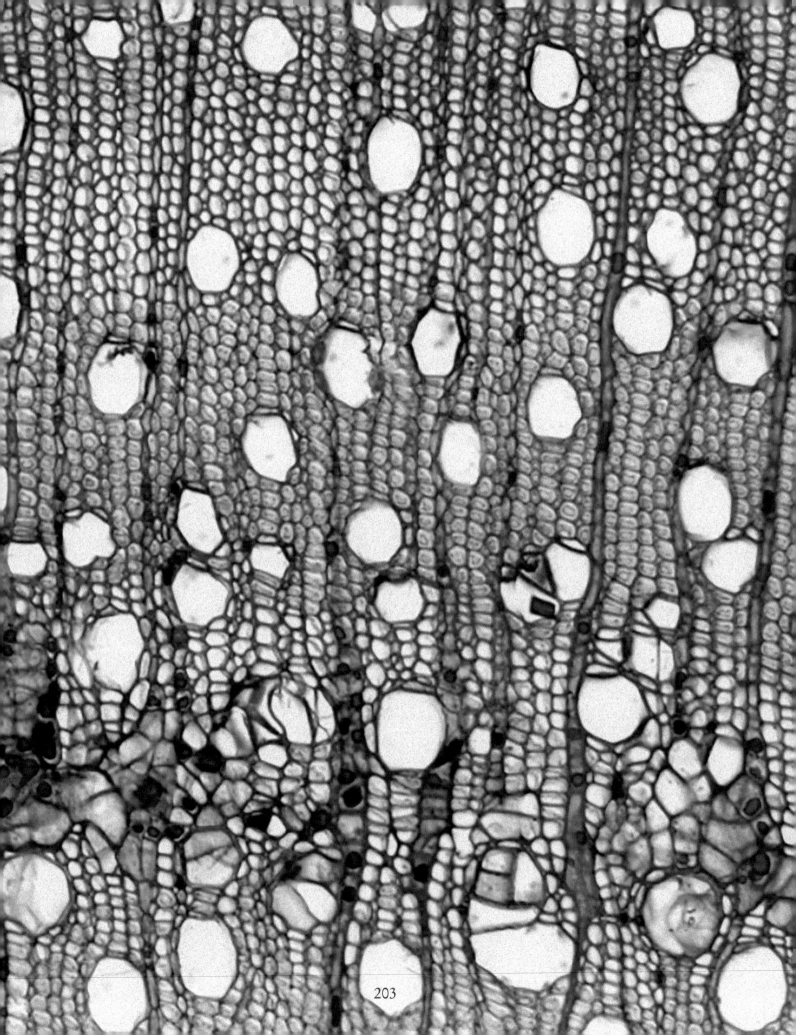

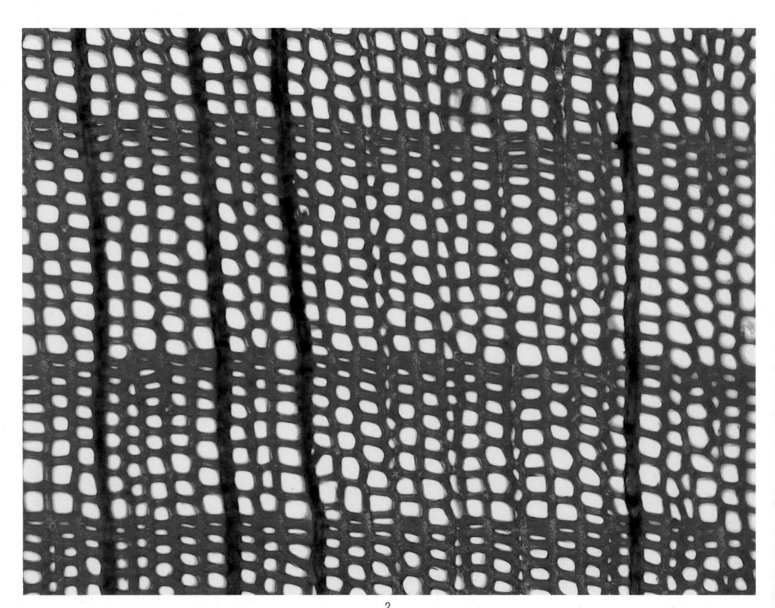

2

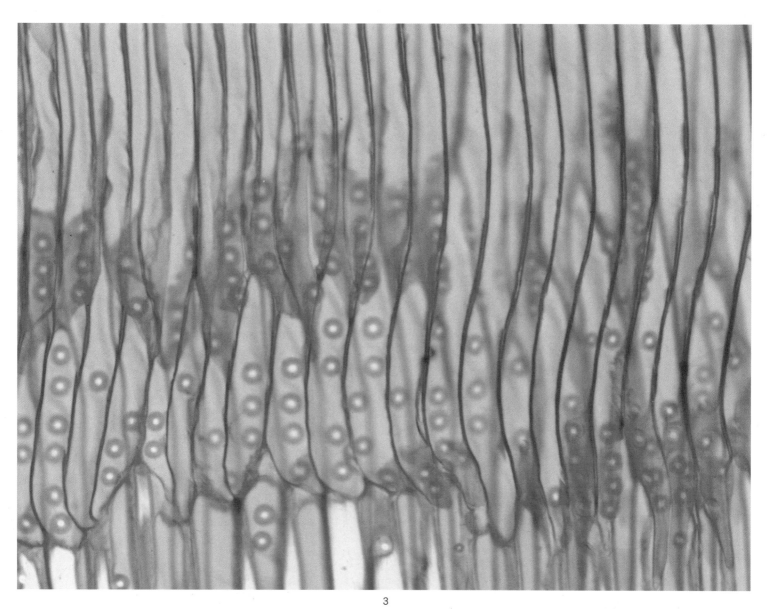

3

(2–3) Section from a conifer wood (juniper) as seen through the microscope at 100 times magnification. The section was obtained by cutting a 20 micrometers thick slice of wood with a special tool called microtome. The red color was artificially added by staining the thin section with safranin, a stain that enhances the presence of lignin in wood cell walls. Conifer wood is composed mainly of tracheids, here seen in their cross-section (2). Tracheids are cells performing both water transport and mechanical support. The water path from roots to leaves is possible because tracheids are connected via pits. Pits are holes in the cell wall connecting adjacent cells (3). | Schnitt eines Nadelgewächses (Wacholder), in 100-facher Vergrößerung durch ein Mikroskop gesehen. Das 20 Mikrometer dünne Schnittpräparat wurde mithilfe eines speziellen Werkzeugs, eines sogenannten Mikrotoms, angefertigt. Die rote Farbe wurde durch künstliche Färbung mit Safranin erzielt, ein Färbemittel, das den Ligningehalt in den Holzzellwänden verstärkt. Nadelholz besteht hauptsächlich aus Tracheiden, die hier im Querschnitt zu sehen sind (2). Tracheiden sind Zellen, die sowohl der Wasserleitung als auch der Festigkeit dienen. Die Wasserleitung von der Wurzel zum Blatt wird durch die Verbindung der Tracheiden durch Tüpfel möglich. Tüpfel sind Löcher in der Zellwand, die die Verbindung zu den Nachbarzellen herstellen (3). © Crivellaro A.

Unlike other building materials that are homogenous in nature, construction wood is a remarkably diverse resource derived from trees.[1] Everybody knows what a tree is: a large woody thing that provides shade. A stricter, more inclusive, botanical definition describes a tree as any plant with a self-supporting, perennial woody stem.[2] Thus, "trees" cover the towering giants over 115 meters through to little sprawling flowering woody plants no more than a few centimeters tall that grow in our gardens such as sage, rosemary, or even oregano. Trees are social; as they tend to grow in forests.[3] A forest describes a community of plants, animals, microbes, and all other organisms interacting together and with the chemical and physical features of their environment.

In our era, the most abundant trees are within the angiosperms (a group of plants producing flowers and enclosed seeds such as oak, beech, eucalyptus) and gymnosperms (plants producing uncovered seeds such as spruce, pine, fir). Industrially, wood obtained from angiosperms is called hardwood, and that from gymnosperms, softwood. Notably, this nomenclature does not necessarily reflect the actual wood properties; balsa (a hardwood) is much softer than average softwood.[4]

The growth of a tree is achieved by two kinds of events, each controlled by specialized parts of the plant. The first is mediated by the shoot apexes and is responsible for stem and branch elongation. Tree stems also have the ability to get thicker. This second growth type is determined by the proliferative activity of vascular cambium, a group of dividing cells located between wood and bark, and responsible for wood production.[5] Because of such mechanism of stem thickening, the oldest wood lies in the center of the stem. The younger, external wood is the water-conducting tissue (sapwood), and it dies and becomes unable to do so in the innermost heartwood. In the heartwood of many trees, a variety of polyphenols protect these dead parts from fungal attack. Worth of notice for construction, heartwood and sapwood have different properties.

Offering limitless construction designs, wood has a high strength to weight ratio thanks to its cellular structure. Several secrets can be revealed by looking at its rarely seen microstructure. First of all, wood shows intricate patterns created by cells of different sizes and shapes. In softwoods (figs. 2–3), tracheids are the predominant wood cell type. They are longitudinally positioned along the stem and constitute the majority of the woody mass. Their functions are both to conduct water and to provide structural support to the tree. Approximately 2–4 millimeters long and roughly 30–60 micrometers wide, they are connected side-to-side via pits to allow water to pass upward. In addition to tracheids, parenchymal cells are also present. The rays, ribbon-like structures positioned radially within the stem, with the main task of carrying plant metabolites (like sugars and starch), are mainly constituted by such parenchymal cells. In hardwoods (fig. 4–6), fibers are the predominant wood

1   See Michael H. Ramage et al., "The Wood from the Trees: The Use of Timber in Construction," *Renewable and Sustainable Energy Reviews* 68 (2017): 333–359.

2   See Peter A. Thomas, *Trees: Their Natural History* (Cambridge, 2014).

3   See Jesus San-Miguel-Ayanz et al., *European Atlas of Forest Tree Species* (Luxembourg, 2016).

4   See Ramage et al., "The Wood from the Trees" (see note 1).

5   See Thomas, *Trees* (see note 2).

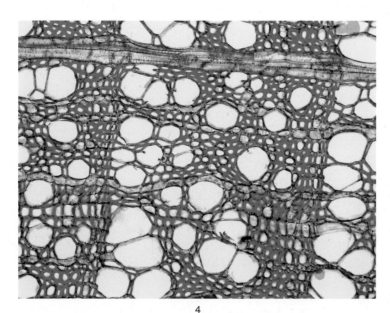

4

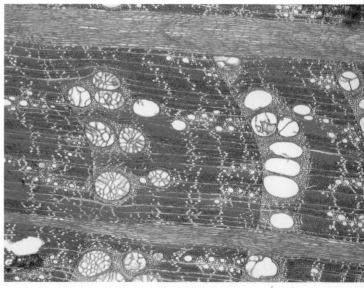

5

Im Gegensatz zu anderen, homogeneren Baumaterialien ist Bauholz[1] ein überaus vielfältiger Rohstoff, gewonnen aus Bäumen. Alle Welt weiß, was ein Baum ist: ein großes Gehölz, das Schatten spendet. Nach einer genaueren und umfassenderen botanischen Definition ist ein Baum jedes Gewächs mit einem selbsttragenden, mehrjährigen verholzten Stamm.[2] „Bäume" reichen demnach von Mammutbäumen mit über 115 Metern Höhe bis zu kleinen, bodennahen, oft nur wenige Zentimeter hohen verholzenden Pflanzen, die wir in unseren Gärten ziehen, wie z.B. Salbei, Rosmarin oder Oregano. Bäume sind soziale Wesen; sie wachsen gern in Wäldern.[3] Ein Wald ist eine Gemeinschaft von Pflanzen, Tieren, Mikroben und anderen Organismen, die miteinander und mit den chemischen und physischen Eigenschaften ihrer Umgebung interagieren.

In unserem Zeitalter fallen die meisten Bäume entweder in die Klasse der Angiospermen oder Bedecktsamer (Blütenpflanzen mit umschlossenen Samen, z.B. Eichen, Buchen oder Eukalyptus) oder in die Klasse der Gymnospermen oder Nacktsamer (Pflanzen mit unbedeckten Samen, z.B. Fichten, Kiefern, Tannen). Das Holz von Angiospermen, also Laubbäumen, wird, vor allem im Englischen, auch als Hartholz bezeichnet, und das von Gymnospermen, also Nadelbäumen, als Weichholz, wobei die englische Nomenklatur nicht unbedingt die tatsächlichen Holzeigenschaften beschreibt; Balsa, ein Laubholz, ist z.B. wesentlich weicher als die meisten Nadelhölzer.[4]

Das Wachstum eines Baums vollzieht sich durch zwei verschiedene Prozesse, die jeweils von spezialisierten Pflanzenteilen gesteuert werden. Einer davon wird durch die Triebspitzen bewirkt und ist für das Längenwachstum von Stamm und Ästen zuständig. Baumstämme können aber auch dicker werden. Diese zweite Art des Wachstums erfolgt durch die Zellvermehrung des faszikulären Kambiums, einer Gruppe sich teilender Zellen zwischen Holz und Rinde, die für die Holzbildung zuständig ist.[5] Dieser Mechanismus des Dickenwachstums hat zur Folge, dass das älteste Holz im Stammesinneren liegt. Das jüngere, äußere Holz bildet das wasserleitende Gewebe oder Splintholz, das allmählich abstirbt und diese Fähigkeit im innersten Kernholz verliert. Im Kernholz vieler Bäume schützt eine Reihe von Polyphenolen die toten Teile vor Pilzbefall. Für die Verwendung als Bauholz ist interessant, dass Kern- und Splintholz unterschiedliche Eigenschaften besitzen.

Die grenzenlosen Entwurfsmöglichkeiten, die Holz bietet, verdankt es seiner hohen spezifischen Festigkeit. Einige ihrer Geheimnisse zeigen sich bei einem Blick in seine wenig beachtete Zellstruktur. Zunächst einmal weist Holz komplexe Muster aus Zellen unterschiedlicher Größe und Form auf. Der vorherrschende Holzzelltyp von Nadelhölzern (Abb. 2–3) sind Tracheiden. Sie sind der Länge nach im Stamm angeordnet und machen den Großteil der Holzmasse aus. Sie fungieren sowohl als Wasserleitung als auch als statisches Gerüst des Baums. Rund zwei bis vier Millimeter lang und rund dreißig bis sechzig Mikrometer dick, sind sie über sogenannte Tüpfel miteinander verbunden, die es dem Wasser ermöglichen aufzusteigen. Neben den Tracheiden finden sich auch Parenchymzellen. Aus ihnen bestehen vor allem die Holzstrahlen, radial im Stamm angeordnete Bandmuster, deren Hauptaufgabe der Transport der Pflanzenmetaboliten (wie Zucker und Stärke) ist. Der vorherrschende Holzzelltyp von Laubbäumen, der auch ihr Traggerüst bildet, ist die Faser (Abb. 4–6). Fasern sind länglich, etwa ein bis zwei Millimeter lang und fünfzehn Mikrometer dick. Für den Wassertransport sind dagegen Gefäße zuständig, die durchschnittlich etwa dreißig Prozent anglospermer Gehölze aus-

1 Vgl. Ramage, Michael H., et al.: „The Wood from the Trees: The Use of Timber in Construction", in: *Renewable and Sustainable Energy Reviews* 68 (2017), 333–359.

2 Vgl. Thomas, Peter A.: *Trees: Their Natural History*, Cambridge 2014.

3 Vgl. San-Miguel-Ayanz, Jesus, et al.: *European Atlas of Forest Tree Species*, Luxembourg 2016.

4 Vgl. Ramage et al.: „The Wood from the Trees" (wie Anm. 1).

5 Vgl. Thomas: *Trees* (wie Anm. 2).

(4–6)

The wood of angiosperms seen through the microscope looks more complicated than the one of conifers. The two thin sections (4, 5) represent only a minimal glimpse of the huge variety in hardwoods' anatomical structure. In here the big empty holes are cross sections of vessels, the water conducting tubes. Smaller and thick-walled cells are fibers. Small bluish cells are those storing sugars and starch. The vertical narrow and wide lines are the rays. When the single cells are divided from each other e.g. to produce paper, the size and shape of each cell are comparable. In this case, all cells stain blue because lignin (which stains red) is missing as it was chemically removed to obtain white paper. | Das Holz von Angiospermen sieht im Mikroskop komplexer aus als das von Nadelhölzern. Die beiden dünnen Schnitte (4, 5) geben nur einen winzigen Einblick die große Vielfalt anatomischer Strukturen bei Laubholz. Die großen Löcher sind Querschnitte der Gefäße: der wasserleitenden Röhren. Die kleineren, dickwandigeren Zellen sind Fasern. Kleine bläuliche Zellen sind solche, die Zuckerverbindungen und Stärke speichern. Die vertikalen schmalen und breiten Linien sind Strahlen. Werden die Einzelzellen, etwa zur Papierherstellung, voneinander getrennt, gleichen sie sich in Form und Größe an. In diesem Fall färben sich alle Zellen blau, weil das (rot färbende) Lignin, das chemisch entfernt wurde, um weißes Papier gewinnen, fehlt. © Crivellaro A.

6

cell type and provide structural support. Fibers are longitudinally oriented, approximately 1–2 millimeters long and 15 micrometers wide. Water conduction is instead assured by vessels, which on average constitute 30 percent of angiosperms wood. Vessel elements are on average 0.2–1.2 millimeters long, 0.05–0.5 millimeters wide, open-ended, and stacked vertically into tubes that can be meters long. Their joining points, called perforation plates, are openings that allow for high roots-to-leaves water conductance. Finally, parenchymal cells are present in hardwoods as well, and the rays which they form play a similar function as in softwoods.[6] Cell distribution patterns reveal a profound difference when comparing woods, as well as determining the visibility of tree stem growth.

Trees' growth is made visible in growth rings. Such rings reflect tree growth in relation to the surrounding environment, with wider rings showing more favorable growing conditions compared to narrower rings. Rapid growth during the spring produces "earlywood," followed later in the season by the slower grown "latewood." Each ring consists of both early and latewood. In softwoods, the two ring portions are easily discernable. Earlywood is less dense and composed of large cells with thinner walls allowing for efficient water transport to support intense photosynthesis. Latewood instead is characterized by more densely packed and smaller cells, production of which stops for winter. In hardwoods, the two portions may or may not be distinguishable by wider earlywood vessels compared to latewood ones, depending on the species. Some lowland tropical trees may not produce rings due to their constant growth in an environment lacking the winter season (fig. 7).[7]

Wood identification is an important knowledge-gathering technique. For example, identifying an unknown piece of wood from the remains of a Neolithic fire allows reconstructing the vegetation surrounding those cavemen who started the fire. Similarly, identifying wood currently traded is important to avoid commercial frauds as well as to combat the trading of protected timber species. Wood identification is a job dealing with different levels of observation of an unknown wood sample. It starts with the observation of macroscopic features visible to the naked eye or through a hand-lens, then it can continue with microscopic observation. The basic tools needed to properly identify wood are a sharp knife, a 10–12 power magnifying lens, and a transmitted light microscope up to 600 times magnification and related equipment.[8] The process is based largely on analyzing the amount, relative proportion, arrangement, wall characteristics, and contents of the different cell types of which wood is composed, many of which also determine its gross appearance to the naked eye. First of all, much can be seen on the cross-section in the clearcut made with a sharp knife. It will reveal sharp details of the patterns of cells exposed in this view. Sometimes, by wetting the cut surface, even better visibility of some structural details will be achieved. Comparing cell size and distribution among woods is like comparing human faces. Human faces have two eyes, a nose, and a mouth. But the variation in size and shape

6   See Fritz H. Schweingruber and Annett Börner, *The Plant Stem: A Microscopic Aspect* (Heidelberg, 2018).

7   See Fritz H. Schweingruber, *Tree Rings Basics and Applications of Dendrochronology* (Dordrecht, 1988).

8   See Flavio Ruffinatto and Alan Crivellaro, *The Hardwood Cross-Sections Book* (Remagen, 2020).

8

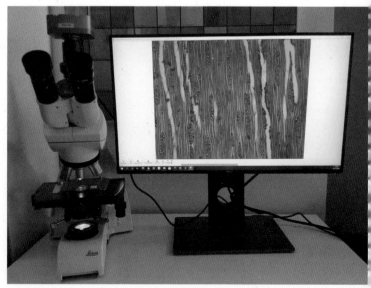

9

machen. Die Gefäßelemente sind gewöhnlich 0,2–1,2 Millimeter lang und 0,05–0,5 Millimeter dick, besitzen offene Enden und sind vertikal zu Röhren gestapelt, die mehrere Meter lang sein können. Ihre Verbindungsstellen, genannt Perforationsplatten, sind Öffnungen, die die Leitung des Wassers über lange Wurzel-Blatt-Strecken ermöglichen. Und nicht zuletzt besitzen auch Laubhölzer Parenchymzellen, und die von diesen gebildeten Strahlen spielen eine ähnliche Rolle wie bei Nadelholz.[6] Vergleicht man verschiedene Hölzer, zeigen sich beträchtliche Unterschiede im Zellverteilungsmuster, was auch Auswirkungen auf die Sichtbarkeit des Stammwachstums hat.

Sichtbar wird das Stammwachstum in den Jahresringen. Es spiegelt sich darin in Abhängigkeit von der Umwelt, wobei breitere Ringe auf günstigere Wachstumsbedingungen verweisen als engere. Das rasche Frühjahrswachstum bildet „Frühholz", worauf später im Jahr das langsamer wachsende „Spätholz" folgt. Jeder Ring besteht sowohl aus Früh- als auch aus Spätholz. Bei Nadelholz sind die beiden Ringteile leicht erkennbar. Frühholz ist weniger dicht und setzt sich aus großen Zellen mit dünneren Wänden zusammen, die einen effizienten Wassertransport zur Unterstützung der intensiven Fotosynthese ermöglichen. Spätholz weist dagegen dichter angeordnete und kleinere Zellen auf, deren Produktion im Winter gänzlich eingestellt wird. Bei Laubhölzern sind die beiden Teile durch vergleichsweise größere Frühholzgefäße unterscheidbar, wenn auch nicht bei allen Arten. Einige tropische Tieflandbäume besitzen aufgrund ihres konstanten Wachstums in einer winterlosen Umgebung überhaupt keine Jahresringe (Abb. 7).[7]

Die Holzbestimmung ist eine wichtige Technik der Erkenntnisgewinnung. Zum Beispiel lässt sich durch die Identifikation eines unbekannten Holzstücks aus den Resten einer neolithischen Feuerstelle die vegetative Umwelt der HöhlenbewohnerInnen, die das Feuer machten, rekonstruieren. Heute spielt die Holzbestimmung eine wichtige Rolle bei der Bekämpfung des illegalen Handels mit geschützten Holzarten. Die Identifizierung eines unbekannten Holzstücks findet auf verschiede-

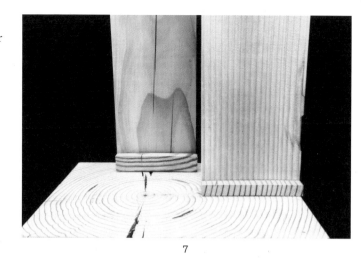

7

Growth rings have a different appearance according to the surface on which they are observed. Actually, only in cross-section they look like "rings" that we could count to estimate the age of the plant. In longitudinal view (as on the surface of a wood board) growth rings appear like "flames" from a fire or as straight parallel lines, and all combinations in between. | Jahresringe unterscheiden sich je nach der Fläche, auf der sie betrachtet werden. Eigentlich sehen sie nur im Querschnitt wie „Ringe" aus, die wir zählen könnten, um das Alter der Pflanze zu bestimmen. Im Längsschnitt (wie z.B. auf der Oberfläche eines Bretts) treten sie in Form von „Flammen" oder parallelen Linien bzw. allen möglichen Mischformen davon in Erscheinung. © Crivellaro A.

nen Untersuchungsebenen statt. Sie beginnt mit der makroskopischen Betrachtung der mit freiem Auge oder einer Lupe erkennbaren Merkmale und kann bis zur mikroskopischen Untersuchung gehen. Grundwerkzeuge für eine fachgerechte Holzbestimmung sind ein scharfes Messer, eine Lupe mit zehn- bis zwölffacher Vergrößerung und ein Durchlichtmikroskop mit bis zu 600-facher Vergrößerung samt Zubehör.[8] Der Prozess

6   Vgl. Schweingruber, Fritz H./Börner, Annett: *The Plant Stem. A Microscopic Aspect*, Heidelberg 2018.

7   Vgl. Schweingruber, Fritz H.: *Tree Rings Basics and Applications of Dendrochronology*, Dordrecht 1988.

8   Vgl. Ruffinatto, Flavio/Crivellaro, Alan: *The Hardwood Cross-Sections Book*, Remagen 2020.

(8–10)

A powerful field identification tool, macroscopic analysis represents the first stage of wood identification (8). In the laboratory, with the aid of a microscope several other patterns and details are revealed, allowing for genus, sub-genus, or species identification depending on the sample (9). Computer vision represents the new frontier of wood identification based on anatomical patterns (10). | Die makroskopische Analyse, ein starkes Bestimmungsinstrument im Feld, ist die erste Stufe der Holzbestimmung (8). Im Labor werden dann mithilfe des Mikroskops viele weitere Muster und Einzelheiten sichtbar, die je nach Probe auch die Bestimmung von Gattung, Untergattung oder Art ermöglichen (9). Die vorderste Front der anatomischen Holzbestimmung bildet derzeit die Computerbildgebung (10). © Ruffinatto F.

10

of these elements allows identifying one person from another.[9] A trained wood anatomist would then deeply examine on carefully cut thin sections the various facets of a wood sample, namely the cross-section, the tangential longitudinal section and the radial longitudinal section. The types of cells present must be ascertained, as well as their relationships to each other, the modifications of their cell walls, their arrangement, number and distribution.

As the external portions of trees differ from species to species, so does the wood. However, closely related woods are so similar that it is impossible to distinguish among them. For example, it is not possible to tell one spruce species from another on the basis of their wood structure. Even more difficult is the identification of the many similar wood species from the tropics. In general practice, nevertheless, it is usually possible to correctly identify most commercial timbers, since many species that look alike are often sold under a common name.[10] However, it should be borne in mind that not all woods are identifiable. This is especially true of non-commercial woods and woods from remote areas, especially if a species was never studied and described.

An important aid in the identification process comes from the so-called "identification keys." A key is most commonly a written device by which woods can be identified by the process of elimination. Basically, by choosing amongst two mutually exclusive statements the user proceeds through successive pairs of options until the wood is identified. Over the past decades, many computer-aided identification keys have been developed, which allow for a more flexible process. Attention must be paid in the choice of the appropriate identification key: each key is restrictive in somehow, as usually indicated in the title: the key to the European woods, the key to whitish woods, and so on.

Many people who are not trained wood anatomists can also recognize wood from its general appearance as in boards, beams, flooring, or furniture pieces. However, in this case, the process is mainly based on specific previous personal experience of the observer, not on stable features deriving from the wood cellular structure.[11] More recently, several advanced identification methods are being introduced such as artificial intelligence and machine learning, DNA, and chemical analysis. However, so far anatomical wood identification is still the most reliable and diffused tool in wood identification (figs. 8–10).

When a microscopic view of sound wood is compared to one of wood decayed by insects and fungi, the origin of weakness in rotten wood is self-explanatory. Wood-boring insects include a huge variety of species tunneling the wood to feed, nest, and protect the offspring. Many insect species are not wood species specific, while others are. Therefore, insects' lifestyle and their interaction with wood make the control of

9   See R. Bruce Hoadley, *Identifying Wood: Accurate Results with Simple Tools* (Newtown, CT, 1990).

10 See Flavio Ruffinatto and Alan Crivellaro, *Atlas of Macroscopic Wood Identification* (Heidelberg, 2019).

11 See Albert J. Constantine, *Know Your Woods: A Complete Guide to Trees, Woods, and Veneers* (Guilford, CT, 2005).

11

12

beruht hauptsächlich auf einer Analyse der Menge, relativen Größe, Anordnung, Wandeigenschaften und Inhalte der verschiedenen Zelltypen, aus denen sich das Holz zusammensetzt und die vielfach auch sein Aussehen für das freie Auge determinieren. Vieles lässt sich bereits in dem mit dem scharfen Messer produzierten Querschnitt erkennen. In ihm zeigen sich die in dieser Ansicht sichtbaren Zellmuster im Detail. Durch Befeuchten der Schnittfläche lässt sich manchmal eine bessere Sichtbarkeit einiger Strukturdetails erzielen. Der Vergleich von Zellgrößen und Zellverteilung in verschiedenen Hölzern ähnelt dem Vergleich menschlicher Gesichter. Sie alle haben zwei Augen, eine Nase und einen Mund, aber aufgrund der Größen- und Formunterschiede zwischen ihnen lässt sich eine Person von der anderen unterscheiden.[9] Ein ausgebildeter Holzanatom bzw. eine ausgebildete Holzanatomin würde danach eine Tiefenuntersuchung an sorgfältig ausgeführten Präparaten von verschiedenen Schnitten der Holzprobe vornehmen: nämlich dem Querschnitt, dem Tangentialschnitt und dem Radialschnitt. Er oder sie würde feststellen, welche Zelltypen vorliegen, in welchem Verhältnis sie zueinanderstehen, welche Veränderungen der Zellwände es gibt, wie hoch die Anzahl der Zellen ist und wie sie angeordnet und verteilt sind.

So wie die äußere Form der Bäume, differiert auch das Holz von Art zu Art. Allerdings sind eng verwandte Hölzer einander so ähnlich, dass sie nicht unterscheidbar sind. Beispielsweise ist es unmöglich, aufgrund der Holzstruktur eine Fichtenart von der anderen zu unterscheiden. Noch schwieriger ist die Identifikation vieler einander ähnlicher Tropenholzarten. Gleichwohl ist es im Allgemeinen möglich, die meisten kommerziell gehandelten Nutzholzarten korrekt zu identifizieren, zumal oft mehrere gleich aussehende Arten unter einem gemeinsamen Namen verkauft werden.[10] Dennoch sollte man im Hinterkopf behalten, dass nicht alle Hölzer identifizierbar sind. Das gilt vor allem für nicht kommerziell genutzte und in abgelegenen Gegenden wachsende Hölzer, besonders bei Arten, die nie erforscht und beschrieben worden sind.

Ein wichtiges Hilfsmittel im Bestimmungsprozess sind sogenannte „Bestimmungsschlüssel". Dabei handelt es sich üblicherweise um eine schriftliche Aufzählung von Merkmalen, anhand derer sich Hölzer durch ein Ausschlussverfahren bestimmen lassen. Im Grunde arbeitet man dabei eine Reihe einander ausschließender Merkmalpaare ab, bis das Holz identifiziert ist. Im Lauf der letzten Jahrzehnte sind überdies zahlreiche computergestützte Bestimmungsschlüssel entwickelt worden, die einen flexibleren Einsatz des Verfahrens ermöglichen. Zu beachten ist die Wahl des richtigen Bestimmungsschlüssels, denn jeder Schlüssel ist eingeschränkt, wie meist schon aus dem Namen ersichtlich ist: Bestimmungsschlüssel für europäische Hölzer, Bestimmungsschlüssel für Weißhölzer usw.

Viele Leute können Hölzer auch ohne holzanatomische Ausbildung anhand ihres allgemeinen Aussehens in Brettern, Balken, Böden oder Möbeln erkennen. In diesem Fall beruht die Bestimmung aber hauptsächlich auf der persönlichen Erfahrung des bzw. der Beobachtenden und nicht auf stabilen, von der Zellstruktur des Holzes abgeleiteten Merkmalen.[11] Neuerdings kommen auch verschiedene avanciertere Bestimmungsmethoden wie künstliche Intelligenz und Maschinenlernen, DNA- und chemische Analysen hinzu. Bislang aber ist das anatomische Verfahren immer noch die verlässlichste und verbreitetste Form der Holzbestimmung (Abb. 8–10).

Vergleicht man eine mikroskopische Darstellung gesunden Holzes mit einer von insekten- oder pilzbefallenem Holz, so erklärt sich der Ursprung der Schädigung von selbst. Insekten, die sich in Holz bohren, um sich davon zu ernähren, darin zu nisten oder ihren Nachwuchs zu schützen, gibt es in einer großen Artenfülle. Viele Insektenarten sind nicht holzart-

9   Vgl. Hoadley, R. Bruce: *Identifying Wood: Accurate Results with Simple Tools*, Newtown, CT 1990.

10 Vgl. Ruffinatto, Flavio/Crivellaro, Alan: *Atlas of Macroscopic Wood Identification: With a Special Focus on Timbers Used in Europe and CITES-Listed Species*, Heidelberg 2019.

11 Vgl. Constantine, Albert J.: *Know Your Woods: A Complete Guide to Trees, Woods, and Veneers*, Guilford, CT 2005.

(11–13)

Many fungi species grow into the wood and produce their fruit body when mature (11–12). The decay caused by wood fungi can result in bluish stains (13) that do not mechanically weaken the wood. | Pilzarten wachsen meist in das Holz hinein und bilden im Reifestadium Fruchtkörper aus (11-12). Der von Holzpilzen verursachte Verfall kann sich in bläulichen Flecken äußern (13), die das Holz aber nicht mechanisch schwächen. © Ruffinatto F.

13

wood-boring species often difficult. Fungi require moisture to grow into the wood, so the durability of timber to this form of decay must be evaluated by looking at both the permeability of the wood and its resistance to the fungus itself. Extractives, when present, give wood natural durability, as most of these compounds are toxic to both fungi and insects.[12] Durable woods can be found among hardwoods and softwoods, as well as non-durable ones. For instance, spruce, a softwood widely used in construction, is not very durable, while larch, a well-known structural timber too, yields better durability.

Timber excels where strength (or stiffness) to weight ratio is more important than absolute strength (or stiffness).

Specific architectural and engineering designs can take full advantage of this distinctive feature, allowing timber buildings to be fundamentally different from steel or concrete buildings in structural and spatial layout.[13] Even simple knowledge about the structure of wood can help to better understand its properties and their variations, as well as decay processes and how to prevent them. Ultimately, we call for more occasions to share knowledge between communities with common interest around wood. ▪

12 See Rodney A. Eaton and Mike D. Hale, *Wood: Decay, Pest and Protection* (London, 1993).

13 See Ramage et al., "The Wood from the Trees" (see note 1).

(14–17) Fungi can completely disintegrate the material creating holes in which wood is completely gone. A more detailed view through the microscope shows fungal decay acting at the cell level, destroying one wood cell after the other. | Pilze können das Material allerdings vollkommen zersetzen und gänzlich holzfreie Löcher hinterlassen. Eine detailliertere Mikroskopansicht zeigt den Pilzzerfall auf Zellebene, die Zerstörung einer Holzzelle nach der anderen. © Ruffinatto F. (18) This cross-section of a piece of wood eaten by insects shows the section of the roundish tunnels dug by the insect larvae. | Querschnittsabbildung eines insektenbefallenen Holzes mit den rundlichen, von einer Larve gegrabenen Tunneln. © Crivellaro A.

Images of the cross-section of the most common woods in constructions as seen through a 10 times magnification hand lens. While conifer woods look very similar (19–22), with pine species having much bigger resin ducts, hardwoods are more distinctive (23–28). | Querschnittsabbildungen der häufigsten Bauhölzer in zehnfacher Lupenvergrößerung. Während Nadelhölzer, mit Ausnahme der größere Harzkanäle bei Kiefern, sehr ähnlich aussehen (19–22), weisen Laubhölzer stärkere Unterscheidungsmerkmale auf (23–28). © Ruffinatto F.

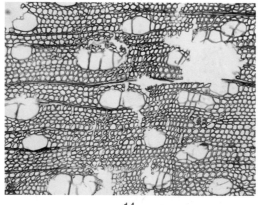

14

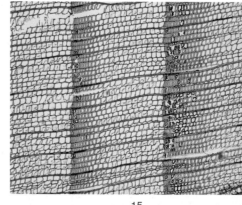

15

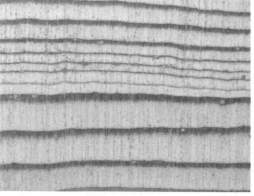

19 Larch | Lärche

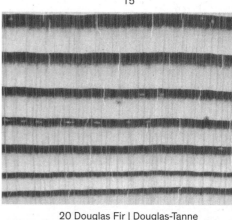

20 Douglas Fir | Douglas-Tanne

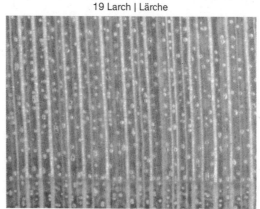

24 Maple | Ahorn

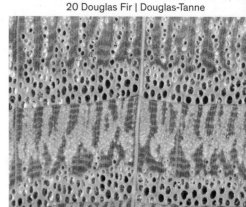

25 Oak | Eiche

spezifisch, andere dagegen schon. Ihre Lebensweise und ihre Interaktion mit dem Holz machen es daher schwer, sie in Schach zu halten. Pilze benötigen Feuchtigkeit, um in Holz hineinwachsen zu können. Um die Beständigkeit von Holz gegen diese Form des Verfalls einschätzen zu können, muss man sich darum die Durchlässigkeit des Holzes ebenso ansehen wie seine Widerstandsfähigkeit gegen den Pilz selbst. Extraktstoffe verleihen Holz eine natürliche Haltbarkeit, da die meisten dieser Stoffe sowohl für Pilze als auch für Insekten giftig sind.[12] Haltbare Hölzer finden sich sowohl unter Laub- als auch unter Nadelhölzern, und das gleiche gilt für unhaltbare. So ist zum Beispiel Fichte, eine im Bau viel verwendete Holzart, nicht sehr haltbar, wogegen die ebenfalls beliebte Lärche beständiger ist.

Holz zeichnet sich dort aus, wo es eher auf die spezifische als auf die absolute Festigkeit (oder Steifheit) ankommt. Architektonische und konstruktive Entwürfe können diese Materialeigenschaft nutzen, lassen sich damit doch Gebäude schaffen, die sich in Tragwerk und Grundriss fundamental von Stahl- oder Betongebäuden unterscheiden.[13] Schon grundlegendes Wissen über die Struktur von Holz kann dazu beitragen, seine Eigenschaften und deren Varianten, aber auch Verfallsprozesse und deren Vermeidung besser zu verstehen. Wir möchten daher dazu anregen, mehr solche Gelegenheiten zum Wissensaustausch zwischen verschiedenen an Holz interessierten Gruppen zu schaffen. ∎

Übersetzung: Wilfried Prantner

12 Vgl. Eaton, Rodney A. und Hale, Mike D.: *Wood: Decay, Pest and Protection*, London 1993.

13 Vgl. Ramage et al.: „The Wood from the Trees" (wie Anm. 1).

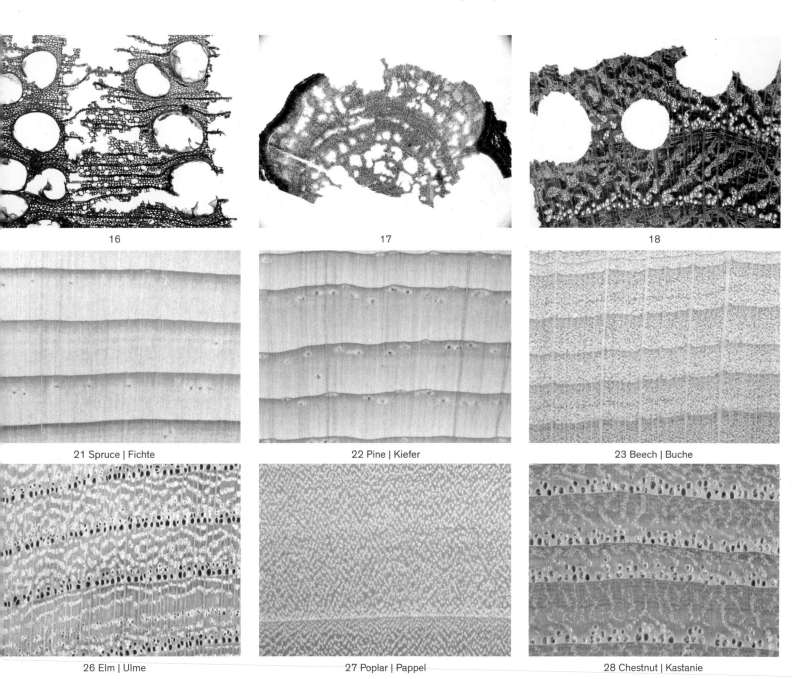

16   17   18

21 Spruce | Fichte   22 Pine | Kiefer   23 Beech | Buche

26 Elm | Ulme   27 Poplar | Pappel   28 Chestnut | Kastanie

213

AutorInnen
Authors

Reyner Banham war ein englischer Architekturkritiker und Historiker, der in seinen Schriften und Vorlesungen das Verständnis von moderner Architektur kritisch in den Blick nahm und einer Neubewertung unterzog. Als Student von Nikolaus Pevsner und Sigfried Giedion fand er später gemeinsame Schnittmengen mit einigen revolutionären kulturellen Bewegungen seiner Epoche, von Brutalismus bis zur Pop-Art. In den 1960er-Jahren reiste er häufig in die USA, wo er sich 1976 schließlich auch niederließ und den Buchklassiker *Los Angeles: The Architecture of Four Ecologies* (1971) verfasste. Er verstarb in London, kurz nachdem er als Sheldon H. Solow Professor of the History of Architecture an das Institute of Fine Arts der New York University berufen wurde.

Reyner Banham was an English critic and historian whose articles, books, and lectures critiqued and revised the understanding of modern architecture. A student of Nikolaus Pevsner and Sigfried Giedion, he would go on to intersect with some of the revolutionary cultural movements of his era, from Brutalist architecture to Pop Art. In the 1960s he frequently visited the United States, where he relocated in 1976, and authored one of the classic books on Los Angeles landscape and urbanism, *Los Angeles: The Architecture of Four Ecologies* (1971). He died in London shortly after being appointed Sheldon H. Solow Professor of the History of Architecture at the Institute of Fine Arts, New York University.

Alan Crivellaro ist Pflanzenökologe und lehrt am Department of Geography der University of Cambridge (UK). Seine Forschungsarbeit konzentriert sich auf die anatomische Beschaffenheit von Pflanzen und positioniert sich an der Schnittstelle zwischen Pflanzenphysiologie und biologischen Aspekten globaler Umweltveränderungen. Er ist Co-Autor von Büchern und Fachaufsätzen, die sich mit den Materialeigenschaften von Holz und ihrer Identifikation beschäftigen, u.a. dem *Atlas of Macroscopic Wood Identification* (gemeinsam mit Flavio Ruffinatto), Springer, 2019.

Alan Crivellaro is a plant ecologist and passionate teacher at the Department of Geography at the University of Cambridge (UK). His research focuses on the anatomical aspects of plants applied at the interface of plant physiology and global change biology. He is the co-author of books and scientific papers on the identification and properties of wood, including the *Atlas of Macroscopic Wood Identification* (in collaboration with Flavio Ruffinatto) Springer, 2019.

Andrea Trimarchi und Simone Farresin sind die Gründer des Studios **Formafantasma** mit Sitz in Amsterdam. Ihr Interesse an Produktdesign wurde an der Design Academy Eindhoven geweckt, wo sie 2009 ihr Studium abschossen. Seitdem entwickeln sie Designprojekte, die durch Materialexperimente und -forschungen und von kritischen Ansätzen zum Thema Nachhaltigkeit geprägt sind. Ihre Arbeiten wurden international ausgestellt, u.a. im New Yorker MoMA, dem Victoria and Albert Museum in London, dem Metropolitan Museum of Art in New York, dem Chicago Art Institute oder dem Pariser Centre Pompidou. Derzeit leiten sie das GEO-Design Department der Design Academy Eindhoven.

Andrea Trimarchi and Simone Farresin are Formafantasma, an Italian designer duo based in Amsterdam. **Formafantasma**'s interest in product design developed at the Design Academy Eindhoven, where they graduated in 2009. Since then, Formafantasma has developed a coherent body of work characterized by experimental material investigations and critical approaches to sustainability. Their work has been presented internationally in museums such as New York's MoMA, London's Victoria and Albert, New York's Metropolitan Museum, the Chicago Art Institute as well as Paris's Centre Georges Pompidou. They are head of the GEO-Design Department at the Design Academy Eindhoven.

Don Fuchs ist freiberuflicher Fotojournalist mit Wohnsitz in Sydney, Australien. Er arbeitet für namhafte Magazine in Australien wie z.B. für das *Australian Geographic Magazine* sowie für andere internationale Zeitschriften und Buchpublikationen. In seinen Arbeiten richtet er den Fokus insbesondere auf Umweltthemen, wie z.B. die Wälder Australiens, Geologie und Vulkanismus. Er hat zahlreiche Bücher über Australien veröffentlicht.

Don Fuchs is a Sydney-based freelance photojournalist. He is a regular contributor to distinguished Australian magazines such as the *Australian Geographic Magazine* but also to international magazines and publications. His work, largely focused on Australian forests and geology, in particular volcanism, has been published widely.

Urs Hirschberg ist Professor für Darstellung der Architektur und Neue Medien an der Architekturfakultät der TU Graz und leitet dort das Institut für Architektur und Medien (IAM). Seit 2013 ist er auch Leiter des TU Graz Field of Expertise „Sustainable Systems". Bevor er an die TU Graz berufen wurde, war er unter anderem Dozent an der ETH Zürich und Assistant Professor of Design Computing an der Harvard Graduate School of Design. In seiner Forschung beschäftigt er sich mit „Augmented Architecture" und der Frage, wie digitale Methoden den Entwurf und die Realisierung von Architektur verbessern können. Er ist Gründungsmitglied der Redaktion von *GAM*.

Urs Hirschberg serves as professor for the Representation of Architecture and New Media at Graz University of Technology. He is the founding director of the Institute of Architecture and Media (IAM) and since 2013 the director of the TU Graz Field of Expertise "Sustainable Systems." Before joining TU Graz, he served among others as lecturer at the ETH Zurich and as assistant professor of Design Computing at the Harvard Graduate School of Design. His research is focused on "Augmented Architecture" and the ways in which digital methods can enhance architectural design and production. He is a founding editor of *GAM*.

Anne Isopp ist freiberufliche Architekturjournalistin und Publizistin. Nach ihrem Architekturstudium an der TU Graz und der TU Delft war sie vier Jahre als angestellte Architektin und Projektleiterin in Hamburg u.a. bei Spengler Wiescholek tätig. Nachdem sie das Aufbaustudium für Qualitätsjournalismus an der Donau-Universität Krems absolviert hatte, war sie von 2009–2020 Chefredakteurin von *Zuschnitt*, einer österreichischen Fachzeitschrift über Holz als Werkstoff und Werke in Holz.

Anne Isopp is a freelance architectural journalist and publicist. After studying architecture at Graz University of Technology and Delft University of Technology, she worked for four years as an architect and project manager in Hamburg, for example at Spengler Wiescholek. She completed a postgraduate degree in quality journalism at Danube University Krems, then from 2009–2020 worked as editor-in-chief of *Zuschnitt*, an Austrian journal focused on wood as a material and wooden products.

Tom Kaden ist seit 2017 Professor für Architektur und Holzbau an der TU Graz und betreibt seit 2015 das Büro Kaden + Lager. Nach seinem Studium an der Kunsthochschule Berlin-Weißensee folgten die Bürogründungen von Architektur Büro Kade

214

1996–2002) und von Kaden Klingbeil Architekten (2002–2013). Mit dem Projekt „E3" erfolgte 2006 der Einstieg in das mehrgeschossige Bauen mit Holz. 2009 wurde er außerdem in den Konvent der Bundesstiftung Baukultur und des Bund Deutscher Architekten (BDA) berufen. Sein erstes Holzhaus realisierte er 1995.

Tom Kaden has served as professor of Architecture and Timber Construction at Graz University of Technology since 2017 and has run the office Kaden + Lager since 2015. After studying at the Weißensee Academy of Art in Berlin, he founded his own architectural firm Architektur Büro Kaden (1996–2002), and then went on to found the architectural firm Kaden Klingbeil (2002–2013). With the "E3" project, he entered the field of multi-story timber construction in 2006. In 2009 he was also appointed as a member of the convention of the Federal Foundation of Baukultur and the Association of German Architects (BDA). He built his first wooden house in 1995.

Thomas Körner (@TOM) zeichnet seit 1991 den täglichen Comicstrip „Touché" für die *TAZ* sowie andere Cartoons, Comics und Illustrationen für namhafte Zeitungen in Deutschland. Er lebt und arbeitet in Berlin.

Thomas Körner (@TOM) has been drawing the daily comic strip "Touché" for the *TAZ* newspaper since 1991, as well as other cartoons, comics and illustrations for well-known newspapers in Germany. He lives and works in Berlin.

Jens Ludloff ist Architekt, Professor für Nachhaltigkeit, Baukonstruktion und Entwerfen und Co-Direktor des Instituts für Baukonstruktion an der Universität Stuttgart. In Lehre und Forschung beschäftigt er sich mit prozessstrukturierten Konstruktionen, die sinnlich wahrnehmbare Scheinräume als Potenziale nutzen und damit digitales Entwerfen und Fertigen neu denken. Die vielfach ausgezeichneten Arbeiten seines Berliner Büros Ludloff Ludloff basieren auf Entwurfstechniken, die nicht von formalen Setzungen, sondern vom wahrnehmenden Subjekt aus gedacht werden.

Jens Ludloff is an architect, professor for Sustainability, Building Construction and design and Co-Director of the Institute for Building Construction at the University of Stuttgart. In his teaching and research, he deals with process-structured constructions that use sensually perceptible illusory spaces as potentials, thus rethinking digital design and fabrication. The award-winning work by his Berlin-based firm Ludloff Ludloff is based on design techniques that are not conceived in terms of formal settings but in terms of the perceiving subject.

Flavio Ruffinatto ist Holzanatom am Institut für Agrar-, Wald- und Lebensmittelwissenschaften (DISAF) der Universität Turin und leitet das Wood Identification Laboratory (WoodIdLab). Sein Forschungsinteresse gilt makro- und mikroskopischen Analysen von Holz sowie forensischen Studien zur Holzidentifikation und zur Erhaltung des kulturellen Erbes von Holz. Auch seine langjährige akademische Lehrtätigkeit umfasst die Fachbereiche Holztechnologie und Holzidentifikation. Er ist Hauptautor des *Atlas of Macroscopic Wood Identification* (Springer, 2019).

Flavio Ruffinatto is a wood anatomist and wood identification expert at the Department of Agricultural, Forest and Food Sciences and Technologies at the University of Turin and directs the Wood Identification Laboratory (WoodIdLab). His professional and research interests include macroscopic and microscopic wood identification, forensic timber identification and wooden cultural heritage conservation. He has extensive experience in teaching wood technology and wood identification to academic students and professionals. He is the leading author of the *Atlas of Macroscopic Wood Identification* (Springer, 2019).

Laila Seewang ist Assistenzprofessorin im Fachbereich Architektur an der Portland State University und Leiterin des Aggregate Architectural History Collaborative, einer Forschungsinitative, die sich der Weiterentwicklung von architekturhistorischer und -theoretischer Forschung und Lehre widmet. Als Architektin und Architekturhistorikerin erforscht sie die Beziehungen zwischen Architektur, Umwelt- und Stadtplanung durch die Linse der Infrastruktur und als Ausdruck einer „Material Assemblage".

Laila Seewang is assistant professor of architecture at Portland State University and a director of the Aggregate Architectural History Collaborative, an initiative dedicated to advancing research and education in the history and theory of architecture. She is a registered architect and an architectural historian whose research uses infrastructure as a lens through which to study the relationships between architectural, environmental, and urban design as a material assemblage.

Kai Strehlke ist Architekt und leitet seit 2015 die digitalen Prozesse der Schweizer Holzbaufirma Blumer Lehmann. Dort ist er für die Produktion komplexer Holzstrukturen verantwortlich. Zuvor war er zehn Jahre lang als Leiter der Abteilung für digitale Technologien bei Herzog & de Meuron beschäftigt. Nach seiner Gastprofessur an der TU Graz 2015 war er von 2016–2020 als Dozent an der Berner Fachhochschule (BFH) tätig.

Kai Strehlke is an architect and has been in charge of digital processes at the Swiss timber construction firm Blumer Lehmann since 2015, where he is responsible for the production of complex timber structures. Before that, he worked as head of Digital Technologies at Herzog & de Meuron for ten years (2005–2015). After his visiting professorship at Graz University of Technology in 2015, he lectured at Bern University of Applied Sciences (BFH) from 2016–2020.

Stephan Trüby ist Professor für Architekturtheorie und Direktor des Instituts für Grundlagen moderner Architektur und Entwerfen (IGmA) der Universität Stuttgart. Zuvor lehrte er Architekturtheorie an der Harvard University (2012–2014) und war Professor für Architektur und Kulturtheorie an der TU München (2014–2018). Zu seinen aktuellsten Büchern gehören *Die Geschichte des Korridors* (2018) und *Rechte Räume. Politische Essays und Gespräche* (2020).

Stephan Trüby is a professor of Architectural Theory and director of the Institute for Principles of Modern Architecture (Design and Theory) at the University of Stuttgart. Previously, he taught architectural theory at Harvard University (2012–2014) and was professor of Architecture and Cultural Theory at the Technical University of Munich (2014–2018). His most recent publications include *Die Geschichte des Korridors* (2018) and *Rechte Räume: Politische Essays und Gespräche* (2020).

Anselm Wagner ist Professor für Architekturtheorie an der TU Graz. Sein Forschungsgebiet umfasst Architektur und Kunst der Gegenwart, kritische Architekturtheorie sowie Institutions- und Wissenschaftsgeschichte. Zu seinen jüngsten Publikationen zählen *Architekturführer Graz* (zusammen mit Sophia Walk, 2019) und *Metamodern Architecture: A Short Introduction* (zusammen mit Robin van den Akker und Timotheus Vermeulen, in Vorbereitung).

Anselm Wagner serves as professor of Architectural Theory at Graz University of Technology. His research interests include contemporary architecture and art, critical architectural theory, and the history of institutions and science. His recent publications include *Architekturführer Graz* (in collaboration with Sophia Walk, 2019) and *Metamodern Architecture: A Short Introduction* (in collaboration with Robin van den Akker and Timotheus Vermeulen, forthcoming).

Stefan Winter ist Professor für Holzbau und Baukonstruktion an der TU München. Seine Forschungsschwerpunkte sind Holzbau, industrielles und energieeffizientes Bauen, Life Cycle Assessment, Brandschutz sowie „Additive Manufacturing". Er ist Gründer und Partner der bauart Ingenieure Gruppe, Prüfingenieur für Holzbau sowie Sachverständiger für Holzbau. Er leitet zahlreiche nationale und internationale Normungsausschüsse, u.a. zum Eurocode 5.

Stefan Winter serves as professor of Timber Structures and Building Construction at the Technical University of Munich. His research areas are focused on timber construction, industrial and energy-efficient construction, life cycle assessment, fire protection, and additive manufacturing. He is founder and partner of the bauart company, check engineer and expert for timber construction. He chairs numerous national and international standardization committees, including for Eurocode 5.

Francesca Zanotto ist Architektin und Postdoc-Wissenschaftlerin im Fachbereich Architektur an der Università Iuav di Venezia. In ihrer Arbeit beschäftigt sie sich mit den ökologischen Verstrickungen von Architektur und der Bedeutung von Konsumverhalten für die Entwurfskultur. Sie ist die Autorin von *Circular Architecture. A Design Ideology* (2020).

Francesca Zanotto is an architect and postdoctoral researcher at the Department of Architecture and Arts at Università Iuav di Venezia (Iuav University of Venice). Her work explores the ecological entanglements of architecture and the implications of consumption patterns for design culture. She is the author of *Circular Architecture. A Design Ideology* (2020).

Faculty News

Aus der Fakultät

„Wenn alles verschwimmt, hängt es enger zusammen."

Anne Femmer (**AF**) und Florian Summa (**FS**) im Gespräch mit Daniel Gethmann und Petra Eckhard (**GAM**)

Anne Femmer und **Florian Summa** besetzen seit dem Wintersemester 2020 die Professur für Integral Architecture an der Fakultät für Architektur der TU Graz. Ihr gemeinsames Büro SUMMACUMFEMMER betreiben sie seit 2015 in Leipzig. Anne Femmer hat nach ihrem Studium an der ETH Zürich bei VON BALLMOOS KRUCKER ARCHITEKTEN in Zürich und de vylder vinck taillieu architecten in Belgien gearbeitet und war danach wieder an der ETH als Assistentin bei Christian Kerez und Jan de Vylder tätig. Florian Summa arbeitete in Zürich und London bei Caruso St John Architects und wechselte danach an den Lehrstuhl von Adam Caruso an die ETH. Zuletzt waren beide GastprofessorInnen an der TU München.

GAM: Ihr seid ein junges Büro und habt 2015 SUMMACUMFEMMER in Leipzig gegründet. Wie würdet ihr die letzten fünf Jahre eurer Bürotätigkeiten parallel mit euren universitären Lehrverpflichtungen beschreiben? Wie bekommt man das in den Griff?

AF: Wir haben beide viel Glück. Weil wir ausschließlich machen können, was uns Spaß macht. Das verbindet sich mit einem starken Gefühl von Freiheit. Auch diese wissen wir sehr zu schätzen, denn die haben wir als EuropäerInnen ja quasi geschenkt bekommen. Schon vor unserer Selbstständigkeit konnten wir an unterschiedlichsten Orten in Europa studieren und arbeiten. Nun haben wir unser Büro in Leipzig und fahren doch fast jede Woche mit dem Zug in andere Städte oder auch Länder – etwa zum Unterrichten nach Zürich, München oder jetzt nach Graz. Wir mögen das Arbeiten im ICE sehr. Manchmal ist man überrascht, dass man nach neun Stunden Fahrt schon angekommen ist.

FS: Wir haben uns dabei immer zum Ziel gesetzt, die Sachen nicht richtig zu trennen – Büro, Lehre und das Drumherum. Oft verwischen die Grenzen und man arbeitet gleichzeitig für die Universität und das Büro. Dazu kommt, dass wir vor einem Jahr eine Tochter bekommen haben. Da kommt dann noch das Familiending hinzu. Wir haben uns bewusst dafür entschieden, alles immer gleichberechtigt zu machen: 50:50. Es gibt keine speziellen Zuordnungen, wir sind beide in allen Bereichen involviert: Jeder von uns unterrichtet, passt jeden zweiten Tag auf die Tochter auf, fährt zu Projekten, auf die Baustelle. Uns gibt das auch eine gewisse Sicherheit, weil wir wissen, dass wir uns jederzeit gegenseitig ersetzen können – aber natürlich ist es ein riesiger Aufwand. Trotzdem wollen wir dieses Konzept ausreizen und auch Anderen die Möglichkeiten vorleben, die hieraus entstehen.

GAM: Die 50:50 Gleichberechtigung ist eine Aufgabenstellung, an der Generationen vor

Anne Femmer & Florian Summa © SUMMACUMFEMMER

euch gescheitert sind, gerade in der Architektur. Wie könnt ihr die programmatische Idee, die hinter dieser strikten 50:50 Aufteilung steht, „ausreizen", wie du sagst – was genau wird da ausgereizt?

AF: Eigentlich geht es um den Luxus der Redundanz. Wir teilen nicht nur, sondern machen auch viel doppelt. Nicht nur bezogen auf uns beide, sondern ganz generell. Vielleicht kann man das an unserem Münchner Bauprojekt erklären, denn das machen nicht nur wir, sondern da sind auch unsere belgischen KollegInnen in Gent beteiligt. Es war unser erstes großes Bauvorhaben – wie auch für das zweite junge Büro – da lief die Bauherrenkommunikation über mich und die FachplanerInnen-Koordination über die belgische Seite. Gezeichnet wurde gleichberechtigt in Leipzig und Gent, diskutiert und gestritten wurde per WhatsApp – und alle zwei Wochen haben sich unsere beiden ICEs am Münchner Hauptbahnhof für den Jour fixe auf der Baustelle getroffen. Klar, das hat nichts mit Effizienz zu tun. Aber effizient zu sein, ist beim Architekturentwurf keine Garantie für das beste Ergebnis, warum sollten wir dann nicht gleich alles Schöne und Nervige mit der Gießkanne verteilen? Jeder will doch auf die Baustelle und keiner möchte gern Bedenkenanzeigen abarbeiten! Also machen alle alles.

FS: Mir scheint, dass das Mischen am Ende paradoxerweise vielleicht sogar effizient ist. Mit einem schreienden Kind an der Backe ist man physisch und nervlich ja bereits zu 90 Prozent ausgelastet. Die verbleibenden zehn Prozent kann man aber durchaus noch in ein Telefonat mit einem ebenfalls schreienden Unternehmer auf der Baustelle investieren. Die Stimmung ist dann ja eh im Keller und man versaut sich nicht gleich zwei Tage. Oder beim Unterrichten: Für die TU München haben wir kurzerhand einen sehr guten Mitarbeiter als Assistent in die Lehre mit eingespannt. Und ehrlich gesagt hat er auch schon ein paar Mal auf unsere Tochter aufgepasst. Im Büro macht er gleichzeitig Wettbewerbe und Bauleitung. Da verschwimmt natürlich auch alles. Dafür sind alle sehr nah dran an den Dingen und die Dinge befruchten sich gegenseitig.

GAM: Das klingt tatsächlich nach viel Aufwand.

FS: Deshalb arbeiten wir lieber an einigen wenigen Projekten und nicht an zehn gleichzeitig. Finanziell funktioniert das oft natürlich überhaupt nicht. Aber wir können

das querfinanzieren, da wir an der ETH, der TU München oder wie jetzt an der TU Graz eine Anstellung haben. Unterm Strich passt es dann wieder. Uns gefällt der Gedanke eigentlich ganz gut, dass die öffentlichen Gelder aus den Lehrgehältern letztlich wieder in gebaute Architektur fließen und diese teilweise überhaupt erst ermöglicht. Wahrscheinlich ist das der Horror eines jeden Architektenverbandes, der um die Auskömmlichkeit des Berufsstandes besorgt ist. Aber ganz ehrlich: Gute Architektur benötigt so viel Zeit- und Energieeinsatz, das kann man wirklich keinem Bauherren bzw. keiner Bauherrin in Rechnung stellen.

GAM: Das ist ein interessanter Punkt. Indem ihr die Dinge vermischt, macht ihr sie überhaupt erst möglich?

AF: Bestimmt. Der Preis für eine Theaterkarte spiegelt ja auch nicht die tatsächlichen Kosten wider sondern wurde quersubventioniert. Große Architekturbüros mögen in der Lage sein, diese Quersubventionierung innerhalb ihres Unternehmens mit lukrativen Großprojekten abzuwickeln. Wir hingegen zapfen die Universitäten an – wissend, dass sie im Gegenzug natürlich auch recht viel von uns bekommen. Lustigerweise kommt es dadurch auch noch zu einer innereuropäischen Umverteilung, denn natürlich kann die ETH Zürich mehr zahlen als eine deutsche Hochschule. Bildlich gesprochen hat es uns die ETH also ermöglicht, dass wir ausreichend Geld übrighatten, um uns fast zwei Jahre mit einem kleinen Haus in Sachsen zu beschäftigen. Das ist doch auch toll!

GAM: Ihr besetzt seit Oktober 2020 die Professur für „Integral Architecture" an der TU Graz. Wie versteht ihr einen integralen Architekturansatz und wie kann man sich seine Umsetzung in der Lehre vorstellen?

AF: Auch hier glauben wir eher an das Verwobene, Verästelte, vielleicht auch Chaotische, als an das Reine und Saubere. Architektur ist für uns nichts Autonomes. Auch wenn Architektur als Form vielleicht eigenständig erscheinen kann und wir das auch sehr schätzen, kann sich Architektur nirgendwo komplett abkoppeln – oder zumindest interessiert uns eine solch isolierte Betrachtungsweise nicht besonders. Was uns hingegen sehr interessiert, sind all die Spuren und Pfade, die am Ende zu Architektur werden können und umgekehrt all die Verästelungen, die von der Architektur auch wieder wegführen.

Im letzten Semester an der TU München, haben wir beispielsweise den Studierenden einige Bücher zur Hand gegeben. Nicht als Teil eines Theorieseminars, sondern als Startpunkt fürs Entwerfen! Gemeinsam war diesen Büchern, dass sie recht provokante Alternativen zu unseren vorherrschenden Lebens- und Gesellschaftsformen skizzieren. Eines dieser Bücher war von Sophie Lewis, die als queerfeministische Denkerin nicht weniger als das traditionelle Bild der Kernfamilie infrage stellt. Wieso, fragt Lewis, wird eigentlich nur die genetische Verwandtschaft als einziges Zeichen von wirklicher Verwandtschaft anerkannt? Da kam sofort die Gegenfrage auf: Was hat denn das mit Architektur zu tun? Sehr viel, denken wir. Denn das klassische Bild der Kernfamilie steckt auch tief in den Köpfen von uns ArchitektInnen drin. Wenn wir für Familien entwerfen, denken wir an die Kernfamilie. Aber das ist doch nur eine mögliche Welt. Und nicht die einzige, die existiert.

FS: Andere Studierende sind mit einem Buch von Donna Haraway in den Entwurf gestartet. Haraway verknüpft darin Anthropologie, Biologie und Science-Fiction, indem sie über neue Formen der Verwandtschaft zwischen den unterschiedlichsten Lebewesen auf dieser Welt spekuliert. Harte Kost zugegebenermaßen, auch für Masterstudierende. Aber es gibt darin unheimlich spannende Momente, die ganz nah an der Architektur sind – auch wenn dieses Wort niemals fällt. Wir sehen es als Aufgabe von uns ArchitektInnen, diese Impulse in unsere eigene Disziplin zu überführen und räumlich-gestalterisch zu verarbeiten. Wenn wir beispielsweise über Nachhaltigkeit sprechen, kann es ja nicht immer nur darum gehen, dass wir die Natur oder unsere Umwelt „schützen". Viel interessanter und relevanter ist doch, wie die Dinge verschmelzen können, wie wir uns einander wirklich annähern können und wie das dann aussieht. Das ist für uns der Kern im Denken von Donna Haraway. Vermutlich ist es ein poststrukturalistisches Denken, dem wir uns überhaupt recht nahe fühlen. Aber am Ende bleiben es natürlich immer fremde Welten, in die wir uns da hineinbewegen. Vielleicht hilft uns hier unser latenter Übermut und ein gewisses Maß an naiver Selbstüberschätzung, dass wir diese Türen überhaupt öffnen.

GAM: Es geht euch also darum, den architektonischen Entwurf, den ihr unterrichtet, nicht als eine abgeschlossene Disziplin aufzufassen, sondern neue Impulse zu integrieren, wie bspw. jenen von Donna Haraway, mit dem man dann in irgendeiner Weise sachdienlich umgehen muss, um in dem „Haraway-Kosmos" nicht komplett zu verschwinden und nie wieder einen Strich zu zeichnen.

AF: Natürlich kann man sich in diesen fremden Territorien verirren. Aber wir wollen auch gar nicht vollständig eintreten in diese Welten, sondern sie eher wie auf einer Reise für eine kurze Zeit besuchen. Um dann von dort aus loszuziehen und die Dinge mit unseren „bekannten" Welten zu verknüpfen. Das ist die Herausforderung in der Lehre. Im Kern betrifft es auch die Frage, was die Studierenden überhaupt in ihrem Architekturstudium lernen sollen. Da sind wir ganz klar: Sie sollten mehr über Form, Ausdruck und Konstruktion lernen als über Anthropologie oder Soziologie. Dies schließt für uns aber nicht aus, dass sie über Form, Ausdruck und Konstruktion *anhand* der Beschäftigung mit Anthropologie und Soziologie lernen – oder umgekehrt. Es ist ein wenig wie im Englischunterricht: Da sprechen wir ja auch nicht nur über die Grammatik des Englischen, sondern auf Englisch auch über ganz andere Dinge. Im Idealfall wird der Chemieunterricht auf Englisch abgehalten.

FS: Damit verlangen wir den Studierenden natürlich viel ab. Andererseits ist es aber auch ein Privileg in der Ausbildung von ArchitektInnen, dass wir sehr intensiv mit den Studierenden zusammenarbeiten können. Wir nutzen die Zeit, damit die Projekte so eigenständig wie möglich werden können. Auch wenn die Ausgangspunkte gleich sein mögen: uns interessieren vor allem die Verästelungen und unerwarteten Pfade, die dann ein Projekt gehen kann. In München hat dies zu sehr überraschenden Ergebnissen geführt.

GAM: Ihr unterrichtet hier in Graz mehrere Entwurfskurse. Werdet ihr da an die Entwurfsprogrammatik eurer bisherigen Lehre anknüpfen?

AF: Ja, wir möchten uns gerne weiter als „AußenseiterInnen" in fremde Welten hineinwagen und schauen, wie diese Welten den architektonischen Entwurf beeinflussen. Jedes Semester betreten wir eine andere Welt, von der wir zugegebenermaßen ebenfalls noch nicht viel kennen. Im gerade laufenden Wintersemester beschäftigen wir uns mit Musik – und das obwohl weder Florian noch ich besonders viel damit am Hut hätten. Die Studierenden

entwerfen auch keine Musiksäle oder Architektur als „gefrorene" Musik. Uns interessieren andere Pfade, zum Beispiel der halluzinatorische Charakter von Post-Punk, das rastlose Streben nach Versinnbildlichung in barocken Oratorien oder die Sturköpfigkeit in der Neuen Musik. Die unterschiedlichen Musikwelten liefern dabei gleichermaßen Assoziationsräume wie auch Strategien, die wir auf das architektonische Entwerfen übertragen.

FS: Schauen wir mal, was am Ende bei herauskommt, es bleibt natürlich ein Experiment. Aber schon jetzt macht es viel Freude mit den Studierenden über Punk, Gordon Matta-Clark und die Möglichkeit von „pöbelnder" Architektur zu sprechen!

GAM: Es ist euch also wichtig, dass Studierende lernen, mit einem theoretischen Kontext zu arbeiten und diesen Kontext auf die Architektur zu übertragen. Welche Kernkompetenzen sollen die Studierenden mit diesen neuen Themen entwickeln?

AF: Im Kern geht es um das eigene Denken. Und dann darf es nicht beim Denken bleiben, sondern es muss zum Handeln kommen. Dazu wollen wir die Studierenden motivieren. Die Hochschulen bilden die ArchitektInnen ja hoffentlich nicht dafür aus, dass sie später treudoof die schlechten Raumprogramme der Wettbewerbsauslobungen in gerade noch akzeptable Formen gießen. Da hat man doch schon etwas mehr Verantwortung und muss die Dinge vielleicht auch mal aus einer anderen Perspektive heraus angehen. Dafür muss man aber eine Vorstellung davon haben, wie viele höchst unterschiedliche Pfade und Nebenpfade schlussendlich in Architektur münden können.

GAM: Wenn ihr auf die Gegenwartsarchitektur schaut, was erscheint euch derzeit wichtig?

FS: Für uns ist Intensität ein wichtiges Qualitätsmerkmal von Architektur. Wenn etwas intensiv ist, wird es meistens interessant. Fülle kann intensiv sein, genauso wie Leere. Wir merken aber, dass es teilweise nicht mehr möglich ist, intensiv zu sein. Vielleicht weil Intensität oft mit dem Extremen, dem Exzessiven verknüpft ist und dadurch schnell als anstößig empfunden wird, wo doch Konsens und Kompromiss das allerhöchste Ziel zu sein scheint. Wir sind trotzdem gelangweilt von dahinsäuselnder Ausdruckslosigkeit und freuen uns über jeden architektonischen Zwischenruf, der überhaupt etwas sagen möchte!

GAM: In einem eurer theoretischen Essays arbeitet ihr mit dem Begriff der „Hauntology" und plädiert dafür, dass Architektur auch von den Geistern der Vergangenheit profitieren kann und ihr diese Geister wecken und neu denken wollt. Wo liegt für euch konkret das Potenzial bei der Arbeit mit historischen Referenzen?

AF: Architektonische Referenzen sind Schätze. Für uns genauso wie für die Studierenden. Spannend finden wir, auf wie viele unterschiedliche Arten sie für das Entwerfen fruchtbar gemacht werden können. Natürlich liefern sie formale, typologische oder konstruktive Anknüpfungspunkte. Uns interessieren aber auch die „ideologischen" Welten hinter diesen Referenzen. Einige davon erscheinen rückblickend als gescheiterte Utopien – aber kann Form wirklich scheitern? Oder kann Form nur zur falschen Zeit am falschen Ort sein? Dann wiederum würde es sich lohnen, auch vermeintlich gescheiterte Utopien kritisch aber wohlwollend zu betrachten und ihnen eine zweite Chance zu geben. Bei unserem Münchner Genossenschaftsprojekt haben wir versucht, solche Geister – oder Gespenster der Vergangenheit in neuer Form wiederauferstehen zu lassen. Unter anderem darf dort das Gespenst des Strukturalismus noch einmal durch die Grundrisse tanzen …

FS: Von mir aus dürften viel mehr Geister wiedererweckt werden. Der Geist des Barocks klopft doch auch schon ganz laut an die Tür, jetzt wo wir alles wegrationalisiert haben und nicht einmal ein zwei Meter auskragendes Gesims machen dürfen, weil damit dann die Baulinie zu weit überschritten würde. Aber schuld können nicht immer die Anderen sein. Wir selbst müssten uns auch mehr trauen. Beim Beispiel des Barocks denke ich da zum Beispiel an die omnipräsente Allegorie, also die bildliche Darstellung eines abstrakten Begriffes. Anne, können wir nicht mal so was machen?

AF: Klar. Bei Marx hat das „Auferstehen" von Gespenstern ja auch mit „Aufstand", also Revolte zu tun. Das wiederum klingt nach Provokation. Und demgegenüber sind wir nicht ganz abgeneigt …

GAM: Wir sind schon gespannt, welche eurer „Gespenster" ihre zweite Chance verdienen. Für heute: Vielen Dank für das Gespräch! ▪

"When Everything's Blurred, It All Merges Together."

Anne Femmer (**AF**) and Florian Summa (**FS**) in Conversation with Daniel Gethmann and Petra Eckhard (**GAM**)

Anne Femmer and **Florian Summa** have held the professorship for Integral Architecture at the Faculty of Architecture of Graz University of Technology since the winter semester of 2020. They have been running their joint practice SUMMACUMFEMMER in Leipzig since 2015. After studying at The Swiss Federal Institute of Technology in Zurich, Anne Femmer worked for VON BALLMOOS KRUCKER ARCHITEKTEN in Zurich as well as de vylder vinck taillieu architecten in Belgium. Afterwards she returned to the Swiss Federal Institute of Technology to work as an assistant for Christian Kerez and Jan de Vylder. Florian Summa worked in Zurich and London with Caruso St John Architects and then moved to join the Chair of Adam Caruso at the Swiss Federal Institute of Technology. Most recently both were visiting professors at the Technical University of Munich.

GAM: You founded your office in 2015. As a fairly young practice, how would you describe combining work at your office with your teaching commitments during the last five years? How do you manage that?

AF: We are both very lucky because we only do what we enjoy, and that is also combined with a strong sense of freedom. We know it is something to appreciate, as that freedom is almost a given as Europeans. Even before we set up our practice, we were able to study and work in all kinds of different places in Europe. Now we are based in Leipzig, but almost every week we take the train to other cities or even countries—such as to teach in Zurich, Munich or now Graz. We quite enjoy working on the train and sometimes you're surprised that you've already arrived after nine hours of traveling.

FS: It has never really been our goal to keep things separate in terms of the office, teaching, and everything in between. The boundaries tend to overlap, and you can be working for the university and your own office simultaneously. We also had our daughter a year ago, then there is the family to think about too. We have consciously decided to do everything on an equal footing: 50:50. There are no special allocations as to who does what, we are both involved in everything. We both teach, look after our daughter on consecutive days, go to various projects or to the construction sites. This also gives us a certain amount of security because we know that we can replace each other at any time—but of course, this takes a huge effort. Nevertheless, we want to fully utilize this concept and show others the possibilities that arise from it.

GAM: The 50:50 equality is a concept that generations before you have failed at, especially in the field of architecture. How can you "fully utilize," as you say, the programmatic idea behind this strict 50:50 division—what exactly is being utilized?

AF: It is actually all about the luxury of redundancy. Not only do we share, but we do a lot of things twice. Not only concerning us two, but actually in general. Perhaps this can be explained by our building project in Munich because we have been running that as a collaboration with our Belgian colleagues in Ghent. It was our first large construction project—as was also the case with our Belgian counterparts—so the communication with the client was handled by me and the coordination of the consultants was done on the Belgian side. Drawings were created both in Leipzig and Ghent, discussions and arguments were held over WhatsApp—and every two weeks our two trains met at Munich Central Station for a briefing regarding the construction site. Of course, this has nothing to do with efficiency. Being efficient is no guarantee for the best results in architectural design, so why not give everyone their fair share of everything—the good, the bad, and the ugly. After all, everyone wants to be there on site, and no one wants to deal with complaints! Therefore, everybody does a bit of everything.

FS: It seems to me that in the end, rather paradoxically, combining tasks is perhaps even efficient. With a screaming child at your side, you are already at 90 percent of your physical and emotional capacity. Therefore, the remaining ten percent can be invested in a phone call to a yelling contractor on site. The mood is already low anyway, so that way you don't ruin two days. Or while teaching: For our job at the Technical University of Munich we have recently engaged a very good employee as an assistant. And to be honest, he has also looked after our daughter a few times. In the office, he deals with both competitions and construction management at the same time. Of course, that's where everything becomes blurred. On the other hand, everyone is very close to all aspects of the job and these aspects mutually enrich each other.

GAM: That sounds like a lot of work.

FS: That's why we prefer to work on a few projects rather than ten at once. Financially, of course, this often doesn't work at all. However, we have been able to balance our finances with other jobs, such as with positions at ETH Zurich, TU Munich, or now, TU Graz. Therefore, everything works out overall. We like the idea that the public money from the teaching salaries will ultimately flow back into built architecture, and that some of it will make this all possible in the first place. That is probably the horror of any architectural association that is concerned about the viability of the profession. Though quite honestly, good architecture requires so much time and energy that no client could possibly manage it themselves.

GAM: That is an interesting point. So, it is by combining things that you make everything possible in the first place?

AF: Definitely. After all, the price of a theater ticket does not reflect the actual costs but was cross-subsidized. Large architectural offices may be able to handle this cross-subsidization within their company with lucrative large-scale projects. We, on the other hand, tap into the universities—knowing that they will of course gain a lot from us in return. Funnily enough, this also leads to redistribution within Europe, because of course, the Swiss Federal Institute of Technology in Zurich can pay more than a German university. Metaphorically speaking, the Swiss Federal Institute of Technology has thus made it possible for us to have enough money left over to occupy ourselves with a small house in Saxony for almost two years, which is also great!

GAM: Since October 2020 you both have held professorships for Integral Architecture at Graz University of Technology. What does an integral architectural approach mean for you and how do you envision its implementation in teaching?

AF: Again, we believe in an interwoven, ramified, perhaps even chaotic approach, rather than a pure and clean one. For us, architecture is nothing autonomous. Even if architecture as a form can perhaps appear autonomous and we appreciate this a lot, architecture can never completely detach itself—or at least we are not particularly interested in such an isolated approach. What we are very interested in, however, are all the traces and paths that can ultimately become architecture and, conversely, all the ramifications that lead away from architecture.

For example, last semester at the TU Munich, we gave some books to the students. Not as part of a theory seminar but as a starting point for designing! What these books had in common was that they sketch quite provocative alternatives to our prevailing ways of life and society. One of these books was by Sophie Lewis, a queer feminist thinker who questions nothing less than the traditional image of the nuclear family. Why, Lewis asks, is genetic kinship recognized as the only sign of real kinship? The counter-question immediately arose: What does this have to do with architecture? A lot, we think, because the classic image of the nuclear family is also deeply ingrained in the minds of us architects. When we design for families, we think of the nuclear family. Though that is only one possible world, and not the only one that exists.

FS: Other students started designing with a book by Donna Haraway. Haraway combines anthropology, biology, and science fiction by speculating on new forms of kinship between the most diverse creatures on this planet. Admittedly challenging, even for master students. However, there are incredibly exciting moments in the book that are very close to architecture—even if the word architecture itself never appears. We see it as our task as architects to transfer this input into our discipline and to process it spatially and creatively. When we talk about sustainability, for example, it cannot always be about "protecting" nature or our environment. What is much more interesting and relevant is how things can merge, how we can come closer to each other, and what that looks like. For us, this is at the core of Donna Haraway's way of thinking. It is probably this poststructuralist thinking that we feel quite close to. Though in the end, of course, there are always foreign worlds into which we move. Perhaps our latent overconfidence and a certain degree of naive overestimation of our abilities help us to open these doors.

GAM: It is, therefore, important for you not to see teaching in architectural design as a closed discipline, but to integrate new input, such as from Donna Haraway. You then have to deal with such input in a relevant way, in order to avoid disappearing completely in the "Haraway cosmos," never to draw a line again.

AF: Of course, you can get lost in these foreign territories. However, we don't want to fully enter these worlds, but rather pay a visit for a short time as if on a journey. Then set off from there and connect aspects with our "known" worlds. That is the challenge in teaching. In essence, it also concerns the question of what students should learn at all in their architectural studies. Here we are quite clear: they should learn more about form, expression, and construction than about anthropology or sociology. For us, however, this does not exclude the possibility that they learn about form, expression, and construction through their study of anthropology and sociology—or vice versa. It is a bit like teaching English: there we don't just talk about English grammar, but using English, we talk about completely different kinds of things. Ideally, even chemistry classes are held in English.

FS: Of course, we demand a lot from the students. On the other hand, it is also a privilege in the training of architects that we can work very intensively with the students. We use the time so that the projects can become as independent as possible. Even if the starting points are the same, we are particularly interested in the outcome and unexpected paths a project can take. In Munich, this has led to very surprising results.

GAM: You teach several design courses here in Graz. Are you continuing the same way of teaching from your previous courses?

AF: Yes, we would like to venture further into foreign worlds as "outsiders" and see how these worlds influence architectural design. Every semester we enter a different world, which admittedly we don't always know much about either. In the winter semester of 2020, we're dealing with music—although neither Florian nor I have anything to do with it. The students do not design music halls or architecture as "frozen" music. We are interested in other paths, for example, the hallucinatory character of post-punk, the restless striving for symbolization in baroque oratorios, or the stubbornness in new music. The different musical worlds provide both associative spaces and strategies that we apply to architectural design.

FS: Let's see how things turn out in the end, it remains an experiment of course. Though already it has been a lot of fun to talk with the students about punk, Gordon Matta-Clark, and the possibility of "rude" architecture!

GAM: That suggests it is important to you that students learn to work with a theoretical context and apply this context to architecture. What core competencies should students develop with these new topics?

AF: At the core, it is about one's way of thinking. Then again, it's not just about thinking, there must be some action too. We want to motivate the students to do both. The universities will hopefully not train the architects so that they will later slavishly follow badly written competition briefs to produce barely acceptable forms. You already have a little more responsibility and perhaps you have to approach things from a different perspective. To do so, however, you have to have an idea of how many different paths can ultimately lead to architecture.

GAM: Looking at contemporary architecture, what do you think is especially important at the moment?

FS: For us, intensity is an important quality feature of architecture. When something is intense, it usually becomes interesting. Fullness can be intense, just like emptiness. Though we notice that sometimes it is no longer possible to be intense. Perhaps because the intensity is often linked to the extreme, the excessive, and is, therefore, quickly perceived as offensive, while consensus and compromise seem to be the ultimate goal. Nevertheless, we are bored by the murmuring lack of expression and are happy about any architecture that makes a statement!

GAM: In one of your theoretical essays, you work with the term "hauntology" and argue that architecture can also benefit from the spirits of the past and that you want to awaken these spirits and rethink them. What exactly do you gain from working with historical references?

AF: Architectural references are treasures, for us as well as for the students. We find it exciting how many different ways they can be made fruitful for designing. Of course, they provide formal, typological, or constructive points of reference. Though we are also interested in the "ideological" worlds behind these references. Some of them appear in retrospect as failed utopias—but can form really fail? Or can form only be in the wrong place at the wrong time? Then again, it would be worthwhile to look at even supposedly failed utopias critically but benevolently, and to give them a second chance. In our cooperative project in Munich, we have tried to revive such spirits—or specters of the past in a new form. Among other things, the specter of structuralism is allowed to dance through the floor plans once again …

FS: Many more specters should be resurrected. The specter of the baroque era is already knocking on the door very loudly, now that we have rationalized everything away and are not even allowed to make a cornice that protrudes two meters, because that would exceed the building line way too much. Though it can't always be the others' fault. We have to dare more. When I think of the Baroque, for example, I think of the omnipresent allegory, the figurative representation of an abstract concept. Anne, can't we do something like that?

AF: Of course. With Marx, the "resurrection" of specters also has to do with "rebellion." That in turn sounds like provocation. Though we are not entirely averse to that …

GAM: We are curious to see which of your "specters" earns their second chance. Thank you very much for taking the time and talking to us today! ∎

Gastprofessur Anna Llonch Sentis

Anna Llonch Sentis © Cierto Estudio

Im Sommersemester 2020 leitete Gastprofessorin Anna Llonch Sentis aus dem jungen in Barcelona ansässigen Architekturbüro Cierto Estudio gemeinsam mit Andreas Lechner die Projektübung am Institut für Gebäudelehre. Cierto Estudio ist ein Team aus sechs jungen Architektinnen, die sich mit einem breiten Spektrum an Projekten befassen, von kollektivem Wohnen bis hin zu Stadtplanung, aber auch mit Möbel- und Produktdesign. Das Büro wurde 2014 von Marta Benedicto, Ivet Gasol, Carlota de Gispert, Anna Llonch Sentis, Lucia Millet und Clara Vidal nach Beendigung ihres gemeinsamen Architekturstudiums an der ETSAB Barcelona gegründet. Das besondere Interesse von Cierto Estudio liegt im Bereich des kollektiven Wohnens. Ihre Entwürfe streben nach typologischer Innovation, um so auf neue Arten des Wohnens zu reagieren, die sich im Einklang mit gegenwärtigen gesellschaftlichen Tendenzen und Bedürfnissen befinden. Mit ihrem Masterplan für einen Häuserblock mit Mehrfachnutzung und sozialer Wohnanlage gewannen sie den ersten Preis des internationalen Wettbewerbs „Illa Glòries". Ihr jüngstes Projekt „Kitch·room", das aus einem Block mit 70 Wohnungen in Masnou bestand, wurde im IMPSOL-Wettbewerb ebenfalls mit dem ersten Preis ausgezeichnet. Die Arbeiten der Architektinnen wurden in Zeitschriften wie

Arquitectura y Diseño, *Neo2*, *Architectural Digest* und *Ginza Magazine* veröffentlicht. Sie lehrten außerdem an Universitäten wie der Architectural Association in London, der School of Architecture der Barcelona ETSAB und der BAU Design School.

Im Rahmen der Projektübung wurde an der Umwandlung eines ehemaligen Militärstandortes im Grazer Bezirk Jakomini mit mehr als 500 Wohneinheiten gearbeitet und damit die Aufgabenstellung und das Ergebnis eines hier kürzlich erfolgten Wettbewerbs einer kritischen Neubewertung unterzogen. Die Projektübung begann mit der Untersuchung von Flexibilitätskonzepten mittels Analyse zahlreicher Wohnbauprojekte, die gemeinsam erörtert, umgestaltet und im Rahmen des Entwurfsprozesses angewandt wurden. Das Ziel von „X-Rooms" war es, festzustellen, wie die Referenz „X" Vorstellungen von Flexibilität im Wohnbau beschreibt, die sich ganz einfach und umkehrbar an die Lebenszyklen anpassen lassen, ohne radikale Veränderungen durchführen zu müssen. Obwohl „X-Rooms" aufgrund der Pandemie als Onlinekurs abgehalten werden musste, gelang es der Gruppe dennoch, mithilfe von Cierto Estudios Methode der Umsetzung eines permanenten Entwurfsdialogs zwischen Außen-, Schwellen- und Innenräumen, innovative und gestalterisch anspruchsvolle Wohntypologien zu untersuchen. ▪

Andreas Lechner (Übersetzung: Alexandra Titze-Grabec)

Visiting Professor Anna Llonch Sentis

In the summer semester of 2020, visiting professor Anna Llonch Sentis from the young Barcelona-based architectural practice Cierto Estudio, led the Integral Design Studio at the Institute of Design and Building Typology together with Andreas Lechner. Cierto Estudio is a team of six young female architects working on a wide range of projects, from collective housing to urban planning, but also furniture and product design. Based in Barcelona, the practice was founded in 2014 by Marta Benedicto, Ivet Gasol, Carlota de Gispert, Anna Llonch Sentis, Lucia Millet, and Clara Vidal after studying architecture together at ETSAB,

Barcelona. Cierto Estudio highlights a special interest in collective housing. Their designs seek typology innovation in order to respond to new ways of inhabiting in line with contemporary social trends and needs. They won first prize in the international competition "Illa Glòries" with their master plan regarding a multi-use city block and the development of a social housing building. Their latest project, "Kitch·room," which involved a block of 70 flats in Masnou, has also recently won first prize in the IMPSOL competition. Their work has been published in magazines such as *Arquitectura y Diseño*, *Neo2*, *Architectural Digest* and *Ginza Magazine*. They have lectured at universities such as the Architectural Association in London, the School of Architecture of Barcelona ETSAB, and Bau Design School.

The Integral Design Studio focused on the conversion of a former military site in the central Graz district of Jakomini, providing over 500 housing units, and the group critically reassessed the brief and outcome of a recent competition on that very site. The Integral Design Studio started by investigating concepts of flexibility through the analysis of numerous reference projects and papers that were collectively discussed, transformed, and applied within the design processes. The goal of "X-Rooms" was to ascertain how the signifier "X" describes notions of flexibility in housing that can easily be adapted to the cycles of life in a reversible way, without making radical changes. Although "X-Rooms" was held as an online course due to the pandemic, the group nevertheless managed to explore innovative housing typologies through Cierto Estudio's methodology of creating a constant dialogue between the housing plan and urbanism. ▪

Andreas Lechner

Gastprofessur Johann Moser

Johann Moser © Renee del Missier/BWMArchitekten

Im Wintersemester 2019/20 konnte das Institut für Gebäudelehre Johann Moser, Gründungspartner des vielfach ausgezeichnetem Wiener Architekturbüros BWM Architekten, als Gastprofessor begrüßen. Gemeinsam mit Andreas Lechner betreute er die Projektübung zum Entwurf eines Neubaus für das Dokumentationsarchiv des österreichischen Widerstandes (DÖW) im ersten Wiener Bezirk. Für diese wichtige Institution mussten die Studierenden ein zeitgemäßes, flexibles Nutzungsprogramm – Multifunktionalität in Form eines Büro-, Archiv- und Ausstellungsgebäudes mit rund 3.000 Quadratmetern Nutzfläche – in eine auch symbolisch angemessene Gestaltung bringen, die als „Protest gegen das Vergessen" (Eric Hobsbawm) auf den allgegenwärtigen Historismus reagieren muss. Nach einer Besichtigung der derzeit in einem Barockpalais im ersten Bezirk untergebrachte DÖW führte Johann Moser durch die von ihm gestaltete Ausstellung zur österreichischen Zeitgeschichte, die als „Haus der Geschichte Österreich" in der Neuen Burg (Hofburg) 2018 zum 100-jährigen Bestehen der Gründung der Republik Österreich eröffnet wurde.

Johann Moser ist der Kopf hinter den Kulturprojekten bei BWM Architekten und mit Daniela Walten und Erich Bernard einer der drei Bürogründer. Als ausgebildeter Künstler wird er oft für Ausstellungsgestaltungen beauftragt, die ein besonderes Finetuning erfordern, wie z.B. beim Literaturmuseum der österreichischen Nationalbibliothek oder beim Ausstellungskonzept für den Österreichischen Pavillon an der EXPO 2017 in Astana, Kasachstan. Auf Vorträgen und Präsentationsreisen bringt er seine Erfahrung auch im Ausland ein.

Visiting Professor Johann Moser

In the winter semester of 2019/20, the Institute of Design and Building Typology welcomed visiting professor Johann Moser, founding partner of the award-winning Viennese architectural firm BWM Architekten. Together with Andreas Lechner, he supervised the Integral Design Studio focused on conceptualizing a new building for the Documentation Centre of Austrian Resistance (DÖW) in Vienna's first district. For this important institution, the students had to consider a contemporary, flexible style—one that is multifunctional, taking the form of an office, archive, and exhibition building with an area of around 3,000 square meters—yet a design that is also symbolically appropriate and that must respond to the omnipresent historicism as a "protest against forgetting" (Eric Hobsbawm). After a tour of the DÖW, currently located in a baroque palace in the first district of Vienna, Johann Moser gave a guided tour of the exhibition he designed on contemporary Austrian history, which opened as the "House of Austrian History" in the Neue Burg (Hofburg) in 2018 to mark the centenary of the founding of the Republic of Austria.

Johann Moser is the brains behind the cultural projects at BWM Architekten, which he founded together with Daniela Walten and Erich Bernard. As a trained artist, he is highly sought-after for exhibition designs that require fine-tuning, such as the Literature Museum of the Austrian National Library or the exhibition concept for the Austrian Pavilion at the EXPO 2017 in Astana, Kazakhstan. He also shares his experience on trips abroad where he gives lectures and presentations. ▪

Andreas Lechner

Digital Teaching

NACHSITZEN

Eine Veranstaltung von **Studierenden aus den Architekturzeichensälen der TU Graz**

© Julian Lança-Gil & Paul Pachner

Nach einem außergewöhnlichen Sommersemester organisierten Studierende der Architekturzeichensäle im Juli 2020 ein offenes Diskussionsforum im Park der Alten Technik. Unter dem Titel „Nachsitzen" wurde Studierenden wie Lehrenden eine Plattform geboten, um sich während der COVID-19-Pandemie von Angesicht zu Angesicht über die Erfahrungen im vergangenen digitalen Semester auszutauschen. Ebenso wurde ein Rückblick auf die Veränderungen des Studiums der letzten Jahre, sowie ein kritischer Ausblick auf die zukünftige Architekturlehre an der TU Graz thematisiert. „Aufgrund des digitalen Semesters war es schwierig, online zu studieren und auch schwierig, online zu evaluieren. Wir möchten hier unsere Perspektive mitteilen, die Meinung der Lehrenden hören und gemeinsam darüber diskutieren. Im Besonderen durch unsere Erfahrungen während des letzten Semesters bemerken wir Veränderungen in der Lehre und möchten gewisse Entwicklungen nicht unkommentiert geschehen lassen. Für die Zukunft wünschen wir uns grundsätzlich eine offenere Kommunikation zwischen Lehrenden und Studierenden. Dafür möchten wir mit der heutigen Veranstaltung einen Anfang setzen", so die Studierenden **Antonia Prohammer** und **Vera Schabbon** in ihrem Eröffnungsstatement. Einerseits gab es durchaus positive Rückmeldungen zur digitalen Lehre: Insbesondere Vorlesungen wurden gut angenommen, durch Onlineaufzeichnungen sei man flexibler und könne diese mehrfach anhören. Andererseits litt für viele Studierende die Qualität der Seminare unter den digitalen Präsentationen der Entwürfe und deren Kritik über Bildschirme. Ähnliches war auch von anwesenden Lehrenden zu vernehmen.

Die Quintessenz lautete: Architekturausbildung braucht Präsenzlehre als Diskussionsgrundlage. Diese muss den Studierenden unter Einhaltung der notwendigen Distanz- und Hygienemaßnahmen in universitären Räumlichkeiten ermöglicht werden, um im Sinne des Lehrkörpers bestmögliche Ergebnisse zu erzielen – auch in Zeiten einer Pandemie, die den Alltag noch länger bestimmen wird. Studierende und Lehrende sollten daher jetzt gemeinsam überlegen, wie essenzielle Präsenzlehre während der COVID-19-Pandemie und das Architekturstudium an der TU Graz ohne Zugangsbeschränkungen zur Universität funktionieren kann. Ein Diskussionsforum um das Architekturstudium zu evaluieren, Anliegen vorzubringen oder auch manches zu kritisieren, sollte weiterhin in regelmäßigen Abständen stattfinden – zum gegenseitigen Austausch zwischen Studierenden und Lehrenden, aber ebenso um den notwendigen, transparenten Dialog innerhalb der Fakultät zu fördern. ∎

NACHSITZEN

An Event Held by **Students from the Architecture Drawing Studios**, **TU Graz**.

After an extraordinary summer semester, students from the architecture drawing studios organized an open discussion event in the park by the "Alte Technik" building in July 2020. At the event "Nachsitzen", students and teachers alike were given the chance to talk face-to-face about their experiences from the past online-based semester during the COVID-19 pandemic. Likewise, a review of how studying has changed in recent years was given, as well as a critical outlook on the future of teaching

architecture at the TU Graz. "It was difficult studying online during the last semester and it is also difficult to evaluate it online. We would like to share our perspective, get the teacher's opinions too, and discuss them together. Especially through our experiences over the last semester, we have noticed changes in teaching methods and do not want to let certain developments happen without addressing them. In the future, we would like to see more open communication between teachers and students. The event today will be a starting point for this," to quote the students **Antonia Prohammer** and **Vera Schabbon** from their opening statement. On the one hand, there was some positive feedback regarding online-based teaching; lectures, in particular, were well received, as online recordings made it possible to be more flexible or listen to them several times. On the other hand, for many students the quality of the seminars suffered due to the digital presentations of designs and the quality on-screen. Similar comments were also heard from the teachers present.

The key finding of the event was that architectural education needs face-to-face teaching as a basis for discussion. This must be made possible for students in compliance with the necessary distance and hygiene measures at the university in order to achieve the best possible results in the interests of the teaching staff—even during a pandemic that will indeed determine our everyday lives for some time to come. Students and teachers should therefore consider how essential face-to-face teaching is during the COVID-19 pandemic, and plan how the study of architecture at Graz University of Technology can go ahead without restrictions to accessing the university site. Such discussion forums that evaluate architecture study programs, and raise concerns or even criticize aspects, should continue to take place regularly—for mutual exchange between students and teachers, and to promote essential and transparent communication within the faculty. ∎

Clemens Haßlinger

„Best Presentation Prize"

Für Lehrende des **Instituts für Architektur und Medien**

„CollabWood" 1:1 Holzstruktur, digital in Echtzeit entworfen | wooden structure, digitally designed in real time
© IAM/TU Graz

Der von der „Education and Research in Computer Aided Architectural Design in Europe" (eCAADe) verliehene und von Bentley Systems gesponserte „Best Presentation Prize" ging 2020 an **Alexander Grasser** und **Alexandra Parger** (IAM) für ihre Präsentation zur Publikation: *Pervasive Collaboration and Tangible Complexity in Realtime Architecture* (Hg. A. Grasser/A. Parger/U. Hirschberg). Die vorgestellte Publikation zeigt eine innovative und spielerische Entwurfs-Plattform, die in Echtzeit digitale Partizipation in der Architektur ermöglicht. Der Preis, der im Rahmen der „Anthropologic – Architecture and Fabrication in the Cognitive Age" Konferenz der eCAADe vergeben wurde, würdigte die von Alexander Grasser entwickelte und programmierte „Realtime Architecture Platform", die einen digitalen Ort ermöglicht, an dem Architektur in Echtzeit entworfen werden kann. Mit der Plattform werden Ideen und Modelle auf spielerische Art digital geteilt und bearbeitet. Lokale sowie globale Entscheidungen werden in virtuellen Räumen und über Audio-Chat kommuniziert. Dieses Konzept ermöglicht eine Architektur, die stets adaptiv und offen ist. Die Plattform wurde zuvor im Rahmen der Projektübung „Collaborative Matter(s)" am Institut für Architektur und Medien gemeinsam mit einer Gruppe von Studierenden als digitale und kollaborative Entwurfsmethode entwickelt und erprobt, um die Möglichkeiten und Potenziale der digitalen Lehre im Architekturstudium auszuloten. Abgehalten wurde die Projektübung im Sommersemester 2020, einem Studienjahr in dem Tele-Präsenz einen besonderen Stellenwert hatte. ∎

"Best Presentation Prize"

For Lecturers at the Institute of Architecture and Media

The 2020 "Best Presentation Prize" awarded by the Education and Research in Computer Aided Architectural Design in Europe (eCAADe) and sponsored by Bentley Systems went to **Alexander Grasser** and **Alexandra Parger** (IAM) for their presentation on the publication *Pervasive Collaboration and Tangible Complexity in Realtime Architecture* (eds. A. Grasser/A. Parger/U. Hirschberg). The presented publication shows an innovative and playful design platform that enables real-time digital participation in architecture. The award, which was presented at eCAADe's "Anthropologic – Architecture and Fabrication in the Cognitive Age" conference, recognized the "Realtime Architecture Platform" developed and programmed by Alexander Grasser, which provides a digital environment where architecture can be designed live. The platform is used to playfully share and edit ideas and models. Local as well as global decisions are communicated over virtual spaces and via audio chat. This concept allows for adaptive and open architecture. The platform was previously developed and implemented as part of the Integral Design Studio "Collaborative Matter(s)" together with a group of students as a digital and collaborative design method to explore the possibilities and potentials of digital tools in architectural studies. The Integral Design Studio was held in the summer semester of 2020, an academic year in which online presence was especially significant. ∎

Alexander Grasser (Translation: Alexander Grasser)

BetreuerInnen | Advisors:
Alexander Grasser, Urs Hischberg, Alexandra Parger, Eszter Katona, Kilian Hoffmann, Nora Hoti
Studio Jury:
Ryan Manning, Manuel Jiménez Gracīa, Daniel Köhler, Jörg Stanzel
Studio PartnerInnen | Studio Partners:
Fifteen Seconds, Exit Games, pro:Holz, Felber Holz
Studierende | Students:
Alina Boss, Angelika Bernhart, Anton Kussinna, Constanze Feitzlmayr, Daniel Buchacher, Donia Elmenshawi, Felix Zitter, Francesco Doninelli, Franciska Kozul, Janine Witzany, Julie Belpois, Kenan Isaković, Kerstin Grangl, Kilian Hoffmann, Maria Matthäus, Max Frühwirt, Sebastian Meisinger, Ronald Tang Pak To, Tilen Sagrković

„Reise durch den Alltag"

Eine Lehrveranstaltung des **Instituts für Grundlagen der Konstruktion und des Entwerfens (KOEN)** organisiert von **Ena Kukić** und **Armin Stocker**

Unter dem Titel „Reise durch den Alltag" reagierte das KOEN auf die COVID-19 Reisebeschränkungen und organisierte im Mai 2020 – als Alternative zum ursprünglichen Reiseziel Kopenhagen – eine Exkursion in die eigenen vier Wände. Im Fokus der ungewöhnlichen Lehrveranstaltung lag die Erforschung des eigenen Lebensraums und der täglichen Abläufe in Hinblick auf architektonische, städtebauliche und landschaftliche Aspekte unter Einbezug der aktuellen Situation einer Pandemie. Unter der Leitung von Armin Stocker und Ena Kukić sowie neun LektorInnen, wurden 128 TeilnehmerInnen mit der Aufgabe konfrontiert, ihren Alltag mittels Skizzen,

„Room with a View", ausgewählte Skizzen | selected sketches
© KOEN/TU Graz

Notizen und Fotografien zu untersuchen. Im Vordergrund stand die Beantwortung der Frage, welche Rolle die bauliche Umwelt im Kontext des täglichen Lebens übernehmen kann und wie sie sich auf den sozialen Raum auswirkt. Ziel dieser Erkundung des eigenen Alltags war es, Sensibilität und Urteilskraft für die gebaute Umgebung zu schulen. Als Ausgangspunkt und Inspiration dienten popkulturelle und literarische Vorbilder, wie zum Beispiel Paul Austers und Wayne Wangs Film „Smoke" Die Ergebnisse werden – flankiert von Textbeiträgen – in einer Publikation des Instituts veröffentlicht. ▪

"A Journey through Everyday Life"

A course at the **Institute of Construction and Design Principles (KOEN)** organized by **Ena Kukić** and **Armin Stocker**.

In response to the COVID-19 travel restrictions in May 2020, and as an alternative to the originally planned destination of Copenhagen, KOEN organized an excursion titled "A Journey through Everyday Life" within their own four walls. The focus of this unusual course was to explore one's own living space and daily routines in terms of architectural, urban planning, and landscape aspects, considering the current situation of a pandemic. Led by Armin Stocker and Ena Kukić working with nine other lecturers, 128 participants were given the task of examining their everyday life by means of sketches, notes, and photographs. The focus was on answering the question of what role the built environment can play in the context of daily life and how it affects social space. The aim of exploring one's own everyday life was to increase sensitivity and judgement for the built environment around us. Pop-cultural and literary models, such as Paul Auster's and Wayne Wang's film "Smoke," served as a starting point and inspiration. The results will be presented in a KOEN publication. ▪

Ena Kukić/ Lea Schuiki/ Armin Stocker

Ferdinand Schuster (1920–1972). Das architektonische Werk: Bauten, Schriften, Analysen

Daniel Gethmann (Hg. | ed.)
Zürich | Zurich: Park Books, 2020
Deutsch, 420 Seiten |
German, 420 pages
ISBN 978-3-03860-183-8
EUR 58,00 | EUR 58.00

Ferdinand Schuster (1920–1972) zählt zu den bedeutendsten Architekten der Nachkriegszeit in Österreich. Seine zahlreichen, vor allem in Kapfenberg und Graz realisierten Kirchen-, Industrie-, Freizeit-, Bildungs- und Wohnbauten sowie seine Vorträge und Essays zur gesellschaftlichen Verantwortung von Architektur haben eine hohe Aufmerksamkeit erreicht. Von 2018 bis 2020 wurde das Werk Schusters in einem OeNB-Forschungsprojekt unter der Leitung von Daniel Gethmann am Institut für Architekturtheorie, Kunst- und Kulturwissenschaften der TU Graz aufgearbeitet. Die Ergebnisse des Forschungsprojekts sind nun in Form einer Monografie über den Architekten erschienen, die auf 420 Seiten Schusters Bauten, seine kommentierten Schriften und Reden sowie zahlreiche Analysen zum gesellschaftlichen, politischen und kulturellen Wirken des Architekten dokumentiert. Die Monografie enthält Beiträge von **Sabine Christian, Lorenzo De Chiffre, Daniel Gethmann, Eugen Gross, Clemens Haßlinger, Heimo Kaindl, Arnold R. Kräuter, Bruno Maldoner, Holger Neuwirth, Felix Obermair, Volker Pachauer, Winfried Ranz, Ferdinand Schmölzer, Antje Senarclens de Grancy, Jörg Uitz** und Fotografien von **Michael Goldgruber** und **Bob Vrablik.** ∎

Daniel Gethmann lehrt Kulturwissenschaft und Entwurfstheorie am Institut für Architekturtheorie, Kunst- und Kulturwissenschaften der TU Graz.

. . .

Ferdinand Schuster (1920–1972) is one of the most significant figures of post-war Austrian architecture. He realized numerous churches, industrial buildings, leisure and educational facilities as well as housing, primarily in Kapfenberg and Graz. Both these projects as well as his talks and essays on social responsibility in architecture attracted widespread attention. Between 2018 and 2020, Daniel Gethmann led an OeNB (Austrian Central Bank) project at the Institute of Architectural Theory, Art History and Cultural Studies, researching Schuster's oeuvre. The results of the research project have now been published as a monograph about the architect, a 420-page publication documenting Schuster's buildings and containing his commented writing and talks as well as numerous analyses of his social, political, and cultural impact. The monograph collects contributions from **Sabine Christian, Lorenzo De Chiffre, Daniel Gethmann, Eugen Gross, Clemens Haßlinger, Heimo Kaindl, Arnold R. Kräuter, Bruno Maldoner, Holger Neuwirth, Felix Obermair, Volker Pachauer, Winfried Ranz, Ferdinand Schmölzer, Antje Senarclens de Grancy,** and **Jörg Uitz** as well as photography by **Michael Goldgruber** and **Bob Vrablik.** ∎

Daniel Gethmann teaches Cultural Studies and Design Theory at the Institute of Architectural Theory, Art History and Cultural Studies at TU Graz.

Translation: Susannah Leopold

Atlas of Digital Architecture. Terminology, Concepts, Methods, Tools, Examples, Phenomena

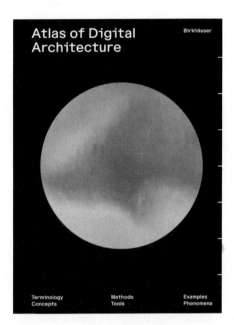

Urs Hirschberg/Ludger Hovestadt/
Oliver Fritz (Hg. | eds.)
Berlin: Birkhäuser, 2020
Englisch, 760 Seiten, kartoniert |
English, 760 pages, paperback
ISBN 978-3-0356-1990-4
EUR 59,95 | EUR 59.95

Digitale Technologien und Architektur sind mittlerweile untrennbar geworden. Neue Ansätze und Methoden verändern nicht nur Arbeitsabläufe und Planungspraxis von ArchitektInnen, sondern mithin auch das Wesen der Architektur selbst. Diese umfangreiche Publikation versammelt Beiträge von zwei Dutzend UniversitätsprofessorInnen und DozentInnen, die ihr breites Fachwissen teilen, welches von einem professionellen Schriftsteller in eine Reihe ansprechender episodischer Kapitel gebracht wurde. In sechs Teile gegliedert, vermittelt der Atlas einen Überblick und gibt wertvolle Orientierungshilfe für die unzähligen zeitgenössischen Anwendungsmöglichkeiten von Computern in der Architektur, darunter 3D-Modellieren und CAD, Rendering und Visualisierung, Skripting, Typografie, Text & Code, digitale Fertigung und Modellbau, GIS, BIM, Simulation, Big Data & Machine Learning und viele weitere. ∎

Urs Hirschberg ist Universitätsprofessor für Darstellung der Architektur und Neue Medien und leitet das Institut für Architektur und Medien an der TU Graz.

. . .

Digital technology and architecture have become inseparable, with new approaches and methodologies not just affecting the workflows and practice of architects, but shaping the very character of architecture. In this compendious work, two dozen university professors and lecturers share their vast range of expertise with a professional writer who assembles this into an array of engaging, episodic chapters. Structured into six parts, the Atlas offers an orientation to the myriad ways in which computers are used in architecture today, such as: 3D Modelling and CAD; Rendering and Visualization; Scripting, Typography, Text & Code; Digital Manufacturing and Model Making; GIS, BIM, Simulation, and Big Data & Machine Learning, to name but these. ∎

Urs Hirschberg is a professor of Architectural Representation and New Media and head of the Institute of Architecture and Media.

Institut für Gebäudelehre. Jahrbuch 18/19

Hans Gangoly (Hg. | ed.)
Graz: Verlag der TU Graz | Publishing
Company of Graz University of
Technology, 2020
Deutsch/Englisch, 400 Seiten,
broschiert | German/English,
400 pages, softcover
ISBN 978-3-85125-726-7
ISBN 978-3-85125-727-4 (E-Book)
EUR 39,00 | EUR 39.00

Die Entwurfslehre setzt in ihrer Komplexität ein hohes Maß an persönlicher Auseinandersetzung und Praxis mit architektonischen Inhalten voraus. Erfahrungen und Lösungsansätze zu strukturellen, typologischen, konstruktiven, materialtechnischen, atmosphärischen und nicht zuletzt darstellungs- und vermittlungstechnischen Fragen müssen sehr unmittelbar und individuell entsprechend den Bedürfnissen der Studierenden in die Lehre eingebracht werden. Die Diskussion im Rahmen der Lehrveranstaltungen, ihre Inputs und Kritiken für die Studierenden und die vielen Gespräche am Rande schaffen Gelegenheit, Fragestellungen im Rahmen der Entwurfslehre zu erweitern. Das Institut für Gebäudelehre an der TU Graz bezieht hier ganz klar Position.

Zudem prägen seit vielen Jahren auch namenhafte GastprofessorInnen durch ihre sehr pointierten Entwurfshaltungen die Entwicklung des Instituts. Das *Jahrbuch 18/19* dokumentiert ausgewählte Ergebnisse der Entwurfslehre am Institut für Gebäudelehre aus dem Studienjahr 2018/19. In dieser ersten Ausgabe der Jahrbuchreihe werden Lehrveranstaltungen aus dem Master- und Bachelorstudium sowie Abschlussarbeiten vorgestellt und damit Einblicke in Themenstellungen, Entwurfsprozesse und Projekte ermöglicht. ▪

Hans Gangoly ist Architekt, Universitätsprofessor für Gebäudelehre und leitet das gleichnamige Institut an der TU Graz.

· · ·

The complexity of design theory requires a high degree of personal involvement and practice with architectural content. Experiences and solutions to structural, typological, constructive, material, atmospheric, and last but not least, representation and mediation issues must very directly be brought into teaching according to the needs of the students. The discussions during the courses, student input and criticism, and the multiple exchanges create the opportunity to expand the field questions within design teaching. The Institute of Design and Building Typology at Graz University of Technology retains their clear position here. For many years now, renowned visiting professors have additionally influenced the development of the institute through their very pointed approaches to design. In the publication *Jahrbuch 18/19* (Yearbook 18/19), the Institute of Design and Building Typology documents a selection of the institute's output in the field of design theory from the academic year 2018/19. The publication presents final theses as well as courses from both the master's and bachelor's degree, providing insights into topics, design processes, and projects. ▪

Hans Gangoly is an architect, university professor, and head of the Institute of Design and Building Typology at Graz University of Technology.

Herbert Eichholzer. Architektur Förderungspreis 2017

Andreas Lichtblau (Hg. | ed.)
Graz: Verlag der TU Graz | Publishing
Company of Graz University of
Technology, 2020
Deutsch, 85 Seiten, kartoniert |
German, 85 pages, paperback
ISBN 978-3-85125-739-7
EUR 27,00 | EUR 27.00

Die einzelnen Wettbewerbsbeiträge können theoretisch in Form eines Essays die Frage nach der politischen Aussage und Auswirkung von Architektur stellen. Daraus abgeleitet werden neue Lösungswege für Erfordernis und Abstimmung von differenzierter „Privatheit" und „Öffentlichkeit" in gebauten Strukturen, oder ein konkreter Entwurf auf Grundlage einer kurzen schriftlichen Positionierung. Ausgehend von Eichholzers Studien zu einem Kollektivhaus in Moskau stellen sich Fragen zu gegenwärtigen sozial relevanten Raumbildungen, um typologische Antworten auf die Frage von differenzierter Privatheit und Öffentlichkeit innerhalb einer Gebäudestruktur und innerhalb von Binnengrundrissen entwickeln zu können. ▪

Andreas Lichtblau ist Architekt, Universitätsprofessor für Wohnbau und leitet das gleichnamige Institut an der TU Graz.

The individual competition entries can pose the question of the political statement and impact of architecture theoretically in the form of an essay. This results in new solutions for the requirement and coordination of differentiated "private" and "public" spheres within built structures, or a precise design based on a brief written statement. Based on Eichholzer's studies of a collective house in Moscow, questions are raised about contemporary socially relevant spatial formations, to be able to develop typological answers to the question concerning differentiated private and public spheres within a building structure and within internal floor plans. ∎

Andreas Lichtblau is an architect, university professor and head of the Institute of Housing at Graz University of Technology.

Institut für Wohnbau. Chronik 2020

Andreas Lichtblau (Hg. | ed.)
Graz: Verlag der TU Graz | Publishing Company of Graz University of Technology, 2020
Deutsch, 96 Seiten, kartoniert |
German, 96 pages, paperback
ISBN 978-3-85425-738-0
Auf Anfrage über das Institut erhältlich |
Available upon request at the institute

Der soziale Wohnbau hat sich von seinen ursächlichen Anliegen, Wohnungen für das Existenzminimum zu schaffen, korrelierend mit der sozialen Entwicklung seit Anfang des 20. Jahrhunderts, zu einem gehobenen Mittelstandswohnen entwickelt. Sicherheitsanliegen von Normen und Gesetzgebungen, eine Optimierung der energetischen Verluste sowie angestrebte Ausbaustandards steigern kontinuierlich die Errichtungsausgaben und damit die Mietkosten von Wohnraum, der für Teile der Gesellschaft nicht mehr leistbar sein wird. Unter dem Aspekt des wirtschaftlichen Wandels und der letzten Finanzmarktkrisen wächst die Zahl der Personen, die in einem prekären Umfeld leben. Allein im europäischen Raum steigt die Zahl der Arbeitslosen, untypisch Beschäftigten, freien DienstnehmerInnen, HeimarbeiterInnen als auch Teilzeit- und Kurzzeitbeschäftigten enorm. Gleichzeitig nehmen Wohn- und Lebenserhaltungskosten, Konsumdruck und Qualitätsansprüche stetig zu. Ein Abbild dieser aufgehenden sozialen Schere stellen auch unsere Städte dar. Die im Rahmen der Schriftenreihe des Instituts für Wohnbau der TU Graz erschienene Publikation basiert auf den gesellschaftspolitisch relevanten Forschungsfragen, die am Institut für Wohnbau thematisiert werden. Die *Chronik 2020* versammelt Beiträge, die sich der langfristigen Sicherstellung der Leistbarkeit von Wohnraum für zunehmend prekäre Lebenssituationen widmen und die räumliche und organisatorische Fragestellungen für das Zusammenleben in solchen Wohnformen behandeln. ∎

Andreas Lichtblau ist Architekt, Universitätsprofessor für Wohnbau und leitet das gleichnamige Institut an der TU Graz.

• • •

Following social development trends since the beginning of the twentieth century, social housing has evolved from its former minimal standard to an upper middle-class standard of housing. Safety concerns regarding norms and legislations, optimizing sources of energy loss as well as higher finishing standards continuously increase construction costs and thus the rental costs of housing that for some groups of society will soon no longer be affordable. Alongside economic change and recent financial market crises, the number of people living under unstable conditions is growing. In Europe alone, the number of unemployed, freelancers, home workers as well as part-time and short-term employees is increasing enormously. At the same time, housing and living costs, consumer pressure, and quality demands are constantly increasing. Our cities are also a reflection of this widening social gap. The publication, which is part of the series of publications at the Institute of Housing at Graz University of Technology, is based on the socio-politically relevant research questions that are addressed at the Institute of Housing. *Chronik 2020* is a collection of contributions that are dedicated to ensuring the long-term affordability of housing for increasingly unstable living situations and that address spatial and organizational aspects of living together in such forms of housing. ∎

Andreas Lichtblau is an architect, university professor, and head of the Institute of Housing at Graz University of Technology.

Bühne und Kostüme. Das Grazer Schauspielhaus als Exempel für Entwerfen im Bestand

Petra Simon/Elemer Ploder/
Martina Thaller (Hg. | eds.)
Graz: Verlag der TU Graz | Publishing
Company of Graz University of
Technology, 2020
Deutsch, 121 Seiten, kartoniert |
German, 121 pages, paperback
ISBN 978-3-85125-762-5
EUR 29,00 | EUR 29.00

Die jüngste Publikation des Instituts für Entwerfen im Bestand und Denkmalpflege trägt den Titel *Bühne und Kostüme* und dokumentiert die studentischen Beiträge zur Lehrveranstaltung „Entwerfen 3", die im Wintersemester 2019/20 unter der Leitung von Petra Simon und Elemer Ploder entstanden sind. Die Studierenden setzten sich am Beispiel des Grazer Schauspielhauses mit dem gesellschaftlichen und historischen Status denkmalgeschützter Gebäude auseinander. Mit Unterstützung der Theaterholding Graz/Steiermark (unter der Geschäftsleitung von Bernhard Rinner), dem Bundesdenkmalamt Steiermark (unter der Leitung von Christian Brugger) und der Intendantin des Grazer Schauspielhauses, Iris Laufenberg, wurden Entwurfsstudien erarbeitet, die aus der Auseinandersetzung mit historischer Bausubstanz, der Integration aktueller Nutzungsprofile sowie einer nachhaltigen Baustruktur hervorgingen. Ziel der Lehrveranstaltung war es, die Spielstätte der Stadtbevölkerung, TheaterbesucherInnen und MitarbeiterInnen des Hauses durch Erweiterung und Umbau zugänglich(er) zu machen und gleichzeitig den kulturellen und historischen Kontext des Hauses im Entwurf zu berücksichtigen. Voraussetzung hierfür war eine interdisziplinäre Vernetzung sowie ein sensibler Umgang der Studierenden mit dem Bestand. Dabei entstanden facettenreiche Ergebnisse mit einer gelungenen Symbiose von Alt und Neu. ▪

Petra Simon und **Elemer Ploder** sind GastprofessorInnen am Institut für Entwerfen im Bestand und Denkmalpflege der TU Graz und Gründer des Architekturbüros epps Ploder Simon ZT GmbH. **Martina Thaller** ist Universitätsassistentin am Institut für Entwerfen im Bestand und Denkmalpflege an der TU Graz.

. . .

The most recent publication from the Institute of Design in Consisting Structure and Architectural Heritage Protection with the title *Bühne und Kostüme* (Stage and Costumes) documents student contributions from the course "Design 3," held during the winter semester 2019/20 by Petra Simon and Elemer Ploder. Using the example of the Graz Schauspielhaus theater, the students looked at the social and historical status of listed buildings. With the support of Theater-Holding Graz/Styria under the management of Bernhard Rinner, the Federal Monuments Authority Austria under the direction of Christian Brugger, and the director of the Schauspielhaus theater Graz, Iris Laufenberg, designs were developed which resulted from the examination of historical building structure, the integration of current usage profiles as well as a sustainable building structure. The aim of the course was to make the venue more accessible for the general public, theater visitors, and employees by means of extension and conversion, while at the same time considering the cultural and historical context of the theater in the design. A prerequisite for this was an interdisciplinary connection and a sensitive approach to the existing building. The result was a multifaceted design with a successful symbiosis of old and new. ▪

Petra Simon and **Elemer Ploder** are visiting professors at the Institute of Design in Consisting Structure and Architectural Heritage Protection and founders of the architecture firm epps Ploder Simon ZT GmbH. **Martina Thaller** is a university assistant at the Institute of Design in Consisting Structure and Architectural Heritage Protection.

Die Wiederentdeckung des olympischen Sarajevo

Alen Čeleketić/Marija Čeleketić
Graz: Verlag der TU Graz | Publishing
Company of Graz University
of Technology, 2020
Deutsch, 207 Seiten, kartoniert |
German, 207 pages, paperback
ISBN 978-3-85125-780-9
EUR 35,00 | EUR 35.00

Die Olympischen Winterspiele 1984 hatten im wirtschaftlichen Sinn einen enormen Einfluss auf die Entwicklung der Stadtinfrastruktur und des Wintertourismus in Sarajevo. Nach der größten Sportveranstaltung Jugoslawiens verblieb der Stadt bedeutsame Architektur, die einerseits die Urbanität des Ortes und die Lebensqualität der Menschen beeinflusste und die andererseits die Berglandschaft um Sarajevo aufwertete. Das Ziel dieses Buches, das aus einer Masterarbeit unter Betreuung von Anselm Wagner (Institut für Architekturtheorie, Kunst- und Kulturwissenschaften) entstand, ist eine intensive Auseinandersetzung mit der olympischen Architektur in Sarajevo. Mit vorhandenen Quellen wurde eine tiefgreifende Analyse der Bauwerke durchgeführt, um auf die Frage des architektonischen Potenzials zu antworten sowie auf die Bedeutung dieser Bauwerke aufmerksam zu machen. Dadurch sollen Erkenntnisse darüber gewonnen werden, ob und warum es auch in Zukunft wichtig wäre, Sarajevos olympische Bauten mit dem nötigen Respekt zu behandeln, sie vor dem Verfall zu bewahren und ihre Rolle für das Gesamtbild der Stadt auszuloten. ▪

Alen und Marija Čeleketić haben an der Technischen Universität in Graz 2016 das Architekturstudium abgeschlossen.

...

The 1984 Winter Olympics had an enormous economic impact on the development of Sarajevo's infrastructure and tourism. After the largest ever sports event in Yugoslavia, the city was left with significant architecture, which on the one hand influenced the urbanity of the city and the quality of life for the people, and on the other hand, enhanced the mountainscape around Sarajevo. The aim of this book, which started out as a master's thesis supervised by Anselm Wagner (Institute of Architectural Theory, Art History and Cultural Studies), is to intensively examine the Olympic architecture in Sarajevo. Based on existing sources, an in-depth analysis of the buildings is carried out to answer the question of architectural potential and to draw attention to the importance of these buildings. The analysis explores whether and why it would be important to treat Sarajevo's Olympic buildings with the necessary respect in the future, to save them from decay, and to evaluate their role for an overall image of the city. ▪

Alen and Marija Čeleketić graduated in architecture at Graz University of Technology in 2016.

Publikationsreihe Cahier
Cahier 4. Kollektive Peripherie – Neue Sichtweisen auf den Freiraum

Institut für Städtebau (Hg. | ed.)
Graz, 2019
Deutsch/Englisch, 16 Seiten, broschiert |
German/English, 16 pages, softcover
EUR 10,00 | EUR 10.00

Urbane Gebiete sind durch eine zunehmende Suburbanisierung gekennzeichnet. Fast 40 Prozent der europäischen Landfläche sind von Gebieten mit mittlerer Bevölkerungsdichte bedeckt, in denen 35 Prozent der Bevölkerung leben. Die Suburbanisierung ist trotz ihres wachsenden Umfangs und ihrer Bedeutung nichts Neues. Es gibt eine lange Tradition, über die Verbreitung der Stadt zu schreiben, allerdings zeichnen sich seit einigen Jahrzehnten Veränderungen in der Art und Zusammensetzung dieser Vorstadtgebiete ab. In anderen Gebieten, in denen die Suburbanisierung das Ergebnis von bürgerlichen Familien ist, die eine ruhige Umgebung wünschen, ist eine wachsende Zahl von Gruppen mit niedrigem Einkommen zu beobachten, die es sich nicht mehr leisten können, in Innenstadtgebieten zu leben – der „Zentrifugal-Effekt" steigender städtischer Immobilienpreise. Ausgehend von städtebaulichen Studien sowie studentischen Projekten zielt dieses Cahier darauf ab, Freiräume in peripheren Gebieten zu untersuchen und zu eruieren, wie diese als Ressourcen für eine neue suburbane soziale und physische Stadtlandschaft genutzt werden können. Ist es möglich Freiräume am Stadtrand kritisch als städtische Kollektivräume zu verstehen, um adäquate Planungsrahmen, Gestaltungsmethoden und -werkzeuge für ihre Qualifizierung zu entwickeln? Das vierte *Cahier* untersucht diese Potenziale und Strategien. ∎

Aglaée Degros ist Professorin und Leiterin des Instituts für Städtebau der TU Graz. **Radostina Radulova-Stahmer** ist Architektin und Universitätsassistentin am Institut für Städtebau der TU Graz. **Sabine Bauer** ist Universitätsassistentin am Institut für Städtebau der TU Graz.

· · ·

Urban areas are characterized by increasing suburbanization. Almost 40 percent of Europe's land is covered by areas of medium population density, where 35 percent of the population lives. Despite its growing scale and importance, suburbanization is nothing new. We have in fact been observing changes in the nature and composition of these suburban regions for several decades. In other areas where suburbanization is the result of middle-class families seeking a quiet environment, we are seeing a growing number of low-income groups who can no longer afford to live in inner-city districts—the "centrifugal effect" of rising urban property prices. Based on urban planning studies as well as student projects, this *Cahier* series aims to investigate open spaces in peripheral areas and how they can be used as resources for a new suburban social and physical urban landscape. ∎

Aglaée Degros is a professor and head of the Institute of Urbanism at Graz University of Technology. **Radostina Radulova-Stahmer** is an architect and university assistant at the Institute of Urbanism at Graz University of Technology. **Sabine Bauer** is a university assistant at the Institute of Urbanism at Graz University of Technology.

LAMA. Das lösungsorientierte Architekturmagazin

© Christina Blümel/LAMA

Christina Blümel/Isabella Fuchs/Philipp Glanzner/Ramona Kraxner/Andreas Maierhofer/Anna Müller/Felix Obermair/ Vera Schabbon (Hg. | eds.)
Graz: Eigenverlag | self-published, 2020
Deutsch, 9 Ausgaben + Sonderausgaben, broschiert | German,
9 editions + special editions, softcover
ISSN 2707-9945
EUR 8,00 | EUR 8.00

LAMA. Das lösungsorientierte Architekturmagazin wurde im Sommer 2019 von vier jungen Architekturstudierenden der Technischen Universität Graz konzipiert. *LAMA* hinterfragt die Architekturdisziplin in Lehre, Praxis und ihrem gesellschaftlichen Stellenwert. Über neun Ausgaben hinweg werden in einem dreijährigen Prozess Schritt für Schritt zukunftsorientierte Lösungsansätze für die Architektur formuliert. Dazu versammelt *LAMA* einen interdisziplinären Pool aus ExpertInnen und LaiInnen, die diese Lösungsansätze gemeinsam ausarbeiten. Als finale Zielsetzung wird ein *Handbuch für eine gesellschaftsbildende Architekturkommunikation* verfasst, welches die bis dahin gewonnenen Erkenntnisse kompakt zusammenfasst. Die erste reguläre Ausgabe wurde im März 2020 unter dem Titel „Ausbildung zur Einbildung – Warum ist die Architekturlehre nicht mehr

gesellschaftsbildend?" publiziert. Darauf folgte im September 2020 eine Sonderausgabe, die sich dem Thema „Innovation statt Isolation – Die Architektur während und nach COVID-19" widmete. Im Dezember 2020 erschien schließlich die zweite reguläre Ausgabe, die sich mit der Architekturpraxis unter dem Titel „Bauen in der Blase – Warum ist die Architekturpraxis nicht mehr gesellschaftsbildend?" auseinandersetzt. Im Frühling 2021 wurde die dritte Ausgabe zum Thema Diskurs „Architektursprache = Architekturbrache – Warum ist der Architekturdiskurs nicht mehr gesellschaftsbildend?" veröffentlicht. ∎

Die *LAMA*-Redaktion besteht aus AbsolventInnen und Studierenden der Technischen Universität Graz. Die Gründungsmitglieder **Philipp Glanzner**, **Andreas Maierhofer**, **Felix Obermair** und **Vera Schabbon** waren zuvor bereits HerausgeberInnen des studentischen Architekturmagazins *SCHAURAUM*. Im Laufe des ersten Projektjahres hat sich das Team um **Christina Blümel**, **Anna Müller**, **Isabella Fuchs** und **Ramona Kraxner** erweitert.

· · ·

LAMA. The idea for the solution-oriented architecture magazine was conceived in summer 2019 by four young architecture students at Graz University of Technology. *LAMA* examines the teaching methods in the architectural discipline as well as its practice and status. Over the course of nine issues, future-oriented solutions for architecture are being formulated step by step over a three-year period. *LAMA* brings together an interdisciplinary group of experts and laypersons who are working to develop these solutions. The final objective is to compile a handbook for socially formative architectural communication that compactly collates all of the insights gained. The first issue was published in March 2020 with the title "Ausbildung zur Einbildung—Warum ist die Architekturlehre nicht mehr gesellschaftsbildend?" (Education for Imagination—Why is the Teaching of Architecture No Longer A Socially Formative Practice?) This was followed by a special issue in September 2020, dedicated to the topic "Innovation statt Isolation—Die Architektur während und nach COVID-19"

(Innovation Not Isolation—Architecture During and After COVID-19). Finally, in December 2020, the second issue was published, addressing architectural practice, with the title "Bauen in der Blase—Warum ist die Architekturpraxis nicht mehr gesellschaftsbildend?" (Building in the Bubble—Why is the Architectural Practice No Longer Socially Formative?). In spring 2021, the third issue was published on the topic "Architektursprache = Architekturbrache—Warum ist der Architekturdiskurs nicht mehr gesellschaftsbildend?" (Architectural Lingo = Architecutral Fallow—How Come the Architectural Discourse is Socially Insufficient? ▪

The *LAMA* editorial team consists of graduates and students from the Faculty of Architecture at Graz University of Technology. The founding members **Philipp Glanzner**, **Andreas Maierhofer**, **Felix Obermair** and **Vera Schabbon** were previously editors of the student architecture magazine *SCHAURAUM*. In the course of the first year of the project, the team expanded to include **Christina Blümel**, **Anna Müller**, **Isabella Fuchs**, and **Ramona Kraxner**.

Stahlbeton- leichtbaudecke — Atelier Hans Kupelwieser

Institut für Tragwerksentwurf

Das Institut für Tragwerksentwurf (ITE) arbeitet in verschiedenen Forschungsprojekten seit Jahren intensiv an der Entwicklung von Bauweisen, die einen ressourcenoptimierten Einsatz von Materialien in der Baubranche ermöglichen. Eine innovative und vielversprechende Methode den konventionellen Stahlbetonbau dahingehend zu verändern ist die additive Fertigung für die Herstellung von Schalungen. Die Technologie für den 3D-Druck mit Beton wurde am Institut in einem vorangehenden Forschungsprojekt (COEBRO) entwickelt und fand seine Anwendung bereits in der Herstellung einer prototypischen um 35 Prozent gewichtsreduzierten Leichtbaudecke unter Verwendung gedruckter Aussparungskörper. Im April 2020 wurde das ITE damit beauftragt, die Bauweise für ein nahezu quadratisches und ca. 100 Quadratmeter großes Deckenfeld für einen Atelierraum im Schloss Seehof in Lunz am See zur Anwendung zu bringen.

Das Projekt umfasste einen in Kooperation mit Hans Kupelwieser entwickelten Entwurf, die komplette Ausführungs- und Detailplanung sowie die Umsetzung des realen Bauprojekts mit 130 unterschiedlichen 3D-gedruckten Aussparungskörpern. Die am Labor für Konstruktiven Ingenieurbau in der Inffeldgasse hergestellten Halbfertigteile wurden im Roboter Design Labor der TU Graz mittels einer neuen 3D-Druckanlage von Baumit unter Verwendung von Baumit PrintCret 230N produziert und mit fachlicher Unterstützung der Firma Gusel auf der Baustelle installiert. Nach einer für alle Beteiligten inspirierenden und außergewöhnlichen Baustellenphase konnte die neuartige Konstruktion Mitte Oktober ausgeschalt werden. Die weitgespannte Deckenkonstruktion steht stellvertretend für eine zukunftsfähige Haltung zur Verwendung von Stahlbeton, welche unter anderem auf wirtschaftliche, digitale Fertigungsmethoden zur Ressourcenschonung setzt. ▪

Stahlbetonleichtbaudecke | Reinforced Concrete Lightweight Ceiling © Robert Schmid/ITE/TU Graz

Reinforced Concrete Lightweight Ceiling – Atelier Hans Kupelwieser

Institute of Structural Design

The Institute of Structural Design (ITE) has been working intensively over the years on various research projects concerning the development of construction methods that enable the optimized use of materials in the building industry. An innovative and promising method to change conventional reinforced concrete construction is additive manufacturing for the production of formwork. The technology for 3D concrete printing was developed at the institute in a previous research project (COEBRO) and this technique was applied in the production of a prototype lightweight ceiling with a weight reduction of 35 percent using printed recess formers. In April 2020, the Institute of Structural Design was commissioned to apply this construction method to an approximately 100 square meter rectangular ceiling for a studio room at the Seehof palace in Lunz am See.

The project was composed firstly of a design, developed in cooperation with Hans Kupelwieser, then the complete execution and detailed planning, as well as the implementation of the building project with 130 different 3D printed recess bodies. The semi-finished parts were produced by the Laboratory for Structural Engineering in Inffeldgasse in the Robotics Lab at Graz University of Technology using a new 3D printing system from the company Baumit, using Baumit PrintCret 230N. The parts were installed on the construction site with the expert support of the Gusel company. After an inspiring and somewhat unusual construction phase, the novel construction could be revealed in mid-October. The wide-span ceiling construction is representative of a sustainable attitude towards the use of reinforced concrete, which, among other things, relies on economic, digital production methods to conserve resources. ∎

Projektlaufzeit | Project duration:
April–Oktober 2020
Projektteam | Project team:
Institut für Tragwerksentwurf | Institute of Structural Design: Stefan Peters, Andreas Trummer, Georg Hansemann, Robert Schmid, Christoph Holzinger, Joshua Paul Tapley
Hans Kupelwieser
Firma | Company Gusel: Hubert Lugbauer
Firma | Company Tröga: Gerald Ottman

ParaSol. Multifunktionale solaraktive Platz- und Straßenüberdachung Leoben

Institut für Städtebau

Ein beträchtlicher Anteil unserer Städte wird von Flächen des fahrenden und ruhenden Verkehrs vereinnahmt. Insbesondere Stellplatzflächen im Freien sind hochgradig unökologisch und flächenintensiv. Sie versiegeln die Böden, begünstigen das Entstehen von sommerlichen Hitzeinseln und sind fast ausschließlich monofunktional nutzbar. In Leoben lotet das Projekt an konkreten Orten aus, welche stadträumlichen Auswirkungen, Synergie- und Energiepotenziale neu zu entwickelnde, solaraktive Platz- und Straßenüberdachungen in Form von weitgespannten Konstruktionen in Leichtbauweise im öffentlichen urbanen Raum mit sich bringen und wie sie sich auf das Stadtbild und die Stadtfunktion auswirken. Im Fokus stehen Stellplatzflächen aber auch langsam befahrene Straßen oder Schienen, wobei weitere Nutzungsszenarien denkbar sind. Mit der Sondierung wird ein nachfolgendes F&E Demoprojekt inhaltlich und strategisch vorbereitet. Dieses F&E-Projekt wird unter Einbeziehung des

ParaSol © stdb/TU Graz

Werkstoffwissens in der Region mit Fokus auf Membran-, Polymer- und Dünnglastechnologien die Anwendung bestehender und neuer Material- und Photovoltaiktechnologien bzw. Technologiekombinationen in der Stadtinfrastruktur in Prototypen demonstrieren und soll in einer marktfähigen Produktentwicklung münden. ▪

ParaSol. Multifunctional Solar Car Park and Street Canopies in Leoben

Institute of Urbanism

A considerable proportion of our cities is occupied by areas of both moving and stationary traffic. Outdoor car parks in particular are highly unecological and space-intensive. They form a seal over the ground, promote heat islands in the summer, and can almost exclusively be used monofunctionally. For the project in Leoben, concrete-heavy areas will be assessed, and urban spatial effects, synergy and energy potential will be highlighted by newly developed, solar-active car park and street canopies in the form of wide-span lightweight constructions in public urban space. It will be explored how these canopies could affect the cityscape and the functioning of the city. The focus is on

car parks but also on slow-moving roads and rail-tracks, although further options would be conceivable. A subsequent R&D demo project is being prepared with regard to content and strategy. This R&D project will demonstrate the application by using prototypes with both existing and new materials and photovoltaic technologies, and combinations of this technology within the urban infrastructure. This process will lead to the development of a marketable product by incorporating material knowledge in the region with a focus on membrane, polymer, and thin glass technologies. ▪

Projektlaufzeit | Project duration:
Januar 2019–Februar 2020
Finanzierung | Funding:
Österreichische Forschungsförderungs-gesellschaft | The Austrian Research Promotion Agency (FFG) (Stadt der Zukunft – City of Tomorrow)
Projektteam | Project team:
Aglaée Degros (Leitung | project leader), Ida Pirstinger, Anna Maria Bagarić, Nina Habe, Mendi Kočiš
ProjektpartnerInnen | Project partners:
FH Salzburg – Smart Building & Smart City Leoben Holding GmbH

Technical Tours Smart Cities 2014–2018

Institut für Städtebau

Beispiel eines Smart City Quartiers | Example of a Smart City Neighborhood © Radostina Radulova-Stahmer/stdb/TU Graz

Weltweit werden in Städten unter anderem Informations- und Kommunikationstechnologien eingesetzt, um den aktuellen urbanen Herausforderungen wie globale Erwärmung, Umweltverschmutzung und Ressourcenknappheit zu begegnen. Der Bedarf nach neuen, modernen, energieeffizienten Stadtquartieren steigt. Sie sollen vieles können: ressourcenschonend, sozialverträglich, kostengünstig, belastbar, energetisch nachhaltig sein und allgemein die Lebensqualität der BürgerInnen erhöhen. Globale Pilotprojekte wie „Songdo" oder „Masdar City" zeigen, dass die einseitige Ausrichtung auf technologische Lösungen zwar die Effizienz im Quartier erhöhen kann, jedoch nicht die räumlichen Qualitäten und damit die Lebensqualität der BürgerInnen steigert. In diesem Kontext fehlt es an einer räumlichen Auseinandersetzung mit dem urbanen Digitalisierungsprozess an der Schnittstelle zwischen Energieeffizienz und Stadtraumgestaltung und macht die Notwendigkeit eines Smart-Spatial-Nexus deutlich. Smart City Konzepte wirken zunehmend auf den urbanen Raum. Die räumlichen Wechselwirkungen zwischen dem physischen Stadtraum und den digitalen Technologien und Energieinnovationen müssen zusammen gedacht werden, um das Potenzial der Energieeffizienz im Quartier ausschöpfen zu können.

Die Publikation *Technical Tours Smart Cities 2014–2018* ist ein Projektbericht, der im Rahmen des Programms „Stadt der Zukunft" entstanden ist; sie fasst die wichtigsten Erkenntnisse der Technical Tours aus den Jahren 2014 bis 2018 zusammen. Ziel war es, dieses Wissen kompakt zu präsentieren und einem erweiterten Publikum zugänglich zu machen. Dabei wurde eine Vielzahl an Beispielen mit umfassenden Qualitäten der Technical Tours publiziert. Zudem wurde auch eine Fotodokumentation der „good practice" Quartiere bereitgestellt, die vor allem die wichtigen räumlichen Qualitäten der Smart City Quartiere zeigt, um die Auswirkungen und Einflussmöglichkeiten auf die Lebensqualität herauszustreichen und somit die Relevanz für den Erfolg von Smart City Quartieren, neben dem Faktor der Energieeffizienz, aufzeigt. ▪

Technical Tours
Smart Cities 2014–2018

Institute of Urbanism

Cities around the world are using information and communication technologies, among other ways, to address current urban challenges such as global warming, pollution, and resource scarcity. The demand for new, modern, energy-efficient urban districts is increasing. They should be highly versatile: able to conserve resources, be socially acceptable, cost-effective, resilient, energy sustainable, and generally improve the quality of life for residents. Global pilot projects such as "Songdo" or "Masdar City" show that the one-sided focus on technological solutions can increase efficiency in the neighborhood, but not the spatial qualities or the quality of life for the residents. In this context, there is a lack of spatial engagement with the urban digitalization process at the interface between energy efficiency and urban planning, which highlights the need for a smart-spatial nexus. Smart city concepts are increasingly impacting urban space. The spatial interactions between the physical urban space, digital technologies, and energy innovations need to be considered simultaneously in order to realize the potential of energy efficiency in the neighborhood.

The publication *Technical Tours Smart Cities 2014–2018* is a project report produced as part of the "Stadt der Zukunft – City of Tomorrow" program; it summarizes the most important findings of the Technical Tours from 2014 to 2018. The aim was to present this knowledge in a compact form and make it accessible to a wider audience. A large number of examples with various qualities from the Technical Tours were published. Photo documentation of the "good practice" neighborhoods was also provided, which primarily shows the important spatial qualities of the Smart City neighborhoods, in order to highlight the effects and possibilities regarding the influence on the quality of life. This, therefore, demonstrates the relevance for the success of Smart City neighborhoods, alongside the factor of energy efficiency. ▪

Projektlaufzeit | Project duration:
Oktober 2016–Februar 2020
Finanzierung | Funding:
Österreichische Forschungsförderungsgesellschaft (FFG) | The Austrian Research Promotion Agency (FFG)
Projektteam | Project team:
Aglaée Degros, Eva Schwab, Radostina Radulova-Stahmer, Nina Habe, Ernst Rainer, Yvonne Bormes, Martin Grabner
ProjektpartnerInnen | Project partners:
Bundesministerium für Klimaschutz, Umwelt, Energie, Mobilität, Innovation und Technologie | Federal Ministry for Climate Action, Environment, Energy, Mobility, Innovation and Technology

Mehr als Wohnen 4.0

Institut für Städtebau

Wanderausstellung in Trofaiach | Traveling Exhibition in Trofaiach © stdb/TU Graz

Herausforderungen für die Lebensqualität der BewohnerInnen von kleinen Städten und Gemeinden sowie Fragen der sozial, ökologisch und ökonomisch nachhaltigen Entwicklung des ländlichen Raums sind vermehrt zum Thema für Politik, Planung und Forschung geworden. Die Komplexität des Themas fordert, dass Zusammenhänge zwischen kleinen und mittleren Städten und ihrer Umgebung, zwischen ländlichen Gebieten, Städten und Metropolen verstanden und die Stärken dieses Netzwerks zur Förderung der ländlichen Entwicklung erkannt und genutzt werden. Innerhalb der Region Obersteiermark Ost gibt es große Unterschiede in Größe und Lage der Gemeinden sowie der Zugänglichkeit von und Ausstattung mit Daseinsvorsorgeeinrichtungen. Dementsprechend manifestieren sich demografische Dynamiken und die Nachfrage nach Wohnraum und Gewerbeflächen in dieser Region unterschiedlich. Dieser Heterogenität steht eine geringe Varianz des Wohnungsangebots gegenüber.

Einerseits bestand das Ziel des Projekts „Wohnen 4.0" darin, die Pilotgemeinden in ihrem Kontext zu verstehen und auf Basis qualitativer Interviews und genauer räumlicher Analysen ihre spezifischen Chancen und Herausforderungen für die Entwicklung zu erkennen. Andererseits mussten Fragen hinsichtlich des Wohnraums und der Innenentwicklung der Gemeinden mit Fragen der Zugänglichkeit zu Einrichtungen, Services und Dienstleistungen als auch der Mobilität gemeinsam gedacht und für jede Pilotgemeinde spezifisch beantwortet werden, um die Lebensqualität in der östlichen Obersteiermark und ihre vorhandenen Potenziale zu stärken. Die Ergebnisse des Forschungsprojekts wurden im Rahmen einer Wanderausstellung von 3. Februar bis 1. März 2020 präsentiert. ∎

More Than Living 4.0

Institute of Urbanism

Challenges to the quality of life for residents of small towns and cities, as well as issues of socially, ecologically, and economically sustainable rural development, have increasingly become a topic for politics, planning, and research. The complexity of the issue demands that connections between small and medium-sized towns and their surroundings, between rural areas, cities, and metropolises are understood and that the strengths of this network for the promotion of rural development are recognized and utilized. Within the region of Upper Styria East there are great differences in the size and location of the municipalities as well as in the accessibility and availability of essential public services. Accordingly, demographic dynamics and the demand for housing and commercial space differ greatly in this region. This diversity contrasts with a low variance in housing supply.

On the one hand, the aim of the project "More Than Living 4.0" was to understand the pilot communities in their context and to identify the future potential and challenges for development on the basis of qualitative interviews and precise spatial analyses. On the other hand, questions regarding housing and the inner development of the communities, accessibility to facilities and services as well as mobility had to be considered simultaneously, and answered specifically for each pilot community in order to increase the quality of life in eastern Upper Styria and its potential. The results of the research project were presented in a traveling exhibition from February 3 to March 1, 2020. ∎

Projektlaufzeit | Project duration:
Januar 2019–Februar 2020
Finanzierung | Funding:
Regionalmanagement Obersteiermark Ost | The Regional Development Agency Upper Styria East
Projektteam | Project team:
Eva Schwab (Leitung | project leader), Sabine Bauer, Cornelia Pregartbauer, Mario Stefan, Aglaée Degros
ProjektpartnerInnen | Project partners:
Kampus Raumplanungs- und Stadtentwicklungs GmbH

Mycera. Der wachsende Baustoff

Institut für Architektur und Medien

Mycera – Verbundene Struktur | Mycera – Connected Structure © Shapelab/IAM/TU Graz

Im Rahmen des genehmigten FWF-Forschungsprojekts „Material- and Structurally Informed Freeform Structures" untersucht das Institut für Architektur und Medien im Sonderforschungsbereich gemeinsam mit acht weiteren Forschungsgruppen der TU Wien und Universität Innsbruck, einen neuartigen Bio-Baustoff. Dieser erhält seine Stabilität durch die Verbindung von Ton und Myzelium, mikroskopisch kleinen Pilzfäden und daraus entstehenden Geweben, sogenannten Hyphen. Ein neuartiges 3D-Druckverfahren von Keramik ermöglicht es nun mittels einer eigens entwickelten Maschinensteuerung die feinen Pilzfäden in verschiedenen Anteilen bereits während dem Druck, oder vor und nach dem Brand der Keramik „einzuimpfen". Die jeweiligen Verfahrenstechniken erlauben somit Baustoffe mit unterschiedlichen statischen und technischen Besonderheiten, die je nach Anordnung ein komplexes und abgeschlossenes Gefüge ergeben können. Durch das gezielte und lenkbare Wachstum durch Zellstoff und Lignin, einem Nebenprodukt aus der Papierherstellung, entstehen Module, die sich durch das natürliche Wachstum fest verbinden und selbst „heilen" können. Diese Module verursachen wenig bis keine Emissionen und sind zu 100 Prozent rückführbar und wiederverwendbar. ∎

Mycera:
The Growing Material

Institute of Architecture and Media

As part of a research project with the Austrian Science Fund (FWF) titled "Material- and Structurally Informed Freeform Structures," the Institute of Architecture and Media are researching a new type of organic building material within a special research field in cooperation with eight other research groups at the Vienna University of Technology and the University of Innsbruck. The material gets its stability from the connections formed between clay and mycelium, microscopic fungal threads and the resulting tissue, so-called hyphae. A new 3D printing process for ceramics now makes it possible, using specially developed machine control, to "inject" the fine fungus threads into various proportions during printing or before and after firing the ceramic. Therefore, the respective process techniques allow for the creation of building materials with different static and technical characteristics, which can result in a complex and self-contained structure depending on the arrangement. Through targeted and controllable growth using cellulose and lignin, a by-product of paper production, modules are created that are firmly bonded by natural growth and can even "heal" themselves; they also cause little to no emissions and are 100 percent recyclable or reusable. ∎

Projektlauftzeit | Project duration:
März 2020–März 2024
Finanzierung | Funding:
Fonds zur Förderung der wissenschaftlichen Forschung Österreichs (FWF) | Austrian Science Fund (FWF)
Projektteam | Project team:
Institut für Architektur und Medien | Institute of Architecture and Media, TU Graz: Julian Jauk, Lukas Gosch, Hana Vasatko, Milena Stavrić

VITALITY District

Institut für Gebäude und Energie

Das Forschungsprojekt „VITALITY District. Optimierte Energiekonzepte in der frühen Planungsphase von resilienten, energieeffizienten Quartieren" hat sich zum Ziel gesetzt, die Planung von Fotovoltaikanlagen bereits in der Entwurfsphase von Gebäudeverbünden und Quartieren auszulegen und zu optimieren. Durch eine integrale Systemplanung auf Quartiersebene, die in Abstimmung mit Verbrauchsprofilen, Gebäudetopologie, Lösungen für „Energy-Communities"-Speicher und Begrünung erfolgt, können Energiespitzen reduziert und Überschüsse in städtischen Energiespeichern gepuffert werden. Zusätzlich können dadurch die Gebäude des Quartiers optimal koordiniert und versorgt und durch Begrünung Kühlungseffekte erzielt werden. Das Projekt soll Möglichkeiten der Stadtplanung für eine quartiersweise Entwicklung hin zu einer „Low-Carbon"-City mit hoher Lebensqualität und guter Resilienz unter Berücksichtigung vorhandener und geplanter Gebäude, Infrastruktur und Nutzung aufzeigen, sowie Parameter zur Entwicklung von Energiegrobkonzepten auf Quartiersebene ausarbeiten und evaluieren. Dies beinhaltet beispielsweise Aspekte wie Energieeffizienz, Raumkomfort, die optimale Platzierung von PV-Modulen oder die Größe des Speichers, um den Eigenverbrauch auf Quartiersebene zu erhöhen.

Als Ergebnis sind Modelle und Werkzeuge zur Simulation von aggregierten PV-Erträgen und Quartieren in der frühen Planungsphase, ein Kriterienkatalog zur Frühplanung und Ausschreibung von energetisch aktiven Quartieren sowie Energieerzeugungsprofile erneuerbarer Energien und Lastprofile unterschiedlicher Gebäudetypen auf Quartiersebene geplant. Angestrebt werden ganzheitliche Lösungsvorschläge für abgestimmte Energienutzung von lokalen Energieressourcen verbunden mit energieeffizienten Komponenten bis hin zu Begrünungskonzepten. Das Projekt kann nicht nur einen umfangreichen Beitrag zur Erreichung der Klimaziele der Stadt Wien und in weiterer Folge der Republik Österreich leisten, sondern auch den entscheidenden Innovationsvorsprung für österreichische StakeholderInnen auf diesem Gebiet schaffen. ∎

VITALITY District

Institute of Buildings and Energy

The research project "VITALITY District – Optimized Energy Concepts in the Early Planning Phase of Resilient, Energy-Efficient Neighborhoods" aims to design and optimize the planning of photovoltaic systems in the design phase of buildings and neighborhoods. Integral system planning at neighborhood level, considering load profiles, building topology, community energy storage solutions, and creating open green areas, can reduce energy peaks and buffer surpluses in urban energy storage. In addition, the buildings in the district can be optimally coordinated and supplied, and cooling effects can be achieved through open green areas. The project explores urban planning options focused on neighborhood specific development, and elaborates and evaluates parameters for the development of energy concepts at neighborhood level, such as energy efficiency, indoor comfort, optimal placement of PV modules, or the size of storage to increase self-consumption. The aim is to create a "low-carbon" city with a high quality of life and good resilience, whilst considering both existing and planned buildings, infrastructure and usage.

As a result, models and tools for simulating aggregated PV yields and neighborhoods in the early planning phase, a set of criteria for early planning and tendering of energy-active neighborhoods, as well as renewable energy generation profiles and load profiles for different building types are planned. The aim is to propose holistic solutions for coordinated energy use, from local energy resources combined with energy-efficient components to creating green areas. The project will not only make an extensive contribution to achieving the climate goals in the city of Vienna and subsequently the Republic of Austria, but also create a decisive innovative edge for Austrian stakeholders in this field. ∎

Projektlauftzeit | Project duration:
September 2020–August 2022
Finanzierung | Funding:
Österreichische Forschungsgesellschaft (FFG) |
The Austrian Research Promotion Agency (FFG)
Projektteam | Project team:
Institut für Gebäude und Energie | Institute
of Buildings and Energy: Brian Cody (Leitung |
project leader), Christiane Wermke,
Anyla Berisha, Martin Kaftan
ProjektpartnerInnen | Project partners:
Austrian Institute of Technology GmbH,
AIT (Koordination | Coordination),
Kontaktperson | Contact person:
Shokufeh Zamini
Architekturbüro Reinberg ZT GmbH
ATB-Becker e.U.
EURAC research – Europäische
Akademie Bozen
FH Technikum Wien
GRÜNSTATTGRAU Forschungs- und
Innovations GmbH, Innovationslabor
SAUTTER ZT – advanced energy consulting

3D WELDING – Optimierte Bauelemente aus dem Metalldrucker

Institut für Tragwerksentwurf/ Labor für Konstruktiven Ingenieurbau/ Institut für Werkstoffkunde, Fügetechnik und Umformtechnik

Seit Januar 2020 arbeitet das Team des Instituts für Tragwerksentwurf, bestehend aus Christoph Holzinger, Stefan Peters, Jana Rieth und Andreas Trummer im Rahmen des Collective Research Projekts „3D Welding: Additive Fabrication of Structural Steel Elements" daran, die Möglichkeiten des 3D-Stahldrucks für das Bauwesen auszuloten. Unter der Projektleitung des Fachverbands Metalltechnische Industrie (FMTI) und in Kooperation mit dem Labor für Konstruktiven Ingenieurbau (Bernhard Freytag) sowie dem Institut für Werkstoffkunde, Fügetechnik und Umformtechnik (Norbert Enzinger) wird untersucht, inwieweit die additive Herstellung metallischer Bauteile im konstruktiven Stahlbau eingesetzt werden kann. Die Technologie ermöglicht sowohl die Herstellung regelmäßiger Geometrien

wie einfache Tragwerksverstärkungen, als auch die Produktion topologieoptimierter Freiformen unter Berücksichtigung von Tragfähigkeit und Gebrauchstauglichkeit.

In der Praxis soll das Stahldruckverfahren auch in der Herstellung von filigranen Bauteilen wie beispielsweise Gitterschalenknoten für Glasfassaden Anwendung finden. Im additiven Herstellungsprozess legt der Roboter Schweißnähte übereinander. „Im Gegensatz zu dem aktuell im Stahlbau noch weit verbreiteten subtraktiven Prozess, in dem Material durch Fräsen oder Bohren abgetragen wird, liegt die Innovationskraft des Stahldrucks in der knapp hundertprozentigen Materialeffizienz". Ein Faktor, der laut Christoph Holzinger nicht nur ressourcenschonend ist, sondern auch zur Kostensenkung beitragen kann. Die erste große Herausforderung, der sich das Forschungsteam zum Projektstart stellt, betrifft die zeitliche Komponente, da nötige Abkühlzeiten in den Druckversuchen einkalkuliert werden müssen. Es sollen Printstrategien gefunden werden, welche die Stehzeiten minimieren bei gleichzeitig möglichst hoher Abschmelzleistung. Bis Dezember 2021 soll das Verfahren soweit erforscht und weiterentwickelt sein, dass dadurch eine Etablierung in der Praxis ermöglicht wird und Empfehlungen für bauwirtschaftliche Normierungen abgegeben werden können. ∎

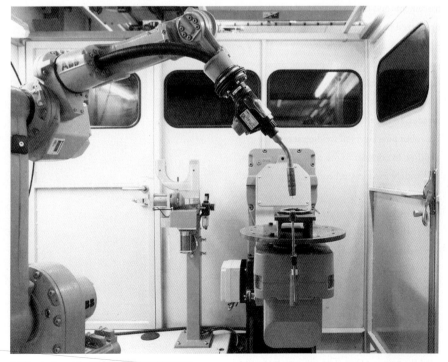

Stahldruckroboter | Steel Printing Robot © ITE/TU Graz

3D Welding. Optimized Components from the Metal Printer

Institute of Structural Design/ Laboratory for Structural Engineering/ Institute of Materials Science, Joining and Forming

Since January 2020, the team from the Institute of Structural Design, including Christoph Holzinger, Stefan Peters, Jana Rieth and Andreas Trummer, have been working on the Collective Research Project "3D Welding: Additive Fabrication of Structural Steel Elements" to investigate the possibilities regarding 3D printed metals within the field of construction.

Under the project management of the Fachverband Metalltechnische Industrie (Metaltechnology Austria) (FMTI) and in cooperation with the Laboratory for Structural Engineering (represented by Bernhard Freytag) and the Institute of Materials Science, Joining and Forming (represented by Norbert Enzinger), the extent to which the additive production of metal components can be used in structural steel construction is being investigated. The technology enables both the production of regular forms such as simple structural reinforcements and the production of topology-optimized free-forms, considering load-bearing capacity and serviceability.

In practice, the steel printing process may also be used in the production of filigree components such as lattice shell nodes for glass façades. In the additive manufacturing process, the robot puts layers of welding seams one over another. In contrast to the subtractive process still widely used in steel construction, in which material is removed by milling or drilling, the innovative advantage of steel printing is its almost one hundred percent material efficiency. According to Christoph Holzinger, this is a factor that not only conserves resources, but can also help to reduce costs. The first major challenge that the research team faced at the start of the project concerns the factor of time, since necessary cooling times must be considered for printing tests. The aim is to find print-ing strategies that minimize downtime, while maximizing deposition rates. By December 2021, the process will have been researched and developed to such an extent that it can be established in practice and recommendations for construction industry standards can be made. ∎

Projektlaufzeit | Project duration:
Januar 2020–Dezember 2021
Finanzierung | Funding:
FFG Collective Research
Projektteam | Project team:
Institut für Tragwerksentwurf | Institute of Structural Design: Christoph Holzinger, Stefan Peters, Jana Rieth, Andreas Trummer
Labor für Konstruktiven Ingenieurbau | Laboratory for Structural Engineering: Bernhard Freytag
Institut für Werkstoffkunde, Fügetechnik und Umformtechnik | Institute of Materials Science, Joining and Forming: Norbert Enzinger
ProjektpartnerInnen | Project partners:
Fachverband für Metalltechnische Industrie | Metaltechnology Austria (FMTI)
Fronius
ABB
Zemann Bauelemente GmbH
Voestalpine Böhler Welding

Ferdinand Schuster (1920–1972). Das architektonische Werk

Im OeNB-Forschungsprojekt „Ferdinand Schuster (1920–1972). Das architektonische Werk" wurden architektonische Dokumente, Abbildungen, Schriften und Pläne erfasst und erschlossen, um den Beitrag von Ferdinand Schuster als Architekt, Theoretiker und Hochschullehrender zur österreichischen Nachkriegsarchitektur zu dokumentieren. Schuster war ab den 1950er-Jahren einer der wesentlichen Vordenker moderner Architektur in der Steiermark, sei es im Sakralbau (z.B. mit dem kirchlichen Mehrzweckraum im Seelsorgezentrum St. Paul-Eiseichsiedlung in Graz), Industriebau (mit den Wärmekraftwerken von Graz und Neudorf-Werndorf) oder im Wohn-, Bildungs- und Städtebau (Schusters prägende Rolle in der Stadtentwicklung Kapfenbergs). In seinen architekturtheoretischen Überlegungen thematisierte Schuster die kulturellen, sozialen und politischen Dimensionen des Bauens. Ab 1964 hatte er den Lehrstuhl für Baukunst und Entwerfen an der Technischen Hochschule Graz inne, und war somit auch als Lehrer prägend für eine ganze Generation an Grazer Architekturstudierenden.

Ziel der Dokumentation von Ferdinand Schusters Schaffen war eine Werkmonografie, die anlässlich seines hundertsten Geburtstags im Jahr 2020 unter dem Titel *Ferdinand Schuster (1920–1972). Das architektonische Werk: Bauten, Schriften, Analysen* erschienen ist. Weitere wichtige Bausteine des Forschungsprojekts waren Interviews mit WegbegleiterInnen Schusters, die bereits abgeschlossene fotografische Dokumentation seiner noch existierenden Bauten und Lehrveranstaltungen, in denen sich Architekturstudierende mit der Architektur und den Schriften Schusters auseinandersetzten.

Vorbereitend auf die Werkmonografie wurden von Oktober 2018 bis März 2019 einige Forschungslabore organisiert, in denen sich ForscherInnen über ihre Erkenntnisse zu Industriebau, Sakralbau, Wohnbau, Architektur + Gesellschaft sowie Bildung + Lehre von Ferdinand Schuster austauschen konnten. ∎

© Holger Neuwirth

Ferdinand Schuster (1920–1972): The Architectural Oeuvre

In the OeNB research project "Ferdinand Schuster (1920–1972): The Architectural Oeuvre," architectural documents, illustrations, written work and plans have been collected and indexed to document Ferdinand Schuster's contribution to Austrian post-war architecture as an architect, theorist, and university instructor. From the 1950s on, Schuster was one of the leading thinkers of modern architecture in Styria, whether in sacred architecture (as with the ecclesiastical multipurpose room in the pastoral care center St. Paul-Eisteichsiedlung in Graz), industrial building (with the thermal power plants of Graz and Neudorf-Werndorf), or in housing, education and urban planning (Schuster's influential role in the urban development of Kapfenberg). In his theoretical reflections on architecture Schuster considered the cultural, social, and political dimensions of building. Beginning in 1964 he was Chair of Architecture and Design at the Technical College of Graz, and as such influenced an entire generation of Graz architecture students.

The monograph entitled *Ferdinand Schuster (1920–1972): Das architektonische Werk: Bauten, Schriften, Analysen*, aiming to document Ferdinand Schuster's work, was published in 2020 on the occasion of what would have been his 100th birthday. Other key components of the research project were interviews with Schuster's companions, the photographic documentation of his buildings still standing today, and courses in which architecture students dealt with Schuster's work. In preparation for the monograph, research labs were organized monthly from October 2018 to March 2019, in which researchers from historic preservation, architectural theory and architectural practice could exchange their findings on Ferdinand Schuster's work in various areas, including in industrial buildings, sacred architecture, housing, architecture + society, and education + teaching. ∎

Projektlaufzeit | Project duration:
März 2018–Februar 2020
Finanzierung | Funding:
Jubiläumsfonds der Österreichischen Nationalbank (OeNB) |
Projektteam | Project team:
Institut für Architekturtheorie, Kunst- und Kulturwissenschaften: Daniel Gethmann (Projektleitung | Project leader), Ajda Goznik, Clemens Haßlinger, Felix Obermair, Ferdinand Schmölzer

Dissertationen
Dissertations

Wolfgang List (2020), *Entwerfen mit Modellen. Untersuchung zur Relevanz analoger Modelle für die Entwurfslehre,* Institut für Grundlagen der Konstruktion und des Entwerfens | Institute of Construction and Design Principles; 1. Gutachterin | 1st reviewer: Petra Petersson, 2. Gutachter | 2nd reviewer: Andreas Lechner, 3. Gutachterin | 3rd reviewer: Margitta Buchert; 255 Seiten | pages, Deutsch | German.

Matthias Raudaschl (2019), *Klettbeton – Analyse und Herstellung verbindungsfähiger Betonstrukturen am Vorbild der Klettverbindung*, Institut für Architekturtechnologie | Institute of Architecture Technology; 1. Gutachter | 1st reviewer: Roger Riewe, 2. Gutachter | 2nd reviewer: Harald Kloft; 155 Seiten | pages, Deutsch | German.

Andrea Redi (2020), *Regeneratives Urbanes Wohnen*, Institut für Wohnbau | Institute of Housing; 1. Gutachter | 1st reviewer: Hansjörg Tschom, 2. Gutachter | 2nd reviewer: Mark Blaschitz; 217 Seiten | pages, Deutsch | German.

Eva Sollgruber (2020), *Die Idee der Großform. Eine neue Sicht auf das Werk des Architekten Oswald Mathias Ungers und die Frage nach einem möglichen Entwurfswerkzeug*, Institut für Gebäudelehre | Institute of Design and Building Typology; 1. Gutachter | 1st reviewer: Hans Gangoly, 2. Gutachterin | 2nd reviewer: Sonja Hnilica; 304 Seiten | pages, Deutsch | German. ∎

Ferdinand Schuster: Symposium zum 100. Geburtstag

Eine Veranstaltung des
**Instituts für Architekturtheorie,
Kunst- und Kulturwissenschaften (akk)**
am 17. und 18. September 2020

© akk/TU Graz

Zum 100. Geburtstag Ferdinand Schusters (1920–1972) widmete die TU Graz dem steirischen Architekten und Hochschullehrer ein zweitägiges Symposium, das eine Rückschau auf sein Wirken mit Analysen seines architektonischen Werks und Reflexionen zu dessen Aktualität verband. Im Anschluss an die Eröffnung durch **Harald Kainz** (TU Graz) und **Elsa Brunner** (Bundesministerium für Kunst, Kultur, öffentlichen Dienst und Sport) hielt **Daniel Gethmann** (akk) einen Eröffnungsvortrag zum Leben und Wirken Ferdinand Schusters. **Bruno Maldoner** (ehem. BDA) sprach im ersten Panel über die denkmalpflegerischen Herausforderungen österreichischer Nachkriegsarchitektur und **Alois Murnig** (BDA, Abteilung Stmk.) behandelte denkmalpflegerische Aspekte am Beispiel des von Schuster entworfenen Pfarrzentrums Leoben-Hinterberg (1965). Eine Podiumsdiskussion der Vortragenden, ergänzt durch die Beiträge von **Sabine**

Christian (Stadtbaudirektion Kapfenberg) und **Holger Neuwirth** (akk), schloss das erste Panel ab. Am Nachmittag wurde die Veranstaltung in Kapfenberg fortgesetzt, wo zahlreiche Bauten Ferdinand Schusters besichtigt wurden.

Der Vormittag des zweiten Tages widmete sich Schuster als Geigenbauer: Der Auftaktvortrag von **Alexander Schwarz** (David Chipperfield Architects Berlin, Universität Stuttgart), seines Zeichens ebenfalls Geigenbauer und Architekt, erörterte Parallelen zwischen Musik und Baukunst. **Jörg Uitz** (Institut für Raumgestaltung) gab als ehemaliger Studierender Schusters einen persönlichen Einblick in dessen Leben und **Elke Chibidziura** (Grazer Philharmonisches Orchester) spielte auf einer Schuster-Bratsche einige Sätze aus Bach-Suiten. Das letzte Panel widmete sich Schusters Architekturlehre: **Eugen Gross** (Werkgruppe Graz) reflektierte persönliche Gespräche mit Schuster in erzählender Form und **Daniel Gethmann** sprach über die Studierenden-Ausstellung „Junge Architektur" im Jahr 1965, an deren Umsetzung Schuster maßgeblich beteiligt war. Den Abschluss des Symposiums bildete ein progressiver Ausblick durch einen Vortrag von **Felix Obermair** (TU Graz), der Schusters Studienplanreform der Technischen Hochschule Graz 1966 den heutigen Curricula gegenüberstellte und damit deutlich machte, dass Schusters didaktische Überlegungen spannende Anregungen für gegenwärtige Aufgabenstellungen enthalten. ▪

Ferdinand Schuster: Symposium Marks 100th Birthday

An Event Held by the **Institute of Architectural Theory, Art History and Cultural Studies (akk)**.

On the occasion of what would have been Ferdinand Schuster's 100th birthday (1920–1972), Graz University of Technology dedicated a two-day symposium (September 17–18, 2020) to the Styrian architect and university teacher, looking back at his life, analyzing his architectural work, and reflecting on its topicality. Following the opening speech held by **Harald Kainz** (Graz University of Technology) and **Elsa Brunner** (Federal Ministry for Arts, Culture,

Civil Service and Sport), **Daniel Gethmann** (akk) gave an opening lecture on Ferdinand Schuster's life and work. In the first panel, **Bruno Maldoner** (former member of the Federal Monuments Authority) spoke about the challenges concerning monument preservation of Austrian post-war architecture, and **Alois Murnig** (Federal Monuments Authority, Styrian department) discussed various aspects of monument preservation using the example of the Leoben-Hinterberg parish center designed by Schuster (1965). A discussion held by the speakers, and the additional contributions from **Sabine Christian** (Building Department Kapfenberg) and **Holger Neuwirth** (akk) concluded the first panel. In the afternoon, the event continued in Kapfenberg, where numerous buildings designed by Ferdinand Schuster were visited.

The morning of the second day was dedicated to Schuster as a violin maker: The opening lecture by **Alexander Schwarz** (David Chipperfield Architects Berlin, University of Stuttgart), also a violin maker and architect, discussed parallels between music and architecture. **Jörg Uitz** (Institute of Spatial Design), a former student of Schuster's, gave a personal insight into his life, and **Elke Chibidziura** (Graz Philharmonic Orchestra) played some movements from Bach's suites on a Schuster viola. The last panel was dedicated to Schuster's teaching of architecture; **Eugen Gross** (Werkgruppe Graz) reflected on personal conversations with Schuster in narrative form, and **Daniel Gethmann** spoke about the student exhibition "Young Architecture" in 1965, in which Schuster was highly involved. The lecture by **Felix Obermair** (Graz University of Technology) concluded the symposium with a progressive outlook; Schuster's 1966 curriculum reform at the Graz University of Technology was contrasted with today's curricula, making it clear that Schuster's didactic considerations contain interesting suggestions for present-day assignments. ∎

Clemens Haßlinger

Am KOEN zu Gast. #digital

Eine Gastvortragsreihe am **Institut für Grundlagen der Konstruktion und des Entwerfens (KOEN)**

Die 2019 ins Leben gerufene Vortragsreihe „Am KOEN zu Gast" wurde ab Mitte 2020 aufgrund der COVID-19-Maßnahmen in den digitalen Raum verlegt. In dem für Vorlesungsübertragungen errichteten Videostudio in der Halle des KOEN gaben die eingeladenen Architektinnen und Architekten den Studierenden des ersten Jahres Einblicke in ihre Entwurfspraxis. Mittels Live-Stream konnte die Teilnahme an den Veranstaltungen einem breiten Publikum zugänglich gemacht werden. Im Anschluss an die Präsentationen wurde die Zuhörerschaft eingeladen, sich via Live-Chat an dem von **Petra Petersson** und **Armin Stocker** moderierten Gespräch mit den Gästen zu beteiligen. ∎

Am KOEN zu Gast. #digital

A Guest Lecture Series at the **Institute of Construction and Design Principles (KOEN)**

The lecture series "Am KOEN zu Gast," launched in 2019, was moved online from mid-2020 due to COVID-19 regulations. In the video studio, set up for broadcasting lectures in the KOEN hall, several architects were invited to give first-year students insights into their design practice. The live stream of the events also allowed for wider audience participation. Following the presentations, the audience was invited to join the conversation with the guests by using the live chat function, and this was moderated by **Petra Petersson** and **Armin Stocker**. ∎

Lisa Obermayer

Vortragende und GesprächspartnerInnen | Speakers and conversation partners:

- 24. Juni 2020 | June 24, 2020:
  Marc Benjamin Drewes (marc benjamin drewes ARCHITEKTUREN, Berlin und | and Vertretungsprofessor FH Erfurt)
- 20. November 2020 | November 20, 2020:
  Nicole Lam (Lam Architektur Studio, Graz)
- 4. Dezember 2020 | December 4, 2020:
  Anne Femmer, **Florian Summa** (SUMMACUMFEMMER Architekten, Leipzig und Professur für Integral Architecture, TU Graz | Professorship for Integral Architecture, TU Graz)
- 16. Dezember 2020 | December 16, 2020:
  Clemens Luser (Hope of Glory Architektur, Graz)
- 15. Januar 2021 | January 15, 2021:
  Alexander Gurmann (agp – Architektur Gurmann und Partner, Graz)

Konzept und Leitung | Concept and direction:
Armin Stocker
Durchführung | Implementation:
Petra Petersson, **Armin Stocker**, **Robert Anagnostopoulos**, das KOEN-Team

Alexander Gurmann am KOEN zu Gast. Moderation: Armin Stocker, Ena Kukić | Alexander Gurmann at "Am KOEN zu Gast" event. Hosts: Armin Stocker, Ena Kukić © KOEN/TU Graz

Infopavillons – Zukunftsträchtige Holzarchitektur

Ein Projekt des **Instituts für Architektur und Medien (IAM)**

Zur Bewerbung der „Erlebnisregion Murau" beauftragte der Verein für Regionalentwicklung „Holzwelt Murau" das IAM mit der Konzeption und Umsetzung von neun Infopavillons. Mit etwas mehr als 27.000 EinwohnerInnen ist Murau sehr dünn besiedelt und hat österreichweit den höchsten Waldanteil. Zu den wichtigsten Wirtschaftszweigen der Region gehört neben dem Tourismus die Holzindustrie. Der Verein wurde auf die aus Holz digital fabrizierten 1:1 Projekte aufmerksam, die am Institut im Rahmen von Lehrveranstaltungen und Forschungsprojekten entstanden waren. Der Entwurf eines solchen Infopavillons war bereits Thema der Projektübung im Wintersemester 2017/18.

Das Resultat der Lehrveranstaltung, der Twist Pavillon, der als Prototyp von den Masterstudierenden im Park der Alten Technik aufgebaut wurde, fand bei den AuftraggeberInnen großen Anklang. Verzögert durch die Pandemie wurden die Pavillons schließlich im Jahr 2020 von Holzbau Horn, einem regionalen Betrieb, fertiggestellt. Auf die neun unterschiedlichen Bauplätze wurde mit drei jeweils kontextspezifischen Bautypen reagiert. Für den Entwurf auf der Basis des Prototyps ebenso wie für die Bereitstellung der Daten für die digitale Fabrikation war **Florian Fend** (IAM) verantwortlich. Die anspruchsvolle Statik, bei der verdrehte Lärchenholzbretter als Tragstruktur zur Anwendung kamen, wurden von Bollinger + Grohmann berechnet. Die digitalen Fräsarbeiten wurden auf der Abbundanlage der Landesberufsschule Murau durchgeführt. Die Infopavillons, die laut Harald Kraxner (Verein Holzwelt Murau) ein „klares Zeichen für eine zukunftsträchtige Holzarchitektur" sind, sollen Einheimische ebenso wie TouristInnen dazu anregen, die Region und ihre Freizeitangebote (besser) kennenzulernen. ∎

Infopavillons Murau | Info-Pavilions in Murau
© IAM/TU Graz

Info-Pavilions – A Promising Sign for the Future of Timber Architecture

A Project Developed by the **Institute of Architecture and Media (IAM)**.

To support the promotion of the diverse region of Murau, the regional development association "Holzwelt Murau" commissioned the IAM to conceptualize and implement nine information pavilions. With just over 27,000 inhabitants, the district of Murau is sparsely populated and has the highest proportion of forest in Austria. In addition to tourism, the timber industry is, therefore, one of the most important economic sectors within the region. The association became aware of the 1:1 projects digitally fabricated from timber that had been created at the institute as part of various courses and research projects. The design of such an information pavilion was already the subject of the Integral Design Studio in the winter semester of 2017/18.

The result of the course, namely the Twist Pavilion, which was built as a prototype by master's students in the park by the Alte Technik university campus building, was very well received by the clients. Delayed by the pandemic, the pavilions were finally completed in 2020 by regional company Holzbau Horn. Three context-specific building types were used in response to the nine different locations. Florian Fend (IAM) was responsible for creating the design, based on the prototype, and for providing the data for digital fabrication. The demanding statics of the twisted larch wood boards, forming the supporting struc-

Infopavillons Murau | Info-Pavilions in Murau © IAM/TU Graz

ture of the pavilions, were calculated by the office Bollinger+Grohmann, and the digital milling work was carried out on the joinery machine at the Murau Vocational School. According to Harald Kraxner (Holzwelt Murau Association), the pavilions are a "promising sign for the future of timber architecture," and they should encourage both locals and tourists to get to know the region and its range of leisure activities better. ∎

Urs Hirschberg

Ringvorlesungen des Kooperationsprojekts KUWI Graz

Das Kooperationsprojekt KUWI Graz veranstaltete im Studienjahr 2020/2021 zwei Ringvorlesungen, die gemeinsam von der **Universität Graz**, der **Kunstuniversität Graz**, des **Grazer Kunstvereins** und der **TU Graz** entwickelt und veranstaltet wurden.

Die Ringvorlesung des Sommersemesters, „**Bitte liebt Österreich! Kunst und Rechtspopulismus**", die aufgrund der COVID-19-Pandemie ab Mitte März 2020 nur mehr online stattfinden konnte, widmete sich aus unterschiedlichen wissenschaftlichen Perspektiven dem Phänomen des Rechtspopulismus, der derzeit weltweit auf dem Vormarsch ist und bis 2019 auch die österreichische Regierungspolitik geprägt hat. Die Ringvorlesung beschäftigte sich mit der Frage, wie rechte Ideologie und rechte Politik in den verschiedenen Künsten einerseits kritisch reflektiert und bekämpft werden, andererseits aber (wie etwa in der Populärkultur) Unterstützung und Verbreitung finden. Unter dem Titel „Bitte liebt Österreich!" veranstaltete Christoph Schlingensief im Rahmen der Wiener Festwochen im Jahr 2000 eine Aktion, in der in einem Container lebende DarstellerIn-

© Paul Poet: Christoph Schlingensief, „Bitte liebt Österreich" | "Please Love Austria," 2000, Wien, Grafik | Graphic design: Viktoriya Yeretska

nen von Asylwerbenden nach dem Reality-TV-Vorbild von „Big Brother" von den ZuseherInnen zur „Abschiebung" hinausgewählt werden konnten. 20 Jahre später schien diese Aktion aktueller denn je. Nach einer Einführung in die Vorlesungsreihe durch **Christa Brüstle** (Kunstuniversität Graz), **Sabine Flach** (Universität Graz) und **Anselm Wagner** (TU Graz), folgten Vorträge von eben denselben, **Karen van den Berg** (Zeppelin-Universität Friedrichshafen), **Stephan Trüby** (Universität Stuttgart), **Monika Platzer** (AzW Wien), **Susanne Sackl-Sharif** (FH Joanneum Graz), **Kristopher Holland** (University of Cincinnati), **Sandro Droschl** (Künstlerhaus Graz) und **Antje Senarclens de Grancy** (TU Graz).

Unter dem Titel „**Der** *material turn* **in den Künsten**" beschäftigte sich die Ringvorlesung des Wintersemesters mit der Frage, inwieweit auch in den Künsten (und in den diese Künste erforschenden Wissenschaften) von einem „material turn" die Rede sein kann. 2006 riefen Dan Hicks und Mary C. Beaudry einen „material turn" in den Kulturwissenschaften aus und rückten damit Gegenstände des Alltags mit ihrer oft komplexen materiellen Herkunft, ihren Funktionsweisen und -verlusten ins Zentrum der wissenschaftlichen Analyse. In der Humangeografie ist von „*nonhuman social partners*", in der Literaturwissenschaft von „*thing theory*", in der Soziologie vom „Akteurnetzwerk" und der „Affordanz", dem Angebotscharakter der Dinge, in der Philosophie von „*vital materialism*" oder „*speculative realism*" die Rede. Für die Kunstwissenschaft gilt das Material der Kunst als zentrale Analysekategorie mit Methoden wie „*object oriented ontology*" und „*strange tools*". **Christa Brüstle** (Kunstuniversität Graz) und **Anselm Wagner** (TU Graz), eröffneten und ergänzten die Ringvorlesung mit eigenen Vorträgen, gefolgt von **Rebecca Grotjahn** (Universität Paderborn), **Rebecca Wolf** (Deutsches Museum München), **Gerhard Nierhaus** (Kunstuniversität Graz), **Peter Scherrer** (Universität Graz), **Jonathan Cane** (University of Johannesburg), **Alexandra Strohmaier** (Universität Klagenfurt/Universität Graz), **Christian Utz** (Kunstuniversität Graz), **Kristopher Holland** (University of Cincinnati), **Klaus K. Loenhart** (TU Graz), **Noëleen Murray-Cooke** (University of Pretoria) und **Carsten Ruhl** (Goethe-Universität Frankfurt a.M.). Die Vorlesungsreihe fand in den Räumen des Grazer Kunstvereins und online statt. ∎

Lecture Series of the Cooperation Project KUWI Graz

Two Lecture Series Organized and Hosted by the **University of Graz**, the **University of Music and Performing Arts Graz**, **Graz University of Technology**, and the **Grazer Kunstverein** in the Scope of the Cooperation Project **KUWI Graz** in the Winter Semester of 2020/21.

The lecture series held in the summer semester, **"Please Love Austria! Art and Right-Wing Populism,"** which due to the COVID-19 outbreak in mid-March 2020 had to take place online, addressed the phenomenon of right-wing populism currently on the rise worldwide and how it shaped Austrian government policy up to 2019 from various perspectives and research areas. On the one hand, the focus was on the question of how right-wing ideology and right-wing politics are both critically reflected and opposed in various art forms, but on the other hand how support and prevalence is gained, such as in popular culture. "Please Love Austria" was the title of the project by Christoph Schlingensief held during the Vienna Festival in the year 2000, in which actors in the roles of asylum seekers living in a cargo container could be selected by the spectators for "deportation" following the "Big Brother" model. Twenty years later this campaign seemed more topical than ever. After an introduction to the lecture series by **Christa Brüstle** (University of Music and Performing Arts Graz), **Sabine Flach** (University of Graz), and **Anselm Wagner** (Graz University of Technology), lectures followed from **Karen van den Berg** (Zeppelin University Friedrichshafen), **Stephan Trüby** (University of Stuttgart), **Monika Platzer** (The Austrian Architecture Museum, Vienna), **Susanne Sackl-Sharif** (University of Applied Sciences, Graz), **Kristopher Holland** (University of Cincinnati), **Sandro Droschl** (Künstlerhaus Graz), and **Antje Senarclens de Grancy** (Graz University of Technology).

© Evan Gardner: „Salon Q", Georg Nussbaumer, Grafik | Graphic design: Viktoriya Yeretska

The lecture series in the winter semester, entitled **"The *material turn* in the arts,"** posed the question of the extent to which the arts (and the sciences exploring these arts) can be called a "material turn." In 2006, Dan Hicks and Mary C. Beaudry declared a "material turn" within cultural studies. The focus of the analysis was on everyday objects with their often-complex material origins, and both the way they function and lose their function. Human geography refers to "nonhuman social partners," literary studies to the "thing theory," sociology to the "network of actors" and "affordance," the character of things as offers, and philosophy refers to "vital materialism" or "speculative realism." For art studies, the material of art is considered a central category of analysis with methods such as "object-oriented ontology" and "strange tools." **Christa Brüstle** (University of Music and Performing Arts Graz), and **Anselm Wagner** (Graz University of Technology), opened the lecture series and each presented their own lectures, followed by **Rebecca Grotjahn** (Paderborn University), **Rebecca Wolf** (Deutsches Museum Munich), **Gerhard Nierhaus** (University of Music and Performing Arts Graz), **Peter Scherrer** (University of Graz), **Jonathan Cane** (University of Johannesburg), **Alexandra Strohmaier** (University of Klagenfurt/University of Graz), **Christian Utz** (University of Music and Performing Arts Graz), **Kristopher Holland** (University of Cincinnati), **Klaus K. Loenhart** (Graz University of Technology), **Noëleen Murray-Cooke** (University of Pretoria) and **Carsten Ruhl** (Goethe University Frankfurt am Main). The lecture series was held at the Grazer Kunstverein and online. ∎

Anselm Wagner

Graz Museum Schlossberg – Modellstudie

Im neuen **Graz Museum Schlossberg** steckt **KOEN Know-how**

Für das neue, vom Architekturbüro Studio WG3 geplante Graz Museum Schlossberg wurde das Institut für Grundlagen der Konstruktion und des Entwerfens (KOEN) damit beauftragt, das Herzstück der multimedialen Ausstellung, ein gläsernes Modell des Schlossbergs zu entwickeln und damit die Vision von **Otto Hochreiter**, dem Direktor des Graz Museums, in ein realisierbares Konzept zu übersetzen. Die Größe und Positionierung im gewählten Ausstellungsraum sowie die Materialität des Modells in Bezug auf seine Funktion als dynamisches, multimediales Ausstellungs-objekt basierten auf einer analytisch-methodischen Machbarkeitsstudie und wurden in zahlreichen Arbeitsmodellen erprobt. Die Werkstücke, die unter der Projektleitung von **Iulius Popa** und der Mitarbeit von **Levita Joao** und **Sonja Kalenjuk** in einem dreimonatigen Arbeitsprozess von Juli bis September 2019 hergestellt wurden, dienten der Überprüfung der räumlichen Verhältnisse und wurden zur Simulation für Materialität und Produktion herangezogen. Die Maßstäbe der produzierten Modelle variierten von einem 1:25 Kartonmodell bis zu einem 1:1 Detailausschnitt. Die Dokumentation der Arbeitsschritte inklusive einer detaillierten Beschreibung des Workflows wurde schlussendlich an die AusstellungsdesignerInnen von Buero41A und die ausführenden Firmen übergeben, um das finale 3,5 × 2 × 0,8 Meter große Modell zu realisieren. Das gläserne Schlossbergmodell kann seit dem 14. September 2020 als Highlight der permanenten Ausstellung besichtigt werden. ∎

Graz Museum Schlossberg – Modellstudie

KOEN Know-How at the **Graz Museum Schlossberg**

For the new Graz Museum Schlossberg, planned by the architectural firm Studio WG3, the Institute of Construction and Design Principles (KOEN) was commissioned to develop the centerpiece of the multimedia exhibition, a transparent model of the Schlossberg; thus, translating the vision of Otto Hochreiter, the director of the Graz Museum, into a feasible concept. The size and positioning in the chosen exhibition space, as well as the material of the model in relation to its function as a dynamic, multimedia exhibition object, were based on an analytical-methodological feasibility study and tests with numerous models. The models, which were produced by project leader Iulius Popa in collaboration with Levita Joao and Sonja Kalenjuk over a three-month period from July to September, 2019, served to verify the spatial proportions and were used to simulate materiality and production. The scales of the models produced varied from a 1:25 cardboard model to a 1:1 detailed model. The documentation of each step including a detailed description of the workflow was finally handed over to the exhibition designers at Buero41A and the production companies in order to create the final 3.5 × 2 × 0.8-meter model. The transparent Schlossberg model has been on display as a highlight of the permanent exhibition since September 14, 2020. ∎

Iulius Popa

Modell Ausstellungsgestaltung, Detail 1:25 | Model exhibition design, detail 1:25 © Ingo Candussi/KOEN/TU Graz

Ringvorlesung Architectural Research 2020

Eine Veranstaltung der **Fakultät für Architektur** vom **Institut für Architekturtheorie, Kunst- und Kulturwissenschaften**

Graz University of Technology
Architectural Research Lecture Series

Pablo von Frankenberg
(Curating Consulting, Berlin)
Thursday, October 15, 2020 19.15, HS II
Architecture / Simultaneity. The Interface of Design and Content

Petra Simon & Elemer Ploder
(TU Graz / epps)
Wednesday, December 16, 2020 17.00, HS L
School Buildings – Learning and Living Environments

Daniel Gethmann
(TU Graz)
Thursday, January 7, 2021 19.15, HS L
Diagrams of the Field

Martino Tattara
(KU Leuven / Dogma)
Thursday, January 14, 2021 19.15, HS L
The Practice of Architecture as Living Thought

Lukas Pauer
(Vertical Geopolitics Lab)
Thursday, January 21, 2021, 19.15, HS L
Objects, Acts, and Imaginaries of Expansionism

TU, akk

© Grafik | Graphic design: Žiga Testen

Die Ringvorlesung Architectural Research bildet einen integralen Bestandteil der Grazer Doctoral School Architektur an der Technischen Universität Graz. Lehrende der TU Graz und internationale Gäste stellen aktuelle Projekte der Architekturforschung hinsichtlich ihrer Konzepte, Methoden und Ergebnisse vor. In Workshops, die in diesem Semester aufgrund der COVID-19-Pandemie teilweise online stattfinden mussten, diskutierten die Vortragenden mit angemeldeten TeilnehmerInnen der Ringvorlesung über ihre Zugänge zur Architekturforschung und die sich daraus eröffnenden Forschungsfragestellungen. Vortragende im Wintersemester 2020/21 waren **Pablo von Frankenberg** (Curating Consulting, Berlin): „Architecture/Simultaneity. The Interface of Design and Content", **Petra Simon** und **Elemer Ploder** (TU Graz/epps): „School Buildings – Learning and Living Environments" und **Daniel Gethmann** (TU Graz): „Diagrams

of the Field". Die Vorträge von **Martino Tattara** (KU Leuven/Dogma): „The Practice of Architecture as Living Thought" und **Lukas Pauer** (Vertical Geopolitics Lab): „Objects, Acts, and Imaginaries of Expansionism" wurden aufgrund der Pandemie in den Herbst 2021 verschoben, in ihren Workshops gaben beide spannende Einblicke in ihre gegenwärtigen Architekturforschungsprojekte. ∎

Architectural Research Lecture Series 2020

An Event at the **Faculty of Architecture** Hosted by the **Institute of Architectural Theory, Art History and Cultural Studies**.

The Architectural Research lecture series is an integral part of the Graz Architecture Doctoral School at Graz University of Technology. In the series, international as well as local scholars and architects present their architectural research projects, introducing research concepts, methods and results. In the workshops, partially held online due to the COVID-19 pandemic, registered participants discussed their approaches to architectural research and research questions with the speakers. In the winter semester of 2020/21 the speakers in the lecture series included **Pablo von Frankenberg** (Curating Consulting, Berlin): "Architecture/ Simultaneity: The Interface of Design and Content," **Petra Simon** and **Elemer Ploder** (Graz University of Technology/epps): "School Buildings – Learning and Living Environments" and **Daniel Gethmann** (Graz University of Technology): "Diagrams of the Field." The lectures by **Martino Tattara** (KU Leuven/ Dogma): "The Practice of Architecture as Living Thought" and **Lukas Pauer** (Vertical Geopolitics Lab): "Objects, Acts, and Imaginaries of Expansionism" have been postponed to autumn 2021 due to the pandemic. In their workshops, both gave exciting insights into their current architectural research projects. ∎

Daniel Gethmann/Christine Rossegger

„Luxembourg in Transition"

Das **Institut für Städtebau** nimmt an internationalem Wettbewerb teil.

Gemeinsam mit dem **AWP Office for Territorial Reconfiguration** (Matthias und Marc Armengaud), dem Büro **One Architecture & Urbanism** (Matthijs Bouw) sowie dem Büro **Taillandier Architecture**, dem **Institute of Landscape Architecture** an der **Harvard Graduate School of Design** (Anita Berrizbeitia), dem **Department of Landscape Architecture** der **Technischen Universität Delft** (Dirk Sijmons) sowie **Arcadis** (Robert de Kort), wurde das **Institut für Städtebau** mit Aglaée Degros ausgewählt, um am internationalen Wettbewerb „Luxembourg in Transition" teilzunehmen, der darauf abzielt, räumliche Visionen für eine kohlenstofffreie und widerstandsfähige Zukunft der Region Luxemburg zu schaffen. Namenhafte StadtforscherInnen und ArchitektInnen, wie Paola Vigano oder Winy Maas, haben auf einen ministeriellen Aufruf zu einer städtebaulichen, architektonischen und landschaftlichen Konsultation in Luxemburg geantwortet. Raumplanerisch soll in dem Wettbewerb mit interdisziplinären Teams aus Planungsbüros und Wissenschaft eine CO_2-neutrale und nachhaltige Großregion Luxemburg entwickelt werden. Die Ergebnisse sollen bestehende Richtlinien und Strategien – wie nationale Energie- und Klimapläne, aber auch den European Green Deal – ergänzen. Generell werden auch Aspekte wie

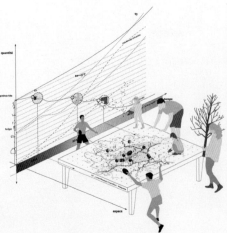

Optimierung der Netzwerke für Luxemburg | Optimizing networks for Luxembourg © AWP Agence de Reconfiguration Territoriale et al.

Energie, öffentlicher Verkehr und Kreislaufwirt-
schaft in die Analyse der Teams einbezogen. ∎

Markus Monsberger (Übersetzung:
Christine Rossegger)

"Luxembourg in Transition"

The **Institute of Urbanism** Competing at
an International Level.

Alongside the **AWP Office for Territo-
rial Reconfiguration** (Matthias and Marc
Armengaud), the office **One Architecture &
Urbanism** (Matthijs Bouw) as well as the office **Taillandier Architecture**, the **Institute of
Landscape Architecture** at **Harvard Graduate
School of Design** (Anita Berrizbeitia), the
Department of Landscape Architecture at
Delft University of Technology (Dirk Sijmons),
and **Arcadis** (Robert de Kort), the **Institute
of Urbanism** with Aglaée Degros was selected
to take part in the international competition
"Luxembourg in Transition." The competition
was aimed at creating spatial visions for the zero-
carbon and resilient future of the Luxembourg
functional region. Well-known urban researchers and architects, such as Paola Vigano and
Winy Maas, responded to a ministerial call for
an urban, architectural, and landscape consul-
tation in Luxembourg. In terms of spatial planning, the aim was to develop a CO_2-neutral and
sustainable Greater Luxembourg Region in a
competition involving interdisciplinary teams
from both planning offices and academia. The
results are to complement existing guidelines
and strategies, such as national energy and climate plans, but also the European Green Deal.
In general, aspects such as energy, public transport, and a circular economy will also be addressed in the teams' analysis. ∎

Markus Monsberger

ia&l Experts' Talks

Eine Veranstaltungsreihe des
Instituts für Architektur und Landschaft

Im Rahmen des Semesterthemas „Dasein
ist Co-Design: Towards Collective Livelihoods
in Post-Pandemic Times" nahm das Institut für
Architektur und Landschaft die gegenwärtige
pandemische Situation zum Anlass, um intensiv über alternative Formen des Zusammenlebens nachzudenken. Dazu wurden führende ExpertInnen aus den Bereichen Ökologie (**Monica
Gagliano**), Philosophie (**Henk Oosterling**), Anthropologie (**Cymene Howe**), Politik (**Marion
Waller**), Klimadesign (**Wolfgang Kessling,
Matthias Ratheiser** und **Maria Feichtinger**)
und Landwirtschaft (**Alex Rudnicki**) zu einer
Reihe öffentlicher Gespräche eingeladen. Die
virtuell abgehaltenen „Experts' Talks" waren
Teil der kollektiv organisierten Projektübung
unter der Leitung von **Klaus K. Loenhart,
Biljana Nikolić, Julian Raffetseder, Christoph
Solstreif-Pirker, Patricia Lucena Ventura,
Tobias Brown** und **Valentin Spiegel-Scheinost**
und stießen auf hohe internationale Resonanz.
Im Sommersemester 2021 wird die Reihe
fortgesetzt. ∎

© ia&l/TU Graz

ly organized Integral Design Studio led by
**Klaus K. Loenhart, Biljana Nikolić, Julian
Raffetseder, Christoph Solstreif-Pirker,
Patricia Lucena Ventura, Tobias Brown,** and
Valentin Spiegel-Scheinost. The discussions
received a strong international response, and
the series will be continued in the summer
semester of 2021. ∎

Christoph Solstreif-Pirker

ia&l Experts' Talks

A Series of Events by the
Institute of Architecture and Landscape

In relation to the topic of focus during
the semester, namely "Existence is Co-Design:
Towards Collective Livelihoods in Post-Pandemic Times," the Institute of Architecture
and Landscape took the current pandemic
situation as an opportunity to intensively consider alternative forms of cohabitation. Leading experts from the fields of ecology (**Monica
Gagliano**), philosophy (**Henk Oosterling**), anthropology (**Cymene Howe**), politics (**Marion
Waller**), climate design (**Wolfgang Kessling,
Matthias Ratheiser,** and **Maria Feichtinger**),
and agriculture (**Alex Rudnicki**) were invited
to a series of public discussions. The "Experts'
Talks," held online, were part of the collective-

Awards

„Breathing Headquarter Grüne Erde" wird mit dem Staatspreis Design Österreich ausgezeichnet

Basierend auf dem von **Klaus K. Loenhart** und seinem Büro terrain: integral designs entwickelten Konzept, kommt im atmenden Hauptquartier der Grünen Erde erstmals eine großflächige „klimatische und atmosphärische Naturperformanz" für das Klima-, Lüftungs- und Kühlkonzept zur Anwendung. In Anlehnung an das Konzept für den Österreichischen Pavillon in Mailand 2015, wird auch im neuen Headquarter der Grünen Erde die umfangreiche Klimatechnik durch Wald- und Pflanzengemeinschaften ersetzt, die in 13 Höfen ihre klimatische und atmosphärische „Pflanzenperformanz" entfalten. Die Pflanzengesellschaften schaffen ein Mikroklima, sorgen für natürliches, lebendiges Licht und versorgen die gesamte Lüftung mit frischem Sauerstoff. Während der Baustoff Holz dabei als nachwachsender Rohstoff eine zentrale Rolle spielt, wird dieser Ansatz durch den fast gänzlichen (98 Prozent) Ersatz erdölbasierter Bauprodukte unterstützt. MitarbeiterInnen und Gäste danken dieser spürbar natürlichen Atmosphäre mit Anerkennung und hohen Aufenthaltszeiten. ∎

"Breathing Headquarters Grüne Erde" Awarded the Austrian National Design Award

Based on the concept developed by **Klaus K. Loenhart** and his office terrain: integral designs, a large-scale "climatic and atmospheric performance of nature" is being used for the first time for air conditioning, ventilation, and cooling in Grüne Erde's "Breathing Headquarters." Based on the design concept for the Austrian Pavilion in Milan in 2015, the extensive air conditioning technology in the new Grüne Erde headquarters will be replaced by thirteen courtyard areas filled with forest and plant communities, creating their climatic and atmospheric "plant-performance." The plant communities create a microclimate, provide natural, living light and supply the entire ventilation system with fresh oxygen. While the building material wood plays a central role as a renewable raw material, this approach is supported by the almost complete (98 percent) replacement of petroleum-based building products. Employees and guests appreciate the noticeably natural atmosphere and take the time to enjoy being in the environment. ∎

Klaus K. Loenhart

Breathing Headquarters Grüne Erde © Jan Schünke

Goldmedaille für das Buch *Entwurf einer architektonischen Gebäudelehre*

Gold Medal for the Book *Entwurf einer architektonischen Gebäudelehre*

At the international competition held by Stiftung Buchkunst (Book Art Foundation), **Andreas Lechner**'s habilitation thesis with the

„The Green Market" gewinnt Wettbewerb

Das Gewinner-Projekt für eine Neugestaltung des größten Platzes Belgiens, dem Grote Markt, ging im Rahmen des offenen Wettbewerbsverfahren „Open Oproep" aus der Kooperation der Büros **Artgineering** (Aglaée Degros, Institut für Städtebau), **LAMA** und **Sweco (ALS_O)** hervor. Der Entwurf für „The Green Market" sieht einen zukunftsträchtigen Ort der Begegnung vor, der nachhaltige Mobilität, die Förderung der lokalen Wirtschaft und klimaschonendes Bauen vereint. Das vier Hektar große Areal wird begrünt und durch einen umfangreichen Mobilitätsplan erweitert, der den Durchgangsverkehr im Zentrum reduzieren und damit mehr Platz für FußgängerInnen und RadfahrerInnen schaffen soll. Die Umgestaltung soll auch den Raum für öffentliche Aktivitäten wie den Donnerstagsmarkt, die Friedensfeierlichkeiten und andere Veranstaltungen attraktiver machen. Mehrere Rasenflächen strukturieren den Platz und verwandeln ihn in einen grünen Park. Auch die Randbereiche des Platzes werden intensiv begrünt; dicht gesetzte Bäume bilden einen Rahmen und schaffen durch Grünflächen und Sitzgelegenheiten qualitative Aufenthaltsflächen an heißen Sommertagen. Wirtschaftstreibende können die Fassadenbereiche gastronomisch aktivieren. Die Neugestaltung beinhaltet auch die Installation von kinderfreundlichen Wasserspielen, die gleichzeitig für Kühlung, Wasserfiltrierung und Klimaregulation des Stadtzentrums sorgen werden. ∎

© Stiftung Buchkunst

Beim internationalen Wettbewerb der Stiftung Buchkunst wurde **Andreas Lechner**s Habilitationsschrift *Entwurf einer architektonischen Gebäudelehre* (Park Books) mit der Goldmedaille ausgezeichnet. Das Buch wurde zuvor als eines der schönsten Bücher Österreichs 2018 prämiert, von CH Studio – **Christian Hoffelner** (Wien/Graz) gestaltet, von Park Books (Zürich) verlegt und in der Medienfabrik (Graz) gedruckt. Andreas Lechners Buch konnte sich in diesem Jahr in einem Feld von über 600 Einreichungen aus 31 Ländern behaupten. Die Kommentare der internationalen Jury aus hochkarätigen GestalterInnen sind eindeutig: „keine farbigen Abbildungen, keine Fotos, nur Text und Zeichnungen auf 500 angenehm dünnen, gräulichen Seiten/nahezu perfekt/über dieses Buch war man sich schnell einig, ohne jegliche Diskussion". Die Preisverleihung im Rahmen der Leipziger Buchmesse wurde aufgrund der Pandemie abgesagt. An der englischen Version des Buchs wird derzeit gearbeitet, sie soll Ende 2021 wiederum bei Park Books erscheinen. ∎

title *Entwurf einer architektonischen Gebäudelehre* (Park Books) was awarded the gold medal. The book was previously awarded for having one of the best book designs in Austria in 2018. It was designed by CH Studio – **Christian Hoffelner** (Vienna/Graz), published by Park Books (Zurich) and printed by Medienfabrik (Graz). Andreas Lechner's book stood out amongst over 600 submissions from 31 countries. The comments from the international jury of distinguished designers are conclusive: "no color illustration, no photo, only text and lines/500 pleasantly thin greyish pages/almost perfect/there was quick general agreement on this book, without discussion." The award ceremony at the Leipzig Book Fair was canceled due to the pandemic. Work is currently underway on the English version of the book, which is scheduled to be published by Park Books in late 2021. ∎

Andreas Lechner

"The Green Market" Wins Competition

The winning project of the open competition named "Open Oproep" that redesigned the largest market square in Belgium, the Grote Markt, resulted from the cooperation between the offices **Artgineering** (Aglaée Degros, Institute of Urbanism), **LAMA**, and **Sweco (ALS_O)**. The design for "The Green Market" envisions a forward-thinking meeting place

„Green Market" © Artgineering

that combines sustainable mobility, the promotion of the local economy, and climate-friendly construction. The four-hectare site will be landscaped and enhanced by a comprehensive mobility plan designed to reduce through traffic in the city center, creating more space for pedestrians and cyclists. The redesign is also intended to make the space more attractive for public activities such as the market on Thursdays, peace celebrations as well as other events. Several grassy areas will structure the square and transform it into a green park. The perimeter areas of the square will also be intensively landscaped; densely planted trees will provide a framework and create comfortable spaces to relax on hot summer days with grassy areas and seating. Gastronomic businesses could also set up on the outskirts of the park. The redesign also includes the installation of child-friendly water features that will simultaneously provide cooling, water filtration, and climate regulation for the city center. ▪

Radostina Radulova-Stahmer

Stuttgarter Leichtbaupreis

Anerkennungspreis für Studierende des Instituts für Tragwerksentwurf (ITE)

Das Studierendenteam bestehend aus **Jana Rieth** und **Lorenz Kastner** erhielt beim Stuttgarter Leichtbaupreis 2019 unter Betreuung von **Christoph Holzinger** (ITE), **Andreas Trummer** (ITE) und **Michael Bader** (Institut für Maschinenelemente und Entwicklungsmethodik) eine Anerkennung für ihr Projekt „ALiS". Ziel der eingereichten Arbeit war die Konzeption und Umsetzung einer adaptiven Struktur in Form eines Pavillons im Maßstab 1:1. Dieser wurde aus 12 aneinander gereihten, aus jeweils elf „Active Bending"-Modulen bestehenden Bögen erstellt. Jedes dieser Module besteht aus zwei 0.9 Millimeter starken Eschenfurnierpaneelen, deren Elementlänge je nach Position im Bogen angepasst ist. Zur Aktivierung der Module wurde ein robustes mechanisches Ansteuerungssystem entwickelt, deren Hauptbestandteile Spannseile, Seilführung, Kurbelwelle und Antrieb sind. Die über ein Rennrad angetriebene Kurbelwelle generiert eine Auslenkung der Zugseile. Dies erhöht die Vorspannung in den „Active Bending"-Modulen und führt zu einer gezielten Verformung der einzelnen Bögen. Besonders positiv bewertet wurde die „zunächst widersprüchliche Erhöhung der Biegebeanspruchung einzelner Bauteile zur Realisierung einer Aktorik in flächigen Strukturen" sowie die Umsetzung des Konzeptes im geforderten Maßstab. ▪

The Stuttgart Lightweight Construction Award

Recognition Prize for Students from the Institute of Structural Design (ITE)

The student team consisting of **Jana Rieth** and **Lorenz Kastner** received recognition for their project "ALiS" at the 2019 Stuttgart Lightweight Construction Award under the supervision of **Christoph Holzinger** (ITE), **Andreas Trummer** (ITE) and **Michael Bader**

PreisträgerInnen Jana Rieth und Lorenz Kastner mit ihrem Projekt „ALiS" | Prizewinners Jana Rieth and Lorenz Kastner with their "ALiS" project © Lorenz Kastner/ITE/TU Graz

(Institute of Machine Components and Methods of Development). The aim of the project was to design and implement an adaptive structure in the form of a pavilion on a scale of 1:1. The structure was created from 12 connected arches, each consisting of eleven "active bending" modules. Each of these modules consists of two 0.9-millimeter-thick ash veneer panels and the element length is adjusted according to their position in the arch. A robust mechanical controlling system was developed to activate the modules, the main components of which are high tension cable, cable guide, crankshaft and propulsion system. The crankshaft, which is operated by bike, generates a deflection of the cables. This increases the pretension in the "active bending" modules and leads to a targeted deformation of the individual arches. The "initially contradictory increase in the bending stress of individual components for the realization of an actuator system in flat structures" and the implementation of the concept to the required scale were rated particularly positively. ∎

Jana Rieth/Lorenz Kastner

GAD Awards 20

Am 15. Oktober 2020 wurden an der Fakultät für Architektur der TU Graz zum 18. Mal die Grazer Architekturpreise verliehen. Die Preisverleihung fand in diesem Jahr digital statt. Erstmals wurden die 36 nominierten Diplomprojekte der Fakultät für Architektur auf einer eigenen Webseite präsentiert und somit nachhaltig für eine breite Öffentlichkeit zugänglich gemacht. Die diesjährige Fachjury, bestehend aus **Karla Kowalski** (SZYSZKOWITZ.KOWALSKI + PARTNER), **Michael Salvi** (Schenker Salvi Weber Architekten) sowie **Bettina Götz** (ARTEC Architekten), traf sich Anfang Oktober zur Jurysitzung an der TU Graz, um nochmals einen Blick auf die Bücher und Modelle zu werfen, um danach die insgesamt sechs Preise zu vergeben.

Der 1. Preis, der in diesem Jahr erstmals vom Land Steiermark, Abteilung 16 – Fachteam Baukultur gestiftet und zweimal verliehen wurde, ging an die Diplomarbeiten von **Jakob Vinzenz Zöbl** („PALIMPSEST") und **Danijel Zorec** („The Living Bridges of Vienna"), zwei, laut Jury, „exzellente Arbeiten, die in ihren jeweiligen, differenten Feldern, sehr entschieden formuliert und in ihrer eigenen Art überzeugend sind". Jakob Zöbls Arbeit, betreut durch **Andreas Lechner** (Institut für Gebäudelehre) beschäftigt sich mit dem architektonischen Potenzial von Infrastrukturbauten im Grenzbereich des Nationalparks Hohe Tauern und zeichnete sich durch eine sensible und poetische Abhandlung aus. Daniel Zorecs Arbeit, betreut von **Roger Riewe** (Institut für Architekturtechnologie) sieht einen urbanen Cluster in Form von mehreren bewohnbaren Brücken über die Donauinsel vor und überzeugte die Jury mit einem radikalen sowie gesellschaftlich relevanten Entwurfsansatz. Der 3. Preis wurde an **Ramona Kraxner** vergeben, die mit ihrer theoretischen Arbeit „Kritik der ideologiefreien Architektur", betreut durch **Anselm Wagner** (Institut für Architekturtheorie, Kunst- und Kulturwissenschaften), einen wertvollen Beitrag zur aktiven Architekturkritik liefert, indem sie in ihrer Analyse die Auffassung von Architektur als Dienstleistung oder als rein pragmatische Handlung scharf kritisiert.

Die Jury vergab weitere drei Auszeichnungen: **Paul Plankensteiner** erhielt den

Siegerprojekt | Winning project „The Living Bridges of Vienna" © Danijel Zorec

Hollomey Reisepreis. Sein Projekt „Die Architektur des Kreises" wurde von **Hans Gangoly** (Institut für Gebäudelehre) betreut. **Jomo Ruderer**, betreut von **Daniel Gethmann** (Institut für Architekturtheorie, Kunst- und Kulturwissenschaften) erhielt für seine Diplomarbeit „Konkrete Utopie im Gemeindebau" den Tschom Wohnbaupreis. Schließlich wurde **Maria Kougias** Projekt „TOPOS. Eine mikroklimatische Landschaft", betreut von **Klaus K. Loenhart** (Institut für Architektur und Landschaft) mit der von der Ziviltechnikerkammer für Steiermark und Kärnten gestifteten Anerkennung für ressourcenschonende und klimagerechte Architektur ausgezeichnet. Alle prämierten Projekte wurden von 15. bis 19. Oktober im Foyer der Alten Technik ausgestellt. Nähere Informationen zu den Arbeiten sowie die Videoaufzeichnungen der Jurystatements finden Sie unter: www.gad-awards.tugraz.at. ∎

GAD Awards 20

On October 15, 2020, the Faculty of Architecture at Graz University of Technology presented the Graz Architecture Diploma awards for the eighteenth time. This year the award ceremony took place virtually. This year and for the first time ever, the 36 diploma projects nominated from the Faculty of Architecture were presented on their own website and were thus accessible to a wider audience. This year's jury of experts, consisting of **Karla Kowalski** (SZYSZKOWITZ.KOWALSKI + PARTNER), **Michael Salvi** (Schenker Salvi

Weber Architekten) and **Bettina Götz** (ARTEC Architekten) met at the beginning of October for the jury meeting at Graz University of Technology to take another look at the books and models in order to then award the six prizes.

First prize was sponsored this year by Land Steiermark, Department 16 – Fachteam Baukultur and awarded to two diploma projects. According to the jury, **Jakob Vinzenz Zöbl** ("PALIMPSEST") and **Danijel Zorec** ("The Living Bridges of Vienna") produced "two excellent projects within their respective fields which are clearly formulated and are both convincing in their own way." Jakob Zöbl's project, supervised by **Andreas Lechner** (Institute of Design and Building Typology), focuses on the architectural potential of infrastructural buildings in the border region of the Hohe Tauern National Park, and is characterized by its sensitive and poetic nature. Daniel Zorec's project, supervised by **Roger Riewe** (Institute of Architecture Technology), depicts an urban cluster in the form of several habitable bridges over the Donauinsel (the Danube Island in Vienna) and it convinced the jury with a radical and socially relevant design approach. Third prize was awarded to **Ramona**

Kraxner for her theoretical project "Kritik der ideologiefreien Architektur," supervised by **Anselm Wagner** (Institute of Architectural Theory, Art History and Cultural Studies). The project makes a valuable contribution to active architectural criticism by heavily criticizing the understanding of architecture as a service or as a purely pragmatic action.

The jury gave three further awards: **Paul Plankensteiner** received the Hollomey Travel Award. His project "Die Architektur des Kreises" was supervised by **Hans Gangoly** (Institute of Building Typology). **Jomo Ruderer** received the Tschom Housing Award for his project "Konkrete Utopie im Gemeindebau," supervised by **Daniel Gethmann** (Institute of Architectural Theory, Art History and Cultural Studies). Finally, the project "TOPOS. Eine mikroklimatische Landschaft" by **Maria Kougia**, supervised by **Klaus K. Loenhart**, was recognized for resource-saving and climate-friendly architecture, a recognition prize made possible through the kind support of the Ziviltechnikerkammer (Chamber of Civil Engineers). All award-winning projects were displayed in the foyer of the Alte Technik building from October 15–19. Further details

on the projects as well as the video recordings of the jury statements can be found on the website: www.gad-awards.tugraz.at. ∎

Petra Eckhard

Siegerprojekt | Winning project „PALIMPSEST"
© Jakob Vinzenz Zöbl

IDEOLOGY AND REGULATIONS.

Jury GAD Awards 20 (v.l.n.r | f.l.t.r.): Michael Salvi, Bettina Götz, Karla Kowalski © GAM.Lab/TU Graz

„Mind the Gap"
Sonderpreis für
Philipp Sattler

Die Diplomarbeit „Portrait of the Bauer. On Architecture and Agronomy of Property" von Philipp Sattler betreut durch Milica Tomić im IZK – Institut für Zeitgenössische Kunst, wurde mit einem Sonderpreis des diesjährigen „Mind the Gap" Award für Gender und Diversität vom Büro für Gleichstellung und Frauenförderung der TU Graz ausgezeichnet. Die Masterarbeit legt die Auswirkungen des bewussten Auflösens von Diversität dar, die Rassismus, Sexismus und Ableismus als strukturelle Diskriminierung ermöglichten. Sattler entpackt die rechtlichen und rhetorischen Konzepte die das Prinzip (Erb-)BauerIn, basierend auf der Ideologie von „Blut und Boden", als Klasse konstituieren. Seine Thesis arbeitet konsequent als performatives Stück, das den LeserInnen ermöglicht die gesellschaftlichen Veränderungen nachzuvollziehen, die sich in den österreichischen Eigentumsverhältnissen bis heute abbilden. Die Arbeit positioniert sich gegen rassistische, patriarchale und faschistische Vorstellungen, die in die architektonische, wie wissenschaftliche Praxis eingeschrieben zu sein scheinen. Auf der Suche nach neuen künstlerischen Formen sieht sich die Arbeit dem Prinzip der Montage, Bertolt Brechts Verständnis des „komplexen Sehens" und Pavle Levis Konzept des „written film" verbunden. ∎

„Mind the Gap" Prize
for Philipp Sattler

The 2020 "Mind the Gap"-Award for Gender and Diversity, organized by the Office for Gender Equality and Equal Opportunity at the Graz University of Technology, was awarded to Philipp Sattler for his master thesis with the title "Portrait of the Bauer: On Architecture and Agronomy of Property," supervised by Milica Tomić at the Institute of Contemporary Art (IZK). The thesis exposes the repercussions of willfully obliviated diversity, enabling racism, sexism, and ableism as

© Philipp Sattler/TU Graz

structural discrimination. Sattler unpacks legal and rhetorical concepts that constituted the "(Erb-)Bauer" as a class, based on the ideology of "Blood and Soil". His thesis consequently works as a performative piece enabling the reader to follow the societal shifts manifesting in property relations of Austria even today: The thesis positions itself against the racial, patriarchal, and fascist notions that seem engrained in architectural as well as scientific practices. While attempting to find new artistic forms, the thesis aligns with principles of montage, Bertolt Brecht's understanding of "complex seeing" and Pavle Levi's concept of "written film." ∎

Philipp Sattler (Translation: Philipp Sattler)

Concrete Student
Trophy 2020

Christian Brügel, Thomas Heinrich und Julia Ober gewinnen mit ihrem Projekt „Capa Verde" den ersten Preis der Concrete Student Trophy. Die Ausschreibung widmete sich der Aufgabe eines Vorentwurfs für ein Hochhaus mit Begrünung in der Seestadt Aspern. Der ressourceneffiziente Entwurf des Siegerteams überzeugte durch die innovative Fassadengestaltung, die Öffnungen in den auskargenden Scheiben zur Unterbringung größerer Bäume vorsieht. Durch die Begrünung und Fassadengliederung verbessert sich die Aufenthaltsqualität in den wohnraumbezogenen Freiräumen, gleichzeitig wird die Überhitzung in den Sommermonaten vermindert. Die Jury, unter dem Vorsitz von Architektin Silja Tillner, lobt auch die ästhetische Qualität des Projekts, da es sich „städtebaulich unaufdringlich, jedoch sehr elegant in die prominente Lage am See einfügt und als attraktiver Wohnturm überzeugt". Der Entwurf wurde im Rahmen der Lehrveranstaltung „Entwerfen spezialisierter Themen" eingereicht, die unter der Leitung von Gernot Parmann (Institut für Tragwerksentwurf), Dirk Schlicke, Thomas Laggner und Christina Krenn (Institut für Betonbau) im Sommersemester 2020 abgehalten wurde.

Nebojša Amidžić, Maximilian Eckart und Katharina Anna Wallner erhielten für ihr Projekt „Green Lakeview Tower" den Anerkennungspreis. Die Jury betonte dabei die mutige und expressive Gebäudeform, die Überlegungen zur Ausarbeitung in UHPC sowie die im Entwurf integrierten großzügigen Grünflächen. Der interdisziplinäre Studierendenwettbewerb wurde von der Vereinigung der Österreichischen Zementindustrie in Zusammenarbeit mit den Technischen Universitäten Österreichs ins Leben gerufen, und fand in diesem Jahr zum 15. Mal statt. ∎

Concrete Student Trophy 2020

Christian Brügel, Thomas Heinrich, and Julia Ober win first prize of the Concrete Student Trophy with their project "Capa Verde." The task for the competition was to draft a

„Capa Verde" © Brügel/Ober/Heinrich/TU Graz

preliminary design for a high-rise building with additional greenery for the urban lakeside district of Aspern. The resource-efficient design from the winning team was convincing due to the innovative façade design, which includes openings in carved-out panes to accommodate larger trees. The greenery and façade structure improve the environmental quality in the residential open spaces while reducing overheating in the summer months. The jury, chaired by architect **Silja Tillner**, also praised the aesthetic quality of the project, as it "blends unobtrusively, yet very elegantly, into the prominent lakeside location in terms of urban planning, and it is a very attractive residential tower." The design was submitted as part of the course "Design of Specialized Topics," which was held by **Gernot Parmann** (Institute of Structural Design), **Dirk Schlicke**, **Thomas Laggner**, and **Christina Krenn** (Institute of Structural Concrete) in the summer semester of 2020.

Nebojša Amidžić, **Maximilian Eckart**, and **Katharina Anna Wallner** received the recognition award for their project "Green Lakeview Tower." The jury emphasized the bold and expressive form of the building, the consideration of the UHPC construction, and the generous green spaces integrated into the design. Taking place for the fifteenth time, the interdisciplinary student competition was initiated this year by the Austrian Cement Industry Association in cooperation with technical universities from all over Austria. ▪

Christine Rossegger

PreisträgerInnen (v.l.n.r.) | Prizewinners (f.l.t.r): Christian Brügel, Julia Ober, Thomas Heinrich © Brügel/Ober/Heinrich/TU Graz

„GORIČKO: country-side revisited"

Eine Ausstellung des **Instituts für Gebäudelehre (IGL)** in Kooperation mit der **Architekturfakultät** der **Universität Ljubljana** und dem **Institut für Architektur und Entwerfen** der **TU Wien** im **Schloss Grad, Slowenien, 12. September bis 4. Oktober 2020**

Goričko, eine entlegene Region im Norden Sloweniens, im Dreiländereck mit Ungarn und Österreich, bildet den Kontext für die Entwurfsarbeiten, die in der Ausstellung „GORIČKO: countryside revisited" gezeigt wurden. Die Ausstellung, eine Kooperation zwischen dem IGL, der Architekturfakultät der Universität Ljubljana und dem Institut für Architektur und Entwerfen der TU Wien, präsentiert mögliche Konzepte eines zukünftigen Lebens und Arbeitens auf dem Land. Der ländliche Raum – als Sehnsuchtsort der Stadtbevölkerung – evoziert seit der Romantik ein Bild der Idylle, das eine Flucht vor den Wirren des städtischen Lebens bieten soll. Die Vorstellung eines ruhigen, naturverbundenen und traditionellen Landlebens, die auch heute noch existiert, steht jedoch im Gegensatz zur Realität des Arbeitens und Lebens auf dem Land. Als Orte der Produktion und der Versorgung der Weltbevölkerung sind ländliche Strukturen – räumliche, infrastrukturelle und soziale – eng mit dem globalen Markt verknüpft und einem steten Wandel unterzogen. So auch die Region Goričko, in der nach Jahren der Abwanderung nun ein steigendes Bewusstsein in der Bevölkerung für regionale Produkte und die eigene Bautradition zu beobachten ist. Es steigt die Zahl der Kleinbetriebe, die auf eine nachhaltige Produktion setzen und mit spezialisierter Verarbeitung von Lehm, Ziegel und Stroh an traditionelles Bauhandwerk anknüpfen.

Die vom IGL ausgestellten Entwürfe einer Teemanufaktur sowie einer Möbelwerkstatt stellen einen weiteren Schritt zur Stärkung dieser Entwicklung dar. Sie zeigen Räume der Produktion, die gleichzeitig durch die Aktivierung der regionalen Bautradition und dem damit zusammenhängenden Einsatz der Materialien auch kulturelle Orte darstellen. Mit der Ausstellung wird zum einen eine positive Vision für die Zukunft der Region Goričko gezeichnet, zum anderen eröffnet sie neue Perspektiven auf eine zeitgenössische Architektur in ruralen Gebieten. ∎

„GORIČKO: countryside revisited"

An Exhibition at Grad Castle, Slovenia, Held by the **Institute of Design and Building Typology (IGL)** in Cooperation with the **Faculty of Architecture at the University of Ljubljana** and the **Institute of Architecture and Design** at the **Vienna University of Technology, September 12 to October 4, 2020.**

Goričko, a remote region in northern Slovenia, in the border triangle with Hungary and Austria, provides the context for the designs presented in the exhibition "GORIČKO: countryside revisited." The exhibition presents possible concepts for the future of living and working in the countryside. Since the Romantic period, the countryside—a place of longing for city dwellers—has evoked an image of idyll that is supposed to offer an escape from the turmoil of urban life. However, the notion of a quiet, close-to-nature, traditional rural life that still exists today contrasts with the reality of working and living in the countryside. As places of production and supply for the world's population, rural structures—spatial, infrastructural and social—are closely linked to the global market and are subject to constant change. This is also the case in the Goričko region, where, after years of migration, there is now a growing awareness among the population of regional products and their own building tradition. There is an increase in the number of small businesses that focus on sustainable production and that link with traditional building trades specializing in processing clay, bricks, and straw.

The designs for a tea factory and a furniture workshop exhibited by the IGL represent a further step towards strengthening this development. They show spaces for production, which at the same time represent cultural places in keeping with the regional building tradition and the use of the materials. On the one hand, the exhibition draws a positive vision for the future of the Goričko region, and on the other hand, it opens new perspectives on contemporary architecture in rural areas. ∎

Eva Sollgruber/Tobias Gruber

Mit Arbeiten von | With works by: **Moritz Aichriedler, Vincent Grömer, Klara Herrmann, Wolfgang Humer, Clara Loidolt, Daniel Lučić, Theresa Mitterdorfer, Fabian Schipflinger, Magdalena Zoller**

„GORIČKO: countryside revisited" © Joana Theuer/IGL/TU Graz

„In|filtration _ Ein|sickerung"

Eine Raum-Klanginstallation und Ausstellung des **Instituts für Raumgestaltung**, im **esc medien kunst labor**, Graz, 31. Juli bis 28. August 2020

„In|filtration _ Ein|sickerung" ist ein interdisziplinäres Projekt und Experiment, das im Rahmen der Auseinandersetzung mit den Wechselwirkungen von Kunst, Wissenschaft und Technologie entstanden ist. Die Klanginstallation ermöglicht bzw. arbeitet mit beharrlichen und unmerklichen Austauschprozessen, bei denen die Oberflächen und Membrane zwischen benachbarten AkteurInnen und Systemen nicht nur als Formen der Abgrenzung betrachtet werden, sondern als teilweise durchlässige Schichten, durch welche sich Vorstellungen, Signale, Materialien, Licht und Klänge ausbreiten und die Identitäten des Getrennten verschmelzen. Ein transluzenter und sensorischer Raumkörper fungiert als Gefäß für Klangstrukturen, die zwischen zwei vermeintlich opaken Computersystemen hin und her wandern.

Die gleichnamige Ausstellung entstand in Kollaboration zwischen dem EU-Projekt MAST (Master Module in Art, Science and Technology) am Institut für Raumgestaltung, dem am Institut für Elektronische Musik und Akustik (IEM)

der Kunstuniversität Graz angesiedelten FWF Projekt „Algorithms that Matter" (ALMAT) und dem esc im April 2019 während des Workshops „Algorithmic Space Studies" indem Entwürfe von Studierenden der Universitäten Nova Gorica (SLO), Madeira (PT) und der TU Graz für eine Rauminstallation entstanden sind. Aus sechs Projekten wurde der Entwurf „filtered" von **Xhylferije Kryeziu**, **Carolina Silveira**, **Feni Sušić** und **Gaja Žnidaršić** ausgewählt, um in Weiterbearbeitung und im Maßstab 1:1 realisiert zu werden. Die visuelle Installation wurde dabei mit einer neuen algorithmischen Klanginstallation von **Hanns Holger Rutz** und **David Pirrò** (ALMAT) verbunden. Die räumliche Umsetzung wurde mit Unterstützung von **Nayarí Castillo** und **Franziska Hederer** erarbeitet und eine Sensorsteuerung wurde von **Richard Dank** entwickelt.

Die Ausstellung war Teil des Graz Kulturjahr 2020 Parcours „Algorithmische Segmente". ∎

"In|filtration _ Ein|sickerung"

A Space-Sound Installation and Exhibition by the **Institute of Spatial Design**, at the **esc medien kunst labor Graz**, July 31 to August 28, 2020

"In|filtration _ Ein|sickerung" is an interdisciplinary project and experiment created as part of an exploration of the interactions between art, science, and technology. The sound installation both enables and works with constant and indiscernible exchange processes, where the surfaces and membranes between neighboring actors and systems are seen not only as forms of differentiation, but as partially permeable layers through which ideas, signals, materials, light, and sounds spread and the identities of the separate aspects merge together. A translucent and sensory spatial body acts as a vessel for sound structures that move back and forth between two supposedly opaque computer systems.

The exhibition of the same name was created in a collaboration between the EU project MAST (Master Module in Art, Science and Technology) at the Institute of Spatial Design, the FWF project "Algorithms that Matter" (ALMAT) based at the Institute of Electronic Music and Acoustics (IEM) at the University of Music and Performing Arts Graz, and the esc in April 2019 during the Algorithmic Space Studies workshop whereby designs for a spatial installation were created by students from the Universities of Nova Gorica (Slovenia), Madeira (Portugal) and Graz University of Technology. Out of six projects, the design "filtered" by **Xhylferije Kryeziu**, **Carolina Silveira**, **Feni Sušić**, and **Gaja Žnidaršić** was selected to be developed further on a 1:1 scale. The visual installation was then combined with a new algorithmic sound installation by **Hanns Holger Rutz** and **David Pirrò** (ALMAT). The spatial implementation was developed with the support of **Nayarí Castillo** and **Franziska Hederer** and a sensor control system was developed by **Richard Dank**.

The exhibition was part of the Graz Kulturjahr 2020 project "Algorithmic Segments." ∎

Franziska Hederer

„In|filtration _ Ein|sickerung" © Hanns Holger Rutz

„On Love Afterwards"

Eine öffentliche Montage von **Milica Tomić** in der **Kunsthalle Wien**, 8. März bis 4. Oktober 2020

„On Love Afterwards" © Srdjan Veljovic

„On Love Afterwards" war eine öffentliche Montage der renommierten Performance- und Medienkünstlerin **Milica Tomić** (Institut für Zeitgenössische Kunst) im Rahmen einer Gruppenausstellung in der Kunsthalle Wien. Tomić rekonstruierte ein symbolisches Monument, das den politischen Imaginationen der Vergangenheit und Gegenwart gewidmet ist und verschiedene Narrative des Widerstands vergleichend gegenüberstellt. Mit Methoden der nicht-linearen Filmmontage hinterfragt sie Gewalt als Reaktion auf Terror und thematisiert das Auslöschen bestimmter historischer Narrative in Hinblick auf TäterInnen und Opfer sowie den Einsatz von zivilem Ungehorsam. Das Foto- und Videomaterial zeigt Tomić mit einem übergroßen Fragment eines Fotos von 25 Staatsführern, das während des ersten Gipfeltreffens der Bewegung der Blockfreien Staaten 1961 in Belgrad aufgenommen wurde. Diese Bewegung, die sich gegen eine binäre Weltpolitik als auch gegen den Einfluss von Kolonialismus und Neokolonialismus richtete, bediente sich jedoch gewaltsamen Auseinandersetzungen, um Emanzipation und Frieden zu bewirken und erinnert an das gewalttätige Vorgehen der AntifaschistInnen in Belgrad während des Zweiten Weltkriegs. Ursprünglich sollte die öffentliche Montage in Wien Tomićs 2009 Performance („One day, instead of one night, a burst of machine-gun fire will flash, if light cannot come otherwise") nachstellen, bei der die Künstlerin mit einem Kalaschnikow-Gewehr und einer Supermarkttasche aus Plastik die Schauplätze antifaschistischer bewaffneter Aktionen in Belgrad aufsuchte. Die Aktion wurde, auch ohne echtes Gewehr, aufgrund von Sicherheitsbedenken der Stadt Wien nicht genehmigt.

„On Love Afterwards" bildete auch den Rahmen einer unkonventionellen Podiumsdiskussion, die am 2. Februar 2020 im Burgtheater Kasino stattfand und bei der u.a. die Studierenden **Budour Khalil**, **Amir Kozman**, **Lung Peng** und **Philipp Sattler** (TU Graz) teilnahmen. ■

Susannah Leopold (Übersetzung: Christine Rossegger)

"On Love Afterwards"

A Public Montage by **Milica Tomić** at **Kunsthalle Wien**, March 8 to October 4, 2020

"On Love Afterwards" was a public montage by renowned performance and media artist **Milica Tomić** from the Institute of Contemporary Art as part of a group exhibition at Kunsthalle Wien. Tomić reconstructed a symbolic, non-material monument dedicated to political imaginations of the past and present, juxtaposing different histories of resistance. By using methods of non-linear film montage, she questions violence as a reaction to terror and addresses the erasure of particular historical narratives around the roles of perpetrator and victim as well as the use of civil disobedience. The photographic material and videos show Tomić carrying an oversized fragment of a photo of 25 state leaders, taken during the first Non-Aligned Movement summit in Belgrade in 1961. This confederation represented a move away from both binary world politics and the influence of colonialism and neo-colonialism. However, the emancipation and peace in the member states was achieved through force, just as Belgrade's anti-Fascists had resorted to violence during the Second World War. Originally this action in Vienna was to replicate Milica Tomić's 2009 performance in Belgrade ("One day, instead of one night, a burst of machine-gun fire will flash, if light cannot come otherwise"), in which she revisited sites of anti-Fascist armed action, carrying a Kalashnikov rifle and a plastic supermarket bag. However, security concerns made this impossible in Vienna, even without a real gun.

"On Love Afterwards" also formed the framework of an unconventional panel discussion that took place on February 2, 2020, in the Burgtheater Kasino and also included student contributions from **Budour Khalil**, **Amir Kozman**, **Lung Peng**, and **Philipp Sattler** (TU Graz). ■

Susannah Leopold

„Topographie des Widerstands in der Steiermark. 1938–1945"

Wanderausstellung des **Instituts für Architekturtheorie, Kunst- und Kulturwissenschaften** zu „75 Jahren Befreiung Österreichs", **9. Juni bis 30. August 2020**

Anlässlich des 75. Jubiläums der Befreiung Österreichs vom NS-Regime haben **Daniel Gethmann** und **Waltraud P. Indrist** vom Institut für Architekturtheorie, Kunst- und Kulturwissenschaften gemeinsam mit Studierenden eine Wanderausstellung zum Thema Widerstand gegen den Nationalsozialismus in der Steiermark erarbeitet. Zu den vier ausgewählten Case Studies – dem KZ-Außenlager Eisenerz im Gsollgraben, der SS-Kaserne in Graz-Wetzelsdorf, der „Kampfgruppe Steiermark" in Deutschlandsberg/Soboth sowie der „Österreichischen Freiheitsfront" in Leoben-Donawitz – wurden die Erkenntnisse der historischen Forschung in Zusammenarbeit mit dem Historiker Heimo Halbrainer ausgewertet und weitere Archivrecherchen in Österreich, Frankreich, Deutschland und Slowenien betrieben. Um das Material in Zusammenarbeit mit der Grafikerin Marie Fegerl visuell aufzubereiten, griff die Ausstellung auf Mittel der forensischen Architektur zurück und zeigte zum Teil gänzlich neue Erkenntnisse: So konnte etwa die konkrete Lage des KZ-Außenlagers Eisenerz erstmals nachgewiesen sowie ein Rekonstruktionsmodell des Lagers erstellt werden. Zu sehen waren die thematisch unterschiedlichen Ausstellungen auf öffentlichen Plätzen in Eisenerz, Graz, Deutschlandsberg und Leoben. Nachdem diese Ausstellungen ein breites (mediales) Interesse erfahren haben, sollen ihre Ergebnisse in einer im Jahr 2021 erscheinenden Publikation dokumentiert werden. ∎

"Topography of Resistance in Styria. 1938–1945"

Traveling Exhibition Hosted by the **Institute of Architectural Theory, Art History and Cultural Studies** Marking **"75 Years since Austria's Liberation," June 9 to August 30, 2020**.

On the occasion of the 75th anniversary of Austria's liberation from the Nazi regime, **Daniel Gethmann** and **Waltraud P. Indrist** from the Institute of Architectural Theory, Art History and Cultural Studies worked together with students to create a traveling exhibition on the topic of resistance to National Socialism in Styria. There were four case studies selected, namely the Eisenerz subcamp in Gsollgraben, the SS barracks in Graz-Wetzelsdorf, the "Kampfgruppe Steiermark" in Deutschlandsberg/Soboth and the "Österreichische Freiheitsfront" in Leoben-Donawitz. The findings of the research were evaluated in collaboration with the historian Heimo Halbrainer and further archival research was conducted in Austria, France, Germany, and Slovenia. In order to prepare the visual material, whilst working in cooperation with graphic designer Marie Fegerl, the exhibition resorted to means of forensic architecture and in some cases presented entirely new findings. For example, the precise location of the Eisenerz subcamp was proven for the first time, and a model reconstruction of the camp was created. The thematically different exhibitions were displayed in various public places in Eisenerz, Graz, Deutschlandsberg, and Leoben. Since these exhibitions have received wide attention, including in the media, the results will be collected and published in 2021. ∎

Waltraud P. Indrist

Mitwirkende Studierende | Student participants: **Lisa-Marie Dorfleitner, Janika Döhr, Ema Drnda, Flora Flucher, Max Frühwirt, Matthias Hölbling, Thomas Lienhart, Lung Peng, Thomas Tunariu, Anna Sachsenhofer, Alice Steiner, Milan Sušić, Katharina Url, Viktoriya Yeretska**, sowie | and **Armin Zepic**

Wanderausstellung | Traveling Exhibition in Leoben (v.l.n.r.|f.l.t.r.) VBgm. | Deputy mayor M. Jäger, M. Hölbling, F. Flucher, K. Url, W. P. Indrist, D. Gethmann) © Leopress

„Wolfsberg *Revisited*"

Eine Ausstellung des **Instituts für Städtebau** in der **Stadtwerkstatt Wolfsberg, 28. Januar bis 12. Februar 2020**

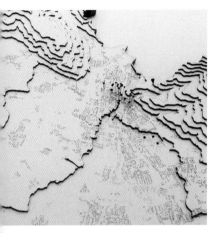

Übersichtsmodell Interventionen Wolfsberg | Model with overview of plans for Wolfsberg © stdb/TU Graz

Wie viele Mittel- und Kleinstädte Österreichs und Europas hat auch Wolfsberg mit den sogenannten Effekten der „Territorial Justice" zu kämpfen. Viele Geschäftslokale und Wohnhäuser im historischen Zentrum stehen leer und die öffentlichen Räume werden hauptsächlich als Parkfläche für PKWs genutzt. Einzelne Projekte der vergangenen Jahre haben jedoch bereits gezeigt, dass eine Belebung der Innenstadt in Wolfsberg möglich ist. Während sich die bisherigen Interventionen zumeist auf die östliche Hälfte der Altstadt (die „Obere Stadt") beschränkt haben, entwarfen die Studierenden der Projektübung unter der Leitung von **Aglaée Degros** und **Sabine Bauer** und der verpflichtenden Wahlfächer „Städtische Infrastruktur" (Leitung **Llazar Kumaraku**) und „Das Fahrrad" (Leitung **Bernhard Wieser**) eine Strategie für das gesamte Stadtzentrum. In enger Zusammenarbeit mit dem Bürgermeisterbüro der Stadt Wolfsberg und dem Grazer Architekturbüro balloon architekten wurden die Potenziale der Stadt erforscht und ein Konzept für die Um- und Neugestaltung des Netzwerkes der Öffentlichen Räume sowie eine nachhaltige Revitalisierung des Zentrums von Wolfsberg und dessen Verbindung mit den umliegenden Gemeinden geplant.

Die Ergebnisse der Projektübung wurden in Form einer Ausstellung in der Stadtwerkstatt und in ausgewählten Leerständen der Innenstadt präsentiert und vom Bürgermeister der Stadtgemeinde Wolfsberg, **Hans-Peter Schlagholz**, den Studierenden und Betreuerinnen der Projektübung eröffnet. Zusätzlich wurden die Strategien und Ideen für Wolfsberg in einer Publikation zusammengefasst und der Stadtgemeinde zur Verfügung gestellt. ▪

"Wolfsberg *Revisited*"

An Exhibition by the **Institute of Urbanism** at the **Stadtwerkstatt Wolfsberg, January 28 to February 12, 2020**

Like many medium-sized and small towns in Austria and Europe, Wolfsberg is struggling with the so-called effects of "territorial justice." Many business premises and residential buildings in the historic center are empty and public spaces are mainly used as car parks. However, individual projects in recent years have already shown that a revitalization of the city center in Wolfsberg is possible. While previous plans have mostly been limited to the eastern half of the old town (the "Upper Town"), the students of the Integral Design Studio, led by **Aglaée Degros** and **Sabine Bauer** and the elective subjects "Urban Infrastructure" (led by **Llazar Kumaraku**) and "The Bicycle" (led by **Bernhard Wieser**), designed a strategy plan for the entire city center, working in close cooperation with the mayor's office in the city of Wolfsberg and the Graz-based architectural firm balloon architekten. The plan explores the potential of the city, redesigns a concept for the network of public spaces, and includes a sustainable revitalization of Wolfsberg city center and its connection with the surrounding communities.

The results of the Integral Design Studio were presented in the form of an exhibition in the Stadtwerkstatt venue and in various locations around the city center. The exhibition was opened by the Mayor of the Municipality of Wolfsberg, **Hans-Peter Schlagholz**, to the students and advisors of the Integral Design Studio.

The strategies and ideas for Wolfsberg were also summarized in a publication and made available to the municipality. ▪

Sabine Bauer

Mitwirkende | Contributors:
Llazar Kumarak, Bernhard Wieser

„Humming Room"

Eine architektonische Klangkunstinstallation von **Milena Stavrić** in **Graz, 24. Juli bis 31. Oktober 2020**

Im Rahmen des Grazer Kulturjahres 2020 verwirklichte die Architektin **Milena Stavrić** (Institut für Architektur und Medien) gemeinsam mit der Künstlerin **Elisabeth Harnik** und der Akustikerin **Jamilla Balint** die Klangkunstinstallation „Humming Room". Die von Milena Stavrić entwickelte begehbare Struktur besteht aus sechs beweglichen, wabenförmigen Wandelementen und ist akustisch mit dem Summen von Honigbienen bespielt. Die dynamische Installation veränderte je nach Konfiguration der Wände das Hörerleben und fungiert als Brücke zwischen realer Architektur und virtuellen Hörimpulsen. Gleichzeitig machte die Installation die Verbundenheit von Mensch und Honigbiene für die BesucherInnen sinnlich erfahrbar. In der letzten Projektphase wurde die Wabenstruktur in ein permanentes Insektenhotel überführt. Die Installation war auf der Grünfläche vor dem Museum der Wahrnehmung in der Friedrichgasse 41 in Graz frei zugänglich. ▪

"Humming Room"

An Architectural Sound Art Installation by **Milena Stavrić** in **Graz, July 24 to October 31, 2020**

As part of the Graz Cultural Year 2020, the architect **Milena Stavrić** (Institute of Architecture and Media), together with the artist **Elisabeth Harnik** and the acoustician **Jamilla Balint**, created the sound art installation "Humming Room." The walk-in structure developed by Milena Stavrić consisted of six movable, honeycomb-shaped wall elements, upon which an acoustic humming of honeybees was played. Depending on the configuration of the walls, the dynamic installation changed the listening experience and acted as a bridge between real architecture and virtual auditory impulses. At the same time, the installation was intended to make the connection between humans and honeybees sensually perceptible to visitors. In the final phase of the project, the honeycomb structure was transformed into a permanent insect hotel. The installation was freely accessible on the area in front of the Museum of Perception at Friedrichgasse 41 in Graz. ▪

Christine Rossegger

„Humming Room" © Jamilla Balint

Erika Petrić und die Faszination der Worte

Ich kann gleich bei ihrer Stimme anfangen, die im März 2013 in einem Raum der TU Graz eines meiner Fotobücher analysierte, treffend, stilsicher, ironisch-elegant, und das alles in nur zehn Sekunden. Diese Fähigkeit, augenblicklich alles zu bewerten, was ihr unter die Augen kam, war typisch für sie. Worte sind wichtig; und sich die Worte eines aus dem anderen entwickeln zu lassen, dabei ganz persönliche Metaphern hinzuzufügen und Fach- und Alltagssprache zu kombinieren, war für Erika nichts Außergewöhnliches. All das entsprang ihrem blitzschnellen, geerdeten und typisch weiblichen Intellekt.

Erika Petrićs Leben war beileibe nicht einfach. Der wahnsinnige Krieg um die Zerstückelung der Nation, in der sie geboren wurde, hat bei ihr Narben hinterlassen. Und die Tatsache, dass sie beschlossen hatte, Österreicherin zu werden („Ich wurde von Österreich großgezogen."), befreite sie nicht von dem Unbehagen, kein Land zu haben, mit dem sie sich identifizieren konnte. In der Fotografie, auf die sie nach einem Lebensabschnitt als Architektin in Wien eher spät gestoßen war, hatte sie rasch ihre eigene Sichtweise entwickelt und jene Elemente ausgemacht, die ihre visuelle Philosophie stützten. Erika Petrić bewegte sich auf zwei Ebenen, oder auf dreien, wenn wir ihre Lehrtätigkeit mit einbeziehen: die Praxis der Fotografie, ihre Interpretationen und schließlich die Theorien, die sie in der Lehre anwandte – mit großem Erfolg, wenn man dem Feedback der Studierenden glaubt. Auf dem ersten Gebiet – dem der Fotografie im eigentlichen Sinn – hatte sie sich aufgrund ihrer Haltung dazu entschlossen, sich eher durch das Bild auszudrücken, statt als Fotografin zu arbeiten. Es ist die Straße des Selbst, die in eine Aufnahme mündet, etwas, das sich so leicht dahinsagt und doch so schwer zu fassen ist. Fotografie ist widerspenstig, sie folgt ihren eigenen inneren Gesetzen. Und im Gegensatz zur allgemein verbreiteten Meinung funktionieren Entfremdung und Teilnahme in der Fotografie sehr gut miteinander; sie sind die wahren chemischen Wirkstoffe des Bildes. In den Fotografien, die Erika Petrić schuf, weist ihr Alter Ego eine Form auf, die gleichermaßen freudig und melancholisch ist, friedfertig und sarkastisch, mitfühlend und bissig.

Mehr als alles andere sind es Worte und Konzepte, die es der Fotografie ermöglichen, in die Welt hinauszutreten und die Erkundung der Umgebung auszulösen; ohne deshalb „in das Loch der Nostalgie zu fallen", um eine ihrer äußerst treffsicheren Metaphern zu bemühen. Und so reicht auch eine glänzende Formulierung aus bloß vier Wörtern wie „What remains of life?", um den Fotografien eines improvisierten Umzugs – mit Möbeln, die mit Seilen auf einen klapprigen Pickup geschnürt wurden, aufgenommen in einer der Städte, die sie häufig besuchte – Sinn zu verleihen. Der Fotografin Erika Petrić, die Anfang der 1990er-Jahre ihren Abschluss in Architektur machte – im nahegelegenen und friedlichen Slowenien (abgesehen von dem brennenden Helikopter, der plötzlich im Hof der Universität aufschlug) –, gelang die Wiederbelebung großer Theorien des 20. Jahrhunderts, deren Kern sie fruchtbar machte, um den Sinn des Bildes zu begreifen.

Die Verbindung zwischen Realität, Phänomen, Erkenntnis und Wahrnehmung war bereits formuliert worden, doch selten noch in so klaren Worten wie in Erikas Texten: „Der Fotograf ist möglicherweise ein Phänomenologe." (aus: „Fotografija kot fenomenološko orodje arhitekturne reprezentacije", *Arhitektov Bilten = Architect's Bulletin* 199–200 (2015), 56–62.) Sicher: Die Husserlsche Phänomenologie hilft jenen, die fotografieren, zu verstehen, was sie tun, ob sie es schaffen, Zugang zur Welt zu erhalten, weil sie sich hinter ihr eigenes Selbst stellen, oder ob sie gezwungen sind, es draußen zu lassen. Der Übergang ist wesentlich: Die äußere Welt existiert, wenn das Bewusstsein sie wahrnimmt, andernfalls bleibt sie unerreichbar; und die Architektur bleibt ein ordentlicher Haufen von Ziegelsteinen. Ohne das Bewusstsein, das das Phänomen enthüllt, entziehen sich Welt und Sprache und verschwinden. Vorhang. In der off_gallery_graz, die vor einigen Jahren von Erika Petrić, Anastasija Georgi und Heinz Wittenbrink gegründet wurde, präsentieren seitdem KünstlerInnen ihre persönliche Sicht einer Welt, die sich vor unseren Augen verändert. Erikas schöne blaue Augen mit den erstaunlich dunklen Pupillen sind nicht länger unter uns, doch ihre Ideen bewegen sich allein weiter. ∎

Paolo Rosselli (Übersetzung: Alexandra Titze-Grabec)

Erika Petrić © Paolo Rosselli

Erika Petrić and the Fascination of Words

And we can start there, from Erika's voice that in March, 2013, could be heard in a room at the TU Graz analyzing a book of my photographs with accuracy, style, and very gracious irony: and that all within the space of ten seconds. It was typical of her; this ability to instantly evaluate anything that she came across. Words are important; and putting them into a sequence while adding highly personal metaphors, mixing specialist language with that of everyday discourse, was normal for Erika, stemming from her lightning-quick, straightforward, and flexible intelligence.

Erika Petrić's life was certainly no walk in the park. The senseless war over the carve-up of the nation in which she was born had left its mark. And even the fact of having chosen to become Austrian ("I was grown up by Austria") did not take away her unease at not having a country with which to identify. In photography, which she encountered rather late after a period working as an architect in Vienna, she rapidly developed a vision of her own, discerning the elements that could sustain her visual philosophy. She moved between two levels, or three, if we consider her teaching: the practice of photography, her interpretations, and finally, the theories that she applied in that teaching activity, something which she carried out with success judging by the feedback from her students. In the first area, that of her photography, she had chosen by disposition to express herself through the image rather than to work as a photographer. It is the path of the self that is poured into an image, something easy to say but difficult to get a hold on. Photography is recalcitrant; it has its own, internal rules. And contrary to what is generally thought, estrangement and participation go very well together in photography; they are the true chemical agents of the image. In the photographs that Erika produced, this photographic alter ego of hers has a form that is both joyful and melancholic, pacific and cutting, compassionate, and caustic.

More than anything else it is words and concepts that help photography to come into the world and set the ball rolling for the exploration of the environment; without as a result "falling down the hole of nostalgia" to use a very apt metaphor of hers. And so a glittering phrase of just four words like "What remains of life?" serves to make sense of the photographs of a makeshift solution of furniture tied with rope onto a rickety pickup taken in one of the cities she frequented. Erika Petrić, who graduated in architecture in the early 1990s in the nearby and tranquil country of Slovenia (apart from that time when a helicopter in flames fell into the courtyard of the university), was able to resuscitate grand theories of the twentieth century and to take the essence of them and use it to understand the sense of an image.

The connection between reality, phenomenon, awareness, and perception had previously been put forward, but not so clearly as it was in Erika's writings: "The photographer is potentially a phenomenologist." (from: "Fotografija kot fenomenološko orodje arhitekturne reprezentacije," Arhitektov Bilten = Architect's Bulletin 199–200 (2015), 56–62.) Certainly. Husserlian phenomenology helps those who take photographs to understand what they are doing, whether they are able to gain access to the world taking their own selves with them or are obliged to leave them outside. The passage is an essential one: the outside world exists if consciousness perceives it, otherwise it remains inaccessible; and architecture remains a tidy heap of bricks. Without the consciousness that reveals the phenomenon, the world and language withdraw and disappear. Curtains. At the off_gallery_graz, founded a few years ago by Erika Petrić along with Anastasija Georgi and Heinz Wittenbrink, artists have succeeded one another for over a year, exhibiting their personal visions of a world that is changing before our eyes. Erika's beautiful blue eyes with their very dark pupils are no longer with us, but her ideas are forging ahead by themselves. ∎

Paolo Rosselli

Reviews

Reviews

**Rethinking Wood. Future
Dimensions of Timber Assembly**

Markus Hudert/

Sven Pfeiffer (Hg. | eds.)

Basel: Birkhäuser, 2019

Englisch, 294 Seiten, 200 Abbil-
dungen Farbe, 38 SW-Abbildungen |
English, 294 pages, 200 color
illustrations, 38 b/w illustrations

ISBN 978-3-0356-1689-7

EUR 49,95 | EUR 49.95

Vielschichtig und Mehrschichtig – Zum Phänomen Holzbau

Armin Stocker

Holz ist im Vormarsch und wird auch bau-
lich immer höher – Deutschlands derzeit höchstes Holzhaus ist das 2019 von Kaden + Lager in
Holzhybridbauweise in Heilbronn errichtete
Saiko mit 34 Metern Höhe. In Österreich erreicht
das von Rüdiger Lainer geplante Wohngebäude
HoHo in der Seestadt Aspern bereits 84 Meter
und Voll Arkitekter errichten aus norwegischem
Brettschichtholz und finnischem Furnierschicht-
holz das derzeit höchste Holzgebäude im norwegischen Brumunddal, ein 85,4 Meter hohes, ge-
mischt genutztes Hochhaus mit Privatwohnun-
gen, einem Hotel sowie Büros und Freizeitein-
richtungen samt Swimmingpool.

Diese Höhenrekorde zeugen nicht nur von
begeisterten Presseaussendungen, sondern, wie
es die vorliegende Publikation umfangreich aus-
führt, von einem ökologogisch motivierten Trend,
der die heutigen Möglichkeiten erst durch die
konsequente Verzahnung von Praxis und Forschung erreichen konnte. Was wir daher anhand
aktueller Forschungsergebnisse auch hinkünftig
für das Entwerfen und Bauen erwarten können,
ist das zentrale Thema von *Rethinking Wood.
Future Dimensions of Timber Assembly*. Diese
Zukunftsperspektive des Entwerfens und Bauens mit Holz unterscheidet das Buch auch deutlich von vertrauten *Best-Of-Publikationen*. Das
Buch richtet sich an eine wissenschaftlich inte-
ressierte Leserschaft, die an Umsetzungsmög-
lichkeiten in der Praxis und an Neu- und Weiterentwicklungen im weiten Feld des ressourcenschonenden und nachhaltigen Bauens und Ge-
staltens interessiert ist.

Die Herausgeber Markus Hudert und
Sven Pfeiffer sind beide sowohl selbstständige
Architekturschaffende als auch in universitärer
Forschung und Lehre tätig und haben mit Unter-
stützung der Aalto University und der Wüstenrot
Stiftung dieses Buch als ein Kompendium her-
ausgegeben, das von Betrachtungen und Heran-
gehensweisen zum Thema Holz in Architektur,

Design und Materialforschung über die Digitalisierung bis hin zu bionischen Gestaltungs- und
Konstruktionsansätzen reicht. Beginnend bei
den Grundlagen des Materials Holz und seiner
Bedeutung im ökologischen Kreislauf, über traditionelle, sortenreine und handwerkliche Konstruktionsweisen bis hin zu neuen, teilweise noch
wenig beforschten Werkstoffen und deren An-
wendbarkeit wird hier der Bogen in fünf thematischen Kapiteln und zwei ausführlichen Vor-
worten bis zur Baubotanik und zur Robotik im
Holzbau gespannt. Sowohl der umfangreiche
Apparat an Literaturangaben als auch die Le-
bensläufe der internationalen AutorInnenschaft
dieser Publikation belegen die Qualität dieses
wissenschaftlichen Sammelbands.

Dennoch liegt dieser Publikation ein eindeutig architektonisches Anliegen zugrunde, das
ex ovo inter- bzw. transdisziplinär angelegt ist,
wenn es sich sowohl dem Bauen als auch den das
Bauen anleitenden Ideen widmet. Entsprechend
geht es ebenso um wissenschaftlich organisiertes
Wissen (etwa „Concepts and Perspectives" ab
S. 16 oder „New Materials and Applications" ab
S. 190) wie auch um praktisch oder handwerk-
lich tradiertes Wissen über den Material- und
Fügungskosmos Holz (etwa „Joinery Culture"
ab S. 56 oder „Reapproaching Nature" ab S. 232),
das hier versammelt wird. Fernab von Material-
romantik oder Nachhaltigkeitssprech ergeben
sich aus dieser Konfrontation von Erkenntnissen
aus Produkt- oder Detailentwicklungen mit Ergebnissen aus experimentellen Ansätzen und
Lösungsversuchen schon zahlreiche, gestalterisch hoch inspirierende Denk- und Entwick-
lungsperspektiven.

Léon Spikker zeigt dazu in seinem Beitrag
über Entwurfs- und Produktionsstrategien von
Studio RAP aus Rotterdam, wie digitale Formfindung und Detailierung mit robotergestützter
Produktion und Endfertigung mit hochwertiger
Gestaltung im Holzbau einhergehen können
(„Bringing Robotic Fabrication Into Practice"
ab S. 151). Nachhaltigkeitsüberlegungen, ent-
werferische Qualität und die Entwicklung des
Gebäudes aus dem konstruktiven Detail heraus
sind bei den Pavillons der Aalto University die
gestalterischen Implikationen, um zeitsparende
Fertigung sowie Abbaubarkeit, Wiederverwer-

tung und gegebenenfalls Recycling gewährleisten zu können („Designing Through Experimentation: Timber Joints at the Aalto University Wood Program", ab S. 61). Die Erscheinung des Materials in seiner Urform, der gewachsenen Pflanze, steht im Fokus der baubotanischen Überlegungen und Entwurfsdokumentation im abschließenden Beitrag der Publikation. Experimentelle Gebäude und Verbindungstechniken im Freilandversuch arbeiten die Optik und Haptik von gewachsenem Holz heraus und zeigen, wie Bauen mit Holz abseits von High-Tech-Produktion und CNC-Fertigung funktionieren kann („Baubotanik: Living Wood and Organic Joints", ab S. 263).

Auf den Ebenen der Atmosphäre, der Behaglichkeit und Emotion scheint Holz in der durchästhetisierten Ökonomie unserer Gegenwart eine unschlagbare Position einzunehmen. Auch die seit geraumer Zeit unter dem Stichwort eines „material turns" vermehrte wissenschaftliche Aufmerksamkeit widmet sich der „Stofflichkeit" der Welt und damit dem zentralen Kompetenzbereich der Architektur. Denn als Expertin für das Gemachtsein der Dinge, für die Stimmung und Ausstrahlung der Bühnen und Hintergründe menschlichen Zusammenlebens braucht die Architektur keine moralische Abkürzung über das Material – unschlagbar nachhaltig mit Holz – zu nehmen. Denn auch wenn

das „Womit?" bereits einen großen Anteil am „Wie?" in der Architektur besitzt, so ziehen die vielschichtigen Bauaufgaben – das „Was?" – der Architektur gesellschaftlich und ökologisch eben auch größere Kreise, für die sich die Lektüre des vorliegenden, vielschichtig ansprechenden Buches außerordentlich lohnt. ∎

Many- and Multilayered: On the Phenomenon of Timber Construction

Wood is on the rise, and in terms of architecture it is getting high and higher—presently, Germany's tallest timber structure is the 34-meter-high Saiko building, erected in 2019 by Kaden + Lager in Heilbronn using a timber-hybrid construction. In Austria, the housing structure called HoHo in the Seestadt Aspern, designed by Rüdiger Lainer, is 84 meters tall. And in the town of Brumunddal, Norway, Voll Arkitekter has built what is currently the tallest timber structure at 85.4 meters in height, made of Norwegian laminated timber and Finnish laminated veneer lumber. It is a multiuse high-rise with private apartments, a hotel, offices, and leisure facilities, including a swimming pool.

Such records in height give rise not only to enthusiastic press releases, but also, as the publication under review here thoroughly explains, attest to an ecologically motivated trend that could only achieve today's possibilities through a resolute combination of practice and research. The central theme of *Rethinking Wood: Future Dimensions of Timber Assembly* deals with what we can thus expect, based on current research results, in the future when it comes to design and construction. The book's focus on the future

prospects of designing and building with wood clearly sets it apart from conventional "best of" publications. The book is addressed to readers interested in scientific aspects, in practice-based implementation possibilities, and in new and further developments in the broad field of resource-saving and sustainable construction and design.

The editors Markus Hudert and Sven Pfeiffer, who are both engaged in work as freelance architects and in university research and teaching, have released this book with the support of Aalto University and the Wüstenrot Foundation. The compendium covers topics ranging from observations and approaches related to timber in architecture, design, and materials research to digitalization and even bionic design and construction approaches. Beginning with the basics of wood as a material and its significance in the ecological cycle, and then exploring traditional, single-variety, and handcrafted construction methods, as well as new materials, some still little researched, and their applicability, five thematic chapters and two detailed forewords explore various topics, such as *Baubotanik* (construction botany) or robotics in timber construction. Both the extensive references and the CVs of the international authors found in this publication attest to the quality of the scholarly anthology.

Nonetheless, this publication is clearly based on an architectural topic that is of inter- and transdisciplinary nature from the outset, devoted as it is both to building and to the ideas that guide building. As such, it deals with scientifically organized knowledge (e.g., "Concepts and Perspectives," pp. 16ff., or "New Materials and Applications," pp. 190ff.), but also with the practical or artisan knowledge that has been passed down about wood and its cosmos of materials and joinery (e.g., "Joinery Culture," pp. 56ff., or "Reapproaching Nature," pp. 232ff.) which has been collected in this volume. Extending well beyond material romanticism or sustainability talk, this confrontation of findings from product- or detail-related developments, featuring results from experimental approaches and attempted solutions, already gives rise to numerous conceptual and development perspectives that are highly inspiring in terms of design.

In this vein, Léon Spikker, in his contribution on the design and production strategies pursued by Studio RAP in Rotterdam, shows how digital form-finding and detailing using robot-enabled production and final assembly can go hand in hand with high-quality design in the context of timber construction ("Bringing Robotic Fabrication Into Practice," pp. 151ff.). In the case of the pavilions of Aalto University, sustainability considerations, quality of design, and building development based on structural details are the design-related implications used to guarantee time-saving production, but also degradability, reuse, and, if applicable, recycling ("Designing Through Experimentation: Timber Joints at the Aalto University Wood Program," pp. 61ff.). The appearance of the material in its original form, that of the grown plant, is the focus of the construction-botanical considerations and design documentation in the final contribution to the publication. Experimental buildings and joinery techniques in field trials explore the look and feel of grown wood, showing that building with wood can be feasible well beyond the context of high-tech production and CNC manufacturing ("Baubotanik: Living Wood and Organic Joints," pp. 263ff.).

In terms of atmosphere, comfort, and emotion, wood seems to occupy an unbeatable position in the thoroughly aestheticized economy of our present. For some time now, under the heading "material turn," scientific attention devoted to the "materiality" of the world, and thus to architecture's main area of competence, has been on the rise. Indeed, as an expert on the constructedness of things, on the mood and emanation of the stages and backgrounds of human coexistence, architecture need not take a moral shortcut by way of materials—in the case of timber, unbeatably sustainable. For even if the "Whereby?" already makes up a large share of the "How?" in architecture, the multilayered building tasks—the "What?"—of architecture make great waves socially and ecologically, for which reason this book, captivating in so many ways, is worth a read. ∎

Armin Stocker (Translation: Dawn Michelle d'Atri)

**Research Culture in Architecture.
Cross-Disciplinary Collaboration**
Cornelie Leopold/Christopher
Robeller/Ulrike Weber (Hg. | eds.)
Basel: Birkhäuser, 2020
Englisch, 375 Seiten, ca. 150 SW-
und Farbabbildungen, broschiert |
English, 375 pages, ca. 150 b/w
and color illustrations, paperback
ISBN 978-3-0356-2014-6
EUR 49,95 | EUR 49.95

Auf dem Holzweg

Stefan Fink

Am 27. und 28. September 2018 fand an der TU Kaiserslautern unter dem Titel „Research Culture in Architecture" eine internationale Konferenz zum Thema Forschung in der Architektur statt, die von der Fakultät für Architektur der TU Kaiserslautern (FATUK) organisiert wurde. Der Anspruch der Veranstaltung war es, den interdisziplinären Charakter dieser Forschung sowie ihre enge Verflechtung mit der Entwurfs- und Planungspraxis herauszuarbeiten. Als weitere Ziele nennt das Booklet zur Tagung die Identifikation von wesentlichen Themenfeldern, die aktuell die Forschung in der Architektur bestimmen. Die 2020 bei De Gruyter erschienene Publikation zur Konferenz wurde von Cornelie Leopold, Christopher Robeller und Ulrike Weber herausgegeben, drei Mitgliedern der FATUK, die auch für die Organisation und Konzeption der Veranstaltung selbst verantwortlich zeichneten.

Nach dem Vorwort von Georg Vrachliotis, Professor für Architekturtheorie am KIT in Karlsruhe, spannen die drei HerausgeberInnen im gemeinschaftlich verfassten Einleitungskapitel einen historischen Bogen bis zu Wissenskulturen gotischer Bauhütten und verorten die Konferenz „Research Culture in Architecture" im Kontext von Konferenzreihen wie „RobArch" („Robotic Fabrication in Architecture, Art, and Design"), „AAG" („Advances in Architectural Geometry") und „FABRICATE" („Digital Fabrication"). Es zeigt sich dabei, dass die Frage, ob es denn überhaupt Forschung bzw. eine Forschungskultur in der Architektur gibt, zurecht als positiv beantwortet vorausgesetzt werden kann – auch wenn sich diese Forschungskultur in vielen Aspekten seit dem 13. Jahrhundert nicht wesentlich verändert hat: „The Gothic period not only symbolizes the complexity of architecture and architectural knowledge, but also the current state of architectural research" (S. 11). Im Gegensatz zur gotischen Epoche sei es gegenwärtig jedoch von großer Bedeutung, dass Architektinnen und Architekten ihre Ergebnisse veröffentlichen und so für andere Spezialisten und vor allem

zukünftige Forschung zugänglich machen. Die einzelnen Konferenzbeiträge selbst werden anschließend in sechs Abschnitten mit jeweils unterschiedlichen thematischen Schwerpunkten und folgenden Überschriften präsentiert: „Digitalization and Robotics", „Timber Construction", „Architectural Practice and Research", „Design Methods", „Sustainability" und „Architectural Space".

Der Abschnitt „Digitalization and Robotics" gibt zu Beginn mit der Keynote von Christian Derix, Partner von Woods Bagot in Sydney und Direktor von SUPERSPACE, unter dem Titel „Paradigm Reversal – Connectionist Technologies for Linear Environments" einen Einblick in den theoretischen Hintergrund sowie die historische Entwicklung der letzten Jahrzehnte im Bereich Digitalisierung und CAAD. Danach beschreibt Sigrid Brell-Cokcan das Projekts „DIANA: A Dynamic and Interactive Robotic Assistant for Novel Applications", bevor sich fünf weitere Beiträge ganz auf den Holzbau konzentrieren und aktuelle Projekte aus den Bereichen Digitalisierung und Robotik in diesem Zusammenhang vorstellen. Der nächste Abschnitt „Timber Construction" steht dann überhaupt zur Gänze im Zeichen des Holzbaus. Die drei enthaltenen Texte zeigen das Potenzial von angewandter Forschung gerade in diesem Bereich: Ein Forschungsprojekt der FATUK und der HTWG Konstanz behandelt die Recyclerbarkeit von Abfällen bei der Sperrholzherstellung, während an der Universität Kassel die Möglichkeiten von textilen Werkstoffen aus Vollholz analysiert werden. Ein weiteres Projekt der FATUK untersucht schließlich den Einsatz von acetyliertem Buchenholz für Tragstrukturen.

Nach diesem Holzbau-Schwerpunkt eröffnet die Keynote von Michael Hensel den dritten Hauptteil der Publikation, der unter dem Titel „Architectural Practice and Research" das Zusammenspiel von gestalterischer Praxis und Forschung thematisiert. Hensel, der seit 2018 das Department „Digital Architecture and Planning" an der TU Wien leitet, stellt am Beginn seines Beitrags unter dem Titel „Developing Research Cultures in Architecture" grundlegende und zentrale Fragen der Konferenz sowie des Architekturdiskurses insgesamt: „What is the state of the discipline of architecture? Is it in transformation and, if yes, in which way? What are the characteristics and impact of current transformations?" (S. 135) Eine Annäherung an diese Fragestellungen erfolgt anhand der Beschreibung von OCEAN, eines interdisziplinären Netzwerks zum Thema Forschung durch Design in Architektur und Städtebau, das 1994 von Hensel mitgegründet wurde. Gerade Konferenzen wie „Research Culture in Architecture" würden das große Potenzial von Architekturforschung an den Hochschulen, aber auch in den Architekturbüros aufzeigen. Tomas Ooms und Charlott Greub untermauern dies im Anschluss anhand des Projekts der Modernisierung des aus den 1960er-Jahren stammenden „Brouckère Tower" in Brüssel bzw. einer Analyse der Architekturausstellung als „An Environment for a Radical Redesign of the Discipline".

Im vierten Abschnitt stehen titelgebend „Design Methods" im Mittelpunkt. Die sechs Beiträge zu diesem Thema spannen inhaltlich den Bogen von aktuellen Ansätzen in der Gestaltungslehre („Werkstücke – Making Objects Into Houses/Understanding by the Way of the Hands in Design Teaching" von Bettina Kraus, Nandini Oehlmann und Mathias Peppler) bis hin zu Analysen von historischer chinesischer Gartenkunst („Exploring Chinese Scholar Gardens as a Paradigm of Lifestyle Landscape Architecture" von Luyi Liu und Luigi Cocchiarella). Von zentraler Bedeutung nicht nur für den Bereich Architektur und Städtebau ist der Aspekt der Nachhaltigkeit, dem sich der vorletzte Abschnitt „Sustainability" widmet. Ein Beispiel für diesbezügliche Architekturforschung sind die Projekte des Natural Building Lab (NBL) an der Technischen Universität Berlin, das dessen Leiter Eike Roswag-Klinge in seiner Keynote unter dem Motto „Designing Natural Buildings" vorstellt. Der letzte Abschnitt „Architectural Space" steht im Zeichen der Wahrnehmung von architektonischem Raum bzw. der körperlichen Interaktion mit diesem Raum, wobei hier unter anderem gleich zwei Forschungsvorhaben herausarbeiten, dass Architektinnen und Architekten architektonischen Raum durchaus auf andere Weise wahrnehmen als Personen ohne facheinschlägigen Hintergrund.

Insgesamt bietet *Research Culture in Architecture* somit einen vielfältigen Überblick der unterschiedlichen Facetten von aktueller Forschung in der Architektur und identifiziert darüber hinaus relevante thematische Schwerpunkte in diesem Bereich. Auffällig ist, wie stark der Holzbau dabei im Fokus steht. Um also Michael Hensels Frage nach dem Zustand der Disziplin Architektur zu beantworten: Diese ist derzeit offenbar verstärkt auf dem Holzweg – im positiven Sinn. ∎

Not Out of the Woods

On September 27 and 28, 2018, an international conference titled Research Culture in Architecture was held at the Technische Universität Kaiserslautern on the topic of research in an architectural context. It was organized by the Faculty of Architecture at the TU Kaiserslautern (FATUK). The event focused on the interdisciplinary character of this research and on its close interrelation with design and planning practice. Other goals, according to the conference booklet, were the identification of essential thematic areasa that are currently influencing research in the field of architecture. The publication of the conference proceedings, released in 2020 by De Gruyter, was edited by Cornelie Leopold, Christopher Robeller, and Ulrike Weber, three faculty members of FATUK who were also responsible for conceptualizing and organizing the conference itself.

Following the preface by Georg Vrachliotis, a professor of architectural theory at the Karlsruhe Institute of Technology (KIT) in Karlsruhe, the three book editors, in their jointly authored introductory chapter, forge a historical bridge to the knowledge cultures of Gothic masons' lodges. They localize the conference Research Culture in Architecture in the context of conference series like RobArch (Robotic Fabrication in Architecture, Art, and Design), AAG (Advances in Architectural Geometry), and FABRICATE (Digital Fabrication). It turns out that the ques-

tion as to whether research or a research culture in architecture even exists can be answered in the affirmative—even if many aspects of this research culture have essentially remained unchanged since the thirteenth century. "The Gothic period not only symbolizes the complexity of architecture and architectural knowledge, but also the current state of architectural research" (p. 11). Yet in contrast to the Gothic age, it is very important in the present day, according to the three editors, for architects to publish their results, thus making this information available to other specialists and, most especially, to future research endeavors. Subsequently, the individual contributions to the conference are presented in six sections, each focused on a different theme and titled as follows: "Digitalization and Robotics," "Timber Construction," "Architectural Practice and Research," "Design Methods," "Sustainability," and "Architectural Space."

The section "Digitalization and Robotics" begins with the keynote address by Christian Derix, a principle of Woods Bagot in Sydney and the director of SUPERSPACE, bearing the title "Paradigm Reversal: Connectionist Technologies for Linear Environments." It provides insights into the theoretical background and the historical development evident in recent decades in the field of digitalization and CAAD. The next contribution is Sigrid Brell-Cokcan's description of the project "DIANA: A Dynamic and Interactive Robotic Assistant for Novel Applications," followed by five other texts which explore the topic of timber construction and introduce current projects in this context that involve digitalization and robotics. The next section, "Timber Construction," is devoted entirely to this building method. The three texts included here demonstrate the potential of applied research in this field in particular: a research project carried out by FATUK and the HTWG Konstanz – University of Applied Sciences deals with the recyclability of waste when producing plywood, while research conducted at the Universität Kassel analyzes applications of textile materials made of solid wood. Finally, another FATUK project examines the use of acetylated beech for load-bearing structures.

After this focus on timber construction, the keynote address by Michael Hensel starts off the book's third main section, which, titled "Architectural Practice and Research," thematizes the interplay between design practice and research. Hensel, who has headed the Department of Digital Architecture and Planning at Vienna University of Technology (TU Wien) since 2018, poses fundamental and pivotal questions relevant to both the conference and overall architectural discourse in his contribution titled "Developing Research Cultures in Architecture": "What is the state of the discipline of architecture? Is it in transformation and, if yes, in which way?

What are the characteristics and impact of current transformations?" (p. 135). An exploration of these questions ensues based on a description of OCEAN, an interdisciplinary network on the topic of research through design in architecture and urban planning, co-founded in 1993 by Hensel. He notes that conferences like Research Culture in Architecture in particular evince the great potential of architectural research at universities, but also in architectural firms. Tomas Ooms and Charlott Greub corroborate this in the next contribution, citing the modernization project of the Brouckère Tower in Brussels, originally constructed in the 1960s, and pinpointing architecture exhibitions as "An Environment for a Radical Redesign of the Discipline."

In the fourth section, the title-giving "Design Methods" take center stage. The six contributions on this topic cover content ranging from current design theory approaches ("Werkstücke: Making Objects Into Houses/Understanding by the Way of the Hands in Design Teaching" by Bettina Kraus, Nandini Oehlmann, and Mathias Peppler) to analyses of historical Chinese garden art ("Exploring Chinese Scholar Gardens as a Paradigm of Lifestyle Landscape Architecture" by Luyi Liu and Luigi Cocchiarella). Of vital importance to architecture and urban planning, as well as to many other contexts, is the aspect of "Sustainability," to which the second-to-the-last section is dedicated. Serving as an example of re-

lated architectural research are the projects of the Natural Building Lab (NBL) at Berlin Institute of Technology (TU Berlin), elucidated by the project head Eike Roswag-Klinge in his keynote address under the banner "Designing Natural Buildings." The last section, titled "Architectural Space," focuses on the perception of and physical interaction with this space. Two of the research endeavors cited here show that architects perceive architectural space in a different way than individuals without a related background.

On the whole, the book *Research Culture in Architecture* offers a varied overview of the different facets of current architectural research and moreover identifies relevant thematic focus areas. Notable here is how strongly the focus is placed on timber construction. So to answer Michael Hensel's question about the state of the discipline of architecture: it clearly won't be out of the woods soon—in a most positive sense. ▪

Stefan Fink (Translation: Dawn Michelle d'Atri)

Eyes That Saw:
Architecture After Las Vegas
Stanislaus von Moos/
Martino Stierli (Hg. | eds.)
New Haven: Yale University Press/
Zürich | Zurich: Scheidegger &
Spiess 2020
Englisch, 503 Seiten, 197 Farb-
und 110 SW-Abbildungen,
Taschenbuch | English, 504 pages,
197 color and 110 b/w illustrations,
paperback
ISBN: 978-1-4008-8020-4
EUR 48,00 | EUR 48.00

Wie die Stadt des 20. Jahrhunderts zu Architektur wurde

Andreas Lechner

Dieser Sammelband geht auf ein Symposium und zwei Ausstellungen zurück, die 2009 an der Architekturfakultät der Yale University in New Haven anlässlich des 40. Jahrestags des legendären Design & Research Studio „Learning from Las Vegas" von Robert Venturi und Denise Scott Brown und ihrem Studienassistenten Steven Izenour veranstaltet wurden. Herausgegeben wird der Sammelband von den beiden Schweizer Kunsthistorikern Stanislaus von Moos und Martino Stierli, die beide intime Kenner von Venturi und Scott Brown und deren vielschichtigem Architekturkosmos sind. So führte von Moos u.a. als Gründer und Herausgeber der Zeitschrift *Archithese* in den 1970er-Jahren die kontroversen Positionen von Venturi und Scott Brown in den Schweizer Architekturdiskurs ein, während Stierli bei von Moos über den kinematografischen Blick in *Learning from Las Vegas* promovierte und seit 2015 Chefkurator für Architektur und Design am Museum of Modern Art (MoMA) in New York ist.

Die zentrale Leistung von *Learning from Las Vegas* wirkt bis heute nach, vor allem in der Architekturlehre. Das Research Studio sprengte nicht nur damalige Konventionen des bürgerlichen Geschmacks, weil es sich dem popkulturellen Glitter der einstigen Glücksspiel- und Amüsiermeile in der Wüste Nevadas widmete. Dabei wurde deren chaotisch-kommerzielle *low culture* mit methodischen Anleihen der empirischen Sozialforschung, der Bildenden Kunst und des Films in einer architektonisch-phänomenologischen Analyse untersucht, und dadurch Werken der *high culture* gleichgestellt. Der akademischen Aufmerksamkeit für Wert befunden, wurde mit *Learning from Las Vegas* nicht nur ein zwielichtiger Stadtraum mit Methoden der Pop-Art analysiert und dokumentiert, sondern die thematischen und methodischen Horizonte eines Mainstreams elegant gelangweilter Kommerzarchitektur gesprengt, der sich im amerikanischen Gefol-

ge Mies van der Rohes bis dahin städtebaulich und gesellschaftspolitisch taub und blind stellen konnte. Was *Learning from Las Vegas* hinter sich ließ und die Gemüter entsprechend erhitzte, war nicht nur die bis heute bekannte Form des Einübens in architektonische Objektgestaltung – Studierende entwerfen im Studio mehr oder weniger nach *trial-and-error* und werden dabei von Meistern korrigiert. Vielmehr richteten sich die in Folge polemisch noch weiter zugespitzten Texte in der zweiten Hälfte der späteren Ausgaben von *Learning from Las Vegas* gegen das gesamte architekturakademische Establishment seiner Zeit: gegen den selbstverliebten Formalismus der Brutalisten („ducks"), gegen den technischen Firlefanz in den britischen Megastruktur-Phantasien (Archigrams „Plug-In-City" etc.), wie auch gegen die akademische Blasiertheit und Realitätsferne utopisch-linker Architekturhaltungen.

Was *Learning from Las Vegas* dem gesamten Establishment vor mittlerweile fünf Dekaden entgegenzuhalten hatte, wird im Sammelband entsprechend umfangreich in vier Kapiteln besprochen, die sich der zeitgeschichtlichen Einbettung („Timelines and Contexts"), dem Feld an Praktiken zur architektonischen Wissensproduktion („Eyes That Saw"), dem gestalterisch-moralischen Gegensatzpaar aus konstruierter Dekoration bzw. dekorierter Konstruktion („On Trial: The ‚Decorated Shed'") und dem Rückblick bzw. der Frage nach der heutigen Relevanz von *Learning from Las Vegas* widmen („What We Learned"). Diese jeweils aus drei bis fünf Aufsätzen gebildeten Kapitel werden von bekannten, mehrheitlich US-amerikanischen ProtagonistInnen der Architektur- und Kunstszene gebildet – AutorInnen der Beiträge sind neben den Herausgebern selbst der 2018 verstorbene Robert Venturi und Denise Scott Brown sowie Architekten wie Stan Allen, Elizabeth Diller und Rafael Moneo, bekannte Architektur- bzw. Kunsthistorikerinnen wie Eve Blau, Mary McLeod oder Beatriz Colomina sowie Künstler wie Peter Fischli und Dan Graham.

Das erste Kapitel führt aus, wie das Las-Vegas-Studio 1968, während der Proteste gegen Krieg und Rassismus, den studentischen Forderungen nach gesellschaftlicher Relevanz nachkommen konnte. *Learning from Las Vegas* ver-

mochte Forschung und Lehrinhalt so in ein neues Lehrformat zu integrieren, dass ein Phänomen des „Anti-Establishments" wissenschaftlich recherchiert wurde, dass Exkursion und Feldforschung mit künstlerischen Dokumentations- und Medientechniken erfolgen konnte und dass die gewonnenen Recherchen, Analysen und Aufzeichnungen kritisch synthetisiert, d.h. als komplexer architektonisch-städtebaulicher Lehr- und Forschungsbeitrag publiziert wurden. Auf die Architekturlehre der folgenden Jahrzehnte sollte *Learning from Las Vegas* auch deshalb maßgeblichen Einfluss ausüben, weil die künstlerischen Strategien der Pop Art – der kommerziellen Welt des Massenkonsums einen vermeintlich nüchtern-kommentarlosen Spiegel vorzuhalten – nun auf einen ganzen Stadtraum ausgeweitet worden war.

Im zweiten Kapitel, „Eyes That Saw", wird diesen Verbindungen zur Pop Art nachgegangen, der Titel bezieht sich aber auch auf Le Corbusiers „Des yeux qui ne voient pas" aus *Vers une Architecture* von 1923. Dessen Plädoyer für die inspirative Zuwendung zur modernen Alltagswelt – bei Le Corbusier noch die Maschinenästhetik technischer Errungenschaften wie Auto, Flugzeug oder Schiff – führte der Realismus von Venturi und Scott Brown als Traditionslinie moderner Architektur fort – sprengte damit aber auch die engen disziplinären Grenzen des guten Geschmacks und der Schicklichkeit nachhaltig. Im dritten Kapitel wird der berühmten Gestaltungspolemik – „ducks" versus „decorated sheds" – nachgegangen. Die plastische Raumskulptur und der dekorierte Zweckbau sind die immobilien-

wirtschaftlichen Optionen in der vollmotorisierten Aufmerksamkeitsökonomie – mehr oder weniger anspruchsvoll gestaltete Einzelobjekte, die ihr Insel-Dasein im modern verstädterten Verkehrsraum fristen. Die Verwirrung von Signifikat und Signifikant ist bei der modernistischen Ente noch eine räumlich-plastische Struktur, die zugleich ihr Ornament bildet, Signifikant und Signifikat fallen – formal gesehen authentisch – ineinander. Beim dekorierten Schuppen werden ornamentale Bildhaftigkeit bzw. sprachliche Zeichen von der das Gebäude selbst tragenden bzw. raum-bildenden Struktur entkoppelt. So können sich Billboards, Ornamente, Grafiken oder Werbepylone überall hin – theoretisch gesehen global wie die Logos entsprechender Konzerne – bzw. über die ganze Oberfläche des Baukörpers oder

How the Twentieth-Century City Became Architecture

This anthology harks back to a symposium and two exhibitions held in the architecture department of Yale University in New Haven, Connecticut, in 2009. They marked the 40th anniversary of the legendary design and research studio "Learning from Las Vegas" by Robert Venturi and Denise Scott Brown and their student assistant Steven Izenour. The anthology is edited by the two Swiss art historians Stanislaus von Moos and Martino Stierli, both of whom possess intimate knowledge of Venturi and Scott Brown's work and their multifaceted architectural cosmos. As founder and editor of the journal *Archithese* in the 1970s, for example, Moos introduced the controversial positions of Venturi and Scott Brown into Swiss architectural discourse, whereas Stierli earned his doctorate with Moos as his advisor on the topic of the cinematographic gaze in *Learning from Las Vegas*. Since 2015 Stierli has been Chief Curator of Architecture and Design at The Museum of Modern Art (MoMA) in New York.

The main achievement of *Learning from Las Vegas* still has impact today, especially in the context of architectural theory. By devoting itself

to the pop-cultural glitter of this gambling and entertainment mile amid the desert of Nevada, the research studio shattered not only the middle-class taste conventions prevalent at the time, but others as well. In the process, the city's chaotically commercial "low culture" was researched with methods borrowed from empirical social research, visual arts, and film in a process of architectural, phenomenological analysis, and thus equated with works of "high culture." Considered worthy of academic attention, *Learning from Las Vegas* inspired not only the analysis and documentation of seedy urban spaces using methods of Pop Art, but also the shattering of the thematic and methodological horizons of elegant yet blasé mainstream commercial architecture, which up to that point had been deaf and blind to urban-planning and sociopolitical issues, along the lines of Mies van der Rohe's American entourage. What *Learning from Las Vegas* left behind, and what accordingly got everyone worked up, was, for one, the form of practicing architectural object design still familiar today: students do design work in a studio more or less according to trial and error and are corrected by masters. Also,

seine Parkierungsflächen ausbreiten. Damit wurde die epistemologische Klarheit der baulichen Struktur, die der Moderne so wichtig war, nachhaltig zerstört. Der ganze Eigentlichkeitsjargon moderner Architektur – das Suchen von absoluten Wahrheiten in Raum und Struktur – verschob *Learning from Las Vegas* in den Bereich von Ornament und Sprachzeichen und übertrug es als Pop- und Werbezeichen auf zweidimensionale Oberflächen. *Learning from Las Vegas* sah keinen Bedarf mehr darin, sich noch länger mit „Räumen" abzumühen – *Space as God* – die sowieso niemand „lesen" konnte. Vielmehr konnten Venturi und Scott Brown mit dem dekorierten Zweckbau behaupten, dass dieser – ganz modern, nicht postmodern (!) – architektonisch Authentizität herstellt, weil er in der Gegenwart

und ihrer Konsumideologie entsprechend gebaute Bilder produziert. Natürlich stimmt das nicht ganz – das ironisch-distinktive Spiel einer Geschmackselite bleibt in den meisten Gestaltungen erkenn- und nachvollziehbar. Was aber durch die polemischen Typen „ducks" und „decorated sheds" mit allergrößtem Nachdruck anschaulich wurde, sind die auf Vollmotorisierung basierenden Raum-, Siedlungs- und Aufmerksamkeitsstrukturen des 20. Jahrhunderts, die zugleich die wichtigsten Raum- und Siedlungsressourcen zur inneren Stadtentwicklung und Nachverdichtung für unsere unmittelbare Zukunft darstellen.

Woran wir weiterbauen werden, ist das, was von *Learning from Las Vegas* im vierten Kapitel, „What We Have Learnt", bleibt. Hier fragt Robert Venturi in seinem posthum erschienenem Beitrag

nach einem „Before Las Vegas" (S. 419): Denn vor Las Vegas untersuchte Venturi in *Complexity and Contradiction in Architecture*, wie ein Lernen von historischer Architektur, von Aalto und von Kahn weniger bauliche Banalitäten produzieren könnte – trotz kommerziellen Drucks. Ein solches manieristischeres, anspielungsreicheres und widersprüchlicheres Weiterbauen an den generischen Kisten der Peripherie steht uns ja bevor und ein Wieder-Zur-Hand-Nehmen eines der wichtigsten Architekturbücher des 20. Jahrhunderts kann dabei nur helfen. Denn *Learning from Las Vegas* ist auch heute noch – und das machen die vielschichtigen Aspekte und Facetten der Beiträge in diesem wunderbar gestalteten Sammelband mehr als deutlich – geistvoll und witzig, inspirierend und unterhaltsam. ∎

in the second half of the later editions of *Learning from Las Vegas*, the more polemically heated texts were directed against the entire architectural establishment of the time: against the narcissistic formalism of the brutalists ("ducks"), against the technical frippery found in British megastructure fantasies (Archigram's "Plug-in City," etc.), and also against blasé academic attitudes and escapist utopian-leftist views of architecture.

Extensively discussed in the anthology is how *Learning from Las Vegas* responded to the entire establishment five decades ago, spanning four chapters respectively dedicated to embedment in contemporary history ("Timelines and Contexts"), the field of practices related to architectural production of knowledge ("Eyes That Saw"), the design- and morals-related contrasting pair of constructed decoration and decorated construction ("On Trial: The 'Decorated Shed'"), and the retrospective view or question of the relevance of *Learning from Las Vegas* today ("What We Learned"). These chapters, each featuring three to five essays, are made up of well-known, mostly American protagonists from the architecture and art scene. Besides the editors themselves,

the contributions are authored even by Robert Venturi (who died in 2018) and Denise Scott Brown, by architects like Stan Allen, Elizabeth Diller, and Rafael Moneo, well-known historians of architecture and art like Eve Blau, Mary McLeod, and Beatriz Colomina, and by artists such as Peter Fischli and Dan Graham.

The first chapter explains how the Las Vegas studio was able to meet student demands for relevance within society in 1968, during the protests against war and racism. *Learning from Las Vegas* succeeded in integrating research and teaching content into a new educational format in such a way that an "anti-establishment" phenomenon could be researched academically, that excursions and field research could be carried out using artistic documentation and media techniques, and that the research, analyses, and recordings thus obtained could be critically synthesized, that is, published as a complex teaching and research contribution on architecture and urban planning. *Learning from Las Vegas* was to exert a decisive influence on the study of architecture in subsequent decades, not least because the artistic strategies of Pop Art—holding up a

supposedly sober, uncommented mirror to the commercial world of mass consumption—had now been extended to all of urban space.

The second chapter, "Eyes That Saw," traces these connections to Pop Art, yet the title also references Le Corbusier's "Des yeux qui ne voient pas" from *Vers une Architecture* of 1923. What eyes should see is the powerful inspiration drawn from engaging with the modern everyday world—in the case of Le Corbusier, this still involved the machine aesthetics of technical achievements like cars, airplanes, or ships—that was continued by the realism of Venturi and Scott Brown as a traditional line of modern architecture. In doing so, however, it also disrupted the narrow disciplinary boundaries of good taste and propriety in a lasting way.

Explored in the third chapter is the famous design polemic "ducks" versus "decorated sheds." The spatial sculpture and the decorated functional building are the economic real-estate options in a fully motorized attention economy—as individual objects with a more or less sophisticated design that carve out an island existence in modern urbanized traffic areas. The confusion of signifier and signified is, in the case of the modernist duck, still that of a spatial structure that simultaneously forms its ornament; signifier and signified coincide, authentically in terms of form. In the case of the decorated shed, ornamental pictoriality or linguistic signs are decoupled from the structure supporting the building itself or forming the space. This allows billboards, ornaments, graphics, and advertising pylons to essentially be placed anywhere—as globally, theoretically speaking, as the logos of the respective companies—or to be spread across the entire surface of a building or its parking areas. Thus, the epistemological clarity of the architectural structure so important to modernism was destroyed for good. All the authenticity jargon of modern architecture—searching for absolute truths in space and structure—was shifted by *Learning from Las Vegas* into the area of ornamentation and linguistic signs, transferring it onto two-dimensional surfaces as pop and advertising symbols. The study no longer saw any need to wrestle with "spaces"—*Space as God*—that no one could even "read" anyway. Rather, Venturi and Scott Brown could assert, by citing

the decorated functional building, that it produces architectural authenticity—in a very modern, not postmodern (!) way—since it creates built imagery in the present according to its consumerist ideology. Of course this is not wholly true; the ironically distinctive game played by the taste elite remains recognizable and plausible in most of the designs. But what became emphatically clear through the "ducks" and "decorated sheds" polemic types were the twentieth-century space, settlement, and attention structures based on complete motorization. These structures count among the most important space and settlement resources for inner-city urban and infill development in our immediate future.

What we will continue to build on is what remains of *Learning from Las Vegas* in the fourth chapter, "What We Have Learnt." Here, Robert Venturi asks in his posthumously released essay about what went "Before Las Vegas" (p. 419). Indeed, before Las Vegas, in his 1966 book *Complexity and Contradiction in Architecture*, Venturi explored how learning from historical architecture, from Aalto and from Kahn, could lead to fewer banal structures

being built—despite commercial pressure. In store for us is, in fact, such a mannerist, more allusive and contradictory continuation of building on the generic boxes of the periphery; and a renewed perusal of one of the most important architecture books of the twentieth century can only be of benefit. Still today, *Learning from Las Vegas* is brilliant and funny, inspiring and entertaining—as is made more than clear by the multilayered aspects and facets of the contributions to this wonderfully designed anthology. ∎

Andreas Lechner (Translation: Dawn Michelle d'Atri)

Die Architekturmaschine:
Die Rolle des Computers
in der Architektur
Teresa Fankhänel/
Andres Lepik (Hg. | eds.)
Basel: Birkhäuser, 2020
Deutsch, 248 Seiten, 230 Farb- und
18 SW-Abbildungen, Hardcover |
German, 248 pages, 230 color and
18 b/w illustrations, hardcover
ISBN 978-3-0356-2155-6
EUR 39,95 | EUR 39.95

Mensch und/oder Maschine

Tobias Gruber

Wie keine andere Erfindung der letzten 70 Jahre versinnbildlicht der Computer die Idee von Fortschritt und Innovation mitsamt allen ihren Konsequenzen und Kontroversen. Eine reflektierte und sachliche Betrachtung über die Geschichte des Computers in der Architektur – losgelöst von SkeptikerInnen und EnthusiastInnen – kann einen wichtigen Indikator bilden, wie dieser auch die Zukunft der Disziplin beeinflussen könnte. *Die Architekturmaschine* tut das als Publikation zur gleichnamigen Ausstellung im Architekturmuseum der Technischen Universität München und gibt einen weit gefächerten, gut geordneten Überblick über die bisherigen Einsatzgebiete der Rechenmaschine in der Architektur. Anhand von vier Kapiteln nimmt das von Museumsdirektor Andres Lepik und der Kuratorin Teresa Fankhänel herausgegebene Buch eine differenzierte Beurteilung des Computers als „Zeichenmaschine", als „Entwurfswerkzeug", als „Medium des Geschichtenerzählens" sowie als „interaktive Plattform" vor. Die Kapitel setzen sich aus Fallstudien und Essays zusammen, die computerbasierte Meilensteine der Architekturgeschichte dokumentieren und ideologische Grundlagen sowie politische Rahmenbedingungen besprechen. Im Anhang werden wichtige Eckdaten und Kategorien noch einmal zusammengefasst und textlich sowie diagrammatisch aufbereitet.

Der Buchtitel *Die Architekturmaschine* bezieht sich auf die „Architecture Machine Group", ein Forschungsprojekt der 1960er-Jahre, das von Leon Groisser und Nicholas Negroponte am MIT ins Leben gerufen wurde. Ausgestattet mit einem Selbstbaucomputer verfolgten die beiden das Ziel, „die Grenze zwischen Mensch und Maschine zu überwinden" (S. 15). Das Experiment konnte einige Erfolge, wie das Ausführen von einfachen Gestaltungsregeln erzielen, scheiterte aber an der grundlegenden Ambition das Gerät lernfähig zu machen.

Die Erwartungen, die auch in Folge an die Entwicklung des Computers herangetragen wur-

den, blieben groß und vielfältig. Eines der bekanntesten Versprechen der Digitalisierung war die Entmaterialisierung. Projekte der 1990er-Jahre wie Bernhard Tschumis „Papierloses Büro" oder Publikationen wie Negropontes „Being Digital" verkündeten die „Befreiung von Papierstapeln und zerknüllten Blättern" (S. 20). Dass es anders gekommen ist, wissen wir heute. Anna-Maria Meister schlägt daher in ihrem Essay „Papier(lose) Architektur. Mediale und institutionelle Überlagerungen" vor, das Materielle und das Digitale als Kategorien zu verstehen, die sich nicht ablösten, sondern wechselseitig antrieben und formten. Sie zeigt am Beispiel der zeitversetzten Entwicklung zweier deutscher Hochschulen, der HfG Ulm und der TU München, zudem die Verquickung institutioneller Vorgänge, die zu nicht-linearen Verläufen führte.

In seinem Essay „Architektur, Computer und technische Unruhe. Zu einer Architekturgeschichte der Angst" beschreibt Georg Vrachliotis die Abwehrhaltung, die ArchitektInnen gegenüber dem Computer als Zeicheninstrument im Entwurf hegten. Eine besonders intensive Dimension erhielt diese Diskussion in den USA, wo 1968 namhafte GegnerInnen und BefürworterInnen aus dem erweiterten Feld der Architektur bei der Konferenz „Computer Graphics in Architecture and Design" aufeinanderstießen. Louis Kahn sah im Computer eine Bedrohung eigenständigen Denkens, die nicht nur den Architekten bzw. der Architektin als alleinige/n EntscheidungsträgerIn, sondern den gesamten Gestaltungsprozess als kulturelle Technik infrage stellte. Dagegen verstand Steven Coons, Ingenieur und einer der Gründungsväter des „Computer Aided Design" (CAD) den Computer als ein ergänzendes Werkzeug im Entwurf, das ungeliebte Arbeitsprozesse übernehmen sollte. Die Frage, ob sich der Designprozess rationalisieren ließe, stellte sich den EntwicklerInnen des CAD grundsätzlich, wie Molly Wright Steenson in „Kreativität und Problemlösung. Herausforderungen des Computergestützten Entwerfens" schreibt. Während Steven Coons Entwerfen als eine „ergebnisoffene, menschliche Tätigkeit" verstand, sah sein Entwicklungspartner Douglas Ross Design als ein formales Resultat vorgegebener Parameter, dessen Entstehungsprozess er automatisieren wollte. Im Kontrast dazu entwickelten ArchitektInnen Visionen um den Entwurfsvorgang anders zu denken. Cedric Price zielte etwa gemeinsam mit John und Julia Frazer in ihrem Projekt „Generator" auf die Veränderbarkeit von Gebäuden ab. Sie wollten eine Architektur schaffen, die sich an wechselnde Erfordernisse durch Hilfe des Computers anpassen würde.

Mollie Claypool knüpft an diese Entwurfsmethodik in „Das Diskrete. Architektur wird digital" an. Kernaspekte des „Diskreten", wie Vorstellungen von Skalierbarkeit, Vielseitigkeit, Offenheit und Verteilung sind architekturimmanente Themen, die sich in „rahmenbasierten" Standardisierungs- und Multiplikationsprozessen der Moderne, in den „modulartigen" Visionen der 50er- und 60er-Jahre oder den „fließenden" Verbindungen parametrischer Architektur wiederfinden. Aber erst durch ein diskretes Denken in Teilen, die wie Voxel (dreidimensionale Pixel) miteinander verbunden wären und sich an verändernde Parameter anpassen, würde es die Architektur schaffen, wirklich im Digitalen anzukommen.

In „Sehen nach Zahlen. Eine kurze Geschichte des Computerrenderings" beschreibt Roberto Botazzi, wie sich digitale Darstellungsmethoden aus analogem Wissen auf Basis der beiden Stränge, geometrischer Konstruktion und der Berechnung von Licht und Schatten entwickelten. Wie auch Teresa Fankhänel in „Bewegung, Zeit, Architektur" für den Bereich der Computeranimation, erzählt er von den technischen Entwicklungshürden, die den Weg von „Wireframe" bis zu „Solid Modelling" maßgeblich verzögerten.

Den Computer als interaktive Plattform besprechen die Texte „Playing Architect. Mit

Computerspielen entwerfen" von Felix Torkar und „Eine Auswahl berechnen. Eigenbau, Konfigurationsmodelle und die Vorstellungswelt der Zahlen" von Theodora Vardouli. Während der erste Essay den „ungeplanten" Einfluss von architekturbasierten Computerspielen auf ArchitektInnen sowie auf eine breite Masse der Gesellschaft offenlegt, zeigt der zweite Essay wie digitale Plattformen Themen von Partizipation, Open Source-Wissen, Eigenbau und Do-It-Yourself-Tendenzen neu verhandeln und in Gebautes übersetzen.

Die Automatisierung und die Erweiterung menschlicher Fähigkeiten und Wahrnehmung, die Entmaterialisierung und Optimierung von Prozessen, neue Formen der Partizipation und bessere Systeme der Vernetzung waren einstige Versprechen der Digitalisierung, die heute zum Teil eingelöst sind und zum Teil schwer einlösbar zu bleiben scheinen. Wie der Computer auch in Zukunft unser Denken und Handeln verändern wird, wie stark er den Gesamtprozess in der Architekturpraxis vom Entwurf bis zur Fertigung prägen wird, können wir aufgrund des „Risikofaktors Mensch" nur vermuten. Dieses Buch zeigt anhand der Geschichte des Computers in der Architekturproduktion, dass es auch in Zukunft keinen linearen Fortschritt geben wird. Digitale Entwicklungen, so bunt und erfindungsreich wie sie einem in den Illustrationen der „Architekturmaschine" entgegenblitzen, werden sich immer wieder einer kritischen Beurteilung unterziehen müssen, um die Architektur davor zu bewahren „die produktive Widersprüchlichkeit des menschlichen Geistes im Effienzversprechen des Computers aufzulösen" (S. 28). ∎

Human and/or Machine

Like no other invention of the last seventy years, computers epitomize the idea of progress and innovation, with all of the related consequences and controversies. A reflected and objective consideration of the history of computers in architecture—at a remove from skeptics and enthusiasts—can be an important indicator of how they might also influence the future of the discipline. *Die Architekturmaschine* (The Architecture Machine) does just this as the book accompanying the eponymous exhibition at the Architekturmuseum of Munich's Technical University. It offers a widely varied, favorably structured overview of previous fields of application of the computing machine in architecture. Edited by museum director Andres Lepik and curator Teresa Fankhänel, the volume offers a differentiated analysis of computers in four chapters, as "Zeichenmaschine" (Drafting Machine), as "Entwurfswerkzeug" (Design Tool), as "Medium des Geschichtenerzählens" (Storytelling Medium), and as an "interaktive Plattform" (Interactive Platform). The chapters are filled with case studies and essays which document computer-based milestones in architectural history and discuss ideological fundaments and political parameters. In the appendix, important key data and categories are summarized once again and presented in both text and diagram form.

The book title *Die Architekturmaschine* pays reference to the "Architecture Machine Group," a research project from the 1960s initiated by Leon Groisser and Nicholas Negroponte at MIT. Equipped with a homemade computer, they pursued the goal of "overcoming the boundary between human and machine" (p. 15). The experiment saw some success, such as the execution of simple design rules, but it fell short of its main ambition of making the device capable of learning.

The expectations subsequently placed on the development of computers remained large and varied. One of the most famous promises of digitalization was dematerialization. Projects carried out during the 1990s like Bernard Tschumi's "paperless studios" or publications like Nicholas Negroponte's *Being Digital* promised "freedom from stacks of paper and crumpled pages" (p. 20). As we know today, things turned out differently. Anna-Maria Meister thus suggests in her essay titled "Papier(lose) Architektur: Mediale und institutionelle Überlagerungen" (Paper[less] Architecture: Mediatic and Institutional Superimpositions) that we view the material and the digital as categories that, instead of replacing each other, have reciprocally driven and shaped each other. Citing the non-synchronous development of two different German universities, the HfG Ulm and the TU Munich, she also demonstrates the fusion of institutional processes that lead to non-linear trajectories.

In his essay "Architektur, Computer und technische Unruhe: Zu einer Architekturgeschichte der Angst" (Architecture, Computers, and Technical Upheaval: On an Architectural History of Fear), Georg Vrachliotis describes the defensive attitude that architects entertained toward computers as a drafting tool in the design context. This debate attained an especially intensive dimension in the United States, where well-known individuals from the broader field of architecture who were for or against this development gathered in 1968 at the conference called Computer Graphics in Architecture and Design. Louis Kahn saw computers as a threat to independent thinking, casting doubt not only on architects as sole decision-makers, but also on the entire design process as a cultural technique. Steven Coons, an engineer and one of the founding fathers of computer-aided design (CAD), on the other hand, viewed computers as a tool supplementing design, one meant to take over unpopular work processes. The question of whether the design process could be streamlined was a

fundamental one for the developers of CAD, as Molly Wright Steenson writes in "Kreativität und Problemlösung: Herausforderungen des Computergestützten Entwerfens" (Creativity and Problem-Solving: The Challenges of Computer-Aided Design). While Steven Coons understood design to be an "open-ended human activity," his development partner Douglas Ross saw design as a formal result of given parameters with processes of creation that he wanted to automate. In contrast to this, architects developed visions meant to rethink the design process. Cedric Price, for example, worked with John and Julia Frazer on their "Generator" project with the intention of enhancing the convertibility of buildings. They set out to create architecture that, with the aid of computers, could adapt to changing needs.

Mollie Claypool takes up this design methodology in "Das Diskrete: Architektur wird digital" (The Discrete: Architecture Goes Digital). Key aspects of "the discrete," such as ideas related to scalability, versatility, openness, and distribution, are topics inherent to architecture, rediscovered in "frame-based" processes of standardization and multiplication during modernism, in the "modular" visions of the 1950s and 1960s, and in the "flowing" connections within parametric architecture. But only by thinking discretely in terms of parts that can interconnect like voxels (three-dimensional pixels) and adapt to changing parameters would architecture manage to truly arrive in the digital realm.

In "Sehen nach Zahlen: Eine kurze Geschichte des Computerrenderings" (Seeing by Number: A Short History of the Computer Rendering), Roberto Botazzi describes how digital methods of representation evolved from analogue knowledge based on the two strands, on geometric construction, and on the calculation of light and shadow. Similar to the area of computer animation as explored by Teresa Fankhänel in "Bewegung, Zeit, Architektur" (Movement, Time, Architecture),

Botazzi speaks of the technical hurdles of development that caused significant lags along the path from "wireframe" to "solid modeling."

Computers as an interactive platform are discussed in the texts "Playing Architect: Mit Computerspielen entwerfen" (Designing with Computer Games) by Felix Torkar and "Eine Auswahl berechnen: Eigenbau, Konfigurationsmodelle und die Vorstellungswelt der Zahlen" (Calculating a Selection: Self-Build, Configuration Models, and the Imaginary World of Numbers) by Theodora Vardouli. While the first essay examines the "unplanned" influence of architecture-based computer games on architects and on much of the populace, the second essay illustrates how digital platforms renegotiate issues like participation, open source knowledge, self-build, and DIY tendencies and translate them into buildings.

Automation and the expansion of human capabilities and perception, the dematerialization and optimization of processes, new forms of participation, and better networking systems were onetime promises of digitalization, which today have been attained in some ways yet seem irredeemable in others. Based on the "human risk factor," we can only guess at how computers will continue to change our thoughts and actions in the future, at how strongly they will shape the process of architectural practice as a whole, from design to assembly. By exploring the history of computers in the context of architectural production, this book shows that linear progress is not to be expected in the future either. Digital developments, as colorful and inventive as they flash before our eyes in the illustrations found in *Die Architekturmaschine*, will ever need to undergo critical evaluation in order to prevent architecture from "dispelling the productive inconsistency of the human spirit in the promise of efficiency held by computers" (p. 28). ▪

Tobias Gruber (Translation: Dawn Michelle d'Atri)

Neues soziales Wohnen.
Positionen zur IBA_Wien 2022
IBA Wien 2022/future.lab (Hg. | eds.)
Berlin: Jovis, 2020
Deutsch 256 Seiten, 150 Farb-
und SW-Abbildungen | German,
256 pages, 150 color and
b/w illustrations
ISBN 978-3-86859-619-9
EUR 35,00 | EUR 35.00

Damit Wohnen besser bleibt?

Sigrid Verhovsek

Seit über hundert Jahren gibt es Internationale Bauausstellungen (IBA), die in unregelmäßigen Abständen und in verschiedenen Städten und Regionen Deutschlands dringliche Themen der Architektur und des Städtebaus im Spiegel ihrer Zeit behandeln und sich dabei auf jeweils aktuelle gesellschaftliche, technische und kulturelle Entwicklungen beziehen. Die IBA 2020 wurde in Basel erstmals außerhalb Deutschlands veranstaltet, für die IBA 2022 hat sich Wien mit dem Thema „Neues soziales Wohnen" beworben. Gerade weil Wien europaweit als Vorreiter im sozialen Wohnbau gilt, ist die Frage nach Innovationen spannend. Gerade in relativ gut funktionierenden Strukturen gibt es Spielräume – für Experimente und das Austesten der Lebbarkeit neuer Modelle, denn „in erster Linie geht es nicht um den Bau von Wohnungen, sondern um das Leben, das sich in den Wohnungen entfalten soll". Was Ferdinand Schuster in seinem Vortrag „Architektur und Politik" aus dem Jahr 1965 statuiert, fasst die aktuellen Leitthemen der IBA_Wien 2022 zusammen. Es geht nicht nur um ökonomisch leistbares Wohnen, sondern um soziale Quartiere, soziale Qualitäten und soziale Verantwortung; wobei sich sozial in diesem Fall nicht vorrangig auf „Einkommens- oder Lebensverhältnisse oder auf die Bedürftigkeit einzelner [bezieht], sondern auf den Aspekt des Gesellschaftlichen und des Zusammenlebens" (S. 326).

Dieses Themenspektrum bedingt, dass ArchitektInnen und StädteplanerInnen Dialoge mit zivilgesellschaftlichen und politischen Ebenen ebenso führen müssen wie mit den fachlich „angrenzenden" Disziplinen Ökonomie, Raumplanung und Soziologie. Als konkrete, architektonische Aufgabe wird dieser Ansatz in neun IBA-Gebieten bzw. 16 Einzelobjekten ersichtlich, für die kreative Ideen und Umsetzungsvarianten gesammelt wurden und die sich nun in verschiedenen Stadien der Umsetzung befinden. Dabei geht es neben Neubau auch um die Weiternutzung, Ertüchtigung oder Erweiterung bestehender Bausubstanz. Dementsprechend endet diese IBA auch nicht im Jahr 2022: Die Projekte sollen nach einigen Nutzungsjahren einer Evaluierung unterzogen werden, die der (sozial)räumlichen und kulturellen Einbindung nachgeht, die daraus gewonnenen Erkenntnisse international publiziert und damit erst den Zweck einer IBA erfüllt sieht.

Als erster Schritt dieses ambitionierten Vorhabens ist der Positionsbericht „Neues Soziales Wohnen" zu sehen, der vom Organisator Kurt Hofstetter und seinem IBA_Wien-Team sowie von Madlyn Miessgang, Kerstin Pluch, Rudolf Scheuvens und Constanze Wolfring vom future.lab der Fakultät für Architektur und Raumplanung der TU Wien herausgegeben wird. Dieser Katalog geht über ein Begleitheft zur Ausstellung im Herbst 2020 weit hinaus, weil es die grundlegenden Ergebnisse der Think-Tanks nachvollzieht. Was „Neues Soziales Wohnen" eigentlich heißen soll, wird in Essays, Interviews und Berichten diskutiert und als Zwischenstände der Forschung, der Projekte und der „IBA-Talks" genannten Werkstattgespräche präsentiert.

Es sind viele prägnante, aber auch sehr unterschiedliche Aufsätze der 59 AutorInnen, die sich wechselseitig so ergänzen, dass viele relevante Aspekte aus verschiedenen Disziplinen und Sparten wie Ökonomie, Soziologie, Politikwissenschaft, Geografie, Urbanistik, Umweltmanagement zueinanderfinden. Beim ersten Durchblättern fällt der Fokus Quartiersentwicklung auf – Binnengrundrisse werden kaum thematisiert, auch kein „Schöner Wohnen". Luftbilder der verschiedenen Quartiere dominieren und werden von stadtraumbildenden Situationen flankiert. Die dabei konsequent und eindringlich betonte Notwendigkeit flexibler Zwischenräume und verschiedener Infrastrukturangebote für nachbarschaftliches Zusammenleben deutet bereits die Vorzüge nahtloser Zusammenarbeit von ArchitektInnen und StadtplanerInnen an und kann das Wissen um die Herstellung räumlicher Atmosphären mit der Einbindung in die reale Welt vernetzen.

Die Einleitung muss die Tradition des Wiener Gemeindebaus selbstverständlich thematisieren, sie geht aber weit über eine Verneigung vor dem Gemeindebau hinaus, weil sie klar die aktuellen Herausforderungen, d.h. die politischen, ökologischen und ökonomischen Schwierigkeiten benennt. Der Hauptteil des Katalogs gliedert sich in die drei Themenblöcke „Dimensionen", „Internationale Perspektiven", und „Interpretationen", auf die noch ein Ausblick folgt. Im ersten und umfangreichsten Teil, den „Dimensionen", werden in drei Panels zu „Wohn- und Bodenpolitik", „Ökologie" und „Gesellschaft" die Grundlagen gebündelt dargestellt. Hier wird das inter- und transdisziplinäre Vorgehen deutlich, wenn Forschung, Planung und Praxis lückenlos ineinander übergehen und sich etwa Tischgespräche unter Erörterungen mischen. So werden immer wieder neue Perspektiven durch Querverbindungen gewonnen, wie bei den „Sozialen Aspekten des Klimawandels", oder den ÖkonomInnen oder JuristInnen, die nicht mehr nur vom leistbaren, sondern vom sozialen oder sogar „guten Wohnen für alle" sprechen bzw. dieses sogar als Recht einfordern. Die Internationalen Perspektiven wirken wie ein Zwischenspiel, hier wären vielleicht mehrere gelungene Beispiele und Entwicklungen interessant gewesen und auch ein Sprung aus Europa hinaus könnte für Impulse sorgen – nicht nur für Zielgruppenplanungen. Die „Interpretationen" behandeln die konkreten Ansätze – thematisiert werden Quartiersentwicklung (bzw. die „Grätzlbildung"), der Umgang mit „Bestandsbauten", die Architektur (und ihr Gestaltungsvokabular), und schließlich verschiedene neue oder auch wiederentdeckte Modelle der Finanzierung, der Partizipation, des Zusammenlebens oder der nachhaltigen Entwicklung.

Ein kurzer Ausblick unter dem Motto „Damit es besser bleibt" fasst den Stand der IBA Wien zusammen, verknüpft einige lose Fäden und wirft nochmals viele interessante Fragen auf, die auch die IBA im Jahr 2022 nicht alle beantworten können wird. Wenn dieser informative und grafisch hochansprechende Katalog zum neuen sozialen Wohnen nur ein Zwischenstand ist, so kann man sich bereits jetzt auf die nächsten beiden Entwicklungsjahre freuen und mit Spannung den mit diesem Wissen angereicherten Projekten entgegensehen. ∎

So Housing Stays Better?

For over a hundred years, international building exhibitions (Internationale Bauausstellungen, IBA) have been held at irregular intervals in various cities and regions across Germany. The idea is to explore pressing issues related to architecture and urban planning as mirrored by their time, while referencing the respective current social, technical, and cultural developments. The IBA 2020 in Basel took place for the first time outside of Germany; and Vienna is contending, with the motto "New Social Housing," for the honor of hosting the IBA 2022. The question of innovation is exciting, especially because Vienna is considered one of Europe's pioneers of social housing. Leeway is found especially in relatively well functioning structures—in terms of experimentation and of testing the livability of new models, for "[i]t is not about the construction of dwellings first and foremost, but about the life that should unfold within these dwellings." The current key themes of the IBA_ Wien 2022 actually summarize what Ferdinand Schuster had asserted in his lecture "Architektur und Politik" (Architecture and Politics) in the year 1965. It is not only about economically affordable housing, but also about social quarters, social qualities, and social responsibility. In this case, however, "social" applies not primarily to "income or living conditions or to the needs of individuals, but to the aspect of society and cohabitation" (p. 326).

This thematic spectrum requires architects and urban planners to engage in dialogue with civic and political bodies in equal measure to with the "adjacent" specialist disciplines of economics, spatial planning, and sociology. This approach as a concrete architectural task is evident in nine IBA areas and in sixteen individual objects, for which creative ideas and forms of implementation were compiled and are now in various stages of realization. In addition to new construction, this also involves the continued use, upgrading, or expansion of existing buildings. As such, this IBA will not end in the year 2022. The projects are earmarked for evaluation after several years of use, at which time the (social-)spatial and cultural integration will be assessed, the resulting knowledge published internationally, and the purpose of an IBA only then arriving at a sense of completion.

The status report *Neues Soziales Wohnen* (New Social Housing) can be viewed as the first step in this ambitious endeavor. The book is edited by Kurt Hofstetter as organizer and his IBA_Wien team, along with Madlyn Miessgang, Kerstin Pluch, Rudolf Scheuvens, and Constanze

Wolfring from future.lab in the Faculty of Architecture and Planning at Vienna University of Technology. This catalogue is far more than a booklet accompanying the fall 2020 exhibition, for it traces the basic think-tank results. What "new social housing" actually means is discussed in essays, interviews, and reports, and also presented as the preliminary results of research, projects, and workshop discussions called "IBA-Talks."

The essays by the fifty-nine authors are concise and well varied, complementing each other in ways that allow many relevant aspects to come together from various disciplines and sectors, such as economics, sociology, political science, geography, urbanism, and environmental management. When skimming through the book, the focus initially falls on the development of districts; interior floor plans are hardly discussed, nor is "beautiful living." Aerial photos of the various districts dominate and are flanked by situations formative for urban space. The consistently and emphatically emphasized necessity of creating flexible interstitial spaces and various infrastructure offerings for neighborly cohabitation already alludes to the merits of seamless collaboration among architects and urban planners. In fact, this can link the knowledge of creating spatial atmospheres with the integration thereof in the real world.

Naturally, the introduction must thematically touch on the tradition of Vienna's *Gemeindebau* (municipal social housing), yet it goes well beyond honoring *Gemeindebau* by clearly pinpointing the current challenges, that is, the related political, ecological, and economic difficulties. The main section of the catalogue is arranged in three thematic blocks called "Dimensionen," "Internationale Perspectiven," and "Interpretationen," followed by a perspective on the future. In the first and most extensive section on "dimensions," the fundamentals are rendered in bundled form in three panels, "Wohn- und Bodenpolitik" (Housing and Land Policy), "Ökologie" (Ecology), and "Gesellschaft" (Society). Apparent here is the inter- and transdisciplinary approach found when research, planning, and practice seamlessly overlap and blend, such as when table talk and debating mix. Thus, ever new perspectives are gained by making cross connections, as in the case of the "Soziale Aspekte des Klimawandel" (Social Aspects of Climate Change) or of the economists and legal experts who no longer advocate affordable housing, or claim it as a right, but rather social or even "good housing for all" instead. The block on "international perspectives" seems almost like an interlude; surely numerous successful examples and developments would have been of interest here. Also, a jump to other regions beyond Europe could be inspiring, and not only for target group planning. The "interpretations" explore concrete approaches, thematizing the development of districts (or *Grätzlbildung*), the treatment of existing structures (or *Bestandsbauten*), architecture (and its design vocabulary), and finally also various new or even rediscovered models of financing, participation, cohabitation, and sustainable development.

A short look into the future under the banner "Damit es besser bleibt" (So It Stays Better) sums up the position of the IBA Wien, ties together some loose threads, and once again raises many interesting questions that the IBA in the year 2022 will not be able to answer in full. If this informative and very graphically appealing catalogue is but an intermediate assessment, then we can already now look forward to the next two formative years and suspensefully await the projects enriched by this knowledge. ∎

Sigrid Verhovsek (Translation: Dawn Michelle d'Atri)

Hans Scharoun und die Entwicklung der Kleinwohnungsgrundrisse. Die Wohnhochhäuser Romeo und Julia 1954–1959 | Hans Scharoun and the Development of Small Apartment Floor Plans: The Residential High-Rises Romeo and Julia, 1954–1959

Markus Peter/Ulrike Tillmann
Mit Fotografien von Georg Aerni und einer Einführung von Eva-Maria Barkhofen in Kooperation mit der Akademie der Künste, Berlin | With photographs by Georg Aerni and an introduction by Eva-Maria Barkhofen in cooperation with the Akademie der Künste, Berlin
Zürich | Zurich: Park Books, 2019
Deutsche und englische Version, gebunden 232 Seiten, 106 Farb- und 152 SW-Abbildungen | German and English editions, 232 pages, hardcover, 106 color and 152 b/w illustrations
ISBN 978-3-03860-156-2 (dt.)
ISBN 978-3-03860-157-9 (en.)
EUR 58,00 | EUR 58.00

Die Wohnung für den geistigen Arbeiter

Waltraud P. Indrist

Das Wertvolle und Besondere an dieser Scharoun-Publikation – soviel gleich vorweg – ist die Verschränkung eines historisch-analysierenden Abrisses zur Entwicklung der Typologie des Kleinwohnungsgrundrisses in den Arbeiten des Architekten Hans Scharoun *mit* der theoretisch-forschenden Auseinandersetzung im Rahmen seiner langjährigen Tätigkeit rund um seinen Städtebau-Lehrstuhl an der TU Berlin. „Romeo und Julia", das Hochhausprojekt in Stuttgart-Zuffenhausen, das 1954–1959 nach Scharouns Plänen errichtet wird, konsolidiert eben dieses über zwei Jahrzehnte andauernde Interesse an der Weiterentwicklung der Typologie des Kleinwohnungsgrundrisses, für das er ein spezifisches Konzept formuliert: „Die Wohnung für den geistigen Arbeiter" (S. 85 ff.). Es zeichnet sich – und darin lässt sich seine Aktualität unschwer erkennen – zum einen durch Scharouns Versuch aus, „Wohnen und Werken" in der Kleinwohnung zu verbinden, da „Werken" und „geistiger Arbeiter" für Scharoun keinen Widerspruch darstellen (S. 93 f.). Zum anderen führt Scharoun in „Romeo und Julia" nun mit Verve aus, was er zum Teil bereits drei Jahrzehnte zuvor – vier Kilometer Luftlinie weiter in der Werkbundsiedlung – zu entwickeln begonnen hatte: Die Maximierung der wahrgenommenen Raumgröße bei kleinster Wohnfläche. Methodisch gelingt ihm das etwa durch den inneren Wohnungsrundgang, durch mehrfache Zugänge zu jeweiligen Bereichen oder durch die Aufweitung des Grundrisses und der Verdoppelung der Haupt-Fassadenabwicklung (S. 112) aufgrund einer polygonalen Raumplanung (S. 172 f.).

Nach Eva-Maria Barkhofens Einleitung und dem Kapitel „Fundstück" – ein Grundriss von „Julia", der zum Ausgangspunkt für den Hauptteil wird – besteht der Hauptteil wiederum aus einer theoretisch-analytischen Auseinandersetzung, die Markus Peter und Ulrike Tillmann in sechs Kapitel gliedern sowie einem Bildteil mit umfangreichen Materialien zum Projekt „Romeo und Julia". Die fadengeheftete Hardcover-Publikation ist hochwertig ausgestattet. Drei Papiersorten differenzieren dabei die Faksimiles der Planmaterialien aus dem Scharoun-Nachlass der Akademie der Künste Berlin (AdK), den Textteil sowie die historisch- und zeitgenössisch-fotografische Dokumentation (Georg Aerni).

Dass Scharouns Entwürfe 1952 „gleichermaßen begeisterte Zustimmung wie echte Schocks" (S. 79) auslösen, liefert einen ersten Eindruck der Diskussionen hinter den Kulissen (s. Kapitel II). Diese spiegeln die berufliche Herausforderung wider, die bis heute im Kunststück einer geglückten Transformation von einer planerischen Idee hin zu seiner Realisierung liegt. Was sich im Falle von „Romeo und Julia" besonders eindrücklich zeigt, ist wie Scharoun gegen jene zunehmenden Normierungsvorschriften im sozialen Wohnbau ankämpft, die noch ein Jahrzehnt zuvor von Architekten wie Ernst Neufert oder Siegfried Stratemann[1] für das NS-Regime ausformuliert worden waren. Dabei handelt es sich etwa um die Anpassung an das Wohnbaugesetz und den damit verbundenen Normierungsanforderungen DIN 18 0 11 über Stellflächen, Abstände und Bewegungsflächen. Die zweigeschossige Wohnung als durchgehende Idee fällt diesen Anforderungen schließlich zum Opfer; die unkonventionelle Lösung der „Wohnung für den geistigen Arbeiter" kann er aber gegen konservative Stimmen 1959 schließlich doch realisieren.

Indem Peter und Tillmann in ausgiebigen Exkursen Scharouns bis dato kaum publizierte Vorlesungen an der TU Berlin aus dem Nachlass der AdK auslegen (s. Kapitel III u. IV), gelingt es ihnen, weit über deskriptive Grundrissbeschreibungen hinauszugehen. Auch weil sie bei ihrer Recherche aus dem Nachlass der AdK und aus dem Durcharbeiten seiner Vorlesungstyposkripte schöpfen. Damit stellen sie einen verdienstvollen Zugang zur Deutung von Scharouns schriftlichem und letztlich entwerferischem Werk bereit: Indem sie etwa Scharouns Auseinandersetzung mit der Grundrissforschung Alexander Kleins aufarbeiten, legen sie im Vergleich zur bisherigen Scharoun-Forschung erfrischende Erkenntnisse vor.

1 Stratemann, Siegfried: *Grundriss-Lehre: Mietwohnungsbau*, Berlin 1941.

„Isolierung und Beziehung" ist dabei Scharouns zentrales Prinzip der „Wohnung des Arbeiters". Bei „Romeo und Julia" entsprechend bedeutet dies: „Unzählige Türen, Doppelflügler, raumhohe Schiebetüren, eine Faltwand, kombiniert mit zwei Einzeltüren und ein Vorhang vor der Schlafkoje der Eltern, erlauben eine dauernde Mutation der räumlichen Beziehungen und damit die gesuchten Möglichkeiten der Isolierung und Bindung" (S. 112). Dabei – so Peter und Tillmann – sehe man insbesondere bei „Julia", dass „keine Entwicklung der Individualität zu erreichen [ist] ohne ihren Widerpart", wie es Scharoun selbst 1950 als „Entwicklung einer echten Sozialität" formuliert (S. 158).

Wie produktiv und nachhaltig die über ein Jahrzehnt andauernde Architekturforschung als Auseinandersetzung mit Scharoun sein kann, zeigen Peter und Tillmann nicht nur anhand dieser Publikation sehr eindrücklich: So veröffentlichte Ulrike Tillmann, Architektin und Architekturhistorikerin, die in ihrer Promotion an der Humboldt-Universität Berlin zum Zusammenhang von Farbwissen und Farbgestaltung bei Bruno Taut forscht, bereits 2008 einen ersten Beitrag zu „Romeo und Julia"[2] und zeichnet für die Grundrissanalysen in der Publikation verantwortlich. Markus Peter ist Architekt und Partner des Schweizer Architekturbüros Meili & Peter sowie Professor für Architektur und Konstruktion an der ETH Zürich und realisierte erst unlängst Stadthäuser in der Münchener Hansastraße, die zweifellos von der Beschäftigung mit Scharouns „Wohnung für den geistigen Arbeiter" inspiriert wurden.

Die Publikation wird schließlich immer wieder mit eigenen visuellen Grafiken (etwa S. 111, 173, 183, Zeichnungen von Tillmann/ ETH Zürich) und Fotografien von Modellen der Kleinwohnungen in „Romeo und Julia" (Cover, S. 84, 98, 146, 160, 178), die im Zuge der Lehre entstanden sind, ergänzt. Ausgehend von diesem spannenden Material wird allerdings deren Analysewert nicht wirklich ausformuliert.

2   Tillmann, Ulrike: „Zum Interpretieren von Architektur. Die Wohnhochhäuser ‚Romeo und Julia' von Hans Scharoun", in: *Wolkenkuckucksheim*, 122, 9 (2008), online unter: https://www.cloud-cuckoo.net/journal1996-2013/inhalt/de/heft/ausgaben/207/Tillmann/tillmann.php (Stand: 10. September 2020).

Dass sich eine Architekturpublikation monografisch und damit ausführlich *einem* Projekt widmet, stellt in der Fachliteratur sicherlich eher eine Ausnahme denn einen Regelfall dar. Dieser Umstand mag vielleicht den einen oder die andere von der Lektüre anfänglich abhalten; wer aber den Banalitäten des Massenwohnungsbaus mit klugen, ressourcenschonenden, ebenso wohnlichen wie kommunikativen Konzepten begegnen will, kann hier ausgiebig fündig werden. ▪

The Dwelling of the Intellectual Worker

What is special about this publication on Scharoun and what makes it worth reading—to make a long story short—is the way it interlaces a historical, analytical outline of the typological development of small apartment floor plans in the work of the architect Hans Scharoun *with* theoretical, research-oriented discussion in the scope of his many years spent in the urban planning department of the TU Berlin. "Romeo und Julia," the high-rise project in the Zuffenhausen district of Stuttgart that was built according to Scharoun's plans from 1954 to 1959, consolidates precisely this interest, lasting over two decades, in the further development of the typology of the small apartment floor plan, for which he formulated a specific concept: the "dwelling of the intellectual worker" (pp. 85ff). On the one hand, this is evident in Scharoun's attempt to link "manual work and brain work" in a small apartment, for in Scharoun's mind "manual work" and "intellectual labor" are not contradictory (pp. 92f.)—and the topicality thereof is quite clear. On the other hand, in "Romeo und Julia" Scharoun executed with verve what he had started developing—four kilometers as the crow flies into the Werkbund Estate—three decades earlier: maximizing the perceived size of the room in the smallest possible living space. Methodically, he succeeded in this, thanks for instance to the inner apartment circuit, to multiple accesses to the respective areas, or to the widening of the floor plan and the doubling of the main façade development (p. 112) according to polygonal spatial planning (pp. 173f.).

The main part of the book, following the introduction by Eva-Maria Barkhofen and the chapter "The Find"—a floor plan from "Julia" that becomes the point of departure for the main part—is comprised of a theoretical-analytical discussion that Markus Peter and Ulrike Tillmann have arranged in six chapters, as well as an image section with extensive material on the project "Romeo und Julia." The thread-bound hardcover publication is of high quality, with three types of paper differentiating the facsimiles of planning material derived from the Scharoun Estate at the Akademie der Künste Berlin (AdK), the text section, and the historical and contemporary photographic documentation (Georg Aerni).

The fact that, in 1952, Scharoun's designs triggered "both enthusiastic approval and genuine shock" (p. 79) is clear in an initial impression of the discussions behind the scenes (see Chapter II). Reflected here is the professional challenge that still today lies in the feat of a successful transformation from a planning idea to its realization. Especially convincing in the case of "Romeo und Julia" is how Scharoun fights against the increasing standardization regulations in the context of social housing that had originally been drafted a decade earlier by architects like Ernst Neufert or Siegfried Stratemann[1] for the National Socialist regime. An example of this is found in the necessary adaptations to the Housing Act and the associated DIN 18 0 11 standardization requirements for parking spaces, distances, and areas dedicated to movement. The two-story apartment as a passing idea ultimately fell victim to these requirements. However, in the face of conservative voices, Scharoun was able to realize the unconventional solution of the "dwelling of the intellectual worker" after all in 1959.

By interpreting, in extensive digressions, Scharoun's lectures from the TU Berlin, which are today found in his estate at the AdK and rarely published (see Chapters III and IV), Peter and Tillmann succeed in going far beyond descriptively detailing the ground plan—not least because their research is drawn from his estate and from a perusal of his lecture typescripts. The authors thus provide commendable access to an interpretation of Scharoun's written work, and ultimately to his design work as well. For example, by reviewing Scharoun's analysis of Alexander Klein's floor plan research, they present refreshing insights as compared to previous scholarship on Scharoun. Here, "isolation and connection" is Scharoun's main principle behind the "home of the worker." In the case of "Romeo und Julia," this means: "the countless doors, double doors, room-high sliding doors, a folding partition combined with two single doors, and the curtain closing off the bed niche in the parents' bedroom make for constantly spatial relations and hence for the desired range of options for isolation and connection" (p. 112). According to Peter and Tillmann, the case of "Julia" particularly illustrates that "there could be no development of individuality without its counterpart," as Scharoun himself phrased it in 1950, calling it the "development of genuine sociality" (p. 158).

Peter and Tillmann have impressively shown, above and beyond this publication, how architectural research that has lasted over a decade can be highly productive and sustainable in exploring Scharoun's work. For example, Ulrike Tillmann—an architect and architecture historian who is conducting doctoral work at the Humboldt-Universität Berlin on the connection between knowledge about color and color design in the work of Bruno Taut—already wrote her first article on "Romeo und Julia" in 2008[2] and is responsible for the floor plan analyses in this publication. Markus Peter—an architect and partner at the Swiss architecture firm Meili & Peter, as well as professor of architecture and construction at ETH Zurich—recently built town houses on Munich's Hansastraße, which were undoubtedly inspired by the study of Scharoun's "dwelling of the intellectual worker."

Finally, the book is supplemented time and again by their own visual graphics (e.g., pp. 111, 173, 183, drawings by Tillmann/ETH Zurich) and photographs of models of the small apartments in "Romeo und Julia" (cover, pp. 84, 98, 146, 160, 178) created over the course of teaching activity. However, despite this exciting material, its analytical value is not really explored in depth.

A monographic architectural publication devoted extensively to *a single* project is surely more of an exception than a rule in specialist literature. Perhaps this circumstance may initially deter a reader or two from picking up the book, but anyone who wishes to see the banal-

ities of mass housing contrasted with clever, resource-saving concepts that are as cozy as they are communicative will find plenty to choose from here. ■

Waltraud P. Indrist (Translation: Dawn Michelle d'Atri)

1   Siegfried Stratemann, *Grundriss-Lehre: Mietwohnungsbau* (Berlin, 1941).

2   Ulrike Tillmann, "Zum Interpretieren von Architektur: Die Wohnhochhäuser 'Romeo und Julia' von Hans Scharoun," *Wolkenkuckucksheim* 12, no. 2 (2008), https://www.cloud-cuckoo.net/journal1996-2013/inhalt/de/heft/ausgaben/207/Tillmann/tillmann.php (accessed September 10, 2020).

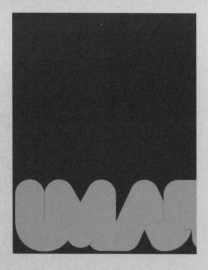

Ludwig Leo: Umlauftank 2

Philip Kurz/Wüstenrot
Stiftung (Hg. | eds.)
Konzeption | concept:
Pablo v. Frankenberg
Grafikdesign | graphic design:
Siyu Mao
Leipzig: Spector Books, 2020
Deutsch/Englisch, 290 Seiten,
140 Farbabbildungen und
80 SW-Abbildungen, Softcover |
German/English, 290 pages,
140 color and 80 b/w illustrations,
softcover
ISBN 978-3-95905-371-6
EUR 28,00 | EUR 28.00 (DE)
EUR 28,80 | EUR 28.80 (AT)

Schaumige Ewigkeit

Sophia Walk

Kobaltblaue und rosafarbene Kornblumen, später zu Hause auf dem Esstisch zu hellgrau und pastellrosa verblasst. Ein frisch aus seiner Verpackung gezogener rosa Küchenschwamm in all seiner noch nicht abgewetzten Schaumigkeit (S. 111).[1] Eine Bettwäschekombination aus dunkelblauem Bettdecken- und rosafarbenem Kopfkissenbezug, die meine Nachbarin zum Trocknen auf ihren Balkon hängt. Der Zeitraum, in dem dieser Text entsteht, ist begleitet von gedanklichen Verknüpfungen zur visuellen und taktilen Wahrnehmung jenes Berliner Bauwerks, dem sich das Buch *Ludwig Leo: Umlauftank 2* widmet.

Die Zeit seit der Fertigstellung 1974 ließ die Bonbonfarben des Mitte der 1990er-Jahre unter Denkmalschutz gestellten und vom Fachgebiet Dynamik maritimer Systeme der TU Berlin als Labor zur Untersuchung von Strömungsdynamiken genutzten Bauwerks verblassen: „Es duckte sich auf seiner Insel wie ein entfernter Verwandter, der einst für seine Exzentrik geliebt, irgendwann aber fallengelassen wurde" (S. 111). Im Zuge der unlängst vorgenommenen Instandsetzung des Gebäudes ist diese Publikation entstanden. Das vom Kurator, Soziologen und Architekturforscher Pablo v. Frankenberg inhaltlich konzipierte Buch geht weit über eine Dokumentation einer Gebäudesanierung hinaus und bildet eine eigenständige Erzählung über dieses geheimnisvolle und mehrdeutige Bauwerk.

In sieben Beiträgen werden Architekturforschung, Stadtbildprägung, Denkmaltheorie und Sanierungspraxis auf technische, historische und literarische Weise miteinander verschränkt. Die eingangs beschriebenen Beobachtungen stellen nicht nur Assoziationen zu dieser Schiffbauversuchsanlage auf der Schleuseninsel im Landwehrkanal am Eingang des Berliner Tiergartens her, sondern auch zur Buchgestaltung, in der die Grafikdesignerin Siyu Mao all diese Fäden miteinander verwebt.

Der Beginn des Buchs ist so enigmatisch wie das Gebäude selbst: Man blättert sich durch einige Fotos, die auf sehr dünnem, Skizzenrollen ähnlichem Papier einzeln für sich stehen und die ebenso erschlossen werden müssen, wie man sich als Betrachterin das Bauwerk erst erschließen muss: „Wenn man weiß, was im Bauch der rundlaufenden Röhre passiert, kann man alle Funktionen von außen ablesen. Wenn man es nicht weiß, starrt man auf ein enigmatisches Gewirr von ausufernder Schaumigkeit, auf die sich ein blauer Block setzt [...]" (S. 111). Dementsprechend bezeichnet auch der britische Architekt und Archigram-Protagonist Peter Cook Leos Umlauftank stimmig als „quizzical test-piece"[2] und sieht es im Zusammenhang mit architektonischen Bezugsobjekten als „eine Anspielung darauf, wie in der Vergangenheit hohe Giebelfelder oder Kirchtürme die Menschen auf ihren Wegen anhielten und sie auf das vorbereiten sollten, was folgen könnte".[3]

Inhaltlich und gestalterisch spürt das Buch dieser Rätselhaftigkeit nach, indem es Charakteristika des Bauwerks nachvollziehbar macht. So zieht sich etwa der rosafarbene Schriftzug „Umlauftank 2", den Siyu Mao eigens für diese Titelgestaltung entworfen hat, in ganz ähnlicher Weise um den Buchumschlag (der durch seine raue Oberflächentextur etwas Schaumigkeit vermittelt), herum, wie die rosa Röhre um den ultramarinblauen kastigen Aufbau der Versuchsanstalt selbst. Und dort, wo sich am Gebäude die rosa Röhre des Umlauftanks durch die Laborhalle windet, verteilen sich mehrere rosafarbige Seiten durch das Buch, auf denen die Schriftstellerin Felicitas Hoppe auf literarische Weise betrachtet, wie „Ludwig Leo ein Schiff [baut]".

Der Architekturhistoriker und -journalist Gregor Harbusch, der zu Ludwig Leo (1924–2012) forscht, ordnet in seinem Beitrag den Umlauftank 2 in Werk und Leben des Architekten ein. Die relativ kurze Werkliste Leos enthält sensibel durchdachte Bauten, denen er „mit minutiöser Detailversessenheit formale und konzeptionelle Mehrwerte ab[rang]" (S. 68). Harbusch stellt Bezüge zu Leos Arbeitsweise

1   Nachdem mir dieses Wort nach der Lektüre im Gedächtnis geblieben ist.

2   Cook, Peter: *Architecture Workbook: Design Through Motive*, Chichester West Sussex, 2016, 106.

3   Ebda., Übers. S.W.

her und zeichnet so die Entstehungsgeschichte der Versuchsanlage nach, deren technische Konstruktion der damals junge Schiffbauingenieur Christian Boës konzipierte und die Leo architektonisch ausformulierte. Bei der Beschreibung der Funktionsweise des sogenannten UT2, die so durchdacht wie komplex ist, kommen sowohl bei Planung und Bau Involvierte zu Wort, als auch diejenigen, die heute den UT2 nutzen.

Herausgeber des Buchs ist Philip Kurz als Geschäftsführer der Wüstenrot Stiftung, die die Sanierung des Umlauftank 2 gefördert hat und die wiederum vom Berliner Büro HG Merz in Zusammenarbeit mit Steffen Obermann (Büro für Architektur, Denkmalpflege und Bauforschung adb) geplant wurde. Die Wüstenrot Stiftung engagiert sich für die Erforschung, den Erhalt und die Vermittlung jenes jüngeren Architekturerbes, das als Bausubstanz der Nachkriegszeit bis herauf in die 1980er-Jahre von der breiten Öffentlichkeit eher übersehen bzw. kaum wertgeschätzt wird. Das Buch *Ludwig Leo: Umlauftank 2* leistet hier einen bedeutenden Beitrag, indem es aufzeigt, wie der Umgang mit Bauten auch aus der zweiten Hälfte des 20. Jahrhunderts aussehen kann, wenn man sie wegen ihres Renovierungsbedarfs nicht einfach abreißt. Entsprechend werden im Buch aber auch grundlegende Fragen zu Originaltreue, Authentizität und Materialgerechtigkeit bei der Instandhaltung/-setzung dieser Bauwerke aufgeworfen: Wie denkmalgerecht mit Alterungsprozessen umgehen, die beim UT2 als „Schaum und Blechpaneele wesentlich für das Denkmal sind …" (S. 130)? Gerade jüngere Baudenkmale wie der Umlauftank 2, die „in [ihrem] ganzen Erscheinungsbild auf Ewigkeitserwägungen [verzichten]" (S. 19) haben es schwer in Rezeption und Einordnung. Materiell liefern sie hinsichtlich der Vergänglichkeit der Baustoffe Herausforderungen und formal richten sich die Gestaltungshaltungen ihrer Architektinnen und Architekten mit Eindeutigkeit nur gegen die Repräsentation und monumentale Schwere der Vorkriegszeit. Wofür stehen sie aber, wenn zu vermuten ist, dass Ludwig Leo selbst wohl nicht für den unbedingten Erhalt des Umlauftanks plädiert hätte (S. 212)?

Dieses Buch liefert Antworten auf die Frage, wie sich dieser Verzicht auf Ewigkeitser-

wägungen in ein Verhältnis mit der Bewahrung jüngerer Baudenkmale setzen lässt. Allerdings setzen diese Antworten ein Verständnis von Denkmalpflege voraus, die auch im 21. Jahrhundert ankommen möchte. Pablo v. Frankenberg und HG Merz fächern in ihrem Beitrag die Bedeutungsebenen des jungen Baudenkmals aus kulturanalytischer Perspektive auf und zeigen, dass der Denkmaldiskurs über seine bisweilen engen disziplinären Grenzen hinaus neuer, indi-

viduellerer und anpassungsfähigerer Methoden und Betrachtungsweisen bedarf: „In dieser Perspektive geht es nicht nur um die korrekte Instandsetzung, sondern auch um die Auseinandersetzung mit den Ideen und Haltungen, die hinter jedem zu sanierenden Material und hinter jeder zu bewahrenden Oberfläche stecken" (S. 125). Denn Bauwerke haben uns weit mehr mitzuteilen als wir ihnen in unserer Gegenwart zuschreiben. ▪

Perpetual Foaminess

Cornflowers in hues of cobalt blue and bright pink, later fading to light gray and pastel pink at home on the dining room table. A pink kitchen sponge fresh from the package in all its fresh, untouched foaminess (p. 137). A combination of bedding, including dark-blue duvet covers and pink-hued pillowcases, hung out to dry on my neighbor's balcony. The time needed to write this text is accompanied by mental associations related to the visual and tactile perception of the Berlin building at the heart of the book *Ludwig Leo: Umlauftank 2*.

Since its completion in 1974, time has caused the candy-colored shades of the Umluftank 2 (Circulating Tank 2) to fade. The structure has enjoyed protection as a historical monument since the mid-1990s and is home to a laboratory for studying hydrodynamics run by the Dynamics of Maritime Systems program at Berlin University of Technology: "It sat bent double on its island in the canal, a distant relative once loved for being eccentric, but at some point forgotten all the same" (p. 137). The publication under review here was created in the course of the recent restoration of the building. Reflecting a concept developed by the curator, sociologist, and architectural researcher Pablo von Frankenberg, the book goes well beyond simply documenting a building restoration process; it offers an independent narrative about this mysterious and ambiguous architectural structure.

In seven contributions, the topics of architectural research, cityscape shaping, monument

theory, and restoration practice are interwoven in technical, historical, and literary ways. The observations described above foster associations not only with this shipbuilding testing facility situated on the floodgate island of Berlin's Landwehr Canal at the entrance to the Tiergarten, but also with the book design, in which the graphic designer Siyu Mao weaves all of these threads together.

The beginning of the book is as enigmatic as the building itself: one flips through several photos positioned alone on very thin paper resembling that of sketching rolls. They must be explored, just as one must first explore the building as a viewer: "Those who know what happens at the heart of the big pink pipe can read all the building's functions from outside. Those who do not know stand bewildered before the enigmatic tangle—overflowing foaminess topped by a blue box …" (p. 137). It is thus fitting that the British architect and Archigram protagonist Peter Cook called Leo's circulating tank a "quizzical test-piece," viewing it, in the context of architectural objects, as "… a reference to how in history the great pediment or church tower would stop people in their tracks and prepare them for whatever might follow."

1   After reading the book, this word remained lodged in my mind.

2   Peter Cook, *Architecture Workbook: Design through Motive* (Chichester, West Sussex, 2016), p. 106.

3   Ibid.

In terms of content and design, the book traces this mysteriousness by making the structure's features comprehensible. For example, the pink-colored lettering "Umlauftank 2," specially developed by Siyu Mao for the book's title design, runs around the cover (which conveys a sense of foaminess through its raw surface texture) in a way that strongly resembles the pink pipes running around the ultramarine-blue, box-like structure of the testing facility itself. And several pink-colored pages run through the book, mirroring how, on the building, the pink tube of the circulating tank winds through the laboratory hall. On these pink pages, the writer Felicitas Hoppe takes a literary approach to exploring how "Ludwig Leo builds a ship."

In his contribution, the architecture historian and journalist Gregor Harbusch, who conducts research on Ludwig Leo (1924–2012), positions the Umlauftank 2 within the life and work of the architect. Leo's relatively concise oeuvre features sensitively designed buildings where he "used meticulous attention to detail to wrestle with each project—and to realize some formal and conceptual added value" (p. 91). Harbusch establishes references to Leo's working methods and thus traces the genesis of the testing facility, its technical construction conceived by the young shipbuilding engineer Christian Boës and architecturally formulated by Leo. In describing the operation of the so-called UT2, which is as sophisticated as it is complex, the individuals involved in the planning

and construction have their say, as do those who use the UT2 today.

The book was edited by Philip Kurz as the director of the Wüstenrot Foundation, which supported the redevelopment of the Umlauftank 2, which in turn was planned by the Berlin-based firm HG Merz in collaboration with Steffen Obermann (Büro für Architektur, Denkmalpflege und Bauforschung adb). The Wüstenrot Foundation is committed to the research, preservation, and mediation of more recent architectural monuments which, as architecture from the postwar period up to the 1980s, tends to be overlooked or hardly appreciated by the general public. In this respect, the book *Ludwig Leo: Umlauftank 2* makes a decisive contribution by showing how buildings in need of renovation, even those from the second half of the twentieth century, can be treated if they are not actually demolished in the first place. Accordingly, the book also raises fundamental questions about remaining faithful to the original, authenticity, and fitting use of materials in the upkeep and restoration of these architectural structures: How can aging processes be dealt with in an appropriate manner, which, in the case of UT2, as "foam and sheet-metal panels were essential in constructing this landmark …" (p. 146)? Especially younger heritage buildings like Umlauftank 2, which "in its appearance quite deliberately dispenses with any aspirations to eternal reverence …" (p. 23), have a hard time being accepted and classified. Materially, such structures prove challenging

due to the impermanent nature of the building materials, and formally, the attitudes of the designing architects were clearly directed primarily against the representation and monumental severity of the prewar period. But what do they stand for, if it can be assumed that Ludwig Leo himself surely would not have advocated the unconditional preservation of the circulating tank (p. 234)?

This publication provides answers to the question of how this abandonment of aspirations to eternal reverence relates to the preservation of more recent architectural monuments. However, such answers presuppose an understanding of the preservation of historical monuments that, for all intents and purposes, has arrived in the twenty-first century. In their contribution, Pablo von Frankenberg and HG Merz analyze from a cultural perspective the levels of meaning that apply to young monuments and illustrate how discourse on monuments needs new, more individual and adaptable methods and approaches beyond its sometimes narrow disciplinary bounds: "This view demands not only careful physical repair, but also the grappling with the ideas and attitudes that inform every piece of material to be refurbished and every surface to be preserved" (p. 144). Indeed, architectural structures have far more to tell us than we give them credit for in our present day. ∎

Sophia Walk (Translation: Dawn Michelle d'Atri)

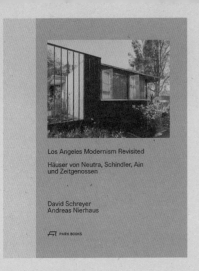

Los Angeles Modernism Revisited. Häuser von Neutra, Schindler, Ain und Zeitgenossen
David Schreyer/Andreas Nierhaus
Zürich | Zurich: Park Books, 2019
Deutsch, 256 Seiten, 199 teilweise farbige Abbildungen und Grundrisse, gebunden | German, 256 pages, 199 illustrations (some in color) and floor plans, hardback
Englisch, 272 Seiten, 263 farbige Abbildungen, gebunden | English, 272 pages, 263 color illustrations, hardback
ISBN 978-3-03860-160-9
EUR 48,00 | EUR 48.00

Ein anti-monumentaler Blick auf Hausbiografien

Ingrid Böck

Bis heute ist das mit Los Angeles am engsten verbundene Medium nicht nur der Film, sondern auch die Fotografie, die mit Aufnahmen von Julius Shulman, vor allem von Richard Neutras Bauten, das Bild der modernen Architektur in dieser Stadt geprägt hat. Diese einflussreichen Vor-Bilder dienten dem Fotografen David Schreyer und dem Kunsthistoriker Andreas Nierhaus zwar als Ausgangspunkt für ihren Band über 19 Häuser der 1930er- bis 1960er-Jahre der kalifornischen Moderne, doch standen die visuellen Ikonen, die „sich längst wie eine blickdichte Folie über die gebaute Wirklichkeit gelegt haben", einem zeitgenössischen Blick auch im Weg (S. 15). Viele Entwürfe Neutras scheinen einen „,Shulman' moment" zu besitzen, da diese gleichsam „eingefrorenen" Fotografien den Eindruck vermitteln, als seien bildwirksame Blickwinkel bereits während des Entwurfsprozesses mitgedacht worden (S. 8 f.).

Schreyer untersucht in seinen Neuinterpretationen etablierte Sehgewohnheiten, wie mit der Übersetzung moderner Architektur ins Medium der Fotografie eine „authentische" und zugleich kanonische Bildersprache des Gebauten erzeugt wurde. Die unterschiedliche Herangehensweise von Shulman und Schreyer spiegelt sich vor allem im Blick auf die BenutzerInnen wider, die sich die funktionalen Bauten angeeignet und sich darin häuslich eingerichtet haben: Während Shulmans Aufnahmen einerseits die „glückliche weiße amerikanische Kleinfamilie im modernen Eigenheim" suggerieren, andererseits jedoch die Bauten „als Kunstobjekte gefangen" nehmen (S. 8 f.), zeigen Schreyers Bilder die kalifornische Moderne als private, oft minimalistisch anmutende Orte des Wohnens.

Schreyer und Nierhaus beschreiben ihre Arbeitsweise als neuen, anti-monumentalen Blick auf Gebrauchsobjekte mit hoher gestalterischer Qualität, die erst durch den gelebten Alltag der BenutzerInnen ihre eigene Atmosphäre ausstrahlen (S. 15). Mit ethnografischen Karten von Los Angeles im Gepäck, die die tiefen gesellschaftlichen Konflikte der städtischen Agglomeration abbilden, begannen die Verfasser ihre Expedition

zu den Privathäusern, in denen die Fotografien entstanden und zeitgleich die Gespräche mit den BewohnerInnen stattfanden. Schreyers Fotografien geben Einblicke in individuelle Hausbiografien, die von einer Konservierung oder Rekonstruktion des Originalzustandes bis hin zu Adaptierungen und Erweiterungen des Entwurfs wegen geänderten Wohnbedürfnissen reichen. Manche Fotografien lassen die Durchlässigkeit und zugleich große räumliche Kompaktheit erkennen, die von den BewohnerInnen als Zurückhaltung und Bescheidenheit wahrgenommen wird. Nierhaus fängt in den kurzen Einleitungstexten zu den einzelnen Objekten die Baugeschichte und individuelle Beziehung zwischen Gebäude und BewohnerInnen ein, die sich manchmal viel Zeit gelassen haben, um in das Haus hineinzuwachsen und mit der „fordernden Strenge" umgehen zu lernen.

In den experimentellen Entwürfen setzen sich die Architekten nicht nur mit Fragen eines funktionalen Raumprogramms, offenen Grundrissen, extremen klimatischen Bedingungen und fließenden Übergängen zwischen Innenraum und umliegender Landschaft auseinander, sondern propagieren auch eine kostengünstige Bauweise mit standardisierten und vorgefertigten Elementen. Neben Neutras neun Bauten (auch aus dem Case-Study-House-Programm) nehmen auch zwei realisierten Entwürfe von Rudolph Schindler, der wie Neutra aus seinem Heimatland Österreich in die USA ausgewandert ist, eine wesentliche Rolle in der Gegenüberstellung der im Band vertretenden Architekturlegenden und ihrer divergierenden Zugänge zur Moderne ein. Ein zentrales Element aller Entwürfe – wie auch der Fotografien – ist die direkte und indirekte Sonneneinstrahlung sowie die Lichtführung im Baukörper, der sich je nach Himmelsrichtung und schattenspendenden Bäumen schließt oder zum Garten hin öffnet. Da sich die Mehrzahl der Häuser an besonderen topografischen Orten, wie an einem stark abfallenden Hang, einer Steilküste hoch über dem Pazifik, innerhalb enger Grundstücksgrenzen oder inmitten eines weitläufigen üppigen Gartens befinden, nimmt die Beziehung zwischen Natur und Baukörper eine wichtige Rolle in der Wahrnehmung des Raumes ein.

Trotz des Anspruchs, den Gebrauch der Häuser im Alltagsleben abzulichten, kommt in den stimmigen Fotografien auch die besondere

Ästhetik der Innenräume zur Geltung: Die schlanken Metallrahmen, die Neutra im Ohara House für Fenster- und Türrahmen einsetzte, lassen die Glaselemente kaum mehr als zarte Membrane erscheinen (S. 17 ff.). Die für die räumliche Ökonomie typischen Einbaumöbel aus Holz, die oft aus kalifornischem Redwood gefertigt sind, schaffen in Neutras McIntosh House nicht nur eine reduzierte Einrichtung und mehr freie Flächen, sondern erzeugen auch einheitliche, großzügig erscheinende Innenräume (S. 48 ff.). Den modernen Entwurfskonzepten gelingt es bis heute, traditionelle Rollenmodelle zu hinterfragen, wie beispielsweise mit der Küche im Daniel House von Gregory Ain, die als offenes Zentrum des Bauwerks funktioniert (S. 101 ff.).

Der hybride Charakter der Buchgestaltung (CH Studio/Christian Hoffelner) mit Fotografien und Texten wird mit Grundrissen im Maßstab 1:200 im Anhang unterstrichen, die eine leichtere Lesbarkeit der geometrisch komplexen Raumstrukturen ermöglichen. Leider fehlen Biografien über die verschiedenen ArchitektInnen, was zu weiteren Recherchen zur systematischen Einordnung der vorgestellten Bauten in den Kontext des jeweiligen Lebenswerkes anregt.

Die dem Schaffen Neutras gewidmete Ausstellung „Richard Neutra. Wohnhäuser in Kalifornien" (13. Februar bis 20. September 2020) im Wien Museum MUSA wurde von Nierhaus kuratiert und zeigte neben Schreyers Fotografien auch bisher unveröffentlichte Dokumente zu Neutras ambivalenter Beziehung zu Wien.

Schreyer, der sich als ausgebildeter Architekt seit 2004 mit Architekturfotografie beschäftigt und an der Universität Innsbruck lehrt, und Nierhaus, Kunsthistoriker und Kurator der Architektursammlung des Wien Museums, gelingt im vorliegenden Band nicht nur, eine atmosphärische Bestandsaufnahme von prototypischen Wohnbauten Mitte des 20. Jahrhunderts durchzuführen, sondern auch die Aktualität eines reduzierten, modernen Wohnideals aufzuzeigen: Mit einem Architekturverständnis, das eine ressourcenschonende, kostengünstige Bauweise, Vorfertigung und Raumökonomie als wesentliche Entwurfsprinzipien erachtet, stellt das empfehlenswerte Buch über die kalifornische

Moderne nicht nur Ikonen von bedeutenden Architekten vor, sondern zeigt auch konkrete, ökologische Modelle für die Zukunft des Wohnens auf. Darüber hinaus vermitteln die Hausbiografien einen sachlichen und zugleich poetischen Blick auf die individuelle Aneignung der Architektur durch die BenutzerInnen und ihre Gebrauchsspuren im gelebten Alltag. ∎

An Anti-Monumental View of House Biographies

To this day, the artistic medium most closely associated with Los Angeles is not just film, but also photography. The latter, with photographs by Julius Shulman, especially of Richard Neutra's buildings, has shaped the image of modern architecture in this city. For the photographer David Schreyer and the art historian Andreas Nierhaus, such influential examples served as the point of departure for their volume about nineteen California modernist houses from the 1930s to the 1960s. Yet these visual icons, "that have long settled like an opaque film over built reality," indeed got in the way of a contemporary gaze (p. 14). Many of Neutra's designs seem like a "Schulman" moment, for these seemingly frozen photographs convey the impression that visually effective perspectives had already been considered during the design process (pp. 8f.).

In his new interpretations, Schreyer examines established viewing habits, such as the "authentic" and simultaneously canonical pictorial language of buildings engendered by a translation of modern architecture into the medium of photography. The different approach taken by Shulman and Schreyer is mirrored most especially in the view of the residents, who have appropriated the functional buildings and turned them into domestic homes. Shulman's photos suggest a "happy, white American nuclear family in their modern, privately owned home," while also "capture them as art objects" (pp. 8f.). Schreyer's pictures, in turn, show California

modernism as private sites of habitation, often with a minimalist flair.

Schreyer and Nierhaus describe their approach as a new, anti-monumental gaze focused on utilitarian objects displaying a high quality of design, which first start radiating their own atmosphere through the everyday lives of those using them (p. 15). Having packed ethnographic maps of Los Angeles, which illustrate the deep social conflicts playing out in this urban agglomeration, the authors began their expedition to the private homes where they took pictures and also engaged in conversation with the inhabitants. Schreyer's photographs offer insight into the individual house biographies, ranging from conservation or reconstruction of the original state to adaptations and extensions of the design due to changed living requirements. Some photos reveal both permeability and great spatial compactness at the same time, which is perceived by the residents as being restrained and modest. In the short introductory texts to the individual objects, Nierhaus captures the architectural history and the individual relationship between the building and its inhabitants, who have at times slowly grown into the house and learned to deal with the demanding austerity.

In the experimental designs, the architects not only deal with issues related to functional space, open floor plans, extreme climatic conditions, and flowing transitions between the interior and the surrounding landscape; they also propagate a cost-effective construction method that uses standardized and prefabricated elements. Aside from Neutra's nine buildings (including the Case Study Houses program), two completed designs by Rudolph Schindler, who, like Neutra, emigrated to the States from his native Austria, play an important role in the juxtaposition of the architectural legends presented in the volume and their divergent approaches to modernism. A main element found in all of the designs—and in the respective photographs—is direct and indirect sunlight, as well as lighting within the structure, which, depending on the cardinal direction and the shade-giving trees, is either closed or else opened to the yard. Since the majority of the houses are situated in special topographical locations—such as on a steep slope, a bluff high above the Pacific Ocean, within narrow property boundaries, or amid a lush, spacious garden—the relationship between nature and building plays a key role in the perception of the space.

Despite the aspiration to capture on film the everyday use of the houses, the photographs do justice to the special aesthetics of the interior spaces: the thin metal frames used by Neutra in the Ohara House to enclose the windows and doors make the glass elements seem like little more than thin membranes (pp. 17ff.). In Neutra's McIntosh House, the built-in furniture fashioned from wood, often California redwood, so typical of the spatial economy not only gives

rise to reduced furnishings and more open spaces; it also creates generous, uniform interiors (pp. 48ff.). Still today, modern design concepts succeed in challenging traditional role models, such as in the case of the kitchen in the Daniel House by Gregory Ain, which serves as an open center within the architectural structure (pp. 101ff.).

The hybrid character of the book design (CH Studio/Christian Hoffelner) featuring photographs and texts is underscored by floor plans at a scale of 1:200 in the appendix, making the geometrically complex spatial structures easier to read. Unfortunately, there are no biographies of the various architects, which encourages further research on the systematic classification of the presented buildings in the context of each architect's respective oeuvre.

The exhibition devoted to Neutra's work, *Richard Neutra: California Living*, which was on show at Wien Museum MUSA in Vienna from February 13 to September 20, 2020, was curated by Nierhaus. It also exhibited, aside from Schreyer's photographs, previously unpublished documents on Neutra's ambivalent relationship with Vienna.

In this volume, the authors—Schreyer, who after graduating from architecture school in 2004 has been focused on architectural photography and on teaching at the University of Innsbruck, and Nierhaus, an art historian and curator of the architecture collection at Wien

Museum—succeed in taking stock of prototypical dwellings in the middle of the twentieth century. Furthermore, they illustrate the topicality of a reduced, modern housing ideal. With an understanding of architecture that considers resource-conserving, cost-effective construction, prefabrication, and space economy as essential design principles, this recommendable book on Californian modernism not only introduces icons by important architects, but also shows concrete, ecological models for the future of housing. What is more, the house biographies impart a factual and also poetic view of the individual appropriation of architecture by those living there, along with their traces of usage, in everyday life. ∎

Ingrid Böck (Translation: Dawn Michelle d'Atri)